T0214861

Communications in Computer and Information Science 1051

Commenced Publication in 2007
Founding and Former Series Editors:
Phoebe Chen, Alfredo Cuzzocrea, Xiaoyong Du, Orhun Kara, Ting Liu,
Krishna M. Sivalingam, Dominik Ślęzak, Takashi Washio, Xiaokang Yang,
and Junsong Yuan

Editorial Board Members

More information about this series at http://www.springer.com/series/7899

Hector Florez · Marcelo Leon ·
Jose Maria Diaz-Nafria ·
Simone Belli (Eds.)

Applied Informatics

Second International Conference, ICAI 2019
Madrid, Spain, November 7–9, 2019
Proceedings

 Springer

Editors
Hector Florez (iD)
Universidad Distrital Francisco Jose de
Caldas
Bogota, Colombia

Marcelo Leon (iD)
Universidad Nacional de Loja
Loja, Ecuador

Jose Maria Diaz-Nafria (iD)
Universidad a Distancia de Madrid
Madrid, Spain

Simone Belli (iD)
Universidad Complutense de Madrid
Madrid, Spain

ISSN 1865-0929   ISSN 1865-0937 (electronic)
Communications in Computer and Information Science
ISBN 978-3-030-32474-2   ISBN 978-3-030-32475-9 (eBook)
https://doi.org/10.1007/978-3-030-32475-9

This Springer imprint is published by the registered company Springer Nature Switzerland AG
The registered company address is: Gewerbestrasse 11, 6330 Cham, Switzerland

Preface

The Second International Conference on Applied Informatics (ICAI 2019) aimed to bring together researchers and practitioners working in different domains in the field of informatics in order to exchange their expertise and discuss the perspectives of development and collaboration.

ICAI 2019 was held at the Universidad Complutense de Madrid in Madrid, Spain, during November 7–9, 2019. It was organized by the Universidad Distrital Francisco José de Caldas, Universidad de Bogotá Jorge Tadeo Lozano, Universidad Complutense de Madrid, Universidad Nacional de Loja, Universidad a Distancia de Madrid, and Bitrum research group. In addition, ICAI 2019 was proudly sponsored by the Information Technologies Innovation (ITI) research group, which belongs to the Universidad Distrital Francisco José de Caldas, and Springer.

ICAI 2019 received 98 submissions on informatics topics such as bioinformatics, data analysis, decision systems, health care information systems, IT architectures, learning management systems, robotic autonomy, security services, socio-technical systems, and software design engineering. Authors of the 98 submissions came from the following 24 countries: Argentina, Austria, Bolivia, China, Colombia, Cuba, Cyprus, Czech Republic, Ecuador, Germany, India, Iraq, Latvia, Lithuania, Luxembourg, Mexico, Nigeria, Poland, South Africa, Spain, Thailand, Turkey, USA, and Vietnam. Moreover, 20 of the 98 submissions are international collaborations.

All submissions were reviewed through a double-blind peer-review process. Each paper was reviewed by at least three experts. To achieve this, ICAI 2019 was supported by 87 Program Committee (PC) members, who hold PhD degrees. PC members come from the following 24 countries: Argentina, Austria, Belgium, Brazil, China, Colombia, Cyprus, Czech Republic, Ecuador, France, Germany, Japan, Latvia, Lithuania, Mexico, Portugal, Romania, Spain, Sweden, Switzerland, Ukraine, UK, USA, and Uruguay. Based on the double-blind review process, 38 full papers were accepted to be included in this volume of *Communications in Computer and Information Science* (CCIS) proceedings published by Springer.

Finally, we would like to thank Jorge Nakahara, Alfred Hofmann, Leonie Kunz, Sanja Evenson, and Manjula Anandan from Springer for their helpful advice, guidance, and support in publishing the proceedings.

November 2019

Hector Florez
Marcelo Leon
Jose Maria Diaz-Nafria
Simone Belli

Organization

General Chairs

Hector Florez   Universidad Distrital Francisco José de Caldas, Colombia
Marcelo Leon   Universidad Nacional de Loja, Ecuador
Jose Maria Diaz-Nafria   Universidad a Distancia de Madrid, Spain
Simone Belli   Universidad Complutense de Madrid, Spain

Organizing Committee

Simone Belli   Universidad Complutense de Madrid, Spain
Manuela Cañizares   Universidad a Distancia de Madrid, Spain
Iris Celorrio   Universidad a Distancia de Madrid, Spain
Jose Maria Diaz-Nafria   Universidad a Distancia de Madrid, Spain
Teresa Guarda   BITrum-Research Group, Spain
Wolfgang Hofkirchner   Institute for a Global Sustainable Information Society (GSIS), Austria
Juan Carlos Revilla   Universidad Complutense de Madrid, Spain
Isaac Seoane   Universidad a Distancia de Madrid, Spain

Steering Committee

Jaime Chavarriaga   Universidad de los Andes, Colombia
Cesar O. Diaz   OCOX AI, Colombia
Hector Florez   Universidad Distrital Francisco José de Caldas, Colombia
Ixent Galpin   Universidad de Bogota Jorge Tadeo Lozano, Colombia
Olmer Garcia   Universidad de Bogota Jorge Tadeo Lozano, Colombia

Workshops Committee

Jaime Chavarriaga   Universidad de los Andes, Colombia
Cesar O. Diaz   OCOX AI, Colombia
Hector Florez   Universidad Distrital Francisco José de Caldas, Colombia
Olmer Garcia   Universidad de Bogota Jorge Tadeo Lozano, Colombia
Teresa Guarda   Universidad Estatal Península de Santa Elena, Ecuador

Publication Chairs

Hector Florez   Universidad Distrital Francisco José de Caldas,
                              Colombia
Sanjay Misra   Covenant University, Nigeria

Program Committee

Fernanda Almeida   Universidade Federal do ABC, Brazil
Francisco Alvarez   Universidad Autónoma de Aguascalientes, Mexico
Gloria Alvarez   Pontificia Universidad Javeriana, Colombia
Cecilia Avila   Fundación Universitaria Konrad Lorenz, Colombia
Oscar Avila   Universidad de los Andes, Colombia
Jorge Bacca   Fundacion Universitaria Konrad Lorenz, Colombia
Verónica Basilotta   Universidad a Distancia de Madrid, Spain
David Benavides   Universidad de Sevilla, Spain
Hüseyin Bicen   Yakin Dogu Üniversitesi, Cyprus
Dominic Bork   Universität Wien, Austria
Paola Britos   Universidad Nacional de Río Negro, Argentina
Robert Buchmann   Universitatea Babes-Bolyai, Romania
Santiago Caballero   Universidad Popular Autónoma del Estado de Puebla,
                              Mexico
Manuela Cañizares   Universidad a Distancia de Madrid, Spain
Patricia Cano-Olivos   Universidad Popular Autónoma del Estado de Puebla,
                              Mexico
Juan Capella   Universitat Politècnica de València, Spain
Iris Celorrio   Universidad a Distancia de Madrid, Spain
Jaime Chavarriaga   Universidad de los Andes, Colombia
Erol Chioasca   The University of Manchester, UK
Helio de Oliveira   Universidade Federal de Pernambuco, Brazil
Cesar O. Diaz   OCOX AI, Colombia
Jose Maria Diaz   Universidad a Distancia de Madrid, Spain
Helga Duarte   Universidad Nacional de Colombia, Colombia
Silvia Fajardo   Universidad de Colima, Mexico
Mauri Ferrandin   Universidade Federal de Santa Catarina, Brazil
Hans-Georg Fill   University of Fribourg, Switzerland
Hector Florez   Universidad Distrital Francisco José de Caldas,
                              Colombia
Ixent Galpin   Universidad de Bogotá Jorge Tadeo Lozano, Colombia
Maira Garcia   Universidad EAN, Colombia
Olmer Garcia   Universidad de Bogotá Jorge Tadeo Lozano, Colombia
Leonardo Garrido   Tecnológico de Monterrey, Mexico
Raphael Gomes   Instituto Federal de Goiás, Brazil
Jānis Grabis   Rīgas Tehniskā Universitāte, Latvia
Annette Grathoff   International Society for the Study of Information,
                              Austria

Contents

Learning Management Systems

Robotic Autonomy

Security Services

Socio-technical Systems

Software Design Engineering

Bioinformatics

Bioinformatics Methods to Discover Antivirals Against Zika Virus

Karina Salvatierra[1]([✉])[iD], Marcos Vera[1], and Hector Florez[2][iD]

[1] Universidad Nacional de Misiones, Posadas, Argentina
karinasalvatierra@fceqyn.unam.edu.ar
[2] Universidad Distrital Francisco Jose de Caldas, Bogotá, Colombia
haflorezf@udistrital.edu.co

Abstract. Zika virus is a member of the *Flaviviridae* virus family, similar to other viruses that affect humans, such as hepatitis C and dengue virus. After its first appearance in 1947, Zika virus reappeared in 2016 causing an international public health emergency. Zika virus was considered a non dangerous human pathogen; however, it is currently considered a pathogen with serious consequences for human health, showing association with neurological complications such as Guillain-Barre syndrome and microcephaly. Then, it is necessary to get antivirals able to inhibit the replication of the Zika virus since vaccines for this virus are not yet available. Zika virus structure is similar to hepatitis C virus structure. This characteristic suggests that anti-hepatitis C virus agents can be used as alternative in treatments against the Zika virus. This work aims to determine a non-nucleoside analogue antivirals that can be considered possible antivirals against Zika virus. In this study, we used computational methods to analyze the Docking and the modeling of the NS5 polymerase of Zika virus and antivirals.

Keywords: Bioinformatics · Zika virus · Antivirals

1 Introduction

The Zika virus (ZIKV) is a pathogen, which is part of the *Flaviviridae* family and is transmitted by mosquitoes, similar to other viruses, such as yellow fever virus (YFV), dengue virus (DENV), West Nile virus (WNV), and Japanese encephalitis (JEV) [2,19]. This virus comes from Uganda, specifically from the Zika forest and was initially identified in 1947, when the Rhesus Macaque monkeys with suspected yellow fever were studied at the Forest Research Institute-Uganda. The presence of the virus in humans, considered initially an occasional host, was confirmed through serological studies in 1952 and it was not until 1968 when the virus was isolated from a patient in Nigeria [5,7].

In America, Zika epidemics occurred from 2015 to 2016, when the World Health Organization (WHO) declared it a public health emergency of international interest. The great epidemic outbreak occurred in Brazil and then quickly spread to other countries in the South American region [2].

© Springer Nature Switzerland AG 2019
H. Florez et al. (Eds.): ICAI 2019, CCIS 1051, pp. 3–14, 2019.
https://doi.org/10.1007/978-3-030-32475-9_1

Among the emerging diseases of the 21st century, ZIKV disease is among the biggest concerns for public health worldwide. Share the same vector, mosquitoes of the genus *Aedes*, with other arboviruses of particular importance to Public Health in the Americas, such as Dengue and Chikungunya, in addition to the Yellow Fever Urban [18].

Currently, there are no vaccines or drugs with an effective license for the treatment of ZIKV infections. Considering the need to mitigate the morbidities associated with ZIKV, it is necessary to provide antiviral against this virus. Consequently, the aim of this work is to determine *in silico* possible drugs with an effective license for the hepatitis C virus as possible drugs for the treatment of Zika infection.

The structure of the paper is as follows: Sect. 2 provides a background related to Zika virus, Sect. 3 presents the related work, Sect. 4 presents the materials and methods used in this research, Sect. 5 reports our results, and Sect. 6 presents the conclusions.

2   Background

2.1   History

No cases of ZIKV were detected for almost 70 years. From October 2013 to March 2014 a major epidemic occurred in French Polynesia, then, during 2014 it was introduced in Brazil from the Pacific Islands [8]. In 2015, Brazil reported an epidemic of ZIKV in the northeast. From this moment, the epidemic was spread very fast to other areas and also it was spread to almost all countries in South America. More than 300,000 cases were confirmed based on laboratory results; however, it is estimated that much more cases occurred because only 15% of cases have symptoms [22].

Its main reservoirs are monkeys and humans, however, serological studies have shown that it could infect other mammals such as rodents, elephants and cats [16]. Its main vector are female mosquitoes of the genus *Aedes* (*Ae.*). The most common being *Ae. Aegypti* and *Ae. Albopictus*, the latter of special interest due to its anthropomorphic habits and high adaptability to them (humans); the vector competence that is associated to the capacity of the virus to multiply to high viral titers within the vector, and the effectiveness of the vector to transfer during the phage process, which makes them a very efficient vector in the transmission of febrile diseases [16].

2.2   Zika Virus

The ZIKV is a particular about 50 nm, which contains (a) an internal nucleocapsid that presents an icosahedral symmetry composed of a positive chain genomic RNA and several copies of the viral capsid protein (C) and (b) the lipid bilayer derived from the host cell external that contains 180 copies of each of two proteins: the viral membrane (M, a cleavage product of the prM protein) and the envelope protein (E) [14].

The genome has a length of 10,794 kb, consisting of positive-sense single-stranded RNA. It is composed by two non-coding regions (5 and 3 NCR) and a single open reading frame (ORF), which together encodes a polyprotein. Furthermore, it is divided into three structural proteins such as capsid (C), envelope (E), membrane precursor (prM) and seven non-structural proteins (NS) [24].

2.3 Pathology

In most cases, infections are asymptomatic or lightly symptomatic. Most of the described symptoms include fever, arthralgia, rash, fatigue, myalgia, conjunctivitis and headache. In humans, the evolution since the bite of the mosquito occurs until the outbreak is between 3 to 12 days [23]. More than 90% of patients present an outbreak of maculopapular eruptions; thus, this symptom allows describing infection by ZIKV [11]. Only about 18 % of the reported cases of ZIKV infections were recorded as symptomatic [26].

2.4 Transmission

ZIKV is mainly transmitted to humans through the bite of infected mosquitoes such as: *Aedes* and *Aedes aegypti*. *Aedes* mosquitoes usually bite during the day, and they also are able to transmit dengue, chikungunya fever and yellow fever [30]. Zika has been detected for prolonged periods in semen and documented cases of sexual transmission are increasing. Intrauterine/perinatal transmission also occurs. In theory, the Zika virus could also be contracted from infected breast milk or organ/tissue transplants [13].

2.5 Treatment

Usually, Zika virus is relatively light and thus, it does not required a specific treatment. Infected patients just need to rest, drink a lot of liquids and take medications against fever. If the patients continues with the symptoms, they must consult the doctor [18], although microcephaly associated with ZIKV and GBS emphasize that antiviral interventions are urgent [25].

An effective vaccine for ZIKV is not yet available, although about 40 candidate vaccines against ZIKV are in the process of being developed. Five of them are close to entering, in the phase I of clinical trials, which evaluates the safety of the vaccine and its effectiveness to produce an immune response [18].

Currently, drug reuse studies have been implemented, where they evaluate the efficacy of medications approved by the Food and Drug Administration (FDA) for antiviral activity against ZIKV infection. Therefore, the systematic screening of drugs approved by the FDA may reveal new agents to treat the infection by ZIKV [1].

The ZIKV structure is very similar to other flaviviruses. Specially, it is similar to the hepatitis C virus (HCV) [25]. Then, it represents an advance in the possible development of treatments against the ZIKV, considered by the WHO as a health emergency. The structure of the ZIKV provides potential regions for a therapeutic treatment, which could be used to evaluate an antiviral [25].

It has been hypothesized that ZIKV uses the NS5 non-structural protein or enzyme RNA-dependent RNA polymerase (RdRp), together with cofactors, to replicate, maintain and express its RNA genome [3].

The predicted three-dimensional structure and the amino acids of the NS5 protein of the ZIKV indicate that the NS5B protein (RdRp enzyme) of HCV shares many residues in common, particularly at the active site, with the NS5 protein of the ZIKV. Therefore, it is possible that certain nucleoside analogues (NA) and non-nucleoside analogues (NNA) that inhibit HCV NS5B protein may have inhibitory potency against ZIKV.

2.6   Antivirals

An antiviral is a type of drug used to treat infections caused by viruses. Viruses, unlike bacteria and other microorganisms, use the biosynthetic machinery of the cell they infect to replicate. Due to this intimate relationship with the host cell they have fewer targets of their own that allow the selective action of a drug. That is why just from the exhaustive study of the mechanisms of viral replication and the recognition of exclusive steps of these agents, antiviral drugs have acquired great interest [32]. The development of new, more effective drugs has been achieved, with fewer side effects, and specifically directed against virus proteins, called direct action antivirals (DAAS) [12].

2.7   Mechanism of Action of Antivirals

To understand the mechanism of action of antivirals, it is necessary to know the complete life cycle of a virus, which comprises 5 steps or stages (adhesion, penetration-loss of the coating, duplication of the genome and viral proteins, assembly and release). Knowledge of these stages has provided scientists with a potential target for antiviral drugs. Each step of the life cycle of a virus is a potential target for inhibitory molecules It should be noted that between these target proteins there are two types, depending on whether they are structural proteins (involved in adhesion) or non-structural proteins (enzymes involved in the multiplication) [21].

Non-nucleoside analogue antivirals act by blocking the enzyme from initiation, through the inhibition of a conformational change necessary to proceed with the elongation of nascent RNA, that is, they bind to less conserved sites outside the active center (allosteric sites), inhibiting the catalytic efficiency of the active center [15].

3   Related Work

Currently, there are some studies that aim to find antiviral molecules. Those studies have been focused on essential enzymes in the infection process.

It is done by two processes: (a) the indirect or direct inhibition of their biological functions or (b) the block of the viral replication [17].

One of the most used targets that is employed for this purpose is the NS2B/NS3 protease and NS5 RNA-dependent RNA polymerase [33]. In addition, flavivirus proteins such as NS2B/NS3 and NS5 have been found essential for viral infectivity and replication.

Some studies are based on a structure-based approach that targets the ZIKV RNA-dependent RNA polymerase (RdRp), which is conducted *in silico* screening of a library of 100,000 small molecules and tested the top ten lead compounds for their ability to inhibit the virus replication in cell-based *in vitro* assays. [20].

Others studies are focused to find the ability of antiviral drugs in preventing vertical transmission of ZIKV in the mouse model by using a well-established flaviviral inhibitor NITD008, an adenosine analog, that has been shown to inhibit the replication by directly inhibiting the RNA-dependent RNA polymerase activity through chain-termination [34], and also shown to reduce viremia in mice infected with ZIKV.

There are many emerging and re-emerging globally prevalent viruses for which there are no licensed vaccines or antiviral medicines. Arbidol (ARB, umifenovir), used clinically for decades in several countries as an anti-infuenza virus drug, inhibits many other viruses. Thus, ARB, was demonstrated by some researchers, which is a broadly acting anti-viral agent with a well-established safety profile, inhibits ZIKV, likely by blocking viral entry. [9]

Therefore, it is currently being studied, not only in the Zika virus, but also in other viruses of the Flavivirus genus such as dengue virus. The purpose of discovering small molecule inhibitors that are suitable as treatment options for the disease.

4   Materials and Methods

According to the literature, the antivirals used for the treatment of HCV that present in their attributes, ideal characteristics for treatment of ZIKV, are those that inhibit the NS5B polymerase of HCV [10]. This enzyme it is essential for HCV replication, since it catalyzes the synthesis of RNA complementary negative chain and subsequent genomic RNA strand positive. The main applicants for ZIKV can probably be established using HCV inhibitors, since NS5B polymerase of HCV [27–29], particularly at the active site, it shares a lot of waste in common with the ZIKV NS5 polymerase, and the structures presented can provide opportunities for intervention strategies to treat ZIKV. For this work, we used the following two antivirals: Dasabuvir and Nesbuvir. These antivirals have possible activity in Zika. In addition, they are used for the treatment of hepatitis C virus. Furthermore, they present in their attributes, ideal characteristics for the treatment of Zika, low toxicity, and potential action against the virus protein. The three-dimensional structures of the possible antivirals proposed were obtained from the DrugBank[1] database.

---

[1] https://www.drugbank.ca/.

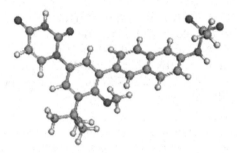

Fig. 1. Dasabuvir molecular structure

Figure 1 presents the Dasabuvir molecular structure that has chemical notation $C_{26}H_{27}N_3O_5S$ with molecular wheight 493.58 [g/mol]. Dasabuvir is a competitive inhibitor of HCV polymerase and inhibits the extension of the RNA chain after incorporation into the RNA of the nascent HCV.

Figure 2 presents the Nesbubir molecular structure that has chemical notation $C_{22}H_{23}FN_{2O5}S$ with molecular weight 446.492 [g/mol]. Nesbuvir joins the pocket of HCV NS5B polymerase palm II site and inhibits the replication of viral genome.

Moreover, we used a docking analysis of ZIKV protein with three-dimensional structure resolved with antiviral. The antivirals proposed were evaluated *in vitro*, by bioinformatics prediction of anti-ZIKV activity. Molecular Docking (computational method) *AutoDock Tools Version* 1.5.6 [31] were use to analyze drug-target interactions (antiviral in interaction with Zika NS5 protein).

Antivirals were represented with the three-dimensional structure of the NS5 protein of the ZIKV using the software *PyMOL Molecular Graphics System*[2], which is an appropriate molecular viewer to produce 3D images of biological molecules, such as proteins, which allows the visualization of multiple conformations.

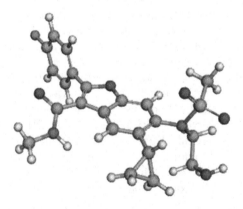

Fig. 2. Nesbuvir molecular structure.

---

[2] https://pymol.org/2/.

The NS5 protein of the ZIKV, extracted from the Protein DataBank (PDB) database from the corresponding identity code (5U04)[3] was used as the working structure.

5 Results

5.1 Molecular Docking Analysis

The NS5 protein of ZIKV was determined *in silico* with the corresponding ligands, i.e., the antivirals: Dasabuvir and Nesbuvir.

A 3D model of the NS5 protein of the ZIKV was created. It was represented by tapes and according to the subdomains were colored as follows:

- blue: the domain corresponding to the thumb
- green: the domain of the fingers
- yellow: the domain corresponding to the palm

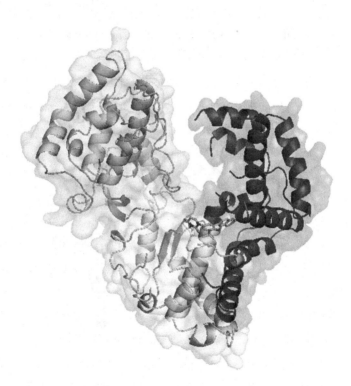

Fig. 3. Three dimensional structure of the Protein NS5 of the ZIKV with the antiviral Dasabuvir. (Color figure online)

---

[3] https://www.rcsb.org.

Fig. 4. Tridimensional view of the docking and interacting of antiviral Dasabuvir in the binding site cavity of zika virus NS5 polymerase. (Color figure online)

In the molecular coupling analysis of the NS5 polymerase of ZIKV and Dasabuvir, the antiviral was located towards the interior of the active site of the NS5 polymerase of the ZIKV. Figure 3 presents the three dimensional structure of the Protein NS5 of the ZIKV with the antiviral Dasabuvir, while Fig. 4 presents the molecular docking of the three dimensional structure of the Protein NS5 of the ZIKV with the antiviral Dasabuvir.

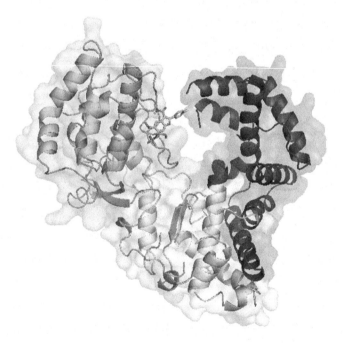

Fig. 5. Three dimensional structure of the Protein NS5 of the ZIKV with the antiviral Nesbuvir. (Color figure online)

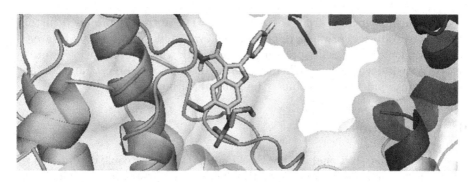

Fig. 6. Tridimensional view of the docking and interacting of antiviral Nesbuvir in the binding site cavity of zika virus NS5 polymerase. (Color figure online)

Finally, the antiviral Nesbuvir was located in the region furthest from the active site (palm) of the NS5 polymerase of ZIKV Fig. 5 presents the three dimensional structure of the Protein NS5 of the ZIKV with the antiviral Nesbuvir, while Fig. 6 the molecular docking of the three dimensional structure of the Protein NS5 of the ZIKV with the antiviral Nesbuvir.

Consequently, the gene coding for RNA polymerase in the *Flaviviridae* family shows the highest degree of conservation. Then, new therapeutic alternatives against hepatitis C virus, especially those that targets viral RNA polymerase, might provide a broader spectrum than other members of the *Flaviviridae* family. With this in mind, the antivirals presented in this work were clinically approved in recent years for the therapeutic intervention against HCV infection. Overall, these results enables studying whether the chemical structures of antivirals have anti-ZIKV activity.

In addition, broad-spectrum antivirals, such as ribavirin, interferon, and Favipiravir are harmful to women and pregnant animal models. Nucleoside analogue anti-HCV drugs, Sofosbuvir, and the non-nucleoside analogues, Dasabuvir and Nesbuvir, have not been associated with teratogenicity [25]. Some previous studies have shown that the antimalarial drug chloroquine and the new nucleoside analogs inhibit the replication of ZIKV [4].

Zmurko *et al.* [35] discovered that the 7DMA viral polymerase inhibitor (7-deaza-2'-C-methyladenosine) inhibits the *in vitro* replication of ZIKV. Therefore, 7DMA can be used as a reference comparator compound in future studies.

Eyer *et al.* [6] demonstrated that nucleoside analogues exert activity against ZIKV under *in vitro* conditions. These compounds provide a basis for optimization based on the structure and rational design of effective prodrugs, which will be further tested in rodent models for the treatment of ZIKV infection. In this work, we show *in silico* that anti-HCV drugs, non-nucleoside analogues, as possible therapeutic agents for ZIKV infection.

In our molecular coupling analysis of the NS5 structure of ZIKV, Dasabuvir was located towards the interior of the active site; whereas Nesbuvir was located in a region further away from the active site. The antivirals proposed in this study were evaluated *in silico*, in order to be evaluated *in vitro* in the future.

Consequently, the results presented in this work will help to provide alternatives of antiviral agents for ZIKV infection, could be used to prevent and contain the emerging epidemic and combat the public health crisis.

6   Conclusions

Based on the computational methods used in this studey, we could determined *in silico* a correct chemical interaction of Dasabuvir and Nesbuvir (non-nucleoside analogue), with the active site of the Zika virus NS5 protein, which allows us to conclude that these drugs have an effective license for the treatment of hepatitis C virus, they can have effects on the inhibition of Zika virus replication. Of the two antivirals analyzed, Dasabuvir, could be more effective for the treatment of Zika virus infection because of its location of binding to the active site of the NS5 protein, while Nesbuvir would be less effective, due to its location in close union to the active site of the NS5 protein that could affect its efficacy.

These results would indicate that an antiviral effect against this flavivirus could be achieved, avoiding the side effects of these viral infections such as microcephaly or congenital malformations associated with ZIKV, when they are not treated in time.

Finally, the absence of specific and efficient treatment protocols (there are no vaccines or drugs with an effective license for the treatment of infections) would allow these drugs to be a potential solution to improve treatments for orphaned or neglected diseases, and to mitigate the morbidities associated with ZIKV. This would imply a progress in the potential treatment against this virus, considered by WHO as a Health emergency and an urgent need.

In this way, antivirals tested in this study are promising to move on to *in vitro* studies and could be use in the future as treatment for ZIKV.

Acknowledgment. Authors are grateful for the support received from Universidad Nacional de Misiones, Posadas (Argentina), and the Information Technologies Innovation (ITI) Research Group, Universidad Distrital Francisco Jose de Caldas, Bogota (Colombia).

References

1. Alam, A., Imam, N., Ali, S., Malik, M.Z., Ishrat, R., et al.: Recent trends in ZIKV research: a step away from cure. Biomed. Pharmacother. **91**, 1152–1159 (2017)
2. Calvet, G., et al.: Detection and sequencing of Zika virus from amniotic fluid of fetuses with microcephaly in Brazil: a case study. Lancet Infect. Dis. **16**(6), 653–660 (2016)
3. Cox, B.D., Stanton, R.A., Schinazi, R.F.: Predicting Zika virus structural biology: challenges and opportunities for intervention. Antivir. Chem. Chemother. **24**(3–4), 118–126 (2015)

4. Delvecchio, R., et al.: Chloroquine, an endocytosis blocking agent, inhibits Zika virus infection in different cell models. Viruses **8**(12), 322 (2016)
5. Dick, G., Kitchen, S., Haddow, A., et al.: Zika virus (II). Pathogenicity and physical properties. Trans. R. Soc. Trop. Med. Hyg. **46**(5), 521–534 (1952)
6. Eyer, L., et al.: Nucleoside inhibitors of Zika virus. J. Infect. Dis. **214**(5), 707–711 (2016)
7. Fagbami, A.: Zika virus infections in Nigeria: virological and seroepidemiological investigations in Oyo state. Epidemiol. Infect. **83**(2), 213–219 (1979)
8. Fauci, A.S., Morens, D.M.: Zika virus in the Americas–yet another arbovirus threat. N. Engl. J. Med. **374**(7), 601–604 (2016)
9. Fink, S.L., et al.: The antiviral drug arbidol inhibits Zika virus. Sci. Rep. **8**(1), 8989 (2018)
10. Florez, H., Salvatierra, K.: Bioinformatics study of mutations of resistance to antivirals in the NS5A gen of HCV. Int. Inf. Inst. (Tokyo) Inf. **20**(9), 6665–6672 (2017)
11. Hamel, R., et al.: Zika virus: epidemiology, clinical features and host-virus interactions. Microbes Infect. **18**(7–8), 441–449 (2016)
12. Kieffer, T.L., Kwong, A.D., Picchio, G.R.: Viral resistance to specifically targeted antiviral therapies for hepatitis C (STAT-Cs). J. Antimicrob. Chemother. **65**(2), 202–212 (2009)
13. Koenig, K.L., Almadhyan, A., Burns, M.J.: Identify-isolate-inform: a tool for initial detection and management of Zika virus patients in the emergency department. West. J. Emerg. Med. **17**(3), 238 (2016)
14. Kostyuchenko, V.A., et al.: Structure of the thermally stable Zika virus. Nature **533**(7603), 425 (2016)
15. Kwong, A.D., McNair, L., Jacobson, I., George, S.: Recent progress in the development of selected hepatitis C virus NS3.4A protease and NS5B polymerase inhibitors. Curr. Opin. Pharmacol. **8**(5), 522–531 (2008)
16. Li, C., et al.: Zika virus disrupts neural progenitor development and leads to microcephaly in mice. Cell Stem Cell **19**(1), 120–126 (2016)
17. Lou, Z., Sun, Y., Rao, Z.: Current progress in antiviral strategies. Trends Pharmacol. Sci. **35**(2), 86–102 (2014)
18. Organization, W.H., et al.: Zika virus research agenda (2016)
19. Pang, T., Mak, T.K., Gubler, D.J.: Prevention and control of dengue–the light at the end of the tunnel. Lancet Infect. Dis. **17**(3), e79–e87 (2017)
20. Pattnaik, A., et al.: Discovery of a non-nucleoside rna polymerase inhibitor for blocking Zika virus replication through in silico screening. Antivir. Res. **151**, 78–86 (2018)
21. Penié, J.B., González-Piñera, J.G., Rodríguez, M.A.R., Alfonso, P.P.P.: Medicamentos antivirales. Acta Médica **8**(1), 86–100 (1998)
22. Petersen, L.R., Jamieson, D.J., Powers, A.M., Honein, M.A.: Zika virus. N. Engl. J. Med. **374**(16), 1552–1563 (2016)
23. Plourde, A.R., Bloch, E.M.: A literature review of Zika virus. Emerg. Infect. Dis. **22**(7), 1185 (2016)
24. Rather, I.A., Lone, J.B., Bajpai, V.K., Paek, W.K., Lim, J.: Zika virus: an emerging worldwide threat. Front. Microbiol **8**, 1417 (2017)
25. Sacramento, C.Q., et al.: The clinically approved antiviral drug sofosbuvir impairs Brazilian Zika virus replication. BioRxiv, p. 061671 (2016)
26. Saiz, J.C., Vázquez-Calvo, Á., Blázquez, A.B., Merino-Ramos, T., Escribano-Romero, E., Martín-Acebes, M.A.: Zika virus: the latest newcomer. Front. Microbiol. **7**, 496 (2016)

27. Salvatierra, K., Florez, H.: Analysis of hepatitis C virus in hemodialysis patients. Infectio **20**(3), 130–137 (2016)
28. Salvatierra, K., Florez, H.: Biomedical mutation analysis (BMA): a software tool for analyzing mutations associated with antiviral resistance. F1000Research **5**, 1141 (2016)
29. Salvatierra, K., Florez, H.: Prevalence of hepatitis B and C infections in hemodialysis patients. F1000Research **5**, 1–6 (2016)
30. Song, B.H., Yun, S.I., Woolley, M., Lee, Y.M.: Zika virus: history, epidemiology, transmission, and clinical presentation. J. Neuroimmunol. **308**, 50–64 (2017)
31. Trott, O., Olson, A.J.: Autodock vina: improving the speed and accuracy of docking with a new scoring function, efficient optimization, and multithreading. J. Comput. Chem. **31**(2), 455–461 (2010)
32. Tuset, M., José, M., Del Cacho, E., Alberdi, A., Codina, C., Ribas, J., et al.: Características de los fármacos antivirales. Enfermedades infecciosas y microbiologia clinica **21**(8), 433–458 (2003)
33. Yang, C.C., et al.: A novel dengue virus inhibitor, BP13944, discovered by high-throughput screening with dengue virus replicon cells selects for resistance in the viral NS2B/NS3 protease. Antimicrob. Agents Chemother. **58**(1), 110–119 (2014)
34. Yin, Z., et al.: An adenosine nucleoside inhibitor of dengue virus. Proc. Natl. Acad. Sci. **106**(48), 20435–20439 (2009)
35. Zmurko, J., Marques, R.E., Schols, D., Verbeken, E., Kaptein, S.J., Neyts, J.: The viral polymerase inhibitor 7-deaza-2'-c-methyladenosine is a potent inhibitor of in vitro Zika virus replication and delays disease progression in a robust mouse infection model. PLoS Negl. Trop. Dis. **10**(5), e0004695 (2016)

Data Analysis

Academic Behavior Analysis in Virtual Courses Using a Data Mining Approach

Dario Delgado-Quintero[1], Olmer Garcia-Bedoya[2]([⊠]) [iD], Diego Aranda-Lozano[1],
Pablo Munevar-Garcia[1] [iD], and Cesar O. Diaz[3] [iD]

[1] Universidad Nacional Abierta y a Distancia, Bogota, Colombia
[2] Universidad de Bogota Jorge Tadeo Lozano, Bogota, Colombia
olmer.garciab@utadeo.edu.co
[3] OCOX AI, Bogota, Colombia
cdiaz@ocox-ai.co

Abstract. Virtual education is one of the educational trends of the 21st century; however knowing the perception of students is a new challenge. This article presents a proposal to define the essential components for the construction of a model for the analysis of the records given by the students enrolled in courses in a virtual learning platform (VLE). The article after a review of the use of data analytics in VLE presents a strategy to characterize the data generated by the student according to the frequency and the slice of the day and week that access the material. With these metrics, clustering analysis is performed and visualized through a map of self-organized Neural Networks. The results presented correspond to five courses of a postgraduate career, where was found that students have greater participation in the forums in the daytime than in the nighttime. Also, they participate more during the week than weekends. These results open the possibility to identify possible early behaviors, which let to implement tools to prevent future desertions or possible low academic performance.

Keywords: Learning management systems · Educational data mining · SOM Networks · Virtual education

1 Introduction

The impact of data mining in the industry is increasingly evident, the proper management of organizational data and how to learn to identify the beneficial information for organizations and turn it into beneficial information for commercial purposes is one of the pillars of its success [6]. Like the other sectors of the industry where data mining has been gaining strength, the educational sector has not been the exception, both in terms of data mining for educational environments, as a research topic or as an innovative factor in the research segment. And also, as an investment in administrative terms, because big data and

Supported partially by Colciencias.

analytics remain top priority for CIOs, due to the return of the invention (ROI) in this kind of projects [9,22].

Educational data mining (EDM) [7] describes the process of converting raw information from a platform or educational system to be used as a knowledge asset for educational entities. EDM seeks to generate value from the information they can gather from the interaction of their students or teachers with their systems. This paper seeks to address the concept of EDM in e-learning platforms, and how data from the interaction records of students or tutors in these platforms can be used to define tools or policies that directly impact the retention and permanence. In traditional learning environments, teachers can obtain feedback of learning through direct interaction with students, enabling a continuous evaluation by teachers [21]. The interaction and observation of students' behavior in the classrooms, as well as the analysis of the history of the courses, give data to estimate appropriate pedagogical strategy to apply in the classroom. However, for work with students in virtual learning environments, this monitoring is more complicated. Tutors should look for other sources than direct observation for audit the learning process of students in the virtual classroom. One of these options is the Web platforms used by educational institutions, which collect large amounts of information automatically from the interaction with their educational systems. The data that these tools collect, after some EDM, can provide multiple dimensions of student behavior to teachers and the institution.

This paper presents a data analytic exercise with the registers (LOGS) coming from a virtual learning platform for higher education programs in virtual mode as an input for the definition of retention and permanence policies. Article is structured as follows: start with the description of the methodology implemented, followed by the exploration and use of data for the recognition of records from educational platforms, and finally the contextualization and use of the same in the definition of student retention and permanence policies.

2 Previous Work

Virtual learning environment (VLEs) or course management systems (CMS) are part of modern pedagogical approaches. These platforms host information about the interaction of the users with these. According to [8,14,23], this information has the potential to improve pedagogical approaches. From this premise, it is found multiple interrelated approaches that seek to exploit the registers or LOGs. In Table 1 is presented different approaches for the analysis of logs in virtual learning environments.

For this particular work, there is special interest in the analysis of the behavior of students and tutors in the VLEs. Taking into account the works related to this topic, Table 2 presents multiple approaches or algorithms centered in different dimensions of student behavior in virtual platforms.

Table 1. Approaches for the analysis of logs in virtual learning environments

Subject	Description	References
Improve the experience in e-learning	Use the Logs of VLEs to identify best practices or policies that allow improving the user experience in these	[3, 12, 20]
Visualization	Log visualization schemes for monitoring and understanding virtual classrooms interactions	[13, 16, 18]
EDM for performance improvement in VLEs	Data mining approaches that allow students to improve academic performance in VLEs	[4, 5, 8, 23, 25]
Platform behavior analysis	Pattern analysis approaches for the analysis of the behavior of students and tutors in VLEs	[1, 2, 10, 14, 15, 17, 19, 24, 25]

Table 2. Mining techniques for the analysis of logs for behavior analysis.

Mining techniques	Algorithm	Description	References
Association rules	Apriori	Find rules of association between behaviors and patterns of records	[14]
Classification	Decision tree, Support vector machines (SVM), NaiveBayes, NearesNeighbours	Design functions to determine the membership of certain classes from patterns in the registers	[14, 25]
Clustering	K-means, Elbow Algorithm, Fuzzy C-Means Clustering	Determine patterns of association between the records of different students	[1, 2, 14, 24]
Process Mining	Heuristic Miner, Fuzzy Miner	Discover underlying processes in event logs	[19]
Intent mining	Viterbi Algorithm, Baum-Welch Algorithm	Model the processes according to the purpose of the actors	[19]
Mining of sequential patterns	Generalized Sequential Patterns (GSP), Sequential Pattern Mining (SPAM), Sequential Pattern Mining Consider, probabilistic models	Find common patterns among the data samples where the values are delivered in a sequence	[15, 17, 19]
Graph mining	Branch-and-bound, On-line Plan Recognition, Recursive Matrix (R- MAT)	Extract patterns (sub-graphics) of interest from the graphs describing the underlying data	[19]

3   Methodology

In this work we seek to develop an approach to identify student behaviors in virtual mode for an academic program using the registers (LOGS) left by them in the virtual learning platforms. The general approach of this work can be summarized by Fig. 1, where:

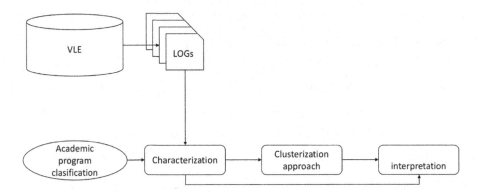

Fig. 1. Academic behavior analysis in academic programs

- Extraction: From the VLE databases a representative sample of the students enrolled in the different courses of an academic program is taken. From these students, once they have finished the courses, their LOGs of interaction with the platforms and their notes are extracted.
- Data Characterization: Once the logs extracted from a sample of students enrolled in an academic program, these records are transformed by formulating metrics related to their behavior that are easily associated with their academic behavior.
- Clustering: Once a database of coded information from the sample drawn from an academic program has been consolidated, an unsupervised clustering algorithm is used to identify the latent behavior patterns in the data sample.
- Analysis and interpretation: The information related to the academic performance of the extracted sample is used to label the different groups identified with the clustering algorithms.

3.1   Data Characterization

In a virtual learning platform (Course Management System - CMS), A log is a sequential file with temporal records associated with all events in an academic course product of the student's interactions with the CMS. For finalized courses, we can obtain a set of records of the students and tutors behavior in an specific configuration of the CMS.

For this work, the CMS configuration is defined as following. The set of activities, $A = \{a_1, a_2, ..., a_n\}$ where n is the number of activities, to performing during a specific course. The set of forums $F = \{f_1, f_2, ..., f_n\}$ defined for each activity, the agenda (interval time) $T = \{[t_1, t_2], [t_3, t_4], ..., [t_{(n-k)}, t_n]\}$ defined for each activity, the evaluative weight $P = \{p_1, p_2, ..., p_n\}$ for each activity where $\sum_{i=1}^{n} p_i = 500$, the course materials, $M = \{m_1, m_2, ..., m_w\}$ where w is the number of folders (folders with books, articles, videos, etc.). The students enrolled in the course, $E = \{e_1, e_2, ..., e_m\}$ where m is the number of students, and the academic ponderation $N = \{n_1, n_2, ..., n_m\}$ for each student. According to the CMS configuration, a course is defined as the function $C(A, F, T, P, M, E) \to N$.

The Logs list $L = \{l_1, l_2, ..., l_m\} \in C$ for each student where $l_i = \{f_i, u_i, ua_i, ec_i, c_i, en_i, o_i, ip_i\} \in e_i$ contains the temporal records of each student, see Table 3.

Table 3. Log structure

Component	Description
f_i	LOG date and time
u_i	User name
ua_i	Interaction with the user
ec_i	Event context
c_i	Course component accessed
en_i	Event name
o_i	Access origin (mobile, web)
ip_i	IP address

Standard logs representation is not enough to contextualize this information in academic terms [3,13]. To transform the logs into academic relevant information we realize a characterization process in order to measure a set of variables that allows realize an academic interpretation of the behavior of students and tutors in the CMS. We propose a set of variables measured using the logs $l_i \in e_i$ for each student, see Table 4.

In a first approximation, $\forall e_i \in E$ we can characterize each student as $g(l_i) \to x_i \mid x_i = \{Tp_i, Tt_i, Ef_i, Er_i, Dp_i, De_i, Vm_i, Nl_i, Ls_i, Lf_i, Ld_i, Ln_i, Pa_i, Fa_i\}$. However, this characterization need a special encoding to approach multiple courses particularities.

3.2 Clustering

Let Σ the database of information encoded for an academic program, define the function $F(\Sigma) \to W$ where $W = [c_1, c_2, ..., c_h]$ are the different types of behavior that students adopt in the CMS. Assuming that it is not known a priori what

Table 4. Logs characterization for each student

Variable	Description
Tp	Total time spent by student in the CMS
Tt	Average time spent by a student in an activity
Ef	Average posts in forums for each student
Dp	Average time (days) spend by each student to participate in an activity
De	Average time (days) spend by each student to send the activity products
Vm	Number of visits to the course materials
Nl	Number of logs generated by the student
Ls	Number of weekday generated logs
Lf	Number of weekend generated logs
Ld	Number of diurnal generated logs
Ln	Number of nocturnal generated logs
Pa	IP ratio
Fa	Access frequency

types of behavior exist, the problem is to classify or segment the behavior inside the virtual courses. Therefore, the type of function proposed is an unsupervised grouping algorithm [26], specifically for this work, the Self-organizing map (SOM) networks proposed by Kohonen [11] following by a hierarchical clustering are used.

SOM networks are an algorithm based on unsupervised neural networks. The main functionality of the SOM networks is their ability to project nonlinear data with high dimensionality in a regular grid of low dimensionality (usually in 2D). The algorithm look for points that are near each other in the input space to be transformed to nearby map units in the SOM.

For our particular case of study, each information element is the vectors, $X_i \in \Sigma$, where each of its components is a variable with a defined meaning. The grid generated by the SOM network can be used as a basis on which vectors with similar characteristics can be projected using a color-based coding, and based on these generated groupings, explain the possible types of behaviors that can be found in virtual courses.

For our study, this topological mapping consists of projecting a set of vectors X k-dimensional in a two-dimensional discrete mesh (2-D) of M positions, see Fig. 2. Each position in the output is characterized by a node $h_j (j = 1, 2, ..., M)$. For each h_i node, a position in the output space is associated by $\boldsymbol{w}$, which is obtained through an optimization process, which reduce the distance between all the inputs and the output in the new space of M positions.

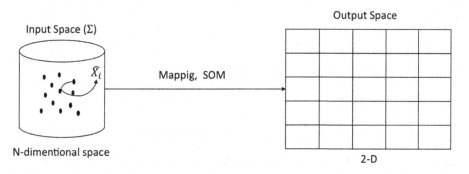

Fig. 2. The SOM mapping pass from a high-dimensional space into a 2-D space.

Starting from the database $\Sigma_{14+(w-1),E}$ (input space), where $14 + (w - 1)$ is the number of characteristics, w the number of classifications within an academic program and E the number of students that have been used to create the database. In Fig. 3 is observed that although the student condition is the same for any sub-classification within an academic program, it is assumed that their behavior may vary depending on the type of subject they are studying.

$\{tp_i, Tt_i, ... Fa_i\}$	0	0	... .	0	0
$\{tp_i, Tt_i, ... Fa_i\}$	0	0	... .	0	0
... .	... .	... .	... .	... .	... .
0	$\{tp_i, Tt_i, ... Fa_i\}$	0	... .	0	0
0	$\{tp_i, Tt_i, ... Fa_i\}$	0	... .	0	0
... .	... .		... .	... .	... .
0	0	$\{tp_i, Tt_i, ... Fa_i\}$	... .	0	0
0	0	$\{tp_i, Tt_i, ... Fa_i\}$	... .	0	0
... .	... .	... .	... .	... .	... .
0	0	0	... .		$\{tp_i, Tt_i, ... Fa_i\}$
0	0	0	... .	0	$\{tp_i, Tt_i, ... Fa_i\}$

Group 1, Group 2, Group 3, ..., Group w

Fig. 3. Input space configuration.

What in terms of the clustering algorithm, will be introduced w primary clusters to which they are looking to perform an additional subcluster, see Fig. 4. To perform this clustering Hierarchical clustering, is used, which is an algorithm that groups similar objects into groups called clusters. The endpoint is a set of clusters, where each one is distinct from the others, and the objects within each cluster are broadly similar.

4   Results

The information of the LOGS and the notes of a semester in five courses of a virtual postgraduate offered by the university was used. The 14 variables already described (Table 4 and N) were obtained, and the students with NaN values in any variable were eliminated. After this preprocessing, the results proposed here are based on a total of 175 students.

Visual Analytics is usually the best way to understand the results of data analytics compared with descriptives techniques, since it facilitates to identify relations between the information. The first exploration, presented in Fig. 5, explore the distribution of the each variable through the diagonal of image table. The distribution of all variables are spread over all the range of data, but some variables can be approximated to some probabilistic distributions. Also, the relation between all the variables of vector X is presented, where it is possible o view some correlation between the variables like is presented in the Fig. 6.

Then, the next step was to obtain a SOM network of dimension five by five. Over this SOM Network the process of grouping, using hierarchical clustering, was done, which allows combining the nodes that are similar and that are side by side in the SOM grid. The results of the grouping with three groups are presented in Fig. 7. To analyze the behavior of each variable, Fig. 9 presents heat maps of the inputs, in which it is possible to analyze the relationship between the clusters and the ranges of the data. Finally, the Fig. 8 presents the histogram of the variable N for each cluster. Both the blue and the green cluster are made up of students with low and medium academic performance, respectively, and are characterized by having little participation in the forums (Ef), low frequency of

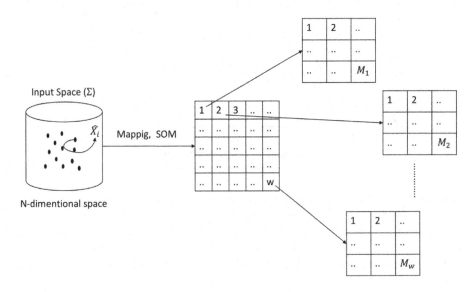

Fig. 4. Clusterization scheme.

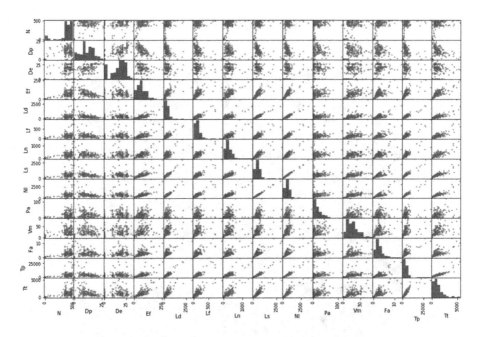

Fig. 5. SOM network 5×5 with cluster using hierarchical clustering of three. (Color figure online)

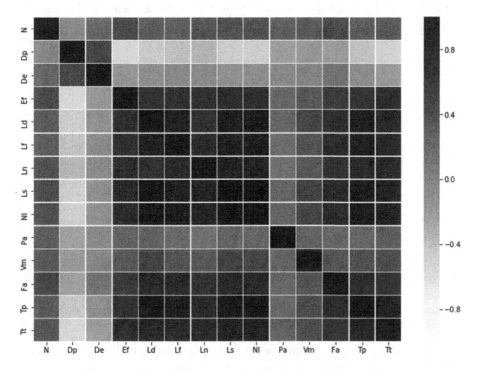

Fig. 6. Correlation of the input data x.

Clusters

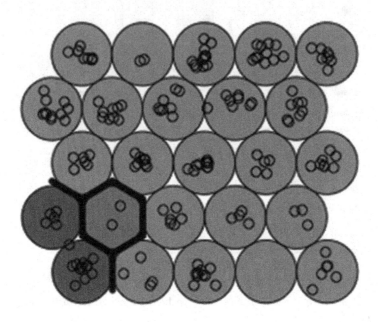

Fig. 7. SOM network 5 × 5 with cluster using hierarchical clustering of three.

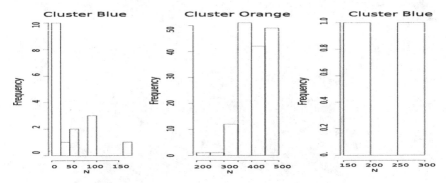

Fig. 8. Histogram of variable Notes (N) for the three clusters.

access (Fa) and little access to the course material (Vm). Otherwise, it happens in the orange cluster, made up of students with the best grades in their majority.

This procedure was repeated for a different number of groups as well as different input variables, which allowed to obtain the following results:

– In the clusters there is a differentiation in a shorter time of participation in the forums (Dp); likewise, there is a more significant number of contributions

between the groups. Regarding the number of logs generated during the week and the frequency of access, certain groups are more abundant.
- Students with low grades, where the total is less than 250 are mainly those who do not participate as much in the activities as in the deliveries and represent 10% of the sample.

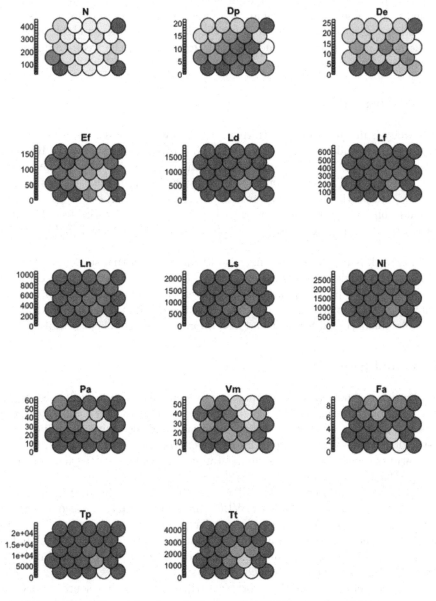

Fig. 9. Heat Maps of each variable over the SOM network architecture.

- The time it takes a student to make the deliveries (Of), as well as the participation in the forums (Dp) does not have an impact on the notes.
- Few contributions in the forums (Ef) and low frequency of access (Fa) to the platform is positively correlated with better grades.
- The variables Ln, Ld, Ls, Lf, Vm, Tt_{min}, Tp_{min}, Nl, and Pa have a weak correlation with the notes.
- Students have greater participation in the forums in the daytime than in the nighttime. Also, they participate more during the week than weekends.
- Students participate about 55% on the day versus 45% at night; however, there is a 76% participation in the platform during the week compared to 24% on the weekend.

5 Discussion

Logs analysis in educational platforms is not a new issue. Even, in terms of characterizing the students' behavior in this kind of technological tools. Research papers as shown in Tables 1 and 2 afford similar approaches like this one. However, the principal contribution of this study is the application of this kind of analysis in a particular population with a socio-economical, cultural, geographical and political environment, in order to afford in future works, use this information to define policies, design new interfaces for technological tools, between others.

This work is framed in the analysis of Colombian virtual students behavior. principally, to understanding how to prevent desertion in virtual high education programs. In this project phase, the characterization approach, and the mining tool was defined, in order to in a future phase use this information to understand the Colombian virtual Student and also improve the technological tools.

6 Conclusion

Teaching or coaching tasks in virtual environments imply new challenges in pedagogy. Virtual Learning environments provide useful tools for the interaction between students, teachers, learning materials, and also with the educational institutions. However, it creates barriers between the players participating in the learning process, such as the understanding of students or teachers behavior beyond the actions in the virtual platforms.

Mathematical approaches that allow continuous monitoring of student behavior according to the logs analysis in VLE, can help to define educational policies in order to take preventive actions in order to reduce the desertion. This also suggests the need to design involving a greater number of variables related to the behavior of the teacher and whose purpose is focused on determining how they affect the performance of their students.

In the development of this work, we will include a representative sample to the analysis of a complete higher educational institution, and also include socioeconomic and geographic information concerning understand particularities of virtual students. Whit this information we want to develop a support tool to aid policies makers to plane in order to reduce desertion and increase the quality of service.

References

1. Alias, U.F., Ahmad, N.B., Hasan, S.: Mining of E-learning behavior using SOM clustering. In: 6th ICT International Student Project Conference: Elevating Community Through ICT, ICT-ISPC 2017, pp. 1–4 (2017). https://doi.org/10.1109/ICT-ISPC.2017.8075350
2. Bara, M.W., Ahmad, N.B., Modu, M.M., Ali, H.A.: Self-organizing map clustering method for the analysis of e-learning activities. In: 2018 Majan International Conference (MIC), pp. 1–5, March 2018. https://doi.org/10.1109/MINTC.2018.8363155
3. Baruque, C.B., Amaral, M.A., Barcellos, A., da Silva Freitas, J.a.C., Longo, C.J.: Analysing users' access logs in Moodle to improve e learning. In: Proceedings of the 2007 Euro American Conference on Telematics and Information Systems, EATIS 2007, pp. 72:1–72:4. ACM, New York (2007). https://doi.org/10.1145/1352694.1352767
4. Charitopoulos, A., Rangoussi, M., Koulouriotis, D.: Educational data mining and data analysis for optimal learning content management: applied in Moodle for undergraduate engineering studies. In: 2017 IEEE Global Engineering Education Conference (EDUCON), pp. 990–998, April 2017. https://doi.org/10.1109/EDUCON.2017.7942969
5. Conde, M., Garca-Pealvo, F., Fidalgo-Blanco,, Sein-Echaluce, M.: Study of the flexibility of a learning analytics tool to evaluate teamwork competence acquisition in different contexts. In: CEUR workshop Proceedings, vol. 1925, pp. 63–77 (2017). ceur-ws.org/Vol-1925/paper07.pdf. cited By 0
6. Dhingra, S., Chaudhry, K.: A study of the impact of data warehousing and data mining implementation on marketing effort. Int. J. Adv. Stud. Comput. Sci. Eng. 7(1), 13–20 (2018)
7. Elaal, S.: E-learning using data mining. Chin. Egypt. Res. J. Helwan Univ. (2013)
8. Gamie, E.A., El-Seoud, M.S.A., Salama, M.A., Hussein, W.: Pedagogical and elearning logs analyses to enhance students' performance. In: Proceedings of the 7th International Conference on Software and Information Engineering, ICSIE 2018, pp. 116–120. ACM, New York (2018). https://doi.org/10.1145/3220267.3220289. Cited by 0
9. Grover, V., Chiang, R.H., Liang, T.P., Zhang, D.: Creating strategic business value from big data analytics: a research framework. J. Manag. Inf. Syst. 35(2), 388–423 (2018)
10. Hernández-García, Á., Acquila-Natale, E., Iglesías-Pradas, S., Chaparro-Peláez, J.: Design of an extraction, transform and load process for calculation of teamwork indicators in Moodle. In: LASI-SPAIN (2018). ceur-ws.org/Vol-2188/Paper7.pdf
11. Kohonen, T.: The self-organizing map. Proc. IEEE 78(9), 1464–1480 (1990). https://doi.org/10.1109/5.58325

12. Kolekar, S.V., Pai, R.M., Manohara Pai, M.M.: Adaptive user interface for Moodle based E-learning system using learning styles. Procedia Comput. Sci. **135**, 606–615 (2018). https://doi.org/10.1016/j.procs.2018.08.226. The 3rd International Conference on Computer Science and Computational Intelligence (ICCSCI 2018): Empowering Smart Technology in Digital Era for a Better Life

13. Konstantinidis, A., Grafton, C.: Using Excel Macros to Analyse Moodle Logs. UK Research.Moodle.Net, pp. 4–6 (2013). http://research.moodle.net/pluginfile.php/333/mod_data/content/1233/UsingExcelMacrostoAnalyseMoodleLogs.pdf

14. Moreira Félix, I., Ambrósio, A.P., Silva Neves, P., Siqueira, J., Duilio Brancher, J.: Moodle predicta: a data mining tool for student follow up. In: Proceedings of the 9th International Conference on Computer Supported Education 1 (CSEDU), pp. 339–346 (2017). https://doi.org/10.5220/0006318403390346

15. Poon, L.K.M., Kong, S.-C., Wong, M.Y.W., Yau, T.S.H.: Mining sequential patterns of students' access on learning management system. In: Tan, Y., Takagi, H., Shi, Y. (eds.) DMBD 2017. LNCS, vol. 10387, pp. 191–198. Springer, Cham (2017). https://doi.org/10.1007/978-3-319-61845-6_20

16. Poon, L.K.M., Kong, S.-C., Yau, T.S.H., Wong, M., Ling, M.H.: Learning analytics for monitoring students participation online: visualizing navigational patterns on learning management system. In: Cheung, S.K.S., Kwok, L., Ma, W.W.K., Lee, L.-K., Yang, H. (eds.) ICBL 2017. LNCS, vol. 10309, pp. 166–176. Springer, Cham (2017). https://doi.org/10.1007/978-3-319-59360-9_15

17. Qiao, C., Hu, X.: Discovering student behavior patterns from event logs: Preliminary results on a novel probabilistic latent variable model. In: 2018 IEEE 18th International Conference on Advanced Learning Technologies (ICALT), pp. 207–211, July 2018. https://doi.org/10.1109/ICALT.2018.00056

18. Raga, R.C., Raga, J.D.: A comparison of college faculty and student class activity in an online learning environment using course log data. In: 2017 IEEE SmartWorld, Ubiquitous Intelligence Computing, Advanced Trusted Computed, Scalable Computing Communications, Cloud Big Data Computing, Internet of People and Smart City Innovation (SmartWorld/SCALCOM/UIC/ATC/CBDCom/IOP/SCI), pp. 1–6, August 2017. https://doi.org/10.1109/UIC-ATC.2017.8397475

19. Ros, S., Lázaro, J.C., Robles-Gómez, A., Caminero, A.C., Tobarra, L., Pastor, R.: Analyzing content structure and Moodle milestone to classify student learning behavior in a basic desktop tools course. In: Proceedings of the 5th International Conference on Technological Ecosystems for Enhancing Multiculturality, TEEM 2017, pp. 42:1–42:6. ACM, New York (2017). https://doi.org/10.1145/3144826.3145392

20. Porras, J.T., Alcántara-Manzanares, J., García, S.R.: Virtual platforms use: a useful monitoring tool. EDMETIC **7**(1), 242–255 (2018). https://doi.org/10.21071/edmetic.v6i2.8696

21. Sheard, J., Ceddia, J., Hurst, J., Tuovinen, J.: Inferring student learning behaviour from website interactions: a usage analysis. Educ. Inf. Technol. **8**(3), 245–266 (2003). https://doi.org/10.1023/A:1026360026073

22. Shim, J.P., French, A.M., Guo, C., Jablonski, J.: Big data and analytics: issues, solutions, and ROI. CAIS **37**, 39 (2015)

23. Smith, S.M., et al.: How might the development of data mining and log analysis systems for the Moodle virtual learning environment improve computer science students' course engagement and encourage course designers' future engagement with data analysis methods for the evaluation of course resources? Ph.D. thesis, University of Lincoln (2017). http://eprints.lincoln.ac.uk/30882/

24. Vega, A.B.: Mejora en el descubrimiento de modelos de minería de procesos en educación mediante agrupación de datos de interacción con la plataforma Moodle. Ph.D. thesis, Universidad de Córdoba (2018)
25. Verma, A., Rathore, S., Vishwakarma, S., Goswani, S.: Multilevel analysis of students' feedback using Moodle logs in virtual cloud environment. Int. J. Comput. Sci. Inf. Technol. **9**, 15–28 (2017). https://doi.org/10.5281/zenodo.2558650
26. Wu, X., et al.: Top 10 algorithms in data mining. Knowl. Inf. Syst. **14**(1), 1–37 (2008). https://doi.org/10.1007/s10115-007-0114-2

Analysis of Usability of Various Geosocial Network POI in Tourism

Jiří Kysela[(✉)]

Metropolitan University Prague, Dubečská 900/10,
100 31 Praha 10, Czech Republic
jiri.kysela@mup.cz

Abstract. The paper deals with an analysis of information usability of Points of Interest across different geosocial networks in tourism. The analysis contains a comparison of data retrieved from Facebook API, Foursquare API and Google Places API. The data was obtained for tourist areas from the smallest towns up to metropolitan cities. This article tries to verify the hypothesis whether or not geosocial networks provide relevant local information to participants in tourism, at least at the equivalent level currently available from traditional information resources used in tourism. In which case, geosocial networks have a potential to be used as a primary information resources in the commercial sector, specifically in local tourism.

Keywords: Geosocial networks · LBS · POI · Tourism · Facebook · Google places · Foursquare · API

1 Introduction

Geosocial networks are a very important segment of Location Based Services (LBS), providing to their users local information in many areas like social services, transport and navigation, tourist attractions, etc. LBS, including geosocial networks, are key milestones in e-tourism, which can significantly change the shape of tourism thanks to quick availability and complete information provided. As a result, they enable a better supply of tourism products for its participants. For geosocial networks, according to the source (GILL, 2008), the exponential growth of information in their databases is typical. This is because very large numbers of participants, who interact with the building of a common information base with high structure flexibility and target-oriented contributions, are characteristic of virtual communities. As published in the source (BUHALIS and WEBER, 2013), the innovative concept of gamification, which applies gaming principles in the tourism environment, also supports the high level of participant interaction. This paper therefore deals with the quality of the information from the POI in the LBS, specifically geosocial networks, which serve as an information resource for local tourism participants, who in turn, expands these geosocial network databases.

The main goal is realized in the Sect. 3 analysis, which maps the availability and quality of these information sources by analyzing the level of completeness of the POI. The related information is provided by the three most widely-used geosocial networks

H. Florez et al. (Eds.): ICAI 2019, CCIS 1051, pp. 32–42, 2019.
https://doi.org/10.1007/978-3-030-32475-9_3

and their Application Programming Interface, that is Facebook API, Foursquare API and Google+/Google Places API. This analysis will try to find the answer to the main research question: *"Do geosocial networks provide relevant local information to tourism participants at least at the equivalent level currently available from traditional tourist information resources?"*. In the positive case, geosocial networks have a potential to be used as a primary information resource in local tourism. The relevance and redundancy of data provided by these API will be taken into account. For the analysis, the categories of restaurants and bars were chosen as points of interest covering the area of hospitality facilities (restaurants and bars) according to the EU statistical methodology (CESTOVNI-RUCH.cz 2009). In the text, the data will be obtained by retrieving data from API of individual geosocial networks and further by field research in the defined area. The outlined circular area (with a diameter of 300 m) was used to select tourist centers of 12 selected towns and cities (see Sect. 2). The benefit of this realized anal-y-sis is to determine the level of completeness of information on tourism subjects provided by geosocial networks. In addition, the hypothesis that the geosocial networks can be used as the primary source of information for tourism participants can be confirmed, due to the higher information completeness of social networks compared with traditional information sources.

2 Methodology with Definition of Examined Areas and Field Research

The evaluation of the quality of tourist information about the POI from geosocial networks was realized on the basis of data obtained within the defined areas, in the historical centers of the below mentioned towns and metropolitan cities. In all these towns and metropolitan cities, the level of completeness of information from the POI of geosocial networks was examined in comparison with other information sources (traditional information resources used in tourism). Moreover the level of completeness of information of the POI of geosocial networks was compared with the current real number of subjects that was empirically found by field research.

In the following towns and cities, the level of completeness of information in the POI of geosocial networks on existing subjects in tourism was analyzed in Sect. 3. The choice of the towns and cities is not random. The first two largest metropolitan cities have a similar population and are neighbouring cities. All the others were selected within two comparable regions, namely Královéhradecký and Pardubický (whose largest cities are the regional cities of Pardubice and Hradec Králové, each with approximately 90,000 inhabitants). These towns and cities were chosen from each region, if possible, corresponding to the number of inhabitants (according to (CZECH STATISTICAL OFFICE, 2017; STATISTICAL OFFICE OF THE SLOVAK REPUBLIC, 2016)).

- Bratislava (approx. 425 900 inhabitants)
  - WGS84 coordinates N 48.143368, E 17.108105,
- Brno (approx. 378 000 inhabitants)
  - N 49.195281, E 16.607797,

- Hradec Králové (approx. 92 900 inhabitants, region of Hradec Králové)
  - N 50.2092658, E 15.8328122,
- Pardubice (approx. 90 000 inhabitants, region of Pardubice)
  - N 50.0385283, E 15.7789706,
- Jičín (approx. 16 400 inhabitants, region of Hradec Králové)
  - N 50.436798, E 15.351683,
- Ústí nad Orlicí (approx. 14 200 inhabitants, region of Pardubice)
  - N 49.973672, E 16.394211,
- Hořice (approx. 8 600 inhabitants, region of Hradec Králové)
  - N 50.368195, E 15.632314,
- Choceň (approx. 8 700 inhabitants, region of Pardubice)
  - N 50.001131, E 16.223798,
- Opočno (approx. 3 100, region of Hradec Králové)
  - N 50.267805, E 16.114996,
- Jablonné nad Orlicí (approx. 3 100 inhabitants, region of Pardubice)
  - N 50.029914, E 16.600118,
- Železnice (approx. 1 300 inhabitants, region of Hradec Králové)
  - N 50.473177, E 15.384998,
- Brandýs nad Orlicí (approx. 1 300 inhabitants, region of Pardubice)
  - N 50.000686, E 16.286851

Author's own methodology for the examined area under investigation determines that the defined areas have a circular shape with a diameter of 300 meters, which includes the central square in the historic city center and the adjacent streets. The center of this circular shape area is always the plague column, which is the unifying reference element in the vast majority of Czech squares. The central square is always identified in accordance with the established methodology. It determines it as a square, captured on historical maps, which are available on Mapy.cz or oldmaps.geolab.cz (maps originating from military mapping in the 19th century, see Fig. 1). The reason for choosing this location is, as the source states (RICHTROVÁ, 2014), that most of the Czech towns were founded with a central square in the middle of the city and the source added: "*A city always has a square where the best and most important events are concentrated - what the city has or needs for its life*" (Fig. 2).

Within these defined circular shape areas, information on all restaurants and bars was obtained, according to the EU statistical methodology (CESTOVNI-RUCH.cz 2009). For the sake of objective comparison, this analysis used data obtained by two independent methods. The first method was field research in all areas studied to obtain primary data by personal identification of objects by the author. In the second method, secondary data was obtained from selected information sources using data mining.

Due to publicly unavailable information about the amount and quality of POI of geosocial networks (in the Czech Republic and in the world), it was necessary to obtain a different way that would provide reliable official results about these POI of geosocial networks. For this reason, the necessary information was obtained by using own data mining from selected API of geosocial networks Facebook, Foursquare and Google+/ Places. In the case of the Google Places API, it has been found to provide different results from Google Maps in the number of POI.

Fig. 1. Historical map of analyzed area-Hradec Králové (Köninggrätz in German) (Source: [8])

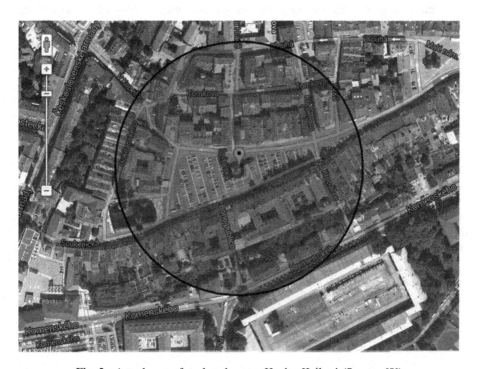

Fig. 2. Actual map of analyzed area – Hradec Králové (Source: [8])

The information was also obtained from the two largest electronic tourism information sources available in Czech Republic. The first was the Czech commercial information source Mapy.cz, belonging to the media house Seznam.cz, owning the largest Czech catalog and search engine. The second was the information source of Google Maps. Because API require coordinates in long WGS84 numeric format, a converter has been used [12].

3 An Analysis of Level of Completeness (Coverage) of POI in Geosocial Networks

Based on an analysis that compares the data obtained from the API (Table 1) of selected geosocial networks (Foursquare, Google+/Places and Facebook) with field research in defined areas (city centers Bratislava, Brno, Hradec Králové, Pardubice, Jičín, Ústí nad Orlicí, Hořice, Choceň, Opočno, Jablonné nad Orlicí, Železnice and Brandýs nad Orlicí), the following information resulted (Table 2).

This information about the coverage of the POI of the geosocial networks (Foursquare, Google+/Places, Facebook) and moreover, the levels of completeness of information of commercial information sources (Mapy.cz, Google Maps) are shown in the following table (Table 2).

As shown in the table (Table 2) and graphs (Figs. 3, 4, 5, 6, 7 and 8), in the defined areas, the Foursquare geosocial network reaches an average of 70% of POI coverage, Google+/Places 62% and Facebook 52%. Data from the commercial information source Mapy.cz, which runs Seznam.cz and Google Maps from Google, were also obtained and included in the comparison. All these geosocial networks offer higher POI coverage compared to Mapy.cz, even up to 24% higher for Foursquare. When compared to the Google Maps, two of the three geosocial networks also achieved higher POI coverage, by up to 9% for Foursquare.

Thus, the research question which was asked: *"Do geosocial networks provide relevant local information to tourism participants at least on the level of completeness of information available to the largest available information sources?"* has a positive result. It should be noted, however, that for example, in the towns of Hořice and Ústí nad Orlicí, geosocial networks did not contain information about several sports bar establishments (i.e. devices primarily with slot machines and a bar), which is certainly not the category of hospitality facilities that tourists would search for on their trips (for this reason, it is also ignored by geospatial users). So, if these sport bars would be subtracted from this study, the average POI coverage would reach higher value.

Table 1. Parameters for data mining through the API Foursquare, Google+/Places and Facebook (Source: [9–11] and author)

Foursquare API	HTTPS GET request: https://api.foursquare.com/v2/venues/search?categoryId=P1&ll=P2&radius= P3&limit=P4&client_id=P5&client_secret=P6&v=P7 P1=venue category (4d4b7105d754a06376d81259=coffee, drinks 4d4b7105d754a06374d81259=food, etc. For details, see https://developer.foursquare.com/docs/resources/categories.) P2=WGS84 coordinates P3=radius in meters P4=number of results P5=user's ID P6=user's secret ID P7=actual date
Google+/Places API	HTTPS GET request: https://maps.googleapis.com/maps/api/place/ nearbysearch/json?location= P1&radius=P2&types=P3&sensor=false&key=P4 P1=WGS84 coordinates P2=radius in meters P3=venue category (for details, see https://developers.google.com/places/supported_types) P4=user's secret key
Facebook API	HTTPS GET request: https://graph.facebook.com/search?type=place&q=P1&center= P2&distance=P3&access_token=P4 Graph API Explorer (https://developers.facebook.com/tools/explorer) request: /search?type=place&q=P1&center=P2&distance=P3 P1=venue category P2=WGS84 coordinates P3=radius in meters P4=user's OAuth access token

Table 2. Comparison results of algorithms to determine the average match of POI names of a real data set (Source: author and "R" statistical computing software)

City/town	Foursquare API	Foursquare coverage [%]	Google + API	Google+/ Places coverage [%]	Facebook API	Facebook coverage [%]	Mapy. cz	Mapy.cz coverage [%]	Google Maps	Google Maps coverage [%]	Real number of subjects
Bratislava	70	89	46	58	70	89	34	43	43	54	79
Brno	43	93	29	63	36	78	22	48	27	59	46
Hradec Králové	31	78	26	65	31	78	18	45	26	65	40
Pardubice	25	86	16	55	27	93	16	55	18	62	29
Jičín	10	71	8	57	9	64	5	36	7	50	14
Ústí nad Orlicí	10	67	6	40	8	53	6	40	7	47	15
Hořice	6	46	4	31	4	31	4	31	4	31	13
Choceň	7	70	6	60	6	60	5	50	6	60	10
Opočno	8	89	6	67	4	44	6	67	6	67	9
Jablonné nad Orlicí	3	50	4	67	2	33	4	67	4	67	6
Železnice	1	50	2	100	0	0	1	50	2	100	2
Brandýs nad Orlicí	2	50	3	75	0	0	1	25	3	75	4
Average POI Coverage		70		62		52		46		61	

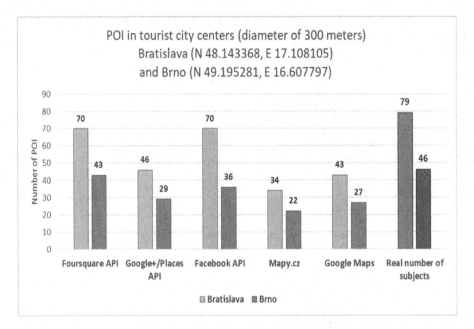

Fig. 3. Comparison of information sources in analyzed area (Source: [4] and author, 2016)

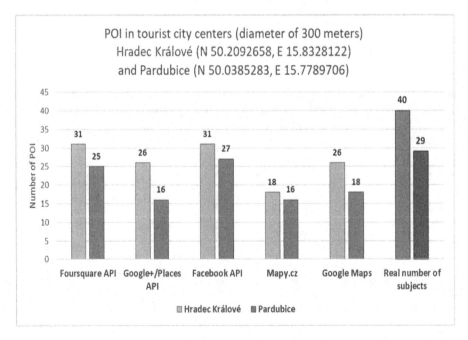

Fig. 4. Comparison of information sources in analyzed area (Source: [4] and author, 2016)

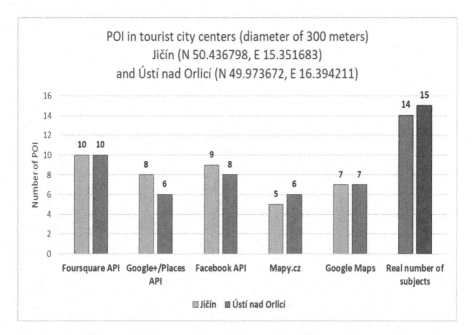

Fig. 5. Comparison of information sources in analyzed area (Source: [4] and author, 2016)

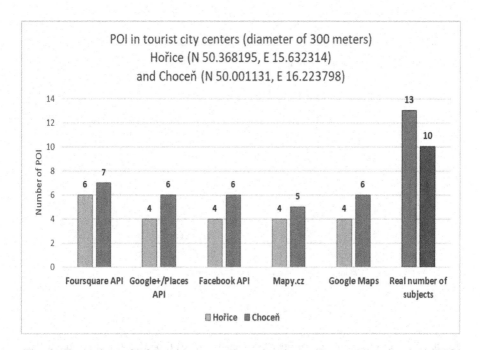

Fig. 6. Comparison of information sources in analyzed area (Source: [4] and author, 2016)

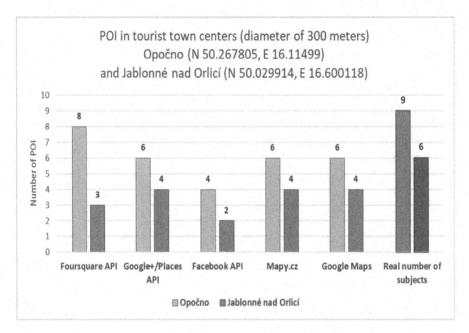

Fig. 7. Comparison of information sources in analyzed area (Source: [4] and author, 2016)

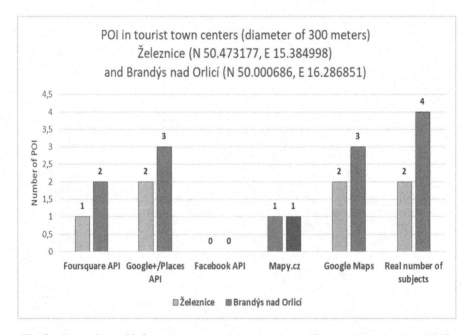

Fig. 8. Comparison of information sources in analyzed area (Source: [4] and author, 2016)

4 Conclusion

LBS, including geosocial networks, are key milestones in e-tourism, which can significantly change the shape of tourism thanks to quick availability and complete information provided. As a result, they enable a better supply of tourism products for its participants.

In this paper, an analysis of the current most important LBS map applications in the Czech Republic was carried out. These services are used as information resources by the participants in tourism. The author found out that Google Maps, on average, covered 61% of the total of 267 existing hospitality facilities, which were ascertained by field research in selected areas (historical centers of 12 cities). Mapy.cz on average covered only 46% of these existing subjects. In any case, both LBS applications do not cover more than 61% of existing subjects in these locations. Thus, neither Mapy.cz nor Google maps are currently able, with sufficient flexibility, to centrally cover dynamically changing local points of tourist interest, such as new subjects of restaurant facilities, accommodation or cultural events such as exhibitions, festivals, etc. So, by these traditional tourism resources not enough complete information about points of interest is provided to tourism participants at the place where they are.

In order to solve this research problem, it was necessary to answer the question *"Do geosocial networks provide relevant local information to tourism participants at least at the equivalent level currently available from traditional tourist information resources?"*. It was therefore necessary to analyze the information quality of geosocial networks, especially their POI with potential of usability as new information resources for local tourism participants. This paper has therefore focused on mapping of the availability and quality of these resources by analyzing the completeness of POI-related information provided by the three selected Facebook, Foursquare and Google+ networks. Based on this analysis, which compared the information obtained by mining data from API of selected geosocial networks with empirical field research in demarcated areas, it was found that Foursquare has an average coverage of 70% of existing hospitality facilities for these areas, Google+ covers an average of 62% of subjects and Facebook has a 52% coverage of the total of 267 existing subjects in each of the selected 12 cities/towns. The best network, Foursquare, therefore had up to 24% higher coverage than Mapy.cz and up to 9% higher coverage than Google Maps.

Thus, the results of the analysis clearly show that geosocial networks offer, on average, a high level of coverage of points of interest in tourism while providing relevant information. They are also more suitable for use as information sources in local tourism compared to the current largest available information sources. This fact also results in a positive answer to the research question, at least on the level of completeness of information available, when compared to the largest available electronic information sources.

Acknowledgements. This publication is the result of Metropolitan University Prague research project no. 68-03 'Public Administration, Law and Industrial Property', which was conducted in 2019 under a grant from the Institutional Fund for the Long-term Strategic Development of Research Organisations.

References

1. Gill, S.P.: Cognition, communication and interaction: Transdisciplinary Perspectives on Interactive Technology. Springer, London (2008). https://doi.org/10.1007/978-1-84628-927-9. ISBN 978-1-84628-926-2
2. Buhalis, D., Weber, J., Xu, F.: Gamification in tourism. In: Xiang, Z., Tussyadiah, I. (eds.) Information and Communication Technologies in Tourism 2014, pp. 525–537. Springer, Cham (2013). https://doi.org/10.1007/978-3-319-03973-2_38. ISBN 978-3-319-03972-5
3. Cestovni-ruch.cz: Kategorizace a klasifikace hostinských zařízení (2009). http://cestovni-ruch.cz/kategorizace/klasrest.php
4. Kysela, J.: Aggregation of Local Information in Tourism Through Geosocial Networks. University of Hradec Králové (2016)
5. Czech Statistical Office: Population of Municipalities (2017). https://www.czso.cz/csu/czso/pocet-obyvatel-v-obcich-see2a5tx8j
6. Statistical Office of the Slovak Republic: Population and migration (2016). https://slovak.statistics.sk/wps/portal/ext/themes/demography/population/indicators/
7. Richtrová, K.: Náměstí jako základní prvek tradiční městské typologie. Czech Technical University in Prague (2014)
8. Mapy.cz: Historická mapa českých zemí z 19. století (2016). https://www.mapy.cz/19stoleti
9. Facebook: Facebook Graph Application Programming Interface. https://graph.facebook.com/
10. Foursquare: Foursquare Places Application Programming Interface. https://api.foursquare.com/v2/
11. Google: Google Places Application Programming Interface. https://maps.googleapis.com/maps/api/place/radarsearch/
12. Earth Point: Tools for Google Earth. http://www.earthpoint.us/Convert.aspx
13. Gentleman, R., Ihaka, R.: The R Project for Statistical Computing. https://www.r-project.org

Application of the Requirements Elicitation Process for the Construction of Intelligent System-Based Predictive Models in the Education Area

Cinthia Vegega[(✉)], Pablo Pytel, and María Florencia Pollo-Cattaneo

Information System Methodologies Research Group,
Universidad Tecnológica de Buenos Aires, Buenos Aires, Argentina
cinthiavg@yahoo.com.ar, ppytel@gmail.com,
flo.pollo@gmail.com

Abstract. Decision-making is an essential process in the lives of organizations. While each member in an organization makes decisions, this process is particularly important for managerial positions in charge of making decisions on resources allocation. These decisions must be based on predictions about time, effort and/or risks involved in their tasks. Currently, this situation is exacerbated by the complex environment surrounding the organizations, which makes them act beyond their traditional management systems incorporating new mechanisms such as those provided by Artificial Intelligence, leading to the development of an Intelligent Predictive Model. In this context, this work proposes the implementation of a process to assist the Information Systems Engineer in the difficult work of collecting, understanding, identifying and registering the necessary information to implement an Intelligent System-based Predictive Model.

Keywords: Intelligent Systems · Machine Learning · Training data · Education and technology

1 Introduction

What is the most favorable option? What will the future bring us? These are questions we ask ourselves whenever we have to make a decision [1]. For this reason, Humanity has always sought mechanisms to make accurate predictions. Such need not only affects individuals but also organizations. Decision-making is an essential process in the life of organizations. While each member of an organization makes decisions, this process is particularly important for managerial positions. Consequently, managers are known as "decision makers" in their tasks of planning, organizing, directing and controlling [2]. Daily, they have to decide how to allocate valuable resources based on predictions [3] about time, effort and/or risks involved in their tasks. This situation is exacerbated by the highly complex and hardly predictable environment of the 21st century [4], which makes organizations act beyond their traditional management systems and incorporate new mechanisms for the "creation and enhancement of the organization's knowledge" such as those provided by Artificial Intelligence [5, 6].

H. Florez et al. (Eds.): ICAI 2019, CCIS 1051, pp. 43–58, 2019.
https://doi.org/10.1007/978-3-030-32475-9_4

An example of these new mechanisms can be found in the area of Predictive Models. Despite the fact that Statistical Techniques and Parametric Models have traditionally been used to generate predictions [7], in the last two decades diverse methods associated to Machine Learning [3, 8] have been incorporated. Consequently, it is possible to build models to find a relation between past and future situations using available historical data. In this sense, Artificial Neural Networks [9, 10] and Bayesian Networks [11, 12] can be mentioned as the main Intelligent Systems architectures to be used for this kind of problems [13–15]. These Intelligent System-based Predictive Models possess very useful features, such as generalization capacities, robustness, and self-organization [16].

However, unfortunately, Predictive Models are usually imprecise [3] or, in some cases, they fail, thus often generating incompatible answers [17]. In this regard, the quality of the information required is highly important to make accurate decisions [18]. It is possible to generate more accurate predictions if lack of knowledge on the problem and its context is reduced. Yet, it is almost impossible to have complete, accurate and precise information to make absolutely accurate predictions. There is always a risk related with trusting the available information to assess the situation so a prediction must be associated to a certain degree of probability [19]. Such probability is affected by what is known about the problem and what is not. Consequently, apart from collecting historical data that will be used to build the Predictive Model, it is also necessary to identify the general characteristics of the domain where the prediction is taking place thus being able to detect situations or events of which there are no data but which the model must consider.

In this context, this work proposes the implementation of a process to assist an Information Systems Engineer in the difficult work of collecting, understanding, identifying and registering the necessary information to implement an Intelligent System-based Predictive Model. For that purpose, Sect. 2 presents a brief summary of the proposed process and Sect. 3 presents the results of the implementation in an undergraduate course. Finally, Sect. 4 describes conclusions and future work.

2   Proposed Process

The proposed process aims to assist with the Information Systems Engineers (in their role of Functional Analyst) involved in the implementation of Intelligent Predictive Models, that is, it seeks to support them during the initial phases of the Project considering its particularities. This proposed Project is limited to contemplating the characteristics of two types of Intelligent Systems applied for the implementation of Predictive Models, Multi-layer Perceptron Artificial Neural Networks (ANN) with error Backpropagation training (BPNN) and Bayesian Networks (BN). Consequently, as a result of this proposal, the objectives, success criterion, constraints and assumptions of the Project are determined in order to identify the available information required to train the Intelligent System and to generate an initial specification of it. These results will help the development team start working on the construction, training and validation of the Intelligent Predictive Model to meet the expectations of the organization. The proposed process is structured into the following five phases:

1. **Project Definition Phase:** it aims to define the stakeholders who collaborate in the Project and its scope based on the objectives to be achieved.
2. **Business Process Elicitation Phase:** its objective is to identify and collect the business processes that are relevant for the project, as well as the expert's task in the case of building a model that emulates their prediction capabilities.
3. **Business Process Data Elicitation Phase:** it seeks to identify the data repositories where the information of the different business processes is stored and to collect information about the characteristics of said repositories.
4. **Business Data Conceptualization Phase:** its objective is to identify and evaluate the representativeness of the data available in the business for the construction of the intelligent predictive model.
5. **Intelligent System Initial Specification Phase:** based on the information obtained in the previous phases, the most appropriate type of architecture to implement the predictive model is determined, as well as a proposal of its initial topology.

Figure 1, shown below, presents the proposed process. Each phase of the process defines a set of activities that apply to a case study within the context of an undergraduate course in Sect. 3.

Fig. 1. Phases of the proposed process.

3   Case Study

This section presents the implementation of the phases of the proposed model in a case in a university setting. Firstly, Sect. 3.1 describes the context of the case study, and then describes the application of each phase of the process along with the activities that are carried out in each one of them. Then, the first phase is described in Sect. 3.2, the second phase in Sect. 3.3, the third phase in Sect. 3.4, the fourth phase in Sect. 3.5 and the fifth phase in Sect. 3.6.

3.1   Context of the Case Study

This case study is developed at Facultad Regional Buenos Aires (FRBA), Universidad Tecnológica Nacional (UTN), Argentina. Specifically, it is carried out in the "Systems and Organizations" course [20], of the first year of the "Information Systems Engineering" undergraduate program. The analyzed course is annual and compulsory for students who have passed the admittance course (with approximately 800 enrolled students) and it is one of the integrative courses of the curriculum. In this context, the aim is to implement an Intelligent System to predict the performance of students throughout the course. Because any error in the predictions can lead teachers or students to make wrong decisions, it is of great importance that the system presents consistent results taking into account the normal behavior of the students in the course.

3.2   Application of the First Phase of Project Definition

The following activities are described: "Identify the Objectives of the Project", "Identify the Project stakeholders" and "Identify the Project Scope".

Activity: "Identify the Objectives of the Project"

In this activity, the first conceptual meeting of the project is held with the "Systems and Organizations" Course Chair, which is the main person in charge of the project. The aim is to understand the objective of the project together with the associated expectations. Furthermore, the Chair's faculty members that will take part of the Project's stakeholders are identified, with whom the initial meeting will then be held. Based on the survey carried out, the information obtained is analyzed and the main objectives of the Project are identified, which are documented in the project objectives form, as shown in Fig. 2.

OBJECTIVES OF THE PROJECT		
ID	*Objective Description*	*Priority*
OBJ1	To implement an Intelligent System to predict the performance of the students in the "Systems and Organizations" course taught at UTN FRBA.	High
Observations		
The priority is considered high because it is the only objective that originates the project.		

Fig. 2. Project objectives form.

Activity: "Identify the Project's Stakeholders"

In this activity, the Functional Analyst, based on the information gathered from the organization, identifies the project participants and creates the form shown in Fig. 3.

PROJECT STAKEHOLDERS			
Position	*Org/ Sector*	*Role in the Project*	*Knowledge Areas*
Course Chair	UTN- FRBA / Course	Person in charge	Generalities Course Theory and Practice Pass Requirements
Teacher 1		Stakeholder	
Teacher 2			
TA Monday Course			Course Theory and Practice Data Repositories
TA Tuesday Course			
TA Thursday Course			
TA Friday Course			

where TA means Teaching Assistant

Fig. 3. Project stakeholders form.

Activity: "Identify the Project Scope"

Based on the collected information, the Functional Analyst defines the success criteria of the project as shown in Fig. 4 and determines the problems to be solved in order to establish what should be included as a result of the project. With this information, the project scope definition form is created, as shown in Fig. 5. This form must be validated by the Course Chair and the business stakeholders. Furthermore, the Functional Analyst also needs to identify the assumptions for the execution of the project. These assumptions include the dependencies on other projects, and all the necessary information that should be available to begin working on the project. This project assumptions form is shown in Fig. 6. Finally, the information restrictions of the project are defined by the project restrictions form, as shown in Fig. 7.

PROJECT SUCESS CRITERIA		
ID	*Criterion Description*	*OBJ-ID*
CE1	To predict the student's performance (including first term exam and make up exams) in the second semester based on data from the first term exam and the first make up exam .	OBJ1

Fig. 4. Project success criteria form.

PROJECT SCOPE DEFINITION		
ID	*Problems to solve*	*OBJ-ID*
P1	To identify students' strengths and weaknesses in order to reinforce what is necessary during the course.	OBJ1
	Problems excluded from the Project	
Concept scores and class-to-class evaluations are excluded. Only term exams and make up exams will be considered for the analysis. In addition, the annual planning of the course is not considered for the analysis, being used only for reference of the topics taught.		

Fig. 5. Project scope definition form.

PROJECT ASSUMPTIONS		
ID	*Assumption Description*	*OBJ-ID*
S1	Either by mail or personally, access to information from teaching assistants and teachers will be unrestricted	OBJ1
S2	Data are considered accurate and complete with the same structure since they were provided by the same teacher.	OBJ1

Fig. 6. Project assumptions form.

PROJECT RESTRICTIONS			
ID	*Type*	*Description*	*OBJ-ID*
R1	Data	There are no data on the student's progress class to class.	OBJ1
R2	Data	Assignment scores cannot be used. This is because such data are not considered representative since they are not standardized across all courses.	OBJ1
R3	Data	Students' first names, last names and file numbers cannot be used because they are considered confidential.	OBJ1

Fig. 7. Project Restrictions Form.

3.3   Application of the Second Phase of Business Process Elicitation

The following activities are described: "Identify Business Processes" and "Collect Business Processes". Since the aim is to implement a Predictive Model based on the knowledge of experts available in the organization, the tasks corresponding to the third activity "Collect the Expert's Tasks" are carried out.

Activity: "Identify Business Processes"
From the minutes of the meetings held with project stakeholders, the Project Objectives form (Fig. 2), the Project Success Criteria form (Fig. 3) and the Project Scope Definition form (Fig. 4), the Functional Analyst defines the most significant business activities for the project and makes a use case diagram that is included in the business process diagram form (Fig. 8).

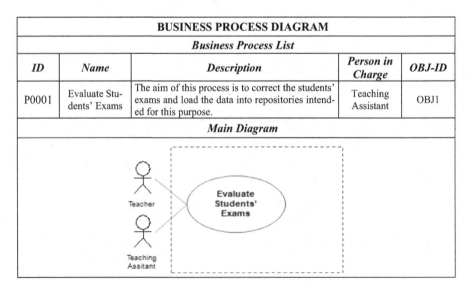

BUSINESS PROCESS DIAGRAM				
Business Process List				
ID	*Name*	*Description*	*Person in Charge*	*OBJ-ID*
P0001	Evaluate Students' Exams	The aim of this process is to correct the students' exams and load the data into repositories intended for this purpose.	Teaching Assistant	OBJ1
Main Diagram				

Fig. 8. Business process diagram form.

Activity: "Collect Business Processes"

Taking into account the collected information associated with the identified business process, the Functional Analyst holds a new meeting with the Course Chair and the course stakeholders. In this way, information is collected to record how this process works and how it is related to data repositories. From the information gathered, the information is registered by documenting it in the business process form, as shown in Fig. 9.

BUSINESS PROCESSES	
P0001 – Evaluate Students' Exams	
Description	The aim of this process is to correct the students' exams and load the data into repositories intended for this purpose.
Actors	Teacher; Teaching Assistant (TA)
Pre-Conditions	Students sat for the exams to be evaluated and they were already distributed among teachers and teaching assistants for their correction
Post-Conditions	The exams were corrected the scores were registered in the course spread-sheet.
Normal Flow	
1 The TA corrects the practice part of the term exams.	
2 The teacher corrects the theory part of the term exams.	
3 The TA holds a meeting with the teacher to deal with doubts during the correction.	
4 The teacher determines the term exam final score.	
5 The TA registers the scores in the course spreadsheet.	
Alternative Flow	
1 In the event that an exam has been inaccurately corrected after the student has analyzed it, the teacher and the teaching assistant will meet again in order to correct it again and define the final score.	
2 Once the score is determined, the teaching assistant registers it in course spreadsheet.	

Fig. 9. Business process form.

Activity: "Analyze the Expert's Tasks"

From previous meetings, it has been detected that the task of determining whether the student passes or not taking into account their characteristics and the result of their exams depends on different types of knowledge that is internalized in the minds of teachers. This means that there are no fixed rules or standard procedures to carry out such task so it is not possible to identify a Business Process. Therefore, it is an expert task and it is decided to analyze it in order to obtain the knowledge applied by the Course Chair. To do this, the Protocol Analysis is selected as the knowledge elicitation technique, thus performing the steps corresponding to the technique according to [21]. Once the steps have been carried out based on the protocol, the Functional Analyst will register the knowledge obtained in the expert's task form, as shown in Fig. 10a and b.

(a)

EXPERT'S TASKS	
TE001 – Evaluate Course Academic Status of the Student	
General Description	The objective is to determine whether the student will or will not pass the course considering their exam results.

Factual Knowledge

Table of Concepts – Characteristics – Values

Concepts	*Characteristics*	*Values*
	FileNumber_Student	Alphanumeric
Student	FullLastName_Student	Alphanumeric
	FullName_Student	Alphanumeric
	Type_Evaluation	Alphanumeric
Evaluation	FinalScore_Theory	Alphanumeric
	FinalScore_Práctice	Alphanumeric

Glossary of Terms

Term	**Description**
Evaluation	It indicates the exam the student is sitting for.
FileNumber_Student	Student's File Number (assigned by the School).
FinalScore_Práctice	Final Score obtained in the practice part of the exams.
FinalScore_Theory	Final Score obtained in the theory part of the exams.
FullLastName_Student	Student's Full Last Name.
FullName_Student	Student's Full Name.
Student	It indicates the student who takes the course, sits for the exams and submits the assignments.
Type_Evaluation	Type of exam, which may be first term exam, second term exam or make-up exams.

Tactical Knowledge

The rules resulting from the Protocol Analysis performed with the Course Chair are as follows:

- If the student passes the theory of the first term exam or the theory of the first make-up of the first term exam or the theory of the second make-up of the first term exam, then the student passes the theory of the first semester.
- If the student passes the practice of the first term exam or the practice of the first make-up of the first term exam or the practice of the second make-up of the first term exam, then the student passes the practice of the first semester.
- If the student passes the theory of the second term exam or the theory of the first make-up of the second term exam or the theory of the second make-up of the second term exam, then the student passes the theory of the second semester.
- If the student passes the practice of the second term exam or the practice of the first make-up of the second term exam or the practice of the second make-up of the second term exam, then the student passes the practice of the second semester.
- If the student passes the theory of the first semester and the practice of the first semester and the theory of the second semester and the practice of the second semester, then the student passes the course.
- If the student does not pass the theory of the first term exam, then it is likely that they will not pass the theory of the second term exam.
  If the student does not pass the practice of the first term exam, then it is likely that they will not pass the practice of the second term exam.

Fig. 10 a. Expert's task form (factual and tactical knowledge) **b.** Expert's task form (strategic knowledge and metaknowledge).

(b)

EXPERT'S TASKS
TE001 – Evaluate Course Academic Status of the Student
Strategic Knowledge
A three-level decomposition tree is drawn in https://bit.ly/2wdk9JF
Metaknowledge
A knowledge map is drawn in https://bit.ly/2HRBz3W

Fig. 10 (*continued*)

3.4   Application of the Third Phase of Business Process Data Elicitation

The following activities are described: "Identify Data Repositories" and "Collect Business Data".

Activity: "Identify Data Repositories"

The Functional Analyst analyzes the information gathered from the interviews conducted with the business stakeholders and from the "Expert's Tasks" form (Fig. 10). As a result, he detects that the main data to be used in the project are in Excel format spreadsheets named *planning_ < course day >* which describe the students' behavior (in relation to their exam, make-up and assignment scores) during the year. These spreadsheets were provided by the Course Chair. After defining such data repositories, the Functional Analyst registers this information and prepares the data repository form shown in Fig. 11.

DATA REPOSITORIES					
ID	**Name**	**Type**	**Description**	**Business Process /Task**	**Person in charge**
P_M	planning_ Monday.xls	Excel spreadsheet	Evaluation results of Monday course students.	P0001; TE001	TA Monday course
P_Tu	planning_ Tuesday.xls	Excel spreadsheet	Evaluation results of Tuesday course students.	P0001; TE001	TA Tuesday course
P_Th	planning_ Thursday.xls	Excel spreadsheet	Evaluation results of Thursday course students.	P0001; TE001	TA Thursday course
P_Fr1	planning_ Friday 1M.xls	Excel spreadsheet	Evaluation results of Friday course 1° module students.	P0001; TE001	TA Friday course
P_Fr2	planning_ Friday 2M.xls	Excel spreadsheet	Evaluation results of Friday course 2° module students.	P0001; TE001	TA Friday course

Fig. 11. Data repository form.

Activity: "Collect Business Data"

The Functional Analyst prepares the data structure form, shown in Fig. 12. Since all the Excel spreadsheets provided have the same format, a generic data structure is obtained, which is valid for all the data repositories.

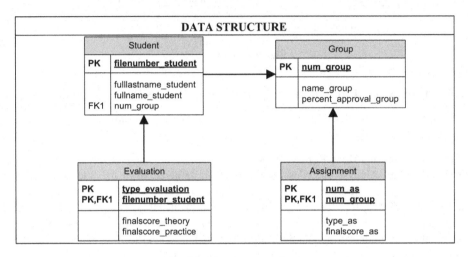

Fig. 12. Data structure form.

3.5   Application of the Fourth Phase of Business Data Conceptualization

The purpose of this phase is to determine whether the data that will be used in the Predictive Model are representative. To do this, in this case study, the two cycles of this phase are conducted, first evaluating the more general initial version of the business data and then a more detailed extended version.

Evaluation of the Initial Version of the Business Data

The evaluation of the initial version of the data is made, completing the tasks corresponding to the activity named "Identify Data to Build the Predictive Model" and then those corresponding to the second activity, i.e. "Validate Data Representativeness".

Activity: "Identify Data to Build the Predictive Model"

Based on the "Data Repository" form (Fig. 11), the "Data Structure" form (Fig. 12) and the information collected in the interviews conducted to the business stakeholders, the Functional Analyst documents the obtained data in the "Available Data" form shown in Fig. 13. In this case, all the spreadsheets identified as data repositories were integrated into a single spreadsheet which includes all the data.

Activity: "Validate Data Representativeness"

Based on the available data obtained in the previous activity, the Functional Analyst analyzes whether such data are representative of the business in order to build the Predictive Model. Due to space constraints, all the tasks performed on the data set are specified in [22]. The conclusions drawn show that the initial version of the data (more

AVAILABLE DATA	
Data Version	Initial Version of the Data (1.0)

The data repositories named *planning_<course day>.xls* have three tabs: "Annual Planning", "Assignments" and "Term Exams". For this project, only the "Term Exams" tab is used, since the data structure includes neither the data related to the assignments nor the data related to the groups of students doing such assignments. This is because such data are not considered representative since they are not standardized across all courses. In addition, students' first names, last names and file numbers cannot be used because they are considered confidential. Both situations are accounted for in the Project Restrictions form (figure 6). After integrating the 5 spreadsheets, identified in figure 10, a single spreadsheet is obtained, from which a sample of 75 records is taken. The integrated data are specified, which includes 14 attributes corresponding to 75 records containing the students' performance in the theory and practice parts of the course exams (term exams and make-ups) as well as the course day and the resulting course academic status.

In this case, two attributes are described as an example.

Attribute:	*COURSE ACADEMIC STATUS*
Description:	Course result, that is, whether the student has passed the course or not or they directly do not appear in the Final Course Records (TPA) due to absenteeism.
Type of Data:	Alphanumeric
Value Range:	- APRUEBA - NO_APRUEBA - NO_TPA

Attribute:	*C1_P_P; C1_1R_P; C1_2R_P*
Description:	Final score of the practice part of the exams (it includes all the practice items of the first semester, which are Process Charts and Organizational Charts), where the prefix means the following: • C1_P: First Term Exam • C1_1R: First Make-up of the First Term Exam • C1_2R: Second Make-up of the First Term Exam
Type of Data:	Alphanumeric.
Value Range:	- AP_dist: Passed with Honors - AP: Satisfactory Pass - AP_err: Passed with some errors - AP_lim: Borderline Pass - NO_AP_lim: Borderline Fail - NO_AP: Failed - NC: Topic Not Answered - AUS: Student Absent in the Evaluation - NA: Topic that the student does not need to answer (this value is used for make-up exams only).
Synonym:	First Semester Practice Score

Fig. 13. Available data form for the initial version of the data.

general and limited) contains biases which generate differences with the relationships preconceived by the teacher of the courses. For this reason, a new version of the data is generated, including more examples and more detail in the attributes used.

Evaluation of the Extended Version of the Business Data

The tasks corresponding to the activity named "Identify Data to Build the Predictive Model" and those corresponding to the second activity, "Validate Data Representativeness" are performed in order to evaluate the extended version of the data.

Activity: "Identify Data to Build the Predictive Model"

In view of the problems detected in the initial version of the data, it is decided to extend them both in number of rows and in detail of the attributes, which are also documented in a new "Available Data" form, shown in Fig. 14.

AVAILABLE DATA	
Data Version	Extended Version of the Data (2.0)
In order to extend the data, a detailed account of the results for each topic of each exam is made (in this way, for instance, in the Practice part of the first term exam, the results for Organizational Charts and Process Charts are indicated). In addition, 51 students' records are added so that the data include a total of 126 rows with 23 attributes. Below, an attribute is described in detail as an example.	

Attribute:	*C1_P_ORG; C1_1R_ORG; C1_2R_ORG*
Description:	Final exam score for the organizational charts topic which is evaluated in the first semester, where the prefix means the following: • C1_P: First Term Exam • C1_1R: First Make-up of the First Term Exam • C1_2R: Second Make-up of the First Term Exam
Type of Data:	Alphanumeric.
Value Range:	- AP_dist: Passed with Honors - AP: Satisfactory Pass - AP_err: Passed with some errors - AP_lim: Borderline Pass - NO_AP_lim: Borderline Fail - NO_AP: Failed - NC: Topic Not Answered - AUS: Student Absent in the Evaluation - NA: Topic that the student does not need to answer (this value is used for make-up exams only).
Synonym:	Score obtained in Organizational Charts in the First Semester

Fig. 14. Available data form for the extended version of the data.

Activity: "Validate Data Representativeness"

Based on the available data obtained in the previous activity, the Functional Analyst once again analyzes whether such data are representative of the business in order to build a Predictive Model. Therefore, all the tasks performed on the data set are described in detail. All the tasks performed on the data set are specified in [22]. Based on the conclusions obtained, the extended version is representative of the students' behavior and therefore it is the version that will be used to build the Predictive Model.

3.6 Application of the Fifth Phase of Initial Specification of the Intelligent System

The following activities are described: "Select the Type of Intelligent System" and "Define Initial Topology of the Intelligent System". In addition, the complete process is specified in [23].

Activity: "Select Type of Intelligent System"
The Functional Analyst answers the questions associated to each characteristic using the meeting minutes written in previous phases, formalizing them in Table 1 as shown below. The possible linguistic values that can be used for each characteristic are "Nothing", "Little", "Regular", "Much" and "All". Once the linguistic values corresponding to each characteristic defined in Table 1 are assigned, the Functional Analyst obtains the values corresponding to each architecture and selects the best architecture for the project. The operations made are presented in the spreadsheet available in [24]. As shown in Fig. 15, the architecture selected in this case is Bayesian Networks. This selection is registered in the predictive model architecture form, shown in Fig. 16.

Table 1. Characteristics evaluated in order to define the most appropriate architecture.

Category	ID	Question associated to the characteristic	Value
Available data	D1	How much confidence is there as to the representativeness of the data?	Much
	D2	To what extent may the data be considered complex and with a nonlinear relationship between their attributes?	Little
	D3	How many examples do the data include?	Regular
	D4	What percentage of data is there with continuous numeric values (in relation to non-numeric values or numeric discrete values)?	Regular
Expected results	R1	To what extent is prediction accuracy considered critical?	Much
	R2	To what extent is it desirable to know and compare the predictions for different possibilities and scenarios?	Much
	R3	To what extent is it important to be able to explain how the results generated were obtained?	Much
Problem domain	P1	How stable is the problem to be solved?	All
	P2	To what extent are the domain experts available to participate in the project?	All
	P3	To what extent it is desirable to be able to manually adjust the network based on the knowledge about the data?	All

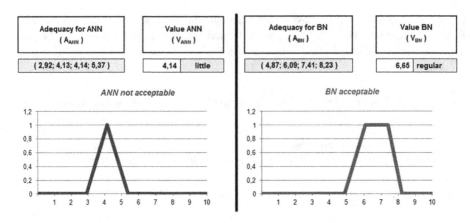

Fig. 15. Appropriateness values for each architecture.

PREDICTIVE MODEL ARCHITECTURE
The most appropriate architecture for this project is Bayesian Networks, while the use of Artificial Neural Networks is discarded for the problem to be solved. The available data include a sufficient number of examples to perform the training and validation of the network, allowing the definition of value ranges for each of them. In addition, there are domain experts available who can contribute their knowledge and participate in the project. Therefore, comparisons between the predictions for different scenarios will be possible as well as knowing how the results were obtained, thus allowing for adjustments in the network that is defined.

Fig. 16. Predictive model architecture form.

Activity: "Define Initial Topology of the Intelligent System"

Once the type of architecture to be used is selected, the Functional Analyst defines the initial characteristics of the topology and documents them in the initial topology of the predictive model architecture form.

For building the model proposed, the Analyst uses the 'Graphical Network Interface' or GeNIe software tool [25], together with the extended version of the data obtained in the previous phase. A simple structure is chosen to be applied, where each node connects with the objective attribute (COURSE ACADEMIC STATUS) and, in the case of the topics, the result of the term exam is associated to the first make-up and the latter with the second make-up. The reason for this linkage is that, as explained by the domain expert, it is thought that the result that a student would obtain in the theory part of the second make-up may be influenced by the results of the first make-up and of the term exam. With such structure, the available data (corresponding to the Extended Version of the Data) are imported so that the tool can determine the a priori probabilities and the conditional probabilities corresponding to each node. As a result of this operation, the probability distribution is obtained, as shown in https://bit.ly/2W1X1gd (the names are displayed in the original language).

Although the implementation of the final Bayesian Network falls outside the scope of this process, in order to confirm whether this initial topology was successfully trained, the validation thereof was performed using the same data with a functionality provided by GeNIe. Despite the fact that in a real project it would not make sense to validate an Intelligent System using the same data as those used to train it (since the accuracy thus obtained is not reliable), in this case we only seek to confirm that the probabilities given by the network can be considered representative of the data used. As a result, the general accuracy of this network is 94%, with 100% of accuracy to predict students that approve the course, 87.5% for students that do not approve and 96,4% for students that do not finish the course. Therefore, it is possible to affirm that this initial topology is useful to be used as a basic prototype of the Intelligent Model to predict the students' behavior in the course.

4 Conclusions

In this work, a proposed process has been applied to predict the performance of students throughout a university course. In the first phase, the objective and requirements of the Predictive Model has been defined. In the second phase, the business process characteristics have been identified. During the third phase, the available data sources have been detected, which then have been evaluated in the fourth phase to retrieve a data set sufficiently representative of the behavior of the students. Finally, in the fifth phase the most appropriate technology to build the Predictive Model has been established to satisfy the project requirements.

References

1. De Kohan, N.C.: Los sesgos cognitivos en la toma de decisiones. Int. J. Psychol. Res. 1(1), 68–73 (2008). ISSN 2011-7922
2. Robbins, S., Coulter, M.: Administración, Décima Edición. Prentice Hall, Upper Saddle River (2010). ISBN: 978-607-442-388-4
3. Mair, C., et al.: An investigation of machine learning based prediction systems. J. Syst. Softw. 53(1), 23–29 (2000)
4. García, F.J.M., Martínez, M.A.P., García, J.S.: Gestión Estratégica del Conocimiento. Asociación Universitaria Iberoamericana de Postgrado (2003)
5. Nilsson, N.J.: Principles of Artificial Intelligence. Morgan Kaufmann, Burlington (2014)
6. Russell, S.J., Norvig, P., Davis, E., Russell, S.J., Russell, S.J.: Artificial Intelligence: A Modern Approach, vol. 2. Prentice Hall, Englewood Cliffs (2010)
7. Shepperd, M., Kadoda, G.: Comparing software prediction techniques using simulation. IEEE Trans. Softw. Eng. 27(11), 1014–1022 (2001)
8. Bontempi, G., Ben Taieb, S., Le Borgne, Y.-A.: Machine learning strategies for time series forecasting. In: Aufaure, M.-A., Zimányi, E. (eds.) eBISS 2012. LNBIP, vol. 138, pp. 62–77. Springer, Heidelberg (2013). https://doi.org/10.1007/978-3-642-36318-4_3
9. Wang, S.-C.: Artificial neural network. In: Wang, S.-C. (ed.) Interdisciplinary Computing in Java Programming. SECS, vol. 743, pp. 81–100. Springer, Boston (2003). https://doi.org/10.1007/978-1-4615-0377-4_5

10. Wang, L., Fu, K.: Artificial neural networks. In: Wiley Encyclopedia of Computer Science and Engineering, pp. 181–188 (2009)
11. Barber, D.: Bayesian Reasoning and Machine Learning. The MIT Press, Cambridge (2012)
12. Premchaiswadi, W. (ed.): Bayesian Networks. In-Tech. (2012)
13. Chatfield, C.: The Analysis of Time Series: An Introduction. CRC Press, Boca Raton (2016)
14. De Gooijer, J.G., Hyndman, R.J.: 25 years of time series forecasting. Int. J. Forecast. **22**(3), 443–473 (2006)
15. Zhang, G., Hu, M.Y.: Neural network forecasting of the British pound/US dollar exchange rate. Omega Int. J. Manag. Sci. **26**(4), 495–506 (1998)
16. Cohen, P.R., Feigenbaum, E.A.: The Handbook of Artificial Intelligence, vol. 3. Butterworth-Heinemann, Oxford (2014)
17. Acquatela, H.: La predicción del futuro: desde el oráculo de Delfos hasta la medicina actual. Gac. méd. Caracas **114**(2), 150–156 (2006). ISSN 0367-4762
18. Rodríguez, M., Márquez Alegría, M.: Manejo de problemas y toma de decisiones, vol. 8. Editorial El Manual Moderno (2015). SBN: 9789684264670
19. Arsham, H.: Tools for decision analysis: analysis of risky decisions (2006)
20. Universidad Tecnológica Nacional – Facultad Regional Buenos Aires. Programa de la carrera Ingeniería en Sistemas de Información (Plan 2008). DISI (2008). https://tinyurl.com/y2kb36xv
21. Gómez, A., Juristo, N., Montes, C., Pazos, J.: Ingeniería del Conocimiento. Centro de Estudios Ramón Areces. S.A. Madrid (1997)
22. Vegega, C., Pytel, P., Straccia, L., Pollo-Cattaneo, M.F.: Evaluation of the bias of student performance data with assistance of expert teacher. In: Florez, H., Diaz, C., Chavarriaga, J. (eds.) ICAI 2018. CCIS, vol. 942, pp. 16–31. Springer, Cham (2018). https://doi.org/10.1007/978-3-030-01535-0_2. ISSN: 1865-0937
23. Vegega, C., Pytel, P., Straccia, L., Pollo-Cattaneo, M.F.: Proceso de Selección de Arquitectura a fin de Implementar un Modelo Predictivo Inteligente. Memorias de 6to. Congreso Nacional de Ingeniería Informática y Sistemas de Información (CONAIISI 2018). Workshop de Aplicaciones Informáticas y de Sistemas de Información (2018). https://tinyurl.com/y6nzhjnv. ISSN 2347-0372
24. Vegega, C., Pytel, P., Pollo-Cattaneo M.F.: Método Evaluador de Arquitectura - Desempeño de Alumnos de Sistemas y Organizaciones (2017). https://bit.ly/2YwE5UM
25. BayesFusion: BayesFusion - Home Page for users of GeNIe. BayesFusion LLC (2015). https://www.bayesfusion.com/

Evaluating Student Learning Effect Based on Process Mining

Yu Wang, Tong Li$^{(\boxtimes)}$, Congkai Geng, and Yihan Wang

Beijing University of Technology, Beijing, China
sallywangyu42@gmail.com, litong@bjut.edu.cn,
{gengcongkai789123,17071121}@emails.bjut.edu.cn

Abstract. As education is taking an increasingly significant role in society today, efficient and precise evaluation of student learning effect is calling for more attention. With recent advances of information technology, learning effect can now be evaluated via mining student's learning process. This paper proposes an interactive student learning effect evaluation framework which focuses on in-process learning effect evaluation. In particular, our proposal analyzes students modeling assignment based on their operation records by using techniques of frequent sequential pattern mining, user behavior analysis, and feature engineering. In order to enable effective student learning evaluation and deliver practical value, we have developed a comprehensive online modeling platform to collect operation data of modelers and to support the corresponding analysis. We have carried out a case study, in which we applied our approach to a real dataset, consisting of student online modeling behavior data collected from 24 students majoring in computer science. The results of our analysis show that our approach can effectively and practically mine student modeling patterns and interpret their behaviors, contributing to assessment of their learning effect.

Keywords: Student behavior analysis · Learning effect evaluation · Frequent sequential pattern mining · Feature engineering

1 Introduction

Student learning effect evaluation has become a great concern today as education is playing a more and more significant role in the new era of information technology. Traditional student evaluation methods regard paper exams, practical experiments, and oral presentations as components of the final grade. However, such traditional methods only focus on evaluating students' final deliverables, but cannot capture and analyze the in-process learning data. With the rapid development in computer science and data analytic techniques [1] like process mining, we argue that a comprehensive and impactful in-process student learning effect evaluation method is of great need to enable a more precise evaluation.

A first challenge to this topic is how to efficiently obtain useful in-process data, which has been ignored by traditional learning effect evaluation methods.

© Springer Nature Switzerland AG 2019
H. Florez et al. (Eds.): ICAI 2019, CCIS 1051, pp. 59–72, 2019.
https://doi.org/10.1007/978-3-030-32475-9_5

Another challenge is concerning how to effectively analyze such in-process data, e.g., identification of meaningful behavior patterns.

Regarding this research topic, relevant researchers mainly use user behavior analysis and frequent sequential pattern mining to help analyze how well the student is performing in the learning process. User behavior analysis is focusing on web log analysis, which is extracting user behavior elements and selecting useful parameters from log data. Capturing characteristics of normal user behaviors is also an important work of user behavior analysis [2]. Considering about the sequential timing characteristic of in-process information, algorithms in frequent sequential pattern mining are showing excellent performance in finding useful insights from data. A suitable and effective algorithm shows both long-term changing trend and short-term violent incident [3].

In this paper, we propose a comprehensive framework for evaluating student learning effect, which focuses on analyzing in-process data. For one thing, we propose to record detailed student modeling behaviors by developing an online modeling platform. For another, we apply and customize process mining techniques [4] to figure out reasonable student behavior patterns and useful insights about student learning effect evaluation. In particular, the contribution of this paper can be concluded as below:

- Propose a student learning effect evaluation framework based on process mining techniques.
- Develop an online modeling platform *BJUTModeling* which can automatically record students' modeling operations.
- Carry out a comprehensive case study based on real in-class data from students in order to evaluate the effectiveness of our proposal.

The rest of paper is organized as follows. Section 2 reviews related work. Related techniques and methodology are presented in Sect. 3. The newly developed online modeling platform is introduced in Sect. 4. We do a case study on real data from students in Sect. 5. At last, we conclude our research in Sect. 6.

2   Related Work

User behavior analysis is widely used in e-commerce marketing strategy evaluation, user experience improvement, website anomalies detection [5]. It collects various types of data, ranges from user demographic information to actual operation parameters. Behavior event analysis model, user retention analysis model, funnel analysis model, user behavior path model, user segmentation, and click analysis model are main models in user behavior analysis [6]. In this paper, we need to apply existing models and methods of user behavior analysis to student learning effect evaluation, in order to realize student behavior analysis.

User logs are often indexed in time order, which is called sequential data. Thus, frequent sequential pattern mining algorithms help us mine the sequential database, looking for repeating patterns that can be used to find associations between different items in the sequential dataset.

Frequent sequential pattern mining algorithms can be sorted into three categories, namely, apriori-based, pattern-growth, and early-pruning algorithms [7]. ArioriAll [8] and GSP [9] algorithms are apriori-based algorithms, with great capability in exploring the complete set of patterns due to its multiple times of scan of the databases. A potentially huge set of candidate sequences may cause great difficulties in mining long sequential patterns in this kind type of algorithm. FreeSpan [10] algorithm is based on pattern-growth, which recursively project sequence databases into smaller projected databases by using frequent items. It then grows subsequences fragments in each projected database. PrefixSpan [11] is also a pattern-growth algorithm, more specifically, a prefix-projected sequential pattern mining algorithm. It makes less projections and quickly shrinking sequence compared with the FreeSpan algorithm.

According to the domain knowledge of this topic, we will use an enhanced PrefixSpan algorithm called PreSeqPat to figure out the useful repeating patterns in the sequential database. This enhanced algorithm can reduce the complexity of the PrefixSpan, details of which will be shown in Sect. 3.

3 An Interactive and Comprehensive Framework for Evaluating Student Learning Effect

3.1 Framework Design

Our proposed student learning effect evaluation framework consists of four modules, online modeling platform, data mining module, feature engineering module, and user behavior analysis module. Details are shown in Fig. 1.

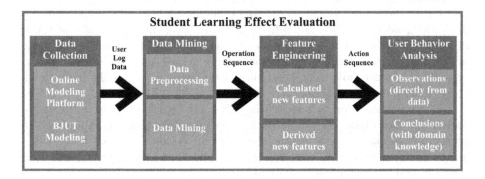

Fig. 1. Student learning effect evaluation framework.

3.2 Data Collection

In this paper, we build up an online modeling platform, whose details will be discussed in Sect. 4. Data are collected from the server of the online modeling platform, consisting of two parts, log data and model data. Log data is recording all user operations on the online modeling platform, including user information and all operation parameters. Model data is recording all elements and links in the diagram, fully representing main structure of the diagram.

Model data mainly shows the final view of the model, and log data contain a great number of in-process information. Thus, we are delivering this research focusing on the log data. Along with the log data, data mining methods and user behavior analysis can be applied to model student behavior, which can bring insightful observations and conclusions from the raw data.

3.3   Data Preprocessing

Data Cleaning and Operation Separation. Raw log data contains plenty of formatting characters, which are meaningless in further data processing. So we re-organize the raw log data and make it as a highly structured dataset. By this data cleaning process, operations are separated from the raw data, resulting in individual operations. This brings great convenience in later data processing.

Noise Removal. Each operation recorded in log data has many columns, including user information, operation information, and operation parameters. Some of the columns are regarded as obviously redundant features, which should be removed as noise to simplify later processes. Remaining columns are vital and useful, avoiding annoying extra information.

3.4   Pattern Mining

Operation Symbolization. According to the design of the online modeling platform, it has several types of operations, such as adding an element, moving an element, adding a link, and editing text of a link. These operations cover all element operations and linkage operations which are essential in modeling and building a diagram. These operations are telling the user behavior in a sequential sequence, so we can symbolize these operations to make it easier in later sequential pattern mining.

The symbolized operation sequences only takes operation types into consideration and can divide the whole dataset by users. By this step, the detailed information of each operation is not considered, because we need to find the general frequent sequential patterns in the dataset first and then do the user behavior analysis individual by individual.

FreSeqPat, an Enhanced PrefixSpan Algorithm. According to the common sense of sequential pattern mining and the specific need in this paper, we develop an algorithm called FreSeqPat based on PrefixSpan, willing to realize the frequent sequential pattern mining in this topic.

PrefixSpan algorithm owns great capability in dealing with items with more than one element inside, which means it needs to consider in-item prefix and suffix. This is vital in online shopping cart analysis and marketing strategy decision process, but not useful in our sequential database. Our sequential dataset does not have any item with more than one element inside. Thus, we improve the PrefixSpan algorithm as the FreSeqPat algorithm to reduce the size of the projected database, resulting in lower space complexity.

FreSeqPat algorithm is able to find the complete set of sequential patterns in the given sequential database. These patterns are with the appearance frequency no less than the preset threshold *min_support*. FreSeqPat checks all patterns in the sequential database with a reasonable size of projections without information loss. The pseudo code of algorithm FreSeqPat is shown in Table 1. The difference between FreSeqPat and PrefixSpan is in the first part. FreSeqPat algorithm does not need to check whether an element is the last one in an item or not, because the sequential database only takes one element per item. Therefore, FreSeqPat can effectively reduce the complexity of PrefixSpan but not lose any frequent pattern from the sequential database.

Table 1. Pseudo code of FreSeqPat.

Algorithm FreSeqPat : Frequent Sequential Pattern Mining
Input: A sequence database S, and the minimum support threshold *min_sup*.
Output: The complete set of frequent sequential patterns.
Parameters: α : a sequential pattern; l : the length of α;
$S\|\alpha$: the α-projected database, if $\alpha \neq <>$; Otherwise the sequence database S.

Method: Call *FreSeqPat (<>, 0, S)*
Subroutine: *FreSeqPat (α, l, $S\|\alpha$)*
Scan $S\|\alpha$;
If item $< b >$ can be appended to α to form a larger sequential pattern, **then**
    put item b into set B;
For each item b in B **do**
    Append b to α to form a sequential pattern α';
    Put α' into set A';
For each pattern α' in A' **do**
    Construct α-projected database $S\|\alpha'$;
    Call *FreSeqPat (α', l, $S\|\alpha'$)*

3.5   Generate New Features from Feature Engineering

As the machine learning and data mining algorithms are being used in more fields, the quality of features is of great concern. It is clear that better features mean better flexibility, simpler data processing models, and better results [12]. Thus, feature engineering methods applied in this paper are of significant value.

Feature engineering results in two kinds of new features, features directly calculated from existing features and features derived from features based on domain knowledge. Both kind of new features are with higher value than the original features of the raw data. New features contain more information along with higher information capacity. These new features can significantly reduce the complexity of modeling and analysis.

3.6 User Behavior Analysis

User behavior on online modeling platform are recorded as operations user log, and user operations have been symbolized as sequential sequences. Along with the pattern mining result of this sequential database, we are now able to perform user behavior analysis on it.

Due to the characteristics of each user, we realize that there huge differences are existing among users. So we need to do case-by-case user behavior analysis in this paper, where each user are regarded as an individual case. In this paper, the behavior even analysis model is used to figure out how each student performs when using the online modeling platform. Also, user behavior path model is also needed in this paper to draw a general overview of online modeling behavior for each student.

4 Online Modeling Platform

4.1 Platform Design

In this project, we develop BJUTModeling[1], an online modeling platform. The modeling page of BJUTModeling is shown in Fig. 2, using data flow diagram as an example. The user interface is clearly shown in the figure, and we can easily see how it works. This platform is the data source of this paper, from where we get the log data of students.

BJUTModeling is designed in the Client/Server mode, where the server records all user operations, including basic user information, operation parameters and other details. It is coded with Html, css, and JavaScript, realizing the online modeling function. It works as a website, where people can sign-up as a user and then log-in to the platform to finish the online modeling behavrior.

4.2 Platform Function

On the online modeling platform BJUTModeling, users can successfully draw a diagram and build up a model. The usability and accessibility of BJUTModeling is guaranteed by test, and its main functions are listed as below:

- User sign-up and log-in.
- Data flow diagram, UML class diagram, and use case diagram.
- Clear view of available elements in diagrams.
- Easy-to-use actions of drag and drop.
- Save and print diagrams.
- Automatically record user modeling operations.

---

[1] http://bjutmodeling.com.

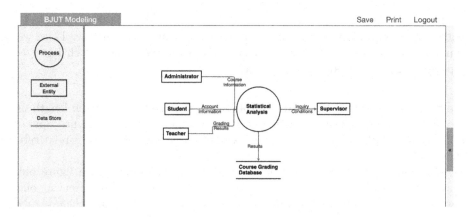

Fig. 2. Online modeling platform BJUTModeling.

5 Case Study

5.1 Case Study Design

Under the design of this student learning effect evaluation method, we apply this method in a real world case analysis. This case analysis is set up in the course *Introduction to Software Engineering*. Users of BJUTModeling are 24 junior students majoring in Computer Science from Beijing University of Technology.

This case analysis is using the log data of the course assignment in structured analysis, requiring students to draw a data flow diagram to model a problem. The case analysis is using a real in-class dataset, consisting of 24 real student online modeling log data. The reliability and practicality of the student learning effect evaluation method is therefore confirmed under this real data case analysis.

5.2 Data Preprocessing

With the raw log data of BJUTModeling on hand, we first analyze all the 16 columns of it. We realize that 6 columns in one operation, which is an entry in log data, is obviously redundant. Thus, we drop these six noise columns in order to get a cleaned log data.

Columns left are renamed as Date, Time, Student Number, Op, Type, OpLevel, and four other operation parameters. These columns are important for data mining procedure later on, which can bring insightful observations and conclusions from this case analysis.

5.3 Pattern Mining

Symbolization of Operations. According to the raw user log data of the online modeling platform BJUTModeling, we can conclude the user operations into 16 types based on columns Op, Type, and OpLevel. In order to analyze the student modeling behavior in a clear and logic way and find the frequent user pattern first, we only take the operation type into consideration now. Thus, we symbolize these user modeling operations into 16 letters, where each letter is representing a user modeling operation.

Re-symbolization of Grouping Operations. It is clear that the length of individual operation sequence is not equally distributed. Some students' operation sequence length is more than 2000, while some students' length is relatively short as 20.

Also, under the design and construction of BJUTModeling, we figure out that some operations can be grouped. Grouping operations are representing one particular action on the online modeling platform. So we can group these highly correlated operations to get much shorter sequences without losing information. In this case, we can group these 16 operations into 8 groups, which are re-symbolized as 8 new actions. The detailed information of grouping operation, actions, and meaning are list in Table 2.

Table 2. Re-symbolization of grouping operations.

Actions	Grouping operations	Meaning
A	mkhcfcd	Add element
M	ecd	Move element
T	fg	Edit text
D	yw	Delete element
L	nvkhab	Add link
C	ab	Change link
E	zvw	Delete link
X	x	Add diagram menu

Frequent Sequential Pattern Mining of Actions. Along with the re-symbolized sequence database, doing frequent sequential pattern mining of actions is now possible. In this case, we need to set a maximum length threshold to the FreSeqPat algorithm to avoid sequence explosion. Otherwise, we will results in a too-long pattern, which is meaningless in this topic. Considering the characteristics of data flow diagram and structured analysis, the maximum length of actions in a single frequent pattern can be set as 20. With this reasonable threshold, we will get interpretable patterns but not overlong patterns.

Also, along with the modeling rules of data flow diagram and domain knowledge in modeling behavior, the parameter min_sup in the FreSeqPat algorithm is set as 4. This is to guarantee the completeness of the frequent patterns, and prevent from pattern explosion. These two constraints can avoid counting patterns with overlong length and exclude anomalies from the action sequences.

5.4   Feature Engineering

By the domain knowledge of software engineering, more specifically, the data flow diagram of structured analysis, we conclude the following new features from the sequential dataset of user log:

1. Operation Time:
   Due to the characteristics of website operations, we can easily find that the operation time is really important in analyzing user behavior. Several observations can be derived from this new feature, such as whether a student is more likely to do online modeling in small steps, whether a user needs to think for a long time between steps.
2. Shifting Distance of Element:
   From the overview of the operation sequence dataset, the importance of calculating a new feature of shifting distance is clear. The raw operation data only records old and new locations of the element shifting operations, but not the shifting distance, so it is in great need to regard this calculation result as a new feature.
3. Fraction of moving right after adding:
   Thinking about the real situation when drawing a data flow diagram, it is significant to consider the fraction that a user moving the newly added element right after the element adding operations. This feature is also a great indicator of a user's online modeling habit.

5.5   Data Analysis Result and Knowledge Interpretation

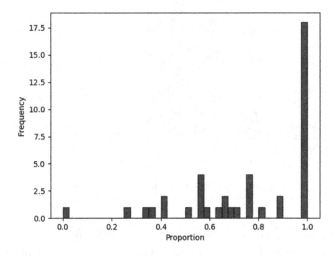

Fig. 3. Proportion of non-operation log-in manipulation.

Proportion of Non-operation Log-in Manipulation. Every log-in manipulation is recorded in raw user log data. Thus, a proportion of non-operation log-in manipulations divided by all log-in manipulations can be calculated. Figure 3 clearly shows the statistical histogram of this proportion.

As we can read from the histogram, 75% of the students has operations in each log-in manipulation. This is a relatively high proportion, showing us that only a few students do the log-in manipulation without any operations. This can be concluded as a user behavior habit of this case analysis focusing on student online modeling behavior.

Types of Operation. According to the 16 types of operation on the online modeling platform, a counting value of appearance frequency of each operation type can be derived to show the importance of each type of operation.

From result shown in Fig. 4, the operation type a, b, c, d, e are important operations. Also we can know that operation a and b are in the same frequency, while operation c, d, and e are almost in the same frequency.

Aside from the absolute values, we can also get some observations from the relative values. Some operations are happening 10 to 20 times more than others, while other operations are only appearing within 100 times. This huge gap between types of operations gives us the necessity to analyze the actual meaning of operations.

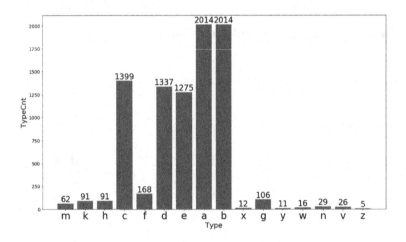

Fig. 4. Frequency of each operation type.

Types of Action. In the re-symbolization procedure, highly correlated operations are grouped as actions. A counting value of appearance frequency of each type of action is a great indicator of its importance. These 8 actions can significantly decrease the processing difficulties and improve the quality of data analysis result.

From Fig. 5 we can know that actions of moving element and changing link are in the highest frequency, which are 12 to 20 times more than other types of action.

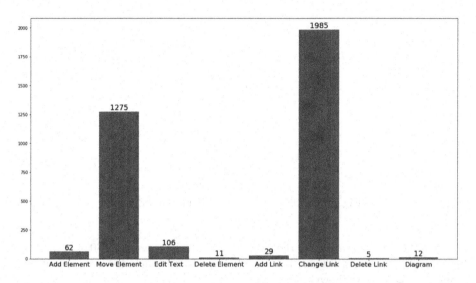

Fig. 5. Frequency of each action type.

According to the proportion value of each type of action, link changing action takes the biggest proportion, which is of 56.96%, and element moving action takes the second largest proportion of actions as 36.59%.

It can be concluded that students are taking more steps in adjusting elements and links rather than creating elements and links. This seems to be a common sense, but the actual user data tells us the truth that the frequency of adjusting elements and links is nearly 13 times more than the frequency of creating and deleting elements and links. This number is extremely high, giving us a great indication that students are actually not so that sure about their modeling actions.

User Behavior Analysis on Action Sequence. According to the user log of each student, a statistical value of the total operation counts can be calculated. It is true that some of the students only own tens of operation, while some students are doing thousands of operations on the online modeling platform.

The range of this operation number per student is 2061, which is too large to be regarded as a convincing statistical value. Also, with this extremely large range, the median, mean, and mode of operation counts are of no use in this case. Thus, we need to do case-by-case analysis in this case analysis to figure out specific user habits for various kinds of students.

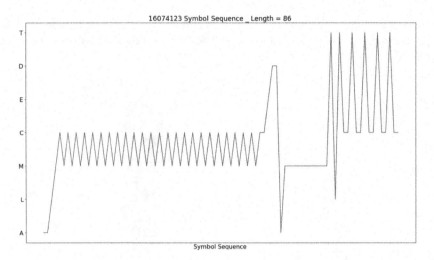

Fig. 6. Action sequence of student 16074123.

Take the action sequence of the student with student number 16074123 shown in Fig. 6, several insightful user behavior habits can be concluded from the action sequences, which are shown as below:

1. Type by type actions:
   Students are more likely to finish all actions in one type first, and then do all actions of another type. As shown in Fig. 6, this student firstly did action sets of changing links and changing elements (shown as action C and M), then did action sets of changing links and editing text (shown as action C and T). These sequential patterns are showing that this student prefers doing the same type of action at one time, then shifting to another type of action.
2. More actions on adjustment:
   Extremely high values are indicating another student modeling behavior pattern. The average value of changing element divided by adding element among the students is 21.2, and the average value of changing link divided by adding link is 21.4. These extremely high values confirm the observation that students tend to do much more adjustment actions after adding an element or a link.

6   Conclusions

This paper proposes an interactive and comprehensive framework focusing on in-process student learning data to evaluate student learning effect. Based on process mining, it uses several advanced techniques including feature engineering, frequent sequential pattern mining, and user behavior analysis. Moreover, we build up an online modeling platform which supports three types of online diagram drawing. It can automatically record user modeling operation data. We also carry out a case study on a real course Introduction to Software Engineering with data collected from the platform. It gives out insightful conclusions about student learning behavior.

In the future, the framework will use more advanced process mining techniques and be applied in various fields to evaluate student learning effect. In addition, more real in-process student learning data will be put into the case study to derive useful conclusions and improve the stability and robustness of the framework.

Acknowledgements. This work is supported by Beijing Education Science Planning Funding (No. CCHA18148), International Research Cooperation Seed Fund of Beijing University of Technology (No. 2018B2), and Basic Research Funding of Beijing University of Technology (No. 040000546318516).

References

1. Baghaei, N., Nehring, N., Dacey, S.: Improving students' performace through gamification: a user study. In: Proceedings of the 10th International Conference on Computer Supported Education, vol. 1, pp. 213–218 (2018)
2. Morita, M., Shinoda, Y.: Information filtering based on user behavior analysis and best match text retrieval. In: Croft, B.W., van Rijsbergen, C.J. (eds.) SIGIR 1994, pp. 272–281. Springer, London (1994). https://doi.org/10.1007/978-1-4471-2099-5_28
3. Cao, H., Mamoulis, N., Cheung, D.W.: Mining frequent spatio-temporal sequential patterns. In: Fifth IEEE International Conference on Data Mining (ICDM 2005), pp. 8–11. IEEE (2005)
4. Van Der Aalst, W.: Process Mining: Discovery, Conformance and Enhancement of Business Processes, 2nd edn. Springer, Heidelberg (2011). https://doi.org/10.1007/978-3-642-19345-3
5. Jansen, B.J., Spink, A., Saracevic, T.: Real life, real users, and real needs: a study and analysis of user queries on the web. Inf. Process. Manag. **36**(2), 207–227 (2000)
6. Agichtein, E., Brill, E., Dumais, S.: Improving web search ranking by incorporating user behavior information. In: Proceedings of the 29th Annual International ACM SIGIR Conference on Research and Development in Information Retrieval, pp. 19–26. ACM (2006)
7. Mabroukeh, N.R., Ezeife, C.I.: A taxonomy of sequential pattern mining algorithms. ACM Comput. Surv. (CSUR) **43**(1), 3 (2010)
8. Agrawal, R., Srikant, R.: Mining sequential patterns. In: International Conference on Data Engineering, pp. 3–14. IEEE (1995)
9. Srikant, R., Agrawal, R.: Mining sequential patterns: generalizations and performance improvements. In: Apers, P., Bouzeghoub, M., Gardarin, G. (eds.) EDBT 1996. LNCS, vol. 1057, pp. 1–17. Springer, Heidelberg (1996). https://doi.org/10.1007/BFb0014140
10. Han, J., Pei, J., Mortazavi-Asl, B., Chen, Q., Dayal, U.: FreeSpan: frequent pattern-projected sequential pattern mining. In: Proceedings of the Sixth ACM SIGKDD International Conference on Knowledge Discovery and Data Mining, pp. 355–359. ACM (2000)

11. Pei, J., Han, J., Mortazavi-Asl, B., Pinto, H.: PrefixSpan: mining sequential patterns efficiently by prefix-projected pattern growth. In: Proceedings 17th International Conference on Data Engineering, pp. 215–224. IEEE (2001)
12. Turner, C.R., Fuggetta, A., Lavazza, L., Wolf, A.L.: A conceptual basis for feature engineering. J. Syst. Softw. **49**(1), 3–15 (1999)

Evalu@: An Agnostic Web-Based Tool for Consistent and Constant Evaluation Used as a Data Gatherer for Artificial Intelligence Implementations

Fernando Yepes-Calderon[1,2(✉)] [ID], Juan F. Yepes Zuluaga[1,2],
and Gonzalo E. Yepes Calderon[1]

[1] GYM Group SA, Carrera 78A No. 6-58, Cali, Colombia
fernando@gym-group.org
[2] Strategic Business Platforms,
417 Heritage Park Tr Nw, Kennesaw, GA 30144, USA

Abstract. Evalu@ is a software development created under the model-view-controller pattern and is meant to be executed in a client-server architecture. It is benefited from the worldwide coverage of the Internet and acts as an evaluating gadget and a data centralizer. Evalu@ is initially conceived as a solution to the lack of assistant tools while running the quality programs in industrial environments. Later, due to its high degree of generalization in the setup of evaluations schemes, the software was successfully flavored to suit the willingness of entrepreneurs in other fields. Recently, some Machine Learning features have been added and are being tested to close the monitoring cycle by not only keeping track of the evaluation items chronologically; but also being capable of classifying and predicting outcomes based on previously gathered data.

Keywords: Data analysis · Artificial intelligence · Research-industry gap diminishing

1 Introduction

In our highly competitive world, commercial and personal work-related activities are pushed to excellence. This tendency seems to be reasonable in a capitalist environment where quality in the services and currency are equally appreciated [11]. However, how to define quality and moreover, how to accomplish it?

During the last century, several regulating organizations were created around the world to provide elements that can lead companies to proceed with high quality. Initially, the principal goal was to provide normalization so all the entities in a particular field not only could speak in the same terms but also, they could have a subtle agreement regarding the form of the delivered, whether it is a service or a product [12]. As everyone wants to have the best for a price, rapidly, the quality initiative became global. Consequently, the International Federation

© Springer Nature Switzerland AG 2019
H. Florez et al. (Eds.): ICAI 2019, CCIS 1051, pp. 73–84, 2019.
https://doi.org/10.1007/978-3-030-32475-9_6

of the National Standardizing Association (ISA) was created in 1926, dissolved during the second world war and re-established as the International Organization for Standardization (ISO) [8]. The ISO defines a group of statements that nowadays go beyond the primary purpose providing the bases for a clear understanding of quality with global traceability. Within the ISO methods, the 'ways of doing' that guarantees clients' satisfaction are defined, while assuring people's integrity and healthy conditions in the creation of a product or a service. Despite the worldwide acceptability of ISO, it lacks a consistent-technological assisting tool that facilitates the application of standards [18]. Designing a tool with enough flexibility to follow a highly dynamic environment that supposes the application of standards in diverse production fields is cumbersome. To assure the desired flexibility, the presented solution breaks the paradigm of *customized solutions* [15] used by software developers, and introduces the agnostic-blackbox (ABlaBo) concept. In the AblaBo, the solutions go from the simple to the complex and get perfectly fitted to particularities while the users interact more time with the tool.

This manuscript presents an Internet-based service available in www. evalualos.com that uses ABlaBo to assist users in the tasks of evaluation, monitoring through time, generation of customized quality criteria, easy visualization, generation of predictions, unlimited creation of indexes and implementation of programmed feedback among many other operative details. The tool is designed to cover all kind of evaluations and to keep historical records of the results chronologically organized. We also present some success cases and introduce the applicability of machine learning (ML) techniques to provide prediction capabilities. With this particular feature, in addition to empowering the tool with an outstanding added value, we shorten the gap between research and real-world applications, while giving to final users the possibility to predict the behavior of their evaluating items; an aspect that traduces to saving resources and capital.

2   Materials and Methods

2.1   Software Designing Pillars and Implementation

2.1.1   EV-Boxes Creation (Containers of e-Items)

In order to provide the desired flexibility so that any group of entities (people or objects) could be evaluated, the design exploits the benefits of the persistence engine by mapping the forms entries into the database. The form-entry mapping is a standard solution used in successful applications like Moodle [3,4] and also in popular content management systems like Joomla or Drupal [10]. The user also defines this form entries through configuration files written in Excel (CSV) files, which gives several advantages including; structural simplicity, reduced size, cross-platform usability, and off-line planning [17]. Besides, in Evalu@, and willing to avoid database transaction overheat, the evaluating items' *(e-items)* descriptors and evaluations *(e-surveys)* are saved as a string containing array-like syntax as generalized in Eq. 1. Furthermore, this text pattern is exploded to be presented to the final users in an organized manner. Also, the users are not limited in any aspect regarding the configuration of e-items and e-surveys. Shortly, the application can host several e-item boxes, where unlimited e-items can be held, and these e-items can be evaluated with unlimited e-survey profiles. No matter how complex the setup scheme is, Evalu@ will continue being fully operative; from here, its agnostic nature. See in Fig. 1 two configuration files to create e-item boxes.

Item to evaluate	Descriptor	ages: photo. For date	Option 1	Option 2	Option 3	Option 4	Option 5
Extinguisher							
A	Serial	IRP-E002					
	Brand	Badger	Ecosan	ABC	Amerex	Zemer	
	Date of purchase	DD/MM/YYYY					
	Capacity	1 kg	2.5 kg	5 Kg	10 Kg		

Item to evaluate	Descriptor	ages: photo. For date	Option 1	Option 2	Option 3	Option 4	Option 5	Option 6
Senior Soccer								
B	Name	Daniel						
	Lastname	Reina						
	DOB	DD/MM/YYYY						
	Position	Goalkeeper	Defense	Midfielder	Attacker			
	Laterality	Right	Left	Ambidextrous				
	Schoolarity	None	Primary	Secondary	BS	MS	MD/PhD	

Fig. 1. Excel files to create two different e-item boxes. In panel A, the e-item box to grouping extinguishers. In panel B the e-item box collects soccer players. Even when the mechanisms of this flexibility are bulky, the system does not create database-transactional overheat

$$F(j) = \begin{cases} [key_j : value_j] & \text{if value exist} \forall key_j \in N \\ Continue & otherwise \end{cases} \tag{1}$$

Where Key_j replaces a descriptor or an evaluation criteria, while $value_j$ holds the corresponding value.

The average time to measure over 100 repetitions querying an entry of $j = 8$ fields organized in the array-like fashion, was of 0.1448 ms. The same exercise with an equivalent data persistence using separated fields (rows) per entry, resulted in 0.1510 ms. Although the time is not considerably different, the used strategy will keep the record in one line, regardless of how many descriptors or evaluation elements are required for a given e-item box. These timing experiments are performed directly at the command line in a Mysql server (Dell, i7 processor) running Ubuntu Linux 16.04 so web latencies timing variations associated with accessing remote database servers are avoided.

2.1.2   Evaluations (e-Surveys) Creation

Regarding the e-surveys, generalization in the construction of the tests is accomplished based on the same mechanism used in the e-items box creation. Several e-survey criteria can be nested in an unlimited category-subcategory structure; these criteria will have a value in the e-survey that is quantitative by nature but can also be presented to final users in qualitative form. Also during the configuration of the e-surveys, the user might define a range of possible values for each criterion by explicitly defining an array of values or implicitly by defining a range in the form *[initial value; step; final value]*. In both cases, the values will be presented in a select box – an HTML-form control – that will be placed in front of every evaluating criteria. The user has one more option regarding the configuration values. When placing an "m" character at the values field in the numeric options (see Fig. 2 - **Panel B**), the system will interpret the entry as used define option, and instead of posting a select box, the HTML-form control will be an input text.

Panel A

Evaluation name	Extinguisher Eval			
Short name	GYM-EV-001			
			Numerical options	
Category	Subcategory	Values or range	Units	Qualitative options
State and facility state		sum	Points	
	Easy access to extinguisher	-10 5 10	Points	No|Partially|Yes
	The tube is firmly connected	-10 10	Points	No|Yes
	The tube is operational	-10 10	Points	No|Yes
	The security pin is in place	0 10	Points	No|Yes
	It is easy to know where the extinguisher is	0 10	Points	No|Yes
Operation		avg	Points	
	OK in hydrostatic test	-10 10	Points	No|Yes
	Is the device charge	-10|2.5|10	Points	Empty|Almost empty|Half level| Almost full|Full
	The security pin releases the system easily	-10 10	Points	No|Yes

Panel B

Evaluation name	CPK n Urea			
Short name	DC-E001			
	Numerical options			
Category	Subcategory	Values or range	Units	Qualitative options	Help messages to the evaluator
CPK		sum	U/L		
	Read of CPK	m	U/L	N/A	Read value for current player as it appears in the screen
Urea		sum	mmol/l		
	Read of Urea	m	mmol/l	N/A	Read value for current player as it appears in the screen

Panel C

Evaluation name	Security in the work place			
Short name	ST-11111-02			
			Numerical options	
Category	Subcategory	Values or range	Units	Qualitative options
Standard 2.1. SBT Policy		sum	Value	
	2.1.1 Policy of the Occupational Health and Safety Management System SG–SST signed; dated and communicated to COPASST / Vigia	10 0	Value	Agree|Disagree
Standard 2.2. SGSST Objectives		sum	Value	
	2.2.1 Defined objectives; clear; measurable quantifiable with goals; documented; revised SG–SST	10 0	Value	Agree|Disagree
Standard 2.3. Initial evaluation SG/SST		sum	Value	
	2.3.1 Evaluation and identification of priorities	10 0	Value	Agree|Disagree
Standard 2.4. Annual work plan		sum	Value	
	2.4.1 Plan that identifies objectives; goals; responsibility; resources with schedule and signed	20 0	Value	Agree|Disagree
Standard 2.5. Documentation conservation		sum	Value	
	2.5.1 Document archive or retention of the Occupational Health and Safety Management System SG–SST	20 0	Value	Agree|Disagree
Standard 2.6. Accountability		sum	Value	
	2.6.1 Performance surrender	10 0	Value	Agree|Disagree
Standard 2.7. Current regulations SST		sum	Value	
	2.7.1 Legal matrix	20 0	Value	Agree|Disagree
Standard 2.8. Communication		sum	Value	
	2.8.1 Mechanisms of self-report communication in Occupational Health and Safety Management System SG–SST	10 0	Value	Agree|Disagree
Standard 2.9. Acquisitions		sum	Value	
	2.9.1 Identification; evaluation; for the acquisition of products and services in the Occupational Health and Safety Management System SG x	10 0	Value	Agree|Disagree

Fig. 2. Excel files to create two different e-surveys. In panel A, An evaluation designed to grade extinguishers. In panel B, an evaluation to follow metabolic variables that may be used in the senior soccer players shown in Fig. 1 - **panel B**. In panel C, an evaluation that follows the literal 2 of the 1111 standard (SG-SST) acronym of "Sistema de gestion, seguridad y salud en el trabajo"

2.2   Association of e-Item Boxes and e-Surveys

Since the e-item boxes and e-surveys are independently created, one can associate an e-survey to several e-item boxes accomplishing re-usability. Another consequence of this assignment freedom, an e-item box can have several e-surveys associated, flexibility appreciated in environments where the e-items are evaluated in more than one aspect, and those aspects need to be analyzed independently (Fig. 3).

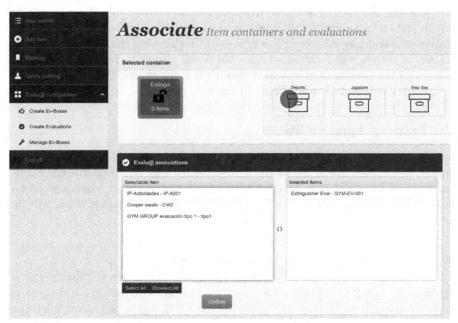

Fig. 3. Association of e-item boxes and evaluations. Here the e-item box of extinguishers is about to be linked to the extinguishers' e-survey that was previously uploaded to the system using the excel template depicted in Fig. 2 - **Panel A**

2.3   Interoperability, and Data Sharing

Evalu@ has a simple but useful module that complies with Remote Procedure Call (RPC) [2]. The protocol to share the information was chosen to be JSON due to both, its transparent translation from native programming objects and its simplicity of treatment in the client console [7]. Through the JSON-RPC specification, other applications may be benefited from the tracking capabilities of Evalu@ and produce their reporting schemes. By the moment of writing this document, Evalu@ can share JSON chains holding individual e-item profiles, including their descriptors and historical records of evaluation. Bulky JSON sharing capabilities are also supported. Besides, Evalu@ can be operated in smartphones and tablets with a responsive cascade style sheet (CSS) design. Also, e-surveys can be posted publicly using permalinks in the evalu@ site and iframes in external URLs [6].

2.4   Classification and Prediction Capabilities

Evalu@ has been given classification and prediction capabilities. These specifications are based on support vector machines algorithm (SVM) [16]. While trying to obtain substantial information from unknown data, one might feed the SVM algorithm with features that do not provide any differentiation power. To avoid the proliferation of useless features, a step of feature reduction is accomplished through an F-test. After the F-test, the K best features are selected and feed to the SVM algorithm. The K value depends on the number of e-items available (not in the system, but the grouping box). This K to number of e-items (N_e) relation is defined by $K = ceil(N_e * exp(-4))$. In this way, the machine learning strategy is always well-formulated since there will always be more samples than features. If the system does not have enough e-items to satisfy the formulation of K, the SVM feature is not offered in the user interface.

2.5   Fields of Applicability

At the moment of writing this manuscript, two fields of applicability that have nothing in common are in use of the system, something that remarks the excellent level of generalization reached by Evalu@ and make us confident of its acceptability and usability. In a further stage, other application fields will be targeted.

2.5.1   Health and Security in the Workplace

Security in the workplace is an essential aspect for companies worldwide and is regulated by the ISO. Despite the directives are self-explanatory, and there is no doubt about the concepts, the applicability is still a pending asset. With the flexibility of Evalu@, an e-item box can be created to group all the e-items by function and then, create different evaluation profiles for each e-item box. Having this centralized information benefits the companies in many aspects, including online management, live reporting, remote monitoring, and the confidence of having the system under control. Also, the prediction capabilities provided through the ML implementation in mode "supervised classification" can suggest when an e-item should be replaced, taken into maintenance or will have high/low performance in case the evaluation is performed on people.

2.5.2   Information Athletes

The process of formation in sports follows some qualification aspects that are strongly associated with the ideology of trainers. Some theory says that players must be evaluated according to the purposes of the microcycles and mesocycles [5] other more pragmatic approaches pretend to form the players in their physical, technical, and overall, mental capabilities [13]. Even though these schemes are associated with soccer, other disciplines are adopting them to educate their prospects. No matter what the approach is, the evaluating stage is of outstanding importance because it says not only the state of the players but their evolution.

By now, coaches and trainers are aware of the state of the players, but few of them can say something about their evolution without incurring in qualitative statements biased by personal perceptions [9]. Even worse, players usually ignore the plan, how they are being evaluated, and their performances according to the evaluation criteria. All these problems are solved with the data centralization and chronological reporting capabilities provided by Evalu@. In this field, the administrators are benefited from the non-supervised classification function, where groups are automatically created among the whole data accordingly to the factors of evaluation [1]. This automatic grouping can be later correlated with overall performance and thus create training plans targeting particular groups necessities, something practically more feasible than individualizing the training.

2.5.3   High-Performance Athletes and Scouting

High-performance athletes of almost any discipline are subject to a market that is continuously looking for excellence. The selection process uses scouts that travel around the world with excel sheets [14]. Then, the information is centralized, and decisions are made with the stored information. This process is expensive, sluggish, and susceptible to human mistakes. With Evalu@, the information is updated instantly, and it is available for administrators and collaborators in the act. Grading responsibilities are evident even in grading sessions that happened time ago. Collaborators can be in any part of the globe as well as the e-items. The administrators are provided with tools compare players on a timing axis to include concepts of regularity in their decisions. Ranking capabilities are also included, and the final user can build filters to profile the ideal player and to create the ranking according to those preferences. The prediction capabilities in this matter are used to define when a prospect is ready to jump to first divisions leagues and when, according to his/her historical performance, it would be better to start the marketing tasks.

3   Results

In this section, some success cases that are currently running are presented. As the system continues gathering the data, the prediction capabilities and other AI-based functions will be enabled.

3.1   Industrial Security

3.1.1   Security Network

A beta-testing stage is currently being executed at a company in the agronomy field that produces sugar as a primary activity and has run diversification tasks to produce paper and fuel. The grouping items in this particular environment consist of fire extinguishers, hydrants, emergency beds, and ambulances. The creation of these boxes was accomplished by the security head officer using the configuration built-in wizard. The company is currently running evaluations

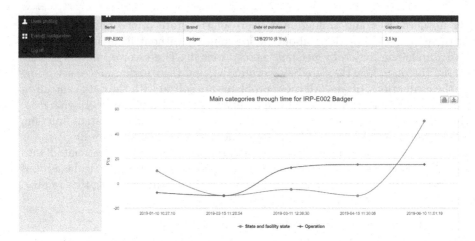

Fig. 4. Evolution in time of an e-item in the extinguishers box. The results correspond to evaluations performed periodically using the e-survey depicted in Fig. 2 - **Panel A**

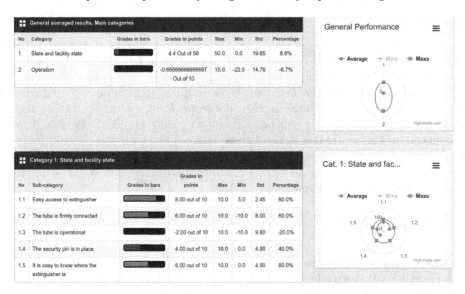

Fig. 5. Part of the average analysis. The data is generated automatically with the information individually shown in Fig. 4

using Evalu@ to certify his security network. See Fig. 4 for extinguishers profiling and evolution in time.

For companies maintaining a security network, it is crucial to report the average analysis as it is shown in Fig. 5. This analysis is provided as a default function by the software.

Fig. 6. Evalu@'s inputting form for the e-survey depicted in Fig. 2 - **Panel C**

3.1.2   Complying with the SG-SST Regulation

Due to the flexibility delivered by Evalu@, it is used in the same company to comply with the regulation SG-SST. The Fig. 6 is a pragmatic evidence of one the uses listed in Sect. 2.5.1.

Within Evalu@, analyzing the strong and weak points of the company, and how the correction measurements impact the performance is easily accomplished by just glancing at the evolution in time report depicted in Fig. 7. Note how the agnostic nature of the software is evidenced.

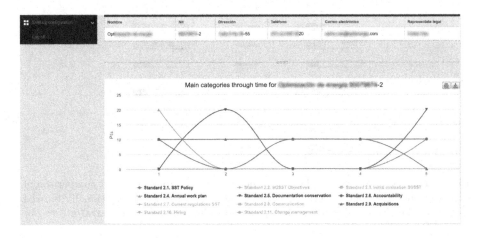

Fig. 7. SG-SST evolution in time for the literal 2 of the standard "Integral operation".

3.2   Sports Scouting

Evalu@ has already passed the first round of tests in an international scouting company where the goal is to have a record of high-performance soccer players. Specific modules such as the versus visualization and the multifeatured ranking help the scouting company to find the right player for a demanding team. Ideally, this activity requires extensive coverage, considering that good players can be anywhere in the world. In this matter, the operation was far away from the desired due to operational problems linked to data transport and data reliability. Now, this aim is feasible due to the inherent global coverage of Evalu@. See the use of the versus mode in Fig. 8.

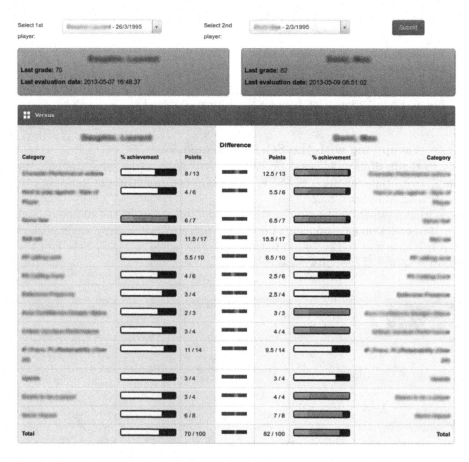

Fig. 8. The versus module has been specifically designed to allow direct comparison of e-items among the e-survey criteria. Some information has been intentionally blurred to protect the evaluation criteria as requested by the company administrator.

4   Discussion

As a response to a recurrent industrial requirement, we have designed and created Evalu@. This system is a powerful tool that reaches a high degree of generalization. The keystone of Evalu@ is strongly related to is flexibility; that makes this solution usable in different fields of application. This tool is still being developed, but its modularity provided by a model-view-controller assures that further development will not affect the correct operation of previously launched specifications. Additionally, Evalu@ provides standard interoperability by implementing the RPC specification. Through the RPC, a simple coded request to evalu@ will return a complete JSON structure that can be used for creating new flavored angles of the same application. An ML implementation is envisaged, and we are strategically collecting more data. The ML approach represents a good step towards narrowing the gap between research and implementation. Evalu@ is being tested in two companies at the moment. They both see potential in this tool for data centralization that will undoubtedly improve their indexes of operation. Regarding success case 1, this is something that saves significant amounts of money currently invested in quality assurance tasks but moreover, the personal costs when the security network fails. Regarding success case 2, the use of this tool increases scouting accuracy that is traduced in credibility, thus profitability. In the following, our team will continue developing associated modules and target the field of athletes in minor divisions, a field that has been already contacted and from which good acceptability has been received.

5   Conclusions

Because of the high coverage provided by the Internet and its associated programming platforms, several applications have migrated from desktop to the browser environments, where a vast range of services are available. Other modern gadgets such as tablets and smartphones facilitate the data generation in almost any daily situation. Data has become massive, difficult to interpret in bulky fashion, but still meaningful. Our job consists of turning this information into valuable leads for companies, that is understandable to final users and provides new features that can assist humans in the decision-making scenario. Evalu@ has been created with all these principles in mind, assisting, to best of our knowledge, an unmet field. Further extensions include the development of hardware gadgets to increase off-line usability. Once data is centralized, AI gadgets can be developed to contribute to the creation of generalized knowledge.

References

1. Barshan, B., Yüksek, M.C.: Recognizing daily and sports activities in two open source machine learning environments using body-worn sensor units. Comput. J. **57**, 1649–1667 (2014)

2. Birman, K.P.: Remote procedure calls and the client/server model. In: Birman, K.P. (ed.) Guide to Reliable Distributed Systems. Texts in Computer Science, pp. 185–247. Springer, London (2012). https://doi.org/10.1007/978-1-4471-2416-0_6

3. Chourishi, D., Buttan, C.K., Chaurasia, A., Soni, A.: Effective e-learning through moodle (2011)

4. Huang, C.-C., Wang, Y.-M., Wu, T.W., Wang, P.A.: An empirical analysis of the antecedents and performance consequences of using the moodle platform. Int. J. Inf. Educ. Technol. 3(2) (2013). https://doi.org/10.7763/IJIET.2013.V3.267

5. Comfort, P., Matthews, M.: An Introduction to Periodisation. Wiley, Hoboken (2010)

6. Florencias-Oliveros, O., et al.: Real-life power quality transients (2017). https://doi.org/10.21227/H2Q30W

7. Ghosh, D., Sheeh, J., Thorup, K.K., Vinoski, S.: Programming language impact on the development of distributed systems. J. Internet Serv. Appl. 3(1), 22–30 (2012)

8. Heires, M.: The international organization for standardization (ISO). New Polit. Econ. 13(3), 357–367 (2008). https://doi.org/10.1080/13563460802302693

9. Hvistendahl, J.: The effect of placement of biasing information. J. Q. 43, 647–654 (1966)

10. Patel, S.K., Rathod, V.R., Prajapati, J.B.: Performance analysis of content management systems- Joomla, Drupal and WordPress. Int. J. Comput. Appl. 21(4), 39–43 (2011)

11. Lambin, J.J.: Capitalism and sustainable development. SYMPHONYA Emerg. Issues Manag. 2, 3–9 (2009)

12. Renard, M.-C.: Quality certification, regulation and power in fair trade. J. Rural. Stud. 21, 419–431 (2005)

13. Mathieu, J.E., Heffner, T.S., Heffner, T.S., Salas, E., Cannon-Bowers, J.A.: The influence of shared mental models on team process and performance. J. Appl. Psychol. 85, 273 (2000)

14. Moore, P.: Scouting an antrhopology of sports. Anthropologica 46, 37–46 (2004)

15. Müller, J., Krüger, J., Enderlein, S., Helmich, M., Zeier, A.: Customizing enterprise software as a service applications: back-end extension in a multi-tenancy environment. In: Filipe, J., Cordeiro, J. (eds.) ICEIS 2009. LNBIP, vol. 24, pp. 66–77. Springer, Heidelberg (2009). https://doi.org/10.1007/978-3-642-01347-8_6

16. Pedregosa, F., et al.: Scikit-learn: machine learning in python. J. Mach. Learn. Res. 12, 2825–2830 (2011). http://dl.acm.org/citation.cfm?id=1953048.2078195

17. Shafranovich, Y.: Common format and MIME type for comma-separated values (CSV) files. RFC 4180, 1–8 (2005)

18. Zeng, S.X.: Overcoming barriers to sustainable implementation of the ISO. Manag. Audit. J. 22, 244–254 (2007)

Model for Resource Allocation in Decentralized Networks Using Interaction Nets

Joaquín F. Sánchez[1]([✉]), Juan P. Ospina[2], Carlos Collazos-Morales[1], Henry Avendaño[1], Paola Ariza-Colpas[3], and N. Vanesa Landero[4]

[1] Universidad Manuela Beltran, Bogotá, Colombia
{joaquin.sanchez,carlos.collazos}@docentes.umb.edu.co,
henry.avendano@umb.edu.co
[2] Fundación Universitaria San Mateo, Bogotá, Colombia
jpabloospina@sanmateo.edu.co
[3] Departamento Ciencias de Computación y Electrónica,
Universidad de la Costa-CUC, Barranquilla, Colombia
pariza@cuc.edu.co
[4] Universidad Politecnica de Apodaca, Apodaca, Nuevo Leon, Mexico
vlandero@upapnl.edu.mx

Abstract. This article presents the description of a model for allocating resources using Interaction Nets and a strategy for playing public goods. In the description of the model first shows the behavior of the allocation of resources towards the nodes depending on the usefulness of the network and the satisfaction of the agents. Then the generalization of the model with Interaction Nets is described, and a simulation of this behavior is made. It is found that there is an emerging behavior condition in the dynamics of the interaction when assigning resources. To test the model, the interaction of sharing the Internet in an ad hoc network is done. The interaction is shown in the general model obtained.

Keywords: Resource allocation · Ad hoc networks · Interaction Nets

1 Introduction

This article shows the design of a model for allocating resources in a decentralized network to its component nodes. The components of the model are, on the one hand, the computational model of Interaction Nets, which is used to formalize the concept of interaction in the context of computation. The second component is the set of public goods as a vision of allocation of resources to the participants of a specific agglomerate.

The control of decentralized networks is an element that differentiates this type of networks because it is from each of the nodes that make up the network [14]. The application of decentralized networks with more significant potential for the design and implementation of solutions in different areas are ad hoc

© Springer Nature Switzerland AG 2019
H. Florez et al. (Eds.): ICAI 2019, CCIS 1051, pp. 85–101, 2019.
https://doi.org/10.1007/978-3-030-32475-9_7

networks [1,5,6]. The operation of these networks is affected by a change in topology and a change in the number of participants as a function of time; since resources are limited, finite, techniques can be explored to optimize the use of these resources [10].

The analogies shown in the literature for assignment in traditional computational models are based on assignment in stable conditions, with centralized control schemes, or in current applications with distributed control schemes [11,12]. However, the change of paradigm of decentralized control in new generation networks makes it necessary to explore new techniques to perform the resources, such as memory, storage, and processing [2,15].

Decentralized networks have signs of complexity, and adaptability schemes to cope with these signs of complexity use various techniques to cope with this phenomenon. One of the possible ways to construct adaptation schemes is to understand the local interactions between network participants [19]. Thus, details of the functioning of decentralized networks can be covered.

The purpose of this work is to show how to generate a model of resource allocation for decentralized networks, the model is based on the game of public goods and is combined with Interaction Nets, looking for implementation in a computer tool (e.g., a programming language). In the real work, the application of the Interaction Net model is described to carry out a coverage expansion, and the resource assignment is the Internet assignment to the nodes that participate in an ad hoc network.

The distribution of the document is as follows: Sect. 2 presents the theoretical considerations of the model, first presents the concept of Interaction Nets, then describes the concept of the set of public goods and finally this the design of the model. Section 3 explains the simulation of the resource allocation model. Section 4 presents the real work. The description of an ad hoc network is presented, expanding the coverage of the Internet signal between the nodes that make up the ad hoc network. Finally, there are the conclusions and recommendations.

2   Theoretical Considerations for the Model

The purpose of this section is to present the relevant concepts that have been worked on for the construction of the resource allocation model. First, the computational model is presented to represent the elements that are part of the experiment. Then the problem of resource allocation is described using the game of public goods; finally, there is the Interaction Nets model.

2.1   Interaction Nets Model

The Interaction Nets model is a conceptual tool that helps to model different systems in engineering. The purpose of understanding and modeling the interactions of the nodes of an ad hoc network.

Interactions in opportunistic networks are a phenomenon associated with the dynamic characteristics of this type of systems [22]. The resulting emergence of these interactions must be modeled and thus controlled by computer systems [7,18]. The idea of the model is the creation of a computational method that contemplates these actions in highly interconnected systems (Environments where IoT networks are deployed or will be deployed) [13].

The model is represented by a graph, the main port, and secondary ports. The exchange of information between different nodes generates a change in the internal states of the nodes. This action is a definition of interaction. The idea of computation as interaction is the basis of this computational model [8,16].

This model is composed of the following elements:

- A set of symbol elements,
- A collection of interaction rules,
- A network of interactions, and active pairs.

A feature of this model uses several models, graphic, for active and function notation.

2.2   The Linear Public Good Game

The problem of the voluntary provision of resources has been usually analyzed using the linear public good game [9]. Nevertheless, due to the nature of open self-organizing systems, this model presents some limitations that need to be considered before applying it in the context of ad hoc networks. For example, it assumes that the public payoff is equally distributed even when it is possible for the appropriation to exceed allocation; that there is a full disclosure of all information required for the process; that there is no cost related to monitoring; that the utility for all resources are the same no matter if they are needed or not. As a consequence, in order to get a more realistic model, we relax some of these conditions using a variation of this game [17]. In this case, n agents form a cluster in which each agent i owns a quantity of some divisible resource and freely decides if contribute or not to the public good. We assume that agents take their decisions under self-interest analysis, and the game is played in consecutive rounds. In each round, each agent i:

- Determines the resources it has available, $g_i \in [0,1]$
- Determines its needs of resources, $q_i \in [0,1]$
- Makes a demand for resources, $d_i \in [0,1]$
- Makes a provision of resources, $p_i \in [0,1]$ $(p_i \leq g_i)$
- Receives an allocation of resources, $r_i \in [0,1]$
- Makes an appropriation of resources, $r'_i \in [0,1]$.

The total amount of resources owned by an agent at the end of the round is given by $R_i = r'_i + (g_i - p_i)$, in which R_i is the sum of resources appropriated by the agent and the ones that it keeps for itself. The contributions of all participants are summed and the payoff u_i for the agent i is given by:

$$U_i = \begin{cases} a(q_i) + b(R_i - q_i) \ if R_i \geq q_i \\ a(R_i) - c(q_i - R_i) \ otherwise \end{cases} \tag{1}$$

where a, b and c are coefficients in $\mathbb{R}$ that represent the relative utility of getting the resources that are needed, getting resources that are not needed, and not getting the resources that are needed.

Furthermore, independent of its utility and the cooperation pattern (the prisoner's dilemma or the linear public good game) each agent i makes a subjective assessment of its satisfaction S_i expressed as a value in $[0, 1]$ according to the relationship between its allocation and its demands. In this regard, we can define the satisfaction level of the agent i in the round $t + 1$ as follows:

$$S_i(t + 1) = \begin{cases} S_i(t) + \alpha\left[1 - S_i(t)\right] & \text{if} \quad r_i \geq d_i \\ S_i(t) - \beta(q_i - R_i) & \text{otherwise,} \end{cases} \tag{2}$$

where α and β are coefficients in $\mathbb{R}$ which determine the rate of reinforcement of satisfaction and dissatisfaction of each agent. As a result, choosing different combinations of α and β allow us to model different behaviors in the agents. For example, high values of α and low values β enable us to model agents with a high level of tolerance to situations in which they do not get what they need. On the other hand, high values of β will make the agents be dissatisfied more quickly, and therefore, they would stop following the institutional rules. This scenario is modeled through a threshold value of τ and an interval value of m. If for m consecutive rounds the agent i evaluate $S_i < \tau$ as true, it will stop cooperate. In the case of the prisoner's dilemma, the agents appropriate several resources greater than the allocated (they turn into free-riders). In the linear public good game, the agent leaves the cluster.

2.3   Distribution Model with Interaction Nets

The purpose of this model is to have a notation that serves to generate functionalities in a programming language, a simple representation of the problem and a perspective to analyze a particular situation. Figure 1 presents the situation of resource allocation from a network to a group of agents. Following the convention described in the problem of public goods, in the interaction the set of Σ agents.

- $\Sigma = \{i, g, q, d, r, r'\}$
- Networks U, S.

The rules of interaction are as follows:

- $i \bowtie g \rightarrow \lambda_1$ Determines available resources.
- $i \bowtie q \rightarrow \lambda_2$ Determines the need for resources.

- $i \bowtie d \to \lambda_3$ Makes a demand for resources to the network.
- $\lambda = \lambda_1 + \lambda_2 + \lambda_3$ The resources of the agent ask to the network.
- $i \bowtie r \to \mu_1$ Receive a resource allocation.
- $i \bowtie r' \to \mu_2$ Makes an appropriation of resources.
- $\mu = \mu_1 + \mu_2$ The resources that the network gives to the agent.

The contribution of the agents to the network and the satisfaction of each agent is the result of interactions between the set of agents and networks U and S. So the system that represents the allocation of resources is given by:

- $(i \bowtie \lambda)^* \to U, S$
- $(i \bowtie \mu)^* \to U, S.$

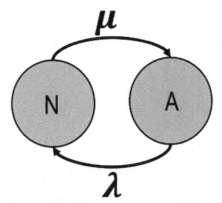

Fig. 1. Model of interactions. N represents the decentralized network, and A represents the collection of agents

Figure 1 shows the concept of interaction for resource allocation. N represents the decentralized network, and A represents the collection of agents. Because a decentralized network has unique features (e.g., decentralized control), it is necessary to review how the model behaves in these cases.

Each interaction between the agents and the network is for a particular scenario. It is considering that there is a variation of nodes in each configuration that varies the time. In each interaction, the usefulness of the contribution of the agents to the network and the satisfaction of the agents varies. Figure 2 shows the variation in the value of the *Utility* and the *Satisfaction* according to the possible configurations that a decentralized network can have. The calculation of each contribution of the participants and the level of satisfaction is exposed. For this we use the model exposed Eqs. 1 and 2.

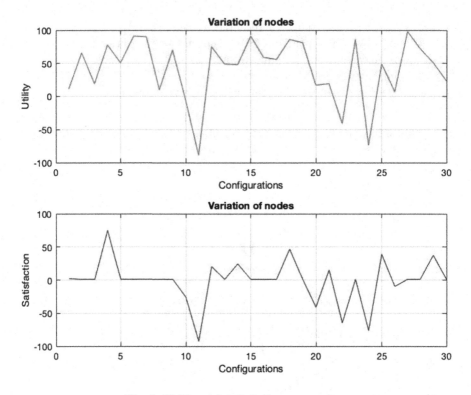

Fig. 2. Utility and satisfaction comparison

The rules of interaction for the general model with different configurations is:

- $(i \bowtie \lambda)^1 \rightarrow U_1, S_1$ and $(i \bowtie \mu)^1 \rightarrow U, S$ Configuration 1
- $(i \bowtie \lambda)^2 \rightarrow U_2, S_2$ and $(i \bowtie \mu)^2 \rightarrow U, S$ Configuration 2
- $(i \bowtie \lambda)^n \rightarrow U_n, S_n$ and $(i \bowtie \mu)^n \rightarrow U, S$ Configuration n.

Figure 3 shows the comparison between the usefulness versus the satisfaction of each agent. It is interesting to note that agent satisfaction is low while network utility is high. This observation indicates that the well-being of the majority is superimposed on that of the individual. One conclusion is that the behavior shown is an emerging characteristic of network behavior as a function of the dynamics of interactions between participants.

3   Tests on the Model

3.1   Simulation

Taking into account the description made in the previous section on the computation model and the resource allocation model, the purpose of this section is to show how to allocate resources from an entity (a network of nodes) to different agents (nodes).

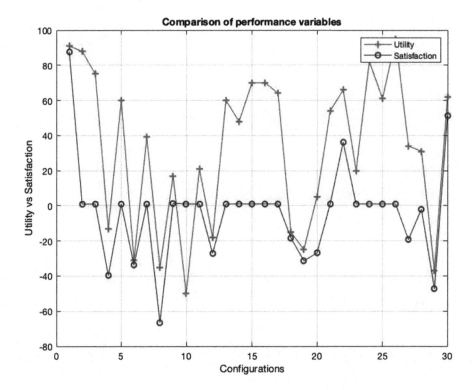

Fig. 3. Comparison of performance variables

NetLogo is used as a platform to simulate, and the variables used are the following: number of agents, degeneration rate, level of satisfaction, agents who do not cooperate.

The purpose of a simulation is to recreate the interactions between agents versus resources. We want to measure in the simulation the evolution of the allocation of resources. The simulation consists of placing a set of agents competing for a resource. The vertical axis corresponds to the amount of resource. The horizontal axis corresponds to the interaction. With the allocation model, resources are guaranteed overtime a necessary feature for performance with quality of service in a data network.

Three scenarios are compared, depending on the number of agents interacting with the network. Figure 4 shows the results of the comparison.

The comparison shows how the allocation of resources is stable from the network to the nodes. Below are the values of the simulation carried out:

- Number of agents: $[10, 30, 50]$
- Rate of degeneration of the resource: $0, 40$
- Scarcity: 1
- Satisfaction level: $S_{th} = 0.1$.

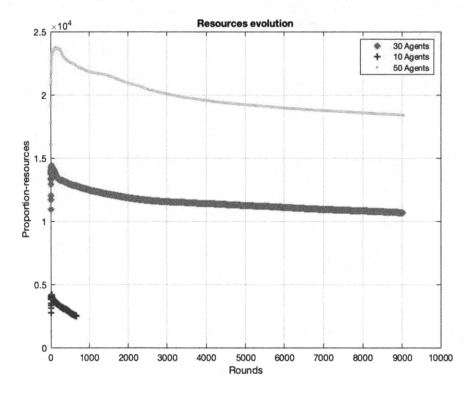

Fig. 4. Model of interactions

The parameter values are used to adjust the simulation to a real situation, for example, an ad hoc network for the generation of a sensor network. In this application, the resource to share in the storage memory.

- Agents equal to nodes.
- The speed at which the power of the nodes decreases (the battery of the devices). The scarcity implies the limit of resources that the agent must maintain.
- The S parameter is the level of times that the node fulfills its function (to take samples with the sensor and to send the information).

3.2   Implementation of an Interaction

The implementation of the interaction is done in the TL language, which is described in [19,20]. Sharing the Internet from one node to the other nodes of the network. This interaction is the most powerful application in the ad hoc network. Several additional services can be offered on the Internet channel to convert the network into a more flexible system and meet the possible user requirements. The code for this interaction is:

```
import mas.__init__
function internet(identifier, description, times)
    x = ExecuteScript()
    x.start()
end
log("test Interaction")
a = internet(1, CycleCallBash, 1000000)
```

For this application, the ExecuteScript agent has been used. In this case the CycleCallBash agent is in charge of executing the native function, which modifies the configuration of the node to create a bridge interface and share the internet service. The graphical view can be seen in Fig. 5.

The interaction is described as follows:

- $internet(A, B) \rightarrow CycleCallBash(A)|ack| \sim (ack)$
- $internet(B, \otimes_n) \rightarrow internet(A, B)|ack| \sim (ack)$
- $CycleCallBash(A, device) \rightarrow ExecuteScript(A, device)$
- $ExecuteScript(A, device) \rightarrow data$

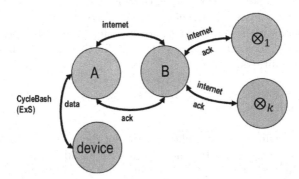

Fig. 5. Agent A shares the Internet with agent B. The interaction of B between the n Nodes of the network is sharing the Internet that comes from the agent A. The function of A is to execute the script as many times as necessary on the device to share the Internet.

The resource that behaves in this application is the Internet (bandwidth). The parameters that intervene in the process are elements described in the previous sections, several nodes of the network, the utility of the network and the satisfaction of the nodes.

- Number of nodes N
- Contribution of the nodes $U(t)$
- Satisfaction of each agent $S(t)$
- Resource: bandwidth, Internet Bw
- WLAN interfaces w_0.

The interaction of this application is:

- $(i \bowtie \lambda)^4 \rightarrow U_4, S_4 : Bw$
- $(i \bowtie \mu)^4 \rightarrow U_4, S_4 : w_0$.

3.3 Approach to Resource Allocation

The purpose of this model is to contribute to understanding decentralized systems as self-organizing systems and how these systems adapt to complexity. The idea of adaptation in self-organizing systems is different from other disciplines like machine learning, statistics or artificial intelligence. In general terms, these disciplines have in mind a single agent acting in an environment that could be unknown, stochastic, partially observable and so on; it could be difficult to find an optimal strategy, but there is a well-defined notion of what an optimal strategy is. In contrast, in the context of self-organizing communication networks, we have systems composed by multiple agents in which everyone is trying to adapt their strategies and achieve their goals at the same time; when an agent adapt its behavior, it is influenced not only by the environment but also by the behavior of other agents. As a consequence, this condition produces a high level of interdependence among the members of the system and makes necessary to provide institutions with adaptive mechanisms that allow them to adjust their parameters in order to react properly to changes in the agents' behavior and the environmental conditions.

4   Real Work

In this section, we will show an implementation of the resource allocation model, expanding the coverage of the Internet signal with an ad hoc network. The purpose is to teach, first, the application using the programming language and second the flexibility of the Interaction Nets model to support different configurations. The resource that is assigned is the bandwidth to route the packets that allow Internet sharing.

The Interaction Nets model considers interactions as computation. In [19,20] there is a definition of this model. A rewriting of the model is done by creating the coverage expansion network. The consideration of the interaction of a network with the following elements:

- A gateway node (Gw)
- Nodes as a proxy server.

Below are the rules of interaction and the graph with which the computational model is represented. This model is carried out by the scripts of the specific programming language for research.

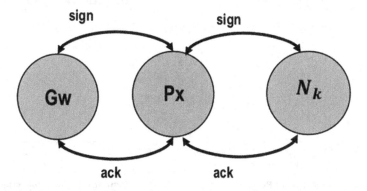

Fig. 6. Interaction graphically proxy

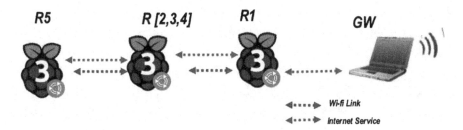

Fig. 7. Straight line configuration

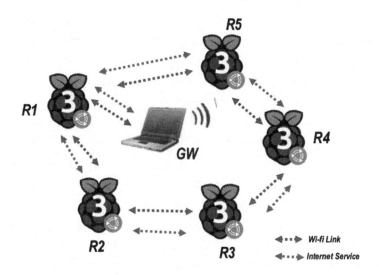

Fig. 8. Radial shape configuration

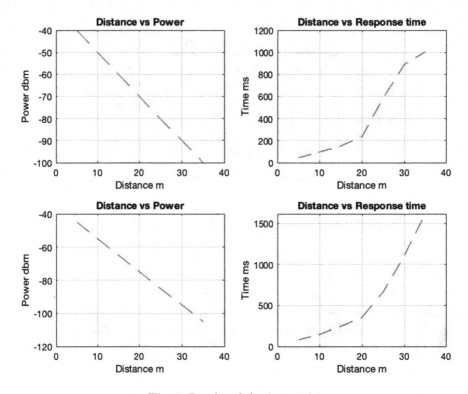

Fig. 9. Results of the 4 scenarios

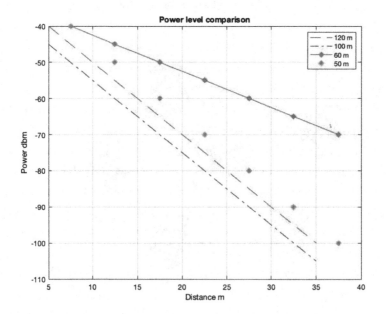

Fig. 10. Power comparison

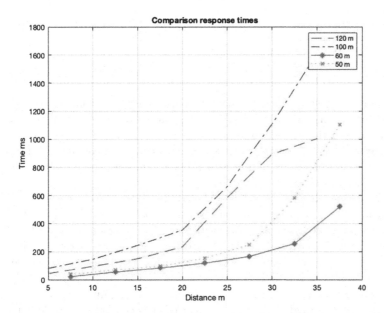

Fig. 11. Lost package comparison

1. $\Sigma = \{G_w, P_x, N_k, sign, ack\}$
2. $G_w \bowtie P_x \rightarrow sign, ack, \ (ack)$
3. $P_x \bowtie N_k \rightarrow sign, ack \ (ack)$
4. $G_w \bowtie P_x \rightarrow P_x \bowtie N_k.$

Figure 6 shows the interaction graphically

From the model, it can be said that item 1 corresponds to the group of agents that make up the interaction. The following agents have been defined for this interaction:

- G_w: agent as Gateway for internet access.
- P_x: agent as Proxy in charge of doing the distribution of the other nodes of the network.
- N_k: agent represents the nodes connected to the ad hoc network.
- $sign$: agent in charge of taking the Internet signal to the nodes of the network.
- ack: an agent with positive or negative response (ack), of the Internet signals in the nodes of the system.

The functioning of the agent modifying the interface of the nodes:

```
#bridge
#!/bin/bash
sudo ifconfig wlan0 down
sudo ifconfig eth0 down
sudo iwconfig wlan0 mode ad-hoc
sudo ifconfig wlan0 mtu 1532
```

```
sudo iwconfig wlan0 mode ad-hoc essid TL_INTERFAZ ap 02:1B:55:AD:0C:02 channel 1
sudo ip link set up dev wlan0
sudo ifconfig eth0 0.0.0.0 up
sudo ip link add name tlon0 type bridge
sudo ifconfig tl0 192.168.2.3 up
```

The previous script is the machine-level operation that is used by the *ExecuteScript*() agent and that allows the configuration of the ad hoc network nodes to expand the internet signal.

Figures 7, 8 show the ad hoc network configuration scenarios – one linear and one radial, with maximum distances of 120 and 60 each. The measured variables are power and response times.

After making the configuration of the ad hoc network, we proceeded to make the measurements of parameters, transmission power, and lost packets. These parameters are contrasted with the distance. The documentation and tests carried out in previous works [3, 4] indicate that at higher distances, more lost packets and less transmission power. In the Figs. 9, 10, 11 it can be seen that these behaviours are fulfilled.

The Fig. 9 shows the different power variations against the distance. The four graphs correspond to the evaluation of power level versus distance and response times versus distance. This is for the first scenario where you have a linear configuration. The behavior of the power and response times is expected, the higher the range, the less power there is from the nodes, and the higher the response times.

With the distance 100 m and 120 m, the thresholds for considering services over the Internet [21], such as e-mail, communication between sensors and sending information to the cloud, are allowed with an acceptable quality of service.

The Fig. 10 shows a comparison between the different power levels for the four distances and scenarios explored. The reference to 25 m is found that the configuration with the least power is for 100 linear meters. Take into account the mobility of the nodes and the consumption of the nodes in a bridge configuration.

In the radial configuration, the power consumption is observed to be lower. This is due to the shorter separation distance. The routing of packages is a strategy to consider in the efficiency in the construction of ad hoc networks, with coverage extension capacity.

The expansion of coverage using ad hoc networks is a viable solution. The results obtained, allow applications over the Internet, can have an acceptable performance? applications such as sensor networks, information exchange between nodes or e-mail.

On the other hand, the operation of the mathematical model (for this research Net Interaction), can generate the modifications to the tool (programming language) to have functions that adapt to the needs of specific applications.

In this way, when reviewing the interaction model so that the nodes have the role of bridges and also to replicate the proxy process, it is proposed to modify the rule where the signal distribution action is generated:

- $G_w \bowtie P_x \rightarrow P_x \bowtie N_k$
- $(G_w \bowtie P_x \rightarrow P_x \bowtie N_k)^+$

This operation seeks to replicate from a configuration with a collection of M nodes in an instant of time $\{t\}$, to a collection of N nodes in an instant of time $\{t+1\}$.

5 Conclusions

This article has shown the process of designing a model for the allocation of resources for a decentralized network using two components, a computational Interaction Nets model and a set of public goods. The model is generalized to the situation where the configurations of the network participants change. The measurements made on the utility of the nodes $(U(t))$ and $S(t)$ reflect a behavior where it is obtained that, the satisfaction of the nodes can be minimal, but the utility of the network is useful or high. However, if the utility is below zero, the satisfaction of the nodes is also low. To complement this analysis, in the description of the evolution of resource allocation, it is also evident that this allocation reaches a stable behavior when its allocation process evolves.

Behavior is the result of the interactions present in the network. There are signs of emerging behavior; this means that if the network can guarantee minimum operating resources, regardless of the level of personal satisfaction of the participants, the behavior of the system will be in good operating points.

On the other hand, the model can be coupled with a computational tool (programming language) and thus develop applications to solve problems in ad hoc networks, such as coverage extension or sensor networks. Some application scripts with the TL programming language are exposed. The results obtained in the real work, indicate that the configuration made gives acceptable results in terms of response times and lost packets. An implementation of a sensor network configured with this tool increases quality and service and decreases implementation time.

References

1. Al-Sultan, S., Al-Doori, M.M., Al-Bayatti, A.H., Zedan, H.: A comprehensive survey on vehicular ad hoc network. J. Netw. Comput. Appl. **37**, 380–392 (2014)
2. Amadeo, M., Campolo, C., Iera, A., Molinaro, A.: Named data networking for IoT: an architectural perspective. In: 2014 European Conference on Networks and Communications (EuCNC), pp. 1–5. IEEE (2014)

3. Chen, Y., Kunz, T.: Performance evaluation of IoT protocols under a constrained wireless access network. In: 2016 International Conference on Selected Topics in Mobile & Wireless Networking (MoWNeT), pp. 1–7. IEEE (2016)
4. Chincoli, M., Syed, A.A., Exarchakos, G., Liotta, A.: Power control in wireless sensor networks with variable interference. Mob. Inf. Syst. **2016**, 10 pages (2016)
5. Conti, M., Giordano, S.: Mobile ad hoc networking: milestones, challenges, and new research directions. IEEE Commun. Mag. **52**(1), 85–96 (2014)
6. De-La-Hoz-Franco, E., Ariza-Colpas, P., Quero, J.M., Espinilla, M.: Sensor-based datasets for human activity recognition-a systematic review of literature. IEEE Access **6**, 59192–59210 (2018)
7. Dressler, F., et al.: Self-organization in ad hoc networks: overview and classification. University of Erlangen, Department of Computer Science **7**, 1–12 (2006)
8. Fernández, M.: Models of Computation: An Introduction to Computability Theory. Springer, London (2009). https://doi.org/10.1007/978-1-84882-434-8
9. Gächter, S.: Conditional cooperation: behavioral regularities from the lab and the field and their policy implications. Technical report. CeDEx Discussion Paper, The University of Nottingham (2006)
10. Ju, H., Zhang, R.: Optimal resource allocation in full-duplex wireless-powered communication network. IEEE Trans. Commun. **62**(10), 3528–3540 (2014)
11. Li, M., Li, Z., Vasilakos, A.V.: A survey on topology control in wireless sensor networks: taxonomy, comparative study, and open issues. Proc. IEEE **101**(12), 2538–2557 (2013)
12. Lin, S., et al.: ATPC: adaptive transmission power control for wireless sensor networks. ACM Trans. Sens. Netw. (TOSN) **12**(1), 6 (2016)
13. Liu, X., Li, Z., Yang, P., Dong, Y.: Information-centric mobile ad hoc networks and content routing: a survey. Ad Hoc Netw. **58**, 255–268 (2017)
14. Lo, C.H., Ansari, N.: Decentralized controls and communications for autonomous distribution networks in smart grid. IEEE Trans. Smart Grid **4**(1), 66–77 (2013)
15. Palechor, F.M., De la Hoz Manotas, A., Colpas, P.A., Ojeda, J.S., Ortega, R.M., Melo, M.P.: Cardiovascular disease analysis using supervised and unsupervised data mining techniques. JSW **12**(2), 81–90 (2017)
16. Perrinel, M.: On context semantics and interaction nets. In: Proceedings of the Joint Meeting of the Twenty-Third EACSL Annual Conference on Computer Science Logic (CSL) and the Twenty-Ninth Annual ACM/IEEE Symposium on Logic in Computer Science (LICS), p. 73. ACM (2014)
17. Pitt, J., Schaumeier, J.: Provision and appropriation of common-pool resources without full disclosure. In: Rahwan, I., Wobcke, W., Sen, S., Sugawara, T. (eds.) PRIMA 2012. LNCS (LNAI), vol. 7455, pp. 199–213. Springer, Heidelberg (2012). https://doi.org/10.1007/978-3-642-32729-2_14
18. Prehofer, C., Bettstetter, C.: Self-organization in communication networks: principles and design paradigms. IEEE Commun. Mag. **43**(7), 78–85 (2005)
19. Sánchez, J.F., Quiñones, J., Corredor, J.M.: Interaction net as a representation model of a programming language. In: Alor-Hernández, G., Sánchez-Cervantes, J.L., Rodríguez-González, A., Valencia-García, R. (eds.) Current Trends in Semantic Web Technologies: Theory and Practice. SCI, vol. 815, pp. 57–83. Springer, Cham (2019). https://doi.org/10.1007/978-3-030-06149-4_3
20. Sánchez, J.F., Quiñones, J.A., Corredor, J.M.: A programming model for decentralised data networks. In: Figueroa-García, J.C., López-Santana, E.R., Rodriguez-Molano, J.I. (eds.) WEA 2018. CCIS, vol. 915, pp. 468–479. Springer, Cham (2018). https://doi.org/10.1007/978-3-030-00350-0_39

21. Sarangapani, J.: Wireless Ad hoc and Sensor Networks: Protocols, Performance, and Control. CRC Press, Boca Raton (2017)
22. Trifunovic, S., Kouyoumdjieva, S.T., Distl, B., Pajevic, L., Karlsson, G., Plattner, B.: A decade of research in opportunistic networks: challenges, relevance, and future directions. IEEE Commun. Mag. **55**(1), 168–173 (2017)

RefDataCleaner: A Usable Data Cleaning Tool

Juan Carlos Leon-Medina and Ixent Galpin[✉]

Dpto. de Ingeniería, Universidad Jorge Tadeo Lozano, Bogotá, Colombia
{juan.leonm,ixent}@utadeo.edu.co

Abstract. While the democratization of data science may still be some way off, several vendors of tools for data wrangling and analytics have recently emphasized the usability of their products with the aim of attracting an ever broader range of users. In this paper, we carry out an experiment to compare user performance when cleaning data using two contrasting tools: RefDataCleaner, a bespoke web-based tool that we created specifically for detecting and fixing errors in structured and semi-structured data files, and Microsoft Excel, a spreadsheet application in widespread use in organizations throughout the world which is used for diverse types of tasks, including data cleaning. With RefDataCleaner, a user specifies rules to detect and fix data errors, using hard-coded values or by retrieving values from a reference data file. In contrast, with Microsoft Excel, a non-expert user may clean data by specifying formulae and applying find/replace functions. The results of this initial study, carried out using a focus group of volunteers, show that users were able clean dirty data-sets more accurately using RefDataCleaner, and moreover, that this tool was generally preferred for this purpose.

Keywords: Usability · Data wrangling · Data cleaning · Reference data

1 Introduction

While attempts have been made to automate, as much as possible, the data wrangling pipeline (e.g., [8,12]), in practice, these steps are most often done manually by experts. This is costly for the organizations involved, given that authors such as [17] and [19] indicate that anomalies are present in around 5% of data, and that an analyst spends 80% of his or her time in the preparation of data, and 20% in the analysis of this data once it has been cleaned and integrated [13]. Given the exponentially increasing volumes of data in the world, it is reasonable to conjecture that organizations may achieve significant savings if tools in a data scientist's pipeline may be effectively used by a broader range of people.

Indeed, the vendors of several tools in a data scientist's data processing pipeline now purport to further the democratization of data science. For example, Tableau conveys this vision through its advertising materials on its website [3], and Exploratory has the marketing slogan *Data Science is not just for*

© Springer Nature Switzerland AG 2019
H. Florez et al. (Eds.): ICAI 2019, CCIS 1051, pp. 102–115, 2019.
https://doi.org/10.1007/978-3-030-32475-9_8

Engineers and Statisticians. Exploratory makes it for Everyone [1]. Furthermore, recently usability workshops have emerged associated with conferences in the data management research community, e.g., HILDA[1] and IDEA[2] co-located with SIGMOD and KDD respectively. This reflects how *usability*, defined by the International Organization for Standardization (ISO) as "the ability of the software product to be understood, learned, used and attractive to the user, when used under certain conditions" [21], is now becoming an ever more important consideration by tool designers.

The problems related to data cleaning and integration encountered during the data wrangling process are varied and require domain expertise, as well as an understanding of issues such as functional dependencies and integrity constraints. Such concepts are not easy to grasp by non-expert users and, as such, there is the risk that tools may be applied incorrectly during this process. Thus, it is a challenge to design tools that are easy-to-use and prevent users from applying the tools incorrectly.

There has been relatively little research into the usability of tools used for data wrangling. In [9], a usability study is carried out of source selection approaches. This work differs from previous work in that it proposes and evaluates the usability of a data cleaning tool.

This paper describes RefDataCleaner, a usable tool to clean dirty data using reference data sets. We design and carry out an experiment in which users are asked to perform various data cleaning tasks using RefDataCleaner and the Microsoft Excel spreadsheet application. We chose Microsoft Excel as a baseline, given that it is a widely-used software tool by organizations throughout the world for a range of purposes, including for tasks for which it was not originally envisioned, such as data cleaning. The results of our experiment show that users perform better with RefDataCleaner for the purposes of diagnosing and repairing data errors. Moreover, we find that RefDataCleaner is preferred by users over Microsoft Excel, despite their increased familiarity with the latter.

This paper is structured as follows. Section 2 presents a brief background. Section 3 describes the RefDataCleaner application. Section 4 presents the experiment design. Section 5 reports the results obtained in the experiments. Finally, Sect. 6 concludes.

2 Background

Data errors may be classified in different ways [4,18] and several taxonomies have been proposed [10,15]. Müller *et al.* [14] classify errors into three groups: syntactic, semantic and contextual. Fan *et al.* [6] define categories of errors pertaining to consistency, duplication, accuracy, existence, conformance and integrity. The focus of this paper is on errors which can be fixed by using reference datasets. A *reference dataset* is a collection of correct and complete data items which make up a subset of the attributes in the dataset being repaired [11]. One such

---

[1] http://hilda.io/2019/.

[2] http://poloclub.gatech.edu/idea2018/.

example would be a lookup table with country names and the respective dialling codes, as used in the illustrated example in Sect. 3. Reference data is used extensively in organizations for data repair during data wrangling. The Colombian tax authority (DIAN) is one such organization, and the tool of choice for this is the Microsoft Excel spreadsheet application.

3   RefDataCleaner Application Description

This section describes RefDataCleaner, a web-based application that we developed using Shiny R which enables error detection and repair rules to be defined and applied to dirty data files. It supports both semi-structured and structured data sets, and operates over diverse file types, including Microsoft Excel, CSV, HTML tables, XML and JSON. We have made our source-code available on GitHub[3]. Furthermore, we have a demo version for readers to try at ShinyApps[4].

RefDataCleaner supports the application of two different types of rules, viz., substitution rules and reference rules. With a *substitution rule*, a user specifies one or more conditions that must hold for a data repair action to be triggered. A condition is a predicate involving an attribute data name, operand, and value, e.g., *country = 'Colombia'*. The data repair action involves one or more assignments of attributes which are required for the data repair action, e.g., *dialling_code ← 57*. In essence, with this option every possible repair value needs to be hard-coded explicitly by the user, and is illustrated in Fig. 1.

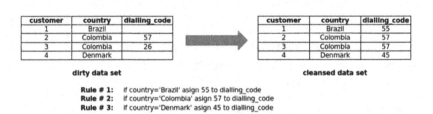

Fig. 1. Using substitution rules.

In contrast, in the case of *reference rules*, a repair is carried out using a reference dataset. For this example, the reference dataset comprises a complete set of records with a country attribute and the respective country code. Thus, for this type of rule, a user specifies a reference data set which can be used for data repair, one or more attributes to be used for an equi-join between the input data set and the reference data set, and one or more assignments of attributes from the reference data set to the input data set. Figure 2 shows an example whereby the *country_code* file is corrected based on reference data.

---

[3] https://github.com/refdatacleaner/version_1_0/.
[4] https://refdatacleaner.shinyapps.io/version_1_0/.

dirty data set

customer	country	dialling_code
1	Brazil	
2	Colombia	57
3	Colombia	26
4	Denmark	

cleansed data set

customer	country	dialling_code
1	Brazil	55
2	Colombia	57
3	Colombia	57
4	Denmark	45

reference data set

country	dialling_code
Brazil	55
Colombia	57
Colombia	57
Denmark	45

Rule # 1: Apply dialling_code from reference data set using country as the join key

Fig. 2. Using a reference rule.

RefDataCleaner consists of four steps, illustrated by the screenshots in Figs. 3, 4, 5, which may be performed in an iterative manner until the user obtains a result that he or she is satisfied with:

1. **Input File Selection.** The user selects the input file with the data set to be repaired. This is uploaded and displayed to the user (see Fig. 3a).
2. **Reference File Selection.** In this optional step, shown in Fig. 3b, the user can add files with reference data. This is only required if the user intends to add reference rules. If several reference files are added, the drop-down menu shown on the top-right enables the user to select the reference data set to view.
3. **Rule Management.** The next step is for the user to manage data repair rules. The plus and minus icons enable rules to be added and removed respectively, and the up and down arrow icons enable rule order to be changed. Figures 4 and 5 show the running example in this section with substitution and reference rules respectively. Note that although not shown in these screenshots, it is possible to mix both types of rules interchangeably.

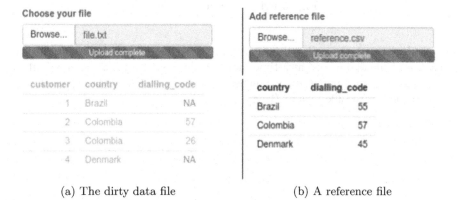

(a) The dirty data file   (b) A reference file

Fig. 3. Uploading the input files to RefDataCleaner.

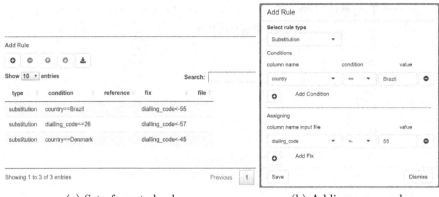

(a) Set of created rules   (b) Adding a new rule

Fig. 4. Substitution rule example.

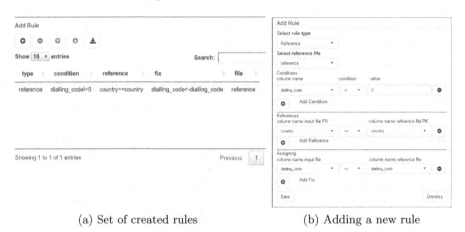

(a) Set of created rules   (b) Adding a new rule

Fig. 5. Reference rule example.

4. **Result Generation.** By clicking on the "Run" icon, the rules are applied to the input file one record at a time, in the order that they have been specified in the Rule Management step. The user may then download the repaired data set in the desired file format (Fig. 6).

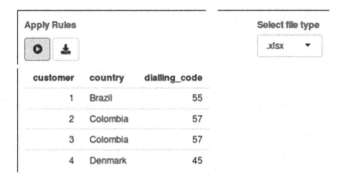

Fig. 6. Apply, look, select and download result file.

4   Experiment Design

In order to evaluate the effectiveness of RefDataCleaner, we carried out an experiment to compare user performance and subjective user preference with the Microsoft Excel 2016 spreadsheet application as a baseline due to its widespread use in organizations throughout the world.

Overview. For the experiment, a focus group comprising an hour-long session was devised as follows:

- Initially, participants are presented with a tutorial on data cleaning for both tools using a practical example [15 min][5].
- Then, using the first tool [20 min]:
  - Users carry out two data cleaning tasks, which involve using tool functionality to correct errors in a data file as explained in the natural language task description (see task descriptions ahead);
  - Users answer a usability questionnaire about the tool.
- The same process, with the same data cleaning tasks, is repeated for the second tool [20 min].
- Finally, a comparative questionnaire is presented to participants in which they give free text answers comparing both tools [5 min].

Participants were divided into two groups. Group A used Microsoft Excel first, and RefDataCleaner second. Group B used the tools in the reverse order. This was done to mitigate any variability which tool order and increased user familiarity with the tasks may cause to the results. The files repaired by the users, and the answers to the usability questions, were all recorded on a Google Form. Users were prompted when the time allocated for each step was reached,

---

[5] In the case of Microsoft Excel, participants are shown how substitution rules may be mimicked using find/replace/copy/paste functionality, and reference rules using VLOOKUP formulae. However, participants are free to use any functionality available in Excel for the data cleaning process.

and asked to upload the repaired data files as they were (even if they were not entirely satisfied with the outcome). This ensured that an equal amount of time was spent using both tools, to enable a fairer comparison.

Task 1: *Repairing the Iris data set.* The first task involves repairing the Iris data set, a well-known multivariate data set introduced by Ronald Fisher in his 1936 paper [7]. This data set comprises 150 records, and five attributes: `sepalLength`, `sepalWidth`, `petalLength`, `petalWidth` and `species`. We randomly deleted 27 data values for the `species` attribute, which the participants were subsequently requested to fix using the decision tree shown in Fig. 7 as a guide. Users were expected to use substitution rules to fix this data set, as this task does not involve a reference data set.

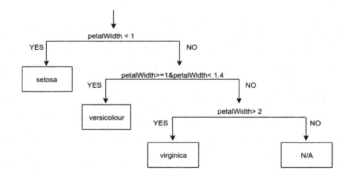

Fig. 7. Iris data set decision tree used to inform data cleaning.

Task 2: *Repairing the Movies Data set.* The second task involves repairing a data set taken from Wikipedia with a list of highest-grossing movies [2]. To make it more manageable, a subset of 46 records are taken from this data set. This data set contains six attributes: `rank`, `title`, `worldwide_gross`, `year`, `director`, and `distributor`. We randomly introduced 92 data errors into the `year`, `director`, and `distributor` attributes.

Furthermore, two reference data sets were made available to participants: (1) *Company*, which contains 8 records with the attributes `distributor_code` and `distributor`, and (2) *Directors*, which contains 56 records with the attributes `title`, `year`, and `director`. Users were expected to use reference rules to fix this data set, by using the reference data sets provided.

Usability Questions. For each tool, we adapted four questions from the System Usability Scale (SUS) [20] to evaluate subjective user preference. We adapted two positive and two negative questions for this purpose, which users answered according to a five-point Likert scale. At the end of the session, we also posed the following three comparative usability questions, which users answered using free text:

- What tool seemed easier to use? Why?
- What tool would you use to clean your data? Why?
- What tool offered you the simplest functionality more simple to clean the data? Why?

4.1 Evaluation Metrics

We have two types of user performance measures, viz., error detection and data repair performance measures. *Error detection* performance measures evaluate how effectively users were able to identify erroneous data using the tools, and *Data repair* performance measures whether erroneous data items were repaired correctly.

Error Detection User Performance. For these measures, we define the following concepts:

- the true positives (TP), i.e., the items of data that are erroneous and were identified as being erroneous.
- the false positives (FP), i.e., the items of data that were not erroneous but were identified as being erroneous.
- the true negatives (TN), i.e., the items of data that are not erroneous and were correctly identified as not being erroneous; and
- the false negatives (FN), i.e., the items of data that are erroneous but were not identified as being erroneous.

For the purposes of these measures, we deem an item of data to have been identified as erroneous when it has been modified. Conversely, if an item of data is not modified, we deem it as having been identified as being correct. Based on this, we define error detection accuracy, precision, recall and specificity as follows [16]:

$$\text{Error detection accuracy} = \frac{TP + FP}{TP + TN + FP + FN} \tag{1}$$

$$\text{Error detection precision} = \frac{TP}{TP + FP} \tag{2}$$

$$\text{Error detection recall} = \frac{TP}{TP + FN} \tag{3}$$

$$\text{Error detection specificity} = \frac{TN}{TN + FP} \tag{4}$$

Data Repair User Performance. Taking into account only the erroneous data, we examine the fraction of records which were correctly repaired. We define the *data repair accuracy* as:

$$\text{Data repair accuracy} = \frac{\text{Records repaired correctly}}{\text{Number of erroneous records}} \tag{5}$$

Usability Score. Apart from user performance, we also compute a usability score to measure subjective user preference. Our approach is based by taking four questions from the System Usability Scale (SUS) [20]. Each question is scored using the Likert scale, where 1 indicates total disagreement and 5 total agreement. The score for each individual question is computed as follows:

- The positive questions take the value assigned by the user minus one.
- The negative questions are 5 minus the value assigned by the user.

The individual scores for the questions are summed, and the total is scaled to give a number between 0 and 100 as follows:

$$\text{Usability Score} = \sum_{i=1}^{N}(score_i) \times \frac{100}{4N} \tag{6}$$

where N is the number of questions (four in this case), $score_i$ is the score awarded to the ith question, and the constant 4 represents the maximum score for any given question.

5   Evaluation Results

We recruited 11 student volunteers familiar with data analysis with experience in Microsoft Excel providing a bonus grade as an incentive for participation to ensure participant engagement. 6 students conformed group A and 5 students group B, resp. In order to ensure equal participation in both groups in our results, we randomly discarded the results obtained from one of the participants in group A. All participants were familiar with Microsoft Excel, and were new to RefDataCleaner. This section reports the results obtained.

5.1   Error Detection Performance

In the first instance we evaluate whether data is correctly diagnosed as being erroneous or correct. Figure 8 presents the error detection performance results obtained, with the results of a paired two-tailed t-test used to determine statistical significance.

For accuracy, shown in Fig. 8a, we observe that more accurate results are obtained for RefDataCleaner than Microsoft Excel for both tasks combined: on average, the accuracy measure is 0.148 higher for RefDataCleaner. This difference is starkest for the Iris Task, where RefDataCleaner average accuracy is 0.241 higher than Microsoft Excel. Moreover, the result is extremely statistically significant, as the p-value obtained is under the commonly-used 0.05 threshold. This result tells us that, overall, the diagnoses made are more likely to be correct with RefDataCleaner than with Microsoft Excel.

The results for error detection precision are shown in Fig. 8b. For both tasks combined, the average precision is 0.306 higher for RefDataCleaner than Microsoft Excel. Once again, this is particularly stark for the Iris task, where the average

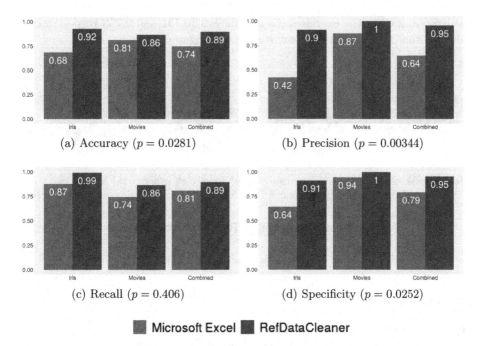

(a) Accuracy ($p = 0.0281$)   (b) Precision ($p = 0.00344$)

(c) Recall ($p = 0.406$)   (d) Specificity ($p = 0.0252$)

■ Microsoft Excel ■ RefDataCleaner

Fig. 8. Error detection performance.

precision is 0.486 higher for RefDataCleaner, and the results are statistically significant. This result indicates that, overall, users were more effective at correctly detecting erroneous data with RefDataCleaner than with Microsoft Excel.

Figure 8c shows the error detection recall. For both tasks combined, the error detection recall is 0.085 greater for RefDataCleaner than for Microsoft Excel. This result suggests that participants were less likely to miss erroneous data items with RefDataCleaner than with Microsoft Excel, although the p-value obtained indicates that this result is not statistically significant.

The results for error detection specificity are similar to the overall trend. The specificity obtained for RefDataCleaner is 0.162 higher for RefDataCleaner than Microsoft Excel, with the difference being starker for the Iris task (0.269). This statistically significant result tells us that participants were more effective at identifying non-erroneous records with RefDataCleaner compared to Microsoft Excel.

5.2 Data Repair

For the second part of the evaluation, we consider the issue of data repair. The results obtained for data repair accuracy are shown in Fig. 9.

The results show that, for both tasks, erroneous data was repaired correctly more often for RefDataCleaner than for Microsoft Excel, equally stark for the Iris task, where the average of data repair accuracy was better. However, the p-value obtained in the exercises iris and movies (0.151 and 0.753 respectively) indicates that these results are not statistically significant.

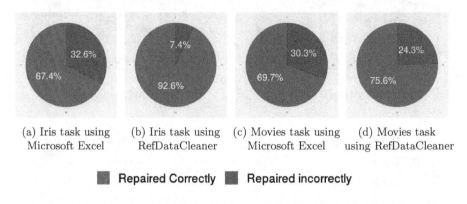

(a) Iris task using Microsoft Excel   (b) Iris task using RefDataCleaner   (c) Movies task using Microsoft Excel   (d) Movies task using RefDataCleaner

■ Repaired Correctly   ■ Repaired incorrectly

Fig. 9. Data repair accuracy.

5.3   Usability

Figure 10 presents the usability scores obtained for each tool. For Microsoft Excel the usability score was 56.3, whereas for RefDataCleaner the usability score was 71.9, approximately 15.6% higher. This result shows that, overall, RefDataCleaner scored higher and was preferred by users. This matches the results obtained for the comparative questions given to participants at the end of the session: 90% percent of participants considered that RefDataCleaner was easier to use, compared to 10% who preferred Microsoft Excel on the basis that it is a familiar tool used in their daily work. Similarly, 90% of participants rated RefDataCleaner as being the more intuitive tool. However, a lower 70% expressed that they would use RefDataCleaner for data cleaning, the justification being that Microsoft Excel provides a broader range of functionality for data cleaning.

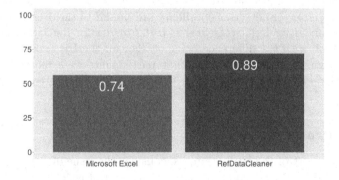

Fig. 10. Usability score ($p = 0.039$)

5.4 Usability Score vs. Error Detection and Data Repaired Accuracy

Finally, when comparing usability score against accuracy, we can observe with RefDataCleaner in Figs. 11c and d a tendency towards the upper right for both error detection and repair.

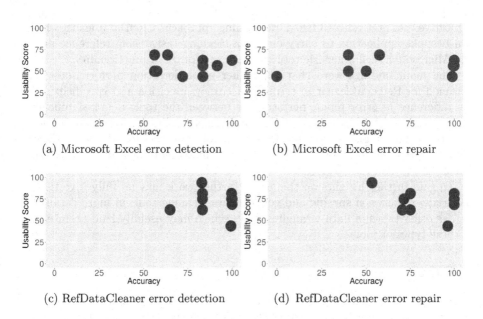

(a) Microsoft Excel error detection   (b) Microsoft Excel error repair

(c) RefDataCleaner error detection   (d) RefDataCleaner error repair

Fig. 11. Accuracy vs. Usability score

This is indicative of the greater performance and subjective user preference exhibited by RefDataCleaner. On the other hand, in Figs. 11a and b we can see that the points are more spread out, an indication that both performance and subjective user preference varied more greatly for Microsoft Excel.

5.5 Qualitative Analysis

We can glean further comparisons between Microsoft Excel and RefData-Cleaner from qualitative analysis of the user answers regarding its usability. Some of the user responses indicating the software application they preferred, and the reasons, were:

- "[I preferred RefDataCleaner as] it is more intuitive."
- "[I preferred RefDataCleaner as] it is optimized to carry out two very useful functions."
- "[I preferred RefDataCleaner as it enables a] faster cleaning processes to be performed."
- "[I preferred Microsoft Excel as it is] more familiar to my daily work.".

6   Conclusions

With the growing development of humanity and the expansion for the need for data management in most everyday fields, it is estimated that some organizations invest up to 40% of their budget in integrating information reliably [5]. Cleaning data is one of the main challenges in this process. This paper reports the results of a preliminary study that shows significant differences on performance and subjective user preference of two data cleaning approaches, RefDataCleaner which is a bespoke application to carry out data cleaning tasks using reference data, and Microsoft Excel, a generic tool with a broad range of functionality.

The main findings were that (1) higher error detection performance was obtained for RefDataCleaner in terms of accuracy, precision and specificity; (2) the difference in error repair performance between the tools is not significant; (3) the preferred tool by users was RefDataCleaner; and (4) usability and performance are more highly correlated for RefDataCleaner than for Microsoft Excel, indicating that performance and usability was much more diverse for Microsoft Excel.

To gain further insights on this issue, further work may usefully investigate the trade-off between specific and generic data cleaning tools in more detail, as well as other types of data wrangling tasks which may usefully lend themselves to these types of tools.

References

1. Exploratory home page. https://exploratory.io/. Accessed 17 June 2019
2. List of highest-grossing films. https://en.wikipedia.org/wiki/List_of_highest-grossing_films. Accessed 14 Apr 2019
3. Tableau website. https://www.tableau.com/learn/whitepapers/make-everyone-your-organization-data-scientist. Accessed 17 June 2019
4. Abedjan, Z., et al.: Detecting data errors: where are we and what needs to be done? Proc. VLDB Endow. **9**(12), 993–1004 (2016)
5. Bernstein, P.A., Haas, L.M.: Information integration in the enterprise. Commun. ACM **51**(9), 72–79 (2008)
6. Fan, W., Geerts, F.: Foundations of Data Quality Management (2012)
7. Fisher, R.A.: The use of multiple measurements in taxonomic problems. Ann. Eugen. **7**(2), 179–188 (1936)
8. Furche, T., Gottlob, G., Libkin, L., Orsi, G., Paton, N.W.: Data wrangling for big data: challenges and opportunities. In: EDBT, pp. 473–478 (2016)
9. Galpin, I., Abel, E., Paton, N.W.: Source selection languages: a usability evaluation. In: Proceedings of the Workshop on Human-In-the-Loop Data Analytics, p. 8. ACM (2018)
10. Kim, W., Choi, B.J., Hong, E., Kim, S.K., Lee, D.: A taxonomy of dirty data. Data Min. Knowl. Discov. **7**(1), 81–99 (2003)
11. Koehler, M., et al.: Data context informed data wrangling. In: 2017 IEEE International Conference on Big Data (Big Data), pp. 956–963. IEEE (2017)
12. Konstantinou, N., et al.: The VADA architecture for cost-effective data wrangling. In: Proceedings of the 2017 ACM International Conference on Management of Data, pp. 1599–1602. ACM (2017)

13. Lohr, S.: For big-data scientists, 'janitor work' is key hurdle to insights. https://www.nytimes.com/2014/08/18/technology/for-big-data-scientists-hurdle-to-insights-is-janitor-work.html. Accessed 15 May 2019
14. Müller, H., Freytag, J.C.: Problems, Methods, and Challenges in Comprehensive Data Cleansing, pp. 1–23. Humboldt-Universität zu, Berlin (2003)
15. Oliveira, P., Rodrigues, F., Rangel Henriques, P., Galhardas, H.: A taxonomy of data quality problems. J. Data Inf. Qual. JDIQ (2005)
16. Olson, D., Dursun, D.: Advanced Data Mining Techniques, 1st edn. Springer, Heidelberg (2008). https://doi.org/10.1007/978-3-540-76917-0
17. Orr, K.: Data quality and systems theory. Commun. ACM **41**(2), 66–71 (1998)
18. Rahm, E., Do, H.H.: Data cleaning: problems and current approaches. IEEE Data Eng. Bull. **23**(4), 3–13 (2000)
19. Redman, T.C.: The impact of poor data quality on the typical enterprise. Commun. ACM **41**(2), 79–82 (1998)
20. Sauro, J.: Measuring usability with the system usability scale (SUS). https://measuringu.com/sus/. Accessed 10 May 2019
21. International Organization for Standardization: Software product quality. https://iso25000.com/index.php/en/iso-25000-standards/iso-25010. Accessed 21 May 2019

Study of Crime Status in Colombia and Development of a Citizen Security App

Raquel E. Canon-Clavijo[1], Cesar O. Diaz[4], Olmer Garcia-Bedoya[2]([⊠])[iD],
and Holman Bolivar[3]

[1] Firefly Energy S.A.S, Cll 15 16 15 T1 604, Facatativá, Colombia
raquel.canon@firefly-e.com
[2] Universidad Jorge Tadeo Lozano, Cra. 4 22 - 61, Bogota, Colombia
olmer.garciab@utadeo.edu.co
[3] Universidad Catolica de Colombia, Bogota, Colombia
hbolivar@ucatolica.edu.co
[4] OCOX AI, Bogota, Colombia
cdiaz@ocox-ai.co
http://www.firefly-e.com

Abstract. The indices of citizen insecurity have been increasing in Colombia in recent years after the signing of the peace agreement. Many of the demobilized guerrilla members have gone to the streets of the country to seek a new direction or occupation and unfortunately have fallen into crime, increasing delinquency levels of crimes such as robbery, extortion, rape, micro-trafficking and personal injury. Added to this, the increase of the migrant population from the neighboring country Venezuela, in conditions of displacement have forced that part of this population with limited employment opportunities to take refuge in crime as it has become their only form of survival. Given this problem, it has become interesting to analyze through this investigation, the behavior of these crimes in the last years and to propose a technological solution that allows detecting the geological sectors and crime type that contribute the most to the social problem. In this way, offer alternatives for the protection of citizens using a mobile application that allows them to face the situation by making them part of the solution.

Keywords: Citizen security · Open data · Big data · Mobile applications · Crime indexes · Data analytics

1 Introduction

Ordinary crime is one of the most complex social problems facing the country with evident growth rates and little control by public entities. The lack of financial resources and public forces destined to take control of this situation is scarce, and the citizenry is increasingly seen with fewer alternatives to face the problem. It is necessary to look for different options that allow the citizen to be a collaborative part of an efficient solution that not only facilitates the processes

© Springer Nature Switzerland AG 2019
H. Florez et al. (Eds.): ICAI 2019, CCIS 1051, pp. 116–130, 2019.
https://doi.org/10.1007/978-3-030-32475-9_9

of reporting and identifying the crime but also leads him to take preventive measures to protect his safety and that of his community [2].

Around the world there are disruptive solutions that protect the citizen and hinder the procedures of the offender; such as, for example, facial biometric recognition and identification that require significant investments in terms of infrastructure, data processing, interconnection and integration between different entities and trained personnel that are capable of understanding, developing, maintaining and using this kind of technology [1]. Right now, there exists open source technology to this type of approach, like identify voice commands [12].

On the other hand, one of the most severe problems in the control of crime refers to the difficulty in reporting, since they are complicated, lengthy and that expose even more the safety of the affected. The criminal processes of judging are also slow, lax, and with doors of escape or minimization of penalties. That is why impunity is another tool, in favor of the delinquent. We also find solutions whose investment in technology and infrastructure are low and achieve to empower the citizen with their resources; in this case, their mobile devices.

According to Asomovil, Colombia has 23.8 million mobile internet users, which is seen as a significant opportunity to use this technology to report incidents and emergencies. With the use of technologies such as data analysis, artificial intelligence, Big Data, cloud computing and the internet of things, it is possible to solve these challenges and respond more intelligently using the ability to predict events. Smart technologies have many purposes, and those, used in the field of safety are building up the Safe City system, which makes part of the smart city concept [7].

The general objective of this research, through the open data available in terms of criminality, consists of providing mechanisms to have current and actual information on their situation regarding crime rates. Additionally, let to propose a mobile solution that can be implemented with its inhabitants to report events that represent a threat to the population.

2 Background

2.1 Diagnosis

Currently, the tools available to the citizen to make complaints regarding actions that affect their own and the community's safety are in an early stage. The affected person must be moved to the local authority institutions to lodge the accusations. Usually, these processes are cumbersome, delayed and ineffective since the citizen tends in many cases to desist not only for the time he loses but also for the lack of effectiveness of the authorities to exercise justice, in addition to the weak mechanisms to follow up the process. Information and communications technology are positively associated with citizens' e-participation [14].

Governments expect big data to enhance their ability to serve their citizens and address significant national challenges involving the economy, health care, job creation, natural disasters, and terrorism [5]. On the other hand, these complaint processes are after the incident, and the immediate attention channels such as the telephone line or the institutional emails are particularly neglected, and timely management of emergencies is not achieved. There exist this problem in multiple society problem like traffic accidents [13].

The Colombian government, through joint actions with the ministry of information technologies and the ministry of defense, are promoting technological innovation solutions to address this problem; make institutions more efficient and provide citizens with access to public information; making government processes more transparent and giving the citizen tools that allow him to take actions of oversight and self-management. That is why Colombia through its open data policy makes public information available to citizens without restrictions of use for the development of research, facilitate decision making, understand and solve the problems of the country and generate value through innovation.

From the scope of this Research Work will be taken as a starting point the open data exposed by public entities to carry out the analysis of the criminal situation of the country and propose alternative solutions that can contribute to improving the environment of the area where we want to implement the pilot.

2.2 Legal Framework

In the legal context of the development of the mobile application for citizen security and the analysis of open data used for the approach of the problem; It is necessary to evaluate the existing Colombian regulations from the perspective not only of compliance but also how we can take advantage of them to leverage the development of our solution.

"Law 1712 of 2014". Law on transparency and the right of access to national public information. The objective of the law is regulating access to public information, procedures, and the exceptions to the publicity of information. This law requires state entities to publish information generated from the different state agencies. Which is used not only for the initial study of descriptive analysis on crime rates in Colombia but also is a guarantee that organizations will use continuously, mechanisms that allow them to have more truthful and reliable information.

"Law 1341 of July 30, 2009". This law determines the general framework for the formulation of public policies that will govern the Information and Communications Technologies sector, its general regulations, the competition regime, user protection, as well as coverage issues. This law defines the quality of service; policies about the promotion of investment in the sector and the development of these technologies; the efficient use of networks and the radio spectrum. Finally, this law facilitates free access and without discrimination of the inhabitants of the national territory to the Information Society. This law promotes and recognizes the development of software as an element for the digital transformation of the country. It also seeks to protect the rights of users, encourages the development of applications, and mentions the importance of information security.

"Law 1581 of 2012. General Provisions of the Protection of Personal Data". Law purpose gives policies of a constitutional right that all persons have to know,

update, and rectify his information. Article 15 of the Political Constitution; as well as the right to information enshrined in article 20 thereof. To comply with the related law 1581 once published in the play store, the terms of use of the application will be increased; which must be accepted by the user before downloading. If the user wishes to unsubscribe and delete the personal information entered in the application, he/she will be able to write to the authorized email of Seguridad Ciudadana to manage their request.

"Law 527 of 1999. Regulates Access and Use of Data Messages, Electronic Commerce, and Digital Signatures". This law talks about data messages and their validity about being legally used as probative acts of an event or obligation and veracity regarding a contract: "The data messages will be admissible as means of proof, and their probative force is granted" in the provisions of Chapter VIII of Title XIII, Third Section, Second Book of the Code of Civil Procedure.

2.3   Review of Available Citizen Security Applications

Therefore, we can see below some options that exist in the market, which have a partially successful implementation. Next, some of the solutions available in the market were evaluated:

- **Seguridad Ciudadana**. Build by 4App Design at Colombia; it is a tool with which you can send alerts and ask for help to all the people that are around you, in this way you will have all the support of the community in case you are in danger or you think an event is happening. Principal functionalities are:
  - Sending alerts
  - Request for help from people around
  - Trusted contacts for sending alerts
  - Physical panic button
  - Call emergency agencies
  - Security groups.

- **SUAP**. Build by Soacha Municipal Hall – Colombia, SUAPP is connected to the emergency system 123 of the National Police and the nearest quadrants, allowing citizens to make complaints and thanks to the cell phone's GPS they can receive the attention of the competent authority in the place where they require it. Principal functionalities are:
  - Alerts and emergencies 123
  - Complaints of crimes
  - Realtime access to private and public security cameras in the town.

- **SOSAFE**. Build by SOSAFE at CHILE; "it is the best way to improve your safety and that of your whole family. Communicate and inform yourself of the emergencies of your loved ones simply and intelligently." SOSAFE sends your location and relevant information to the attached security services and your contacts simultaneously, ensuring timely and efficient service when you need it most. Principal functionalities are:

- Report theft and suspicious activity.
- Ask for help from your neighbors, security, fire and other services.
- Collaborate with the community.
- Report and find lost pets.
- Realtime checking about what happens in your locality.

– **Sinesp Ciudadana.** The SINESP citizen is a module of the National Public Security System. The information that allows Brazilian citizens direct access to the National Secretariat for Services of extraordinary public security Ministry of Public Security. Principal functionalities are:
  - Check stolen vehicles
  - See Order of Detention
  - consult missing persons.

– **Mi policia.** Build by Secretary of public security at Mexico, the application brings the citizen interactively to the information of their respective Quadrant, providing a quick way to make a call in case of emergency and graphically know the location of the Quadrants of Mexico City [9]. Principal functionalities are:
  - Quadrant realtime notifications
  - Emergency call
  - Check of quadrants in Mexico City.

– **REACH.** Build by Epicasoft at Peru; Reach is a social security network, which allows you to prevent the dangers that lurk in your environment, as well as provide you with the opportunity to receive immediate help in emergencies. Principal functionalities are:
  - Report an anonymous crime
  - Alerts people close to the area about a crime
  - Reliable emergency contacts
  - Alert of lost people
  - Request the current location to your contacts
  - Alerts in realtime about the routes required by the police in the area to get to the scene
  - Exchange of comments and multimedia.

– **bSafe.** Build by SMobile Software AS at Norway, in the fight against rape and sexual abuse, bSafe provides pioneering features such as activating the voice alarm, live streaming, and audio automatically and recording video. Bsafe allows parents to locate the whereabouts of their children at any time, as long as they keep their mobile phones on [6]. Principal functionalities are:
  - Activation of the SOS with voice.
  - Live broadcast.
  - Audio automatically and video recording.
  - Alarm to trusted contacts.
  - Shared route tracking with trusted contacts.

– **Citizen.** Build by Sp0n Inc. at the USA; It offers joining the Citizen safety network will give you instant access to information about the crimes in your area. Citizen technology will send push notifications in realtime to alert you of the crimes that are nearby. Principal functionalities are:
  - Access to crime in the area
  - Realtime notification of crimes in the area
  - Chat with close citizens.

– **NAMOLA.** Build by Namola EMS Group in the USA, Namola is the fastest way to request emergency help. By using the GPS location, the application can respond with nearby agents, know who you are and where you are. Principal functionalities are:
  - Ask for emergency help
  - Telephone answer by the local police
  - Emergency contact alert
  - Realtime query of the location of an emergency contact.

3   Descriptive Analysis of the Status of Delinquency in Colombia

The task of adequately measuring crime rates is a challenging exercise since several factors significantly affect the reality of these measurements [11], one of the biggest problems is to achieve an adequate classification of crimes as an international consensus. Therefore the consolidation and homologation of the type of crime is a difficult task. Therefore, in 2015, the United Nations Statistical Commission adopted the new International Classification of Crimes for Statistical Purposes (ICCS), and through the UNODOC (United Nations Unit on Drugs and Crime) a manual was prepared for the implementation of this classification and added to this problem, lack of denunciation by citizens, a correct or non-existent collection of data by the authorities regarding the victimization of citizen security incidents.

Colombia has had a significant improvement in terms of safety indexes and the positive perception of other countries in this aspect have made our country reactivate some industries such as tourism and exports. However, it is crucial to analyze with open data, how has been the evolution of our country and what is the current state in the different typified crimes.

The data sources used for the study come from the sites *Datos.gov.co* and the official sites of the entities: General Prosecutor of Colombia, Chamber of Commerce of Bogota, government of Cundinamarca, National Police of Colombia, organization of the united nations, organization of the American states and, Office of the United Nations against drugs and crime. Figure 1 presents the architecture used to process the data.

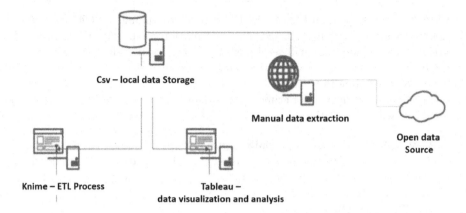

Csv – local data Storage

Manual data extraction

Open data
Source

Knime – ETL Process

Tableau –
data visualization and analysis

Fig. 1. Deployment diagram for data analytics

3.1 Visual Analytic

The Fig. 2 shows the behavior during the years 2000 to 2016 of the countries with
the highest number of homicide reports (it does not take into account the population), however it shows us clearly that Brazil, for example, has significantly
increased the reports of homicides and Colombia after occupying a 4 place in
the year 2000 today has happened to be in position 8.

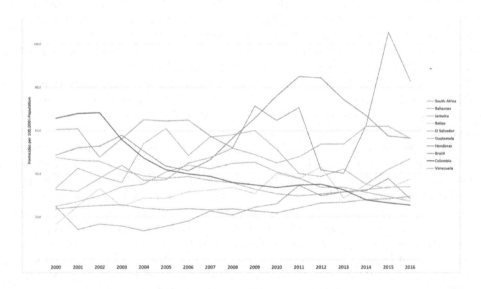

Fig. 2. Most insecure countries by homicide rate

About Colombia, [3] presents an analysis that concludes that the predomi-
nance of spatial-environmental factors in the occurrence of homicide, backed by

variables of the theory of disorder, territoriality, routine activity, and the defendable space. In Fig. 3, we see the ten crimes that most affect the citizen security of the country. The first three places are occupied: theft, personal injury, and intrafamily violence. This analysis can show us the way of how a mobile application focused on the reporting and prevention of this group of crimes can help citizens to contribute to the improvement of these indexes and provide the tools of self-protection and prevention.

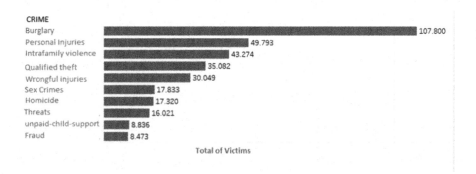

Fig. 3. Top 10 of the most common crimes in Colombia

Figure 4 allows us to see the increase in the number of victims in the year 2017 and 2018 in the crime of theft. This behavior is based on the criminology investigations of the national police to be associated with two very important political and social factors in the country; the first and most relevant is the demobilization of the FARC guerrilla; This episode in Colombian history explains the phenomena that we have observed so far, the drop in homicide rates and the increase in crimes such as theft; Given that people have abandoned their weapons in a large percentage, they have not found a way to rejoin civil society in an easy way, and they have had to resort to crime as a means of survival.

The other factor of great influence in the increase of crime is the great mobilization of immigrants to the country that largely do not find opportunities in Colombia and incorporates theft as a livelihood mechanism. It is also important to analyze how people such as personal injuries and intrafamily violence are increasing considerably over the years that has become a history of intolerance and aggression within our communities.

Figure 5 a review of the five municipalities with the most related reports according to the nation's attorney general's office. Facatativá is within the five municipalities with the highest number of reports, and all of them reflect a progressive increase in behavior over the last four years. Being Soacha the municipality with a stronger trend of crime growth since 2015 approximately. However, these data reflect the situation of the municipalities directly related to the number of inhabitants; since these five municipalities are also those that contribute

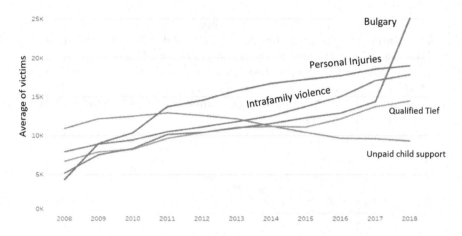

Fig. 4. Evolution of types of crime in Colombia

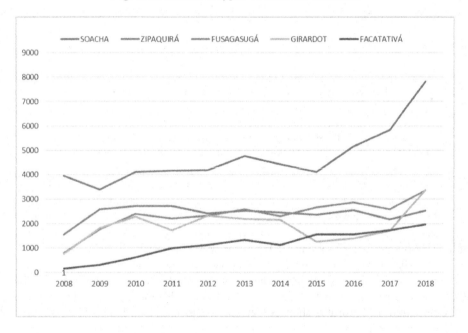

Fig. 5. Annual average number of crimes per municipality in Cundinamarca

more population to the department of Cundinamarca. It is, therefore, appropriate to evaluate this same indicator but taking into account the population rate.

The Fig. 6 shows us a slightly more accurate picture of Cundinamarca, where the highest rates of victims are reflected according to the number of inhabitants. Of the 116 municipalities that the department has, we see in the previous graph the 30 with the highest levels of delinquency. In this case, our municipality under study; Facatativá occupies a place 21. Being the place where the pilot will be carried out for the introduction of the Citizen Security App, this graphic can help us make future decisions about which municipalities should continue with the implementation of the tool, where it would surely be to attack the problem in the municipalities of Ubate, La Vega, Girardot, and Tocancipá.

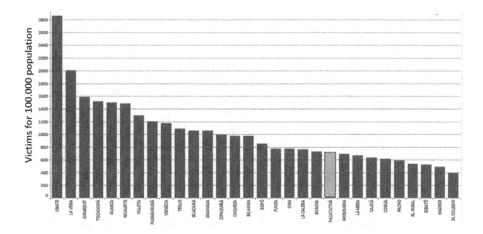

Fig. 6. Crime rate per 100,000 population in Cundinamarca 2018

Another of the points of study on crime in Colombia is the analysis of information regarding the public security personnel assigned to attend to the problems of each department of the country. According to the UN, a recommendation is that for every 100,000 inhabitants, there should be at least 300 policemen. Colombia has an average of 311 police officers per 100,000 inhabitants, which apparently indicates that this indicator is adequate; however, next, we will review the distribution of agents by the department to have even more interesting conclusions.

Figure 7 shows the distribution of public order personnel in the National territory behaves, evidencing that the departments with the highest crime rate (according to the analysis of the previous graph), are below the recommended index (300 agents) with the exception of the department of Santander that has 319. In a special way, we can see how the municipality of Cundinamarca, which is the object of our analysis, has a police deficit of 83 per 100,000 inhabitants, which would indicate that for the municipality of Cundinamarca it would be necessary to assign approximately 2300 agents for compliance with the indicator. These analyses show that the public force is not sufficient to meet the needs of citizens in the region and, therefore, the mechanisms for reporting and attention to citizen security can not be focused solely on delegating management responsibility to the agencies public. It is evident that it is necessary to implement mechanisms that allow citizens to self-manage.

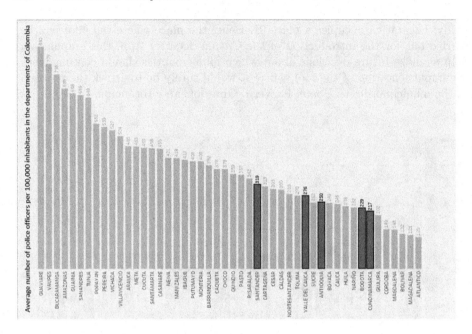

Fig. 7. Average number of police officers per 100,000 population

3.2 Analysis of Results for Descriptive Analysis

The results of the analysis of transnational crime information obtained from the statistical information from the UNODC and the UN show a positive panorama of Colombia, according to the behavior of recent years. While it is true; some crimes have been increasing; the most severe, such as homicide, has decreased significantly; this has made the international communities see the country with different eyes and is deciding to invest in Colombia, this fact has reactivated industries such as tourism and in general has helped to reactivate the economy. More significant efforts must be made in terms of the mechanisms for standardizing crime worldwide. Because With the information available, the only thing clear is that homicide is a crime in all countries. Other crimes can be classified in a wide range of categories that do not allow to determine a correspondence to make conclusions. For example, theft has more than 300 types or categories depending on the amounts stolen to the way the crime has proceeded. This lack of unity in the classification makes an assertive analysis very complicated.

Although the policy of open data and transparency in Colombia has helped to take a massive step in terms of knowledge of critical information in the country, we still have problems associated with the standardization of information, data quality, information gathering and, in some cases, veracity. Therefore, there is a generalized culture of non-denunciation, due to several factors: Fear to be identified; repression of the victim; the lack of confidence of the citizen towards institutions; the inability to impart justice. These reasons lead us to question ourselves about what should be the adequate mechanisms to obtain more reliable information from the institutions and what tools to improve the reporting and judgment channels.

Currently, according to the analysis of the year 2018; The crimes with higher incidence and growth in the country are: theft (in all its categories), personal injuries, domestic violence, qualified robbery, and sexual crimes. Therefore, it is recommended that government policies can focus on the prevention and care of these crimes. Especially those that have shown more significant growth since 2017, such as theft and personal injuries. The analysis of the information showed surprisingly, that although the country has a policy rate per number of inhabitants acceptable according to the recommendations of the UN. The distribution within the country is not adequate since the departments with higher crime rates are those that are mostly devoid of police presence. Therefore, it is useful to know that other factors influence the distribution of authorities in the country to achieve more significant balance at this point.

4   Perspective and Requirements of the Mobile App Build

Although solutions similar to the one in this project are found in the market, we see that the differentiating components are focused on the implementation of emerging technologies such as Big Data and Machine Learning, technologies that can offer indicators by analyzing the information obtained and predictions that facilitate security work not only to the authorities but to the citizenry. However, although technology has its benefits, it does not help much if the human factor that intervenes in the processes does not make efficient use of it or if there is no sufficiency and efficiency in the treatment of crime and the exercise of justice. Having said this, we will now reveal the most relevant conclusions through the work done not only in the survey of the state of the art of similar solutions but also in the architecture and technology decisions used as a basis for the construction of the tool:

- The first observation is about the stakeholders that would be involved not only in use but in the use of the App. In this sense, the App has citizenship as a user of report and consultation about the incidents of insecurity. It must take into account the skills of the population for the use of technology, minimize the possibility of false reports or information and the ease of use of the tool so that it actually takes advantage as it should be. A second stakeholder is the local authorities, who will consult and receive the reports of the citizens. It is very important to clarify that the support of the authorities for the success of the project is decisive; given that it implies that the government organization has the personnel available to be able to attend the reports and the citizens really feel that this is a useful and quick channel for managing their needs in the face of crime.
- Given the results of the exploration of the solutions that solve similar problems, it is necessary to understand that the attention to the incidents should

not be left solely in the hands of the authorities because the personnel for the attention is insufficient. That is why some of the initiatives has failed. Therefore, the involvement of the citizen as a resource that can also give attention and help to their community is of the utmost importance and is a differentiating factor of this tool compared to others.

- In Colombia, some solutions also failed because although the initiatives were supported by local authorities with the change of government or officials, the continuity of the process was lost. Therefore, the question arises: How to make this solution transcend political interests? This is something difficult to control, but a mitigating factor is that citizenship is also part of the attention.

- A very marked problem in Colombia in terms of reporting are the processes and channels that are difficult to access. The application Adenunciar! [10] of the prosecution seeks to improve that process but also that it is a tool of poor usability, it eventually falls or does not work, this makes people not use it, and it generates a bad reputation of the tool and the institution. It is very important, once our application is going to massive ensure stability and usability tests to ensure it is the most intuitive and easy for the citizen.

- The infrastructure and architecture supported by the application must be prepared for significant growth if the pilot is successful and can be implemented in more populations. That is why we chose a robust, secure and versatile cloud solution such as Google Cloud Platform, prepared not only for the current needs of the tool but to integrate with more powerful solutions for big data, machine learning, and analytics. Introduced a Machine Learning approach to automate and help crime analysts identify and work on cases where they can make a difference [4]. The construction of the tool was ready and integrated with Big Query for future integration with analytics tools. It is also important to mention that Cloud providers support this type of social innovations with preferential costs in the use of its services with visibility in the start-up ecosystem.

- Firebase as a platform for the development of mobile applications simplifies the development process, making the developer a little disinterested in the problems associated with the infrastructure. It also offers a set of Apis and libraries that facilitate the use of features such as geo-referencing, handling, and synchronization of messaging, security, and authentication. Particularly, and having had the opportunity to develop in other platforms, The use of this type of technologies allows obtaining much more agile results and take fewer risks in the development process.

- The solution must go beyond and provide not only the notification of an event but must also allow unified control panels and dashboards to draw conclusions and determine generalized improvement actions.

5 Conclusions and Future Work

Below are the recommendations to give continuity to the implementation of the pilot and subsequent phases of the tool.

5.1   Functional Recommendations

- Achieve adequate coordination with the control agencies so that the attention of the mobile channel is immediate and promotes use in the population.
- The implementation project should seek to mitigate the risk of lack of continuity due to change of administration in the local mayor's office.
- It is necessary to explore with the local mayor's office the possibility of having additional police personnel for the attention of the reports that arrive through the canal, since there is evidence of lack of this resource.
- Promote in the target population of the prototype the consolidation of local communities for monitoring, attention, and control; This is because the tool seeks to make the citizen participation in the care and safety of the community. The process can be supported by Whatsapp groups for the continuous communication of the communities.
- Validate, as a subsequent phase of the project, the integration of IoT components to report other types of incidents; Example: fire alarms, burglar alarms, seismographs, and weather stations [8].

5.2   Technical Recommendations

- Perform machine learning processes on the information collected during the time that the pilot test of the tool is put into production with the Cloud ML Engine components that were mounted on the Firebase architecture of the solution.
- Perform usability tests with the population selected for the pilot and thus find improvement factors in the App.
- Carry out simulated load tests before massifying the solution and in this way correctly size the infrastructure.
- Implement additional functionalities in the mobile application to facilitate communication between the communities formed. For example, a messaging tool. For this, it is important to see the results of the use of WhatsApp between the communities and to validate if it makes sense to implement this functionality in the mobile application.

References

1. Barra, S., Castiglione, A., De Marsico, M., Nappi, M., Choo, K.K.R.: Cloud-based biometrics (biometrics as a service) for smart cities, nations, and beyond. IEEE Cloud Comput. 5(5), 92–100 (2018)
2. Carlo Bertot, J., Jaeger, P.T., Grimes, J.M.: Promoting transparency and accountability through ICTS, social media, and collaborative e-government. Transform. Gov. People Process. Policy 6(1), 78–91 (2012)
3. Céspedes, E.N., Vargas Espinosa, N.M., Avendaño Prieto, B.L., Rincón, H., Ospino, M.A.: Criminología ambiental y homicidio en la ciudad de bogotá (colombia). Revista de Estudios Sociales 63, 55–71 (2018)

4. Ghosh, D., Chun, S., Shafiq, B., Adam, N.R.: Big data-based smart city platform: Real-time crime analysis. In: Proceedings of the 17th International Digital Government Research Conference on Digital Government Research, pp. 58–66. ACM (2016)
5. Kitchin, R.: The real-time city? Big data and smart urbanism. GeoJournal **79**(1), 1–14 (2014)
6. Kvalnes, Ø.: Risky Play, pp. 1–20. Springer, Cham (2017). https://doi.org/10.1007/978-3-319-63318-3_1
7. Lacinák, M., Ristvej, J.: Smart city, safety and security. Procedia Eng. **192**, 522–527 (2017)
8. Lin, J., Yu, W., Zhang, N., Yang, X., Zhang, H., Zhao, W.: A survey on internet of things: architecture, enabling technologies, security and privacy, and applications. IEEE Internet Things J. **4**(5), 1125–1142 (2017)
9. Luccisano, L., Macdonald, L.: Guns and butter. Violence in Latin America and the Caribbean: Subnational Structures, Institutions, and Clientelistic Networks, p. 132 (2017)
10. Rodríguez-Ortega, J.D., Mejía-Londoño, D., Caro-Zambrano, L.d.P., Romero-Hernández, M., Campos-Méndez, F.: Implications of the integration process of the administrative records of criminality between the SPOA (oral accusatory criminal system) of the attorney general's office (FGN) and the SIEDCO (statistical, delinquency, offenses and operations information system) of the national police of Colombia (PONAL), and the implementation of the "iADenunciar!" app on crime figures. Revista Criminalidad **60**(3), 9–27 (2018)
11. Walsh, A., Jorgensen, C.: Criminology: The Essentials. Sage Publications, Thousand Oaks (2017)
12. Wanumen, L., Florez, H.: Architectural approaches for phonemes recognition systems. In: Florez, H., Diaz, C., Chavarriaga, J. (eds.) ICAI 2018. CCIS, vol. 942, pp. 267–279. Springer, Cham (2018). https://doi.org/10.1007/978-3-030-01535-0_20
13. Wanumen, L., Moreno, J., Florez, H.: Mobile based approach for accident reporting. In: Botto-Tobar, M., Pizarro, G., Zúñiga-Prieto, M., D'Armas, M., Zúñiga Sánchez, M. (eds.) CITT 2018. CCIS, vol. 895, pp. 302–311. Springer, Cham (2019). https://doi.org/10.1007/978-3-030-05532-5_22
14. Zheng, Y.: Explaining citizens' e-participation usage: functionality of e-participation applications. Adm. Soc. **49**(3), 423–442 (2017)

University Quality Measurement Model Based on Balanced Scorecard

Thalia Obredor-Baldovino[1], Harold Combita-Niño[2],
Tito J. Crissien-Borrero[3], Emiro De-la-Hoz-Franco[2(✉)],
Diego Beltrán[4], Iván Ruiz[5], Joaquin F. Sanchez[5],
and Carlos Collazos-Morales[5]

[1] Departamento de Gestión Industrial, Agroindustria y Operaciones,
Universidad de la Costa, Barranquilla, Colombia
[2] Departamento de Ciencias de la Computación y Electrónica,
Universidad de la Costa, Barranquilla, Colombia
edelahoz@cuc.edu.co
[3] Departamento de Humanidades, Universidad de la Costa,
Barranquilla, Colombia
[4] Facultad de Ingeniería, Escuela Colombiana de Ingeniería, Bogotá, Colombia
[5] Vicerrectoría de Investigaciones, Universidad Manuela Beltrán,
Bogotá, Colombia

Abstract. A Higher Education Institution (HEI) has the responsibility to track the processes through indicators that guarantee the measurement of the results in almost real time. This article presents the design of a management and quality model of the processes in a university, through the integration of a Balance Scorecard (BSC) and the implementation of an information system. For which it was required: a review of existing tracing and monitoring systems in the academic sector, definition of the requirements of the proposed technological, a diagnosis of the current measurement system of the HEI analyzed, identify measurement indicators and develop a technological tool. The designed model presents a precise and clear methodological guide that can be replicated in any HEI to monitor its processes.

Keywords: Quality measurement model · Higher education institution ·
Balance scorecard · Information system · Academic software · Decision making

1 Introduction

Higher Education contributes to the social, economic and political growth of the countries, because it trains future professionals who will generate different solution alternatives aimed at solving social problems. Universities in Colombia materialize this contribution through the definition of policies aligned to the institutional teleological component, and the design and operationalization of action plans that contribute to the improvement of the quality of the training process and of all administrative processes to support it. With the intention of promoting the acquisition and development of both generic and professional skills and competences, [45] proposes a proposal in this regard.

© Springer Nature Switzerland AG 2019
H. Florez et al. (Eds.): ICAI 2019, CCIS 1051, pp. 131–144, 2019.
https://doi.org/10.1007/978-3-030-32475-9_10

The Colombian university system has implemented different strategies, leading to improve the service offered, as evidenced in [42, 45]. Understanding that their quality, accessibility and efficiency depend both on the economic development of the geographical area and on human capacities [5]. Despite the commitment to quality shown by the Colombian Ministry of National Education (primarily in the last two decades), in terms of definition and implementation of such strategies, many HEIs still do not have effective monitoring and accountability systems (that allow them to evaluate the performance of their strategic areas), which does not contribute to the improvement of the processes and is contrary to the quality criteria required by higher education for the training of qualified professionals.

The use of an appropriate management tool provides the opportunity to increase academic, scientific and cultural quality by facilitating the process of competing with leadership in the increasingly demanding university education market [1]. Given this, it is relevant to have clarity about the internal purposes as an institution and to have alignment with the external requirements or parameters through which the quality of education is determined. In this paper the process of building a system for tracking and monitoring the strategic areas belonging to a university is showed. The paper is made up of five sections: the first section shows an introduction, the second section details the evaluation of the management and quality of processes in HEI, the third section shows the design of the management model and quality of the methodology defined by the management system of the BSC, the fourth section describes the information system that supports the model and each of the modules that constitute it, finally the conclusions and references are presented.

2   Evaluation of the Management and Quality of Processes in HEI

In the High Education Institutions, the evaluation of the management and quality of processes will be strategically addressed from: the analysis of the Indicators system (based on a global perspective), the mechanisms of quality assurance in education (based on the normative reference defined in the Republic of Colombia, by the Ministry of National Education) and the Balance Scorecard (as an integrating tool that facilitates the decision making).

2.1   Indicators System

The management of processes in any organization is a complex task that must be developed under a review approach at both micro and macro level to be able to cover all the needs of the areas that compose the organization. Once management maintains a continuous and permanent task, should be measured the quality of its processes and subsequently take actions that allow to optimize its resources and increase the impact of its activities. The HEI as organizations, are no stranger to this, because the quality of higher education must cover all its functions and activities with reference to teaching, programs, research, staff, students, infrastructure and services to the community and the university world, as raised [6]. This implies, that management in education integrates policies in a practical way through the purposes of the organization, by means of planning its procedures and the permanent evaluation of these [2]. It also implies that those responsible for carrying out the management, recognize the need to treat the information at the inputs, during its processing and at the outputs, so as to facilitate decision-making in coherence with the purposes of the university, according to [3].

Educational planners must pay attention to quality [3], so that strategic planning and performance evaluation play an essential role in consolidating a better future for society [4]. Recognition of key performance indicators is one of the main steps in performance evaluation [7]. Indicators have become an essential tool for describing and understanding the quality of a system. They are instruments of observation and monitoring of a system, designed from the relation of variables of the system. The measurement of these variables and their subsequent comparison with the established goals, allows to determine the achievement of the system and its trend of evolution [8].

From the cybernetics and control concepts, described in [8], the following steps are defined to establish an indicator:

- Have objectives and strategies
- Identify critical success factors
- Establish indicators for each critical success factor
- Determine for each indicator, the status, the threshold and the management range
- Design the measurement and source of information.

In [6] defines the "System of Indicators", within the context of education, as the coherent set of indicators, combined or not, according to a system of variables and categories that represent the management or operation of a unit of analysis for a given function, for example: teaching, research, extension or institutional service.

The evaluation of higher education systems and the measurement of the objectives achieved is a complex task. For this reason, many measurement methods have been proposed with opinions differ on which are the most appropriate indicator systems, some of those proposals are: [10–14]. These tools have been designed to perform or support certain functions and the debate focuses more on its use than on the way they are designed and implemented. In [15] and [16] indicators structures have been proposed, in order to have a more organized construction and obtain a very close and reliable representation of the interests and projection of the organization. These structures have grouped indicators considering results, internal organizational processes, integrative criteria, organizational culture, and capacity for change, linkage between resources and results, technical aspects of the organization, and relationship of the organization to human factors.

In Latin America has been observed in a significant use of indicators, according to the quality of: curriculum components, process related to educational management (human resources, material resources and didactic factors), immediate results related to the training acquired by students, services and integration [3]. Such indicators have been categorized in academic, research and support, and based on the characteristics of the Analytical Hierarchy Process (AHP), trend analysis and comparative data, as manifested in [17]. In Colombia, a recent study presents a list of indicators related to processes and activities carried out in planning, teaching, research, social responsibility, welfare, internationalization, management and resources [18]. On the other hand, there are evaluation tools that have been used by the education sector to maintain sustainable monitoring and benchmarking [19].

In the European continent, the application of indicators has developed much more. Since the end of the twentieth century, different universities have implemented information management systems based in indicators, which support to decision making in the development of academic processes that were mainly oriented toward teaching, research and management. The above, has facilitated the integration of indicators with a set of quality improvement tools, that were developed in subsequent years, as evidenced in [20–22]. It should be noted that there is no marked trend in the use of any quality management tool. However, the philosophy of Total Quality Management (TQM) has been used as a conduit to achieve the objectives of Quality Management for organizations [24].

Asia has not been alien to these structures, considering that BSC-based indicators have been constructed for university education centers through information systems and academic monitoring, as referenced in [25–28].

In different world scenarios, proposals are being developed to strengthen the measurement of quality in Universities. In [46] the interaction between the organizational structure/managerial and organizational value/ psychological elements that impact on the quality of education was evaluated. Based on this, a route analysis was carried out on the data collected from the academics with teaching coordination functions. The study recommended the creation of policies and institutional strategies aimed at improving educational quality through the consolidation of collaborative teaching/learning communities with an explicit concern for morality, participation and development. In [47] a committee for quality assurance (QAC) is proposed within Italian universities in order to identify if, as happened in other New Public Management (NPM) reforms, to detect the key variables that promote a satisfactory QAC functioning; based on both the analysis of the composition and the role of QAC in all the Italian public universities and significant case studies.

2.2 Mechanisms of Quality Assurance in Education

When an organization refers to the term of quality, it is associated to the satisfaction of the expectations according to defined criteria that are objectively evaluated, allowing to have greater proximity to degrees of excellence. The concept of quality in education has arisen because governments, educational institutions and society have identified the importance of permanently improving academic training processes that lead to a better economic development of society.

The concept of quality applied to the public service of higher education refers to the synthesis of characteristics that allow to recognize a specific academic program or institution of a certain type and make a judgment about the closeness between how the institution or the academic program provides this service and how it should be provided [29]. This situation has given rise to a growing social requirement to improve and ensure the quality of universities and their undergraduate and graduate programs. In response to the above, both the State and the institutions themselves have generated quality assurance mechanisms, in order to give greater guarantees to users and the general public regarding compliance with minimum standards of quality and the levels of performance of graduates [30].

Colombia began its experience of quality improvement of higher education through the accreditation of high quality that appears in Law 30 of 1992 [31]. Taking into account the requirements of the society, the mechanism was created to obtain a qualified register of obligatory character, coordinated by the National Commission for the Quality Assurance of Higher Education (Comisión Nacional de Aseguramiento de la Calidad de la Educación Superior - CONACES); and guidelines for high-quality accreditation of voluntary nature governed by the National Accreditation Council (Consejo Nacional de Acreditación - CNA).

In order to offer and to develop an academic program of higher education, in the address of an HEI, or in another place, it is necessary to have previously the qualified registry of the mentioned program [32]. While the central purpose of accreditation is to promote continuous improvement and to determine whether an academic institution has quality in general or respect of one or more of its careers or educational programs, if it is able to demonstrate that it is progressing continuously and systematically with the use of adequate strategies, procedures and resources to achieve its mission and objectives, reasonably fulfilling the established criteria and quality standards [33].

In most of the countries at the global level, national accreditation systems are created, which seek to ensure that HEIs that are part of these systems meet the highest quality requirements to offer programs that can meet the labor demand. In Colombia, the accreditation process does not arise within the framework of state inspection and oversight, but rather in the promotion, recognition and continuous improvement of quality [34]. Considering the above, it can be affirmed that both the obtaining of the qualified registry and the guidelines for the high accreditation, seek the recognition and the quality of the academic programs. The first is the way to achieve the basic operating conditions for the offering of the programs and the second continually seeks to improve processes to achieve academic excellence.

2.3   Balance Scorecard

In 1992 Kaplan and Norton of Harvard University, revolutionized business management with a proposal known as the Balance Scorecard (BSC) to align the company towards achieving organizational strategies through tangible goals and indicators. Kaplan states that "Managers, like pilots, need an instrument that measures their environment and performance to lead the journey towards future excellence".

The BSC is a management tool that assists decision making, by providing periodic information on the level of compliance with the objectives, previously established through indicators, the latter include both financial and non-financial aspects. The BSC favors transparency in management and the establishment of a balance between immediate actions and strategic lines, by integrating four perspectives or key areas and relating them to the mission, vision and objectives. The four perspectives are financial, training, internal processes and the relationship with customers/users.

In the BSC, it is preferable that the indicators be of a numerical nature, as this will allow the establishment of tolerance levels. According to their nature, there are indicators that measure: efficiency, economy, effectiveness, excellence and environment

[35]. Management through performance measurement, has historically been an important aid in enabling managers to diagnose a situation and learn more about it. In the 1960s and 1970s, Target Management became a widely used management tool to align management actions with organizational objectives. In addition, BSC has a huge impact on knowledge creation and provides greater interactivity, since it helps to communicate strategy involving different levels of the organization [36]. On the other hand, the Balanced Scorecard provides models and processes for measuring and supervising the performance of human resources and their impact on the strategic success of the company [37].

For example, Universidad Centroccidental Lisandro Alvarado (UCLA), in the implementation of its BSC has established as perspectives the state, society, internal processes, and organizational development and learning. Its implementation was supported on the systems of control of management like accounting and budget, taking into account that the institution belongs to the public sector [38].

The BSC proposes to obtain relevant information about the main factors that can lead to the achievement of the objectives of the universities. It is also very useful for communicating the strategy to the entire university community and for the goals of each employee to be consistent with those of the university itself [39].

The implementation of a BSC through information systems, provide organization, dynamism and decrease the margin of error in making decisions, by enhancing the analytical, organizational, operational and financial capacities of each company. On the other hand, it provides the environment, structure and language to communicate mission and strategy, using measurements to inform employees about the causes of current and future success [40]. Organizations are becoming increasingly sensitive to the need for management information systems, largely due to the changing environment and globalization. In addition, universities have a complex organizational structure, characterized by a high dispersion of authority for decision making in various bodies. Therefore, the BSC reaches its maximum expression when it is designed and implemented through the use of new information technologies [41].

3 Design of the Management Model and Quality

It is important to highlight that the methodology defined by the management system of the BSC was established for the construction of indicators. For the review of the tracing and monitoring systems applied in HEIs, it was considered that they would have the recognition of institutional accreditation that guarantees an academic organization with high quality standards. In this way the different indicators created according to each type of institution were identified, reflecting the characteristic situation of the institution and the approach to which each one contributed. Subsequently the requirements defined for the design of the system were determined, establishing the starting point for the creation of the technological tool. The classification of these requirements was relevant to define in more detail the types of requirements necessary to have accurate and truthful information of the system.

In order to construct an informative diagnosis in relation to the current measurement system of the HEI studied, the strategic map scheme was designed, which consolidated the structure of the institution's vision in relation to its processes and procedures. Subsequently, the required indicators were elaborated according to the objectives established in the perspectives defined in the strategic map, thus relating indicators-objectives-perspectives. For each indicator the following items were defined: the associated objective, name, display order, description, formula, unit of measure, orientation (if desired to maximize or minimize), tolerance levels, target, frequency of collection, information source, data quality, periodicity of the goal, accreditation factor, collection manager (s), performance manager (s), version, version update date.

With the articulation between: the Institutional Educational Project (IEP), the Program Educational Project (PEP), the interests of the management, the national regulations established for minimum quality conditions for higher education programs, and the policies established by the National System of Accreditation, it was possible to construction a strategic map as shown in the Fig. 1, which grouped and organized in a structured way the main objectives in order to obtain concrete results that generate value in the HEI.

The perspective of Academic Processes is related to the integrality and flexibility of the curriculum, interdisciplinarity, teaching and learning strategies, the student evaluation system, and academic and teaching support resources. The Visibility perspective focuses on the insertion of the program in national and international academic contexts, for which it seeks to increase the visibility of the University at a national and international level, and strengthen the academic and administrative management of the graduate Department. The Self-regulation perspective aims at the permanent evaluation of the programs through the existence of an efficient, effective and sustainable management of resources, articulated with the IEP. The Research perspective ensures that high quality programs, according to their nature, are recognized for the effectiveness of their research training processes, and for their contributions to scientific knowledge and innovation, an interesting implementation of this perspective is presented in [44]. Finally, the Extension perspective is related to the positive influence of academic programs on their environment, promoting the link with the various sectors of society.

To achieve the objectives, 63 indicators were divided among the five perspectives previously mentioned. These indicators are obtained and measured by users in the critical areas of Academic Management, Internship Management, Financial Management, Publications Management, Research and Innovation Management, and Administrative Management.

When consolidating the indicators, it was observed that the perspectives of Academic Processes and Research represent 51% and 35% of the measurement system, respectively. This indicates that the HEIs currently concentrate their efforts on maintaining a quality education by guaranteeing procedures and adequate resources for both students and the teaching staff so that updated tools and corresponding competencies are provided for adequate job placement.

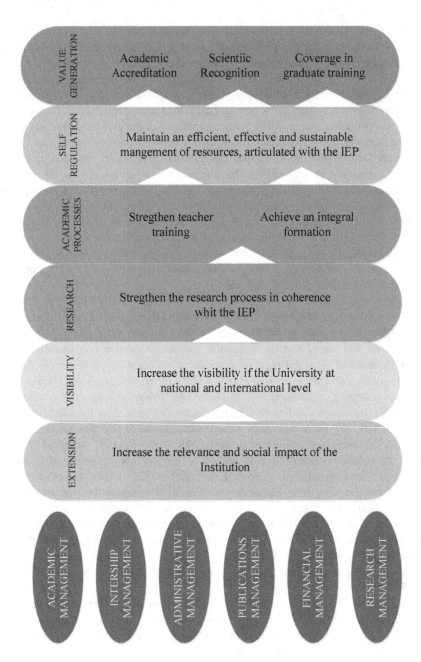

Fig. 1. University strategic map

4   Information System

The model of management and quality of the university processes was implemented through a software, which integrates: a transactional system for the recording of the measurements of the indicators and an interface with visual reports for the decisions making. The Information System includes modules that allow: the parameterization of the software, the management and the generation of reports for decision making. The main interface presents a web desktop (see Fig. 2), to access different windows and view essential information of the BSC through widgets. In addition, it has a main menu to access the different functionalities of the software.

The desktop allows the opening of several windows at the same time and navigate among them through the web desktop. The default view of the web desktop is enabled for the visualization of widgets and direct access to the functions most used by the logged in user.

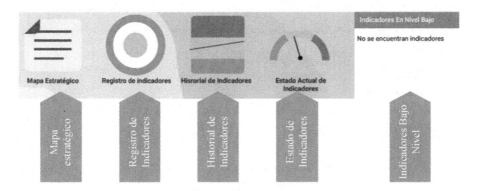

Fig. 2. Screenshot of login and web desktop

4.1   Parameterization Module

The information system allows the definition of different parameters, such as the assignment and denial of permits, for the access of user groups to the different modules. Similarly, within the system, user profiles and all their associated information are managed. Areas of university and academic programs can also be defined. On the other hand, for the implementation of the BSC is necessary to make the configuration of the strategic map. First, the perspectives are defined and then the objectives associated with each of them.

The life cycle of an indicator consists of seven moments, from its creation and configuration to its measurement and visualization, these moments are: creation of the indicator, definition of goals, definition of performance managers, definition of collection manager, activation of the indicator, recording of measurements and visualization of the indicator.

4.2　Management Module

At the transactional level, this module is important, since it allows to carry out the measurement records of each one of the indicators by each academic program. It means, the value that an indicator can take at a specific time may be different for each academic program. Depending on the user who has logged into the platform, the indicators that can be obtained will be displayed, presenting them in a panel according to the frequency of the collection. Depending on the formula of the indicator, the user will see how to enter it. Future periods cannot be recorded, but it is possible to insert all periods prior to the current date. After three (3) days of the indicator registration deadline, an alert will be generated by email to the user. In addition, for each measurement period the user can attach a support document (Fig. 3).

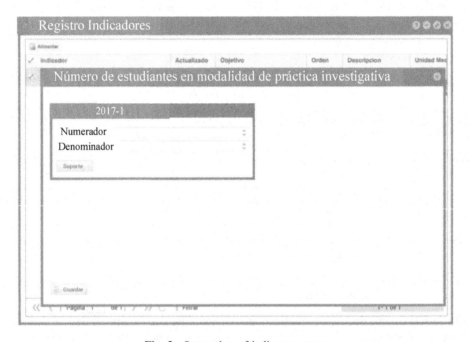

Fig. 3. Screenshot of indicators entry

4.3　Reports Module for Decisions Making

Within the information system, three key reports can be found in order to trace and make decisions based on the results of the management: the strategic map, the history of the indicators and the current state of the indicators.

The strategic map lists the defined perspectives, the objectives of each perspective and the indicators of each objective. For each indicator its current value or state can be seen, through a semaphore (red: bad, Yellow: normal, Green: fine), each time the indicator is updated, the last measurement period and other indicator information is displayed. This panel serves to identify bad indicators and to know what objective is not being met in the institution. Reporting is done in two layers, in the first layer the measurements can be seen at the institutional level, but also can be seen the detail of each indicator, identifying the measurement of that indicator by program. In this way, it can be known, which program is lowering or increasing an indicator, to make decisions about it.

On the other hand, there is a report on the indicators history, where the different measures that an indicator has had throughout its existence are displayed on a graph. This allows to know if the indicator is growing or decreasing, in order to take corrective measures or to design strategies that allow to achieve the goals. For this reason, in this report the goal to be achieved can be seen, in each one of the graphs of the indicator. Finally, Fig. 4 shows the report of the current status of the indicators, where a semaphore is displayed that indicates the limits of the tolerance ranges of the indicator and its current measurement.

Fig. 4. Screenshot of indicators display (Color figure online)

5 Conclusions

All HEI requires a tool to measure and control its processes in order to evaluate the impact of its activities and compete in the market. For this, it requires great support and commitment from the areas involved for the process of constructing indicators that reflect their need and maintain the objectivity of the evaluation.

There is no accurate measure of indicators to evaluate a university, but there are references of quality that guide the creation of these towards compliance and control of processes. In this way national accreditation guidelines and guidelines for obtaining qualified registration are an essential starting point for effective measures in the education sector.

In designing the tracing and monitoring model, it was possible to define that the main purposes in which the system should be focused were to achieve an integral formation in the students of the different academic programs of the University, in line with the challenges of high quality, by strengthening: the teachers' plant (consolidating the programs of admission, promotion, permanence and graduation of the student population with relevance and quality, and increase the visibility of the University at national and international level), the academic and administrative management of the graduate department (keeping an efficient, effective and sustainable management of resources, articulated with the IEP), the research process (in coherence with the IEP and the needs of the environment) and increase the relevance and social impact of the Institution.

At the same time, the most relevant perspectives that concentrate the functionality of the HEI are the Academic Processes and the Research, concentrating the Universities their efforts in maintaining a quality education by guaranteeing procedures and resources that are appropriate both for students and the teaching staff so that updated tools and corresponding competencies are provided for adequate job placement. Also, it is of great importance to maintain a continuous process of knowledge flow that allows to generate the evolution and the transcendence of the science. Finally, the importance of the use of an information system for the implementation of educational quality measurement systems is highlighted, considering that it is necessary to have three indispensable requirements for decision making: integrity, reliability and availability.

References

1. Bustos, J., Zapata, M., Ramírez-Valdivia, M.: Beyond strategic management for universities: a Balance Score Card application. Oikos **12**(26), 95–114 (2008)
2. Costa Morosini, M., et al.: Quality of higher education and the complex exercise of proposing indicators. Revista Brasileira de Educação **21**(64), 13–37 (2016)
3. Vidal García, J.: Plan nacional de evaluación de la calidad de las universidades. In: España, M.D.-G. (ed.) Indicadores en la universidad: información y decisiones. España (1999)
4. Jalaliyoon, N., Taherdoost, H.: Performance evaluation of higher education; A necessity. Procedia – Soc. Behav. Sci. **46**, 5682–5686 (2012)
5. González López, M.J., Cácerez Salas, J.: Hacia una gestión estratégica de los departamentos universitarios propuesta de un cuadro de mando integral. Auditoría pública: revista de los Órganos Autónomos de Control Externo **35**, 55–72 (2005)
6. Megnounif, A., Kherbouche, A., Chermitti, N.: Contribution to the quality assessment in higher education: the case study of the faculty of technology, Tlemcen, Algeria. Procedia Soc. Behav. Sci. **102**, 276–287 (2013)
7. Azma, F.: Qualitative Indicators for the evaluation of universities performance. Procedia Soc. Behav. Sci. **2**(2), 5408–5411 (2010)
8. Rios Giraldo, R.M.: Seguimiento, medición, análisis y mejora en los sistemas de gestión. Enfoque bajo indicadores de gestión y Balanced Scorecard (Tercera ed.). Bogotá, Colombia: ICONTEC (2013)
9. Cabeza, M.A.: Indicadores de gestión en la educación superior como herramienta de la planificación estratégica. Revista Venezolana de Análisis de Coyuntura **X**(2), 105–116 (2004)
10. Chinta, R., Kebritchi, M., Elias, J.: A conceptual framework for evaluating higher education institutions. Int. J. Educ. Manage. **30**(6), 989–1002 (2016)
11. García-Aracil, A., Palomares-Montero, D.: Examining benchmark indicator systems for the evaluation of higher education institutions. High. Educ. **60**(2), 217–234 (2010)
12. Larrondo Petrie, M.M., Medina García, V.H., Méndez Giraldo, G.: Modelo de Registro y Acreditación de Instituciones de Educación Superior basado en el Modelo CMMI. Seventh LACCEI Latin American and Caribbean Conference for Engineering and Technology (LACCEI'2009), pp. 1–8. San Cristóbal, Venezuela (2009)

13. Abadie, P.: Estudio sobre indicadores y costos en la educación superior. Recuperado el 17 de January de 2018, de Universidad.edu.uy (2001). http://www.universidad.edu.uy/pmb/opac_ css/doc_num.php?explnum_id=29
14. Rodriguez Rodriguez, R., Alfaro Saiz, J., Ortiz, B.A.: Quantitative relationships between key performance indicators for supporting decision-making processes. Comput. Ind. **60**(2), 104–113 (2009)
15. De Miguel Díaz, F.M.: Modelos de investigación sobre organizaciones educativas. Revista de Investigación Educativa, RIE **7**(13), 21–56 (1989)
16. Pérez Juste, R., García Ramos, J.M.: Diagnóstico, evaluación y toma de decisiones. Tratado de educación personalizada No. 9. Madrid, España: Ediciones Rialp (1989)
17. Suryadi, K.: Key performance indicators measurement model based on analytic hierarchy process and trend-comparative dimension in higher education institution. Int. Symp. Anal. Hierarchy Process (ISAHP) **3**(12), 1689–1695 (2007)
18. Sánchez Quintero, J.: A proposal of quality indicators to self-assessment and accreditation of undergraduate programs in management. Estud. Gerenciales **30**(133), 419–429 (2014)
19. Cronemberger, H., Magrini, A.: Higher education institution sustainability assessment tools: considerations on their use in Brazil. Int. J. Sustain. High. Educ. **17**(3), 322–341 (2016)
20. Andrés Fernández, M.A.: Propuesta de indicadores del proceso de enseñanza/ aprendizaje en la formación profesional en un contexto de gestión de calidad total. RELIEVE. Revista Electrónica de Investigación y Evaluación Educativa **11**(1), 63–82 (2005)
21. Gurban, I., Sudakova, A.: The Development of Higher Education in Russia: An Assessment Methodology. Procedia Soc. Behav. Sci. 596–605 (2015)
22. Scheffel, M., Drachsler, H., Stoyanov, S., Specht, M.: Quality indicators for learning analytics. Educ. Technol. Soc. **17**(4), 117–132 (2014)
23. García-Aracil, A., Palomares-Montero, D.: Indicadores para la evaluación de las instituciones universitarias: validación a través del método Delphi. Revista Española de Documentación Científica **35**(1), 119–144 (2012)
24. Sanchez, A., Neira, D., Cabello, J.: Frameworks applied in quality management - a systematic review. Revista Espacios **37**(9), 17 (2016)
25. Indrayani, E.: Management of Academic Information System (AIS) at Higher Education in the City of Bandung. Procedia Soc. Behav. Sci. **103**(26), 628–636 (2013)
26. Law, N., Niederhauser, D.S., Christensen, R., Linda, S.: A multilevel system of quality technology-enhanced learning and teaching indicators. J. Educ. Technol. Soc. **19**(3), 72–83 (2016)
27. Ong, M.Y., Muniandy, B., Ong, S.L., Tang, K.N., Phua, K.K.: Comparing the acceptance of key performance indicators management systems on perceived usefulness and perceived ease of use in a higher education institution in Malaysia. Int. J. Mod. Educ. Comput. Sci. (IJMECS) **4**(10), 9–16 (2012)
28. Wu, H.Y., Lin, Y.K., Chang, C.H.: Performance evaluation of extension education centers in universities based on the balanced scorecard. Eval. Program Plann. **34**(1), 37–50 (2011)
29. CNA: Lineamientos para la Acreditación de Programas de Pregrado. Recuperado el 15 de January de 2018, de Consejo Nacional de Acreditación (2013). https://www.cna.gov.co/ 1741/articles-186359_pregrado_2013.pdf
30. González, L.E.: El impacto del proceso de evaluación y acreditación en las Universidades de América Latina. Recuperado el 15 de January de 2018, de Universidad Estatal a Distancia (Costa Rica) (2005). https://www.uned.ac.cr/academica/images/igesca/materiales/12.pdf
31. Restrepo Gómez, B.: Tendencias actuales en la educación superior: rumbos del mundo y rumbos del país. Revista Educación y Pedagogía **18**(46), 79–90 (2006)

32. MEN: Decreto No 1295. Recuperado el 15 de January de 2018, de Mineducación, 20 de April de 2010: https://www.mineducacion.gov.co/1621/articles-229430_archivo_pdf_decreto1295.pdf

33. Borroto Cruz, E.R., Salas Perea, R.S.: Acreditación y evaluación universitarias. Educación Médica Superior 18(3), 1 (2004)

34. MEN: Ley 30 de diciembre 28 de 1992 (Servicio público de la Educación Superior en Colombia). Recuperado el 15 de January de 2018, 28 de December de 1992. https://www.cna.gov.co/1741/articles-186370_ley_3092.pdf

35. Kaplan, R.S., Norton, D.P.: El cuadro de mando integral: the balanced scorecard. (G. 2000, Ed.) Harvard Business School Press (2016)

36. Ballvé, A.M.: Creando conocimiento en las organizaciones con el Cuadro de Mando Integral y el Tablero de Control. Revista de Contabilidad y Dirección 3, 13–38 (2006)

37. Rodrigues Quesado, P., Aibar Guzmán, B., Portela Lima Rodrigues, L.M.: El cuadro de mando integral como herramienta de gestión estratégica del conocimiento. Perspectivas em Gestão and Conhecimento 2(1), 70–102 (2012)

38. Bastidas Bermúdez, E.L., Moreno Freitez, Z.: El cuadro de mando integral en la gestión de las organizaciones del sector público: El caso Universidad Centroccidental Lisandro Alvarado. Revista Universo Contábil 2(3), 105–118 (2006)

39. Salas, O.A., García, P.S.: Histórico del perfil de contratante. Recuperado el 16 de January de 2018, de Universidad de Cantabria (1999). http://historicosweb.unican.es/perfilcontratante/OriolAmat.doc

40. Portela Lara, L.: El cuadro de mando integral y la gestión de información. Ciencias de la Información 35(2), 33–47 (2004)

41. Ripoll Feliu, V.M., Aparisi Caudeli, J.A.: El Cuadro de Mando Integral, una herramienta para el control de gestión. Partida doble (114), 54–63 (2000)

42. Sanz Del Vecchio, D.A., Crissien-Borrero, T.: "Respondability" in higher education institutions. Cultura, Educación y Sociedad 3(1), 147–156 (2012)

43. Villasmil Molero, M., Crissien-Borrero, T.: Change of paradigm in the university management based on the theory and praxis of reengineering. Económicas CUC 36(1), 261–274 (2015)

44. Combita-Niño, H., Ariza-Colpas, P.: Análisis y desarrollo de un software web para la gestión y fomento de la investigación en instituciones de educación superior en Colombia: "educaras cloud". INGENIUM 32, 71–88 (2016)

45. Romero Díaz, C., Villarreal Villa, S., Samper Ibáñez, J., Ospino Rihaza, I.: Fortalecimiento de las competencias ciudadanas a partir de la lectura crítica en escenarios virtuales. Revista virtual - Universidad Católica del Norte 51, 216–232 (2017)

46. Bendermacher, G., Oude Egbrink, M., Wolfhagen, H., Leppink, J., Dolmans, D.: Reinforcing pillars for quality culture development: a path analytic model. Studies in Higher Education, Artile in Press (N/A), pp. 1–20, 26 de October de 2017

47. Agasisti, T., Barbato, G., Dal Molin, M., Turri, M.: Internal quality assurance in universities: does NPM matter. Studies in Higher Education, Article in Press (N/A), 1–18, 23 de November de 2017

Decision Systems

Algorithmic Discrimination and Responsibility: Selected Examples from the United States of America and South America

Musonda Kapatamoyo[1]([⊠]), Yalitza Therly Ramos-Gil[2], and Carmelo Márquez Dominiguez[2]

[1] Southern Illinois University Edwardsville, Edwardsville, IL 62025, USA
mkapata@siue.edu
[2] Pontificia Universidad Católica Del Ecuador Sede Ibarra,
Cdla "La Victoria" - Código Postal:, Ibarra 100112, Ecuador
{ytramos,camarquez}@pucesi.edu.ec

Abstract. This paper discusses examples and activities that promote consumer protection through adapting of non-discriminatory algorithms. The casual observer of data from smartphones to artificial intelligence believes in technological determinism. To them, data reveal real trends with neutral decision-makers that are not prejudiced. However, machine learning technologies are created by people. Therefore, creator biases can appear in decisions based on algorithms used for surveillance, social profiling, surveillance, and business intelligence.

This paper adapts Lawrence Lessig's framework (laws, markets, codes, and social norms). It highlights cases in the USA and South America where algorithms discriminated and how statutes tried to mitigate the negative consequences. Global companies such as Facebook and Amazon are among those discussed in the case studies. In the case of Ecuador, the algorithms and the lack of protection of personal data for citizens are not regulated or protected in the treatment of information that arises in social networks used by public and private institutions. Consequently, individual rights are not strictly shielded by national and international laws and or through regulations of telecommunications and digital networks. In the USA, a proposed bill, the "Algorithmic Accountability Act" would require large companies to audit their machine-learning powered automated systems such as facial recognition or ad targeting algorithm for bias. The Federal Trade Commission (FTC) will create rules for evaluating automated systems, while companies would evaluate the algorithms powering these tools for bias or discrimination, including threats to consumer privacy or security.

Keywords: Algorithmic discrimination · Algorithmic responsibility · Privacy · Dirty data · Machine learning

© Springer Nature Switzerland AG 2019
H. Florez et al. (Eds.): ICAI 2019, CCIS 1051, pp. 147–157, 2019.
https://doi.org/10.1007/978-3-030-32475-9_11

1   Introduction

All over the world, people are concerned about machines making life-changing decisions on their behalf [1, 2, 38]. It cannot be deduced when the worldwide concern about the growing loss of control of personal data began, nor the list of unsolved problems about the analysis of algorithms in the field of computation, machine learning, and artificial intelligence. However, observers, practitioners, and scholars have raised the alarm since computer-mediated communications became mainstream [3, 4]. Presently, many case studies and theoretical frameworks allow us to think about how the consensuses of algorithmic analysis and treatment are carried out. Understandably, algorithms play an ever-increasing role in our daily lives due to the proliferation of automated decision-making systems whose impact, unfortunately, may lead to negative aspects such as discrimination. This has become the paradox typical of the human race and has renewed the call to make the algorithms more transparent and accountable [5]. The way out of these scenarios has been to draft bills, which in some way regulate the responsibility of Internet users and intermediaries; and to increase transparency and apportion blame where it is lacking [2, 6].

According to Silva and Kenney [7] an algorithm is essentially "a process or set of rules that are used by computers in calculations or other problem-solving operations." (p. 11). According to Diakopoulos [1] "machine-learning algorithms enable other algorithms to make smarter decisions based on learned patterns in data. Human input may lead to uncertainty of decisions in some instances" (p. 3).

Many countries have adopted the European Union's General Data Protection Regulation (GDPR) description of algorithmic discrimination. According to the GDPR, algorithmic discrimination refers to discriminatory effects on natural persons based on special categories such as racial or ethnic origin, political opinion, religion or beliefs, trade union membership, genetic or health status or sexual orientation, or that result in measures having such an effect [8].

There is agreement among international, political, economic, cultural, and institutional regulatory frameworks that support the Universal Declaration of Human Rights on the protection of personal data. The evolving system remains "a certainly imperfect system, affected by errors and faults that should be corrected and based on categories whose meaning and scope is not yet established in an absolute and indubitable way" [9] as a system surrounded by critical constants that underline its insufficiency to eradicate the violations of human rights in the world.

The principles of the free circulation of knowledge and information in South America are governed by initiatives that do not grasp the real trends in non-discrimination. Therefore, the battle of rights and the protection of data is essentially a struggle to expand personal protection in the context of social networks and other areas of communication and interactions with authorities.

The current challenges on social networks and their resulting global expansion, occur throughout the Latin American hemisphere [2, p. 11]. There, as seen in other places, new developments and innovations are encouraged in the technology field, leading to diffusion of automated decision-making systems. Most often, decision-making automated systems use algorithms for data mining that rely on data that is supplied from other systems. Sometimes, as Won Kim et al. [10] describe, that data may be flawed. They termed this dirty data, a term that denotes "missing data, wrong data, and non-standard representations of the same data" (p. 81).

Richardson et al. [11] expanded the definition of dirty data to include data that is "derived from or influenced by corrupt, biased, and unlawful practices" (p. 195). Biases may come from societal stereotypes. The dirty data may also come from records of arrests innocent people [12]. They further state that dirty data incorporates successive uses of data especially if that data has been manipulated by others. This further complicates discerning what is bad or good data. Dirty data, in other circumstances, confirms what Mayson [13] referred to as bias in – bias-out.

1.1   Trust in the Machine

When interacting with algorithms, most people look at the tools and machines for decision making that are built by humans, as fair as humans themselves. They are bestowed with an algorithmic responsibility without absolute form or definition to solve theoretical problems that are fuzzy, anonymous, and complex. The fact that the automated decision-making system resolves some issues does not necessarily mean that it works for the good of society [14]. Decision making, using algorithms, follows a set pattern of prioritization, classification, association, and filtering. Diakopoulos [1] explains that prioritization is ranking or ordering to emphasize certain things over others; classification refers to putting things in categories based on similar features; association about linkages or relations between subjects; and finally, filtering is a process that deals with including or excluding information according to a recognized criterium. Therefore, if dirty data was input in the first place, auditing becomes a considerable challenge in the aftermath.

On a global scale, dirty data means that a lot of decisions are made that reflect the wrong interpretation of analyzed data. Compounding this problem is the belief by many people that information is clean and neutral, hence the resulting decisions are neutral as well. However, many scholars have indicated that unarticulated beliefs and goals of creators are sometimes consciously or unconsciously embodied in technologies [14, 15]. According to Seaver [16] and Piskorski [17], discussed theories about dating sites. Algorithmic choices of dating sites shape the user's choices by recommending matches that appear scientifically chosen.

This paper shows attempts in the USA and South America at identifying lacunas in data collection and analysis; as well as machine learning and explores ways different communities or governments are seeking remedies by curating a sense of responsibility in the creators.

1.2   Problem Statement

Dirty data, when employed in machine learning, has implications on social, economic, and political aspects of individuals, and affect fairness, equity, and justice. Laws mandating vigorous auditing, and cleaning of data to create a sense of fairness are lagging. Many scholars such as [1] have written about algorithm accountability from the standpoint of architectural design. Architectural designs may be infused with bias.

By use of examples from two continents, we suggest ways that responsibility should rest in the individuals whose biases may influence the design.

2 Algorithmic Discrimination, Bias, and Mitigating Laws in the United States

The following section discusses examples of algorithm-generated discrimination in the public sector. In the United States of America, it is common for bad data to be blamed for adverse policing outcomes [11, 12]. Bad data ends up in machine learning processes that are used by the algorithms blamed for specific discriminatory practices based on race and other categories identified in the GDPR above. For example, police rely on data for predictive policing. Following widespread complaints, companies, police departments as well as the US Congress have attempted to mitigate the fall out by instituting policies, best practices, and laws that call for transparency in predictive policing and other services.

3 Predictive Policing

US police departments have adopted mainly predictive policing with data fashioned after old practices and software created by the private sector, such as Azavea's HunchLab, PredPol, and Palantir. Richardson et al. [11] describe predictive policing as "use of systems to analyze available data to predict the location where a crime will likely happen or the possible perpetrators (p. 198). The data used in these systems come from police departments and may contain inaccuracies and bias.

The New York Police Department (NYPD) has used Azavea to collate data used in predictive policing. Azavea creates software and data analytics using geospatial expertise to aid clients to address complex civic, social, and environmental problems [18]. HunchLab is a another popular web-based proactive patrol management application that was created by Azavea. It uses statistical models to predict locations and times of potential crimes. It features tools to help patrols prioritize where to add resources [19].

Similar to NYPD, the Baltimore Police Department (BPD) uses a machine-learning algorithm for predictive policing. Their vendor, PredPol uses a machine-learning algorithm to calculate predictions based on three data points that include: the type, the location, and the date/time of a crime. The technology purports to show where and when specific crimes are most likely to occur. BPD, in turn, uses that data to allocate resources and proactively patrol highlighted areas and to help reduce crime rates and victimization [20].

The New Orleans Police Department (NOPD) also practices predictive policing in their processes. They have used the database-heavy platform called Palantir Law Enforcement that features an intuitive, user-friendly interface that allows any agent, detective, or investigator to access all the available information in one place quickly. The system is simplified so that users login one time and can conduct one search for a suspect, target, or location through a single portal and retrieve data from all relevant systems. The system integrates NOPD's case management systems. It also includes the warrant and arrest records, as well as data from their Computer Aided Dispatch (CAD). The system also gathers data from federal databases such information about gangs, and vehicle license plates [21].

The above examples are reflective of a common trend among well-resourced police departments, of which hundreds used some form predictive policing. The common thread amongst them is that they employed data from human entries, artificial intelligence platforms, as well as aggregated data from disparate databases. The different systems and standards of data management may create some adverse effects on populations whose data is misapplied. As stated above, casual observers may think the data used is neutral of bias and in some cases scientifically applied. However, as Moraff [40] says, people outside of these police department and intelligence authorities have no idea that predictive policing relies on data that is unilaterally provided individual police agencies themselves, or by the firms peddling software to them. This affects the data's reliability. It is also noteworthy that some of these jurisdictions have been accused of bias; been reported or investigated by the Department of Justice and entered into some remedial programs [11].

4   Algorithmic Responsibility in South America

As is the case in the United States of America, South American authorities have been concerned about algorithmic discrimination as well, especially as it pertains to personal data. Ortiz Frueler and Iglesias [6] reviewed the context report carried out by the Latin American Open Data Initiative (ILAPD) in 2017, in which Tim Berners-Lee, the founder and inventor of the WWW, expressed his concerns about the lack of control of personal data and urged research to create methods, think about the risks, and look at the opportunities that improve the use of personal data.

Countries such as Argentina, Brazil, Colombia, Peru, Mexico, and Uruguay have moderate results according to specific indicators and international parameters for personal data protection [2, p. 11]. In recent decades, South America governments have contributed to producing and maintaining digital records. The large communication and telecommunications groups continue to use technology, laws, software and smart devices, to overwhelm culture and control data. Except for Ecuador, where over 90% of the population are connected in networks, the redefinition of including oneself in a digital world based on a new economy and security of digital platforms is far from comparative reality.

Platforms created by new digital media that take advantage of social networks generate content that allows users to share information on their mobile devices. However, these platforms do not guarantee the legal mechanisms on the right of communication that all people have, individually or collectively. These instruments are the same mechanisms used to ensure plural information. This counterproductive situation reveals, in this case, that platforms specialized in social networks are inherent in the discriminatory bias of their creators. Likewise, this same citizenry that participates in the virtualization of content elevates the informative legality of the data and violates the right of users to become a legitimate practice. Some smartphone applications, such as WhatsApp, which is one of the most used services from social networks, are created without any possibility of avoiding discriminatory content. Consequently, they used for illegal practices by users who do not know their functional use. Informative data practices become a free, plural, and democratic character in the culture and individual thinking of citizens, as subject and audience in a context of algorithmic discrimination.

Going forward, the utilization of this data will be the basis for legal advances and new regulations, and strategies in the sanctions of organic communication laws and telecommunications, especially for Facebook, Twitter, or Instagram, which are some of the many social networks that affect millions of users. Since they are presented as tools of a tremendously promise of freedom and yet are contrary to the right to the protection of personal communications.

South America countries faced little success in creating policies that effective enough to audit algorithms. This has led to challenges in establishing tools or processes that "go beyond the field of data science and constitutional frameworks" [6]. For example, in Argentina there is a growing interest in the use of open data, and the making of algorithms through the creation of a model whose predictive capacity is capable of; (a) modernizing public and private institutions; (b) predicting school dropout; (c) predicting adolescent pregnancies, and (d) identifying business opportunities through a map.

In the case of Uruguay, Ortiz Freuler and Iglesias [6] explain that the most striking use of algorithms deals with an automatic learning models to predict crimes. The models define and update "hot zones" on a map that was used to direct police assets.

In an analysis of Ecuador, the Center for Latin America's [2] "Data, algorithms, and policies. The redefinition of the digital world " and the "Algorithms and Artificial Intelligence in Latin America" reports showed that the foundation World Wide Web is somehow discouraging. According to the Ministry of Telecommunications and the Information Society [39], 91% of Ecuadorians use social networks on their smartphones, whether for the dissemination of information of a commercial, educational, cultural or personal nature. But digital inequalities in public and private institutional services are born and die on the mobile phone. They are distributed in the absence of topics on knowledge bases, normative frameworks, human talent, technological infrastructure, financing, and enabling external conditions.

The Ecuadorian government through its legislative bodies, the Organic Law of Telecommunications [22], the Organic Law of Communications [23], and the current Law Amendments of 2019, have constitutional principles that regulate the mediatization of content and the media industry. However, still unprotected are the individual and inherent collective rights of human dignity in any field that occurs on the internet and its consequent algorithmic responsibility concerning the implementation of automated decision-making systems. So, the current legal and regulatory regime does not respond to a digital commitment that is configured in prospective studies that monitor digital social rights in human behavior.

However, Ecuador has adapted technical guidelines to prevent and combat discrimination due to sexual diversity and gender identity in the educational field. It is a project carried out between the Ministry of Education, the National Council for Gender Equality and the Flemish Association for Development Cooperation and Technical Assistance. Taking into account international guidelines to combat hate speech against the gay, lesbian, bisexual, transgender and intersex) (GLBTI) population and discrimination against children and adolescents of school age, such as the technical recommendations of the Inter-American Commission on Human Rights and the United Nations Children's Fund (UNICEF) and the Yogyakarta Principles [24]. It is also true that the instrument only guarantees the diversity and inclusion of the GLBTI community. A guide, which responds to the integration of crucial concepts, based on rights, of what to do when presented with a case of discrimination and awareness-raising activities. However, social networks and media diffusion do not have an algorithm of bias and protection in this GLBTI community.

5 Theoretical Analysis

Since Lessig [25] introduced us to the idea that code could be a law unto itself in the 1990s, cyberspace became a reality that governments could not directly control and would be self-governing. However, he cautioned that control would nonetheless happen through "an invisible hand, through commerce, [that is] constructing an architecture that perfects control –an architecture that makes possible highly efficient regulation" (p. 6). Lessig [25] tried to answer fundamental questions such as "will cyberspace promise privacy or access?" (p. 7).

The internet changed our view of identity. Whereas identity in real space included fewer variables such as how you look, in the cyberspace Lessig [25] expanded the variables to include where you live, name, sex, education, driver's license number, social security number, online purchases, occupation, and so on" (p. 31). One's identity is revealed in real life, whether one wants to or not because many facts about a person are self-evident when someone looks at you. In cyberspace, the expanded variables could now be layered to create intricate patterns about groups of people of individuals.

On the internet, authenticating a user is the process by which aspects of your identity become known when you reveal them to gain access to something. Therefore, identification and authentication are different because of the design based on internet protocols that require a starting and ending address that is needed by web servers. Technically the webserver does not know the identity of the user. It only knows that a user is located at an IP address is complaint with the Transmission Control Protocol (TCP). At this basic design level, data and people are unidentified. Where different data are combined and used for machine learning is where algorithms can use dirty data and lead to discriminatory practices.

Lessig [25] declared that "architecture is a kind of law: it determines what people can and cannot do" (p. 59). Further, William Mitchell [37] stated that "control of code is power": "For citizens of cyberspace,...code... is becoming a crucial focus of political contest. Who shall write that software that increasingly structures our daily lives?" (p. 79).

Despite the above observations, technology determinists would view data used in predictive policing as accurate and in turn, judge decision-making algorithms that learn from that data as neutral. However, the reality is more nuanced, as Richardson et al. and others have stated, that it is a "common fallacy that the police data is objective and reflects criminal behavior, patterns, or other indicators of concern to the public safety in a given jurisdiction." (p. 201). Others claim that "in reality, police data reflects the practices, policies, biases, and political and financial accounting needs of a given department" [26, p. 474; 29].

6 The Basis for Algorithmic Responsibility

Relying entirely on confirmation feedback loops obfuscates realities, influences public policy, and can skew decision-making. Therefore, cultivating responsibilities in the parties involved should take a different approach, such as the ones we suggested or approved below.

Levinson-Waldman [27] of the Brennan Center for Justice suggested some approaches to algorithmic responsibility, such as (1) Ensure public transparency for all datasets and databases used by governments; protect first amendment rights of citizens' from government intrusion; expand the public's oversight over the National Counterterrorism Center; and mandate robust and regular inspection of protocols used in collection, retention, and use of Americans' information.

Further, the U.S. Congress through Senators Cory Booker (D-NJ) and Ron Wyden (D-OR), together with Rep. Yvette D. Clarke (D-NY) introduced the Algorithmic Accountability Act. Expressly, the bill would mandate the Federal Trade Commission (FTC) to audit their sensitive automated decision systems. The law would also require them to insure that including training data is accurate, fair, non-discriminatory and ensures privacy and security of individuals. Lastly, the law would require that companies immediately correct any issues discovered during impact assessments. [28]. The thrust for this legislation is that law influences the behavior of its citizens in various ways. As Scott [29] stated, "imposing sanctions or granting subsidies, the law either expands or contracts the horizon of opportunities within which individuals can satisfy their preferences" (p. 1603). Primarily these rules stimulate changes in the costs of certain behaviors.

The laws are applied in order of first to third to achieve the highest compliance. The first order is banning a behavior or practice; the second order is empowering peers to ridicule or criticize, and the third order is sanctioning behavior with consequences.

Literature on social norms shows that laws can also have indirect effects on incentives. For example, people are motivated to stop smoking or clean up after their pets via a legal ban on smoking in public places or a "pooper-scooper" law respectively. This is a first order enforcement because the state has not invested any resources [29, 30]. Further, second order enforcement happens when neighbors and peers ridicule an offender into behavior change [31, 32]. The third order, and most sustainable enforcement occurs when citizens internalize the legal rule and are deterred by the prospect of guilt, hence the correct behaviors become inherent [33–35].

According to Scott [29] effectively applying these laws is complex because a shaming sanction is only effective if normative structure can influence predictable manifestation of social meaning of the favored or disfavored activity. Consequently, self- sanctions rely on the even more complex phenomenon of internalization of normative behavior [29, p. 1604].

International treaties should take into consideration a lot of aspects. Among them are the deontological norms referring to human dignity, the protection of the data, and free culture in computer law. Human dignity demands that the diffusion of contents, images, symbols, and iconographic representations, Gif, memes, and phrases that allude to discriminatory comments, sexism, and prejudice, as part of the data have not been ignored in the Safeguarding of Human Rights and Fundamental Freedoms.

But what is meant by personal data in the dignity of human rights? We must first understand as a basis, the inherence of data protection on the condition of freedom in order to accurately answer this question. In consequence, protection becomes a computer right, which is, at the same time, a contradiction to human dignity, while the data define sufficient individualizing force, which reveals aspects of a particular person [36]. Data protection, guided by way of understanding the digital consumer in cyberspace, should be without limits. The marked use of social networks and the pervasive digital communication will give thanks to knowledgeable public and private democratization of those who can establish technological trajectories.

According to Ortiz Freuler and Iglesias [6], legal, political, or practical effects of an algorithm are some of the most relevant considerations in creating laws and norms to discourage algorithmic discrimination. They state that "legitimacy stands as a parallel challenge, which requires a series of tools and processes that go beyond the field of science" (p. 6); A good framework that in its algorithmic design and implementation operate with intelligent decisions should be humanly intelligent.

7 Conclusions and Implications

In the above examples, it is evident that Lessig's four ideas about regulation hold. Code (or algorithms) is law in and of itself, adjudicating an ever-increasing array of aspects of our lives. Due to the broad acceptance by people that algorithms do not make mistakes, there is a general lack of clarity about the power of algorithms. It is also influenced by markets as can be seen in the number of police departments that have adopted technologies predictive policing, despite some concerns. The architecture of the code can be exclusionary or even discriminatory, as seen in the above examples from the USA and South America. Lastly, social norms dictate the role of technologies, where social determinism, rather than technology determinism, is the driving force.

Our recommendation is for governments to be proactive in mandating serious algorithm audits, without stifling innovations. The focus should be on behavior change on the part of developers so that their creations are vetted for adverse outcomes. Specifically, values such as controllability, responsibility, responsiveness, transparency, and sense of liability ought to be front and center when developing machine learning approaches. Laws ought to promote technology designs whose incentive is to create favorable conditions for people to choose how they want to participate in their communities and work together. Algorithms that discriminate, inherently go against that norm. Similarly, in South America, the push for control of algorithms must be focused on human decisions to correct future behavior.

References

1. Diakopoulos, N.: Algorithmic accountability. Digit. Journalism **3**(3), 398–415 (2015)
2. Cepal. Data, algorithms, and policies the redefinition of the digital world (2018). https://repositorio.cepal.org/bitstream/handle/11362/43477/7/S1800053_es.pdf
3. Katyal, N.K.: Digital architecture as crime control. Yale Law J. **112**(8), 2261–2289 (2003)
4. Lessig. L. The Code 2.0. (2009). www.articaonline.com/wp-content/uploads/…/Elcódigo-2.0-Lawrence-Lessig.pdf. Accessed 17 June 2019
5. Angwin, J. Make Algorithms Accountable. The New York Times, August 2016. http://www.nytimes.com/2016/08/01/opinion/make-algorithms-accountable.html. Accessed 16 June 2019
6. Ortiz Freuler, J., Iglesias, C.: Algorithms and artificial intelligence in Latin America. In: A Study of Implementation by Governments in Argentina and Uruguay. Foundation World Wide Web, pp. 9–167 (2018). https://webfoundation.org/docs/2018/09/WF_AI-inLA_Report_Spanish_Screen_AW.pdf. Accessed 17 June 2019
7. Silva, S., Kenney, M.: Algorithms, platforms, and ethnic bias: an integrative essay. Phylon **55**(1 & 2), 9–37 (2018)
8. European Convention on Human Rights, Article 14 (2010). https://www.echr.coe.int/Documents/Convention_ENG.pdf. Accessed 17 June 2019
9. Asprino, M., Márquez-Domínguez, C., Ramos-Gil, Y.: Human rights and the concept of dignity in the digital society. In: Rocha Á., Guarda T. (eds) Proceedings of the International Conference on Information Technology & Systems (COISINT 2019) (2019)
10. Kim, W., Choi, B.-J., Hong, E.-K., Kim, S.-K., Lee, D.: A taxonomy of dirty data. Data Min. Knowl. Discov. **7**(1), 81–99 (2003). https://doi.org/10.1023/A:1021564703268
11. Richardson, R., Schultz, J.M., Crawford, K.: Dirty Data, Bad Predictions: How Civil Rights Violations Impact Police Data, Predictive Policing Systems, and Justice, New York University Law Review, vol. 192, pp. 204–217 (2019)
12. Brantingham, P. J. The Logic of Data Bias and Its Impact on Place-Based Predictive Policing, 15 OHIO ST. J. CRIM L. 473, 485 (2018). https://www.booker.senate.gov/?p=press_release&id=903
13. Mayson, S.G.: Bias in, bias out. Yale Law J. **128**(8), 2122–2473 (2019)
14. Winner, L.: Do artifacts have politics? Daedalus, **109**, 121–136 (1980)
15. Noble, D.: Forces of Production: A Social History of Industrial Automation. Routledge, New York (2017)
16. Seaver, N.: Algorithmic Recommendations and Synaptic Functions, Limn **1**(2) (2012). https://escholarship.org/uc/item/7g48p7pb
17. Piskorski, M.J.: A Social Strategy: How We Profit from Social Media. Princeton University Press (2014). http://www.jstor.org/stable/j.ctt6wpzxq
18. Azavea: Next City Coverage of First Comprehensive NIJ Study on Predictive Policing Highlights HunchLab. December 17th, 2014. Accessed 19 June 2019
19. Cheetham, R.: Why We Sold HunchLab. 23rd January 2019. https://www.azavea.com/blog/2019/01/23/why-we-sold-hunchlab/. Accessed 17 June 2019
20. PredPol (2019). https://www.predpol.com/. Accessed 17 June 2019
21. Palantir Law Enforcement (2019). https://www.palantir.com/solutions/law-enforcement/. Accessed 17 June 2019
22. Ley Orgánica de Telecomunicaciones. Quito. Asamblea Nacional (2015). https://www.telecomunicaciones.gob.ec/…/Ley-Orgánica-deTelecomunicaciones.pdf. Accessed 16 June 2019

23. Organic Law of Communication. Quito. Asamblea Nacional (2013). www.arcotel.gob.ec/wpcontent/uploads/.../2013/07/ley_organica_comunicacion.pdf. Accessed 17 June 2019
24. Yogyakarta Principles plus 10. http://yogyakartaprinciples.org/wpcontent/uploads/2017/11/A5_yogyakartaWEB-2.pdf. Accessed 20 June 2019
25. Lessig, L.: Code and Other Laws of Cyberspace. Basic Books, New York (1999)
26. Armacost, B.E.: Organizational culture and police misconduct. George Wash. Law Rev. **62**(1), 1–68 (2009). http://www.jstor.org/stable/40379719
27. Levinson-Waldman, R.: What the Government Does with Americans' Data. The Brennan Center for Justice (2013). https://www.brennancenter.org/publication/whatgovernment-does-americans-data. Accessed 17 June 2019
28. Booker, C., Wyden, R., Clarke, Y.D.: Introduce Bill Requiring Companies to Target Bias in Corporate Algorithms, 10 April 2019. https://www.booker.senate.gov/?p=press_release&id=903. Accessed 17 June 2019
29. Scott, R.E.: The limits of behavioral theories of law and social norms. Va. Law Rev. **86**(8), 1603–1647 (2000). Symposium: The Legal Construction of Norms
30. Ellickson, R.C.: A critique of economic and sociological theories of social control. J. Legal Stud. **16**, 67 (1987)
31. Bishop, D.: Legal and extra-legal barriers to delinquency: a panel analysis. Criminology **22**, 403 (1984)
32. Jacob, H.: Deterrent effects of formal and informal sanctions. Policy Implementation 69 (1980)
33. Tyler, T.R.: Why People Obey the Law 42 (1990)
34. Wrong, D.H.: The oversocialized conception of man in modem sociology. Am. Soc. Rev. **26**, 183–191 (1961)
35. Robinson, P., Darley, J." The utility of desert. Nw. U. L. Rev. **91**, 453, 468-77 (1997)
36. García, J.F.: The protection of personal data. Right Ecuador.com (2011). https://www.derechoecuador.com/la-proteccion-de-datos-personales
37. Mitchell, W.J.: City of Bits: Space, Place, and the Infobahn. MIT Press, Cambridge (1996)
38. Goodman, B.: A step towards accountable algorithms: algorithmic discrimination and the european union general data protection. In: 29th Conference on Neural Information Processing Systems (NIPS 2016), Barcelona, Spain (2016)
39. Ministerio de Telecomunicaciones y de la Sociedad de la Información. https://www.telecomunicaciones.gob.ec/91-de-ecuatorianos-utiliza-las-redes-socialesen-su-telefono-inteligente/. Accessed 17 June 2019
40. Moraff, C.: The Problem with Some of the Most Powerful Numbers in Modern Policing, 15 December 2014. https://nextcity.org/daily/entry/predictive-policing-crime-statsdata-measure. Accessed 15 June 2019

Continuous Variable Binning Algorithm to Maximize Information Value Using Genetic Algorithm

Nattawut Vejkanchana[✉] and Pramote Kucharoen

National Institute of Development Administration, Bangkok, Thailand
nattawut.vej@stu.nida.ac.th, pramote@as.nida.ac.th

Abstract. Binning (bucketing or discretization) is a commonly used data pre-processing technique for continuous predictive variables in machine learning. There are guidelines for good binning which can be treated as constraints. However, there are also statistics which should be optimized. Therefore, we view the binning problem as a constrained optimization problem. This paper presents a novel supervised binning algorithm for binary classification problems using a genetic algorithm, named GAbin, and demonstrates usage on a well-known dataset. It is inspired by the way that human bins continuous variables. To bin a variable, first, we choose output shapes (e.g., monotonic or best bins in the middle). Second, we define constraints (e.g., minimum samples in each bin). Finally, we try to maximize key statistics to assess the quality of the output bins. The algorithm automates these steps. Results from the algorithm are in the user-desired shapes and satisfy the constraints. The experimental results reveal that the proposed GAbin provides competitive results when compared to other binning algorithms. Moreover, GAbin maximizes information value and can satisfy user-desired constraints such as monotonicity or output shape controls.

Keywords: Binning · Genetic algorithm · Data pre-processing · Information value · Constrained optimization

1 Introduction

1.1 Binning

In predictive modeling, binning or discretization is performed to transform a continuous variable into intervals. Each binned interval can be assigned by a value that represents its interval characteristic. The purpose of binning is to (1) increase the stability of the predictive continuous variables, (2) reduce statistical noises and complexities in the variables, (3) reduce the influence of outliers, and (4) standardize both categorical and continuous variables by replacing each binned range with a standardized representative value.

For predictive models in applications that use scorecards such as credit scoring or predictions in healthcare industry, the final scorecard can be used and understood easily since there are less levels in each variable.

© Springer Nature Switzerland AG 2019
H. Florez et al. (Eds.): ICAI 2019, CCIS 1051, pp. 158–172, 2019.
https://doi.org/10.1007/978-3-030-32475-9_12

A well-known statistic to measure independent variables predictive power is the Information Value (IV) [1]. The larger IV indicates the higher predictive power of a variable. Therefore, IV can be used to measure the predictive power of a binned variable. A good binning algorithm should bin a variable to have a good IV after binned. We discuss IV in more details in the next section.

There are several binning algorithms. However, to our knowledge, none of them directly aims to maximize the IV. The existing algorithms are further discussed in more details in the related work section.

In this paper, the authors propose a new binning algorithm using a genetic algorithm for continuous variables in binary classification problems. It can achieve good binning characteristics [2] which are (1) missing values are binned separately, and (2) each bin should contain at least 5% percent observations. In addition, the new algorithm can satisfy user-desired constraints such as monotonicity or output shape controls and maximize a desired statistic, IV.

1.2 Information Value (IV)

One of the main statistics we use to analyze predictive variables is the Information Value (IV). This statistic evaluates the association between possible predictors and target variable (e.g., bad loan in credit scoring or churn in churn prediction). The IV measures how much a predictor can differentiate between good and bad instances. The higher IV indicates a stronger relationship between the predictors and the target. Before we calculate IV, we need to separate data into bins (i.e. categories or groups). The following formula is used to calculate the IV.

$$IV = \sum_i (\%Good_i - \%Bad_i) \times \ln\left(\frac{\%Good_i}{\%Bad_i}\right) \qquad (1)$$

where

$\%Good_i$ = number of good instances in i^{th} bin out of total number of good instances
$\%bad_i$ = number of bad instances in i^{th} bin out of total number of bad instances

The log component in the IV formula is the Weight of Evidence (WoE) which measure the strength of a grouping for separating good and bad instances.

$$WoE_i = \ln\left(\frac{\%Good_i}{\%Bad_i}\right) \qquad (2)$$

The higher WoE value in absolute term, the stronger the separation between good and bad instances. WoE value can be interpreted as follows:

- WoE = 0: Good and bad instances distributed equally in a particular bin
- WoE < 0: Distribution of bad instances is greater than the distribution of good instances in a particular bin
- WoE > 0: Distribution of good instances is greater than the distribution bad instances in a particular bin.

Generally, the values of the IV statistic can be interpreted as in Table 1 [1]:

Table 1. IV interpretation

IV	Predictive Power
<0.02	Not useful
[0.02, 0.1)	Weak predictor
[0.1, 0.3)	Medium predictor
≥ 0.3	Strong predictor

2 Related Work

There are commonly used binning methods. We review eight well-known methods and categorize them into four groups. This first group is an unsupervised method i.e. it does not use the target variable's information to bin an input variable. On the other hand, the rest are supervised.

1. Unsupervised binning. The equal-width and equal-size binning [2] are in this group. For the equal-width, a continuous variable is divided into a user-defined number of equal-width intervals. Therefore, an equal-width binned output is obtained. For equal-size, the output has roughly the same number of observations. This group does not handle any desired constraints, nor does it aim to optimize any statistics.
2. Supervised, iterative merging. The optimal-binning [3] and Chi-Merge [4] methods belong to this group. These algorithms aim to find cut points for intervals. The number of output bins is not pre-defined. The number of output bins depends on a user-defined threshold. For the optimal-binning, it uses chi-square test's p-value. The other one uses the chi-square test statistic directly. The algorithms repeatedly merge pairs which contain two similar bins according to the statistics into a bin. Again, the group does not handle any desired constraints, nor does it aim to optimize any statistics.
3. Supervised, tree-based greedy search. This group has the multi-interval discretization [5], conditional inference tree-based binning [6], CAIM [7], CACC [8], and Ameva discretization [9] as examples. These algorithms aim to find cut points for intervals by adopting the greedy best first search algorithm. They start by finding a cut point on the whole range and creating two children nodes. Then, they continue to recursively split children nodes until a stopping criterion is reached. The first method uses entropy as heuristic. The second uses a two-sample permutation test statistic. The other three methods use Class-Attribute Interdependence Maximization (CAIM), Class-Attribute Contingency Coefficient (CACC), and Ameva coefficient respectively. This group does not directly aim to handle constraints nor optimize the output's statistics.
4. Supervised, monotone merging. There are two methods that could be categorized to this group which are the Maximum Likelihood monotonic coarse classifier (MLMCC) [2] and monotone optimal binning [10]. These algorithms aim to obtain

monotonic binned outputs. The main idea is that they split the input variable into many intervals and try to merge bins into a fewer number of monotonic bins. After obtaining monotonic bins, the algorithms iteratively merge adjacent bins based on a statistic. The cumulative bad rate is used for the MLMCC. For the latter, it uses the two-sample z-test's p-value statistic. In addition, the latter can handle the minimum observation in each bin constraint by forcefully merging violated bins to their adjacent. However, both methods do not directly aim to maximize output's statistics.

The algorithms incline to use supervised methods. The existing algorithms split a variable into intervals using a statistic (e.g., p-value or bad rate) to find cut points. Cut points separate two adjacent bins that are considerably different in term of the statistic used. The results from these algorithms are bins which have different characteristics based on their chosen statistics. Moreover, a main drawback of existing methods is that they ignore business knowledge. Business rules can be viewed as constraints and should be handled by binning algorithms. These algorithms do not facilitate adding new constraints. This leads us to implement a new method which we can easily choose output shape, constraints and a statistic to be optimized.

3   Implementation

3.1   Fine and Coarse Classing

In general, the binning process can start by firstly bin a continuous variable into many small bins. This is called fine classing. For example, a continuous variable from the HELOC (home equity line of credit) dataset from FICO [11], income can be binned into fine bins. Figure 1 shows WoE values of each bin. The bins with large WoE values contain more good instances than bad ones. The output in Fig. 1 is strange and difficult to explain why the bin [2424, 2435] is better than [1510, 2418].

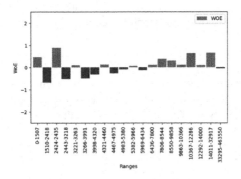

Fig. 1. Fine classing bins

A reason that could cause the fluctuation is insufficient samples in the bins. To stabilize the variable or to make it more explainable, practitioners may apply a domain knowledge that the larger the income, the higher chance of good instances. We use the knowledge to group the small adjacent bins together to obtain an output as in Fig. 2. This is called coarse classing. The result is more explainable. We can further use the binned output variable as an input variable for a classification problem. One way to do that is to simply use the WoE of each bin as a representative value.

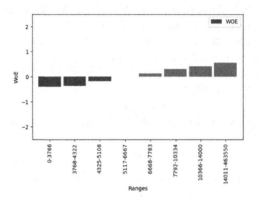

Fig. 2. Coarse classing bins

From the example above, binning can be viewed as a process to merge adjacent bins together or find cut points to obtain a good set of output bins. We use the criteria of good binning as described in the introduction section. The criteria are constraints. It is also a good idea to incorporate other constraints such as monotonicity, allowing only one local maximum, and minimum for output shape controlling. For a variable in the binning problem, there can be many output solutions that pass all the constraints. To decide which solution is the best one, we use IV as a heuristic. At this stage, we view the binning problem as a constrained optimization problem.

3.2   Search Space

Let us consider the search space of the problem. As an example, we assume the starting number of bins is four, the expanded search tree is shown in Fig. 3. The numbers 1, 2, 3 and 4 represent the nth bins. The root level shows that we start with four individual bins. The second level or the level that each node has three bins. The first node means

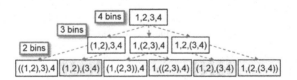

Fig. 3. Exhaustive search without pruning

we group the 1st and 2nd bins of the parent node together and leave the 3rd and 4th bins as they are. The bins in parentheses are in the same binned group. The number of leaf nodes in the expanded tree is factorial of N-1 when N is the starting number of bins. It is a huge number when N is big. Fortunately, at the last level or the 2-bins level, we can see that the second and fifth nodes are identical. This also happens to the fourth and sixth nodes. It means that we can prune the search tree to reduce the search space.

The problem can also be viewed this way. Starting with four separated bins, we group them into three bins by selecting a pair of adjacent bins which are (1, 2), (2, 3) and (3, 4) and grouping them together. The result is illustrated in Fig. 4. Therefore, the number of nodes generated in this level is 3, i.e. choosing a pair from three available pairs or $\binom{3}{1}$. The same approach can be applied to generate the two-bins nodes by choosing two from the starting three pairs and getting $\binom{3}{2}$ or 3 nodes. In total, with the starting bins of four, we generate seven nodes. As a result, if we have the starting bins of N, we generate $2^{N-1} - 1$ nodes. To summarize, the actual search space is an exponential function with base 2. Assuming we have an upper bound of the starting bins of 20 then the search space is 524,287 nodes. The 20 or N starting bins could be initially transformed from a continuous range into bins from the equal-size or equal-width binning algorithm. We could finish running it in a timely manner with a parallel brute force program with a commodity CPU. However, with the assumption, it is hardly believed that the solution has the best possible IV.

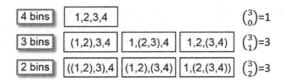

Fig. 4. Output nodes after pruning

3.3   Binning Algorithm Using Genetic Algorithm

This paper proposes a new binning algorithm using a genetic algorithm which we call "GAbin" to solve the constrained optimization problem. The success of using a genetic algorithm depends on two key components: (1) gene representation and (2) fitness function [12].

Gene Representation. We use cut points as the gene representation. With a binned output e.g., 1, (2, 3), 4, we have three output bins. The cut points are written as gene representation of 101. The gene representations are called individuals or chromosomes. Solutions produced from a genetic algorithm called individuals. An individual contains a series of 1s and 0s. A single bit is a gene. The "1" and "0" state cut and no cut points respectively. The "0" means we do nothing. The "1" means we group all prior consecutive 0s (if any) and itself together into a bin. In this case, we group bin 2 and bin 3 together. N bins have N-1 cut points because the last bin is always a cut point (end). We cut the four initial separated bins at the first and third positions. The below figures depict on how the gene representation is used in a genetic algorithm. In Fig. 5, we create a hypothetical continuous variable and initially bin it into 5 bins. We assume that it should be increasing monotonic. We start with five bins and its gene representation is 1111 (every bin is a cut point). The output contradicts the prior knowledge of monotonicity.

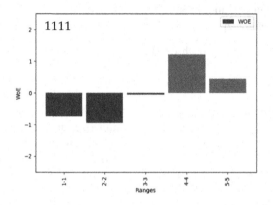

Fig. 5. Five bins of a hypothetical continuous variable

In Fig. 6, we bin the 1st and 2nd bins together and its gene representation is 0111 (the 1st bin is not a cut point). We could see that the output represents a good monotonicity in the range from one to four (the first three output bins).

In Fig. 7, we bin the 4th and 5th bins together and its gene representation is 1110. We could see that the output represents a good monotonicity except the first bin in the output. We could see that the two outputs are good at some bins. The 0111 and 1110 outputs are good for the bins on the left and right sides respectively. Combining them and producing new good outputs could be naturally done by the genetic algorithm's crossover operation. The crossover operation randomly picks two individuals at a time.

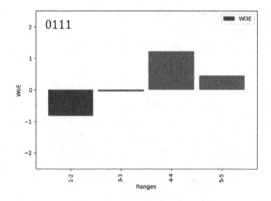

Fig. 6. 0111 gene representation

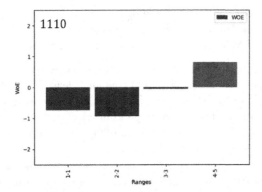

Fig. 7. 1110 gene representation

For each picked individual, cut it into two chunks at a random position (gene). Combine chunks from each individual to form a new individual (offspring). In this case, assume that we cut the first 0111 individual to 011 and 1. Cut the second 1110 and get 111 and 0. By combining the genetic codes (the first's 011 and the second's 0), we obtain 0110 and it is an increasing monotonic output as illustrated in Fig. 8. This shows that using cut points as a genetic representation in a binary-coded genetic algorithm could bin and control the shape of the binning problem. In our GAbin, an individual is randomly initialized to N-1 binary digits where N is the number of starting bins. The maximum number of 1s in an individual is 19 since it is said that in every output bin should contain at least five percent of samples. Therefore, the maximum number of output bins is 20.

Starting Bins. To bin a continuous variable, it is suggested that we bin its continuous range into starting bins using the equal-size or equal-width binning algorithm. However, deciding on how many starting bins is problematic. The output of the binning process by combining bins using cut points depends on starting bins. We could not change the so-called cut points inside the starting bins. This leads us to use unique

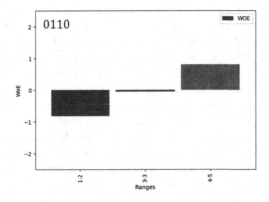

Fig. 8. 0110 gene representation

values of the continuous value as our starting bins. For example, for the FICO dataset, the age values are from 19 to 99. There are 81 unique values and they are our starting bins. This gives the GAbin full control over selecting cut points.

Fitness Function. GAbin's objective is to maximize IV subject to given constraints. The guidelines suggest that each bin should contain at least 5% percent observations. This could be treated as a constraint. We also add other constraints such as (1) each bin should contain at most two times of average samples in each bin to avoid having too many samples in a bin, (2) output's shape controlling constraints (monotonicity, one or two local maxima). The constraints in GAbin are optional. Users can select which constraints to use. Moreover, business rules can be also viewed as constraints and easily incorporated to GAbin. To summarize, our GAbin use IV as the objective function subject to two main groups of constraints which are (1) number of samples in each bin or constraint group 1, and (2) shape controlling constraints or constraint group 2.

The GAbin uses the static penalty approach to handle constraints in the genetic algorithm. This means the fitness function is independent of the current generation number [13].

This is an example of a binning option. With a continuous variable, the constraints are (1) each bin contains at least 5%, (2) at most two times of average samples in each bin, and (3) monotonicity.

We have three main penalty types:

1. Death penalty. We give a death penalty (−10,000) to an individual with more than 19 cut points to avoid too many useless output bins after crossover.
2. Constraint group 1's penalty. The penalties for the first and second constraints are how many samples are more or less than the acceptable threshold. Let us consider an example. A variable has a total number of samples of 400. The 5% threshold is 20 samples. A small bin has only five samples then the penalty is 15.
3. Constraint group 2's penalty. The penalty for the shape controlling constraint is the total number of samples in the bins that violate the constraint. When we try to control the monotonicity, there is a bin of five samples that violates the monotonicity while other bins are satisfied. The penalty for this case is 5.

A bin cannot violate the first and second constraints at the same time. However, a bin can violate both the number of samples in each bin and shape controlling constraints. We use a double-counting approach. For example, a small bin of five samples violates the first and third constraints. This means it has too few samples and breaks the monotonicity. With the 5% threshold of 20, the total penalty for this bin is 15 + 5 = 20. The mentioned penalties reflect two key properties of a good constraint handling penalty function [13]. The first property is to represent the number of violated constraints. This demonstrates in the double-counting approach. The penalty function counts the violated samples for each constraint. The second property is to represent the distance to feasibility. This is the reason we count how far away from the acceptable threshold. Therefore, we create the fitness function for GAbin as Eq. 3. In addition, to control the output shape of one local maximum or minimum (excluding the first and last bins), we use a similar penalty taking care of the monotonicity. If the constraint is violated, the penalty function counts numbers of samples in each violated bin.

$$\text{fitness}(X) = IV - w_1 \sum\nolimits_{j=1}^{c} \sum\nolimits_{i=1}^{k} N_{1i} - w_2 \sum\nolimits_{i=1}^{k} N_{2i} \qquad (3)$$

where

IV	Information Value described in Eq. 1.
w_1	penalty coefficient of constraint group 1 (default: 1)
w_2	penalty coefficient of constraint group 2 (default: 2)
c	number of group 1 constraints
k	number of output bins
N_{1i}	samples that violate the acceptable threshold for the jth group 1 constraint in i^{th} bin
N_{2i}	samples in i^{th} bin that violate the constraint group 2

Algorithm. We summarize the algorithm for the GAbin in Algorithm 1. The default values of hyper parameter are from experiments.

Algorithm 1 GAbin: Binning Algorithm to Maximize Information Value using genetic Algorithm

Inputs:

1. A continuous variable with a binary target variable $D = \{(x_i, y_i)\}_{i=1}^{N}$
2. f(x), A fitness function according to Equation 3.
3. $|P|$, size of the population in each generation (default: 3,000)
4. PB_{CX}, the probability with which two individuals are crossed (default: 0.5)
5. PB_{mu}, the probability for mutating an individual (default: 0.1)
6. PB_{i_mu}, the probability for mutating a gene (default: 0.05)
7. $|T|$, tournament size (default: 3)
8. G_{ND}, maximum number of generations with no development (default: 20)
9. G_{max}, maximum number of generations (default: 300)

Initialization

Initialize:

1. g ← 0 #generation number
2. Count unique values for x_i and its associated numbers of good and bad samples. These unique values become the starting input bins.
3. Create an initial population, P_g. The individuals in the population are from a generator that randomly initialized to N-1 binary digits where N is the number of starting bins. The maximum number of 1s in an individual is 19.

Evaluate:

4. Evaluate the entire population using f(x).

Main loop

while $g < G_{max}$ and the no f(x) develops $< G_{ND}$ do

1. Select:　individuals in P_g to offspring set, S_g based on its f(x) and the $|T|$.
2. Crossover: Randomly select pairs two individuals in S_g with the probability of PB_{CX} and crossover them. This is a processed S_g called S'_g.
3. Mutate:　individuals in S'_g with the probability of PB_{mu} and PB_{i_mu}. This is a processed S'_g called S''_g.
4. Evaluate: Evaluate the entire S''_g using f(x).
5. Update: Replace S''_g to P_{g+1}, $g \leftarrow g + 1$ and count the no development generations.

end while

return individual with the largest f(x) in P_g.

The time complexity for a genetic algorithm could be considered by numbers of fitness function evaluations. It is $O(|P| \times G_{max})$. For GAbin, it is $3{,}000 \times 300$ or $900{,}000$ regardless the number of starting bins.

4　Experiment and Results

For demonstration purpose, we implemented the GAbin and used it to bin the HELOC (home equity line of credit) dataset from FICO [11]. It was a binary classification problem. The target variable stated a defaulted or non-defaulted loan. We binned a continuous dependent variable, LTV (Loan to value ratio). We believed that LTV could have a decreasing monotonic relationship with the default. Larger LTV means more money to repay. We first split the dataset into training and testing datasets. We used the training dataset to bin the variable using three binning options:

1. Each bin contains at least 5% and at most two times of average samples in each bin. Furthermore, the adjacent bins must have minimum WoE difference of 5 percent of the maximum WoE. (Basic constraints).
2. The basic constraints plus monotonic (increasing or decreasing).
3. The basic constraints plus allowing only two local maxima (excluding the first and last bins).

After binned the training data, we applied the binned ranges to the test data and calculate its IV. The summarized result is shown in Table 2. As expected, output with

Table 2.　Binning result for LTV

Option	IV in training	IV in testing	Output's bins
1	0.2346	0.1971	8
2	0.2183	0.1551	5
3	0.2249	0.1621	10

only basic constraints had the highest IV. It was because the genetic algorithm could find any solution to maximize IV with fewer restrictions. The same reason is applied to the other options. Option 2 had tighter restrictions than option 3.

We placed outputs for each option in training and testing datasets in Figs. 9, 10 and 11. Figure 9 had the loosest constraints, so the shape in test data was different from train data. This could mean unstable output bins. Figure 10 shapes were stable. This could mean that the monotonic assumption suits LTV well. Figure 11 shapes had roughly one minimum and one maximum point or two peaks in both train and test data. This demonstrated that GAbin could produce user-desired output shapes.

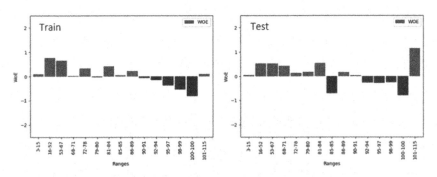

Fig. 9. Option1 result for train and test datasets

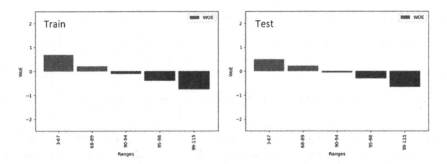

Fig. 10. Option2 result for train and test datasets

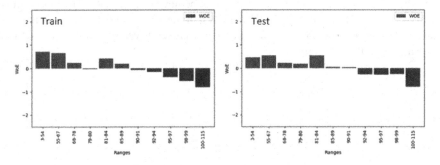

Fig. 11. Option3 result for train and test datasets

Comparing results with other binning algorithms mentioned in the related work section are shown in Fig. 12. The GAbin with only basic constraints achieved the best IV in both train and test set. It showed that the GAbin can truly optimize the target function, IV. However, looking at only IV can be misleading. The result shape should be explainable and non-fluctuating. Therefore, it was dubious to use the first option in real-world applications. Its output shape could not sustain in the test set. This was also the case for MLMCC. The method aimed and was able to obtain monotonic bins in the train set but not in the test. The GAbin with 2 peaks (option 3) achieved high IV in train and test set. In additional to that, the output shape in the test set was roughly similar. Also note that the outputs for GAbin monotonic and monotone optimal binning are identical for this variable.

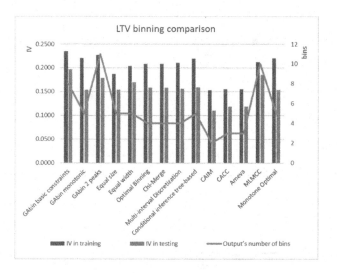

Fig. 12. LTV binning comparison

Another example to show that output shape controlling was useful. We binned the prior custom score variable and compared with other methods. The comparison is showed in the Fig. 13. The Chi-Merge had the highest IVs in train and test set, but the output shapes were different and fluctuating. While others' outputs are monotonic, we found that allowing the variable to have a peak achieved higher IVs. The output bins from GAbin were shown in Fig. 14. It showed that the output shape sustains in the test dataset. This led us to believe that the prior custom score variable is more suited the one-peak shape than monotonic.

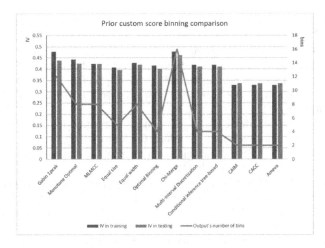

Fig. 13. Prior custom score comparison

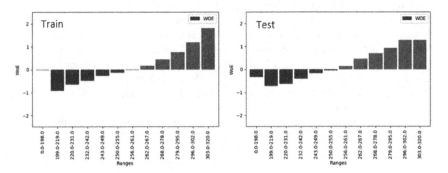

Fig. 14. GAbin's prior custom score in train and test datasets

5 Conclusion

GAbin is a supervised binning algorithm. Three main advantages of the GAbin are (1) users obtain IV-optimized results for classification problem, (2) users can choose the output shapes, and (3) all constraints are handled. Experiment results show that output bins can achieve high IVs, satisfy constraints and produce good results in test data. Using a genetic algorithm in GAbin demonstrates its powerfulness. GAbin can constrained-optimize IV while it does not require any number of starting bins, output bins or predefined statistic thresholds. However, it does require hyper parameters for the genetic algorithm. Tuning hyper parameters is possibly an area for improvement. At this stage, it can be used for only a binary classification because of its fitness function, IV. GAbin's structure can support other supervised learning by changing its fitness function to a suitable one.

Acknowledgments. This research was partially supported by Taskworld Inc.

References

1. Siddiqi, N.: Credit Risk Scorecards, pp. 79–82. Wiley, Hoboken (2013)
2. Thomas, L., Edelman, D., Crook, J.: Credit scoring and its applications, pp. 131–139. SIAM, Society for industrial and applied mathematics, Philadelphia (2002)
3. Refaat, M.: Credit Risk Scorecards: Development and Implementation Using SAS. Lulu.com, Raleigh (2011)
4. Kerber, R.: ChiMerge: discretization of numeric attributes. In: The Tenth National Conference on Artificial Intelligence, San Jose, California (1992)
5. Fayyad, U.M., Irani, K.B.: Multi-Interval Discretization of Continuous-Valued Attributes for Classification Learning. In: IJCAI (1993)
6. Jopia, H.: Scoring Modeling and Optimal Binning. (2019). https://cran.r-project.org/web/packages/smbinning/smbinning.pdf. Accessed April 2019
7. Kurgan, L., Cios, K.: CAIM discretization algorithm. IEEE Trans. Knowl. Data Eng. **16**(2), 145–153 (2004)
8. Tsai, C., Lee, C., Yang, W.: A discretization algorithm based on class-attribute. Inf. Sci. **178** (3), 714–731 (2008)
9. Gonzalez-Abril, L., Cuberos, F., Velasco, F., Ortega, J.: Ameva: an autonomous discretization algorithm. Expert Syst. Appl. **36**(3), 5327–5332 (2009)
10. Mironchyk, P., Tchistiakov, V.: Monotone optimal binning algorithm for credit risk modeling. Researchgate (2017). https://www.researchgate.net/publication/322520135_Monotone_optimal_binning_algorithm_for_credit_risk_modeling. Accessed April 2019
11. FICO: Home Equity Line of Credit (HELOC) Dataset. FICO. https://community.fico.com/s/explainable-machine-learning-challenge?tabset-3158a=2. Accessed April 2019
12. Russell, S., Norvig, P.: Artificial Intelligence: A Modern Approach, 3rd edn, pp. 126–129. Prentice Hall, Upper Saddle River (2010)
13. Coello, C.A.C.: Constraint-handling Techniques used with evolutionary algorithms. In: The Genetic and Evolutionary Computation Conference Companion, Kyoto, Japan (2018)

CVRPTW Model for Cargo Collection with Heterogeneous Capacity-Fleet

Jorge Ivan Romero-Gelvez[(⊠)], William Camilo Gonzales-Cogua, and Jorge Aurelio Herrera-Cuartas

Universidad de Bogotá Jorge Tadeo Lozano, Bogotá, Colombia
jorgei.romerog@utadeo.edu.co

Abstract. This work shows the application of the Capacitated Vehicle Routing Problem with Time Windows (CVRPTW) to collect different cargo-demand in several locations with low time disponibility to attend any vehicle. The objective of the model is to reduce the routing time in a problem with mixed vehicle-fleet. The initial step is the creation of a distance matrix by using the Google Maps API, then cargo capacities for every vehicle and time-windows for every demand point are included in the model. The problem is solved with Google-OR tools using as firt solution aproximated algoritm and as second solution one metaheuristic algorithm for local search.

Keywords: CVRPTW · Routing · Distribution · Heterogeneous capacity-fleet

1 Introduction

Planning and managing transportation activities plays a fundamental role in the modern supply chain. Two categories are well known to address the problem, those who are related to long-distance cargo transport and other related with pick-up and delivery of packages in short distances [16]. The first category consists most of the cases in assignment related formulations with linear restrictions. By the other hand, the initial formulation of vehicle routing problems is proposed by Dantzing & Ramser as a generalisation of Flood's travelling salesman problem [13] in their work [11] proposed a matching-based heuristic for its solution. The vehicle routing problem objective is finding the best routes for delivery minimising a linear cost function over a set of nodes or clients, usually diverse and disperse forming an integer and combinatorial optimisation-problem. Years later, several heuristic solutions to VRP problem appeared including, savings, proximity, matchings, and intra-route inter-route improvement [20]. The most prominent savings algorithm is the Clarke and Wright savings heuristic, it has remained until now, due to its simplicity and speed for implementation [10]. Exact solution algorithms appear in the 80's whit two works proposed

© Springer Nature Switzerland AG 2019
H. Florez et al. (Eds.): ICAI 2019, CCIS 1051, pp. 173–184, 2019.
https://doi.org/10.1007/978-3-030-32475-9_13

by Chistofides et al. the first one is a dynamic programming formulation [8] and the second one a mathematical programming formulation making use of q-paths and k-shortest spanning trees [9]. Later, Laporte et al. propose a VRP algorithm based on the solution of linear relaxation of an integer model [19]. Since then, several exact formulations appear but in most cases are solved by branch-and-cut. Also, its posible to formulate VRP as a partitioning problem like the successfull applications [5,14]. Modern heuristic development is related to the last years, here we highlight the works in tabu search based algorithms [15,28,32]. According with [20] vehicle some algorithms were over-engineered and the best meta-heuristic procedure must have a broad and in-depth search of the solution space and can solve several variants of the problem [23]. This work addresses the problem of a classical formulation of capacitated vehicle routing problem with time windows; the case study refers to a cargo company who have to pick packages in 25 locations or nodes. They also count on 13 vehicles with different capacity. The capacity of the vehicles and the demand show kg as cargo units. The structure of the paper show first a short literature review about the CVRPTW and some applications in a similar context in Colombia, later presents de methodological approach and the model design including mathematical formulation, software and hardware used for solve the model. Finally, shows the results and a short discussion about the benefits and difficulties of this approach to solve CVRTW. The main contribution of this article is to show how a complex problem such as CVRPTW can be solved efficiently and simply, allowing the use of different vehicle capacities, which in the classical formulation is not easy to handle.

2   Literature Review

In this item, the work shows relevant and similar applications of vehicle routing problems in Colombia. As designed, the VRP applications solve instance for develope routes in short-haul transport; the particular characteristics of urban development in Colombia, do not allow parking on the street for a long time and also presents demand points without cargo bays. Along whit, present themselves the recurrent issues in cargo transportation as traffic, road maintenance, new works, small roads, among others. The incremental relevance of the CVRPTW in academic literature shows a rise of publications in this problem among last years, from a search in Scopus®. The results show 1429 documents only in the maim formulation over CVRP; including the time windows restrictions, the number of documents in Scopus® gives 722 document results (Fig. 1).

In Colombia the CVRP and his generalization CVRPTW aplies in many contexts, but in litterature can be highligted the works in collection of food donations [4], also in distribution patterns [7] and school bus routing [26]; also there are interesting works applied in other simmilar countries for pharmaceutical distribution [18]. From the same search in Scopus, notice that there are 10 Documents, 6 original articles and 4 proceedings since 2015 [3,6,12,17,21,22,24,25,27,29].

3   The CVRPTW Model Design

The family of VRP models and his study is extensive. The most study model in their taxonomy is the capacitated vehicle routing problem CVRP; the time windows restrictions form a generalisation of this model named VRPTW. The approximation in this work includes the capacity and time windows constraints simultaneously. Fist, we describe and show the mathematical formulation of the model, later also present the solution algorithms and tools to solve the problem.

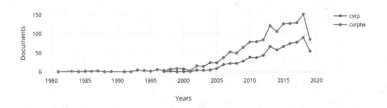

Fig. 1. Documents per year

3.1   Mathematical Formulation to CVRPTW

The mathematical formulation for modelling CVRPTW shows as follows and its described according [30, 31, 33].

$$Min \sum_{k \in K} \sum_{(i,j) \in A} c_{ij} x_{ijk} \tag{1}$$

subject to

$$\sum_{k \in K} \sum_{j \in \Delta+(i)} x_{ijk} = 1 \qquad \forall \, i \in N, \tag{2}$$

$$\sum_{j \in \Delta+(0)} x_{0jk} = 1 \qquad \forall \, k \in N, \tag{3}$$

$$\sum_{i \in \Delta+(j)} x_{ijk} - \sum_{i \in \Delta+(j)} x_{jik} = 0 \qquad \forall \, k \in N, \, j \in N, \tag{4}$$

$$\sum_{i \in \Delta-(n+1)} x_{i,n+1,k} = 1 \quad \forall \, k \in K, \tag{5}$$

$$x_{ijk}(w_{ik} + s_i + t_{ij} - w_{jk}) \leq 0 \quad \forall \, k \in K, (i,j) \in A, \tag{6}$$

$$a_i \sum_{j \in \Delta+(i)} x_{ijk} \leq w_{ik} \leq b_i \sum_{j \in \Delta+(i)} x_{ijk} \quad \forall \, k \in K, \, i \in N, \tag{7}$$

$$E \leq w_{ik} \leq L \quad \forall \, k \in K, \, i \in \{0, n+1\}, \tag{8}$$

$$\sum_{i \in N} d_i \sum_{j \in \Delta+(i)} x_{ijk} \leq C \quad \forall \, k \in K, \tag{9}$$

$$x_{ijk} \geq 0 \quad \forall\, k \in K,\ (i,j) \in A, \tag{10}$$

$$x_{ijk} \in \{0,1\} \quad \forall\, k \in K,\ (i,j) \in A. \tag{11}$$

The objective function 1 refers to minimize the total cost expressed like distance units in the distance matrix. Constraints 2 restric the assignment of each customer to exactly one vehicle route. Next, constraints 3–5 characterize the flow on the path to be followed by vehicle k. Additionally, constraints 6–8 and 9 guarantee schedule feasibility with respect to time considerations and capacity aspects, respectively. Note that for a given k, constraints 7 force $W_{ik}=$ 0 whenever customer i is not visited by vehicle k. Finally, conditions 11 impose binary conditions on the flow variables.

3.2   Solution Method

- **googleDistance Matrix API:** The CVRPTW is solved using google maps distance matrix API [1], and for solve the algorithm this work use google or-tools [2] for developers.
- **googleORTools:** OR-Tools is open source software for combinatorial optimization, which seeks to find the best solution to a problem out of a very large set of possible solutions.
- **Routing Options:** Time spend in every search of 100 s, fist solution strategy cheapest insertion, local search objective tabu search.
- **IDE:** IPython/Jupyter notebooks.

The distance matrix C_{ij} is created by calling google maps distance matrix API, with units as distance in meters using the directions for every client from the Table 1 and represented in the Fig. 2.

Each client has different demands, the entire fleet is available, but they have different cargo capacity. The first module for the main program developed in python 3.0 is the data creation module, as we say before we use the google distance matrix API, then we add time window constraints with an initial time at 2:00 pm.

The time windows data is a set of pairs with initial time and final time for each time window in every pair into the set.

The vehicle capacities are added as another set of data in the first module of data creation. The second module calculates the distance between directions using the distance matrix created before.

The velocity for every truck is added as a mean velocity for vehicles at the day in Bogota, Colombia (25 km/h). An exciting and useful characteristic of the Google API is the possibility of getting the distance matrix data in real time.

All vehicle capacities must be greater than the sum of every demand nodes. Otherwise, the problem has no feasible solution. The use of heuristics helps to find a feasible (but not always the best) solution with faster development in the time of execution for the algorithm previously selected. The imput information for the first module of data creation in our program is Table 3

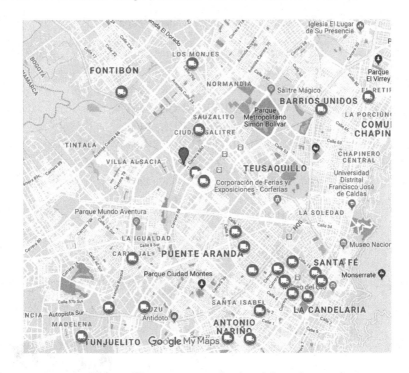

Fig. 2. Clients map - nodes for pick packages

The CVPTW presents in each node a time window expressed as the initial time i_t and the final time f_t when a truck can visit a demand node at a time v_t as we show as follows (Table 2):

The vehicle routing problem with time-windows (CVRPTW) reffers to: As can bee seen in the Fig. 3 a fleet of shipping cars with uniform capability must serve clients with known demand and opening hours for a single commodity.

Table 1. Geographical coordinates for the demand nodes: Lat = Latitude, Lon = Longitude

Node	Lat	Long	Node	Lat	Long	Node	Lat	Long
DEPOT	4,644074	−74,120507	C8	4,61009	−74,090002	C16	4,617141	−74,101125
C1	4,63816	−74,114188	C9	4,588141	−74,106311	C17	4,588499	−74,154815
C2	4,64093	−74,116914	C10	4,597977	−74,133829	C18	4,613504	−74,137859
C3	4,675887	−74,117909	C11	4,609671	−74,09831	C19	4,606171	−74,07572
C4	4,62192	−74,103876	C12	4,612365	−74,085213	C20	4,6012	−74,080275
C5	4,666847	−74,141226	C13	4,661076	−74,075602	C21	4,602244	−74,085227
C6	4,597748	−74,145742	C14	4,654545	−74,1156	C22	4,665044	−74,059959
C7	4,608708	−74,077771	C15	4,596786	−74,095874	C23	4,587774	−74,099263
						C24	4,606273	−74,08787

Table 2. Fleet with heterogeneous capacity

Code	Brand	Class	Capacity
4020	HINO	TRUCK	8500
4033	HINO	TRUCK	5400
4036	CHEVROLET	TRUCK	5400
4037	CHEVROLET	TRUCK	5400
4041	CHEVROLET	TRUCK	5400
4042	HINO	TRUCK	4600
4043	HINO	TRUCK	4200
4044	HINO	TRUCK	4200
4039	HINO	TRUCK	4000
4040	HINO	TRUCK	4000
4035	HINO	TRUCK	4000
4034	HINO	TRUCK	4000
4031	CHEVROLET	TRUCK	3500

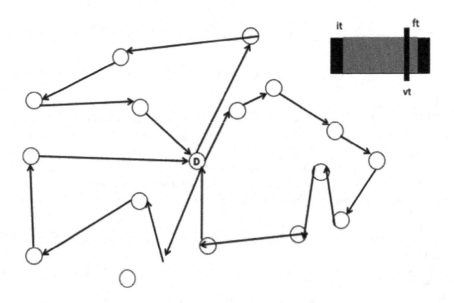

Fig. 3. VRPTW representation of time windows

At a D depot node, the cars begin and end their paths. Only one car can serve each client. The goals are to minimize the fleet size and assign a sequence of customers to each fleet truck minimizing the total distance traveled so that all customers are served and the total demand served by each truck does not exceed its capacity. The time windows are represented as the time interval vt from it to ft in which each customer can receive deliveries (Table 4).

4   Results

The solution of the problem was performed using the algorithm of Objective tabu search and includes time window constraints and capacity constraints simultaneously. The performance of the algorithm was measured, given a solution at a time execution of 0.09 s.

The routes for the Trucks contains load in every node, total time and total distance for each. The total distance for every route was 10044 m, the total time of every route was 2174 min, but the more significant time for every rout was 333 min for truck number 4039. Also, we can plot every route, as can see the first two of them as follows:

Table 3. Time windows in minutes starting at 2:00 pm and demands for everey client

Node (client)	Tw (start)	Tw (end)	Demand
D	0	0	0
C1	0	50	391
C2	30	100	71
C3	60	80	36
C4	120	160	2519
C5	150	270	248
C6	210	227	478
C7	180	200	589
C8	210	235	1105
C9	210	225	55
C10	240	255	237
C11	240	255	235
C12	240	265	908
C13	240	270	1473
C14	240	255	24
C15	270	285	144
C16	270	285	181
C17	270	290	564
C18	270	295	764
C19	300	330	1386
C20	300	345	4034
C21	300	320	669
C22	330	345	361
C23	330	355	1113
C24	360	405	4271

Table 4. Results for the CVPTW

Item	performance results
Total Distance of all routes	10044 m
Total Load of all routes	21856
Total Time of all routes	2174 min
Algorithm performance	0.09801173210144043 s

As can be seen in Table 5a it is possible to obtain the routes of each vehicle where the first row shows the route that each vehicle must follow starting from the deposit and returning to it.

Table 5. Solution for the CVRPTW

(a) Route 1-Truck 4041

Route 1	D	2	12	20	D
Load (Kg)	0	71	908	4034	0
Total Load	5013				
Total Distance	1296				
Total time	302				

(b) Route 2-Truck 4042

Route 2	D	11	24	D
Load (Kg)	0	235	4271	0
Total Load	4506			
Total DIstance	1131			
Total time	362			

(c) Route 3-Truck 4039

Route 3	D	8	9	15	23	D
Load (Kg)	0	1105	55	144	1113	0
Total Load	2417					
Total Distance	1811					
Total time	333					

(d) Route 4-Truck 4040

Route 4	D	1	7	19	21	D
Load (Kg)	0	391	589	1386	669	0
Total Load	3035					
Total Distance	1325					
Total time	302					

(e) Route 5-Truck 4035

Route 5	D	6	10	17	18	D
Load (Kg)	0	478	237	564	764	0
Total Load	2043					
Total Distance	1706					
Total time	272					

(f) Route 6-Truck 4035

Route 6	D	4	16	D
Load (Kg)	0	2519	181	0
Total Load	2700			
Total Distance	761			
Total time	271			

(g) Route 7-Truck 4031

Route 7	D	3	5	14	13	22	D
Load (Kg)	0	36	248	24	1473	361	0
Total Load	2142						
Total Distance	2014						
Total time	332						

The second row shows the load collected at each point, rows 3 and 4 show the total load collected by each vehicle and the total route time (Figs. 4 and figura4).

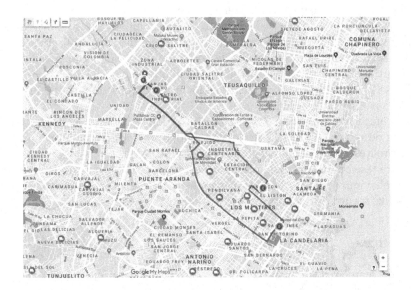

Fig. 4. Route 1 - Route generator in google maps

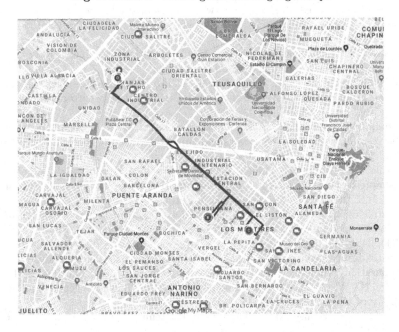

Fig. 5. Route 2- Route generator in google maps

5   Conclusions

The use of google optimization tools allows to solve optimization and meta-heuristic problems efficiently and also allows its integration with visualization tools such as google maps for a better understanding of the results.

The routing problem in a real case for a Bogota company is solved by reducing the delivery time and the fleet required to carry out the cargo collections.

The biggest contribution of google tools in this case is the possibility of changing the loading capacity of trucks in a simple way.

The solution time is very efficient, achieving a response in a short time for a complex metaheuristic problem.

The company do not need 6 trucks of 13; the demand is satisfied with 7 trucks as it was described in the last item. The model provides dynamic planning for delivery routes using a heterogeneous capacity fleet.

Future research can include machine learning algorithms to add human preference behaviour to chose how to accomplish the routes, including perception aspects like security or comfort.

References

1. Clients map - google's maps api. https://drive.google.com/open?id=1_MxV75hs_qlFENsXIhh0HJDYZkcu7pJ-&usp=sharing
2. Google's or-tools. https://developers.google.com/optimization/
3. Aguirre-Gonzalez, E., Villegas, J.: A two-phase heuristic for the collection of waste animal tissue in a colombian rendering company. Commun. Comput. Inf. Sci. **742**, 511–521 (2017)
4. Arenas, I.G.P., Sánchez, A.G., Armando, C., Solano, L., Medina, L.B.R.: Cvrptw model applied to the collection of food donations
5. Baldacci, R., Christofides, N., Mingozzi, A.: An exact algorithm for the vehicle routing problem based on the set partitioning formulation with additional cuts. Math. Program. **115**(2), 351–385 (2008)
6. Bernal, J., Escobar, J., Paz, J., Linfati, R., Gatica, G.: A probabilistic granular tabu search for the distance constrained capacitated vehicle routing problem. Int. J. Ind. Syst. Eng. **29**(4), 453–477 (2018)
7. Carrillo, M., Felipe, A.: Modelo de ruteo de vehículos para la distribución de las empresas laboratorios veterland, Laboratorios Callbest y Cosméticos Marlioü París. B.S. thesis, Facultad de Ingeniería (2014)
8. Christofides, N., Mingozzi, A., Toth, P.: Exact algorithms for the vehicle routing problem, based on spanning tree and shortest path relaxations. Math. Program. **20**(1), 255–282 (1981)
9. Christofides, N., Mingozzi, A., Toth, P.: State-space relaxation procedures for the computation of bounds to routing problems. Networks **11**(2), 145–164 (1981)
10. Clarke, G., Wright, J.W.: Scheduling of vehicles from a central depot to a number of delivery points. Oper. Res. **12**(4), 568–581 (1964)
11. Dantzig, G.B., Ramser, J.H.: The truck dispatching problem. Manag. Sci. **6**(1), 80–91 (1959)

12. Escobar-Falcon, L., Alvarez-Martinez, D., Granada-Echeverri, M., Willmer-Escobar, J., Romero-Lazaro, R.: A matheuristic algorithm for the three-dimensional loading capacitated vehicle routing problem (3l-cvrp). Rev. Fac. de Ing. **2016**(78), 9–20 (2016)
13. Flood, M.M.: The traveling-salesman problem. Oper. Res. **4**(1), 61–75 (1956)
14. Fukasawa, R., Longo, H., Lysgaard, J., de Aragão, M.P., Reis, M., Uchoa, E., Werneck, R.F.: Robust branch-and-cut-and-price for the capacitated vehicle routing problem. Math. Program. **106**(3), 491–511 (2006)
15. Gendreau, M., Hertz, A., Laporte, G.: A tabu search heuristic for the vehicle routing problem. Manag. Sci. **40**(10), 1276–1290 (1994)
16. Ghiani, G., Laporte, G., Musmanno, R.: Introduction to Logistics Systems Planning and Control. John Wiley & Sons, Hoboken (2004)
17. Herazo-Padilla, N., Montoya-Torres, J., Nieto Isaza, S., Alvarado-Valencia, J.: Simulation-optimization approach for the stochastic location-routing problem. J. Simul. **9**(4), 296–311 (2015)
18. Jacobo-Cabrera, M., Caballero-Morales, S.-O., Martínez-Flores, J.-L., Cano-Olivos, P.: Decision model for the pharmaceutical distribution of insulin. In: Florez, H., Diaz, C., Chavarriaga, J. (eds.) ICAI 2018. CCIS, vol. 942, pp. 75–89. Springer, Cham (2018). https://doi.org/10.1007/978-3-030-01535-0_6
19. Laporte, G., Desrochers, M., Nobert, Y.: Two exact algorithms for the distance-constrained vehicle routing problem. Networks **14**(1), 161–172 (1984)
20. Laporte, G., Toth, P., Vigo, D.: Vehicle routing: historical perspective and recent contributions (2013)
21. Lenis, S., Rivera, J.: A metaheuristic approach for the cumulative capacitated arc routing problem. Commun. Comput. Inf. Sci. **916**, 96–107 (2018)
22. Lopez-Santana, E., Mendez-Giraldo, G., Franco-Franco, C.: A hybrid scatter search algorithm to solve the capacitated arc routing problem with refill points. Lect. Notes Comput. Sci. (including Subseries Lect. Notes Artif. Intell. Lect. Notes Bioinform.) **9772**, 3–15 (2016)
23. Pisinger, D., Ropke, S.: A general heuristic for vehicle routing problems. Comput. Oper. Res. **34**(8), 2403–2435 (2007)
24. Quintero-Araujo, C., Bernaus, A., Juan, A., Travesset-Baro, O., Jozefowiez, N.: Planning freight delivery routes in mountainous regions. Lect. Notes Bus. Inf. Process. **254**, 123–132 (2016)
25. Rivera, J., Murat Afsar, H., Prins, C.: Mathematical formulations and exact algorithm for the multitrip cumulative capacitated single-vehicle routing problem. Eur. J. Oper. Res. **249**(1), 93–104 (2016)
26. Santana, L., Ramiro, E., Carvajal, J.D.J.: A hybrid column generation and clustering approach to the school bus routing problem with time windows. Ingeniería **20**(1), 101–117 (2015)
27. Solano-Charris, E., Prins, C., Santos, A.: Local search based metaheuristics for the robust vehicle routing problem with discrete scenarios. Appl. Soft Comput. J. **32**, 518–531 (2015)
28. Taillard, É.: Parallel iterative search methods for vehicle routing problems. Networks **23**(8), 661–673 (1993)
29. Toro, E., Franco, J., Echeverri, M., Guimaraes, F.: A multi-objective model for the green capacitated location-routing problem considering environmental impact. Comput. Ind. Eng. **110**, 114–125 (2017)
30. Toth, P., Vigo, D.: Models, relaxations and exact approaches for the capacitated vehicle routing problem. Dis. Appl. Math. **123**(1–3), 487–512 (2002)

31. Toth, P., Vigo, D.: The Vehicle Routing Problem. SIAM, Philadelphia (2002)
32. Toth, P., Vigo, D.: The granular tabu search and its application to the vehicle-routing problem. Informs J. Comput. **15**(4), 333–346 (2003)
33. Toth, P., Vigo, D.: Vehicle Routing: Problems, Methods, and Applications. SIAM, Philadelphia (2014)

Evaluation of Transfer Learning Techniques with Convolutional Neural Networks (CNNs) to Detect the Existence of Roads in High-Resolution Aerial Imagery

Calimanut-Ionut Cira$^{(\boxtimes)}$ ⓘ, Ramon Alcarria ⓘ,
Miguel-Ángel Manso-Callejo ⓘ, and Francisco Serradilla ⓘ

Universidad Politécnica de Madrid, 28031 Madrid, Spain
cira.calimanut-ionut@alumnos.upm.es

Abstract. Infrastructure detection and monitoring traditionally required manual identification of geospatial objects in aerial imagery but advances in deep learning and computer vision enabled the researchers in the field of remote sensing to successfully apply transfer learning from pretrained models on large-scale datasets for the task of geospatial object detection. However, they mostly focused on objects with clearly defined boundaries that are independent of the background (e.g. airports, airplanes, buildings, ships, etc.). What happens when we have to deal with more complicated, continuous objects like roads? In this paper we will review four of the best-known CNN architectures (VGGNet, Inception-V3, Xception, Inception-ResNet) and apply feature extraction and fine-tuning techniques to detect the existence of roads in aerial orthoimages divided in tiles of 256×256 pixels in size. We will evaluate each model's performance on unseen test data using the accuracy metric and compare the results with those obtained by a CNN especially built for this purpose.

Keywords: Transfer learning · Convolutional neural networks · Remote sensing · Road detection

1 Introduction

The success of deeper CNN architectures in solving computer vision problems (AlexNet [1], VGGNet [2], GoogLeNet [3], Resnet [4] and Inception-ResNet [5]) incentivized a new wave of research in the remote sensing community. These deeper networks achieve great success in imagery classification tasks [6] and address the problem of the vanishing gradient by replacing the traditional sigmoid & tanh activation functions with the rectified linear unit (ReLU) activation function and the overfitting problem by applying batch normalization for optimization or dropout for stronger regularization [7]. These improvements enhance the performance while making the models more generalizable.

Researchers in the field of remote sensing have successfully applied transfer learning from models pretrained on large-scale datasets (ILSVF challenge) for geospatial object detection or for land use analysis in large-scale satellite imagery data [8].

© Springer Nature Switzerland AG 2019
H. Florez et al. (Eds.): ICAI 2019, CCIS 1051, pp. 185–198, 2019.
https://doi.org/10.1007/978-3-030-32475-9_14

Mathematically, transfer learning works by initializing the weights of a network from an already trained (and accurate) value to cause a better convergence. When applying feature extraction, we use the base of a pretrained convolutional network and only train the new classifier added on top, so that we can repurpose the feature maps learned previously for our dataset. When applying fine-tuning technique, we unfreeze a portion of the layers from the model's convolutional base and retrain them together with the new classifier added on top, making the representations learned by the pretrained model more specific for our task [9].

One of the hot research topics is related to object detection in remote sensing imagery. The authors of [10] propose a framework for detecting airports which integrates features extraction and object localization and is validated with data collected from Google Earth. In [11], a comparative analysis between four CNNs was conducted using refined open-source data to extract building footprints across the United States. The authors of [12] propose a framework for multi-class geospatial object detection tasks (including bridges, ships, tennis courts) using transferred knowledge from remote sensing image classification tasks and supervision from scene tags.

These papers have in common objects with clearly defined boundaries that are independent of the background. What happens when we have to deal with more difficult, continuous objects like roads? We need to consider that using aerial imagery can be challenging because of the noise, obstructions and complexity of the scenes and that roads can be structured (clear marked highways and city roads) or unstructured (no obvious borderers), which further complicates their detection.

Hutchison et al. were among first to approach the problem of road detection by using unsupervised training to obtain filters that improved the performance of the road detector on manually tagged data [13]. The authors of [14] and [15] focus on extracting roads from aerial images and propose neural networks for semantic segmentation tested on a dataset containing public roads where they demonstrated great performance.

In [16], a network consisting in five convolution layers, with Global Average Pooling (GAP) replacing Fully-connected (FC) layers, is proposed to extract roads and build geometries on challenging urban datasets. In [17], the authors recognize the complexity of road detection in real-world applications and study the efficiency of state-of-the-art CNNs for road segmentation from satellite imagery, obtaining precision levels of maximum 70%.

The authors of [18] propose RoadNet composed of three CNN based on VGGNet's architecture to predict road surfaces, edges, and centerlines. Other works approached this task from temporal perspective by adding a temporal processing block on top a deep CNN trained for image segmentation [19]. Automatic road detection from remotely sensed imagery can play an important role in infrastructure monitoring, digital geospatial data integration or vehicle navigation [20].

The goal of this paper is to evaluate the performance of four of the best-known CNN architectures (VGGNet, Inception-v3, Xception, Inception-ResNet) in learning the relationships between the training inputs and their correspondent categories using supervised learning and transfer learning techniques. We will evaluate each network's performance using the accuracy obtained on unseen data and compare the results with those obtained by a CNN built for this purpose.

2 Methodology

This project tackles a computer vision problem applied to remote sensing, the specific machine-learning problem being binary classification. The variables studied are the pixels of high-resolution orthoimages divided in tiles of 256×256 pixels in size, the research having a quantitative approach.

This section provides information about the methodology applied and describes the workflow followed for the classification task.

2.1 Building the Datasets

The data was labelled using a WMS-based cartographic viewer implemented to tag the tiles by visually comparing the aerial orthoimage to existing cartographic support. During the labelling operation we used the same zoom level, for consistency reasons. We considered different areas in Spain, each with a representative type of vegetation coverage that may affect the network's capability in detecting geospatial elements for the whole territory.

The tiles containing road tags were merged into a single dataset (category 2 - road), while the tiles not containing any roads were merged into another dataset (category 1 - No road). These categories will allow the CNNs to learn about the existence/non-existence of roads in tiles (samples from these datasets can be seen in Fig. 1).

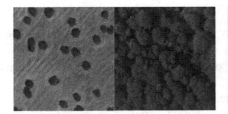 

Fig. 1. Tiles extracted from "No road" category (left)" and "Road" category (right)

We obtained approximately 9000 tiles of 256×256 pixels (0.07 MP) in size, occupying a disk volume of approximately 1.2 GB. The tiles were split according to the conventions in the literature [21, 22]: $\sim 50\%$ for training (to perform the weights initialization), $\sim 25\%$ for validation (used for tuning the model's hyperparameters and analyzing their impact on performance) and $\sim 25\%$ for testing (used to test the performance after selecting the parameters).

2.2 Tiles Preprocessing

The tiles must be preprocessed from png files to tensors before being fed into the CNNs. The images were decoded into RGB grids of pixels and their vales (between 0 and 255) were rescaled between 0 and 1.

Given that our dataset contains a low number of samples (i.e. compared to ImageNet), we augmented the training samples via several transformations (random rotations, horizontally and vertically translations and flipping, etc. – as seen in Fig. 2). The augmentation was applied automatically during training, the iterator returning one batch of images augmented in-memory (not stored on the disk) for each iteration.

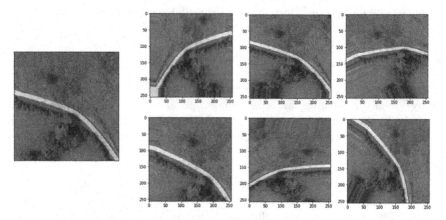

Fig. 2. Data augmentation transformations applied to a random tile

2.3   CNN Architecture

We opted for building a 12-hidden-layers CNN and decided to pass the tensors through four convolutional layers, containing filters with a 3×3 receptive field. In [23] we considered other configurations, but this particular architecture showed a higher computational efficiency.

After every convolutional layer we added max-pooling layers with a 2×2-pixel window. At the end of the model we have two Fully-Connected layers: the first contains 512 units, while the second contains 1 unit (where it performs the classification).

Our task is a binary-classification problem; therefore, we had to end our network with a dense layer of size 1 and a sigmoid activation function encoding the probability of a class or the other. As activation functions we used ReLU non-linearity for the convolutional layers and the first dense layer and sigmoid for the last Fully-Connected layer.

Given that we ended the network with a sigmoid unit, we used binary crossentropy as loss function for training the model and Adam [24] as optimizer (it is considered to be the fastest to converge) [25].

To address the problem of overfitting, we applied data augmentation to the training dataset to "generate" more training data (and expose the network to more aspects of data) and added a dropout layer before the classifier (fully connected layers). The dropout operation randomly sets a rate of input units (50% in our case) to 0 at each training update to avoid neurons developing co-adaptations among themselves.

2.4   Network Training

The training is based on the convolution operation performed on the input data, where filters (of size 3 × 3 in this case) slide over the input to produce feature maps by performing a matrix multiplication at every location and summing the result onto the feature map.

The goal of this paper is to evaluate the performance of transfer learning techniques with respect to CNNs especially built for a given task. To achieve this, we will first train a network from scratch using random initialization. Next, we will apply transfer learning techniques which consist of using the weights of pre-trained networks as initializers: when applying feature extraction, we will train only the classifier added on top of the convolutional base, while in fine-tuning we will unfreeze a portion of layers from the model's convolutional base and retrain it together with a newly added classifier. A number of 100 epochs was chosen as standard for training the models. However, if the loss was still decreasing and the model was still learning, the CNN was trained for longer (200–300 epochs) to observe how its behavior is changing. In the next three subchapters we'll see how CNNs are behaving in different training scenarios:

Method 1: CNN Built from Scratch

In this case, we pass the inputs through four convolutional + max-pooling stages, and because we started from inputs of size 256 × 256, the feature maps decrease to 14 × 14 pixels while their depth increases from 32 to 128 just before the GAP/Flatten layer.

First, we trained the model without data augmentation and achieved a classification accuracy of 96% on the training set and 90% on the validation set. The network showed characteristics of light overfitting, adapting to the training data despite applying a dropout layer with a large rate before the FC layers.

In the second scenario, by adding data augmentation and training the model using the same hyperparameters, we were no longer overfitting (training and validation curves were closely following each other – Fig. 3). This time, we have reached an accuracy of almost 91% both on the training and on the validation set, the network showing a stable behavior.

In the previous two scenarios, the convolutional layers were followed by a GAP layer and resulted in models having little over 300,000 total parameters. However, it is known that by having many parameters we can represent much more complicated functions, so we decided to try a Flatten layer instead of the GAP layer. By adding a Flatten layer after the convolutional layers, the number of parameters increased to over 13 million. In this scenario, the network achieved a classification accuracy of around 96% on the training set and 92% on the validation set. We could find again characteristics of overfitting, where the training loss was heading towards 0, whereas the validation loss reached its minimum after 150 epochs and then stalled. It means that the network is again adapting too well to the training data, probably due to the high number of parameters. We should apply additional regularization or tune the model's parameters (e.g. number layers in the CNN or number filters per convolution layer) to control this behavior.

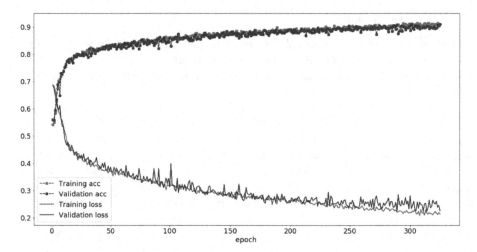

Fig. 3. Training and validation accuracy & loss curves: built CNN with data augmentation

Method 2: Feature Extraction

Next, we applied transfer learning techniques which consist of using pre-trained network weights as initializers. We imported the convolutional bases of four of the best-known architectures (VGGNet, Inception-v3, Xception and Inception-ResNet) pre-trained on ILSVRC (ImageNet Large Scale Visual Recognition Competition) and added a new classifier on top of the models. The new classifier will consist of a GAP layer, a Dropout layer and two Dense layers. It is important to freeze the convolutional base (to prevent its weights from being updated) before we compile and train the model. This way only the weights from the two Dense layers added will be trained. For training the models, we applied the same regularization techniques used in the previous method (same data-augmentation configuration and dropout layer) together with the same Adam optimizer with its default learning settings.

First, we trained VGGNet with the newly classifier added on top and reached classification accuracies of 87% on the training set and 88% on the validation set. The validation loss stood stable for most of the training, while the training loss had a slower decreasing evolution. Our model performed better on the validation data; one of the reasons for this might be the use of augmentation on the training data, which made it harder to predict in comparison to the unmodified validation samples. A small difference between training and validation is considered to be normal.

Next, our classifier was added on top of Inception-v3's convolutional base. The model achieved a classification accuracy score of around 86% on both sets but started to minimize the loss on the training data. We should consider there is 50 + % increase in the number of parameters when compared to VGGNet and apply stronger regularization.

Xception and Inception-v3 have the same number of parameters, but Xception slightly outperforms Inception-v3 on the ImageNet dataset, while vastly outperforms it on a classification dataset containing 17,000 classes, which implies a greater computational efficiency [26]. Using Xception, we achieved a classification accuracy of 88%

on both the training and the validation set and we observed a more stable learning process when compared to the previous scenario.

Residual connections allow shortcuts in the model and enabled researchers to successfully train even deeper neural networks, leading to the best result on ILSVRC competition. In this case, we froze Inception-ResNet's convolutional base and trained the classifier added on top for 100 epochs. The network achieved a classification accuracy of around 86% on the training set and 90% on the validation set (Fig. 4). Looking at the evolution on the values, we can see the validation's loss stood below 0.3 for most of the training, while the training loss had a slower decreasing and more stable evolution. After 100 epochs the loss was still decreasing; the network could be trained for a longer period to observe its evolution.

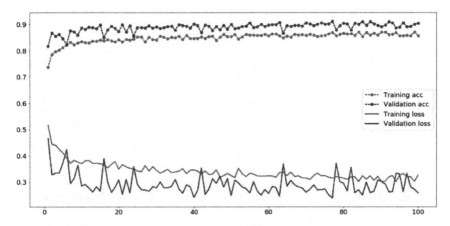

Fig. 4. Training and validation accuracy & loss curves: feature extraction – inception-ResNet

Method 3: Fine-Tuning Pre-trained Models

The other transfer learning technique is fine-tuning where the premise is that the top layers of deep CNNs are probably too specialized and may not be the best candidates for solving a new given task. By unfreezing some top layers of a frozen model and retraining them with a newly added classifier (the same used for feature extraction, consisting in a GAP layer, a Dropout layer and two Dense layers), we can fine-tune the model to make the representations learned more specific for our task. We can fine-tune as many layers as we want, but we must keep in mind that the more parameters we are training, the risk of overfitting increases. We decided to train the top, middle and bottom blocks of the convolutional bases analyzed in the previous subchapter and observe their evolution.

We started with fine-tuning VGGNet's last convolutional block. The number of trainable parameters increased from 250,000 during feature extraction to 7.3 million. The model achieved accuracies of around 97% for training and 94% for validation. When plotting the loss curves, we can find again characteristics of a light overfitting, which is normal considering the model is training and adapting to the training set and the overfitting does not cause the validation accuracy to fall to levels that make it useless (Fig. 5). On the other hand, when trying to fine-tune lower blocks of convolution, the accuracy levels dropped below 70%, the training appearing to harm the representations learned by the model. This might be due to VGGNet's compact architecture which can make it sensible to updating the weight of its lower convolutional blocks. Nonetheless, the results obtained are much better when compared to feature extraction, as we are seeing an 7% absolute improvement in accuracy (from about 88% to around 95%). It is worth mentioning that training time per epoch is considerably longer (10%–30% increase).

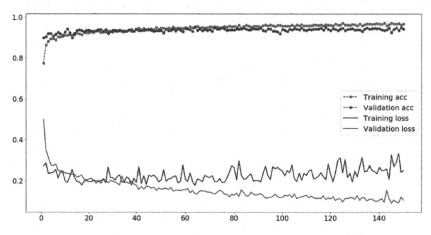

Fig. 5. Training and validation accuracy & loss curves: fine-tuning VGGNet's last conv_block

Next, we fine-tuned (or updated the weights of) the last three Inception-v3's blocks. The overfitting behavior was observed from the beginning, obtaining a training accuracy of around 98% while the validation accuracy remained at 91%. We should employ stronger regularization and a smaller learning rate to prevent overfitting. The authors of [27] studied the transferability of learning in CNN and observed that fine-tuning a pre-trained model with a large number of parameters on a small dataset may result in overfitting. When we went deeper into the architecture and updated the weights of earlier blocks, the training time increased, and the network showed a very unstable behavior, the overtraining being even more pronounced. The training accuracy reached nearly 100%, with the loss almost dropping to 0, whereas the validation loss surpassed 0.8.

Afterwards, we fine-tuned the last two convolutional blocks of the Xception architecture, the behavior of overfitting from the start being present here as well (thing to be expected given its almost identical architecture to Inception-v3). The training accuracy reached 98%, while the validation accuracy dropped to 91%. When we updated the weights starting with lower layers and with a smaller optimization rate (0.0001), the training time increased and the network showed more pronounced overfitting characteristics.

Finally, we fine-tuned the last part of Inception-ResNet model and reached classification accuracies of 97% on the training set and 91% on the validation set. The network showed a more stable behavior, probably due to its architecture containing residual blocks (which skip connections and propagate larger gradients to initial layers so the initial layers can learn as fast as the final layers during backpropagation). When trying to fine-tune lower layers the time/epoch increased too much (1.5–2x times) and training became intractable on the available GPU.

3 Results and Discussion

In binary-classification problems, a model's classification accuracy on the test dataset is considered to be an appropriate measure of performance. Classification accuracy is the number of correct predictions made divided by the total number of predictions made on unseen data. The recommended approach for obtaining a model's classification accuracy is by predicting the output using training input and then evaluate the performance by comparing it against the test output.

The results obtained are presented in Table 1 for all the models trained in subchapter 2.4. We can see that accuracy levels stand above 90% in most cases; the best result being obtained by fine-tuning the last convolutional block of VGG16 model. This may be due to VGGNet's compact architecture designed to gradually increase the semantic complexity.

However, in our view, the best approach for solving the task was by building a CNN from scratch and using regularization techniques. By applying data augmentation, training the model for a longer period and using a high number of parameters, the network was able to learn about the complexity of the road network's characteristics and reached accuracy levels of almost 93% (Fig. 6 and Table 1).

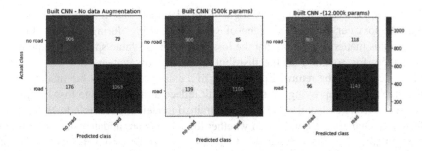

Fig. 6. Confusion matrices of ConvNets trained under the scenarios presented in Method 1.

We could further tweak some of the hyperparameters (smaller learning rate, number of filters per convolution layer, filter size) to improve the performance, but accuracy levels are very high nonetheless considering the simplicity of the model's architecture.

As for the training process, in transfer learning (especially fine-tuning) the loss curves showed signs of overfitting. Transfer learning proved to be a powerful tool, initializing the weights with transferred features instead of random weights improved the generalization performance (VGGNet obtained the highest score), but we should to apply additional regularization techniques to control the overfitting.

Table 1. Accuracies obtained on test data (unseen by the networks)

Model	Test accuracy	Training time/epoch (s)	Parameters (millions)	Trainable parameters
Built CNN – No data augmentation	92.07%	31	0.3	100.00%
Built CNN – Data augmentation	91.82%	75	0.3	100.00%
Built CNN – Higher number of parameters	92.79%	89	13.1	100.00%
Feature extraction – VGGNet	87.96%	112	15	1.76%
Feature extraction – Inception-v3	87.88%	100	22.9	4.59%
Feature extraction – Xception	89.85%	129	21.9	4.79%
Feature extraction – Inception-ResNet	92.53%	101	55.1	1.43%
Fine-tuning – VGGNet	94.09%	130	15	49.02%
Fine-tuning – Inception-v3	91.19%	125	22.9	60.69%
Fine-tuning – Xception	92.20%	148	21.9	35.62%
Fine-tuning– Inception-ResNet	91.28%	159	55.1	20.05%

The accuracies on test data were higher than 91% in all fine-tuning scenarios, even though the loss curves showed signs of strong overfitting during training. Looking more into this matter, we found that the loss is an average value specific to a point and what matters for accuracy is the distribution of the loss values, not their average, because accuracy is the returned probability of a class predicted by the model and the model may still be improving even if this isn't reflected in the average loss [9]. In fine-tuning scenarios, we also observed that pre-trained models are sensible to changes, the performance changing depending on whether the weights are updated starting from the bottom, middle, or top of the network. Retraining the lower levels of the network lowered the performance and the cause of it might be that earlier layers could have co-adapted to obtain the characteristics and changing their weights damaged the features learnt.

Feature extraction resulted to be the option with poorer results in our case but has the advantage of being less computational expensive when compared to fine-tuning. Seems that adapting the representation learned by an existing model to a new and very different dataset by only changing the classifier on top is not sufficient. When dealing with a dataset similar to ILSVRC categories, it could be the preferred technique.

The time required for training the models was highly dependent on their architecture and the number of trainable parameters. For this reason, during fine-tuning we needed more computing power, and the training time/epoch increased longer considerably (especially in the case of models containing more than 20 million parameters). The number of parameters is defined by the number of layers in the network, the number of units in every layer and the input's dimensionality. The choice of layers also influences the number of parameters: as seen in the third scenario, using a flatten layer dramatically increased the number of parameters, with the benefit of obtaining 1% gains in accuracy. Using Flatten layer instead of GAP on our top classifier from transfer learning could have led to better transfer learning performance (at the cost of more computational power). When dealing with large number of parameters, we need to apply stronger regularization.

Another noticeable result is that when evaluating the models with test data from areas with dense vegetation and data from the Mediterranean (drier) areas separately, we can observe a considerable difference in performance (7–10%). One of the reasons could be the fact that there was more data from areas with dense vegetation, so the model is better there. It could also mean that for the models trained it is easier to detect roads in images with vegetation. Another reason could be that the difference in road/no road ratios can introduce a bias in the model (for example in forested area the ratio is 1.4 compared to just over 1 in the Mediterranean area); the model can try to check if there are more false positives in the forest images and may think that the green vegetation increases the probability of a road. These differences in performance mean that we can specialize the models (no one-can-fit-all-the-Spanish-territory model) and separate the tiles in forested areas/Mediterranean areas (with the criteria of similar background colors).

As a side note, we often consider deep learning models as "black boxes" and that the representation they learn are impossible to be understood by humans. However, this is not true in the case of CNNs, the characteristics they learn are in fact representation of real visual concepts (earlier portions of a network contain more generic, while latter layers contain specific representations). We can visualize the intermediate activations (the output of convolutional + maxpooling layers = feature maps) to understand how an input is transformed into the filters learned by the CNN. For example, in Fig. 7, we can visualize the feature maps obtained from the network trained in Method 1 (subchapter 2.4) and we can see that it "learned" that a road is probably a straight continuous line. This aspect can be particularly useful in transfer learning, because we can understand what levels of complexity may not be useful for a particular task, and what parts of a network might need to be fine-tuned. Another application of could be to verify the low-level filters when we are building a network from scratch and see if they correspond to those trained with bigger image datasets.

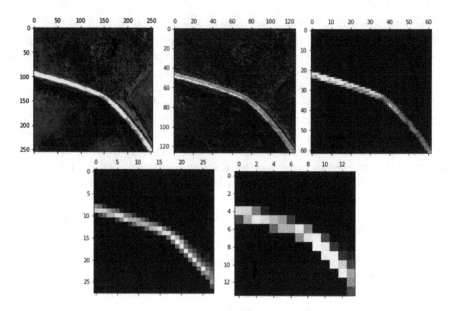

Fig. 7. Intermediate activation of the tile presented in Fig. 2

4 Conclusions and Future Lines of Investigation

Convolutional neural networks proved to be a powerful tool for analyzing remotely sensed image data. The results show that very deep CNNs are not always necessary for achieving high performance metrics on challenging datasets. In our case, by training an 11-hidden-layers model from scratch on a small dataset (i.e. when compared to ImageNet) we obtained high performance metrics by only using data augmentation and dropout to fight overfitting.

It is easy to reuse an existing model on a new dataset. In our opinion, if the new dataset has categories similar to those in ILSVRC, the best choice is feature extraction. However, in our case, fine-tuning achieved better results and improved the CNN performance by adapting the previously learned representation to our task. A model with higher number of parameters can better represent complicated mappings, with the downside of needing more computational resources and being more prone to overfitting. We need stronger regularization to prevent this behavior (extensively encountered during our training). Fine-tuning the lower and middle parts of a model generally lowered its performance metrics.

Next, we plan to plan to increase the number of samples and balance the datasets. This will provide much more variation in the data and counterbalance the disadvantage of highly correlated data resulted from data augmentation. Furthermore, we want to specialize the models for different vegetation coverage areas. In the end, we want to apply segmentation techniques to extract the geometry of the roads in the form of vector data layers. We hope to obtain a model deployable for real-world cases that will reduce human participation in detecting changes in cartography.

Acknowledgments. This research received funding from the Cartobot project, in collaboration with Instituto Geográfico Nacional (IGN), Spain. We thank all Cartobot participants for their help in generating the dataset.

References

1. Krizhevsky, A., Sutskever, I., Hinton, G.E.: ImageNet classification with deep convolutional neural networks. In: Pereira, F., Burges, C.J.C., Bottou, L., Weinberger, K.Q. (eds.) Advances in Neural Information Processing Systems 25, pp. 1097–1105. Curran Associates Inc, Red Hook (2012)
2. Simonyan, K., Zisserman, A.: Very Deep Convolutional Networks for Large-Scale Image Recognition, ArXiv14091556 Cs, (September 2014)
3. Szegedy, C., et al.: Going Deeper with Convolutions, ArXiv14094842 Cs, September (2014)
4. He, K., Zhang, X., Ren, S., Sun, J.: Deep Residual Learning for Image Recognition, ArXiv151203385 Cs, December (2015)
5. Szegedy, C., Ioffe, S., Vanhoucke, V., Alemi, A.: Inception-v4, Inception-ResNet and the Impact of Residual Connections on Learning, ArXiv160207261 Cs, February (2016)
6. Pritt, M., Chern, G.: Satellite image classification with deep learning, In: 2017 IEEE Applied Imagery Pattern Recognition Workshop (AIPR), pp. 1–7. Washington, DC, USA (2017)
7. Zhou, W., Newsam, S., Li, C., Shao, Z.: PatternNet: a benchmark dataset for performance evaluation of remote sensing image retrieval. ISPRS J. Photogramm. Remote Sens. **145**, 197–209 (2018)
8. Albert, A., Kaur, J., Gonzalez, M.C.: Using convolutional networks and satellite imagery to identify patterns in urban environments at a large scale. In: Proceedings of the 23rd ACM SIGKDD International Conference on Knowledge Discovery and Data Mining - KDD 2017, pp. 1357–1366. Halifax, NS, Canada, 2017
9. Chollet, F.: Deep Learning with Python. Manning Publications Co, Shelter Island (2018)
10. Cai, B., Jiang, Z., Zhang, H., Zhao, D., Yao, Y.: Airport detection using end-to-end convolutional neural network with hard example mining. Remote Sens. **9**(11), 1198 (2017)
11. Yang, H.L., Yuan, J., Lunga, D., Laverdiere, M., Rose, A., Bhaduri, B.: Building extraction at scale using convolutional neural network: mapping of the United States. IEEE J. Sel. Top. Appl. Earth Obs. Remote Sens. **11**(8), 2600–2614 (2018)
12. Li, Y., Zhang, Y., Huang, X., Yuille, A.L.: Deep networks under scene-level supervision for multi-class geospatial object detection from remote sensing images. ISPRS J. Photogramm. Remote Sens. **146**, 182–196 (2018)
13. Hutchison, D., et al.: Learning to detect roads in high-resolution aerial images. ECCV 2010. LNCS, vol. 6316, pp. 210–223. Springer, Heidelberg (2010). https://doi.org/10.1007/978-3-642-15567-3_16
14. Zhang, Z., Liu, Q., Wang, Y.: Road Extraction by Deep Residual U-Net. IEEE Geosci. Remote Sens. Lett. **15**(5), 749–753 (2018)
15. Wang, Q., Gao, J., Yuan, Y.: Embedding Structured Contour and Location Prior in Siamesed Fully Convolutional Networks for Road Detection. IEEE Trans. Intell. Transp. Syst. **19**(1), 230–241 (2018)
16. Alshehhi, R., Marpu, P.R., Woon, W.L., Mura, M.D.: Simultaneous extraction of roads and buildings in remote sensing imagery with convolutional neural networks. ISPRS J. Photogramm. Remote Sens. **130**, 139–149 (2017)

17. Henry, C., Azimi, S.M., Merkle, N.: Road segmentation in SAR satellite images with deep fully-convolutional neural networks. IEEE Geosci. Remote Sens. Lett. **15**(12), 1867–1871 (2018)
18. Liu, Y., Yao, J., Lu, X., Xia, M., Wang, X., Liu, Y.: RoadNet: learning to comprehensively analyze road networks in complex urban scenes from high-resolution remotely sensed images. IEEE Trans. Geosci. Remote Sens. **57**(4), 2043–2056 (2019)
19. Luque, B., Morros, J.R., Ruiz-Hidalgo, J.: Spatio-temporal road detection from aerial imagery using CNNs, In: Proceedings of the 12th International Joint Conference on Computer Vision, Imaging and Computer Graphics Theory and Applications,, pp. 493–500. Porto, Portugal (2017)
20. Woźniak, M., Damaševičius, R., Maskeliūnas, R., Malūkas, U.: Real time path finding for assisted living using deep learning. JUCS - J. Univers. Comput. Sci. **24**(4), 475–487 (2018)
21. Xu, Y., Goodacre, R.: On splitting training and validation set: a comparative study of cross-validation, bootstrap and systematic sampling for estimating the generalization performance of supervised learning. J. Anal. Test. **2**(3), 249–262 (2018)
22. May, R.J., Maier, H.R., Dandy, G.C.: Data splitting for artificial neural networks using SOM-based stratified sampling. Neural Netw. **23**(2), 283–294 (2010)
23. Cira, C.I., Alcarria, R., Manso-Callejo, M.A., Serradilla, F.: A deep convolutional neural network to detect the existence of geospatial elements in high-resolution aerial imagery. Proceedings, **19**(1), 17 (2019)
24. Kingma, D.P., Ba, J.: Adam: A Method for Stochastic Optimization, ArXiv14126980 Cs, (December 2014)
25. Chen, X., Liu, S., Sun, R., Hong, M.: On the Convergence of A Class of Adam-Type Algorithms for Non-Convex Optimization, ArXiv180802941 Cs Math Stat, (August 2018)
26. Chollet, F., Xception: Deep Learning with Depthwise Separable Convolutions, ArXiv161002357 Cs, (October 2016)
27. Yosinski, J., Clune, J., Bengio, Y., Lipson, H.: How transferable are features in deep neural networks?, ArXiv14111792 Cs, (November 2014)

Predicting Stock Prices Using Dynamic LSTM Models

Duc Huu Dat Nguyen[✉], Loc Phuoc Tran, and Vu Nguyen

Faculty of Information Technology, University of Science,
Vietnam National University, Ho Chi Minh, Vietnam
{1512125,1512302,nvu}@fit.hcmus.edu.vn

Abstract. Predicting stock prices accurately is a key goal of investors in the stock market. Unfortunately, stock prices are constantly changing and affected by many factors, making the process of predicting them a challenging task. This paper describes a method to build models for predicting stock prices using long short-term memory network (LSTM). The LSTM-based model, which we call dynamic LSTM, is initially built and continuously retrained using newly augmented data to predict future stock prices. We evaluate the proposed method using data sets of four stocks. The results show that the proposed method outperforms others in predicting stock prices based on different performance metrics.

Keywords: LSTM · Stock price prediction · Dynamic models

1 Introduction

Predicting stock prices is one of the most complex financial problems because there are many surrounding factors that directly affect the price fluctuation of the stock market. On the one hand, several authors argue that future stock prices are impossible to predict. Malkiel and Fama show that all new information is reflected on the stock price without delay, and thus, future stock price movement is not dependent on past and present information [1]. On the other hand, technical analysts argue that it is possible to capture important information about stock growth or decline according to information gathered from the historical stock data. Hence, if moving trends of a stock for a period can be captured, its prices are predictable.

In addition, Kai et al. have shown that the evolution of the stock market is directly affected by many factors such as: general economic conditions, political events, corporate policies, commodity price index, bank rate, exchange rate, investor expectations, other stock market movements, and investor sentiment [2].

Different models have been explored to use past stock values including Moving Average (MA), Exponential Smoothing, Exponential Moving Average (EMA), Autoregressive Integrated Moving Average (ARIMA) [3], and Vector Autoregression (VA). These models are used to find signals for future values of the target stock [4].

Recently with the development of large data processing capabilities based on upgraded hardware, scientists have developed several stock prediction models using approaches such as Artificial Neural Networks (ANN), fuzzy logic, and Genetic

© Springer Nature Switzerland AG 2019
H. Florez et al. (Eds.): ICAI 2019, CCIS 1051, pp. 199–212, 2019.
https://doi.org/10.1007/978-3-030-32475-9_15

Algorithms (GA) [5]. One application of deep learning for stock prediction is the time-series prediction, which predicts the future value of a stock at a certain time. Prediction can be mainly classified as short-term (prediction for stock prices in seconds, minutes, and days ahead) and long-term (prediction for more than one year or beyond) [6].

In previous studies on ANN, indicators for stock prices are computed to capture temporal information or patterns and then used as input features for ANN [7–11]. Chen et al. investigated an LSTM-based model to predict stock prices on the Chinese stock market [12], suggesting that this model has the potential to predicting stock prices as it leads to improvements in stock prediction accuracy. Nelson et al. developed an LSTM-based method to predict stock prices and evaluated it with baseline methods such as random forest, multi-layer perceptron, and pseudo-random models [13]. They show that the LSTM-based model generates comparatively favorable predictions. Li et al. investigated the use of investor sentiment extracted forum posts as an input for a network along with historical market data to predict CSI300 (China Securities Index 300) and sentiment [14]. They show that the other model trained with numerical data and textual representations produced higher profits than did the model trained with only numerical data [15].

Several the recent development in the analysis of time-series involved the use of deep neural networks such as Convolution Neural Network (CNN), Recurrent Neural Network (RNN), and LSTM networks [16, 17]. Previous studies used LSTM-based models to predict stock prices [15, 18]. However, this prediction model, which we call *static LSTM*, is built using a fixed training data to predict test data, and the models are not retrained when new data is available. Thus, such models may not capture the most recent information existing in the new data to predict a stock's prices.

In this study, we proposed a method, which is called *dynamic LSTM*, to predict stock prices using LSTM by continuously augmenting the most recent data to the LSTM network to predict new prices. By this, the LSTM network is continuously updated with new actual stock prices to predict the future ones. We evaluate the method on the data set collected from the Apple (AAPL) stock prices during a 10-year period, General Electric (GA), China Petroleum & Chemical Corporation (SNP), and Facebook (FB) during a 5-year period. The results show that the proposed method outperforms others similar methods including the static LSTM method in predicting closing prices of the four stocks based on different performance metrics.

2 Long Short-Term Memory Network

LSTM was first introduced in 1997 to address several problems in previous networks such as the absence of notion of order of time in Feed Forward Neural Networks (FFNN) [19] and the *vanishing gradient* problem in RNN. This problem occurs when the gradient becomes smaller with each layer and turns out to be too small to have any effect in the deepest layers. The memory cell in LSTM allows to have a continuous gradient flow that helps address this vanishing gradient problem. A LSTM model can have one or many LSTM hidden layers. An LSTM network can be considered an enhanced version of RNN. RNN allows information to persist in the network by making use of feedback loop.

As shown in Fig. 1, in an LSTM network, current inputs and previously learned inputs are taken into consideration. An LSTM network consists of units called Memory cell unit or memory cell in the place of hidden layers. These cells have three gates including input gate, forget gate, output gate. These gates in an LSTM cell regulates the cell ability to add or remove information from cell state. Through memory cells and gates, an LSTM network can learn long-term dependencies. Recent studies investigated the use of LSTM networks to learn and capture temporal patterns for time-series analyses [20–22].

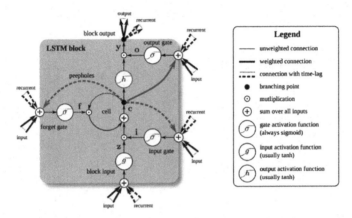

Fig. 1. An LSTM unit [23]

3   LSTM-Based Stock Price Prediction Methods

In this section, we describe the methods for constructing LSTM networks to predict stock prices. The methods consist of basic steps such as data collection and preprocessing, model building and training, and evaluation of prediction from the LSTM models.

The first part of our method is like the LSTM model for predicting stock prices proposed in [15]. The second part involves training the LSTM model with new actual stock prices. This part enables the model to capture the trend of the data in the closest time to the predicted time. Each of these steps is explained in these sections.

For the experiment purpose, closing prices of daily trading data are predicted. Flowcharts of the steps involved in predicting stock prices using LSTM models are shown in Fig. 2.

3.1   Model Flowcharts

Two methods are investigated in this study, the static and the dynamic models. The static model is not rebuilt when the stock price of the recently predicted date is available while the dynamic model is rebuilt using the stock price of the recently predicted date. The flowcharts of two models shown in Fig. 2 consist of three phases (data collection, data processing, and evaluation) with the dynamic model having an additional phase (rebuilding model).

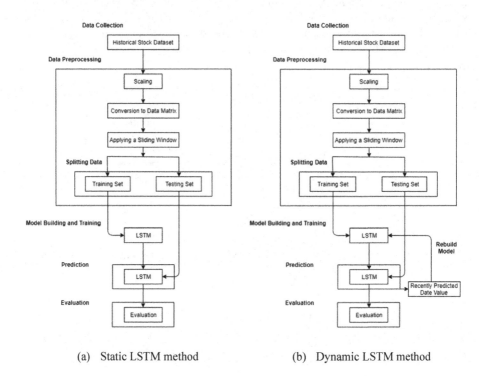

(a)   Static LSTM method   (b)   Dynamic LSTM method

Fig. 2. Flowcharts of the static and dynamic LSTM methods

- **Data Collection**: this phase is focused on retrieving and achieving data from sources such as Yahoo! Finance.
- **Data Preprocessing**: a linear transformation is applied to normalize the closing price and obtain the values between 0 and 1 for faster computation. The data is then converted into a matrix to which the sliding window approach is applied. The sliding window approach uses a window of n trading days of which the first $n-1$ days are used as input, and the last day (the nth day in the window) is used as output for the LSTM network. The window is then moved forward one day, and the input and output for the network are determined accordingly.
- **Evaluation**: when the training step is completed, the resulted models are used to generate predictions for the test set. The models are then evaluated using four performance measures which are defined in Sect. 4.4.
- **Rebuilding Model**: the recently predicted date's stock price will be added to the training set to rebuild the model.

4   Experimental Design

4.1   Dataset Preparation and Preprocessing

The stock data is collected automatically from Yahoo! Finance [24]. For a given stock collected, each data point consists of the date collected, trade volume, opening, closing, high, low, and adjusted closing prices. In this study, the closing price is used for prediction, and the sliding window approach is used for training the neural networks [18].

We collect and use data from four stocks listed in the NASDAQ stock market [25], including Apple (stock symbol AAPL), General Electric (GE), China Petroleum & Chemical Corporation (SNP), and Facebook (FB). For AAPL, the dates collected range from 05/21/2009 to 05/20/2019 (about 10 years) or 2511 data points each presenting a working day. The data of Apple stock prices is represented in Fig. 3 with the x-axis showing the number of trading days and the y-axis showing the closing price. For GE, SNP, and FB, the stock data is collected from 05/21/2014 to 05/20/2019 (5 years).

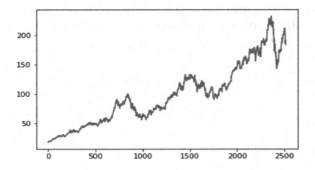

Fig. 3. Historical AAPL dataset

A linear transformation is applied to the stock price to normalize the value to the range between 0 and 1. The data is then converted into matrix for faster computation, and the sliding window approach is applied to the matrix.

Each stock dataset is split into 80% for training and 20% for testing. The training set is further divided into the training set (80%) and validation set (20%). After the preprocessing step, the sequential deep neural network models are developed and trained using the training data.

For the static LSTM method, the model is built once and is not updated with recently available stock data (see Fig. 2(a)). This model is used to predict stock prices for all days in the testing set.

For the dynamic LSTM method, the actual closing price of the recently predicted date is added to the training dataset to rebuild the model to make predictions for data in the testing set.

4.2   Framework and Hardware

In our experiments, we use Kensas and TensorFlow for implementing the LSTM network. Kensa is a high-level neural network API. Tensorflow is an open-source machine learning framework on which Keras is based. We use Python version 3.6.4, TensorFlow version 1.12.0, and Keras version 2.2.4 [26]. The PC platform used for training is Intel Core i7 8700 with RAM 16.00 GB, GPU NVIDIA Quadro P2000 with 5 GB VRAM. The models are trained for 7 days, about 158 h and 43 min, in normal conditions without interruption.

4.3   Training

For finding the best results in predicting stock prices, we decided to conduct training with different conditions and adjustments:

- Epoch ranging from 10–180 for the static LSTM model and 10–30 for the dynamic LSTM model.
- Experimenting 4 time periods to build training and testing models with the Apple stock: 10-year (05/21/2009 to 05/21/2019), 5-year (05/21/2014 to 05/20/2019), 2-year (05/21/2017 to 05/20/2019), 1-year (05/21/2018 to 05/20/2019) (all cases are divided into 80% training set and 20% testing set).
- Sliding window ranging from 5–30.

In building the LSTM model, we use hyper-parameters for layers of LSTM network as follows:

- Size of the cell state: 256
- Dense: 1
- Optimizer: 'ADAM' [27]

ADAM is an algorithm which is used to update the network weights during training which for different parameters an adaptive learning rates are computed. To prevent over-fitting in the neural network, a regularization technique known as dropout is used with the dropout rate representing the percentage of nodes dropped for each iteration.

4.4   Performance Measures

In this paper, we use the following measures including Mean Absolute Error (MAE), Mean Absolute Percentage Error (MAPE), Mean Squared Error (MSE), and relative Root Mean Squared Error (rRMSE) to evaluate the performance of prediction models. These measures are often used in the evaluation of stock price prediction [10]. These performance measures are computed as:

$$MAPE = \frac{1}{n} \sum_{t=1}^{n} \frac{|y_t - x_t|}{|y_t|} \times 100 \tag{1}$$

$$MAE = \frac{1}{n}\sum_{t=1}^{n}\frac{|y_t - x_t|}{|y_t|} \qquad (2)$$

$$rRMSE = \sqrt{\frac{1}{n}\sum_{t=1}^{n}\left(\frac{y_t - x_t}{y_t}\right)^2} \qquad (3)$$

$$MSE = \frac{1}{n}\sum_{t=1}^{n}(y_t - x_t)^2 \qquad (4)$$

Where y_t is the actual value at time t, x_t is the predicted value at time t, n is the number of days predicted.

5 Experimental Results

This section represents the implementation details, observations, results obtained from the experiment.

5.1 Performance of the Dynamic Model with Different Time Periods

This provides the results from our experiment using the dynamic model with different periods. We report performance measures in MAE, MAPE, rRMSE, and MSE. We train and test the model on four periods of data, 10-year (05/21/2009 to 05/21/2019), 5-year (05/21/2014 to 05/20/2019), 2-year (05/21/2017 to 05/20/2019), 1-year (05/21/2018 to 05/20/2019). The model is trained with the number of epochs increasing from 10 to 30.

Table 1 describes the prediction accuracy based on MAE, MAPE, rRMSE, and MSE obtained from the dynamic model for four periods. The first column shows the statistics, and the second to the fifth column show the values for four performance measures.

Table 1. Prediction performance of the static model

Statistics	MAE	MAPE	rRMSE	MSE
Max	0.0212	2.1201	0.0299	29.5886
Min	0.0144	1.4429	0.0212	14.9390
Mean	0.0169	1.6905	0.0242	19.7096
Median	0.0167	1.6642	0.0238	19.0654

Figure 4 depicts prediction accuracy based on MAPE, MAE, rRMSE, and MSE from the static model on 5-year period of the AAPL stock data for different epoch values and sliding window sizes. The x-axis represents the values of four performance measures, and y-axis represents the sliding window size (from 5 to 30).

The prediction accuracy from the model trained with the AAPL stock's 5-year period is more stable than those with other time periods using different epochs and sliding window sizes. As shown in Fig. 4, the dynamic model using the epoch of 30 generally produces better prediction performance than using other epoch values on the AAPL stock data. The window size of 5 days also results in the lowest error. Thus, we will use 5-year period, the epoch of 30, and the sliding window size of 5 days for further analysis.

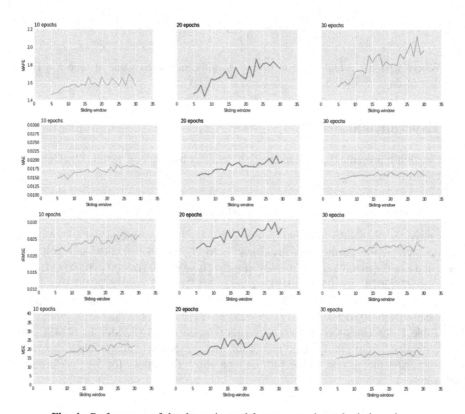

Fig. 4. Performance of the dynamic model across epochs and window sizes

5.2 Comparison Between the Static and Dynamic LSTM Models

The static and dynamic LSTM models are both built using the AAPL stock data for 5-year period from 05/21/2014 to 05/20/2019 and the epoch of 30. The results from these models are presented in Table 2 with the last two columns showing prediction accuracy in terms of MAPE and MSE. The dynamic model improved prediction accuracy significantly over the static model, reducing mean MAPE by 0.82 or 31.2% and mean MSE by 19.41 or 45.9%.

Table 2. Performance of the static and dynamic models

Model	Statistics	MAPE	MSE
Static	Min	1.77	21.57
	Max	4.02	97.64
	Mean	2.63	42.25
	Median	2.51	34.86
Dynamic	Min	1.55	16.72
	Max	2.12	29.59
	Mean	1.81	22.84
	Median	1.82	22.66

Average MAPE and MSE values across window sizes obtained by the models are depicted in Fig. 5, using the 5-year AAPL stock data and the epoch of 30. MAPE and MSE values produced by the dynamic model are much lower than those by the static model across almost window sizes. The dynamic model tends to be less dependent on window sizes than does the static model with the MAPE and MSE results from the latter fluctuating significantly across window sizes. MAPE ranges from 1.55 to 2.12 and MSE from 16.73 to 29.59 for the dynamic model while MAPE ranges from 1.77 to 4.02 and MSE from 21.57 to 97.64 for the static model.

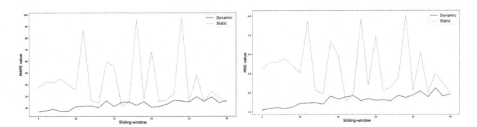

Fig. 5. MAPE and MSE from the static and dynamic models across sliding window sizes

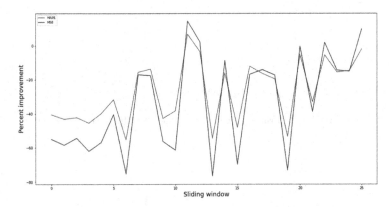

Fig. 6. Percent improvement in MAPE and MSE by the dynamic model over the static model, using the epoch of 30.

Figure 6 depicts percent improvements in MAPE and MSE across window sizes of the dynamic model over the static model using 5 year AAPL stock data and the epoch of 30. MAPE for the dynamic model decreases up to 55% while MSE for this model decreases up to 78% over the static model. These results show that the improvements in MSE are larger than those in MAPE by the dynamic model over the static model.

Actual and predicted closing prices of the AAPL stock are shown in Fig. 7 with those by the static model depicted in Fig. 7(a) and those by the dynamic model depicted in Fig. 7(b). The predicted closing prices by the dynamic model are closer to the actual prices than those by the static model. The predicted closing prices by the static model seem to fluctuate more significantly than those by the dynamic model. This observation is clearly reflected in MAPE and MSE results shown in Fig. 5.

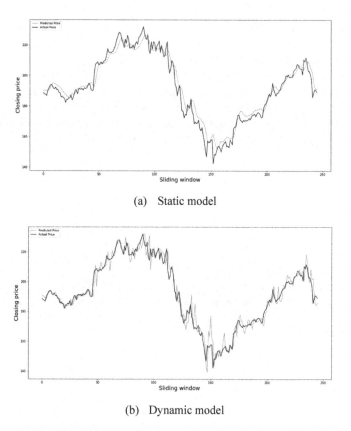

(a)   Static model

(b)   Dynamic model

Fig. 7. Actual and predicted closing prices by the models for the AAPL stock (30 epochs and window size of 5 days)

5.3 Comparison Between the Dynamic Model and Linear Methods of Prediction

We choose two linear methods including Standard Averaging (SA) with the sliding window of 5 days and Exponential Moving Average (EMA) with the decay of 0.5 to compare with the dynamic model. SA and EMA are computed using the following formulas:

$$\text{SA: } x_n = \frac{1}{w} \sum_{n-w}^{n-1} x_i \tag{5}$$

$$\text{EMA: } x_n = x_{n-1} \times (1 - d) + d \times EMA_{n-2} \tag{6}$$

Where x_n is the predicted value at the nth time, w is the size of sliding window in trading days, and d is the decay value.

Table 3. Performance measures obtained by three methods

Method	MAPE	MAE	rRMSE	MSE
SA-5	1.7984	0.0240	0.0395	21.3490
EMA-0.5	1.6424	0.0274	0.0305	17.7174
Dynamic LSTM model (30 epochs, sliding window size of 5)	1.5519	0.0155	0.0222	16.7154

Table 3 shows the prediction performance based on MAPE, MAE, rRMSE, and MSE of three methods using four-year AAPL stock prices for training and the following year for testing. The results for the dynamic LSTM model are the mean values obtained from using 30 epochs and the sliding window of 5 days.

As shown in Table 3, the dynamic model produces better predictions based on four performance measures than SA-5 and EMA-0.5. This model reduces MAPE, MAE, rRMSE, and MSE by 13.7%, 35.4%, 43.8%, and 21.7% over SA-5, respectively. Similarly, the model also reduces these performance measures by between 5.5% and 43.4% over EMA-05.

5.4 Evaluating the Methods Using GE, SNP, and FB Stock Prices

In this analysis, we run four models on GE, SNP, and FB stock data instead of APPL. The closing prices of these stocks are for 5-year period from 05/21/2014 to 05/20/2019.

The results from this analysis are shown in Table 4. The first column shows three stocks, the second columns shows for models, and the remain columns show the values for four performance measures.

Table 4. Prediction performance measures of the models on three stocks

Stock	Model	MAPE	MAE	rRMSE	MSE
GE	Dynamic model	**2.5722**	**0.0257**	**0.0359**	**0.2051**
	Static model	3.6577	0.0366	0.0474	0.2114
	SA-5	2.6805	0.0288	0.0415	0.2078
	EMA-0.5	2.6107	0.0268	0.0392	0.2062
SNP	Dynamic model	**1.6186**	**0.0162**	**0.0215**	**3.4050**
	Static model	1.6872	0.0169	0.0219	3.5745
	SA-5	1.7904	0.0182	0.0331	5.6721
	EMA-0.5	1.6748	0.0177	0.0308	4.2368
FB	Dynamic model	**1.9031**	**0.0190**	**0.0275**	**20.9702**
	Static model	1.9471	0.0195	0.0302	25.0147
	SA-5	2.9013	0.0278	0.0358	28.2258
	EMA-0.5	2.7281	0.0215	0.0311	25.3692

Across the stocks, the dynamic model consistently outperforms the other models based on all four performance measures. This model improves between 2% to 30% of MAPE, MAE, rRMSE, and MSE over the static model on three stocks. The reductions in prediction error by the dynamic are even higher when comparing to SA-5 and EMA-0.5. The static model outperforms SA-5 and EMA-0.5 when predicting SNP and FB, but it performs worse than these model on the GE stock. This result shows that this model is not consistent across stocks.

6 Conclusions

The proposed work involves the use of the dynamic LSTM model by retraining the model using newly added data for short-term prediction of stock prices. We comparatively evaluated this approach with the static LSTM model that is not retrained throughout the prediction process. The dataset of daily closing prices of four stocks including AAPL, GE, SNP, and FB was used for analysis.

The results show that stock prediction accuracy based on MAE, MAPE, rRMSE, and MSE obtained by the dynamic LSTM model is much better than that by the static LSTM model across four stocks investigated. The dynamic model also consistently outperforms the linear models SA-5 and EMA-0.5 when predicting four stocks. This model improves prediction accuracy by 45.9% on average based on MSE and 31.2% based on MAPE over the static model when predicting the AAPL stock.

Unlike the static model which is not designed to take advantage of the temporal information, the dynamic LSTM model takes into account both spatial and temporal information of a stock to predict its prices. This is a possible explanation for the advantage of this model in terms of prediction accuracy over the other models investigated in this study.

This study offers evidence that the LSTM network designed to incorporate temporal information has the potential for stock price prediction. Updating the LSTM network continuously with recently available data is a relevant approach to incorporating temporal information for the network.

As a future research direction, we plan to improve the dynamic LSTM model by using more stock-related factors and indicators such as simple moving average, momentum, relative strength index, and volume [28]). We are also interested in making predictions for longer time such one to ten days ahead of time.

References

1. Malkiel, B.G., Fama, E.F.: Efficient capital markets: a review of theory and empirical work. J. Finan. **25**(2), 383–417 (1970)
2. Miao, K., Chen, F., Zhao, Z.-G.: Stock price forecast based on bacterial colony RBF neural network. J. Qingdao Univ. (Nat. Sci. Ed.) **2**, 011 (2007)
3. Bollerslev, T.: Generalized autoregressive conditional heteroskedasticity. J. Econ. **31**, 307–327 (1986)
4. Box, G.E., Jenkins, G., Reinsel, G., Ljung, G.: Time Series Analysis: Forecasting and Control. John Wiley & Sons, Hoboken (2015)
5. Hadavandi, E., Ghanbari, A., Abbasian-Naghneh, S.: Developing an evolutionary neural network model for stock index forecasting. In: Huang, D.-S., McGinnity, M., Heutte, L., Zhang, X.-P. (eds.) ICIC 2010. CCIS, vol. 93, pp. 407–415. Springer, Heidelberg (2010). https://doi.org/10.1007/978-3-642-14831-6_54
6. Jain, S., Dr. Roopam, G., Dr. Asmita A.M., Stock price prediction on daily stock data. Int. J. Neural Netw. Adv. Appl., 5 (2018)
7. Göçken, M., Özçalıcı, M., Boru, A., Dosdoğru, A.T.: Integrating metaheuristics and artificial neural networks for improved stock price prediction. Expert Syst. Appl. **44**, 320–331 (2016)
8. Kim, K.-J., Han, I.: Genetic algorithms approach to feature discretization in artificial neural networks for the prediction of stock price index. Expert Syst. Appl. **19**, 125–132 (2000)
9. Lendasse, A., de Bodt, E., Wertz, V., Verleysen, M.: Non-linear financial time series forecasting - application to the Bel 20 stock market index. Eur. J. Econ. Soc. Syst. **14**(1), 81–91 (2000)
10. Patel, J., Shah, S., Thakkar, P., Kotecha, K.: Predicting stock market index using fusion of machine learning techniques. Expert Syst. Appl. **42**, 2162–2172 (2014)
11. Ticknor, J.L.: A bayesian regularized artificial neural network for stock market forecasting. Expert Syst. Appl. **40**, 5501–5506 (2013)
12. Chen, K., Zhou, Y., Dai, F.: A LSTM-based method for stock returns prediction: a case study of China stock market, In: 2015 IEEE International Conference on Big Data (Big Data) (2015)
13. Nelson, D.M.Q., Pereira, A.C.M., Oliveira, R.A.d.: Stock market's price movement prediction with LSTM neural networks. In: 2017 International Joint Conference on Neural Networks (IJCNN) (2017)
14. Chiang, W.-C., Enke, D., Wu, T., Wang, R.: An adaptive stock index trading decision support system. Expert Syst. Appl. **59**, 195–207 (2016)
15. Baek, Y., Kim, H.Y.: ModAugNet: a new forecasting framework for stock market index value with an overfitting prevention LSTM module and a prediction LSTM module. Expert Syst. Appl. **113**, 457–480 (2018)
16. Hochreiter, S., Schmidhuber, J.: Long short-term memory. Neural Comput. **9**(8), 1735–1780 (1997)

17. LeCunn, Y., Bengio, Y.: Convolutional networks for images, speech, and time-series, The Handbook of Brain Theory and Neural Networks. MIT Press, Cambridge (1995)
18. Selvin, S.: Stock price prediction using LSTM, RNN and CNN-sliding window model, In: International Conference on Advances in Computing, Communications and Informatics (ICACCI) (2017)
19. Svozil, D., Kvasnicka, V., Pospichal, J.: Introduction to multi-layer feed-forward neural networks. Chemom. Intell. Lab. Syst. **39**, 43–62 (1997)
20. Lipton, Z.C., Kale, D.C., Elkan, C., Wetzel, R.: Learning to diagnose with LSTM recurrent neural networks, In: ICLR 2016 (2016)
21. Sak, H., Senior, A., Beaufays, F.: Long short-term memory recurrent neural network architectures for large scale acoustic modeling, In: INTERSPEECH 2014 (2014)
22. Sundermeyer, M., Schlüter, R., Ney, H.: LSTM neural networks for language modeling, In: INTERSPEECH 2012 (2012)
23. Greff, K., Srivastava, R.K., Koutník, J., Steunebrink, B.R., Schmidhuber, J.: LSTM: a search space odyssey. IEEE Trans. Neural Netw. Learn. Syst. **28**, 2222–2232 (2017)
24. Finance, Y.: Yahoo! Finance. https://finance.yahoo.com/
25. Nasdaq, "Nasdaq". https://www.nasdaq.com/
26. Keras, "Keras". https://pypi.org/project/Keras/
27. Kingma, D.P., Ba, J.: Adam: a method for stochastic optimization. In: The 3rd International Conference for Learning Representations, San Diego (2014)
28. Kara, Y., Acar Boyacioglu, M., Baykan, Ö.K.: Predicting direction of stock price index movement using artificial neural networks and support vector machines: the sample of the Istanbul stock exchange. Expert syst. Appl. **38**, 5311–5319 (2011)

Health Care Information Systems

Hyperthermia Study in Breast Cancer Treatment Using a New Applicator

H. F. Guarnizo Mendez[1(✉)], M. A. Polochè Arango[2],
J. F. Coronel Rico[1], and T. A. Rubiano Suazo[1]

[1] Universidad El Bosque, Bogotá, Colombia
{hguarnizo, jcoronelr, trubianos}@unbosque.edu.co
[2] Universidad de San Buenaventura, Bogotá, Colombia
mpoloche@usbbog.edu.co

Abstract. A study about effects obtained by implementing an electromagnetic hyperthermia (EM) treatment model are presented. The study focus is the breast cancer treatment; this study is perform using an electromagnetic simulation model. A breast was modeled using the conductivity and permittivity of tissues such as fat, skin, lobules and muscle. The distribution of the power density was analyzed for two cases, first the applicator is not aligned with the tumor; second the applicator is aligned with the applicator. The distribution of the power density was analyzed inside the breast model when it was irradiated with two applicators at 2.45 GHz and 5 GHz. The second applicator proposed it is a new prototype of applicator developed in the Groove Gap Waveguide technology (GGW). The power density obtained in lobes, tumor and fat is compared and it was observed that tissues overheating that are close to the tumor can be avoided by optimizing the applicator location. The preliminary results indicate that with the new prototype of applicator developed in the Groove Gap Waveguide technology (GGW) is possible to focus the EM energy. Moreover, the tissues close to the tumor obtain a lower concentration of power density.

Keywords: Heat flow · Hyperthermia · Radiation · Applicator · Groove gap waveguide · Tissues

1 Introduction

The advances in cancer treatment have diminished the mortality rate, however breast cancer is leading reasons of death in the world [1]. The breast cancer death has the highest mortality rate among women [2]. In this field, the main treatments used are radiotherapy, immunotherapy, surgery (lumpectomy, mastectomy and axillary lymph node dissection), chemotherapy, drug and stem cells [3–5]. In addition to these methods, there is another method known as hyperthermia. The hyperthermia treatment involves raise the temperature of the body tissues affected by the cancer cells, one of the objectives of this treatment is that healthy tissues have a minimum temperature increase. In humans, this treatment is still under development [6] and in breast cancer cell lines [5]. In non-invasive electromagnetic hyperthermia, it is important to focus the electromagnetic field on the tissue affected by cancer, while damage surrounding

© Springer Nature Switzerland AG 2019
H. Florez et al. (Eds.): ICAI 2019, CCIS 1051, pp. 215–229, 2019.
https://doi.org/10.1007/978-3-030-32475-9_16

tissues is avoided [7, 8]. In the treatment of cancer with hyperthermia, tissue temperature is increased (up to 45 °C). Therefore, to obtain a more effective treatment and avoid temperature increase in other tissues, it is important to know the distributions of power density and the temperature. As reference, the temperature distribution obtained from a 3D model of a breast is presented in [7–9]. In the context of the breast cancer treatment with hyperthermia, the radiotherapy, hyperthermia, taxol and mastectomy were combined in a therapeutic program in [10]. In this therapeutic program, it was observed that tumor reoxygenation can be obtained with hyperthermia. In [11] is presented a treatment in which hyperthermia is used as neoadjuvant. In patients with breast cancer that is locally advanced, this treatment is a viable and well-tolerated strategy. In the work carried out by Tamer Refaat [12] on locally advanced or recurrent breast cancer, it was observed that when radiation therapy is implemented together with hyperthermia, the effectiveness of the treatment increased by 50%.

With the aim of improving the cancer treatment, new treatments have been perform combining current techniques, in [13] is mentioned that it was obtained a response of 39.8% in a treatment against the cancer with radiotherapy, while it was obtained a response of 54.9% when the treatment was carried out with hyperthermia and radiotherapy. In [14] hyperthermia is combined drugs therapies and some antibiotics, in this treatment was obtained more than an additive death of the cancer cells. In [15] hyperthermia is combined with irradiation and nanoparticles, this combination induces cell apoptosis. In [16] hyperthermia and chemotherapy are combining, the response of treatment improved from 61% (chemotherapy alone) a 76%. The chemotherapy and hyperthermia combination show an improvement in the remission percentage and the prognosis of patients' life. According to Sugimachi [17] the effectiveness of chemotherapy for esophageal cancer is 18.8% while combined with hyperthermia this is 41.2%.

In the hyperthermia treatment based on electromagnetic energy, waveguides or applicators (antennas) are used to couple the electromagnetic energy to the tissues. The applicators used are the array tapered microstrip patch antenna, array antipodal tapered slot, array of rectangular patch elements, antipodal Vivaldi antennas, miniaturized cavity-backed patch antenna, antenna with an embedded EBG structure, and applicators based on metamaterial technology [9, 18–25].

In this study, the distribution of power density in an electromagnetic model of breast radiated by microwaves at 2.45 GHz and 5 GHz is analyzed. The influence of the position of applicator, and the possible undesired effects by increases of temperature in the other parts of the breast is analyzed too. Two different applicators are presented, the first applicator is a waveguide, and the second applicator is a new prototype of applicator developed in the GGW (*Groove Gap Waveguide*) technology. The characteristics of the electromagnetic simulation are presented. The power density was obtained for two cases, first the applicator is placed at 2 cm over the breast, and 90° above the breast; Second the applicator is placed at 2 cm over the breast, and 135° above the breast.

2   Methodology

Breast's models have been implemented using different models. For example the breast model in [20] was carried out with skin, fatty and fibro-glandular tissue, muscle and tumor, in [26] the breast model was carried out with skin, muscle, glandular and fat and the breast model was carried out by Erdal [18] used skin, fat, lobes and tumor. In this paper, the lobes, fat, muscle and skin were used to create the breast model, so, the finite element method (FEM) solver of ANSYS Electronics® was used to carried out the electromagnetic simulation as show in [27]. The radius of the breast model was of 6.5 cm. The cube shape was chosen to represent the tumor model. The cube wide, high and large were selected to 0.8 cm. In the Table 1 is presented the simulation setup.

Table 1. HFSS configuration setup

Properties	Values
Maximum number of passes	10
Maximum delta S	0.01
Minimum converged passes	3
Order of basis function	Mixed order

To improve both the mesh accuracy and the convergence of the simulation, the values of the maximum delta S and minimum converged passes are presented in the Table 1 were chosen. Because the breast has different tissues and different electrical properties (permittivity (ε) and conductivity (σ)), mixed order basis function was chosen. *Mixed order assigns base function elements based on the need greater precision in different parts of the model.* Figure 1 shows the flow chart of the simulation process perform in HFSS®.

The electrical properties of the breast tissues [28, 29] for a frequency of 2.45 GHz are presented in the Table 2. These electrical properties are used in the electromagnetic simulation.

The electrical properties of the breast tissues [28, 30, 31] for a frequency of 5 GHz are presented in the Table 3. These electrical properties are used in the electromagnetic simulation.

3   Applicators at 2.45 GHz and 5 GHz

A waveguide WR340 is used like the first applicator at 2.45 GHz.

Figure 2 presents the second applicator at 2.45 GHz. The GGW (*Groove Gap Waveguide*) technology was used for the design of this applicator. The design procedure presented in [32, 33] was used to design the new prototype of applicator in GGW technology. The radiation system of the new prototype of applicator developed in the GGW technology is not shown in Fig. 2 because it is in patent process.

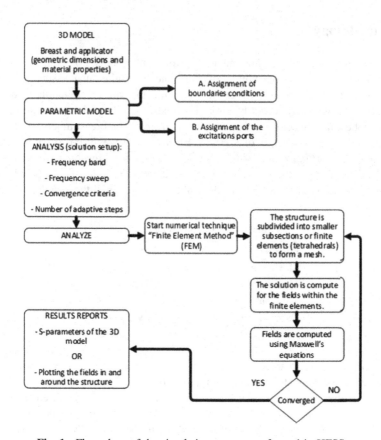

Fig. 1. Flow chart of the simulation process performed in HFSS.

Table 2. Electrical properties of the breast tissues

Tissue	Permittivity	Conductivity (S/m)
Muscle	52.7	1.7
Tumor	56	1.8
Fat	5.3	0.3
Skin	38	1.5
Lobes	35	1

Table 3. Electrical properties of the breast tissues

Tissue	Permittivity	Conductivity (S/m)
Muscle	50	4
Tumor	48	5.6
Fat	12	1
Skin	23	4
Lobes	29	3

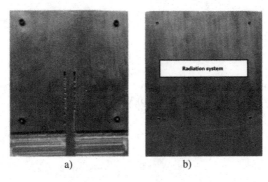

a)   b)

Fig. 2. GGW technology applicator at 2.45 GHz. (a) Top view, (b) Bottom view

4 Results

For the algorithm created, two positions of applicators have been analyzed. First, with the objective to consider the case where the applicator isn't aligned with the tumor, the applicator was situated at 90° over the breast (see Fig. 3). Then, the alignment between the applicator and the tumor was considered, that is, the applicator was situated at 135° over the breast (see Fig. 10). The two applicators were exited with a power of 1 W. Figure 3 shows the case when the applicators are 90° over the breast.

The breast was subdivided in 4 levels. In the level 1 are the fat, skin and a lobe. In the level 2 are the skin, fat and 5 lobes. In the level 3 are the fat, skin, 5 lobes and the tumor and in the level 4 are the skin, fat and 5 lobes (see Fig. 4).

From Figs. 5, 6, 7, 8 and 9 the first case is presented, that is, the applicator is 90° over the breast.

Figure 5 shows the power density obtained on the fat in the level 3 (see Fig. 4) at 2.45 GHz when the applicator was located 2 cm over the breast, the tumor is not aligned with the applicators.

In Fig. 5, it is observed that the highest level of power density is obtained with the waveguide applicator, the highest power density concentration is obtained with the waveguide applicator. However, the power density is more focused on the fat with the new prototype of applicator developed in the GGW technology.

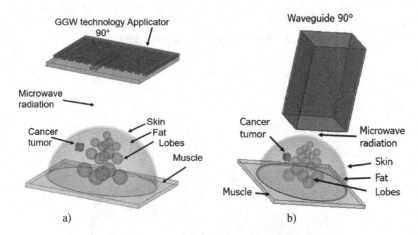

Fig. 3. 3D model for the applicators at 90° over the breast, the tumor is not aligned with the applicators. (a) GGW technology applicator, (b) Waveguide applicator.

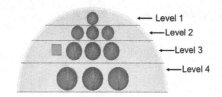

Fig. 4. 3D model and levels inside the breast.

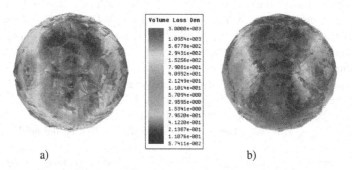

Fig. 5. Power density [kW/m³] in the level 3 (see Fig. 4) at 2.45 GHz. (a) new prototype of applicator developed in the GGW technology at 90°, (b) waveguide applicator at 90°.

In the Fig. 6, it is presented the power density on the lobes and tumor in the level 3 (see Fig. 4) at 2.45 GHz when the applicator was located 2 cm over the breast and the tumor is not aligned with the applicators.

Figure 6 shows that the highest power density was obtained on the lobes. This concentration of power density is observed in the Fig. 5 too. The highest power density

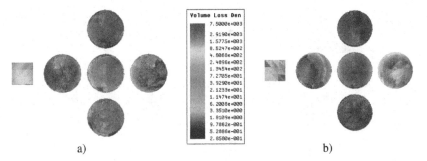

Fig. 6. Power density [kW/m³] in parts of the level 3 (see Fig. 4) at 2.45 GHz. (a) new prototype of applicator developed in the GGW technology at 90°, (b) waveguide applicator at 90°.

concentration (on the lobes) is obtained with the waveguide applicator. However, the highest power density on the tumor was obtained with the new prototype of applicator developed in the GGW technology and the lowest power density concentration on the lobes is obtained with the new prototype of applicator developed in the GGW technology also.

Figure 7, it is presented the power density on the fat in the level 4 (see Fig. 4) at 2.45 GHz when the applicator was located 2 cm over the breast, the tumor is not aligned with the applicators.

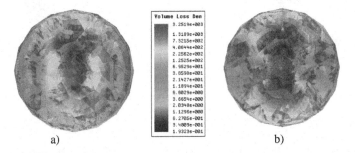

Fig. 7. Power density [kW/m³] in the level 4 (see Fig. 4) at 2.45 GHz. (a) new prototype of applicator developed in the GGW technology at 90°, (b) waveguide applicator at 90°.

In the Fig. 7, it is observed that with the new prototype of applicator developed in the GGW technology the power density is more focused. This power density focalization is important because most of the tissues below level 3 (see Fig. 4) will have lower levels of irradiation.

In the Fig. 8, it is presented the power density on the fat in the level 3 (see Fig. 4) at 5 GHz when the applicator was located 2 cm over the breast, the tumor is not aligned with the applicators.

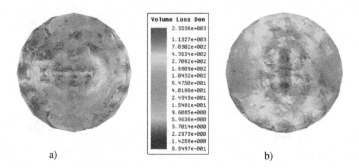

Fig. 8. Power density [kW/m³] in the level 3 (see Fig. 4) at 5 GHz. (a) new prototype of applicator developed in the GGW technology at 90°, (b) waveguide applicator at 90°.

Figure 8 shows that the highest power density was obtained with the waveguide applicator, this power density is obtained on the lobes. However, the power density is more focused on the left side of the fat with the new prototype of applicator developed in the GGW technology, in this side the tumor is located.

In the Fig. 9, it is presented the power density obtained on the lobes and tumor in the level 3 (see Fig. 4) at 5 GHz when the applicator was located 2 cm over the breast and the tumor is not aligned with the applicators.

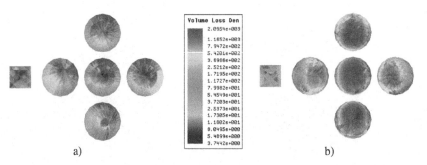

Fig. 9. Power density [kW/m³] in parts of the level 3 (see Fig. 4) at 5 GHz. (a) new prototype of applicator developed in the GGW technology at 90°, (b) waveguide applicator at 90°.

In Fig. 9(b), it is exhibited that the highest power density was obtained on the lobes at 5 GHz. This power density is observed in the Fig. 8 too. The highest power density on the lobes is obtained with the waveguide applicator, in this case the tumor obtains a lower concentration of power density. The highest power density concentration on the tumor is obtained with the new prototype of applicator developed in the GGW technology and the lowest power density concentration on the lobes is obtained with the new prototype of applicator developed in the GGW technology also.

Now, Figs. 11, 12 and 13 present the second case, that is, the applicator is 135° over the breast.

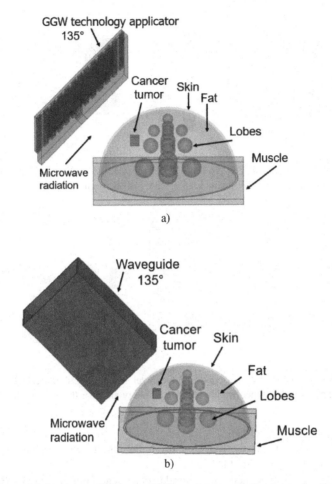

Fig. 10. 3D model for the applicators at 135° on the breast, the tumor is aligned with the applicators. (a) GGW technology applicator, (b) Waveguide applicator.

The case where the applicator is 135° over the breast is presented in the Fig. 10, the tumor is aligned with the applicators.

Figure 11 shows the power density obtained on the fat in the level 3 (see Fig. 4) at 2.45 GHz when the applicator was located 2 cm over the breast, the tumor is aligned with the applicators.

In the Fig. 11, it is displayed that the highest power density was obtained with the waveguide applicator. This power density is in the tissue situated directly below of the applicator.

In the Fig. 12, it is presented the power density obtained on the lobes and the tumor in the level 3 (see Fig. 4) at 2.45 GHz when the applicator was located 2 cm over the breast, the tumor is aligned with the applicators.

In the Fig. 12, it is displayed that the highest power density is obtained with the waveguide applicator. This power density is in the tumor. However. In the case of the

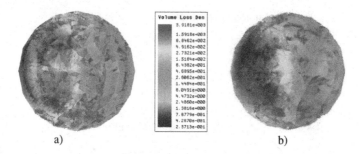

a)   b)

Fig. 11. Power density [kW/m^3] in the level 3 (see Fig. 4) at 2.45 GHz. (a) new prototype of applicator developed in the GGW technology at 135°, (b) waveguide applicator at 135°.

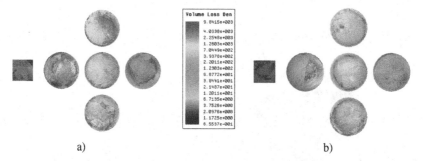

a)   b)

Fig. 12. Power density [kW/m^3] in parts of the level 3 (see Fig. 4) at 2.45 GHz. (a) new prototype of applicator developed in the GGW technology at 135°, (b) waveguide applicator at 135°.

waveguide applicator, the tissues that are close to the tumor obtain a high concentration of power density too (see Fig. 11).

In the Fig. 13, it is presented the power density on the fat in the level 4 (see Fig. 4) at 2.45 GHz when the applicator was located 2 cm over the breast, the tumor is aligned with the applicators.

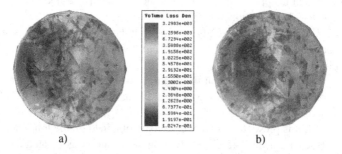

a)   b)

Fig. 13. Power density [kW/m^3] in the level 4 (see Fig. 4) at 2.45 GHz. The applicators are located 2 cm over the breast, the tumor is aligned with the applicators. (a) new prototype of applicator developed in the GGW technology at 135°, (b) waveguide applicator at 135°.

In the Fig. 13, it is observed that the power density is more focused with the new prototype of applicator developed in the GGW technology. This power density focalization is important because most of the tissues below level 4 (see Fig. 4) will have lower levels of irradiation.

Figure 14 shows the power density obtained on the fat in the level 3 (see Fig. 4) at 5 GHz when the applicator was located 2 cm over the breast, the tumor is aligned with the applicators.

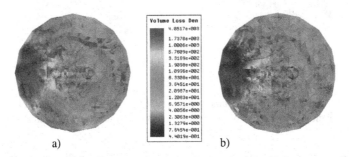

a)   b)

Fig. 14. Power density [kW/m³] in the level 3 (see Fig. 4) 5 GHz. (a) new prototype of applicator developed in the GGW technology at 135°, (b) waveguide applicator at 135°.

In the Fig. 14, it is observed that with the waveguide applicator is obtained the highest power density. This power density is in the tissue (fat and skin) located below of the applicator.

In the Fig. 15, it is presented the power density on the lobes and the tumor in the level 3 (see Fig. 4) at 5 GHz when the applicator was located 2 cm over the breast, the tumor is aligned with the applicators.

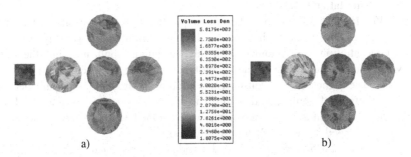

a)   b)

Fig. 15. Power density [kW/m³] in parts of the level 3 (see Fig. 4) at 5 GHz. (a) new prototype of applicator developed in the GGW technology at 135°, (b) waveguide applicator at 135°.

In the Fig. 15, it is observed that with the waveguide applicator is obtained the highest power density. This power density is in the tumor. However. In the case of the waveguide applicator, the tissues that are close to the tumor obtain a high concentration of power density too (see Fig. 14).

In the Fig. 16, it is presented the power density on the lobes and the tumor in the level 4 (see Fig. 4) at 5 GHz when the applicator was located 2 cm over the breast, the tumor is aligned with the applicators.

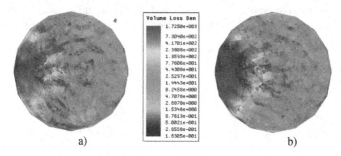

a)   b)

Fig. 16. Power density [kW/m^3] in parts of the level 4 (see Fig. 4) at 5 GHz. (a) new prototype of applicator developed in the GGW technology at 135°, (b) waveguide applicator at 135°.

In the Fig. 16, it is observed that with the waveguide applicator is obtained the highest power density. However, in the case of the new prototype of applicator developed in the GGW technology the power density is more focused. This power density focalization is important because most of the tissues below level 4 (see Fig. 4) will have lower levels of irradiation.

5 Conclusions

This paper presented the power density concentration on a breast affected by cancer when it is radiated with two applicators. The results show that highest power density is absorbed for the fat and the lobes.

At 2.45 GHz and 5 GHz and when the applicator is not totally aligned with the tumor, the lobes absorb the highest power density concentration. The highest power density concentration was obtained with the waveguide applicator, but the power density was more focused with the new prototype of applicator developed in the GGW technology. The highest power density concentration on the tumor was obtained with the new prototype of applicator developed in the GGW technology and the lowest power density concentration on the lobes was obtained with the new prototype of applicator developed in the GGW technology also.

At 2.45 GHz and 5 GHz and when the applicator is aligned with the tumor the highest power density concentration was obtained with the waveguide applicator. The highest power density concentration is obtained in the tissue located below of the applicator. This power density was obtained on the tumor, but in the case of the waveguide applicator, the tissues that are close to the tumor obtain a high concentration of power density too. The power density was more focused with the new prototype of applicator developed in the GGW technology.

The results indicate that with the new prototype of applicator developed in the GGW technology, it is possible to obtain the best EM energy focus at 2.45 GHz and 5 GHz for the two cases, that is, the applicator is 90° over the breast and it is aligned with the tumor and the second case, the applicator is 135° over the breast and it is aligned with the tumor. Moreover, in the case when the new prototype of applicator developed in the GGW technology is used, the tissues that are close to the tumor obtain a lower concentration of power density in comparison with the concentration of power density in the tumor.

Additionally, in the 2 cases, it is observed to improve the treatment effectiveness with hyperthermia, the applicator location is important because the damage to healthy cells can be avoided.

Currently, the process for the miniaturization of the new prototype of applicator developed in the GGW technology is being designed.

Then, an array of miniaturized new prototype of applicator developed in the GGW technology will be carried out in order to obtain a higher concentration of the electromagnetic energy.

The new prototype of applicator developed in the GGW technology at 5 GHz is in manufacturing process.

References

1. Jemal, A., Bray, F., Center, M.M., Ferlay, J., Ward, E., Forman, D.: Global cancer statistics. Ca-Cancer J. Clin. **61**(2), 69–90 (2011)
2. Bray, F., Ferlay, J., Soerjomataram, I., Siegel, R.L., Torre, L.A., Jemal, A.: Global cancer statistics 2018: GLOBOCAN estimates of incidence and mortality worldwide for 36 cancers in 185 countries. CA Cancer J. Clin. **68**(6), 394–424 (2018)
3. Naz, S., Shahzad, H., Ali, A., Zia, M.: Nanomaterials as nanocarriers: a critical assessment why these are multi-chore vanquisher in breast cancer treatment. Artif. Cells, Nanomedicine Biotechnol. **46**(5), 899–916 (2018)
4. Chalakur-Ramireddy, N.K.R., Pakala, S.B.: Combined drug therapeutic strategies for the effective treatment of Triple Negative. Breast Cancer **38**(1), BSR20171357 (2018)
5. Lee, T.H., Bu, J., Kim, B.H., Poellmann, M.J., Hong, S., Hyun, S.H.: Sub-lethal hyperthermia promotes epithelial-to-mesenchymal-like transition of breast cancer cells: implication of the synergy between hyperthermia and chemotherapy. RSC Adv. **9**(1), 52–57 (2019)
6. Chicheł, A., Skowronek, J., Kubaszewska, M., Kanikowski, M.: Hyperthermia - description of a method and a review of clinical applications. Rep. Pract. Oncol. Radiother. **12**(5), 267–275 (2007)
7. Nguyen, P.T., Abbosh, A.M.: Focusing techniques in breast cancer treatment using non-invasive microwave hyperthermia. ISAP **2015**, 1–3 (2015)
8. Iero, D.A.M., Crocco, L., Isernia, T., Korkmaz, E.: Optimal focused electromagnetic hyperthermia treatment of breast cancer, In: 2016 10th European Conference Antennas Propagation, EuCAP 2016, pp. 1–2 (2016)
9. Merunka, I., Fiser, O., Vojackova, L., Vrba, J., Vrba, D.: Utilization potential of balanced antipodal Vivaldi antenna for microwave hyperthermia treatment of breast cancer. In: 8th European Conference Antennas Propagation, EuCAP 2014, vol. 6, no. EuCAP, pp. 706–710 (2014)

10. El, J., et al.: Thermochemoradiotherapy improves oxygenation in locally advanced breast cancer. Clin. Cancer Res. **10**(13), 4287–4293 (2004)
11. Vujaskovic, Z., et al.: A phase I/II study of neoadjuvant liposomal doxorubicin, paclitaxel, and hyperthermia in locally advanced breast cancer. Int. J. Hyperth. **26**(5), 514–521 (2010)
12. Refaat, T., et al.: Hyperthermia and radiation therapy for locally advanced or recurrent breast cancer. Breast **24**(4), 418–425 (2015)
13. Nguyen, P.T., Abbosh, A., Crozier, S.: Microwave hyperthermia for breast cancer treatment using electromagnetic and thermal focusing tested on realistic breast models and antenna arrays. IEEE Trans. Antennas Propag. **63**(10), 4426–4434 (2015)
14. Kampinga, H.H.: Cell biological effects of hyperthermia alone or combined with radiation or drugs: a short introduction to newcomers in the field. Int. J. Hyperth. **22**(3), 191–196 (2006)
15. Ghaleh, H.E.G., Zarei, L., Motlagh, B.M., Jabbari, N.: Using CuO nanoparticles and hyperthermia in radiotherapy of MCF-7 cell line: synergistic effect in cancer therapy. Artif. Cells Nanomed. Biotechnol. **47**(1), 1396–1403 (2019)
16. Hurwitz, M., Stauffer, P.: Hyperthermia, radiation and chemotherapy: the role of heat in multidisciplinary cancer care. Semin. Oncol. **41**(6), 714–729 (2014)
17. Kitamura, K., Sugimachi, K.: Thermo-radiotherapy combined with Chemotherapy for Esophageal Tumors. In: Thermoradiotherapy and Thermochemotherapy, 2nd edn., 85–94 (1996)
18. Korkmaz, E., Isık, O., Sagkol, H.: A directive antenna array applicator for focused electromagnetic hyperthermia treatment of breast cancer. In: 2015 9th European Conference Antennas Propagation, vol. 1, pp. 1–4 (2015)
19. Chakaravarthi, G., Arunachalam, K.: Design and characterisation of miniaturised cavity-backed patch antenna for microwave hyperthermia. Int. J. Hyperth. **31**(7), 737–748 (2015)
20. Curto, S., Ruvio, G., Ammann, M.J., Prakash, P.: A wearable applicator for microwave hyperthermia of breast cancer: performance evaluation with patient-specific anatomic models. In: Proceedings 2015 International Conference Electromagnetic Advance Application ICEAA 2015, pp. 1159–1162 (2015)
21. Merunka, I., Fiser, O., Vojackova, L., Vrba, J., Vrba, D.: Microwave hyperthermia treatment of neck cancer using eight UWB antennas. In: European Microwave Week 2014: Connecting the Future, EuMW 2014 - Conference Proceedings; EuMC 2014: 44th European Microwave Conference, pp. 790–793 (2014)
22. Li, J., Wang, X.: Comparison of two small circularly polarized antennas for focused microwave hyperthermia. In: 2019 13th European Conference Antennas Propagation, no. EuCAP, pp. 5–8 (2019)
23. Stang, J., Haynes, M., Carson, P., Moghaddam, M.: A preclinical system prototype for focused microwave thermal therapy of the breast. IEEE Trans. Biomed. Eng. **59**(9), 2431–2438 (2012)
24. Vrba, D., Vrba, J.: Applicators for local microwave hyperthermia based on metamaterial technology. In: 8th European Conference Antennas Propagation, EuCAP 2014, no. EuCAP, pp. 68–71 (2014)
25. Tao, Y., Wang, G.: Conformal hyperthermia of superficial tumor with left-handed metamaterial lens applicator. IEEE Trans. Biomed. Eng. **59**(12), 3525–3530 (2012)
26. Nguyen, P.T., Abbosh, A.M., Crozier, S.: Realistic simulation environment to test microwave hyperthermia treatment of breast cancer. In: IEEE Antennas Propagation Society AP-S International Symposium, pp. 1188–1189 (2014)
27. Guarnizo Mendez, H.F., Pochè Arango, M.A., Pantoja Acosta, J.J.: Hyperthermia Study in Breast Cancer Treatment. In: Figueroa-García, J.C., Villegas, J.G., Orozco-Arroyave, J.R., Maya Duque, P.A. (eds.) WEA 2018. CCIS, vol. 916, pp. 256–267. Springer, Cham (2018). https://doi.org/10.1007/978-3-030-00353-1_23

28. Porter, E., Fakhoury, J., Oprisor, R., Coates, M., Popovic, M.: Improved tissue phantoms for experimental validation of microwave breast cancer detection. In: Antennas Propagation (EuCAP), 2010 Proceedings Fourth European Conference, pp. 1–5 (2010)
29. Nikita, K.S.: Handbook of Biomedical Telemetry, 1st edn. John Wiley & Sons Inc, Hoboken (2014)
30. Miklavčič, D., Hart, F.X.: Electric properties of tissues. Wiley Encycl. Biomed. Eng., 1–12 (2006)
31. Gabriel, S., Lau, R.W., Gabriel, C.: The dielectric properties of biological tissues: II. Measurements in the frequency range 10 Hz to 20 GHz. Phys. Med. Biol. **41**(11), 2251–2269 (1996)
32. Bohórquez, J.C., et al.: Planar substrate integrated waveguide cavity-backed antenna. IEEE Antennas Wirel. Propag. Lett. **8**, 1139–1142 (2009)
33. Nawaz, M.I., Huiling, Z., Kashif, M.: Substrate integrated waveguide (SIW) to microstrip transition at X-Band. In: 2014 International Conference Circuits, System Control, pp. 61–63 (2014)

Manual Segmentation Errors in Medical Imaging. Proposing a Reliable Gold Standard

Fernando Yepes-Calderon[1]([✉]) [ID] and J. Gordon McComb[1,2] [ID]

[1] Neurosurgery Division, Children's Hospital Los Angeles,
1300N Vermont Ave, 90027 Los Angeles, CA, USA
fernandoyepesc@gmail.com
[2] Keck School of Medicine, University of Southern California,
1975 Zonal Ave, 90033 Los Angeles, CA, USA

Abstract. Manual segmentation is ubiquitous in modern medical imaging. It is a tedious and time-consuming process that is also operator-dependent and due to its low reproducibility, presents to specialist a challenge to reach consensus when diagnosing from an image. In the diagnosis of several abnormalities, geometrical features such as distances, curvatures, volumes, areas, and shapes are used to derive verdicts. These features are only quantifiable if the measuring structures can be separated from other elements in the image. The process of manual segmentation provides the analysis with a response to the question of the limits, and those limits are not easy to identify. Despite all the mentioned drawbacks, manual segmentation is still used in medical imaging analysis or employed to validate automatic or semi-automatic methods. Intending to quantify the operator variability of the process, we have created a controlled environment and run segmentations on known volumes scanned with Magnetic Resonance. The strategy proposed here suggests a mechanism to establish gold standards for geometrical readings in medical imaging; thus measuring instruments can be analyzed and certified for the task.

Keywords: Segmentation standards · Medical image quantification · Repeatable segmentations

1 Introduction

In medical imaging, radiologists have to identify the boundaries of structures present in the visual information. The work is performed in a cognitive process that involves apriori knowledge of the form, variations associated with the point of view, understanding of the possible pathogenic causes of deformation, textures, intensities, modalities, consideration of the concept of scale and awareness of the changes in the image introduced by modifications of the acquisition protocols [4]. Naturally, in the presence of this abundant set of qualitative factors,

© Springer Nature Switzerland AG 2019
H. Florez et al. (Eds.): ICAI 2019, CCIS 1051, pp. 230–241, 2019.
https://doi.org/10.1007/978-3-030-32475-9_17

verdicts are operator dependent and diverse [6,8,11], a fact that may mislead treatments and negatively affect the health of the patients. Unification of concepts is desired, but utopic. One possible strategy consists in minimizing the qualitative insights and use more deterministic features [10,13]. Ideally, when all the criteria used in a verdict are turned into deterministic features, the final verdict will also be deterministic and, as in mathematical formulation, each possible scenario will have one and only one outcome. One instrument created as a consequence of including deterministic facts in the creation of verdicts is the manual segmentation (Mseg). In Mseg, an operator delineates the boundaries of the analyzing structures, and this definition of limits provides the quantifying elements with the necessary starting and stopping conditions. Currently, Mseg is a standard in radiology units when quantifications are needed; moreover, scientists have proposed a myriad of automatic and semi-automatic segmentation methods [1,3,9] and used MSeg as a validation mechanism. Far of being perfect, the Mseg also involves uncertainty due to the involvement of all qualitative factors previously mentioned by the moment of defining where the separating line should go. Automatic segmentation approaches may have the desired repeatability but, since only Mseg is used as a gold standard to test the accuracy, automatic and semi-automatic methods are also dubious.

Here we demonstrate how Mseg can yield results in that the uncertainty moves the readings around important decision boundaries that might mislead the course of treatments and also, we propose a strategy to measure the accuracy of automatic and semi-automatic segmentation instruments, other than the time-consuming and operator-dependent Mseg.

2   Materials and Methods

Randomly selected images of the brain lateral ventricles were manually segmented to create 3D models of the structure. The volume of the 3D models was estimated using an electronic device that reads water displacement (WD). The 3D models were used to create MRI phantoms that were scanned using a 3T Phillips Scanner using isometric voxels of 1 mm. Four trained operators performed Mseg in the three views, using an assisting software that allows the operator to focus solely on the drawing tasks. Modality variability was calculated using the volume of the 3D models – estimated by WD – as gold standards. Since the WD device plays a crucial role in the determination of Mseg errors, details of its construction are provided.

2.1   Mseg Assisting Software

The MSeg process involves tasks that are not related to drawing but are also essential to accomplish the activity. These collateral activities refer to loading images, moving through slices, saving the mask obtained from the current slice, concatenating the masks, and saving the created volume. Since our purpose is to qualify and quantify the process of segmentation, the mentioned collateral activities are fully automated; therefore, the operator is forced to be concentrated in finding and delineating the region of interest in every slice. Besides, we have accounted for operator fatigue with timers that allow the operator to work 30 min and force a 10 min rest before restarting the segmentation. These values were empirically chosen after receiving feedback from operators regarding their exhaustion times. The software monitors some activities performed by the operator and records the times provided before and after every taken action. The Listing 1.1 shows the main function of the Mseg assisting tool.

```
1  function main(dir , nfiles , myDir)
2  {
3      mtime = getTime();
4      list = getFileList(dir);
5      for (i=0; i<list.length; i++)
6      {
7          showProgress(i, nfiles);
8          path = dir+list[i];
9          print("Dealing with subject "+list[i]+" in "+path);
10         if (isOpen("Log"))
11         {
12             selectWindow("Log");
13             setLocation(0,0);
14         }
15         views = newArray("AX","SG","CR");
16         runPatient(path , myDir , views);
17     }
18 }
```

Listing 1.1. Main javascript code to automate collateral tasks of Mseg

The main function receives a pointer to the folder where the images are saved ($ndir$), the number of images in the directory ($nfiles$) and a path where the masking results are going be saved ($myDir$). In line 4, the name of the images are extracted and put in a list. In line 5 the for loop visits every image in the given folder. In line 10, the backup for consistent recovery after duty cycle is applied. In line 15 a switch to define the views to be visited and finally, in line 16, the system launches the processing of the selected image, named patient within the code.

2.2   Brain Ventricles 3D Models and Phantoms

The Fig. 1 shows the process of 3D modeling and MRI phantom creation for a normal subject and two cases of hydrocephalus. The ventricles are segmented from a T1 image of randomly selected subjects. The resulting masks are moved to stereolithography (STL) format. Next, the STL files are loaded in Cura using a resolution of 0.1 mm in all axis. Then, the models are moved to gcode format before printed in a Monoprice Ultimate 3D printer Device using 0.1 mm of precision and 20% for structural filling. From this moment, a physical-measurable object exists with dimensions in the real world; however, its form is complex, and analytical-measuring methods are unpractical. With the physical models, MRI phantoms are created. The process consists in suspending the volume in a solution jelly:water (1g:3ml). The inert material of the 3D model surrounded by the watery fixation creates the needed contrast on an MRI scanner from where images are obtained. From this point on, all geometric measurements done on the images can be referred to the ones done in the physical volume. The brain-ventricular models were extracted from healthy patients in ages [1, 6, 15, 24, 48, 66, 78, 96, 114] months old. Additionally, two hydrocephalus patients underwent the same process.

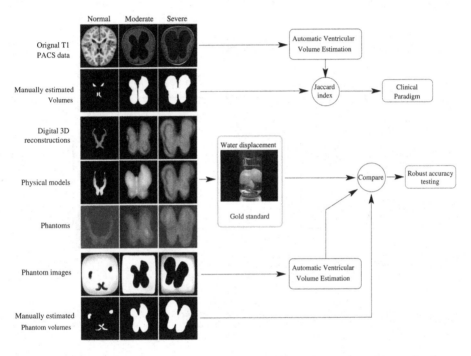

Fig. 1. Phantom creation process. The clinical paradigm (on top) is the standard procedure to validate automatic or semiautomatic segmentation tools. Below, the scheme of a more reliable gold standard and its use.

2.3   The Water Displacement Measuring Device

The water displacement (WD) was chosen as the method to measure the irregular volumes of the 3D reproduced ventricles. The conceptual design of the device is shown in the Fig. 2. The montage consists of a measuring [MR] and a sample recipient [SR] both hosting electrical water pumps [WP-01] and [WP-02]. The recipients rest on digital scales [DS-01] and [DS-02] with a precision of 0.1 ml. The [SR] has a non-contact-level sensor [NC-LS] which works as a digital switch. The [NC-LS] is on when water reaches or exceeds the sensor level; it is off otherwise. The pumps are connected to two pipes in a way that depleting one recipient fills the other. The tube that drains [SR] is connected to a flow sensor [FS] that produces pulses when the water moves. The [FS] is specified to read fluxes in the range of 0.1–3 L/min. This hardware is controlled with a Beagle Bone Black (Programmable device) that recovers logical TTL signals in its sensor ports (magenta lines) and use the control ports (black lines) to activate/deactivate the pumps over the residential power distribution (120 V-60 Hz) through transistorized power interfaces.

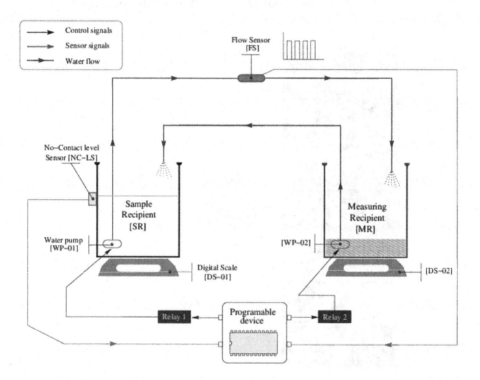

Fig. 2. Design of the water-displacement-measuring device.

To start, the water level in [SR] is below the [NC-LS] sensor; thus, [NC-LS] sends a 0 through its sensor line. Then [WP-02] is activated to push water on [SR] until the water reaches the [NC-LS] level. At this moment the programmable device will see a logic 1 in the [NC-LS] sensor line. Next, [WP-01] is activated to deplete water from [SR] to find the zero-level. At that moment, the programmable device sees a zero in the [NC-LS] line. Then, the sample is submerged in [SR] raising the water level above the [NC-LS] sensor forcing a logic 1 in the sensor line. Next, the [WP-01] is turned on, and the programmable device activates the pulse counting in the [FS] sensor line. The water pumping from [SR] will continue until the water level reaches the zero-level. The volume of the displaced water is equal to the volume of the submerged object, and it will be captured by the pulsating pattern yielded by the [FS] sensor (See Fig. 3-A). Because the 3D volumes are built with gaps in their internal structure, sinkers are needed to eliminate the buoyancy.

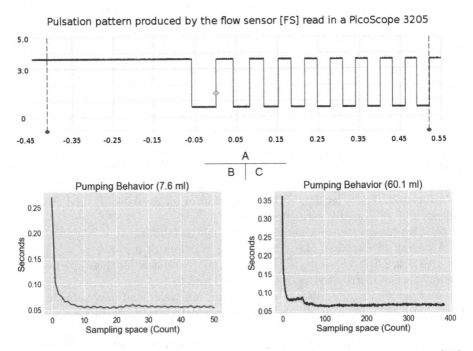

Fig. 3. The pulsation pattern of the flow sensor. In panel A, the signature of the [FS] device. In panels B and C, plots of the timing-slots of two different volumes showing the irregular pumping performance of the WP-01 device.

2.4 Water-Displacement-Device's Precision Estimation

Marbles of different sizes are utilized to accurately estimate the water's flux traversing the [FS] device. The marbles' volume is determined analytically by measuring the diameter (D) with a caliper of precision 0.1 mm and using $V = \frac{1*\pi*D^3}{6}$. The uncertainty of the device is estimated by measuring known volumes –the marbles– in the range of the studied ventricles. Each uncertainty point is calculated by averaging five readings.

2.5 Tuning Strategy

In Fig. 3-B,C, The pump [WP-01] does not uniformly move the water. The strategy consists of dynamically estimating the variations of flux that are captured by our system as timing deviations in the pulsating pattern given by [FS]. To this purpose, we have created a tuning routine that consists of measuring all the available volumes and combinations of them to cover the working range. In every experiment, the challenge dwells in estimating the flux per time slot, so the small contributions per slot reach the known volume. In every tuning experiment, we end by having a timing scheme and a flux per slot. We combine all contribution of the supervised tests in two histogram-look-up tables where each bin is loaded with the mean value of all its contributors for timing and flux. Further unknown volumes will produce a timing scheme that will be translated to an estimated volume through the previously created look-up tables.

In each marble's timing array T_p, it is possible to estimate the flux ($F_p[i]$) in the timing slot ($tslot_i$) by

$$F_p[i] = \frac{tslot_i}{time_{total}} * RV \ \forall \ i \in len(T_p) \tag{1}$$

Where RV corresponds to the analytically estimated volume of the tuning marble.

At the end of this process, every timing array T_p has an array of fluxes F_p associated. Then, let T_{up} be the collection of all available T_p and F_{up} the collection of all available estimated fluxes F_p.

Now we can create the timing look-up table as follows.

An array of distances A_d is built using K_i slots of distances $d = \frac{1}{2^{2j}}$ for $j = [1, 1.5, 2, 2.5, 3, 3.5]$ and $i = [1, 2, 2, 4, 8, 16]$. Note how all these fractions of the unity when distributed as ordered by K_i add to 1.

Next, let m_u, t_{min} and t_{max} be the mean, min value and max value in T_{pu}. From here, the distances $d1$ and $d2$ are calculated as $d_1 = m_u - t_{min}$ and $d_2 = t_{max} - m_u$.

The timing look-up table T_{lut} is created by concatenating the arrays $A_1 = d_1(A_d)$ and $A_2 = d_2(A_d)$.

For the flux look up table, assume $R_{(a,b)}$ to be all indexes i where $T[i]_{pu} \in range(a, b)$, where a,b are times in T_{lut}, then:

$$F^{a,b}[i] = \sum F[i]_{up} \ \forall \ i \in R_{(a,b)} \tag{2}$$

When $F^{a,b}$ cover all possible ranges in T_{lut}, it becomes F_{lut}.

From this point on, it is possible to estimate any new volume by obtaining its pulsating pattern with the WD device and using the look-up tables T_{lut}, F_{lut}.

3   Results

3.1   Instrument Tuning Data

The Tables 1 and 2 should be observed together. The Real Vol value is obtained analytically using the diameter of the marble, and its associated uncertainty is related to the propagation of the caliper's precision. The records on these tables correspond to calculations done on the marbles (distinct). Bigger volumes can be reached by submerging several marbles per experiment.

One can calculate the average flux per slot produced by the flow sensor thanks to the analytically estimated volume (Real Vol in the tables) of the object.

Table 1. Marbles' volumes, pulse counting in the flux sensor and estimated fluxes.

Count (pulses)	Model	Real Vol (ml)	MeanFlux (ml/s)	Mean Flux/Slot (ml)
61	Ma1	8.1 ± 1.0	4.4 ± 0.5	0.133 ± 0.016
58	Ma2	8.0 ± 1.0	4.5 ± 0.5	0.138 ± 0.017
66	Ma3	7.3 ± 0.9	3.5 ± 0.4	0.111 ± 0.014
65	Ma4	7.6 ± 0.9	3.7 ± 0.5	0.117 ± 0.014
63	Ma5	7.9 ± 1.0	4.1 ± 0.5	0.125 ± 0.015
252	Ma6	35.6 ± 0.9	4.7 ± 0.04	0.141 ± 0.001
445	Ma7	60.1 ± 0.9	4.4 ± 0.03	0.135 ± 0.001

Table 2. Marbles' volumes and time slot statistics per experiment

Count (pulses)	Model	Real Vol (ml)	Max time	Mean time	Min time	Std time
61	Ma1	8.1 ± 1.0	0.037157	0.030073	0.027922	0.000779
58	Ma2	8.0 ± 1.0	0.037157	0.030398	0.025835	0.000993
66	Ma3	7.3 ± 0.9	0.037157	0.031326	0.027922	0.000707
65	Ma4	7.6 ± 0.9	0.037157	0.031458	0.027922	0.001300
63	Ma5	7.9 ± 1.0	0.037157	0.030483	0.027922	0.000795
252	Ma6	35.6 ± 0.9	0.033232	0.029899	0.025774	0.000930
445	Ma7	60.1 ± 0.9	0.034960	0.030765	0.026517	0.000837

The differences in the time per pulse – time stats in Table 2 – suggest an irregular operation in the pumping device that tends to stabilize itself when the pump is operative for extended periods. We use the timing records per slot in a strategy that creates a look-up-table. During volume estimation, the look-up table is queried with a time – slot time – to retrieve the displaced water in milliliters.

3.2 Estimated Precision in the Working Range

The device's precision is summarized in Fig. 4. The comparisons with the real volumes suggest an exponential adjustment; however, the reader should consider that the x-axis has been equalized to favor the visualization. In the current approach, the uncertainty has been used constant depending on the read value, e.g., if the estimated volume is 18 ml, the uncertainty is 4.7%. Also, observe in the absolute-error columns how the obtained values are below the precision of the scales.

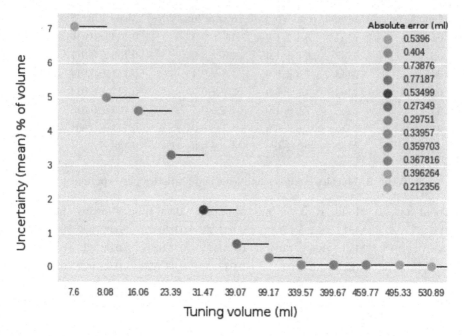

Fig. 4. After estimating the volumes with the look-up tables, it is possible to calculate the absolute and percent errors on each experiment by comparing the reading with the analytically obtained volume. Note how the device is more precise while the analyzed volume is bigger.

3.3 Volume Measurements and Clinical Comparisons

See in Table 3, the estimated volumes for the created 3D objects.

Once the physical volumes are estimated (Vols - Sinker column), the results are compared to the volumes estimated by manual segmentation. The values presented in each view in Table 4 are the averages of the manual segmentation performed by the four trained experts. Recall that AX, SG and CR are contractions for Axial, Sagittal and Coronal respectively and refer to views in medical imaging.

The presented strategy and device has been conceived as a validating tool and proposes an alternative to the unreliable manual segmentation.

Table 3. Records of read volumes in physical 3D models by water displacement using the device previously tunned with the marbles.

Structure	Est Vols (ml)	Sinker used	Vols - sinker (ml)
sinker 1	13.9 ± 0.8	–	–
sinker 2	12.8 ± 0.6	–	–
v1mo	17.3 ± 0.4	1	3.4 ± 0.9
v6mo	21.2 ± 0.4	1	7.3 ± 0.9
v24mo	24.4 ± 0.5	1	10.5 ± 0.9
v15mo	24.7 ± 0.5	1	10.8 ± 0.9
v48mo	27.2 ± 0.6	1	13.3 ± 1.0
v66mo	21.9 ± 0.5	1	8.0 ± 0.9
v78mo	25.4 ± 0.5	1	11.5 ± 1.0
v96mo	24.8 ± 0.5	1	11.0 ± 0.9
v114mo	33.5 ± 0.7	1	19.7 ± 1.1
vHmod	349.9 ± 0.2	1, 2	323.8 ± 0.9
vHsev	494.5 ± 0.3	1, 2	468.4 ± 0.9

Table 4. Preliminary comparison between the physical volume of the 3D models and the volume estimated from the images in the three views.

Structure	Physical-WD (ml)	Manual AX (ml)	Manual SG (ml)	Manual CR (ml)
v1mo	3.4 ± 0.9	3.2 ± 1.5	3.8 ± 1.0	3.3 ± 1.4
v6mo	7.3 ± 0.9	9.8 ± 1.3	8.6 ± 1.2	7.0 ± 1.2
v24mo	10.5 ± 0.9	10.1 ± 1.0	9.6 ± 1.3	10.1 ± 1.0
v15mo	10.8 ± 0.9	13.2 ± 1.1	8.2 ± 1.3	8.9 ± 1.1
v48mo	13.3 ± 1.0	11.4 ± 1.5	10.9 ± 2.0	9.6 ± 1.8
v66mo	8.0 ± 0.9	11.2 ± 1.1	11.6 ± 1.3	10.8 ± 1.6
v78mo	11.5 ± 1.0	10.2 ± 1.3	8.7 ± 2.1	10.5 ± 1.2
v96mo	11.0 ± 0.9	8.8 ± 1.2	8.0 ± 1.1	8.8 ± 1.3
v114mo	19.7 ± 1.1	17.0 ± 1.2	20.4 ± 1.6	18.3 ± 1.5
vHmod	88.4 ± 0.9	$77.2.7 \pm 6.3$	83.1 ± 7.0	75.9 ± 6.5
vHsev	115.9 ± 0.9	99.5 ± 8.0	105.2 ± 8.9	102.8 ± 7.3

4   Discussion and Conclusions

When quantifications are needed in hospitals and clinics, the operators not only deal with the tedious, time-consuming, and always operator-dependent manual segmentation. The task is also strongly regulated by the Health Insurance Portability and Accountability Act (HIPAA); therefore, images are only available under Institutional Review Board (IRB authorization). Such as procedure may introduce days or even months to the process before the data are anonymized and authorized to be taken out of the hospital repository so images can be feed to third-party developed software. Recall that some clinical procedures demand immediate attention. Such a scenario suggest the implementation of automatic methods that, besides to yield reliable and repeatable results, are compliant with the regulations.

In several other human activities, extracting quantifiable features from a qualitative process is crucial. If something can be measured, it can be improved. For this reason, there exists patterns or gold standard for almost all critical measurements that we execute [2, 7, 14] and, in some industries, the measuring instruments are periodically taken to a certification process [5, 12] where a stamp is given only if the device measures within the specifications for the task. As the use of technology is progressively augmenting in hospitals and clinics, those almost artisan activities involving human interaction tend to disappear and be replaced by automation that will need to be tested for precision and accuracy and will need to be adjusted periodically. We are anticipating these events and propose the water-displacement device along with a strategy, that even in its prototype stage provides better specifications than manual assessments.

References

1. Bae, K.T., Giger, M.L., Chen, C.-T., Kahn Jr., C.E.: Automatic segmentation of liver structure in ct images. Med. Phys. **20**, 71–78 (1993)
2. Dyjack, D.T., Levine, S.P.: Development of an ISO 9000 compatible occupational health standard: defining the issues. Am. Ind. Hyg. Assoc. J. **56**, 599–609 (1995)
3. Admiraal-Behloul, F., et al.: Fully automatic segmentation of white matter hyper-intensities in MR images of the elderly. NeuroImage **28**, 607–617 (2005)
4. Fenster, A., Chiu, B.: Evaluation of segmentation algorithms for medical imaging. IEEE EMB, January 2006
5. Duca, D., Riva, G., Foppa, E., Toscano, P.G.: Wood pellet quality with respect to EN 14961–2 standard and certifications. Fuel **135**, 9–14 (2014)
6. Fukuda, Y., Terada, Y., Yoshioka, H., Yu, H.J., Chang, A.: Comparative study of intra-operator variability in manual and semi-automatic segmentation of knee cartilage. Abstr./Osteoarthr. Cartil. **24**, 296–297 (2016)
7. Jovanović, B., Filipović, J.: ISO 50001 standard-based energy management maturity model-proposal and validation in industry. J. Clean. Prod. **112**, 2744–2755 (2016)
8. Kim, H., et al.: Quantitative evaluation of image segmentation incorporating medical consideration functions. Med. Phys. **42**(6), 3013–3023 (2015)
9. Moeskops, P., Viergever, M.A., Mendrik, A.M., de Vries, L.S., Benders, M.J.N.L., Išgum, I.: Automatic segmentation of MR brain images with a convolutional neural network. Fuel 9–14 (2014)
10. Pohle, R., Toennies, K.D.: Segmentation of medical images using adaptive region growing. In: Proceedings of Medical Imaging, vol. 4322, July 2001
11. Rana, M., et al.: Development and evaluation of an automatic tumor segmentation tool: a comparison between automatic, semi-automatic and manual segmentation of mandibular odontogenic cysts and tumors. J. Cranio-Maxillo-Fac. Surg. **43**, 355–359 (2015)
12. Wei, W., Ramalho, O., Mandin, C.: Indoor air quality requirements in green building certifications. Build. Environ. **92**, 10–19 (2015)

13. Yan, P., Kassim, A.A.: Medical image segmentation using minimal path deformable models with implicit shape priors. In: IEEE EMB, October 2006
14. Yao, J., Warren, S.: Applying the ISO/IEEE 11073 standards to wearable home health monitoring systems. J. Clin. Monit. Comput. **19**, 427–436 (2005)

IT Architectures

A Proposal Model Based on Blockchain Technology to Support Traceability of Colombian Scholar Feeding Program (PAE)

Carol Cortés[ID], Alejandro Guzmán[ID], Camilo Andrés Rincón-González[ID], Catherine Torres-Casas[ID], and Camilo Mejía-Moncayo[✉][ID]

Universidad EAN, Calle 79 # 11-45, Bogotá, Colombia
{ccortes39062,jguzman05553,crincon99291,ctorres38223,
cmejiam}@universidadean.edu.co

Abstract. Given the development of Blockchain technology and its advantages of immutability and traceability to provide traceability in the control and management of transactions the present work exposes a model based on Blockchain technology to support traceability and control of the resources of the Colombian Scholar Feeding Program PAE (in Spanish Programa de Alimentación Escolar – PAE). This proposal tries to promote a technological approach to face corruption linked with this kind of programs; providing PAE with tools that could reduce the risk to lost resources or facilitate the identification of the people responsible of corruption cases. The steps of the proposed model are described providing their advantages and limitations.

Keywords: Blockchain · Traceability · Smart contracts · Social programs · Scholar feeding program

1 Introduction

The humanitarian and social programs have been a tool to help the most impoverished and needy communities on the planet; being in some cases, the only support from governments or international organizations. In Colombia, a well-known example is the scholar feeding program (in Spanish Programa de Alimentación Escolar - PAE) which provides food rations to childhood and youth scholar population.

PAE emerges as a government strategy to improve the quality of life of the most vulnerable population for the reduction of malnutrition, extreme poverty, and school desertion rates. Unfortunately, the mishandling of the contracting and execution of the program has led to the corruption taking over a part of these resources [16].

In this sense, immutability, traceability, and transparency of Blockchain technology could play a crucial role; improving transparency among participants,

© Springer Nature Switzerland AG 2019
H. Florez et al. (Eds.): ICAI 2019, CCIS 1051, pp. 245–256, 2019.
https://doi.org/10.1007/978-3-030-32475-9_18

since "it allows the creation of a decentralized environment where cryptograph-ically validated transactions and data are not under the control of any third party organization" [6].

Currently, Blockchain 2.0 is in developing, which unlike the 1.0 that has its core in cryptocurrencies, it is focused more on supply chain [3,5,11] and smart contracts for production processes or other applications [10], increasing efficiency, reducing barriers and costs and automating control and monitoring.

PAE has been selected as a study case of this contribution. In which, the main concerns of the program actors are the transparency and delivery of resources to those who should be the final beneficiaries. In this sense, the Blockchain tech-nology could be evaluated as an alternative to control the resources allocated to this program and guarantee its timely delivery, given its ability to store data immutably without relying on a central authority, which allows it to preserve its integrity and avoid tampering attempts [1]. Thus, this technology could help promote transparency, generate confidence, and improve the efficiency of trans-actions in humanitarian projects [9], generating social, economic, and political transformations.

There are several studies on the implementation, advantages, and challenges of Blockchain technology in the financial sector [2,7,20], however, its uses in other scenarios have not been widely studied. In this way, this work seeks to promote the potential use of this technology in social programs as PAE.

This document starts with a brief analysis and description of the Blockchain technology Sect. 2, its main uses, and its evolution. We will talk about Blockchain 2.0 and its application with smart contracts in logistics processes in different sec-tors. Next, we will talk about PAE Sect. 3, its operation, and its main weaknesses. Section 4 describes the research methodology and finish this contribution with the proposed model Sect. 5 and conclusions.

2 Blockchain Technology

According to Tapscott [17], Blockchain is a data structure in which the infor-mation contained is grouped into blocks, to which meta-information is added relative to another block of the previous chain in a timeline. Thanks to crypto-graphic techniques, the information contained in a block can only be repudiated or edited by modifying all subsequent blocks. In other words, it is a distributed records database or public accounting book of all transactions or digital events that have been executed and shared among the participating parties. Each trans-action in the public ledger is verified by consensus of the majority of the par-ticipants in the system. Once entered, the information can never be erased. The Blockchain contains a specific and verifiable record of each transaction made.

The most famous example of this technology is Bitcoin, the decentralized coin between p2p pairs, created by Satoshi Nakamoto in 2008 [15]. It works as a means of payment and merchandise but has been subject to considerable controversy [4].

Beyond Bitcoin, Blockchain technology has shown excellent performance not only in financial matters but in other fields. Leading it to be cataloged as the most important invention after the internet, due to has the potential to change the functioning of the current world [4].

Pilkington [13] exposes an immense potential of Blockchain technology to be implemented in a wide range of areas, by the interest generated in different sectors. In which there are great possibilities in their operating benefits given cost savings due to efficiency improvements. In this sense, Blockchain 2.0, goes beyond cryptocurrencies and is involved with Smart Contracts, which are mostly a computer protocol designed to facilitate, verify, or enforce the negotiation or execution of a contract digitally. These contracts allow the realization of credible transactions without third parties and are stored under the Blockchain technology [4].

Blockchain is revolutionizing the digital world from the monetary field up to applications that until a few years ago seemed impossible. It is raising a considerable revolution not only in our economy but in all kinds of areas. For example, open-source companies such as Ethereum allow using smart contracts under a custom Blockchain. In which is possible creates digital tokens which can be used as currency, asset, proof of ownership in contracts. Thereby, smart contracts will be the base for numerous application in government, independent banks, crowdfunding, and humanitarian programs. Based on the above, Blockchain also could be the next disruptor of humanitarian assistance [14], under the modality of smart contracts could provide significant benefits when is used to transfer aid resources or in the traceability of it.

There has been a growing interest in Blockchain technology that has been gaining ground in these projects [19]. An example of this is the United Nations Children's Fund (UNICEF), which is already investing in early blockchain startups to explore possible applications of technology for humanitarian causes [8]. Currently, different blockchain platforms can be adapted for humanitarian programs [8]. In the same way, those interested in implementing Blockchain can take examples of new technologies that are being adopted in this sector. For instance, humanitarian actors may consider the adoption of mobile banking as an example of how Blockchain and digital currencies can be used for humanitarian needs [13].

3 Programa de Alimentación Escolar - PAE

The scholar feeding program (in Spanish Programa de Alimentación Escolar - PAE) is a scholar feeding policy that provides food supplement to children and adolescents throughout the Colombian territory [12]. PAE is part of thereat government strategy to increase schooling rates (coverage and quality) in the country. The PAE was designed in two ways; On the one hand, encourage the permanence of children, adolescents, and youth in the education system, and on the other provide nutritional support for this population [12]. PAE contributes to the permanence of students in the school system and provides them with nutrients in the percentages defined for each modality.

PAE process starts by identifying and prioritizing Educational Institutions with the most needs. It is done through the Social Policy Committee or the Committee on Childhood and Family or Food and Nutrition Security of each town. It is pertinent to mention that in each of these instances, it is mandatory the representation of the parents.

The Educational Institutions are classified primarily by their geographical location [18]. Educational Institutions in rural areas that only have one teacher, Educational Institutions that exclusively serve ethnic communities (indigenous, Afro-Colombian, Raizales, and gypsies).

In third place, the Educational Institutions with a high concentration of population with scores of SISBEN[1] 48.49 for the 14 biggest cities and 45.34 for remainder (locality, sector, neighborhood, commune).

In the latter, are prioritized the Educational Institutions that provide the level of preschool education, then essential primary and those that offer training to ethnic groups with a high proportion of population victim of the armed conflict or both.

After the selection of the Educational Institutions, they proceed to select the beneficiaries of the program, although it is already clear what the target population is, unfortunately, the program does not cover this population in its entirety. The staff of Educational Institutions participates in the allocation of quotas for the selection of beneficiaries, as parents who have an active role in the oversight. In the rural area and for the ethnic population, 100% of the enrolled students who are attending preschool and primary school must be met, the students who are victims of the armed conflict must be attended to in their entirety regardless of the degrees in which they are enrolled [18].

After having selected the Educational Institutions and the population that will cover the program, it is necessary to establish the food component with which the PAE will be executed. The food component is the daily supply of at least one food ration during the school calendar. These must be delivered to educational establishments for immediate consumption, guaranteeing the existence of infrastructure and quality conditions in the processes of purchase, storage, production, and distribution of food.

The above must be done in time and form by the operator, but this is not the only one that intervenes in the PAE, in which families and caregivers of children and adolescents, the community, Educational Institutions, Territorial Entities (District/Municipal Mayors) take part. Secretaries of Education and Committees and spaces of agreement, Ministries of Education, Health and Social Protection, ICBF, and last but not least, children and adolescents [12].

The PAE works thanks to the different funding sources that have been arranged both at the National level and at the local level; Mainly it is the resource stipulated annually by the MEN [12], according to the budget established for the provision of food service to children and adolescents, then we find the funds from the General Participation System - SGP where these are transferred to the territorial entities, are the royalties and own resources of each Department, towns, and districts, and finally are the resources assigned by the private sector, cooperative or non-governmental.

---

[1] The SISBEN is the Identification System of Potential Beneficiaries of Social Programs that, through a score, classify the people according to their socio-economic conditions.

However, the PAE has severe deficiencies in its operation that have made it inefficient. Of the 127 territorial entities covered by the program, approximately 40% of them (31) have no certainty about coverage in the attention to students receiving school feeding [18]. It indicates that there is no relationship between the three dimensions involved in the universal coverage framework: students, rations, and days attended, a situation that leads to the low results of the PAE.

There is no control towards the program operators. Some have stopped providing food service for long periods when 100% of the contract has already been paid, others have been paid for on non-working days. There is no control over the users registered to SIMAT[2]. Rations payments have been provided and made to students not registered in the platform as well as to students enrolled in private schools.

The quality to provide the foodservice is not met. Some Education Institutes do not have the infrastructure required to provide the service in optimal physical, sanitary, and quality conditions. There are shortages in the rations delivered by the operators, especially in the protein (meat, chicken, fish) and fruits and vegetables. Besides, the portion served does not correspond to the weight and volume previously defined in the standard minimum.

In summary, the above shows the severe deficiencies that the PAE has monitoring the program development, in breach of the goals of coverage promised by the national government. Although the MEN has defined the conditions and mechanisms to operate and control the program [12], this not was enough to avoid that corruption takes advantage of the significant number of intermediaries between the resources and the final beneficiaries and the enormous information generated in the bidding, hiring, and operation of the program. In this sense, Blockchain technology could support the program by mean of smart contracts and the registry of the principal transactions to help audit process, reducing the system vulnerabilities.

4   Methodology

The scope of this contribution is to expose how a model based on Blockchain technology could facilitate the resources traceability and control in social programs such as the PAE. For this, a non-experimental research design has been selected to identify the implications, advantages, and opportunities for implementing a model based on Blockchain technology for the control of social program resources. The methodology applied to achieve the above had three stages; In the first stage, to identify the main advantages, challenges, and needs of the implementation of Blockchain technology in social programs or humanitarian aid projects a bibliographic review was carried out. In the second stage, the supply chain of humanitarian projects was analyzed, with their respective actors and control points, identifying the inconveniences in the delivery and traceability

---

[2] SIMAT is the integrated registration system of the Colombian Education Ministry.

of resources destined for these projects. Finally, based on the information collected, a general model for the management and control of social resources has been defined, focused in PAE.

5 Proposed Model

Currently, PAE works as a Program that helps to fight school desertion providing a food supplement for the comprehensive care to children and adolescents in rural and urban areas of different ethnic groups registered in the enrollment system SIMAT as official students [12]. However, in many cases, the resources were executed without fulfilling the minimum quality conditions, generating that the children and adolescents are not fed correctly [16]. These situations expose that the most significant PAE weakness is achieving to establish capable mechanisms to control its processes and make that the clauses of the contracts are being fulfilled.

Considering the above the model proposed in this contribution tries to provide to PAE automated tools to minimize their vulnerabilities against these issues; by mean of a structure based on Blockchain technology, using its immutability, transparency, and distributed structure to support a more reliable operation.

PAE was defined by the Colombian Education Ministry since its creation [12] (see Sect. 3). Due to it, the proposed model will be focused on the integration of Blockchain technology by mean of smart contracts. Firstly it is convenient to take into consideration that the value of the information lies in its accuracy. In this sense, the control process has to be automated, including the principal transactions that will be included in Blockchain technology and will be managed by means of smart contracts.

The characteristics mentioned above previously are incorporated in the model schema shown in Fig. 1. The model is divided in six layers: actors, processes, information, transactions, smart contract, and Blockchain registries, which are described as follow:

- Actors are the people related to each operation in the different levels of the system, taking into consideration three main actors: who manage, who makes and who verify each process and transaction.
- The process is the set of administrative, financial, productive, logistic, and control operations needed to satisfy the goals of the program. The process has actors, procedures, and specific criteria of fulfillment, which are included in the transaction.
- Information includes all the documents associated with each process (contracts, invoices, technical sheets, requirements, procedures etc.).
- Transactions are the data needed in a smart contract to validate or verify the process fulfillment.
- The smart contract is an automated mechanism to verify the process fulfillment regarding transaction data.

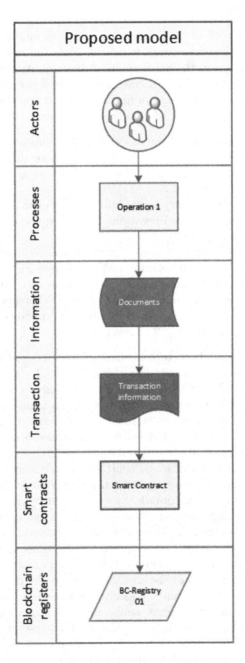

Fig. 1. Schema of proposed model PAE

– Blockchain registries is an encrypted and distributed database in which all system transactions are stored.

Given the complexity of PAE program in its operation, it is essential to develop the technological framework which supports the model; given that the ideal configuration requires the automation of the majority of the processes and transactions. In this sense, firstly is necessary to develop a set of phases which allows us to characterize the program in each location and then implement the proposed model as is shown in Fig. 2 and described next:

1. It is essential to define the resource sources, the managers which control the resources, and the profile of the beneficiaries. These three steps (see Fig. 2 in yellow) provides the origin and the end of the program, and the people responsible for the control of it.
2. In each location, it is necessary to describe the processes and the actors of the supply chain, including all the operations, people, equipment, and information needed to satisfy the goals (see Fig. 2 in blue).
3. The rules of smart contracts (process fulfillment criteria) need to be defined including the budget execution information flow (see Fig. 2 in orange); these two steps will allow structuring a public Blockchain with smart contracts and a book of the supply chain under a platform like Ethereum.
4. The implementation of the model and supply chain supported by a Blockchain system are final steps (see Fig. 2 in green).

Once the program is characterized, it is possible to execute steps 8 and 9 of Fig. 2. In which the model core is materialized, under smart contracts and Blockchain. With the Blockchain technology, smart contracts can be used to code and encapsulate the rules and processes that govern transactions between the PAE actors (see Fig. 3). When the transaction is processed, the smart contract automatically performs actions and verifies compliance according to the rules that have been established at steps 6 and 7 (see Fig. 2).

In this way, the definition of smart contract and the supply chain (steps 4 to 7) establish the deliverable, allowing that when a previously programmed condition is fulfilled, the contract automatically executes the corresponding clause. It is essential to regard that the participants must agree on how the transactions, data, and rules that govern these transactions are achieved. Then, it is crucial to express these rules accurately, explore possible exceptions, and define a framework for resolving disputes. Additionally, it is necessary to take into account the revision of the rules, the test of the controls rules on the transaction data, the simulation of scenarios to guarantee a safely and transparently Blockchain.

Consequently, the smart contract would contain information on the coverage of the program, that is, the number of children and adolescents who access food, the exact amount of food that should be served, the frequency with which it will be consumed weekly and data about their growth, healthy and academic performance, in other aspects (information of steps 1 to 3). For example, a smart contract would be made between the MEN and the territorial entities, which would define the general conditions of the school canteens, the needs for

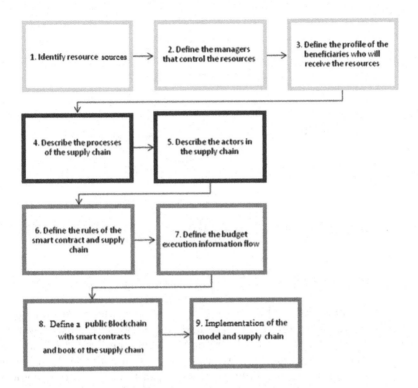

Fig. 2. Steps to implement the proposed model (Color figure online)

attention, program coverage, available public resources, and the requirements that allows identifying the most suitable children and adolescents, according to their conditions. When this step has been finished, the smart contract could enable the start of the tender to define the operators.

In the end, closing the loop, Blockchain will allow a record of transactions among parties involved, dates, location, status, and quality of the product and percentage of program execution, which could be audited easily. It is imperative to highlight that the MEN and other actors, such as the beneficiaries themselves, could review the terms and clauses of the contract, executing monitoring and control over the transactions which are registered in Blockchain. Thanks to the unchangeable and cryptographic nature of it, which makes this tracking reliable.

However, it is essential to note that there are some limitations to the implementation of this model. Firstly, it is necessary to develop the technological infrastructure for the application of the model. Second, the parties involved need agreeing in the use of technology. Likewise, the technical and regulatory challenges that allow reaching maturity must be taken into account to guarantee the adequate implementation of the model and the accessibility to the technology.

Finally, Blockchain technology could reduce the risk of loss of resources and facilitate the audit of the system, but the human factor is always the weak link

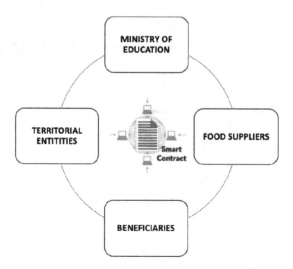

Fig. 3. PAE smart contract scheme

and is the main limitation of this proposal. In the case in which a criminal agent can add a corrupt definition of the rules and transactions for smart contracts. Although the system may work, the results may not be desired because the setting could include the approval of transactions that are outside the minimum acceptance levels or that never happen. However, in the system, they could be accepted and then paid, allowing the loss of resources. This because these issues are hiding under the sight of all the people without a clue of it.

6   Conclusions

Taking into consideration the advantages of disintermediation, traceability, and immutability of Blockchain, in this contribution is presented a model based on this technology to support the Colombian scholar feeding program PAE. The main objective o this proposal is formulated a reliable structure, in which the principal transactions are registered in Blockchain and smart contracts take control over the verification of the processes fulfillments.

The proposed model to be implemented need the development of the legal framework and technological infrastructure to support their processes. These elements could be used in the future not only for PAE, even could serve as a government seed to establish an automated tool for other programs of great social impact, promoting the digitalization of the state and helping to increase citizen participation in the control of this kind of programs.

References

1. Al-Saqaf, W., Seidler, N.: Blockchain technology for social impact: opportunities and challenges ahead. J. Cyber Policy **2**(3), 338–354 (2017). https://doi.org/10.1080/23738871.2017.1400084. https://www.tandfonline.com/doi/full/10.1080/23738871.2017.1400084

2. Beck, R., Avital, M., Rossi, M., Thatcher, J.B.: Blockchain technology in business and information systems research. Bus. Inf. Syst. Eng. **59**(6), 381–384 (2017). https://doi.org/10.1007/s12599-017-0505-1. http://link.springer.com/10.1007/s12599-017-0505-1
3. Bettín-Díaz, R., Rojas, A.E., Mejía-Moncayo, C.: Methodological approach to the definition of a blockchain system for the food industry supply chain traceability. In: Gervasi, O., et al. (eds.) ICCSA 2018. LNCS, vol. 10961, pp. 19–33. Springer, Cham (2018). https://doi.org/10.1007/978-3-319-95165-2_2. http://link.springer.com/10.1007/978-3-319-95165-2_2
4. CCrosby, M., Pattanayak, P., Verma, S., Kalyanaraman, V.: BlockChain technology: beyond Bitcoin. Technical report (2016). http://scet.berkeley.edu/wp-content/uploads/AIR-2016-Blockchain.pdf
5. Dasaklis, T.K., Casino, F., Patsakis, C.: Defining granularity levels for supply chain traceability based on IoT and blockchain. In: Proceedings of the International Conference on Omni-Layer Intelligent Systems - COINS 2019, pp. 184–190. ACM Press, New York (2019). https://doi.org/10.1145/3312614.3312652. http://dl.acm.org/citation.cfm?doid=3312614.3312652
6. Holotescu, C.: Understanding blockchain opportunities and challenges. In: The 14th International Scientific Conference eLearning and Software for Education, pp. 275–284, March 2018. https://doi.org/10.12753/2066-026X-18-253
7. Hyvärinen, H., Risius, M., Friis, G.: A blockchain-based approach towards overcoming financial fraud in public sector services. Bus. Inf. Syst. Eng. **59**(6), 441–456 (2017). https://doi.org/10.1007/s12599-017-0502-4. http://link.springer.com/10.1007/s12599-017-0502-4
8. Ko, V., Verity, A.: Blockchain for the humanitarian sector: future opportunities. Technical report (2016). www.digitalhumanitarians.com. https://reliefweb.int/report/world/blockchain-humanitarian-sector-future-opportunities
9. Kshetri, N.: Will blockchain emerge as a tool to break the poverty chain in the Global South? Third World Q. **38**(8), 1710–1732 (2017). https://doi.org/10.1080/01436597.2017.1298438. https://www.tandfonline.com/doi/full/10.1080/01436597.2017.1298438
10. Lund, E.H., Jaccheri, L., Li, J., Cico, O., Bai, X.: Blockchain and sustainability: a systematic mapping study. In: Proceedings of the 2nd International Workshop on Emerging Trends in Software Engineering for Blockchain, pp. 16–23 (2019). https://doi.org/10.1109/WETSEB.2019.00009. https://dl.acm.org/citation.cfm?id=3355360
11. Mann Zurich, T.: A survey on blockchain and IoT based implementations for supply chain management. Technical report. http://www.csg.uzh.ch/
12. Ministerio de Educación Nacional (MEN): Lineamientos Técnico Administrativos y Estándares del Progrma de Alimentación Escolar (PAE) (2013). www.mineducacion.gov.co
13. Pilkington, M.: Blockchain technology: principles and applications. In: Research Handbook on Digital Transformations, pp. 225–253 (2015). https://doi.org/10.4337/9781784717766.00019. http://www.elgaronline.com/view/9781784717759.00019.xml
14. Purvis, K.: Blockchain: what is it and what does it mean for development? – Global Development Professionals Network – The Guardian. https://www.theguardian.com/global-development-professionals-network/2017/jan/17/blockchain-digital-technology-development-money
15. Nakamoto, S.: Bitcoin: a peer-to-peer electronic cash system, p. 9 (2008). https://bitcoin.org/bitcoin.pdf

16. Semana: Corrupción en el Programa de Alimentación Escolar. https://www.
    semana.com/educacion/articulo/corrupcion-en-el-programa-de-alimentacion-
    escolar/579501
17. Tapscott, D., Tapscott, A., Salmerón, J.M.: La revolución blockchain : descubre
    cómo esta nueva tecnología transformará la economía global. Deusto (2017)
18. Unión Temporal G–Exponencial CINDE: Evaluación de Operaciones y Resultados
    para Determinar el Grado de Efectividad del Programa de Alimentación Esco-
    lar - PAE. Technical report (2013). https://www.icbf.gov.co/sites/default/files/
    informe_final_eval_pae.pdf
19. de Vrij, A.: Blockchain in humanitarian aid: a way out of poverty and famine?
    Ph.D. thesis (2018). https://openaccess.leidenuniv.nl/handle/1887/67036
20. Yoo, S.: Blockchain based financial case analysis and its implications. Asia Pac.
    J. Innov. Entrep. **11**(3), 312–321 (2017). https://doi.org/10.1108/APJIE-12-2017-
    036. http://www.emeraldinsight.com/doi/10.1108/APJIE-12-2017-036

Capacity of Desktop Clouds for Running HPC Applications: A Revisited Analysis

Jaime Chavarriaga[1]([envelope]) [ID], Carlos E. Gómez[1,2] [ID], David C. Bonilla[1] [ID], and Harold E. Castro[1] [ID]

[1] Systems and Computing Engineering Department,
Universidad de los Andes, Bogotá, Colombia
{ja.chavarriaga908,ce.gomez10,dc.bonilla10,hcastro}@uniandes.edu.co
[2] Universidad del Quindío, Armenia, Colombia

Abstract. Desktop Clouds, such as UnaCloud and CernVM, run scientific applications on desktop computers installed in computer laboratories and offices. These applications run on virtual machines using the idle capacities of that desktops and networks. While some universities use desktop clouds to run bag of tasks (BoT), we have used these platforms to run High Performance Computing (HPC) applications that require coordination among the nodes and are sensible to communication delays. There, although a virtual machine with 4 virtual cores on computers released in 2012 may achieve more than 40 GFLOPs, the capacity of clusters with tens or hundreds of virtual machines cannot be determined by multiplying this value. In a previous work, we studied the capacity of desktop clouds for running applications non-intensive on communications on our computer labs. This paper presents a revisited analysis, focused on the capacity of desktop clouds for running HPC applications. The resulting information can be used for researchers deciding on investing on HPC clusters or using existing computer labs for running their applications, and those interested on designing desktop clusters that may achieve the maximum possible capacity.

Keywords: Desktop clouds · LINPACK · Computing capacity

1 Introduction

In universities and research centers, computers are typically underutilized most of the time [4]. Several solutions aims to harvest such idle capacity and provide computing resources to run scientific applications [1]. For instance, solutions for Volunteer Computing, such as *BOINC* [2] and *Condor* [11], and for Desktop Clouds, such as UnaCloud [17] and CernVM [19], exploit these capabilities to run scientific applications using specific libraries or customized virtual machines. Nowadays, research center such as CERN, run software for their research using a combination of computers in dedicated datacenters with desktops distributed through all its campus [19].

© Springer Nature Switzerland AG 2019
H. Florez et al. (Eds.): ICAI 2019, CCIS 1051, pp. 257–268, 2019.
https://doi.org/10.1007/978-3-030-32475-9_19

Desktop clouds (DC) offer cloud computing services by running virtual machines on desktop computers that are idle or used below their capacity [1]. In contrast to other solutions, DCs such as *cuCloud* [13] and *UnaCloud* [17] allow researchers to run clusters of customized virtual machines. Therefore, researchers can use these platforms to run more complex distributed applications such as LINPACK[1], GROMACS[2] and many other MPI-based software[3] at lower costs that the required if they bought specialized HPC hardware.

Previous work have been focused on determining the idle capacity of desktops on university campuses [4,7,16] and their potential for running scientific applications [18]. Regretfully, they have been considering *Bag of Tasks (BoT)* applications where the computing work is divided in chunks that can be processed independently. In these applications, the computing potential can be determined by multiplying the the number of computers by the capacity of each. These studies do not show the potential capacity for parallel processing where the work is distributed across multiple nodes to be processed at the same time.

This paper extends existing work by (1) analyzing the potential processing capability of desktop clouds to run MPI-based parallel applications, (2) presenting some considerations to deploy virtual clusters for MPI-based applications on desktop clouds, and (3) discussing use cases and designs where desktop clouds can be used instead of buying specialized (and expensive) HPC hardware.

The rest of this paper is organized as follows. Section 2, gives a background on HPC, desktop clouds and MPI-based applications. Section 3 talks about the related work. Section 4 presents an evaluation of the capacity of desktop clouds using the well-known LINPACK benchmark, and Sect. 5 discusses the results and propose some hints for designing virtual clusters. Finally, Sect. 6, concludes the paper and discusses future work.

2   Background

This section introduces some concepts used in our work. Here we define desktop clouds, describe some applications that can run on these platforms and specify the MPI-based applications we are interested to run on our solution.

2.1   Desktop Cloud Systems

A DC combines volunteer computing and cloud computing [1,3]. They use idle computing resources of the participant computers, like volunteer computing platforms, and offer virtual machines for on-demand processing or infrastructure as a service, like cloud computing platforms.

Considering the type of applications they can run, we identify two types of DCs: (1) DCs oriented to run *Bag of Tasks (BoT)* applications and (2) DCs that support virtual clusters.

---

[1] https://www.netlib.org/benchmark/hpl/.

[2] http://www.gromacs.org/.

[3] https://www.mpi-forum.org/.

DCs oriented to BoT are solutions [3,12,19] based on volunteer computing platforms such as *BOINC* [2] and *Condor* [11]. These platforms use an agent in each computer that, when it detects some idle capacity, requests a task to the platform and runs a VM or a container to do it. There, these tasks can run independently and do not require interactions among the nodes.

DCs supporting virtual clusters, such as *cuCloud* [13] and *UnaCloud* [17], provide infrastructure as a Service (IaaS) and allow researchers to run their own virtual machines and configure their clusters. In these platforms, the agent in the computer does not run tasks. Instead, it runs customized virtual machines that can be joined to a virtual cluster. Although these clusters can run BoT applications, they are well-suited to run parallel applications where each node must interact with the others.

2.2   MPI-based Applications

Among the applications that can be run on virtual clusters, we can mention the MPI-based applications.

Message Passing Interface (MPI) is a standardized and portable set of specifications to create programs that may function on diverse parallel computing architectures[4]. MPI defines not only a programming API, but also a protocol and semantics describing how they behave in any implementation. Nowadays, it is a *de-facto* standard for parallel programs running on distributed memory systems, it is used in many of the TOP-500 supercomputers[5], is implemented by several libraries (e.g.MPICH2 and Open MPI) and can be used in diverse languages (such as C, C++, Fortran, Java and .Net languages).

There are many MPI-based scientific applications. For instance, researchers can use *BLAST* and *mpiBLAST* to analyze DNA sequences and proteins, *COMSOL Multiphysics* to simulate physics, *ARPS* to model and predict weather, *GROMACS* to simulate bio-chemical and molecular dynamics, and *GNU Octave*, *Maple* and *ATLAS* to perform different numerical computations.

2.3   Running MPI on Desktop Clouds

We have been using desktop clouds to run MPI applications. In previous works we have reported some experiences running GROMACS on UnaCloud [5,6].

A virtual cluster to run MPI-based applications comprise two types of nodes:

Multiple processing nodes that run the application. Each node run an instance of the program and interact with the other nodes. In our clusters, these nodes are virtual machines using Ubuntu 16,04 Linux with the MPI libraries. In addition, all the nodes have a common user account (e.g.**mpiuser**) that can connect to the others using SSH keys.

---

[4] https://www.mpi-forum.org/.

[5] https://www.top500.org.

A NAS server that provides a shared disk where all the processing nodes access the MPI-based software and the data to process. In our clusters, this server can be a high-availability server on a physical machine or a Ubuntu-based server on a virtual machine.

Once the nodes in the cluster are running, the common user account can run the MPI-based applications using different techniques and tools. The simplest way is (1) to create a `hosts` file with the IP addresses of all the nodes and (2) execute the application using the `mpirun` command.

2.4 LINPACK

LINPACK is an MPI-based application extensively used to benchmark super-computers.

The *HPL-Linpack benchmark (LINPACK)* reflects the performance of a system for solving a dense system of linear equations. It measures the number of floating point operations (FLOP) that the system can perform per second. Results are shown in MFLOPs (10^6 FLOPs), GFLOPs (10^9 FLOPs) and TFLOPs (10^{12} FLOPs).

Parameters. The benchmark can be configured with a set of parameters: N, or the *problem size*, represents the matrix size for the underlying system of linear equations to solve. *NBs* defines the block size used in the computations. P and Q, or the *process grid*, represent the number of processes and nodes that will perform the tests.

In order to achieve the optimal performance, these parameters must be defined to obtain the largest possible problem size. There are many applications that may calculate these parameters given the number of nodes, and the number of cores and memory per node[6].

System Efficiency. LINPACK is used to determine the efficiency of a system. Using *Rpeak*, the *peak theoretical performance* given the specifications of the CPU processor, and *Rmax*, the maximum performance obtained in the benchmark, the efficiency *RPeak%* is the value of ($Rmax/Rpeak * 100$). Typically, supercomputers have an efficiency greater than 60–70%[7].

System Scalability. LINPACK can be also used for evaluating the scalability of a system. The *Speedup* denotes the absolute speedup achieved after adding nodes or processors/cores to the system.

3   Related Work

There are other works that have analyzed the idle capacity of desktop computers in computer labs and the potential capacity of desktop grids and desktop clouds running on them.

---

[6] e.g. https://www.advancedclustering.com/act_kb/tune-hpl-dat-file/.

[7] https://www.top500.org/statistics/efficiency-power-cores/.

Domingues et al. [4] analyzed the usage of resources of 169 computers in 11 classrooms with computers during 77 consecutive days. They noted that these computers had, in average, 97,9% CPU idle and 42.1% unused memory. In their study, more than one third of the time, the machines remained without an interactive session and completely available. Considering only the computers with an interactive session, the CPUs were 94.2% idle in average. They conclude that these labs can be used for implementing desktop grids, where a set of these desktop is roughly equivalent to a cluster with half of the size.

Oviedo [16] analyzed the idle capacity of computer labs in Universidad de los Andes in 2011. Gómez et al. [7] updated this analysis in 2015 after the computer labs were updated. They analyzed 70 computers in 2 independent computer labs during the three busiest weeks in a semester. They found that the average use of CPU and memory were less than 5% and 25% respectively. They estimated that a desktop cloud can harvest around 24 GFLOPs without affecting the normal usage of these labs. However, they considered only BoT applications where each node work without interacting to the others but not MPI-based applications.

Many authors have compared public and private cloud platforms for running HPC applications [10, 14, 15].

For instance, He et al. [10] compared Amazon, GoGrid and IBM public cloud running a weather simulation application in 2010. They noted that typical nodes in Amazon and IBM did not scale. While a single node (8 cores and 7 GB RAM) exhibited 57 GFlops and three nodes went to 64 GFLOPs, a cluster with 4 or 5 nodes performed less than 60 GFLOPs per node. In contrast, the specialized GoGrid cloud platform increased monotonically from 55 to 165 GFlops for clusters going from 1 to 5 nodes (6 cores and 8 GB RAM).

In 2018, Mohammadi et al. [14] compared more recent offerings from cloud vendors. They compared clusters of virtual machines running in Amazon, Azure, Rackspace and SoftLayer using 1 to 32 nodes with 16 to 32 cores each one. In contrast to previous evaluations, they found providers offering clusters using high performance networks[8] that may increase their performance monotonically. For instance, Amazon clusters increased from 0.30–0.64 to 8.59–10.68 TFLOPs and Azure increased from 0.61 to 17.26 TFLOPs. Clusters in Rackspace had less scalability going from 0.16 TFLOPs in one node to 3.04 TFLOPs in 32 nodes. In contrast, SoftLayer, that relied on non-specialized networks, failed to scale. While the cluster with one node achieved 0.57 TFLOPs, the cluster with four nodes got 0.44 TFLOPs and the cluster with 32 nodes got only 2.46 TFLOPs, i.e.it obtained an increment of only 4.33 times instead of 18.55–28.94 times obtained in the other providers.

Please note that, at mid of 2019, while the VMs used in the He et al. evaluation [10] may cost \$ 0.074 USD/hour, the specialized VMs used in the Mohammadi et al. study [14] goes from \$ 0.796 to \$ 3.168 USD/hour[9], i.e.specialized VMs may cost around 43 times more.

---

[8] https://docs.microsoft.com/en-us/azure/virtual-machines/windows/sizes-hpc.

[9] https://azure.microsoft.com/en-us/pricing/details/virtual-machines/linux/.

4 Evaluation

We are interested on determining the capacity of desktop clouds to run MPI-based HPC applications. Therefore, in contrast to other studies, we must consider the impact of the network and the interactions among the computers to determine the potential capacity. This section describes our considerations, the tests we performed and the results obtained in one of our computer labs.

4.1 Overview

As mentioned before, there are many factors that may affect the processing capacity of a desktop cloud. On the one hand, the use of virtual machines may reduce the computing processing of each node. On the other hand, the use of non-dedicated high performance networks mat affect the coordination and passing of messages among the nodes. We defined two tests to evaluate how these factors interact and limit the capability.

T1: Efficiency of LINPACK running on virtual machines. A test to compare the theoretical capacity of the used computers with the value achieved in LINPACK. This provides hints on the impact of running scientific applications on virtual machines instead of on the "bare-metal".

T2: Scalability of LINPACK on desktop clouds. A test to evaluate the impact, to the overall performance, of introducing new nodes into a cluster. Its results provide hints on the impact of using the computer lab network for our clusters.

4.2 Results

We performed our tests in the "Networking lab" in the Universidad de los Andes, Colombia. There, we can configure different network topologies using diverse models of routers and computers. For these tests, we used two sets of computers. On the one hand, 20 computers with Intel Core i7-4770 CPU @3.40 GHz (released at June 2013) with 20 MB RAM and, on the other hand, 20 computers with Intel Core i7-7700 CPU @3.60 GHz (released at January 2017) with 16 MB RAM.

LINPACK Efficiency on Virtual Machines. To determine LINPACK efficiency, we must determined first *Rpeak*, the theoretical performance of the CPU, and the *Rmax*, performance of the virtual machines.

Peak Performance. Intel publishes GFLOPs information for their CPUs in their report of *Export Compliance Metrics*[10]. According to them, the maximum performance for the Intel Core i7-4770 CPU @3.40 GHz is 127.6 GFlops.

---

[10] https://www.intel.com/content/dam/support/us/en/documents/processors/APP-for-Intel-Core-Processors.pdf.

Theoretically, peak performance can be calculated using the following formula:

$$Rpeak = \text{CPU GHz} * \# \text{ cores} * \text{vector ops(AVX)} * \text{special instr(FMA3)}$$
$$= 3.4 \; Ghz * 4 \; cores * 8 \; DP \; vector \; ops * 2 \; FMA3$$
$$= 217.6 \; GFlops$$

We ran LINPACK using 8 cores (to excercise all the cores) and 11 GB RAM on the "bare-metal". We achieved a maximum performance $Rmax$ of 144.47 GFlops. That means that our desktops have a 66,39% efficiency $Rpeak\%$.

For the Core i7-7700 CPU @3.60 GHz, according to Intel, $Rpeak$ is 230.4 GFLOPs.

Performance on VMs. In our virtual clusters, we use VMs with the *large* profile in UnaCloud, i.e. VMs with 4 cores and 8 GB RAM. We selected this profile because it consumes near to the 50% of the available computing power to the desktop cloud (e.g.the half of the CPU threads) and leave space for the applications running by the users. We ran LINPACK inside these VMs to determine what performance we can achieve there by using 1 to 4 virtual cores. Table 1 shows the results.

Table 1. Performance running LINPACK on VMs

# procs	Intel Core i7-4770 ($Rpeak$ = 217.6 GFlops)				Intel Core i7-7700 ($Rpeak$ = 230,4 GFlops)			
	Rmax GFLOPs	per core GFLOPs	Speedup	Rpeak%	Rmax GFLOPs	per core GFLOPs	Speedup	Rpeak%
1	12,56	12,56	1.0	5,77%	15,43	15,43	1.0	6,70%
2	21,59	10,80	1,718	9,92%	28,24	14,12	1,830	12,26%
3	30,83	10,28	2,454	14,17%	40,59	13,52	2,630	17.62%
4	39,92	9,98	3,178	18.35%	53,88	13,47	3,491	23,39%

Note that VMs using near to the 50% of the computing power achieve 39,9 to 53,8 GFlops. This means that our *large* profile VMs achieve an $RPeak\%$ efficiency of 18,35 to 23,39%, i.e. less than 1/4 of the real computing power of the hardware.

LINPACK Scalability on Desktop Clouds. When these VMs are configured into a virtual cluster, applications running on them interchange messages using the local network. We ran LINPACK using different combinations of nodes and number of virtual cores in each node to evaluate the scalability of the platform and explore the impact of the network and the coordination tasks on the performance.

Table 2. Performance running LINPACK on VMs with 1 core

# nodes	Intel Core i7-4770 (Rpeak = 217.6 GFlops)				Intel Core i7-7700 (Rpeak = 230,4 GFlops)			
	Rmax GFLOPs	per core GFLOPs	Speedup	Rpeak%	Rmax GFLOPs	per core GFLOPs	Speedup	Rpeak%
1	12,56	12,56	1.0	5,77%	15,43	15,43	1.0	6,70%
2	20,62	10,31	1,641	4,74%	25,42	12,71	1,647	5,52%
3	30,48	10,16	2,426	4,67%	38,46	12,82	2,492	5,56%
4	38,59	9,65	3,072	4,43%	52,76	13,19	3,419	5,72%
5	44,70	8,94	3,550	4,11%	60,80	12,16	3,940	5,28%

Scalability Using 1-Core VMs. We ran some LINPACK using just VMs with a single core but varying the number of nodes. Table 2 shows the results varying the number of nodes from 1 to 5.

Note that varying the number of nodes decrease faster the number of GFLOPs than we increased the cores. For instance, using 1 node with the Intel Core i7-4770 and 4 processes (4 cores), we achieved 47,10 GFLOPs but using 4 nodes with 1 core we got 38,59 GFLOPs. Using the Intel Core i7-7700, we got 53,88 GFLOPs using 1 node and processes and 52,76 using 4 nodes and 1 processing core. Basically, the message passing among cores in a single node is faster than the passing through the network.

Considering the theoretical peak of performance, *Rpeak*, as the number of nodes multiplied by the maximum of a node, the cluster that used only one core in each node remained with an efficiency below the 5 to 6%.

Scalability. We ran LINPACK varying both the number of nodes and the number of cores in each node to evaluate the scalability of our clusters. Table 3 and Fig. 1 show the results of scaling the cluster using the Core i7-4770 CPU.

Table 3. LINPACK Scalability on multiple VMs with multiple cores

Rmax for Intel Core i7-4770

# cores	Nodes in the cluster							
	1	2	3	4	5	10	15	20
1	12,64	20,75	30,48	38,59	45,80	50,33	71,82	96,25
2	21,59	33,67	46,42	58,14	68,49	52,89	82,20	107,70
3	30,83	32,41	56,26	65,70	74,71	52,27	71,79	90,17
4	39,92	48,11	37,34	69,72	71,79	44,77	66,00	89,95

Note that clusters using nodes with a single core scale by increasing the number of nodes. The clusters using two or more cores have scalability problems around 10 nodes. While clusters with 1 to 5 nodes increase their performance

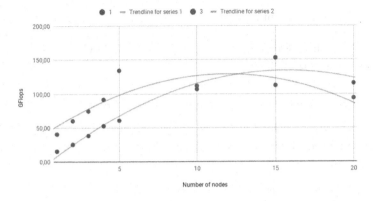

Fig. 1. LINPACK Scalability

monotonically, clusters with 7–12 nodes decrease their performance. The performance increase again after 13–15 nodes.

Table 4. LINPACK Scalability on multiple VMs with multiple cores

$Rmax$ for Intel Core i7-7700							
# cores	Nodes in the cluster						
	1	2	3	4	5	10	15	20
1	15,43	25,42	38,46	52,76	60,80	106,82	152,76	115,68
2	28,24	47,68	64,53	79,89	104,10	91,77	132,02	126,86
3	40,59	60,10	74,70	91,73	134,31	111,60	112,40	93,92
4	53,88	71,29	91,00	112,21	156,23	89,53	78,97	90,64

Table 4 shows the results for the Intel Core i7-7700. Note that the these clusters fail to scale after 6–7 nodes. The scalability is better with less processes per nodes: While the clusters with 1-core nodes achieve top performance around 15 nodes, the clusters with 4-core nodes achieves it around 7 nodes. However, the performance of a cluster with 5 nodes with 4-core each one is better than the obtained with a cluster with 15 nodes with 1 core each one.

5   Discussion

We are using the results of our evaluation to propose hints regarding how to design virtual clusters in our computer labs.

5.1   Comparison to Other Platforms

Our evaluation shown virtual clusters using Core i7-4770 CPUs (released at 2013) achieving 100–160 GFLOPs. This performance is comparable to the #215 of the TOP500 supercomputers at November 2001[11]. It is similar than the performance obtained in "normal" VM instances in Amazon and IBM [10], but slower than the obtained using "specialized" instances in GoGrid [10], Amazon, Azure, Rackspace and SoftLayer [14].

5.2   Designing Virtual Clusters on Desktop Clouds

Desktop clouds can run MPI-based applications on computers labs. To achieve the maximum performance, researchers must design their virtual clusters following some recommendations:

- Each virtual node must be configured using the largest VM profile. In our evaluation, VMs achieve almost 1/4 of the computing power of the desktop where they run.
- Virtual cluster must be configured using 7–15 VMs. These clusters achieve an 4–6% efficiency. Larger clusters have less capacity.
- Use the fastest possible network. MPI-applications interchange messages among the cluster nodes and will benefit of faster communications. If it is possible, install faster network switches in the computer labs where the clusters will run.
- Use the fastest possible NAS server. Depending on the application, the MPI-based application may store files during processing and, therefore, their performance may benefit of using faster file access. If it is possible, install specialized hardware or install NAS software in a dedicated computer in the same network segment of the computer labs where the clusters will run.
- Use tools for resuming the work after a fault. MPI applications fail when a node fails and, in desktop clouds, the VMs are volatile. While applications such as GROMACS create checkpoints to resume the work, other applications do not include these options. Additional software, such as *Checkpoint/Restore In Userspace (CRIU)*[12], can be used to resume some interrupted work. Furthermore, desktop clouds such as Unacloud have extensions for creating global snapshots [8], i.e. for checkpointing all the system.

6   Conclusions

The potential capacity for running HPC applications and for running Bag of Tasks (BoT) applications on desktop clouds is not the same. HPC applications, more specifically MPI-based software, coordinate the work of multiple nodes by passing messages across the network. The capacity and performance of these applications are not only determined by the capacity of each node and processor, but also by the capacity of the network were they interchange data. Desktop clouds do not use high velocity or dedicated networks and, therefore, introducing new nodes to a clusters may reduce the overall capacity instead of increase it.

---

[11] https://www.top500.org/statistics/efficiency-power-cores/.
[12] https://criu.org/.

The capacity of virtual cluster on desktop clouds depends on the application, the number of nodes in the cluster and the memory and number of processes (cores) running in each node. Our evaluation shows that, using desktops with CPUs released at 2013 (Intel Core i7-4770), these clusters may achieve a capacity between 100 to 160 GFLOPs on the LINPACK benchmark. Using VMs configures with a half of the CPU threads, the efficiency is near to 4–6% in the cluster (22–23% in each machine) because the impact of using a hypervisor instead of running applications "on-bare metal" and the impact of using normal networks. The resulting performance is comparable to more than 100 of the Top500 HPC computers of November 2001 and June 2002. In addition, this performance is better than the obtained using "normal" VM instances in cloud computing providers such as Amazon and IBM, and it is similar to the obtained in "high-performance" VM instances in GoGrid in 2010.

We suggest people designing virtual clusters on desktop clouds, to configure each node with the largest number of cores and memory allowed by the platform and avoid clusters with more than 15 nodes. We consider that desktop clouds can be used extensively to teach MPI programming and to test custom applications without using specialized HPC hardware. In addition, universities can use them to run preliminary tests of scientific experiments. Finally, while small-to-medium institutions can complete their experiments on these platforms, large institutions may prefer to run further work on specialized hardware or use cloud computing resources instead.

We are working on improving Unacloud to support GPUs, containers and improve its reliability [17]. For instance, We have been extending the platform to support checkpoints, fault recovering and migration of applications that do not include these features [9]. Future work is planned to evaluate the performance and reliability of running MPI-applications for large periods of time using desktop clouds with our extensions.

References

1. Alwabel, A., Walters, R.J., Wills, G.B.: A view at desktop clouds. In: International Workshop on Emerging Software as a Service and Analytics (ESaaSA 2014), Barcelona, Spain, pp. 55–61. ScitePress (2014)
2. Anderson, D.P.: BOINC: a system for public-resource computing and storage. In: Proceedings of the 5th IEEE/ACM International Workshop on Grid Computing, pp. 4–10. IEEE Computer Society (2004)
3. Cunsolo, V.D., Distefano, S., Puliafito, A., Scarpa, M.: Volunteer computing and desktop cloud: The Cloud@Home paradigm. In: Eighth IEEE International Symposium on Network Computing and Applications (NCA 2009), Cambridge, MA, USA, pp. 134–139. IEEE (2009)
4. Domingues, P., Marques, P., Silva, L.: Resource usage of windows computer laboratories. In: 2005 International Conference on Parallel Processing Workshops (ICPPW 2005), Oslo, Norway, pp. 469–476. IEEE, June 2005
5. Garcés, N., et al.: Analysis of Gromacs MPI using the opportunistic cloud infrastructure UnaCloud. In: Sixth International Conference on Complex, Intelligent, and Software Intensive Systems (CISIS 2012), pp. 1001–1006 (2012)

6. Garcés, N., Sotelo, G., Villamizar, M., Castro, H.: Running MPI Applications over Opportunistic Cloud Infrastructures. In: 2012 Seventh International Conference on P2P, Parallel, Grid, Cloud and Internet Computing (3PGCIC), Victoria, BC, Canada, pp. 309–314. IEEE (2012)

7. Gómez, C.E., Díaz, C.O., Forero, C.A., Rosales, E., Castro, H.: Determining the real capacity of a desktop cloud. In: Osthoff, C., Navaux, P.O.A., Barrios Hernandez, C.J., Silva Dias, P.L. (eds.) CARLA 2015. CCIS, vol. 565, pp. 62–72. Springer, Cham (2015). https://doi.org/10.1007/978-3-319-26928-3_5

8. Gómez, C.E., Chavarriaga, J., Bonilla, D.C., Castro, H.E.: Global snapshot file tracker. In: Florez, H., Diaz, C., Chavarriaga, J. (eds.) ICAI 2018. CCIS, vol. 942, pp. 90–104. Springer, Cham (2018). https://doi.org/10.1007/978-3-030-01535-0_7

9. Gómez, C.E., Chavarriaga, J., Castro, H.E.: Fault characterization and mitigation strategies in desktop cloud systems. In: Meneses, E., Castro, H., Barrios Hernández, C.J., Ramos-Pollan, R. (eds.) CARLA 2018. CCIS, vol. 979, pp. 322–335. Springer, Cham (2019). https://doi.org/10.1007/978-3-030-16205-4_24

10. He, Q., Zhou, S., Kobler, B., Duffy, D., McGlynn, T.: Case study for running HPC applications in public clouds. In: 19th ACM International Symposium on High Performance Distributed Computing (HPDC 2010), Chicago, Illinois, pp. 395–401. ACM (2010)

11. Litzkow, M.J., Livny, M., Mutka, M.W.: Condor-a hunter of idle workstations. In: 8th International Conference on Distributed Computing Systems, pp. 104–111. IEEE (1988)

12. Marosi, A., Kovács, J., Kacsuk, P.: Towards a volunteer cloud system. Futur. Gener. Comput. Syst. **29**(6), 1442–1451 (2013)

13. Mengistu, T.M., Alahmadi, A.M., Alsenani, Y., Albuali, A., Che, D.: cuCloud: Volunteer Computing as a Service (VCaaS) system. In: Luo, M., Zhang, L.-J. (eds.) CLOUD 2018. LNCS, vol. 10967, pp. 251–264. Springer, Cham (2018). https://doi.org/10.1007/978-3-319-94295-7_17

14. Mohammadi, M., Bazhirov, T.: Comparative benchmarking of cloud computing vendors with high performance linpack. In: 2nd International Conference on High Performance Compilation, Computing and Communications (HP3C), pp. 1–5. ACM (2018)

15. Napper, J., Bientinesi, P.: Can cloud computing reach the top500? In: Proceedings of the Combined Workshops on UnConventional High Performance Computing Workshop Plus Memory Access Workshop (UCHPC-MAW 2009), pp. 17–20. ACM (2009)

16. Oviedo, A.: UnaCloud MSA: Plataforma basada en UnaCloud para la generación y análisis de alineamientos múltiples de secuencias. Master's thesis, School of Systems and Computing Engineering (2011)

17. Rosales, E., Castro, H., Villamizar, M.: UnaCloud: opportunistic cloud computing infrastructure as a service. In: Second International Conferences on Cloud Computing, GRIDs, and Virtualization (CLOUD COMPUTING 2011), pp. 187–194. ThinkMind (2011)

18. Ryu, K.D.: Exploiting idle cycles in networks of workstations. Ph.D. thesis, University of Maryland, College Park (2001)

19. Segal, B., et al.: LHC cloud computing with CernVM. In: 13th International Workshop on Advanced Computing and Analysis Techniques in Physics Research (ACAT 2010), Jaipur, India, p. 004. PoS (2010)

Migration to Microservices: Barriers and Solutions

Javad Ghofrani[1](✉) and Arezoo Bozorgmehr[2]

[1] Department of Informatics/Mathematics,
HTW Dresden University of Applied Sciences, Dresden, Germany
javad.ghofrani@gmail.com

[2] General Practice and Family Medicine, University Hospital Bonn, Bonn, Germany
arezoo.bozorgmehr@ukbonn.de

Abstract. Microservices architecture (MSA) has been emerged over the past few years. Despite standardization efforts, migrating large-scale legacy applications into microservices architecture remains challenging. This study presents the results of seventeen interviews about obstacles and suggested solutions in migration to microservices. We analyzed the results of interviews using Jobs-to-be-done framework in literature and classified the barriers into three categories—inertia, anxiety and context. This work provides a categorization and a framework to overcome the barriers based on the advises of experts in this field. The results can be a reference for future research directions and advanced migration solutions.

Keywords: Microservices · Migration · Cloud · Interview

1 Introduction

Microservices Architectures (MSA) addresses the strong modularization of the complicated systems into small services, called microservices. Each microservice operates within its own isolated process frame, known as the share-nothing philosophy, and allows a system to be designed and implemented by loosely coupled microservice components, realizing the system functionality cooperatively [25]. Scalability, resilience, and reliability are the features that motivate system engineers and companies, such as Amazon and Netflix, to adopt and advance MSA.

Besides MSA based system development, plenty of legacy applications intend to profit from the advantages of MSA without losing their functionalities. As a result, migration from traditional architecture to MSA is receiving closer review.

Microservices were initially presented by Fernandez et al. in their research paper [4]. Since 2014, when microservices have aroused great interest among researchers, various works have been published. Jamshidi et al. [12] and Alshuwayran et al. [1] tried to investigate and characterize the proposed challenges and solutions in microservices architecture. Later, Ghofrani and Lübcke [7] introduced some of the challenges in the practical aspects of microservices architecture as well. While their result offers a general perspective to microservices,

H. Florez et al. (Eds.): ICAI 2019, CCIS 1051, pp. 269–281, 2019.
https://doi.org/10.1007/978-3-030-32475-9_20

our work focuses on the migration processes. We try to determine the challenges within the migration processes.

Besides the new development of enterprise systems using MSA, migration to MSA is another common scenario in enterprise systems [25]. MSA promises more scalability, flexibility, resilience of systems, automation through the continuous pipelines, and reliability when facing changes. Many enterprise systems tend to migrate their monolithic architectures into MSA due to these advantages. Most monolithic systems used by enterprises are commonly in the form of web applications, which provide some services. Not only are these systems of huge internal complexity, they are also implemented over the years, subjected to different programming skills, requirements, and architectural styles. There exits a considerable amount of monolithic systems operating based on primitive mechanism or remaining in their migration phase.

In order to investigate particularities, challenges, barriers, and problems, which harden or even prevent the migration to microservices, we have carried out a qualitative survey. The interviewees of the survey are experts in microservices who contributed valuable insights on the perceived obstacles and potential solutions of MSA migration. They are selected based on their publications on authoritative journals, and proceedings of workshops and conferences.

The paper consists of four parts. Related work is presented in Sect. 2. We then propose our research methodology in Sect. 3 and discuss the analytic results of the interviews in Sect. 4. In Sect. 5 we will discuss some issues and explain the limitations of our research. Section 6 concludes our work and proposes the future work and our research direction.

2   Related Work

A number of secondary studies have been published on the topic of microservices. Two secondary studies of Alshuqayran et al. [1] and Vural et al. [23] are systematic mapping studies on microservices architecture, however, they did not directly address the migration towards microservices architecture in their works. Taibi et al. [21] performed a questionnaire survey on migration towards microservices architecture, filled by 21 practitioners. On the contrary, our research is an in-depth investigation of migration activities and challenges. We perform a deep analyze of each phase in respect of inertia, anxiety, and context. We also propose solutions for overcoming the barriers. Taibi et al. [21] analyzed some aspects of migration such as motivations and benefits behind migration to microservices architecture. However, they do not investigate the barriers and offer any solution for migrating to microservices architecture.

Konche et al. [15] conduct an interview among experts in Germany about drivers and barriers towards adopting microservices. Their work is limited to the experts in Germany and their analysis is based on runtime performance and transactionality.

There are also some primary studies that addressed certain aspects of the MSA migration, including techniques, approaches, analyses, and experience reports [8,14,16]. On the contrary, we aim at identifying more generalizable insights from an academic perspective, while the focus of the primary studies was typically on specific case study or domains.

3   Research Methodology

The research questions are carefully designed to examine barriers and investigate solutions for MSA migration

- **RQ1: What are the main barriers which hinder or make it difficult to migrate into microservices?**
- **RQ2: What are the solutions and suggestions?**

We searched for qualified interviewees with knowledge and experience on MSA migration by a systematic literature review. Through a two-phase searching process, we managed to identify suitable candidates who have published related research papers or had experience in reports on peer-reviewed journals.

First Phase: In the first phase, we followed the guidelines of Kitchenham et al. [13] and Peterson et al. [19]. Based on our research questions, the following search string was generated:

> (decomposition OR clustering OR module OR modularization OR extraction OR recovery OR evolution OR migrate OR migration OR integrate OR integration) AND (enterprise OR container OR legacy OR large scale OR application OR system OR architecture) AND (microservice OR cloud OR service)

We submitted this search string on different scientific databases. Some of these data sets do not accept the exact phrase of the search string. The keywords and binding phrases had to be adopted and passed to *advanced search* functionalities provided by these data sets. Table 1 lists the selected data sets in addition to the number of papers that we found in them. The results were captured in March 2018.

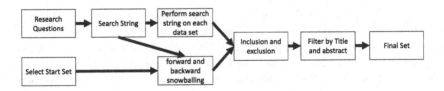

Fig. 1. Work-flow of collecting the papers

Table 1. Selected data sets and their returned results based on our search string

Digital library	Found papers
IEEE Xplore	82
ACM Digital Library	42
ISI Web of Knowledge	104
ScienceDirect	479
Wiley InterScience Journal Finder	5

Second Phase: In the second phase, we performed forward and backward snowballing [24] to gain a comprehensive overview of the research objective. The snowballing method began with specifying a set of studies with a certain level of relevance to the topic. Our starting set consists of [5,9,17], and [2]. In each iteration of snowballing, we compared the search string with title and abstract of the found paper. Once the search string passed to the title or abstract, we included the paper in basis set for next snowballing iteration. After 6 iterations of snowballing, 87 studies were found.

Final Set: We added the results of our first and second phases together and started the screening of papers via inclusion and exclusion criteria, listed in Table 2. Figure 1 illustrates the work-flow of collecting the scientific papers. Through the search, 56 papers remained in the final set. Due to the lack of space, we will discard the list of papers in our final set. The final set is available online [6].

We interviewed the authors of the selected paper via email from March 10th to March 20th, 2018. Fourteen researchers responded with their perspectives on the research questions and three of them offered an opportunity to conduct a further interview.

4   Results

We filtered and categorized the email responses. Since the answers of emails are saved in written and digital form, it facilitates the coding, categorizing and searching process.

Figure 2 depicts the model that we adopted to analyze our results. This model was used in other researchers to analyze forces that prevent the usage of agile methods in model based software engineering. All these researches were referring to the Customer Forces Diagram by Maurya[1] and the Forces Diagram by Moesta and Spiek from the Jobs-to-be-done framework[2] as origin of this model. In the context of our study—migration to microservices—the model classifies the forces into six different categories. In the case of a change in a system, the

---

[1] https://leanstack.com/science-of-how-customers-buy/.
[2] http://jobstobedone.org.

first three forces "trigger", "push", and "pull" motivate the system to migrate from the current area to a new area—from monolithic architecture to MSA. On the contrary, the other three forces "inertia", "anxiety", and "context" play the role of pull factors which hinder the migration.

In our research, we focus on the preventing forces, namely inertia, anxiety, and context. We explain these forces briefly and introduce the corresponding challenges and solutions referring to the interviewing responses. Due to the acceptance of this method among researchers [10,22], and possibility to adapt existing solutions from other fields of research, we selected this method to analyze our findings.

4.1 Inertia

The inertia is the intention of people doing the same thing that they have been doing before. For instance, the developers who have worked with specific technologies for years tend to continue working with them as no serious changes are necessary. We found 6 main issues pointing to inertia among our answers. One interviewee suggests that "The existing companies are built around a particular technology stack. Hence, it creates a problem when migrating, because most of their employees have expertise in that particular technology stack".

Another interviewee addresses the effect of microservices on architecture of monolith, "In many cases we have a much more unfavourable situation with older monoliths, like those from procedural programming of the past. So, the migration effort to services would be much complicated, leading often to completely new software architecture, designs, and programs". Software system transformation is not the only change required during the migration process, as being pointed out, "take the advantage of this benefit means re-organizing the development team."

Among the interview responses, we notice that the transition to a new thinking process is a main obstacle. One of our interviewees mentioned "It is much easier to version and control one system than many microservices. We have used to version the entire system and now we need to version each microservice. If you have one team that works with many services (it is my reality), they have difficulties to consider each service as a 'system' with its own version and configuration. It is not our reality to have many teams and each of them working in only one microservice at each time".

In order to overcome these challenges and help the people to change their habits in fronting new architectures, some solutions are also suggested by our interviewees. At the first level, explaining the benefits of new architecture and data models would be helpful in addition to defining some guidelines. These guidelines would be eventually used as the enforcement to change the team culture. Furthermore, solutions such as "More research and better guidance for the organizational, team-related aspects of microservice development" are suggested.

Table 2. Inclusion and exclusion criteria

Inclusion criteria	Exclusion criteria
– Studies in form of Peer-Reviewed scientific works	– The paper was written before 2010 (Since MSA didn't exist before 2010)
– The paper discusses extraction of microservices from traditional disturbed or centralized architectures	– Do not explicitly discuss the MSA
– The paper discusses the refactoring, migration to the MSA	– The paper is not accessible
– The paper discusses techniques, tools or frameworks to extract or speed up the microservices extraction of monolithic architectures	– Do not propose a method technique or a tool to facilitate a microservices extraction task since
– The paper is written in English	– Editorial, abstract or short papers
– The paper describes experiences, solutions, or evaluation of microservices extraction	– A study that does not specifically propose a solution for migration. (there are enough references to discuss the theoretical challenges in migration or splitting systems into microservices, e.g., [18])
– A study that is developed by either of academics and practitioners. Rationale: Both academic and industrial migration approaches are relevant to this study	– Studies that propose implementation of a new system using microservices architecture
	– Plain migration (the so called "lift and shift"), which moves the application into one functional entity such as, a server or a container to mimic a microservices architecture [11]

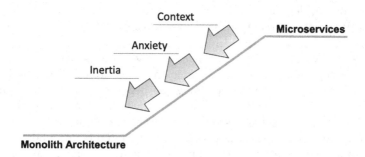

Fig. 2. Preventing forces on migration to microservices

Table 3. Summary of challenges and solution in migration to microservices architecture regarding inertia, anxiety, and context forces

Forces	Challenges	Suggested solution
Inertia	– Complicated design and implementation procedure for a new architecture	– Declaring the benefits of splitting the domain model and data model
	– To convince the teams to split the database or domain models and share it with other team members	– Enforcing cultural changes in teams and improving governance processes (e.g., utilizing DevOps, setting team members by people who have a good background in microservices)
	– To convince the teams to consider each service as a "system" with its own version control and configuration	– Establishing guidelines
	– Difficulties in re-organizing the development team specializing in particular technology stack	
Anxiety	– Lack of understanding of hidden complexities of microservices and negative returns on small scaled systems	– Provisioning of better prototypes, documentations and quick start guides
	– Giving permission to the development team to maintain the database	– Better automated support for setting up an initial microservices architecture
	– Lack of good guidance, technical expertise, knowledge of domain and its related standards, documentation on system decomposition and building microservices architecture	– Utilizing informal guidance on decomposition techniques
	– Challenges in handling storage and splitting data files and big data	– Providing some white papers about standards in modeling
	– Organizational alignment, security, automated deployment and aggregated monitoring	– Training, training and training
		– Using MDD and DDD to ease the business-dependent decomposition
		– Adopting patterns such as distributed transactions, polyglot databases
Context	– Institutional issues rather than technical	– Providing a comparison framework for different types of technologies for implementing microservices
	– Complex testability due to technical limitation of hardware and software systems	– Relying on approaches that are more efficient than HTTP, e.g., Web-sockets, or using shared persistence storages
	– Network communication among microservices can be cause a bottleneck	– Allowing developers to build automated deployment pipelines and design specialized dashboards for monitoring the deployed application
	– It is really difficult to implement DevOps in parallel of change of paradigm from monolith to microservices architecture	

4.2 Anxiety

The anxiety is the fear of unforeseen or unexpected events that could happen during new experiences.

We have extracted 11 points related to anxiety from results of our interviews. Various reasons have been mentioned by our interviewees which leads to anxiety. "Microservices is an abstract concept with multiple moving parts. It has a high learning curve, negative returns on small scale systems, and the concepts only become clear through experience", "The stack of implementation technologies exhibits a certain complexity, while not being always very well documented. Hence, it requires some effort to setup a prototype to work on", and "Increased management complexity". These comments from our interviewees reveal the lack of knowledge about the new architecture, which leads to an underestimation of the complexities behind it. Despite automation tools and approaches which help the system experts to decompose a monolith to microservices, "there is still a lack of good guidance on how to decompose your monolith" remarked by an interviewee.

The reluctance of making changes exists not only among the software engineers for monolithic systems, but database experts also share the anxiety. Two of our interviewees placed the emphasis on concerns regarding handling the database. Their anxiety is splitting and storing big data while allowing the development team to handle the databases. One of our interviewees brought up the concerns on operational level that the operation experts are not ready to handle the deployment and maintenance of system with new architecture. Interviewees obliviously mention the need of knowledge to overcome most of factors which lead to anxiety. According to three of interviewees, providing the knowledge in either a formal and informal way can be achieved by creating some prototypes and quick start guides, publishing white papers about some common standards, and training the staff. Model-Driven Development (MDD) [20], Domain Driven Design (DDD) [3], and informal guidelines can be used to ease the decomposition of the systems into microservices, as mentioned by two other interviewees. These methods would help to reduce the occurrence of some unexpected manner by dividing the system into smaller architectural and organizational units. In order to handle the unknown complexity of applying microservices, our interviewees suggested to adopt the patterns such as distributed transactions and polyglot databases.

4.3 Context

The context factors are considered as forces that prevent experiencing something new in an established architecture because of the boundaries and structure of the architectures. Violating these boundaries is in most cases, impossible or harmful for existence of a system. In an established monolith, the related boundaries to the fixed structures on the organizational and architectural level are categorized as context factors, which is acknowledged by the interviewees in their comments.

Our interviewees have mentioned 7 issues as context among their answers to the influencing facotrs. We have analyzed the answers of our interviewees with regard to the boundaries and structural barriers which prevent the migration to microservices. We divided these factors into two stages. The first stage corresponds to the technical complexity in handling the testability, as well as network communications among microservices. Second stage includes the institutional issues over the technical issues. On the subject of these issues, one of our interviewees mentioned that "Budgeting the time for a substantial refactoring extremely difficult to justify, even in an academic environment, that in commercial production environments it may be even harder". Furthermore, the organizational barriers affect the DevOps implementation while performing a migration to microservices. In order to overcome the mentioned obstacles in the first stage, our interviewees recommended to provide an overview of existing technologies. A framework for comparing different types of technologies could support the developers by overcoming the technical complexities. Furthermore, they suggested to take approaches such as web-sockets and shared persistent storage, which make it more efficient to solve the technical challenges. The second stage requires more flexibility in development teams. For this reason, it has been suggested to encourage the teams to build their own deployment pipelines as well as developing specialized tools for monitoring the production environment.

4.4 Summary

According to the responses collected from our interviewees, migration to the microservices challenges organizations on a broader level than splitting databases or system architecture into smaller parts. Migration to the microservices involves the cultural, development and organizational aspects of companies. Rather than a transformation of the entire system from horizontal layers into vertical units, MSA migration should be considered as a revolution of the system. Even with good knowledge to the system complexity, the development team should lay more emphasis on an in-depth investigation towards the character of stakeholders to assess their readiness for a revolution and their threshold of tolerance. Only through such an investigation can the system engineers and architects decide about cost and gains of migration to microservices. Some of the barriers are organizational issues (i.e., team skills, guidance, ownership of code and database). Therefore, a discussion of good practices can be beneficial in migration to MSA. Furthermore, since DevOps and microservices architectures usually come together, main part of the identified factors appear to be related to the introduction of DevOps practices in the development organization (e.g., continuous delivery, testability, independent versioning, and deployment of individual services). However, investigation on impact of each technology independently is out of scope of this paper.

5 Discussion

We introduced two parties of factors which prevent and push the system engineers towards a migration to MSA. Note that in this paper, we only focus on preventing factors of migration to MSA for the following reasons: (i) Although we mentioned the pushing factors (i.e. Trigger, Push, Pull) as a part of reference model that we use for evaluation our results, they are not impeding but helping the migration process. An extensive presentation of these factors could lead to misunderstanding and distraction from our research. (ii) Since our answers are collected via emails, we had the fear that asking too many questions reduce the chance of receiving any answer from our participants. Therefore, we limited our research questions to two focusing on the pull factors. However, the limited number of participants and responses is admittedly a drawback for getting a more comprehensive understanding. (iii) The focus of our work is set on preventing factors. Motivation factors are out of scope of our research, since other researchers (e.g.,Taibi et al. [21]) have already investigated motivation factors behind migration to microservices.

Migration to a new type of architecture with more flexibility is the most important aspect of our work, which is currently named as microservices. The same concept could be promoted to other terminologies in near future (e.g., server-less computing, or function as a service, etc.). In such cases, regardless of the name of the newly developed architecture, the idea behind our work applies to the re-engineering of monolithic architectures to adapt the new technologies with less effort and costs. Books on MSA written by respected authors such as Sam Newmann [18] and Eberhard Wolff [25] provide a detailed explanation of MSA. However, our research is not about building microservices, but it is about migrating to microservices architecture. Our idea is to have a migration with less effort instead of creating a new system based on functionalities of a monolithic architecture through some iterations. The objective of our systematic method is to ascertain the authors who have investigated the migration to MSA and experienced the barriers and challenges closely. Trying to get an interview with famous authors is the next problem that we faced. Most of them did not have enough time to answer to the interview emails. Due to the limitations of place and time, we could not test all existing methods to reach candidates.

Some of the proposed solutions are very abstract or high level. It could be the case that problems in the real life scenario cannot be solved solely based on these answers (e.g., "Establish some guidelines"). Because of the complicated and context-dependent nature of the issue, our research fails to provide detailed solutions for individual cases. Alternatively, we proposed a general but expert thinking process when encountering the MSA migration problem.

In some cases, it is difficult to determine whether some action/statement is caused by inertia or anxiety (e.g., the "lack of good guidance" statement could also be due to the inertia to put in a lot of effort to learn new things). We tried to perform a voting mechanism between three experts to decide on categorization of such statements.

Internal Validity: We face the challenge of validation with our small sample size—number of interviewees—in our research. We have selected the experts based on their reputation with reference to their peer-reviewed publications. We managed to elevate the quality of answers by upholding the knowledge level of participants. Therefore, the target set of the potential interviewees were small. The main objective of our research is not have a significant correlation between answers of a statistical survey. Our main goal is to present an overview of the comments and propositions from the experts on preventing factors to migrate from monolithic architectures into microservices. Therefore, collecting the empirical results from a survey is out of the scope of this paper.

External Validity: In order to hinder the bias of the researchers through analysis of results, three researcher have evaluated the answers and categorized them based on inertia, anxiety, and context. We captured the answers in emails to prevent loss or misinterpretation of data. Since our selected data sets utilize different search mechanisms, in some cases we had to adapt our search string to the syntax of search tool. Therefore, there is a possibility of bias in the selected papers.

6 Conclusion and Future Work

In this paper, we addressed the challenges of migrating traditional architectures to microservices. We gathered the factors which prevent the migration to microservices based on the interviews with some experts. Finally, we provided a classification of factors based on scientific models. Table 3 summarizes the comments and suggestions of experts while answering our research questions. Based on our results, anxiety as most mentioned factor by interviewees should be considered more than other factors. We are going to use these results as a starting point for our further research. We will start with testing and evaluating the quality of the proposed solutions. For a thorough evaluation, we will need proper metrics to measure the quality of these solutions.

Acknowledgements. This paper is co-financed with funds on the basis of the budget adopted by the deputies of the Saxon state parliament.

References

1. Alshuqayran, N., Ali, N., Evans, R.: A systematic mapping study in microservice architecture. In: 2016 IEEE 9th International Conference on Service-Oriented Computing and Applications (SOCA), pp. 44–51. IEEE (2016)
2. Dragoni, N., et al.: Microservices: yesterday, today, and tomorrow. Present and Ulterior Software Engineering, pp. 195–216. Springer, Cham (2017). https://doi.org/10.1007/978-3-319-67425-4_12
3. Evans, E.: Domain-Driven Design: Tackling Complexity in the Heart of Software. Addison-Wesley Professional, Boston (2004)

4. Fernández Villamor, J.I., Iglesias Fernandez, C.A., Garijo Ayestaran, M.: Microservices: lightweight service descriptions for REST architectural style (2010)
5. Furda, A., Fidge, C., Zimmermann, O., Kelly, W., Barros, A.: Migrating enterprise legacy source code to microservices: on multi-tenancy, statefulness and data consistency. IEEE Softw. **35**, 63–72 (2017)
6. Ghofrani, J., Bozorgmehr, A.: Online material for the paper of migration to microservices: barriers and solutions (2018). https://doi.org/10.6084/m9.figshare.7461215.v1
7. Ghofrani, J., Luebke, D.: Online material for survey on challenges of microservices architecture (2018). https://doi.org/10.6084/m9.figshare.5852598
8. Gouigoux, J.P., Tamzalit, D.: From monolith to microservices: lessons learned on an industrial migration to a web oriented architecture. In: 2017 IEEE International Conference on Software Architecture Workshops (ICSAW), pp. 62–65. IEEE (2017)
9. Granchelli, G., Cardarelli, M., Di Francesco, P., Malavolta, I., Iovino, L., Di Salle, A.: Towards recovering the software architecture of microservice-based systems. In: 2017 IEEE International Conference on Software Architecture Workshops (ICSAW), pp. 46–53. IEEE (2017)
10. Hohl, P., Münch, J., Schneider, K., Stupperich, M.: Forces that prevent agile adoption in the automotive domain. In: Abrahamsson, P., Jedlitschka, A., Nguyen Duc, A., Felderer, M., Amasaki, S., Mikkonen, T. (eds.) PROFES 2016. LNCS, vol. 10027, pp. 468–476. Springer, Cham (2016). https://doi.org/10.1007/978-3-319-49094-6_32
11. Hwang, J., Vukovic, M., Anerousis, N.: FitScale: scalability of legacy applications through migration to cloud. In: Sheng, Q.Z., Stroulia, E., Tata, S., Bhiri, S. (eds.) ICSOC 2016. LNCS, vol. 9936, pp. 123–139. Springer, Cham (2016). https://doi.org/10.1007/978-3-319-46295-0_8
12. Jamshidi, P., Pahl, C., Mendonça, N.C.: Pattern-based multi-cloud architecture migration. Softw. Pract. Exp. **47**(9), 1159–1184 (2017)
13. Kitchenham, B.: Procedures for performing systematic reviews. Keele UK Keele Univ. **33**(2004), 1–26 (2004)
14. Knoche, H.: Sustaining runtime performance while incrementally modernizing transactional monolithic software towards microservices. In: Proceedings of the 7th ACM/SPEC on International Conference on Performance Engineering, pp. 121–124. ACM (2016)
15. Knoche, H., Hasselbring, W.: Drivers and barriers for microservice adoption-a survey among professionals in germany. Enterp. Model. Inf. Syst. Arch. (EMISAJ) Int. J. Concept. Model. **14**(1) (2019)
16. Linthicum, D.S.: Practical use of microservices in moving workloads to the cloud. IEEE Cloud Comput. **3**(5), 6–9 (2016)
17. Mazlami, G., Cito, J., Leitner, P.: Extraction of microservices from monolithic software architectures. In: 2017 IEEE International Conference on Web Services (ICWS), pp. 524–531. IEEE (2017)
18. Newman, S.: Building Microservices: Designing Fine-Grained Systems. O'Reilly Media Inc., Sebastopol (2015)
19. Petersen, K., Feldt, R., Mujtaba, S., Mattsson, M.: Systematic mapping studies in software engineering. In: EASE, vol. 8, pp. 68–77 (2008)
20. Schmidt, D.C.: Model-driven engineering. Comput. IEEE Comput. Soc. **39**(2), 25 (2006)
21. Taibi, D., Lenarduzzi, V., Pahl, C.: Processes, motivations, and issues for migrating to microservices architectures: an empirical investigation. IEEE Cloud Comput. **4**(5), 22–32 (2017)

22. Vogelsang, A., Amorim, T., Pudlitz, F., Gersing, P., Philipps, J.: Should i stay or should i go? on forces that drive and prevent MBSE adoption in the embedded systems industry. arXiv preprint arXiv:1709.00266 (2017)
23. Vural, H., Koyuncu, M., Guney, S.: A systematic literature review on microservices. In: Gervasi, O., et al. (eds.) ICCSA 2017. LNCS, vol. 10409, pp. 203–217. Springer, Cham (2017). https://doi.org/10.1007/978-3-319-62407-5_14
24. Wohlin, C.: Guidelines for snowballing in systematic literature studies and a replication in software engineering. In: Proceedings of the 18th International Conference on Evaluation and Assessment in Software Engineering, p. 38. ACM (2014)
25. Wolff, E.: Microservices: Flexible Software Architecture. Addison-Wesley Professional, Boston (2016)

Towards a Maturity Model for Cloud Service Customizing

Oscar Avila$^{(\boxtimes)}$, Cristian Paez, and Dario Correal

Department of Systems and Computing Engineering, School of Engineering,
Universidad de los Andes, Bogotá, Colombia
{oj.avila, co.paez, dcorreal}@uniandes.edu.co

Abstract. In last years, more and more cloud providers are making great efforts to offer personalized services that fully match customers' needs. However, it is not always easy because of the maturity level that requires their customization capabilities in order to design, implement, operate and improve personalized services. Furthermore, there is a lack of tools to help cloud providers to understand what is the current maturity level of their customization processes and the path to improve them. In this context, this work presents our progress for building a maturity model for the customization of cloud services. The model is proposed from a literature review in the area and two interviews to industry experts. The model, that includes two dimensions (customization capabilities and maturity levels) aims at helping researchers to develop new contributions in this research area and practitioners to develop their customization capabilities.

Keywords: Cloud computing · Customization · Personalized · Configurable · SaaS · PaaS · IaaS · Capability model

1 Introduction

Cloud computing is helping organizations to provide an increased experience to customers in all industrial sectors through its characteristics that include elasticity, broad network access, and on demand self-service, among others [1, 2]. However, the possibility of taking such advantage depends directly on the cloud provider capabilities to customize the service characteristics in order to match customer needs. Such requirements can range from security and access changes to workflow and business process logic modification, creating a large scope of options when we refer to cloud customization. However, providing customized services that fully satisfy customer needs is very hard for cloud providers because of several reasons, among which are: (i) the investment level required to design personalized services considering the number of clients and the diversity of their needs and (ii) the high costs involved in managing personalized services during the operation considering the differences in their design and the request for change raised by customers [2].

Regardless of these issues, cloud providers are making great efforts to offer customization possibilities to customers in order to best serve their needs and in this way improve their experience in two ways: during the customization and implementation of the service and during its consumption. However, this purpose is difficult to attain as it

© Springer Nature Switzerland AG 2019
H. Florez et al. (Eds.): ICAI 2019, CCIS 1051, pp. 282–294, 2019.
https://doi.org/10.1007/978-3-030-32475-9_21

requires complex and mature capabilities in order to design, implement, operate and improve personalized services. In addition, there is a lack of evaluation frameworks allowing cloud providers to measure the maturity level of such capabilities. Assessing maturity levels can help them to improve the performance of their processes and in turn of the services they provide to customers [3].

In this context, this paper presents our progress towards the construction of a maturity model for customization of cloud services based on a literature review in the area and two interviews with experts of the industry. The objective of this model is twofold: (i) provide practitioners with a maturity model that can help them place their customization process on a scale that describes their maturity level, what serves as a basis to improve such processes and (ii) identify research opportunities in the field of cloud customization for researchers.

This work is organized as follows: Section two presents our research approach. Section three describes the literature review methodology, application and results. Section four presents the industry perspective that describe the results of the interviews to cloud experts. Section five describes the maturity model, describing its dimensions. Finally, section six presents the conclusions and future work.

2 Research Design

We propose the method described in Fig. 1 in order to design the maturity model. As said in the introduction, we consider that cloud providers need to improve their life-cycle process in order to fulfil customer needs in better way. Consequently, the first step of our method consists in identifying what are the main stages of the customization process on which maturity needs to be assessed to make the process more performant. Then, our proposition consists in defining research questions for each one of the stages (second step) in order to gather contributions concerning how such stages are performed at different maturity levels. The application of first and second steps are described in the next subsection. As our aim is to collect both research contributions and industry insight, we use to this end the research questions within a systematic literature review (third step) and two interviews with experts from the cloud industry (fourth step). Third and fourth steps are presented in the Sects. 3 and 4 respectively. Finally, we design the maturity model from the collected contributions by using a two-dimensional structure (capabilities and maturity levels) which are very common in the academy and the industry [3, 4]. The application of this last step is detailed in Sect. 5.

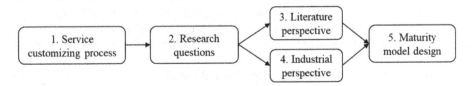

Fig. 1. Method for designing the maturity model

2.1   Service Customizing Dimensions and Research Questions

Assessing maturity levels and managing relevant processes can help organizations to improve their visible and invisible performance [5]. We consider thus that the customizing lifecycle process contains and organizes the aspects on which organizations need to improve and evolve in maturity in order to fulfil customer needs. According to [5] the customizing process includes the following stages: (i) Customization analysis and design, where aspects like the scope of the customization and architecture are defined, (ii) Customization implementation, where the aspects previously planned and designed are implemented and put into practice, (iii) Customization assessment, where measurements of the already working cloud service are made to evaluate customization effectiveness (iv) Customization improvement, were new characteristics that fulfill emerging needs are analyzed and implemented.

As described in the research method, we define research questions linked to the customizing process stages to lead the design of the maturity model from literature and the industry perspectives. The research questions that we propose are described as follows:

1. Customization analysis and design: How is the customization scope defined? Which are the tools (models, languages or notations) employed to express requirements and the architecture design of the service?
2. Customization implementation: How is the customization implementation process defined? In which degree customization implementation is made in an automatic, semi-automatic or manual way?
3. Customization assessment: How is customization effectiveness measured?
4. Customization improvement: How is the improvement of the service made?

3   Literature Review Perspective

We propose the following steps to carry out the literature review: (i) planning, (ii) conducting and material collection, and (iii) reporting. The description and application of these steps are presented as follows:

(i) Planning: it consists in the definition of the criteria and the query to conduct the search and validate the selected works. It aims at identifying the relevant contributions in the research field. In the case of this study, we used the following criteria:

- Cloud Services Search Terms: IT Service or ICT service or Cloud Service or Cloud Computing or Cloud Management or Cloud Sourcing or Software as a Service or Platform as a Service or Infrastructure as a Service.
- Customization terms: Customizing or Personalize or Customized or Adapted or Adjusted or Custom-build or Custom-made or Tailor-made or Made-to-order or Tailored or Configurable or Configuration.
- Search Area: Computer Science.
- Document type: Conference paper or Journal paper.
- Search field type: Title.

(ii) Conducting and Material Collection: this step is related to perform an exhaustive search for primary approaches by using the criteria previously defined. It also validates and assesses the found approaches with respect to the research questions. The goal of this step is to select a final set of works. We used thus the defined criteria in the Scopus search engine by introducing the following query:

TITLE (("information and communication technology service" OR "information technology service" OR "IT service" OR "ICT service" OR "cloud service" OR "saas" OR "paas" OR "iaas" OR "cloud computing" OR "cloud management" OR "cloud sourcing" OR "software as a service" OR "platform as a service" OR "infrastructure as a service" OR "software-as-a-service" OR "platform-as-a-service" OR "infrastructure-as-a-service") AND ("multi tenant"OR multitenant OR multi-tenant OR customizing OR customizing OR personalize OR personalise OR customized OR personalized OR adapted OR adjusted OR custom-build OR custom-made OR tailor-made OR made-to-order OR "made to order" OR tailored OR configurable OR configuration)).

This search returned 279 candidate articles as a result. To reduce the number of articles to be included in the analysis, firstly, a review of the articles titles was carried out. This filter reduced the number to 89. Secondly, a reading of articles abstracts was undertaken to filter those works that do not present evidence of answering any of the analysis questions. This filter limited the number of articles to 31. Thirdly, a complete reading of the articles was performed to select the final works set, made up of 25 articles [6–30] which were identified and included in the analysis.

(iii) Reporting: this step presents a synthesis of the answers for each research question. A material analysis and interpretation is presented as follows.

Which are the tools employed to express requirements and the architecture design of the service?

In our analysis we found that the expression tools range from undocumented meetings to semiautomatic tools using a mixture of languages that show how graphical models are commonly used to express requirements and architecture design. Specifically, we found that 9 papers used Flow Charts, 9 papers used Feature Models, 7 papers used the UML standard, 6 papers used Architectural models, 3 papers used Trees models, 3 papers used Components Models and 2 used meetings, interviews, and text documents.

How is the customization scope defined?

We found several methods for scope definition that includes case-by-case customization following an ad-hoc approach, customization following a set of options, and semi automatic or automatic configuration. We classify such methods as follows: *New modules* (5 papers) that consists in developing new functional modules following and ad-hoc approach as the client request them, in some cases reusing modules made in the past for efficiency. Selectable Modules (6 papers), it uses an approach that allows the customer to pick from a predefined list of already developed modules to use in his application, making the assembling of modules in real time. System Structure (2 papers), it is used to personalize the workflow and structure of the application through an interface that allows user to reconfigure their single instance according to their needs. Feature Selection Aid (8 papers) in this cloud services help users choose the features they need to get their desired service by mapping their requirements to the potential services through automatic matching algorithms.

How is the customization implementation process defined?

In our analysis we found that this aspect ranges from manual, sporadic and ad-hoc processes to architecture definition processes with customization aspects, extension points, and characteristics such as reutilization and automatization. We classified the contributions in: SPL techniques (10 papers) that include the domain analysis of the product to be developed, the development of assets that can be connected to a base application and a set of rules for the development and assembling of assets for new configurations. Development of new Architectures (6 papers) in which the objective is to develop a new architecture with customization in mind by defining all the major architectural components and a general workflow. Function customization (5 papers), that focus on the customization of short pieces of code (usually functions) in order to customize specific functionalities and improve user experience. Finally, Implementation of Algorithms (4 papers), that run algorithms that automate or aid users with their customization process.

In which degree customization implementation is made in an automatic, semiautomatic or manual way?

In our study, we found that in 17 papers the implementation process was completely manual, 5 used semiautomatic tools and procedures in certain stages and 3 used automatic tools and methods in some of activities. Concerning manual processes, they concern mainly Software Product Lines (SPL) related methods and their variations. The semiautomatic processes are mostly related to the use of semiautomatic tools for defining new architectures and customization, and the automatic processes are mostly related to the implementation of algorithms to automate or aid users with the customization process without interacting with IT developers or analysts.

How is customization effectiveness measured?

We found 5 papers that mention the need for establishing service-level agreements (SLA) with well-defined metrics in order to define the operation expectative of users. Service levels usually are related to the availability of the service (3 papers), and some of them refer to other quality and technical aspects such as capacity or security (2 papers). The real performance of the service needs then to be measured in order to determine if service levels are being achieved. The papers argued that service level achievement is narrowly related to customization effectiveness. We did not find measurement aspects related to the service functionality.

How is the improvement of the service made?

We found 17 papers addressing the improvement of customized services through the development of new functionality or the improvement of the current one. Those works can be classified in two groups: the works of the first group, that we call *development of independent modules and services*, propose methods for the development of modules case by case depending on user's requests and needs. In such case, each tenant of the service has a different set of modules that cannot be reusable with other tenants. The works of the second group, that we call *integration of reusable modules and components*, consist in preexisting configurable modules, role adaptable modules, graphical and work flow templates and architectures with extension points that allow each tenant's instance to incorporate new modules depending on their needs.

The base of such propositions is mainly an adaptable architecture compatible with all instances and a system to keep already created modules updated so they can be used when needed.

4 Industry Perspective

We carry out two separate interviews for about 90 min each one to two expert consultants working in two different international companies that provide cloud services mainly in Europe and Latin America. We used the research questions and the results of the literature review to get insight from them. The main results are described as follows:

- *Which are the tools employed to express requirements and architecture design?* Both consultants responded they use a tool to track customer customizing requests such as Pivotal Tracker and Jira. To model functional and technical requirements they use several types of diagrams by using manual tools such as Draw.io. They agreed with the literature review results concerning the range of tools and stated that more advanced maturity levels should involve automated tools and graphical models.
- *How is the customization scope defined?* Consultant 1 responded that in her company the scope is defined through a predefined set of configuration options. Consultant 2 said that the scope is not determined by options but it depends on customer needs and follows an ad-hoc approach. Both experts agreed with the literature review results and argued that maturity levels in this capability should evolve from defining the scope case-by-case following ad-hoc approach to automatic and standardized configuration of service characteristics depending on customer needs.
- *How is the customization implementation process defined?* Consultant 1 stated that one important aspect in the implementation in her organization was standardization of customization process activities. In addition, she argued that this aspect should be assessed through all the capabilities of the model in order to determine the standardization level at each stage. Consultant 2 stated that in addition, to the literature review results, highest levels of maturity should involve the integration or aggregation of external and internal services and/or the use of multi-cloud.
- In which degree customization implementation is made in an automatic, semi-automatic or manual way? Both consultants agreed with the relevance of this aspect during the customization life-cycle process and the results of the literature review. Consultant 2 argued that his company tries to automate as much as possible the implementation process activities. For example, new functionalities are automatically deployed through development, staging (quality control) and production environments, and services have automatic error detection and auto-repair capabilities (automatic rollback to return to previous version). Both consultants were emphatic in the fact that automation should be assessed not as an isolated capability but through the other capabilities of the model in order to determine the automatic or hand operated level of each stage.

- *How is customization effectiveness measured?* Both experts agreed with the importance of using metrics such as service time response, availability and incident number per period among others. They argued that maturity in the measurement should evolve to standardized and automatic processes.
- *How is the improvement of the service made?* Consultant 1 said they make improvement not only on functional aspects but on quality aspects (availability, security and continuity) as well by using operation metrics as main source of information. Consultant 2 said they carry out improvement from information automatically collected and analyzed in an analytics platform.
- *Do you think that other capabilities should be considered?* Consultant 1 expressed that communication channels with customers are very important especially during the design stage in order to interact and receive and clarify requirements. She said as well that quality control is very important during service operation. Consultant 2 said customer satisfaction is very important to measure effectiveness and classical measurement channels includes surveys, reports regarding accomplishment of metrics, as well as mail, phone and other channels to receive claims. He also argued that more sophisticated ways include the use of analytics platforms to collect and analyze information concerning user behavior when using the service to establish service usability and customer experience, user comments by using service functionality, sentiment analysis on social networks comments and download platforms (e.g. playstore).

5   Towards a Maturity Model for Service Customization

5.1   Capabilities

The capabilities of the maturity model, that are based on the results of the literature review and the industry perspective analysis, are classified on the stages of the customizing process (see Sect. 2.1 service customizing dimensions and research questions) as follows:

1. Customization analysis and design: we define three capabilities to be evaluated in this stage: *scope definition and expression tools* (from the literature review), and *communication channels* (from the interviews).
2. Customization implementation: we define two capabilities in this stage, *customization implementation process* (from the literature review) and *quality control* (from the interviews).
3. Customization assessment: we suggest one capability in this stage, *customization effectiveness measurement* (from the literature review).
4. Customization improvement: we propose only one capability, namely, *service improvement* (from the literature review).

5.2 Maturity Levels

Our maturity model evaluates capabilities in five maturity levels that represent the continual improvement of a cloud provider. To define such levels, we consider recommendations and insights from in the industry perspective section. In particular, we did not include a capability regarding the implementation process automation level but instead we decided to include this aspect within the levels in order to measure automation maturity in each capability. We propose thus that the more automatic is the way in which the provider perform the capability, the more mature is the process in such capability. We made the same with standardization, so that, the more standardized is the way in which the provider perform the capability, the more mature is the process in such capability. The maturity levels that we consider are described as follows:

- Level 1 - Initial/Ad Hoc. There is evidence that the provider has recognized the need for customization. However, there are no standardized procedures; instead, there are ad hoc approaches that tend to be applied on an individual or case-by-case basis.
- Level 2 - Repeatable. Service customization is addressed by defined procedures but not standardized procedures. There is no formal training and there is a high degree of reliance on knowledge of individuals.
- Level 3 - Standardized. Service customization is addressed by standardized and documented procedures, which are adopted through training. However, the procedures are not sophisticated, but are the formalization of good existing practices.
- Level 4 - Managed. Procedures are defined, standardized, and under constant improvement and provide good practice. Service Customization is clearly understood and semi-automatic.
- Level 5 - Optimized. Procedures are based on the results of continuous improvement and maturity modeling in comparison with other organizations. The service customization is automatic and provides tools to improve quality and effectiveness.

In general terms, while the capabilities escalate maturity levels, the customizing process acquires greater automation, standardization, improvement implementation which leads to a better service to customers.

5.3 The Maturity Model

In Table 1 we described the model by using the capabilities and maturity levels previously defined. In the intersection between those dimensions, we describe the characteristics of the capability depending on the level achieved by the provider in that capability. We explain below some of the capabilities, their intersections with the maturity levels and the rational used to define such intersections.

Scope definition assesses both the extent to which the provider is able to offer variants of the cloud service to the customer and the means the provider provides to the customer to build or select such variants. In this dimension, the customization scope ranges from customization made individually (case by case) by request following a manual ad-hoc approach (level 1) to automatic customization depending on user's needs and characteristics (level 5). As a result, for instance, a customizable service with

Table 1. A maturity model for cloud service customization

Stage	Capability	Level 1 - Initial/Ad hoc	Level 2 - Repeatable	Level 3 - Standardized	Level 4 Managed	Level 5 Optimized
Customization Analysis and Design	Customization Expression Tools	Customization is defined through undocumented meetings. Usage of such tool is sporadic.	Informal Text Documents are used to describe service customization. Expression tools are defined but only used for some services.	Formal text forms are used to describe service customization. These techniques are standard for all services.	Graphical languages are used to describe the customization requirements. Expression Tools are semi-automatic.	
	Team Communication Channels	Verbal Communication channels are used, which are informal. Miscommunication is common.	Communication channels (email, chat, document management systems) are defined and only used in some customization projects.	Communication channels are standardized across all customization projects.	Communication is made through an omni channel strategy tailored to client's needs.	
	Scope definition	Customization is only made by request and sporadically for each service following an ad hoc approach.	Users can select among predefined variants or configurations to customize services.	Users can define their own configurations or config-vices from options following a standard process. Such configurations are not predefined.	Values for configuration options are automatically recommended to users by a recommendation system based on their needs and characteristics. Customization is semi-automatic.	Customization is automatic depending on user's needs and characteristics. This process is monitored to ensure efficiency.
Customization Implementation	Customization implementation Process	The customization implementation process is manual, sporadic and made following an ad-hoc approach.	The customization implementation process is defined but only used in some customization services.	The customization implementation process is standard for all customization services and reuse components.	The customization implementation process follows a semi-automatic and standardized approach and aggregates internal and external services.	The customization implementation process automatically implements customization components, follows a standardized approach, and aggregates multi-cloud services.
	Quality Control	Quality Control is informal and sporadic.	Quality Control processes are defined and aligned with project management, but only used in some services.	Quality Control processes are an standard across all services which ensure customization quality	Quality control is semi-automatic and based on knowledge of the service's customization.	Quality control is automatic and focused in continuous improvement.
Customization Operation	Effectiveness measurement	Measurement of service level achievement is informal and made following an ad hoc approach.	Measurement of service level achievement is defined but only used in some services.	Measurement of service level achievement is an standardized and planned process for all services.	Measurement of service level achievement is an semi-automatic process that uses application statistics.	Measurement of service level achievement is automatic and monitored to ensure efficiency.
	User's satisfaction measurement	Processes that measure satisfaction are informal and sporadic.	Processes that measure satisfaction are defined but only used in some services.	Processes that measure satisfaction are standard across all services and uses classical communication channel with the user.	Processes that measure satisfaction are semi-automatic.	Processes that measure satisfaction are automatic and monitored. It includes the use of analytic platforms to collect and analyse user behaviour, sentiments and preferences.
Customization Improvement	Emerging Needs management	The evolution management is informal and made following an ad hoc approach. Evolution is only performed when requested and develop functional independent modules for each case.	Service evolution is a defined process but not made for all Customization Services. Formal sources of information to define improvement plans are not established.	Service evolution is planned and standard for all services. Customization Services. It re-uses existing functional modules in a manual way. It uses metrics of service operation to define improvement plans.	Service evolution re-uses existing modules in a semi-automatic way. It uses analytics platforms to define improvement plans.	

a maturity level 2 allows the user to select among already predefined variants that cannot be individually changed (see Table 1). These services allow personalization only by selecting another predefined variant with different preconfigured options.

Expression tools assesses the tools used by the organization to express the functional and non-functional characteristics for the personalization of services. In our model, we describe this capability from maturity level 1 to 4 ranging from oral and undocumented meetings to semi-automatic tools that offer tailored graphical languages.

We consider for example that an expression tool is in a maturity level 4 when it generates graphical templates (graphical models with base information) in a semi-automatic way according to the service customization context (see Table 1). Such utility can help analysts reduce time and improve efficiency when creating models to express customization requirements. Also, we consider that this dimension does not have a maturity level 5, since in current tools input from users are necessary and we do not see for the moment a clear evolution to full automation.

Customization implementation process assesses the degree of standardization, automation and service aggregation of the provider's customization process. This capability ranges from manual, sporadic and ad hoc approaches (level 1) to a process that automatically implements predefined customization components and aggregates services from multi-cloud sources through a standard approach (level 5) (see Table 1). To illustrate this, an implementation process with a maturity level 3 is standard for all services, however, it does not bring any degree of automation or service integration/aggregation.

User's Satisfaction Measurement assesses the automation, standardization and monitoring degree of the process that measures user's satisfaction through the personalization life-cycle. This criterion also assesses the means deployed and used by the provider to allow customers express their experience during the personalization process. Our maturity model describes from maturity level 1 to 5 this dimension, ranging from an informal and sporadic measurement process to an automatic, standard and monitored measurement process. For example, as shown in Table 1, a process with maturity level 3 has a regular and constant communication channel with users which allows the provider to directly measure satisfaction and receive complaints and recommendations for potential improvement. At this level, the process is standardized for all services, which ensures consistency and quality, however, it does not bring any degree of automation and monitoring.

6 Conclusions and Perspectives

We contributed in this paper a maturity model from a literature review and two interviews with industry experts. The literature review allowed us to define the basis and main characteristics of cloud service customization from the contributions and advances in this topic made in the academy. The industry analysis allowed us to gain insight from two expert consultants in order to validate the previously gathered basis and characteristics, enrich them with current practices in the industry and sort them in maturity levels. This last analysis also allowed us to get in-deep knowledge in the model capabilities.

As further work, first, the model needs to be validated and improved through additional interviews, focus groups and other validation techniques involving industry representatives. Second, a method to use the model is to be designed and validated in order to facilitate cloud providers its application. Third, a road map is to be proposed to allow providers to move from a current maturity level to a higher one. Fifth, the model is to be validated by applying it to several case studies in different industries. Last, further research is necessary to identify the benefits that cloud service customization can provide to customers in several areas such as Business and IT alignment [31] as well as to understand the implications it can bring to organizations in important subjects such as information security [32].

References

1. Armbrust, M., et al.: A view of cloud computing. Commun. ACM **53**(4), 50–58 (2010)
2. Zhang, Q., Cheng, L., Boutaba, R.: Cloud computing: state-of-the-art and research challenges. J. Internet Serv. Appl. **1**(1), 7–18 (2010)
3. Becker, J., Knackstedt, R., Pöppelbuß, J.: Developing maturity models for IT management. Bus. Inf. Syst. Eng. **1**(3), 213–222 (2009)
4. C. P. Product Team: CMMI for Development, version 1.2 (2006)
5. Ehrhardt, R.: Cloud build methodology. In: Handbook of Research on End-to-End Cloud Computing Architecture Design, pp. 105–129. IGI Global (2017)
6. Khan, K.M., Jiang, Z.: Managing client-specific customised functions in multitenant software-as-a-service. In: 2017 IEEE International Conference on Software Quality, Reliability and Security Companion (QRS-C), pp. 108–113 (2017)
7. Tizzei, L.P., Nery, M., Segura, V.B., Cerqueira, R.: Using microservices and software product line engineering to support reuse of evolving multi-tenant SaaS. In: Proceedings of the 21st International Systems and SPL Conference. pp. 205–214. ACM (2017)
8. Hajlaoui, J.E., Omri, M.N., Benslimane, D.: Multi-tenancy aware configurable service discovery approach in cloud computing. In: 2017 IEEE 26th International Conference on Enabling Technologies: Infrastructure for Collaborative Enterprises, pp. 232–237 (2017)
9. Zhou, Y., Hoffmann, H., Wentzlaff, D.: Cash: supporting IaaS customers with a sub-core configurable architecture. In: 2016 ACM/IEEE 43rd Annual International Symposium on Computer Architecture (ISCA), pp. 682–694 (2016)
10. Bobak, M., Hluchy, L., Tran, V.: Tailored platforms as cloud service. In: 2015 IEEE 13th International Symposium on Intelligent Systems and Informatics (SISY), pp. 43–48 (2015)
11. Cao, Y., Lung, C.H., Ajila, S.A.: Constraint-based multi-tenant SaaS deployment using feature modeling and XML filtering techniques. In: 2015 IEEE 39th Annual Computer Software and Applications Conference, vol. 3, pp. 454–459 (2015)
12. Kriouile, H., Mcharfi, Z., Asri, B.E.: Towards a high configurable SaaS: to deploy and bind auser-aware tenancy of the SaaS. In: ICEIS 2015 - Proceedings of the 17th International Conference on Enterprise Information Systems, vol. 2, pp. 674–679 (2015)
13. Kumara, I., Han, J., Colman, A., Kapuruge, M.: Runtime evolution of service-based multi-tenant SaaS applications. In: Basu, S., Pautasso, C., Zhang, L., Fu, X. (eds.) ICSOC 2013. LNCS, vol. 8274, pp. 192–206. Springer, Heidelberg (2013). https://doi.org/10.1007/978-3-642-45005-1_14
14. Khalil, E., Enniari, S., Zbakh, M.: Cloud computing architectures based multitenant IDS. In: 2013 National Security Days (JNS3), pp. 1–5 (2013)

15. Tsai, W.T., Sun, X.: SaaS multi-tenant application customization. In: 2013 IEEE Seventh International Symposium on Service-Oriented System Engineering, pp. 1–12 (2013)
16. Lee, W., Choi, M.: A multi-tenant web application framework for SaaS. In: 2012 IEEE Fifth International Conference on Cloud Computing, pp. 970–971 (2012)
17. Schroeter, J., Cech, S., Gotz, S., Wilke, C., Aßmann, U.: Towards modeling a variable architecture for multi-tenant SaaS-applications. In: Sixth International Workshop on Variability Modeling of Software- Intensive Systems, pp. 111–120 (2012)
18. Liu, G., Zhang, W., Li, D., Zhou, S., Zhu, Z.: BPEL based service process configuration in SaaS application. In: Wu, Y. (ed.) Advances in Computer, Communication, Control and Automation. LNEE, vol. 121, pp. 157–164. Springer, Heidelberg (2011). https://doi.org/10.1007/978-3-642-25541-0_21
19. Kang, S., Kang, S., Hur, S.: A design of the conceptual architecture for a multitenant SaaS application platform. In: 2011 First ACIS/JNU International Conference on Computers, Networks, Systems and Industrial Engineering, pp. 462–467 (2011)
20. Wang, H., Zheng, Z.: Software architecture driven configurability of multi-tenant SaaS application. In: Wang, F.L., Gong, Z., Luo, X., Lei, J. (eds.) WISM 2010. LNCS, vol. 6318, pp. 418–424. Springer, Heidelberg (2010). https://doi.org/10.1007/978-3-642-16515-3_52
21. Mietzner, R., Leymann, F., Papazoglou, M.P.: Defining composite configurable SaaS application packages using SCA, variability descriptors and multi-tenancy patterns. In: 2008 Third International Conference on Internet and Web Applications and Services, pp. 156–161 (2008)
22. Müller, J., Krüger, J., Enderlein, S., Helmich, M., Zeier, A.: Customizing enterprise software as a service applications: back-end extension in a multi-tenancy environment. In: Filipe, J., Cordeiro, J. (eds.) ICEIS 2009. LNBIP, vol. 24, pp. 66–77. Springer, Heidelberg (2009). https://doi.org/10.1007/978-3-642-01347-8_6
23. Jumagaliyev, A., Whittle, J., Elkhatib, Y.: Evolving multi-tenant SaaS cloud applications using model-driven engineering. In: CEUR Workshop Proceedings, vol. 1706, pp. 60–64 (2016)
24. Walraven, S., Borger, W.D., Vanbrabant, B., Lagaisse, B., Landuyt, D.V., Joosen, W.: Adaptive performance isolation middleware for multi-tenant SaaS. In: 2015 IEEE/ACM 8th International Conference on Utility and Cloud Computing (UCC), pp. 112–121 (2015)
25. Khan, K.M., Nhlabatsi, A., Khan, N.: A process model for customisation of software in multi-tenant SaaS model. In: 2015 IEEE/ACM 8th International Conference on Utility and Cloud Computing (UCC), pp. 418–419 (2015)
26. Sun, W., Zhang, X., Guo, C.J., Sun, P., Su, H.: Software as a service: configuration and customization perspectives. In: 2008 IEEE Congress on Services Part II (Services-2 2008), pp. 18–25 (2008)
27. Correia, A., Penha, J.R., Da Cruz, A.M.R.: An architectural model for customizing the business logic of SaaS applications. In: ICSOFT 2013 - Proceedings of the 8th International Joint Conference on Software Technologies, pp. 162–168 (2013)
28. Jamshidi, P., Pahl, C.: Orthogonal variability modeling to support multi-cloud application configuration. In: Ortiz, G., Tran, C. (eds.) ESOCC 2014. CCIS, vol. 508, pp. 249–261. Springer, Cham (2015). https://doi.org/10.1007/978-3-319-14886-1_23
29. Walraven, S., Van Landuyt, D., Truyen, E., Handekyn, K., Joosen, W.: Efficient customization of multi-tenant software-as-a-service applications with service lines. J. Syst. Softw. 91(1), 48–62 (2014)
30. Schroeter, J., Mucha, P., Muth, M., Jugel, K., Lochau, M.: Dynamic configuration management of cloud-based applications. In: Proceedings of the 16th International Software Product Line Conference - Volume 2, SPLC 2012, pp. 171–178 (2012)

31. Avila, O., Garcés, K.: Change management contributions for business-IT alignment. In: Abramowicz, W., Kokkinaki, A. (eds.) BIS 2014. LNBIP, vol. 183, pp. 156–167. Springer, Cham (2014). https://doi.org/10.1007/978-3-319-11460-6_14

32. Rueda, S., Avila, O.: Automating information security risk assessment for IT services. In: Florez, H., Diaz, C., Chavarriaga, J. (eds.) ICAI 2018. CCIS, vol. 942, pp. 183–197. Springer, Cham (2018). https://doi.org/10.1007/978-3-030-01535-0_14

Towards an Architecture Framework for the Implementation of Omnichannel Strategies

Nestor Suarez and Oscar Avila[(⊠)]

Department of Systems and Computing Engineering, School of Engineering,
Universidad de los Andes, Bogotá, Colombia
{nl.suarez,oj.avila}@uniandes.edu.co

Abstract. New technological trends and disruptive technologies are allowing companies from multiple sectors to define and implement omnichannel strategies to provide a better customer experience. The implementation of such strategies consists of supporting marketing and sales activities through interrelated and coherent channels in order to reach target markets. Although this approach has allowed companies to exploit digital technologies to get competitive advantages, its implementation involves harmonizing marketing, sales, delivery and service processes as well as the underlying information and technology infrastructures supporting them for the correct operation of the company. However, as far as we know, there is no approach dealing with the alignment of these different aspects which are at different organisational levels. To deal with this lack, we present in this paper our advances towards an architecture framework to fit business and information and technology aspects related to omnichannel development. The framework is applied to a case study in the educative sector.

Keywords: Enterprise architecture · Digital services · Customer journey · Customer understanding · Multichannel

1 Introduction

New technological trends and disruptive technologies are allowing companies from multiple sectors to implement omnichannel strategies to provide a better experience to customers. Such strategies consist in developing the customer relationship through multiple digital channels (social networks, virtual stores, mobile applications, sensors, etc.) and traditional channels (warehouses, distribution points, home delivery, etc.) by achieving integration between them [1, 2]. This context implies a great complexity related to the harmonization and synergy needed between business strategy and processes, information and technology for the incorporation and operation of channels. That is why the implementation of omnichannel strategies involve defining, implementing and aligning elements at different organizational levels such as business, data, application and infrastructure levels. This is where enterprise architecture approaches become important as they provide the methodology to align in a holistic manner business and Information Technology (IT) elements [3, 4]. However, in a preliminary

© Springer Nature Switzerland AG 2019
H. Florez et al. (Eds.): ICAI 2019, CCIS 1051, pp. 295–309, 2019.
https://doi.org/10.1007/978-3-030-32475-9_22

literature review, we did not find research works supporting the development of omnichannel strategies considering the specific characteristics of this kind of initiatives. Such characteristics include:

Physical channels vs digital channels: On the one hand, traditional bricks-and-mortar businesses that deploy digital channels may require to integrate them to traditional channels to efficiently execute logistic processes in order to control inventories and meet delivery expectations to both physical and digital customers [1]. On the other hand, exclusively digital organizations that open showrooms and face-to-face stores may require changes in the operation and processes dynamics, forcing them to harmonize distribution and delivery strategies [2].

Integration of information: the second characteristic relates the integration of information that flows through the deployed channels. Channels managed independently cannot achieve efficiencies in the marketing, sales, delivery and service chain, opening thus a door to nonconformities when customers do not perceive the same performance through the different channels and coherence between them [5].

Channel choosing: Although business and digital strategies are efficiently aligned within the organization, omnichannel strategies are directly related to the interaction of the organization with the customer and other third-parties. Organizations must thus select and provide the most efficient channels according to the characteristics of the target market segment in order to provide a positive experience [6]. When organizations interact with partners and suppliers, the most adapted channels to ensure the production and distribution need to be selected in a synergistic manner [7].

Culture of change: due to the close relationship of this kind of approaches with technology, organizations must be aware of changes in the technology environment and develop a culture of constant change allowing them to transform organizational operation and processes and hence the business and digital strategies [8].

To fulfil this lack of research works dealing with this specific characteristics, our aim is to propose an architecture framework for the development of omnichannel environments. This work is organized as follows: Section two presents related work. Section three presents the architecture framework. Section four presents the case study. Finally, section five describes the conclusions and future work.

2   Omnichannel Related Work

We carried out a literature review including research works [1, 2, 5–27]. In this review, we identified a lack of architecture frameworks and research works dealing with the definition, implementation and alignment of IT and business elements for implementing omnichannel strategies in considering the particularities of such type of initiatives. In particular, the literature review delivered the results summarized below in form of four issues.

1. There are no frameworks, models or methodologies to help companies implement IT for adopting omnichannel environments. Organizations deploy channels without considering a guiding model helping them include and synchronize business and technology requirements.

2. We did not find research works supporting information integration when using different IT services to support deployed channels. Specific IT services are implemented each time a channel is deployed and organizations face too complex information management.

3. There are no frameworks, models or methodologies that allow organizations to adopt omnichannel environments based on customer behavior. Channel deployments are due to specific market pressures and not to an established business strategy that contemplates the customer journey and in general the customer behaviour.

4. No contributions were found in the literature regarding technology identification and forecasting in the adoption of omnichannel environments. However, new technologies are very important in the adoption of such environments and it should be considered as a constant activity to identify them in order to be aware of potential threats and opportunities they may represent.

3 Towards an Architecture Framework

Among the enterprise architecture approaches and propositions in the literature, four frameworks have been the most predominately used: Zachman Framework [28], TOGAF [29], FEA [30] and Gartner [31]. These frameworks share a common objective which is the identification, analysis and integration of the organizational elements involved in business and technology strategy implementation. However, there is an attribute that differentiates TOGAF of the other frameworks: TOGAF sets a collaborative environment and capabilities for its integration with other reference frameworks and best practices such as ITIL, CMMI, COBIT, PRINCE2, PMBOK and MSP [32]. In addition, it offers several advantages due to its flexibility and implementation methodology (the Architecture Development Method - ADM) [32]. These reasons have made TOGAF the leading and the most used enterprise architecture framework [33]. It is why we have chosen TOGAF as the base approach to build our omnichannel architecture framework. Considering that TOGAF is an architecture framework for generic purposes, it does not deal with all the specific problems described in Sect. 2. In particular, the following aspects are not addressed:

- Technology forecasting: although the TOGAF framework provides guidance for technology adoption and implementation through the ADM, it does not provide tools to help organizations identify emergent and disruptive technologies that could be implemented to improve communication and relationship with customers.
- Customer understanding: although the TOGAF framework provides building blocks to gather and analyse requirements, constrains and assumptions of customers, it does not provide elements to help organizations understand behaviour and preferences of customers. This information is important in order to define the characteristics of the omnichannel strategy.

We propose thus to adapt TOGAF in order to address the points not covered by this framework. A general description of TOGAF content framework structure is described in Sect. 3.1 and the adaptations are described Sect. 3.2.

3.1 The TOGAF Content Framework

The TOGAF content framework [29] provides a structural model for architectural content that allows organisations to consistently define, structure and present the work products or outputs resulting of executing the ADM. Such products include process flows, architectural requirements, project plans, architecture diagrams and views, project compliance assessments, etc.

The content framework includes three categories to describe the type of architectural work product:

- *Deliverables*: they represent the output of projects. Deliverables are saved into an Architecture Repository structured by following the reference model structure.
- *Artefacts*: an artefact is an architectural work product that describes an aspect of the architecture. Artefacts are generally classified as catalogues, matrices, and diagrams. A deliverable contains one artefact or several of them.
- *Building blocks*: a building block represents an enterprise component that can be combined with other building blocks to deliver architectures and solutions. They can be classified in Architecture Building Blocks (ABBs) that typically describe enterprise capabilities (e.g. billing, shipping, customer service) and Solution Building Blocks (SBBs) that represent components (software, processes, data) that will be used to implement ABBs. Artefacts describe building blocks.

The relationships between deliverables, artefacts, and building blocks are shown in Fig. 1.

Fig. 1. The TOGAF content framework structure categories

The TOGAF content framework [29] defines all the types of building blocks that may exist in an architecture. Such definition includes the description of a set of entities and the relationship between them. Main building blocks include:

- *Architecture Principles, Vision, and Requirements* entities are intended to capture the surrounding context of formal architecture models, including general Architecture principles, strategic context and requirements.
- *Business Architecture* entities capture architectural models of business operation, looking specifically at motivational factors, organisation structure, and organization capabilities.

- *Information Systems Architecture* entities capture architecture models of information systems, looking at applications and data in line with the TOGAF ADM phases.
- *Technology Architecture* entities capture technology infrastructure assets that are used to implement and realize information system solutions.
- *Architecture Realization* entities capture change roadmaps showing transition between architecture states and binding statements to govern architecture implementations.

3.2   Adaptations to TOGAF

Adaptations to the TOGAF for adoption of omnichannel environments are made by adding new entities in order to address the aspect no covered by the original content framework. Those modifications are described as follows.

Coverage Matrix of Issues Identified in the Literature. Solutions to problems 1 and 2 are proposed by means of TOGAF blocks and entities. This framework helps organizations align business and IT objectives, integrate IT services and data components and implement IT. However, in order to adequately address issues related to the customer behavior and the organization's IT environment exposed in problems 3 and 4, it is proposed to extend to the original architectural framework since this framework does not propose specific elements for the solution of such problems. The resolution of problems through the original TOGAF and the proposed extensions are presented in Table 1. Such extensions are presented in the following subsections.

Table 1. Problems, extensions and modifications

Extensions and modifications	Problem 1: there are no frameworks, models or methodologies that help companies adopt IT to implement omnichannel environments	Problem 2: No research works supporting information integration when using different IT services to support deployed channels	Problem 3: Lack of contributions that allow organizations to adopt omnichannel environments based on customer behavior	Problem 4: No contributions regarding technology forecasting in the adoption of omnichannel environments
Original TOGAF	X	X		
M1: IT environment forecasting				X
M2: customer understanding			X	

Adaptation 1. Inclusion of the *IT environment forecasting* entity to the *Architecture Principles, Vision, and Requirements* building block. This entity is intended to continuously capture technological advances and trends that may negatively or positively impact communication and relationship with customers. Such advances, including analytics, IoT, artificial intelligence, and soon, may improve customer understanding and customer journey identification processes that in turn may help organizations define omnichannel strategies. For the IT environment forecasting entity to be included within the TOGAF framework, we follow the same structure in which inputs, processing and outputs are defined (see Fig. 2). Inputs refer to internal and external sources of information such as analysis of expert consulting companies in the area. Processing relates the steps to analyse inputs in order to define omnichannel strategies. Outputs concern reports with the results of the analysis undertaken. These elements are described below.

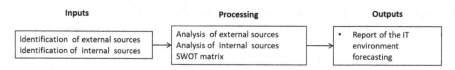

Fig. 2. Inputs, processing and outputs of the IT environment forecasting

Goals: The objectives of the IT environment forecasting entity are [34]:

- Review the external technological environment to identify those technological agents and trends that may impact organizations either positively or negatively.
- Review the internal environment, identifying internal needs by interacting with all areas of the organization.
- Deliver technological information to the organization that allows it to compete and evolve.

Inputs: Those are classified in external and internal inputs. Regarding types of external elements, we consider the following [34]:

- External actors: technology-based actors that can impact the organization through their IT services.
- External needs: It represents the demand side of the organisation environment. Actually, changing user needs may require changes into the companies in order to adapt them to these needs.
- External issues: current or future events that significantly influence the organization's environment and impact the achievement of the proposed objectives such as merge of companies, acquisition of companies, changes in sector regulation, etc.

We consider the following types of internal sources [34]:

- Internal actors: Because of their political power, the impact of their decisions and their capacity to lead transformation, internal actors should be considered.

- Internal needs: It is defined as the evolution of the internal requirements. It includes evolving needs from internal customers or departments.
- Internal issues: It involves events or other forthcoming developments (e.g., political factors, development in organizational culture and government etc.).

Processing Activities: For this entity we include the following processing activities:

- Analysis of external sources: It relates the analysis of external inputs from academic and industrial environments described before.
- Analysis of internal sources: It relates the analysis of internal inputs from internal areas described before.
- SWOT matrix elaboration: It consist in describing a SWOT (strengths, weakness, opportunities and threats) matrix from the analysis activities made before.

Outputs: Only one output is considered, namely, the IT environment forecasting report. It should contain the analysis performed to external and internal sources together with the analysis of the SWOT matrix. It should contain information about new technologies, actors, issues and other environment aspects and their respective potential impact for the organization.

Adaptation 2. Inclusion of the *customer understanding* entity to the *Architecture Requirements* building block. This entity is intended to capture customer understanding regarding behaviour and preferences when interacting through different contact points offered by the organisation. Such understanding includes the customer journey and requirements related to the interplay of customer through physical and digital channels. For the customer understanding entity to be included within the TOGAF framework, we follow the same structure in which inputs, processing and outputs are defined (see Fig. 3).

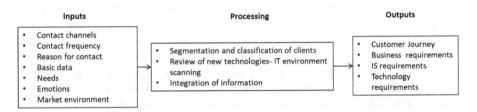

Fig. 3. Inputs, processing and outputs of the customer understanding

Goals: The objectives of the customer understanding entity are described as follows:

- Understand how the client behaves through the different contact points offered by the organization and generate the customer journey.
- Define according to the customer characteristics, the underlying business and IT requirement that will serve for the definition of the rest of architecture layers or building blocks.

Inputs: We consider the following inputs for this entity:

- Contact channels: Identify which are the contact channels used by customers during the different interaction stages.
- Frequency of contact: It can be used to be improve business processes related to logistics and inventories.
- Identification: Customer identification guarantees the strategies to be implemented by the organization meet customer requirements.
- Reason for contact: This can help the organization determine marketing, selling and service strategies and best practices.
- Needs: the organization must understand what the client needs. Needs can be directly expressed in the reasons for contact, however there are needs that cannot be explicit expressed and are part of the general analysis of the customer behaviour.
- Emotions: There are several ways to capture these emotions, ranging from qualitative analysis from observation to highly complex software to analyse word syntax and voice frequencies.
- IT environment forecasting: the outputs generated by the IT environment forecasting entity must be reviewed in order to identify which market trends and forces and which new technologies can impact customer relationship scenarios.

Processing: For this entity we include the following processing activities [23]:

- Storage: The organization must create and maintain a database containing the aforementioned identification, contact and additional specific data as required by the organization.
- Classification: based on inputs, the organization must undertake a classification of customers in order to design relationship strategies tailored to each customer category. Each organization must determine the most convenient parameters for this classification. The most recurrent are the age, the contact channel, the preference for a good or service and the amount of revenue generated by each client. This classification can be made manually or automatically by using the "K-means" or other algorithms [23].
- Customer Journey: It consist in describing a map of how the customer interacts with the different channels or touchpoints. In addition, it is also necessary to identify and understand the customer sentiments and experience when using such touchpoints [35]. Such understanding can help organisations improve omnichannel strategies [35]. For organizations that have never described a customer journey, it is proposed to find the current path followed by customers during marketing, sales and service activities by using the current deployed channels.

Outputs: We consider the following outputs for this entity:

- Business requirements: list of business requirements to support the customer journey and the omnichannel strategy.
- Information system requirements: list of requirements for the total integration of information, regardless of the channel through which it is generated.
- Technology requirements: list of technology infrastructure, network and security requirements necessary for the operation of the omnichannel strategy requirements.

Omnichannel Architecture Framework. Figure 4 shows the structure of the proposed architecture framework which contains the minimum set of building blocks and respective entities for the implementation of an omnichannel strategy. In this diagram, the *customer understanding* and *IT environment forecasting* entities capture specific requirements discussed before for the implementation of the omnichannel strategy. From these inputs, changes in business and logistics processes, roles and skills necessary to adopt the omnichannel environment are captured through the *Business Architecture* entities. Then, from the analysis of the new processes, the requirements to develop the IT applications and services that will support the channels to be deployed are captured by using the *Information Systems Architecture* entities. These applications must be synchronized with business processes and structured to handle information in a consistent manner no matter which channel the client is using. Finally, IT applications and services that will support the channels or touchpoint are deployed on the technological infrastructure represented in the architecture by the *technological architecture* entities.

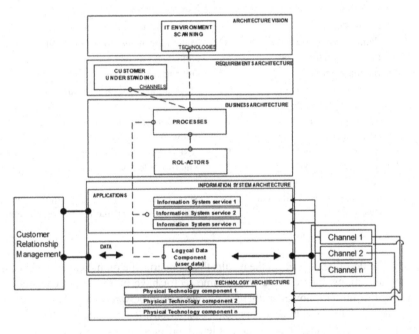

Fig. 4. Omnichannel architecture framework

4 Case Study

The case study concerns a private education institution with more of 20 years of existence in the market. It is recognized in the sector for their personnel training programs in the aeronautical domain. The institution wants to improve the relationship it has with current and potential students by improving their current customer relationship strategy and including new channels.

4.1   Architecture Vision - IT Environment Forecasting

Inputs: For external sources, institutions that provide similar education programs were analysed by accessing their website, requesting information by telephone and using any other channel deployed to identify the following information: deployed channels, omnichannel management, programs offered, cost of the programs, location advantages, additional benefits. In addition, the existing state regulation and commercial offers of software and IT service providers were reviewed. For internal sources, surveys were conducted to the internal stakeholders that form the organization.

Processing: An analysis of external and internal sources was performed. In addition, the following SWOT matrix was developed. In this matrix, S represents strengths, O represents opportunities, W represents weakness and T represents Threats.

Table 2. SWOT Matrix of the case study

	Internal factors		External factors
S1	High staff demand	O1	Implement technological advances
S2	Academic programs aligned with airlines requirements	O2	Make agreements to complete the preparatory cycle
S3	International Training	O3	Offer new programs
S4	Teachers with extensive experience in the sector	O4	Make alliances with new airlines
W1	Inefficient physical infrastructure	T1	Failure to comply with quality standard renewals
W2	Educational tools and bibliography - outdated or insufficient	T2	Lost support from the holding company to which it belongs
W3	Non-centralized data, different databases	T3	New regulations asking for requirements that are not accessible to the organization

Outputs: We describe as follows the results that concerns the omnichannel architecture work. Organizations that compete in the same sector have more contact channels that the analysed institution, however, there is no integration between such channels so that they are not able to provide an omnichannel experience to customers. The programs offered by the organization have been implemented in a very similar by the competition. No added value is generated to customers in comparison to other institutions. It is necessary to improve the efficiency of the physical infrastructure since the organization is distributed in two distant locations. Technological tools used in the pedagogical process are outdated respecting to the ones used by the competition. In addition, physical and digital bibliographic resources are scarce. Regarding the IT infrastructure, a centralization of data must be implemented to have a single source of information for all the organization dependencies.

4.2   Requirement Architecture - Customer Understanding

Inputs: We proceeded to prepare a template document with the necessary fields (see adaptation 2 in Sect. 3.2) to be applied to all channels deployed by the organization to collect customer information.

Processing: Data collected from the organization channels was standardized, unified and stored in a central database for the next processing steps. For customer classification, it was necessary to determine by interviewing different stakeholders which were the most important classification parameters. As a result, the parameter selected was the program, what allows us to classify potential and current students in three groups. The first group includes any program excepting the flight attendant program. The second group includes the flight attendant program. The third group includes the business training program. The customer journey for the student registration process, which is one of the core processes of the organization, is presented in Fig. 5 and described as follows. Users request information through four main channels deployed by the organization for this effect: Facebook, Twitter, mail and telephone. Payments made by users in an external site of a third party (usually banks). The rest of the activities, it is to say, documentation, registration, scheduling and training, are carried out by the students through the web channel and the physical site as presented in the figure, by following a unique path without the possibility of choosing alternative channels. In addition, there is no coherence between deployed channels.

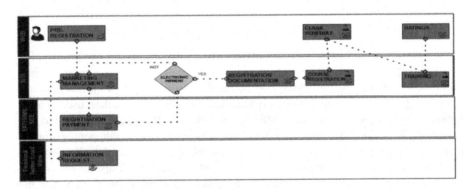

Fig. 5. Customer journey As-is

Outputs: The following requirements were formulated by the organization:

1. Information standardization and integration through all deployed channels: Web page, physical site, telephone, Facebook, Twitter, etc.
2. Execution of any activity of the registration process through any of these two different channels: the physical site and the web page.
3. Changes to software application and infrastructure and acquisition of new IT capabilities is necessary in order to support the omnichannel environment.
4. Changes need to consider economic and technical resources of the organization.

From these requirements, a To-Be customer journey map (see Fig. 6) was elaborated, where the customer can use any of the two required channels regardless of the last point of contact used. This strategy is intended to increase the use of the website and decrease demand on the physical site.

4.3 Business Architecture – Processes and Roles

Regarding processes, the registration process changes since the payment is made electronically through the website. The electronic payment also allows the organization to collect and updated user's information, which eliminates the preparation manual reports. As repetitive operational tasks decrease, the role of administrative assistants is concentrated in the management of the payment system that becomes a vital support to the marketing.

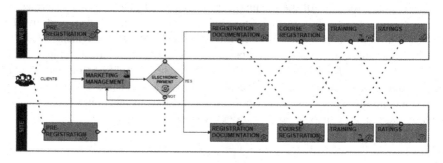

Fig. 6. Customer journey to-be

Regarding processes, the registration process changes since the payment is made electronically in the website avoiding physical records and bank reconciliations. Electronic payment also allows the organization to collect and update user's information, which eliminates manual fulfilling of formats. Regarding enrolment documentation, it is done automatically with the data collected in the pre-registration without human intervention. As repetitive operational tasks decrease, the administrative assistant role, that was before involved in payment and enrolment operations, is concentrated now in the payment system management and becomes a vital support to the marketing activities.

4.4 Information Systems Architecture – Applications and Data

From the analysis made in IT environment forecasting, customer understanding, processes and roles entities, the following design decisions were defined:

1. Applications supporting deployed channels must be integrated and data unified within a unique database. This will enable agility and integration of core processes.

2. The electronic payment service must be implemented on the website and payment terminal service must be offered on the physical site. Data form both payment methods need to be integrated to the unique database.
3. The pre-registration web application is to be archived and a functional extension is to be developed within the IS that support registration documentation and course registration. Data collected during the pre-registration process is to be standardized as it will feed the registration process.
4. The standardization of data collection also applies to the data collected from social networks that will feed a unified database for social networks.

4.5   Technology Architecture – Physical Technology Components

The technology architecture to support the requirements generated by the business architecture and information systems architecture must implement connectivity with the electronic payment and payment terminal services, enhance the servers of the registration IS by adding RAM to support the pre-registration process and make the connection to the unified database. To this end, it is necessary to extend the internet channel bandwidth to 20 megabytes in order to ensure agility in transactions. The necessary adjustments must be made to allow access to the process on the website through mobile devices.

5   Conclusions and Future Work

From a literature review, we identified a lack of frameworks and research works to help companies define, implement and align elements at different organizational levels such as business, data, application and infrastructure in order to implement omnichannel strategies. To address this lack, we propose an architecture framework by adapting the TOGAF content framework. Indeed, the original TOGAF is intended for general business and IT contexts and do not provides tools to tackle the specific characteristics of omnichannel initiatives. To this end, we proposed two adaptations or extensions: the first consists of integrating the IT environment forecasting capability and the second of adding the customer understanding capability. The framework was applied to a case study in which requirements generated by the new entities were considering in all the architecture layers (business, data, application and infrastructure) in order to support the omnichannel environment proposed for the organization.

   As further work, first, the adapted architecture model needs to be validated through interviews, focus groups and other validation techniques involving industry represen-tatives and architects. Second, an application method is to be proposed to allow companies to move from its current state to a desired state by using the framework. Such method could be an adaptation of TOGAF ADM. Last, strength and weakness of the model are to be identifying by applying it to several case studies in different type of industries.

References

1. Gao, F., Xuanming, S.: omnichannel retail operations with buy-online-and-pick-up-in-store. Manag. Sci. **63**(8), 2478–2492 (2017)
2. Bell, D.R., Gallino, S., Moreno, A.: Offline showrooms in omnichannel retail: demand and operational benefits. Manag. Sci. **64**(4), 1629–1651 (2018)
3. Avila, O., Goepp, V., Kieffer, F.: Understanding and classifying information systems alignment approaches. J. Comput. Inf. Syst. **50**(1), 2–14 (2009)
4. Avila, O., Goepp, V., Kieffer, F.: A framework to analyse is alignment approaches: towards the definition of underlying alignment mechanisms. In: Proceedings of MoDISE-EUS 2008, pp. 79–90 (2008)
5. Lee, C.K.H.: A GA-based optimisation model for big data analytics supporting anticipatory shipping in Retail 4.0. Int. J. Prod. Res. **55**(2), 593–605 (2017)
6. Park, A., Park, A., Lee, K.: Service design based on IoT and technology comparison for fine art gallery. In: Proceedings of the 14th International Joint Conference on e-Business and Telecommunications - Volume 4: ICE-B, (ICETE 2017), pp. 138–143 (2017)
7. Oh, W., Lee, S., Lee, K., Jung, D., Son, H., Ko, J.: Implementation of product oriented omni channel technology using multi-modal information. In: International Conference on Information and Communication Technology Convergence (ICTC), Jeju, 2017, pp. 296–300 (2017)
8. Peltola, S., Vainio, H., Nieminen, M.: Key Factors in developing omnichannel customer experience with finnish retailers. In: Nah, F.F.-H., Tan, C.-H. (eds.) HCIB 2015. LNCS, vol. 9191, pp. 335–346. Springer, Cham (2015). https://doi.org/10.1007/978-3-319-20895-4_31
9. Kim, J.-C., Chun, S.-H.: Cannibalization and competition effects on a manufacturer's retail channel strategies: implications on an omnichannel business model. Decis. Support Syst. **109** (2018), 5–14 (2018)
10. Shen, X.-L., Li, Y.-J., Sun, Y., Wang, N.: Channel integration quality, perceived fluency and omnichannel service usage: the moderating roles of internal and external usage experience. Decis. Support Syst. **109**, 61–73 (2018)
11. Zhang, M., Ren, C., Wang, G.A., He, Z.: The impact of channel integration on consumer responses in omnichannel retailing: the mediating effect of consumer empowerment. Electron. Commer. Res. Appl. **28**, 181–193 (2018)
12. Hosseini, S., Merz, M., Röglinger, M., Wenninger, A.: Mindfully going omnichannel: an economic decision model for evaluating omnichannel strategies. Decis. Support Syst. **109**, 74–88 (2018)
13. Luo, J., Fan, M., Zhang, H.: Information technology, cross-channel capabilities, and managerial actions: evidence from the apparel industry. J. Assoc. Inf. Syst. (2015). Research Paper No. 2016-056
14. Yadav, V.S., Tripathi, S., Singh, A.R.: Exploring omnichannel and network design in omni environment. Cogent Eng. **4**(1) (2017)
15. Thamm, A., Anke, J., Haugk, S., Radic, D.: Towards the omni-channel: beacon-based services in retail. In: Abramowicz, W., Alt, R., Franczyk, B. (eds.) BIS 2016. LNBIP, vol. 255, pp. 181–192. Springer, Cham (2016). https://doi.org/10.1007/978-3-319-39426-8_15
16. Mirsch, T., Lehrer, C., Jung, R.: Transitioning to an omnichannel approach: a dynamic capability perspective. In: 2016 International Conference on Information Systems, ICIS 2016 (2016)
17. Härtfelder, J., Winkelmann, A.: Opportunities and challenges for local retailing in an environment dominated by mobile internet devices - Literature review and gap analysis. In: Multikonferenz Wirtschaftsinformatik, MKWI 2016, vol. 1, pp. 33–44 (2016)

18. Notomi, N., Tsukamoto, M., Kimura, M., Yamamoto, S.: ICT and the future of the retail industry - consumer-centric retailing. NEC Tech. J. **10**(1), 38–41 (2015)
19. Kang, J.-Y.M.: Showrooming, webrooming, and user-generated content creation in the omnichannel era. J. Internet Commer. **17**(2), 145–169 (2018)
20. Gao, F., Su, X.: Omnichannel service operations with online and offine self-order technologies. Manag. Sci. **64**(8), 3595–3608 (2018)
21. Togawa, T., Sato, T., Saito, J.: Media processing technologies for affective digital marketing. Fujitsu Sci. Tech. J. **53**(5), 38–46 (2017)
22. Carnein, M., et al.: Towards efficient and informative omni-channel customer relationship management. In: de Cesare, S., Frank, U. (eds.) ER 2017. LNCS, vol. 10651, pp. 69–78. Springer, Cham (2017). https://doi.org/10.1007/978-3-319-70625-2_7
23. Reis, J., Amorim, M., Melão, N.: New ways to deal with omni-channel services: opening the door to synergies, or problems in the horizon? In: Za, S., Drăgoicea, M., Cavallari, M. (eds.) IESS 2017. LNBIP, vol. 279, pp. 51–63. Springer, Cham (2017). https://doi.org/10.1007/978-3-319-56925-3_5
24. Schütte, R.: Information systems for retail companies. In: Dubois, E., Pohl, K. (eds.) CAiSE 2017. LNCS, vol. 10253, pp. 13–25. Springer, Cham (2017). https://doi.org/10.1007/978-3-319-59536-8_2
25. Liu, J., Abhishek, V., Li, B.: The impact of mobile adoption on customer omnichannel banking behavior. In: 2016 International Conference on Information Systems, ICIS 2016 (2016)
26. Li, Q., Luo, H., Xie, P.X., Feng, X.Q.: Enterprise networks integration in a sensing environment: a case study. In: Meersman, R., et al. (eds.) OTM 2014. LNCS, vol. 8842, pp. 265–274. Springer, Heidelberg (2014). https://doi.org/10.1007/978-3-662-45550-0_27
27. Ervasti, M., Isomursu, M., Mäkelä, S.-M.: Enriching everyday experience with a digital service: case study in rural retail store. In: 27th Bled eConference: eEcosystems – Proceedings (2014)
28. Zachman, J.: A framework for information systems architecture. IBM Syst. J. **26**(3), 276–292 (1987)
29. The Open Group: The TOGAF Standard, Version 9.2. https://publications.opengroup.org/downloadable/customer/products
30. Wang, X., Zhou, X., Jiang, L.: A method of business and IT alignment based on enterprise architecture. In: IEEE International Conference on Service Operations and Logistics, and Informatics, Beijing, vol. 1, pp. 740–745. IEEE (2008)
31. Scott Bittler, R., Kreizman, G.: Enterprise Architecture Process: Evolution 2005, Gartner Research Publication ID Number: G00130849 (2005)
32. Lim, N., Lee, T.-G., Park, S.-G.: A comparative analysis of enterprise architecture frameworks based on EA quality attributes. In: 10th ACIS Conference on Software Engineering, Artificial Intelligence, Networking and Parallel/Distributed Computing, SNPD 2009, pp. 283–288 (2009)
33. Sessions, R., De Vadoss, J.: A comparison of the top four enterprise-architecture methodologies (2014). http://download.microsoft.com/download/6/1/C/61C0E37C-F252-4B33-9557-42B90BA3E472/EAComparisonV2-028.PDF
34. Avila, O., Garcés, K.: Change management contributions for business-IT alignment. In: Abramowicz, W., Kokkinaki, A. (eds.) BIS 2014. LNBIP, vol. 183, pp. 156–167. Springer, Cham (2014). https://doi.org/10.1007/978-3-319-11460-6_14
35. Segura, M., Barragán, J., Alarcón, G.: The Customer Service Pathway, an alternative started tool kit for service improvement and innovation. Int. J. Good Conscienc. **13**(1), 14–27 (2018)

Learning Management Systems

Connecting CS1 with Student's Careers Through Multidisciplinary Projects. Case of Study: Material Selection Following the Ashby Methodology

Bruno Paucar, Giovanny Chunga, Natalia Lopez, Clotario Tapia, and Miguel Realpe$^{(\boxtimes)}$

ESPOL Polytechnic University, Escuela Superior Politécnica del Litoral, ESPOL, Guayaquil, Ecuador
{bpaucar,gchunga,nplopez,vtapia,mrealpe}@espol.edu.ec

Abstract. This paper describes the implementation of an open-source software developed using Python, which facilitates the materials selection process commonly used in engineering. This software has been developed by non-CS students (Materials Engineering, Food Engineering and Chemistry Engineering), as a project course of their 1st-year cross-curricular course of CS1 ("Programming Fundamentals"), in order to connect their CS1 learning process with core subjects related to their careers, aiming to motivate both, the use of computer programming in their personal development and also, their interest in their professional career. The program developed allows choosing between different types of materials, based on specific characteristics required by the user; furthermore, this program enables the visualization of the Michael Ashby methodology for materials selection, which allows non-CS students to solve a problem related to their career, while it gives upper-level students a new tool to learn in class. The dataset used covers approximately 10000 distinct materials, classified by its features as ceramics, metals, polymers, wood/natural materials, pure elements and other advanced engineering materials. As a part of the outcome of this project, a public access repository has been created containing the implemented algorithms and the dataset used. The code developed can be modified and reused under license "GNU General Public License". Finally, a report on the perception of non-CS students taking CS1 and the perception of upper-level students taking "Material selection" subject is described and analyzed.

Keywords: CS1 · Ashby methodology · Materials selection · Computer science education · Project Based Learning · PjBL · Self-efficacy

1 Introduction

The world is constantly changing and so is the higher education. Over the years the teaching and learning processes have undergone several breakthroughs to satisfy the society and industry needs, by enabling engineering graduates to recognize and solve both social and technical challenges. Low et al. [1] affirms that, nowadays, not only

© Springer Nature Switzerland AG 2019
H. Florez et al. (Eds.): ICAI 2019, CCIS 1051, pp. 313–326, 2019.
https://doi.org/10.1007/978-3-030-32475-9_23

technical skills are needed to be developed in the new generations of engineers, on the contrary, soft skills are compulsory to be formed, in accordance to the NEA guidelines [2]. These soft skills are consistent with the attainment of the 21st century skills, in which critical thinking, problem solving, communication, collaboration, creativity and innovation are highlighted as highly relevant for modern engineers.

The 21st century skills are meant to be developed during the student's higher education learning. Methodologies such as Problem Based Learning (PBL) and Project Based Learning (PjBL) have been developed as part of the solution to help the new generations of engineers improve their soft skills needed in the new era [3]. Khair et al. [4] analyzed the PBL and PjBL methods, and their studies proposed that PBL is more suitable for medicine and intern practitioners; on the contrary, PjBL approach has the conditions for the development of soft skills in engineering student and working life, due to its relationship to a final product as objective in which several tasks are deployed to be solved in order to reach an expected solution.

Teamwork is foresight as one the most important soft skills to be developed in undergraduate students, therefore the multidisciplinarity factor has been introduced to reinforce social skills. Hirsch et al. [5] state that the projects carried out by multidisciplinary teams generate, in general, higher quality final outcomes, mainly because the problems are tackled in an integral way and not only analyzed from one point of view, biased by a specific scope of knowledge. Additionally, according to the authors, the interaction with real-clients during the project development process reinforces their communication abilities, teamwork and problem solving skills.

Wing [6] mentioned that computational thinking is a necessary tool for any engineering student. The author highlighted the involvement of several mental tools directly related to problem solving. In addition, problem solving skills are the fundamental structure of programming [7] and several authors affirm that the implementation of software programming in the curricula improves students' cognitive abilities [8, 9]. Consequently, the students may develop the ability to solve problems of any kind by the application of their software programming abilities. On the other hand, Plass et al. [10] state that the burden of problem-solving tasks by using programming skills might be too heavy for novice students, recommending an introductory preparation course for freshmen students. The technical and soft skills acquired through problem solving and executed within a multidisciplinary group environment with a final product as a goal seeks to prepare students for real-life engineering challenges, in which senior students and graduates are expected to generate valuable solutions, considering different and complementary points of view by the applications of their technical and social skills in a particular teamwork, where several areas of knowledge come together.

In this context, the Escuela Superior Politécnica del Litoral (ESPOL) has integrated CS1 to its careers curricula (since 2016 for engineering and since 2017 for all careers). During these years some adjustments have been made in order to adapt the content and the methodology of the subject to non-CS students and their careers' needs, e.g. a biannual non-CS focused Hackathon has been implemented since second semester of 2017 [11].

With the aim of improving the students' self-efficacy, teachers and experts from diverse careers were consulted and chosen as tutors of a final course project. Four different multidisciplinary projects were proposed based mainly on the tutor's expertise. After that, the class was divided into groups of diverse careers whose curricula include a subject related to each project. Then, each group was assigned the project best related to the students' careers and the relation with that subject. Finally, five different stages were defined were the students had to progressively complete the project. One of these projects was "Material selection following the Ashby Methodology". The project was successfully completed by the students and was proposed and tested as a learning tool for upper-level students of the Materials Engineering career.

2 Material Selection Following the Ashby Methodology

2.1 Material Selection

The "Material selection following the Ashby Methodology" project consisted of implementing the Ashby Methodology through different phases where the students had to apply the content of the CS1 course in synergy with the acquisition of domain-specific skills. At the end of the course, a survey on the perception of students was performed with the objective of knowing their experience. Also, students of "Material selection" subject tested the software developed and gave their opinions about it and about the utility of learning CS1. During the project the students had to apply the knowledge acquired in classes and had to self learn new concepts related to material engineering and to CS. In order to facilitate the explanation of the case of study, the use and development of the Ashby graph of elasticity vs. density module is detailed. The use is manifested in the filtering of materials according to specific values of density and modulus of elasticity, through vertical and horizontal lines, respectively. Furthermore, it allows the selection of materials based on the performance index of this graph for values of specific rigidity in wires, beams and panels in flexion, which allows the user a selection in three levels, like the one proposed by commercial software.

The selection of materials is an integral part of the product design and development process. In general, the criteria for selecting materials are defined by the function, purpose and constraint of the components. Due to the wide variety of materials available, this selection can be a challenging task. In fact, it is essential to use a systematic material selection process, in order to avoid an inadequate selection by the designer or to overlook a better alternate material.

Each material has properties that result from the physicochemical interactions at the atomic or structural level, such as density, mechanical resistance, impact resistance, thermal conductivity, among others. On the other hand, a design for an application demands a certain profile of the materials, such as low density, high strength, good resilience, recyclability, low cost, among others. Due to the wide variety of available engineering materials and respecting the iterative spirit of the design process, a methodology should be established to facilitate the material selection process among the many available options.

Numerous material selection techniques have been developed over the years, all of which are based on a huge dataset of materials and their properties. The two key steps in the choice of materials are selection and classification. The first one allows to quickly reduce the field of possible materials to a few manageable, while the second restricts even more options and evaluates and classifies the options to identify the optimal materials [12].

2.2 Properties of Materials

The density is defined as the weight of the substance per unit volume. Its units in the international system of units are $Kg/(m^3)$ and it is usually represented by the Greek letter ρ.

The modulus of elasticity or Young's modulus defines the ability of the material to retain its elastic behavior. Its units in the international system of units are Pascal (Pa), although due to the rank it is usually expressed as Megapascals (MPa) and it is represented with the letter E [13]. The modulus of elasticity is related to the stiffness of the bonds of the atoms and the packing density of these.

There are characteristics that depend on their interaction with others, which generates a change in the behavior and performance of a material. This is true particularly in the stiffness index of the material, which is the modulus of elasticity divided by density. The relationship that leads to the stiffness value may vary, depending on the performance required by the material, and is generally used to optimize/minimize the weight in some particular application. To minimize the mass of a lightweight taut bar is an application that can be replicated in different ways in particular designs of mechanical or civil engineering. This is obtained through the calculation of the specific stiffness, given by Eq. (1). On the other hand, a typical situation is to arrange a material in the state of flexion instead of tension, which is modeled according to Eq. (2). Likewise, the mathematical modeling of a panel in flexion is estimated according to Eq. (3) [14].

$$R = \frac{E}{\rho}. \tag{1}$$

$$R = \frac{E^{1/2}}{\rho}. \tag{2}$$

$$R = \frac{E^{1/3}}{\rho}. \tag{3}$$

2.3 Ashby's Methodology

Ashby's methodology compares the relative performance of a variety of materials for a specific constructive function using performance indexes as design criteria. The selection of materials, based on these performance indexes, is best done by plotting the performance indexes that are usually a mathematical combination of material properties on each axis of a materials selection chart [13]. In this graph it is demonstrated that the properties of the different kinds of materials can vary in wide intervals, forming groups that are located in closed areas, zones or distinguishable fields. That means the same family of materials can have an appreciable variation in their properties, in the numerical sense strictly. In these charts, properties such as resistance, modulus of elasticity, density, tenacity, conductivity, diffusivity and thermal expansion, costs, among others are plotted in order to deploy a range of materials based on a particular pair of properties and their derived performance indexes [15].

Figure 1 shows the Young's Modulus (E) vs. Density (ρ) chart. As it can be seen, ceramic materials are plotted and grouped in the yellow bubble at the top-right and have modules of up to 1000 (GPa). Similarly, the metals are in the reddish zone near the top right. On the other hand, polymers are found in the dark blue bubble in the center. Elastomers can be visualized below the polymers, in the lighter blue zone. The materials with lower density, which are presented in this Ashby graphic, are man-made foams and natural cellular structures, such as wood. It is evident that this presentation of the diverse families of the materials offers a general view that shows where the families and their members are in the space E $-$ ρ. This helps during the design challenge since the selection of material for applications of limited rigidity is commonly related to the minimization of weight [16].

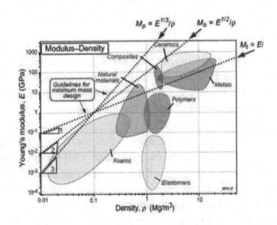

Fig. 1. Ashby's graph: Elasticity modulus vs. Density.

2.4 Python Programming Language

Python is a programming language with an open-code open for general purposes, optimized for quality, productivity, portability and integration. It is used by hundreds of thousands of developers around the world, in areas such as internet scripts, systems programming, data analysis, scientific research, user interfaces, product customization and more [17]. Python language can be easily accessed and used by the most experienced programmers, and also by the beginners, as there are many Integrated Development Environments (IDE) that facilitate the development and debugging of code in a single environment, as well as containing various functions and libraries clearly documented.

Python has many advantages, such as its gratuity, simplicity and extensive documentation, which allow anyone who has the motivation of learning computer programming to use it according to their own needs. Another advantage is that it facilitates modularization, which simplifies code maintenance and avoids redundancy, since different parts of the program can be modularized without having to repeat the same code several times. Another advantage is that libraries, lists and dictionaries that help the programmer achieve their final goal in a well-organized manner can be freely downloaded [18].

3   The Project Implementation

The final objective of the program is to create two graphs in Ashby's methodology, the first graph containing all the materials in the database, differentiated in colors and symbols, while the second graph should only contain the elements that meet the design restrictions imposed by the user. In addition, both graphs show the vertical module lines, the horizontal density and the stiffness line with their respective slope. For this, Python 3.7 has been used in the IDC PyCharm Community 2018 and the software has been organized in different modules, each with a specific purpose. The total process is subdivided into small functionalities, which facilitates the maintenance of the code and allows the reusability of parts of the program in other similar applications. The result can be downloaded in [19].

The software is composed of five modules and a main program (in addition to an extra web scraping script). The "information extraction" module contains a function that reads a csv file and organizes the information of the materials into a dictionary-type collection for general use. The second module "filter" contains functions that extract information about the materials that meet the requirements of the user. The third "graphic" module is responsible for making two graphs, one of all the materials from the database and another that only displays the materials that meet the user's requirements. The fourth "interface" module interacts with the user in order to set the problem's restrictions. Figure 2 shows the flow diagram that follows the modules of the program. The fifth "escribirArchivos" module puts together all the filter materials' data in a csv file in order to allow the user to see the data in Excel.

In order to obtain the information of the materials, the "MatWeb" webpage was scraped using the Selenium library [20] with a minute pause for each request in order to avoid overloading the Matweb server. The graphical interface is a data entry panel that contains options to select and enter values that are represented as limits in the Ashby chart. The interface allows selecting the slope or indexing according to the geometry of the material, it also allows enter a value for the limits of the properties (stiffness, density and modulus of elasticity) and a threshold condition for each of the selected properties. The families of materials (Metals, Ceramics, Polymers, Carbon, Wood and Natural Materials, Pure Elements, Fluids and Other Engineering Materials) were classified based on the information provided by the MatWeb webpage. In addition, it contains an information button "Info" to fill all the parameters, and another message on the button "Submit" to help the interpretation of the chosen values as depicted in Fig. 3.

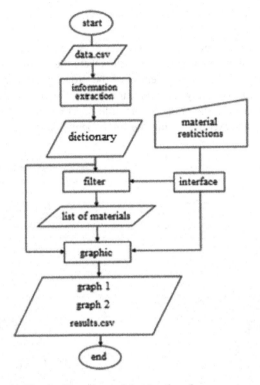

Fig. 2. Flowchart of the developed program.

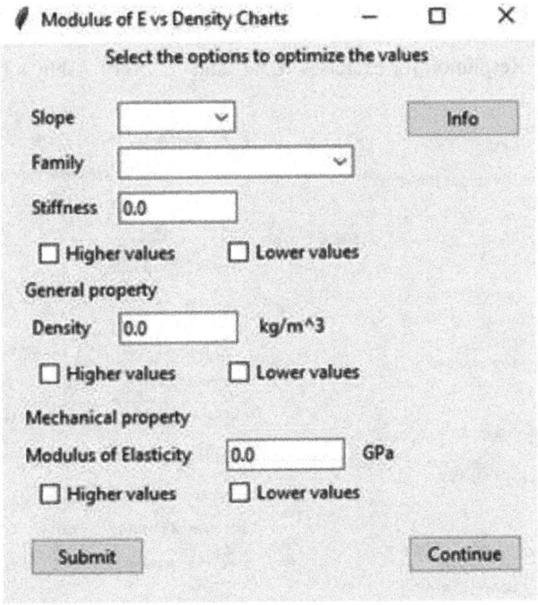

Fig. 3. Graphical interface for parameter input.

4   Project's Experimental Results

Tests were carried out following the specific rules of Ashby's book [13]. Two exercises were chosen and solved using the software; results were then compared with the book's solutions in order to verify the effectiveness of the program. Results provided by the software and results provided by the book are shown below. Figure 4 describes the approaches and solutions in the book. Meanwhile, the Figs. 5, 6, 7, 8 show the resolution sequences of said exercises using the implemented software.

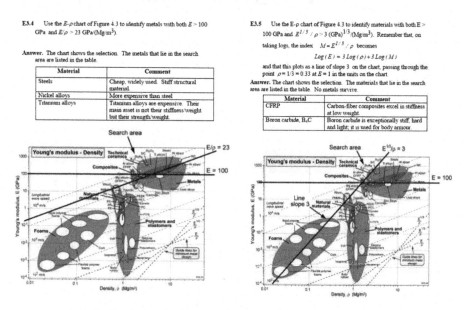

Fig. 4.   Resolution for exercises 'E3.4' and 'E3.5' of Ashby's book.

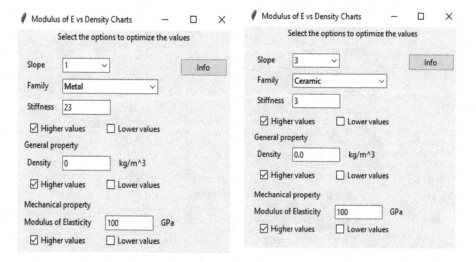

Fig. 5.   Interface with the book's restrictions for exercises 'E3.4' and 'E3.5'.

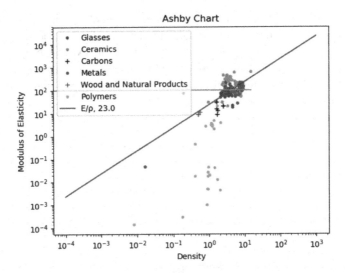

Fig. 6. Ashby's graphic for all materials from the database, including slope 1 ('E3.4').

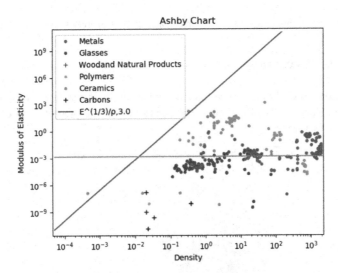

Fig. 7. Ashby's graphic for all materials from the database, including slope 3 ('E3.5').

In the first exercise, 237 materials were found that comply with the book's restrictions. The following materials and its data can be found in the csv file written by the software: "TIMETALÂ® 6-2-4-6 Titanium Alloy (Ti-6Al-2Sn-4Zr-6Mo)", "Titanium Ti-6Al-4V ELI (Grade 23)) "," Titanium Ti-10V-2Fe-3Al (Ti 10-2-3) Solution Treated 850Â ° C (1560Â ° F) "," TIMETALÂ® 3-2.5 Titanium Alloy (Ti-3Al-2.5V; ASTM Grade 9) CWSR "," among others; materials that belong to the family of "Titanium alloys" mentioned in the resolution of the example proposed by the book.

In the second exercise, one material that meets the book's restrictions was found. This exercise shows a limitation of the software developed, which needs to receive a particular type of family to carry out the filtering, while the exercise of the book does not specify what type of material; However, in the solution given by the book, "Boron Carbide" can be seen as a filtered material, material that also was found by the software, as shown in Fig. 8 (right).

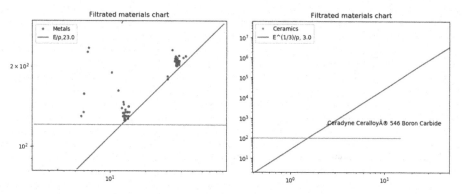

Fig. 8. Ashby Graphic that shows filtered materials, for exercises 'E3.4' and 'E3.5'.

5   Students Perceptions

57 (of a total of 60) CS1 students were consulted about their perception of many topics of the course. The results of the questions related to all the projects and course perception are shown next.

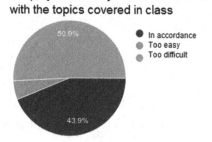

Open comments about the project

Fueron agradables, te llevaban a investigar más para mejorarlo y sobretodo que los temas van de acuerdo a la carrera que seguimos, sin embargo, me hubiera gustado trabajar con inteligencia artificial.

El segundo proyecto estuvo muy complicado.

en el segundo proyecto pude notar que la dificultad del que le tocó a mi grupo estaba bastante elevada en comparación con los demás proyectos; quizá sólo se trataba de explicar mejor de lo iba el proyecto, nunca me quedó muy claro realmente.

El proyecto final se me complicó un poco, pero cuando ya se le pudo dar solución fue woww, ya que el proyecto era muy interesante

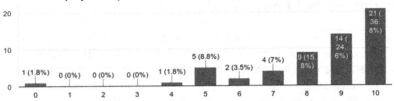

The project helped me to understand better the course's topics

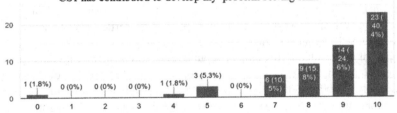

CS1 has contributed to develop my problem solving skills

Additionally, the developed software was tested with 12 students of the subject "Material selection" (from a course of 18). The students were asked to solve the exercises 'E3.4' and 'E3.5' using the traditional approach and using the software and then their opinions were asked. Some results are shown below.

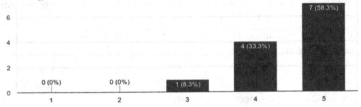

Do you think that the use of the software would optimize the learning process of the Ashby Methodology? 12 responses

Do you consider Computer Programming as a useful tool for the learning process in you career? 11 responses

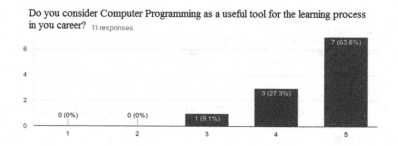

6 Conclusions and Future Works

The use of open source software developed in Python to facilitate the process of material selection according to the Ashby methodology turns out to be a valid option to replace those with a private license, given that it allows free access to the source code in order to make adjustments according to the needs of each user or application. Additionally, the presented software can be integrated into the classroom as a tool that helps to understand the Ashby methodology more easily.

The open source program allows to make graphics of "Modulus of Elasticity vs. Density", however future works, such as more pairs of properties, may be developed by students taking "Material selection" subject.

As part of the results of this project, a public access repository with the algorithms implemented and a dataset with the values of density and modulus of elasticity of approximately 10000 materials has been created [19] which can be useful for students and professionals who require similar exercises for the selection of materials.

The projects using this approach were perceived as difficult by half of the students. However, 87.6% of the students had a positive opinion in relation to the influence of the project for understanding the course topics. Many students commented that the projects were challenging and they were forced to learn extra libraries, such as csv, selenium, folium, opencv, etc. that were not included in the syllabus, and despite the initial "feeling of hopelessness" they feel increased mastery experiences after the project was completed.

As a future work a "tracking" of the students' progress in their careers is suggested. Furthermore, in order to really take advantage of the 1st-year cross-curricular course of CS1 a more synergistic relationship between CS1 and other subjects of the upper-levels in all the careers is needed. Regarding this, many teachers and experts consulted while searching for tutors declared they would like to introduce more CS related topics, exercises, projects or applications to their subjects, but they think that they or their students lack of the abilities needed for that.

References

1. Low, S.M.: Developing undergraduate students' multi-engineering skills through projects on embedded. In: 2006 7th International Conference on Information Technology Based Higher Education and Training (2006)
2. National Education Association: National education association, National Education Association [En línea]. http://www.nea.org/assets/docs/A-Guide-to-Four-Cs.pdf. [Último acceso: 28 July 2019]
3. Kolmos, A.: Problem-based and project-based learning institutional and global change, University Science and Mathematics Education in Transition, pp. 261–280 (2009)
4. Noordin, M.K., Md. Nasir, A.N., Ali, D.F., Nordin, M.S.: Problem-Based Learning (PBL) and Project-Based Learning (PjBL) in engineering education: a comparison. In: Proceedings of the IETEC 2011 Conference, Kuala Lumpur, Malaysia, pp. 1–14 (2011)
5. Hirsch, P.I., et al.: Engineering Design and Communication: The Case for Interdisciplinary Collaboration
6. Wing, J.J.M.: Computational thinking. Commun. ACM **49**(3), 33–35 (2006)
7. Beaubouef, T., Lucas, R., Howatt, J.: The UNLOCK system: enhancing problem solving skills in CS-1 students. SIGCSE Bull. **33**(2), 43–45 (2001)
8. Feurzeig, W., Papert, S., Bloom, M., Grant, R., Solomon, C.: Programming Language as a Conceptual Framework for Teaching Mathematics. Bolt Beranek & Newman, Cambridge (1969)
9. Ross, P., Howe, J.: Teaching Mathematics Through Programming. North Holland, Amsterdam (1981). Lewis R. & Taggs D
10. Plass, J.L., Moreno, R., Brünken, R.: Cognitive Load Theory. Cambridge University Press, New York (2010)
11. Bonilla, R.I., Lozano, E., Granda, R.: Pyweekend: not your typical Hackathon. In: 2019 IEEE Global Engineering Education Conference (EDUCON), Dubai, United Arab Emirates, pp. 853–858 (2019)
12. Shah, D.U.: Natural fiber composites: comprehensive Ashby-type materials selection charts. Mater. Des. (2014). https://doi.org/10.1016/j.matdes.2014.05.002
13. Ashby, M.F.: Materials Selection in Mechanical Design, vol. 3, p. 665. Elsevier, New York (1999). https://doi.org/10.1017/CBO9781197415324.004
14. Ashby, M.F.: Materials Selection in Mechanical Design. Materials Science and Engineering A, 3rd edn., vol. 53 Suppl. Pergamon Press 1992 (2005). https://doi.org/10.1016/b978-1-85617-663-7.00011-4
15. González, H.Á., Mesa, D.H.: Artículo-La importancia del método de selección de materiales (24), 175–180 (2004)
16. Ashby, M.F., Ferreira, P.J., Schodek, D.L.: Material property charts and their uses. In: Nanomaterials, Nanotechnologies and Design, pp. 147–176 (2009). https://doi.org/10.1016/b978-0-7506-8149-0.00007-6
17. Lutz, M.: Programming Python, 4th edn. O'Reilly Media, Inc., Sebastopol (2010). (J. Steele, Ed)
18. Ozgur, C., Colliau, T., Rogers, G., Hughes, Z., Myer-Tyson, B.: MatLab vs. Python vs. R. J. Data Sci. **15**(3), 357–358

19. Chunga, G.E., Paucar, B.G., Miguel, R.: OpenMaterialsSelector - Open Source Software for Material Selection using Ashby Method, March 2019. Retrieved from GitHub: https://github.com/mrealpe/OpenMaterialsSelector
20. Muthukadan, B.: Selenium Bindings 2 documentation, March 2019. https://selenium-python.readthedocs.io
21. Granta material inspiration: User Manual & Getting Stated Guide CES EduPack 2017 (2017). http://www.grantadesign.com/dowload/pdf/edupack2017/CES_EduPack_2017_Getting_Started_Guide.pdf

Development of Online Clearance System for an Educational Institution

Oluranti Jonathan[1], Sanjay Misra[1(✉)], Funmilayo Makinde[1],
Robertas Damasevicius[2], Rytis Maskeliunas[2], and Marcelo Leon[3]

[1] Covenant University, Ota, Nigeria
{jonathan.oluranti,
sanjay.misra}@covenantuniversity.edu.ng,
teny_bunper@yahoo.com, robertas.damasevicius@ktu.lt
[2] Kaunas University of Technology, Kaunas, Lithuania
{robertas.damasevicius,rytis.maskeliunas}@ktu.lt
[3] Universidad Nacional de Loja, Loja, Ecuador
marceloleonll@gmail.com

Abstract. It is mandatory for graduating students of an educational institution to exit the system in an orderly manner. The students usually do this through the mandatory clearance process. The manual process is time-consuming and stressful as the students have to move from place to place to get their clearance document endorsed. It has also been found to be vulnerable to fraud and other vices. The few automated ones also exhibit some limitations in their functionalities such as non-user-friendly interface, lack of adequate information to user, non-prioritization of processes and so on. This study therefore proposes a system that overcomes the issues with manual processing while improving on the identified automated ones. The study adopts a case study approach of a complete manual system for a leading institution of learning in Southwest Nigeria, with a view to evolving a working prototype. First a thorough understanding of the existing procedure is carried out. A new system that is web-based is built using Hypertext Markup Language (HTML) along with PHP for business logic layer, CSS for proper rendering of display pages of the front end and MySQL for the data layer. The new system will reduce the amount of time and efforts wasted on students' clearance as well as reduce cost incurred on paper by the institution. Another advantage is that students can also initiate and monitor their clearance status from any location they are thereby eliminating the need to travel or be physically present.

Keywords: Clearance · System · Web-based · Student · Institution · Online

1 Introduction

The Oxford Advanced Learner dictionary defines the word 'clearance' as a formal authorization, permitting access to classified information, documents etc. No one should be granted access to classified information solely because of their position or rank in an organizational level, but once a clearance is obtained, access to the requested information will be granted. However, in the context of an educational institution, we

H. Florez et al. (Eds.): ICAI 2019, CCIS 1051, pp. 327–339, 2019.
https://doi.org/10.1007/978-3-030-32475-9_24

consider clearance as a mandatory process that all graduating students or workers exiting a system must undergo. Although the results of carrying out clearance in most institutions are the same, the modalities for the clearance may vary from institution to institution. For instance, in Covenant University, Southwest Nigeria, the clearance is mandatory for all graduating students and must be done before proceeding on the mandatory one-year National Youth Service Corps (NYSC) programme of the Federal Government. A number of students have missed the opportunity to participate in the programme due to their inability to complete the clearance process. The major reason given is the absence of personnel responsible for the task of clearing the students at the time the students need them. At some other institution, clearance is done mostly at the point of final exit or collection of final results. It is however sad to note that most institutions still conduct this vital activity using manual means. There are several concerns when it comes to the issue of manual clearance. According to [1], some of the issues with current manual clearance include: (i) the unavailability of the clearing officer as at when needed, (ii) the offices and departments to visit are quite many requiring so much effort moving around, (iii) the process is time and effort-consuming, (iv) clearing officer may cleverly delay expecting some kind of gratification from the students, (v) the queue for clearance may be quite long, students becoming wearied while waiting, (vi) inability to check system for student records due to power failure or faulty system and a host of other reasons.

Considering all these factors, there is therefore the need to develop a system that mitigates all limitations mentioned above. This work leverage on the current advances in technology to solve the issues highlighted as regards existing clearance system. A web-based clearance application that has the advantage of web-based information processing over those of the traditional or manual systems is designed and developed. Thus, an online clearance system allows users to check their clearance status and find out whether there is anything standing against their being cleared such as balance of fees to be paid for tuition, medical or utility, borrowed books that are yet to be returned to the library, among others. The expected benefits of the online system are enormous. The online system saves a lot of time, allows for ease of use, faster information processing, and reduction in the cost of labor and stationery for institution [2]. Moreover, the issue of delayed youth service as a result of inability to complete the tedious manual process of clearance would be drastically curtailed.

Other sections of this work include related works where a thorough study of existing traditional methods of clearance is presented. There is also the section for the design of the new system to overcome the limitations or issues identified. The new system is web-based and was built using Hypertext Markup Language (HTML) along with PHP for business logic layer, Cascading Style Sheets (CSS) for proper rendering of display pages of the front end and MySQL for the data layer. The study will help reduce the amount of time and efforts wasted on students' clearance as well as reduce cost incurred on paper by the institution. Another advantage is that students can also initiate and monitor their clearance status from any location they are thereby eliminating the need to travel or be physically present for clearance.

2 Related Works

A clearance system means different things in different contexts. In this study, the term clearance refers to the procedure that is meant to be followed by students who are graduating from an institution after having written their final exams in the institution. Traditional methods of manual clearance have a lot of setbacks as highlighted in the preceding section. Nowadays, a number of institutions of learning are gradually sub-scribing to the use of modern technology to improve their operations [3–5]. There seems to be an overall drive towards online systems given the need for flexibility in scheduling and the daily emergency of communication technology and capabilities [6]. Online system is presented as a means of conveying instruction to an extensive learning community in any place and at any time. Indicates that adequate designated online learning as the driving force and model for transformation in teaching, learning and formal schooling online course has the potential to provide a learner individualized attention by the instructor, which is impossible in a large classroom environment (environmental education and training partnership 2006).

A number of works have done with regard to the development of online clearance system for an institution of higher learning. [7] developed an online clearance system using Active server pages (ASP) to create the application interface. [8] in 2015, also developed a web-based database-driven students' clearance system. The system was developed using PHP and MySQL. The aim of the wok was to eliminate the delays associated with the manual process of final clearance. However, the interface provided by the work is not user-friendly as it is difficult to navigate. In [9], an online clearance system for final year clearance of a state government-owned institution in Eastern Nigeria was developed. They made use of PHP, Javascript, Cascading style sheets (CSS), Apache and MySQL for the database. The system was able to process data with great speed and also replaced the error-prone manual clearance system. However, the application is not informative enough as it does not provide room for the student to know which of the departments was still pending. It only presents the status as pending. [1] presented a portal based approach for the development of student clearance system. The system enabled authorized officers to access the students' clearance page and clear the student without the student needing to visit the officer. This system is also con-figured to send email reminders as well as sms-alerts to all concerned in the process of clearance. The portal was developed using the HTML and PHP packages while the database was implemented using the MySQL database package. However, the system has similar limitation as the one describe in [9] above.

There are several other related works [20–22] where authors tried to develop systems for academic institutions. In [20] authors have presented an academic research management system for higher education institutions and demonstrated their imple-mentations. In another paper [21], authors developed a mobile-based emergency sys-tem which report and response in case of emergencies in academic institutions. This system is developed specially for developing countries. In another work a mobile system was developed for academic advisory [22]. This system helps the higher sec-ondary students to choose their program based on their right skill an interest. In all these works authors tried to develop e-systems for covering different aspects of the academic organization but not considered the online clearance systems.

Based on the reviewed work, it is certain that online clearance applications have continued to evolve in order to satisfy the ever-growing needs of users. However, for the few systems reviewed, we have identified a number of shortcomings which our new system has tackled. First, existing systems do not show on their platforms for clearing officers, the departments that have so far cleared the students. This in our opinion shows that such applications are informative enough as the students have to report this verbally. The clearing officer is left to believe the report of student in order to clear him or her. Also identified is the issue of restrictions. There are no restrictions as to which departments/units should precede the other during the clearance process. This refers to a situation where clearance is being done for a department that requires the student to have been cleared by another department first. For instance, the academic department clearance should proceed only after the library clearance has been done. This is not the case presently for most systems reviewed. All these and more are the additions that our system has introduced in the design and implementation as improvement over existing systems.

3   Theoretical Framework for Online Clearance System

The design and implementation of the online clearance system is premised the model of input-process-output model (IPO). The model can be used to describe the working of the our application in the following ways: the students' clearance requirements serve as the input to the online clearance system for processing while the end product is the clearance the student receives from the school. This is as illustrated in Fig. 1 below with the three main stages involved. It should be noted however, that the end product type is dependent on the type or form of the requirements (input) supplied to the system.

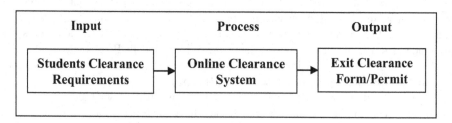

Fig. 1. Input-Process-Output (IPO) model of online clearance system

4   System Requirements

The system requirements are captured in two categories namely functional and non-functional requirements [10] which will be discussed as with respect to the clearance system.

4.1   Functional Requirements

i. Students, clearance officers and administrators must login to access the services.
ii. The system should provide a notification to students, clearance officers and administrators showing success or failure of their transaction.
iii. The system should be able to display units/departments for which students have already been cleared for the purpose of transparency.
iv. The system should ensure that the right order of clearance is followed by all clearing officers.
v. The system should keep transaction history.

4.2   Non-functional Requirements

Non-functional requirements elaborate the performance characteristics of the system which assures the efficiency and effectiveness of the system [11]. Some of the non-functional requirements of the application include;

(i) Usability Requirement: should have a clear, friendly, ergonomic and easy to navigate interface. The users should be able to interact with the system with ease.
(ii) Security Requirement: system should prevent malicious attempts and attacks by requesting all users, and students login using their unique IDs numbers.
(iii) Performance Requirement: The system is expected to have a short response time (the time a request is submitted until the first response it produced).
(iv) Reliability Requirement: The system should be readily available and should with good fault tolerance mechanism.
(v) In case of attacks, the system should be able to have a backup to prevent the loss of data and information.
(vi) Scalability Requirement: The system capacity will be made to accommodate sufficient large number of users such that no matter the number of users using the system at the same time, the clearing process would not be slowed down.

5   System Design and Modeling

In system design, components, interfaces, modules and their various architectures are designed in order to satisfy the requirements of the system. System design may also refer to the application of systems theory to product development [12, 13]. Modeling is done to help a system analyst understand the functionalities of the system. It can also be used to validate the software requirements by examining from a different point of view [14, 15]. Modeling is used to design a software application before coding begins. The Unified Modeling Language (UML) is used in this paper to describe the system from various perspectives.

5.1   Class Diagram

Figure 2 below represents the class diagram of the application with a full description of the set of objects that share the same attributes, operations, relationships and semantics [16]. The Fig. 2 shows that there are four classes – USER, STUDENT, ADMIN OFFICER and ADMINISTRATOR. All the attributers and functions are shown in the class diagram.

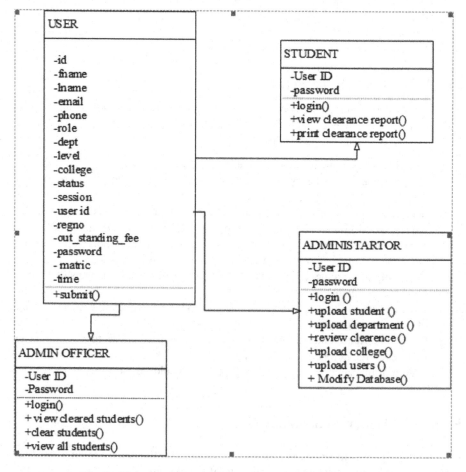

Fig. 2. Class diagram representing the student clearance system

5.2   Sequence Diagram

A sequence diagram is an interaction diagram that emphasizes the time ordering of message. It shows a set of objects and the messages sent and received by those objects [17]. It is used to represent the work flow, message passing and how elements in general conjoin over time to achieve a result [18].

Figure 3 below describes the sequence diagram of how the operations are carried out in the system with student, clearing officers and the administrator.

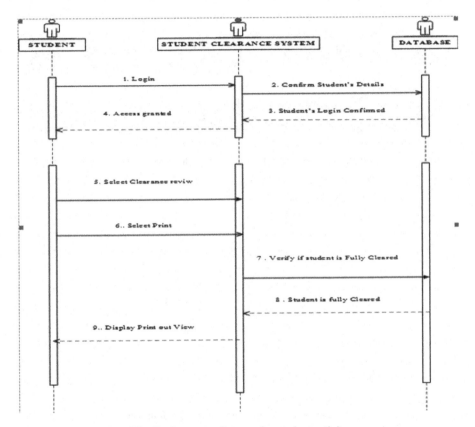

Fig. 3. Sequence diagram for student activity

6   System Implementation

The purpose of system implementation is to create a new system or modify an existing system in compliance to stakeholder's requirements [19]. The system was implemented using HTML (Hypertext Markup Language), PHP (Hypertext Preprocessor) and JQuery. They facilitate the development of web based applications. MySQL server was used for the database management. The figures that follow represent some of the captured interfaces of the new application. Figures 4 and 5 below represent the user management window and student management window respectively of the admin panel. The windows are available only to those that possess admin privileges and show the list of all registered users and the uploaded students respectively. The administrator clicks on Upload Students then select the session and he also selects the excel document (.csv file) which contain all the students and their information then he clicks on upload. The information automatically gets updated on the database.

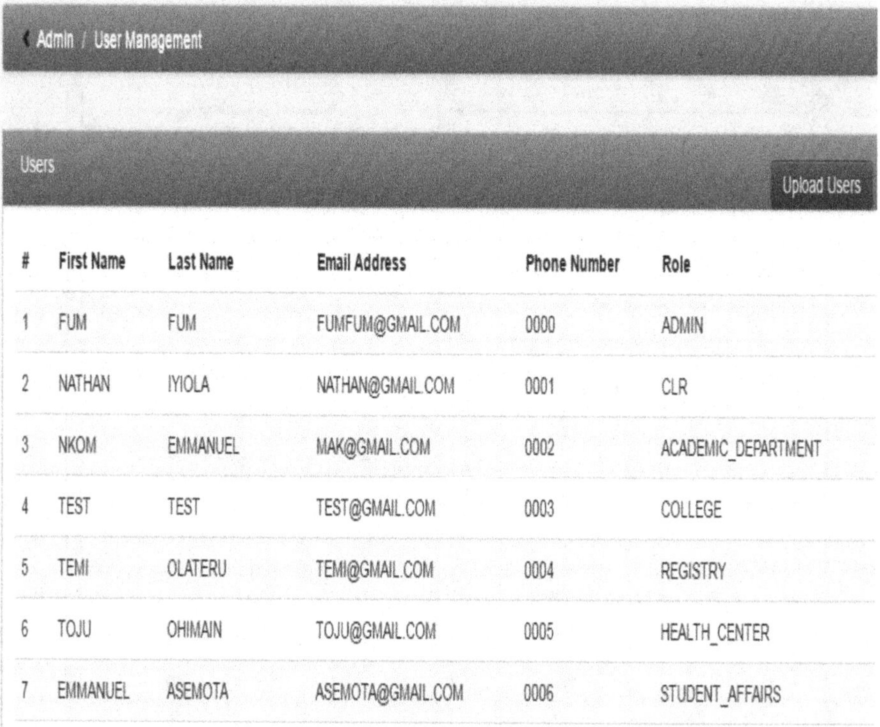

#	First Name	Last Name	Email Address	Phone Number	Role
1	FUM	FUM	FUMFUM@GMAIL.COM	0000	ADMIN
2	NATHAN	IYIOLA	NATHAN@GMAIL.COM	0001	CLR
3	NKOM	EMMANUEL	MAK@GMAIL.COM	0002	ACADEMIC_DEPARTMENT
4	TEST	TEST	TEST@GMAIL.COM	0003	COLLEGE
5	TEMI	OLATERU	TEMI@GMAIL.COM	0004	REGISTRY
6	TOJU	OHIMAIN	TOJU@GMAIL.COM	0005	HEALTH_CENTER
7	EMMANUEL	ASEMOTA	ASEMOTA@GMAIL.COM	0006	STUDENT_AFFAIRS

Admin / User Management — Users — Upload Users

Fig. 4. User management window of the admin panel

Figure 6 below shows the screenshot of the students' view on his portal. The student sees the progress of his clearance. In the existing system we are benchmarking, this view is not available to clearing officers so they are not aware which departments have cleared the student and which have not. When the student is cleared from all units and departments, he or she will then be able to print a copy of the clearance report.

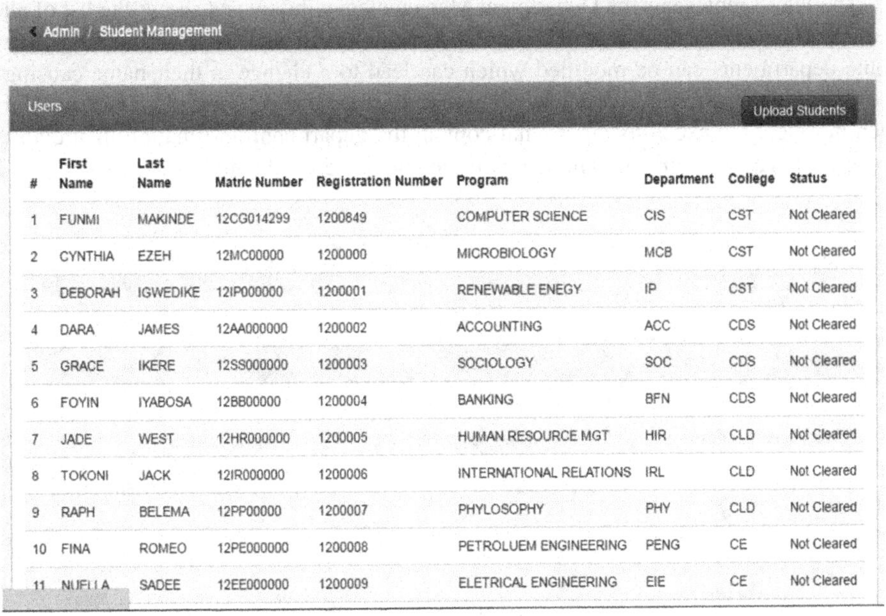

‹ Admin / Student Management

Users   Upload Students

#	First Name	Last Name	Matric Number	Registration Number	Program	Department	College	Status
1	FUNMI	MAKINDE	12CG014299	1200849	COMPUTER SCIENCE	CIS	CST	Not Cleared
2	CYNTHIA	EZEH	12MC00000	1200000	MICROBIOLOGY	MCB	CST	Not Cleared
3	DEBORAH	IGWEDIKE	12IP000000	1200001	RENEWABLE ENEGY	IP	CST	Not Cleared
4	DARA	JAMES	12AA000000	1200002	ACCOUNTING	ACC	CDS	Not Cleared
5	GRACE	IKERE	12SS000000	1200003	SOCIOLOGY	SOC	CDS	Not Cleared
6	FOYIN	IYABOSA	12BB00000	1200004	BANKING	BFN	CDS	Not Cleared
7	JADE	WEST	12HR000000	1200005	HUMAN RESOURCE MGT	HIR	CLD	Not Cleared
8	TOKONI	JACK	12IR000000	1200006	INTERNATIONAL RELATIONS	IRL	CLD	Not Cleared
9	RAPH	BELEMA	12PP00000	1200007	PHYLOSOPHY	PHY	CLD	Not Cleared
10	FINA	ROMEO	12PE000000	1200008	PETROLUEM ENGINEERING	PENG	CE	Not Cleared
11	NUFLLA	SADEE	12EE000000	1200009	ELETRICAL ENGINEERING	EIE	CE	Not Cleared

Fig. 5. Student management window of the admin panel

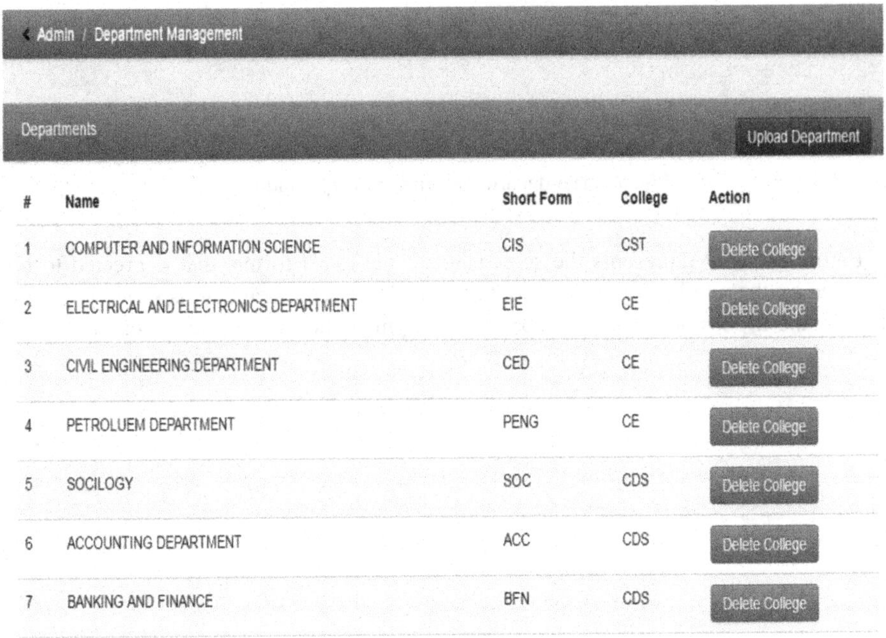

‹ Admin / Department Management

Departments   Upload Department

#	Name	Short Form	College	Action
1	COMPUTER AND INFORMATION SCIENCE	CIS	CST	Delete College
2	ELECTRICAL AND ELECTRONICS DEPARTMENT	EIE	CE	Delete College
3	CIVIL ENGINEERING DEPARTMENT	CED	CE	Delete College
4	PETROLUEM DEPARTMENT	PENG	CE	Delete College
5	SOCILOGY	SOC	CDS	Delete College
6	ACCOUNTING DEPARTMENT	ACC	CDS	Delete College
7	BANKING AND FINANCE	BFN	CDS	Delete College

Fig. 6. A student view page

The Fig. 7 represents the Department Management window and shows the list of all the departments in the institution. The department can change on rare conditions like some departments can be modified which can lead to a change in their name causing the former department to be deleted. The administrator clicks on Upload department then he select the excel document that contain the department information then clicks on upload. The information automatically gets updated on the database.

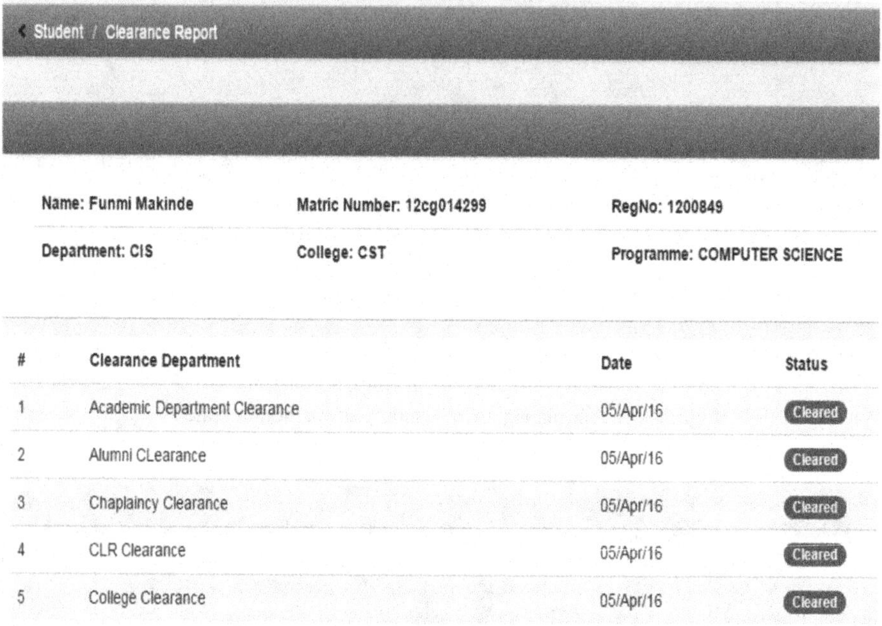

| ‹ Student / Clearance Report |

Name: Funmi Makinde   Matric Number: 12cg014299   RegNo: 1200849

Department: CIS   College: CST   Programme: COMPUTER SCIENCE

#	Clearance Department	Date	Status
1	Academic Department Clearance	05/Apr/16	Cleared
2	Alumni CLearance	05/Apr/16	Cleared
3	Chaplaincy Clearance	05/Apr/16	Cleared
4	CLR Clearance	05/Apr/16	Cleared
5	College Clearance	05/Apr/16	Cleared

Fig. 7. The department management window

Figure 8 below represents the screenshot of the excel format that is created to be uploaded by the administrator into the database. The excel document is saved as a .csv file to make it possible for the database to recognize and upload the document.

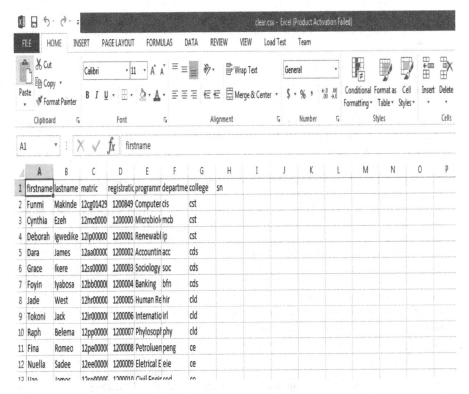

Fig. 8. A screenshot of an excel document to upload students

7 Conclusion and Future Work

The online student clearance application developed in this work is an improvement on existing systems especially in the terms of features and functionalities. This work represents an improvement over existing systems in the following ways; better performance, more user-friendly, easy to use, among others. On the whole the application mitigates most of the shortcomings the manual process earlier highlighted. The application was properly tested with standard testing methods applied. This was done while developing the various modules of the system as well as when the final application was ready. The local errors found during the unit testing were resolved and while issues with the interface were mitigated during the integration testing.

Presently the application has been deployed for use on the portal of the institution selected as case study. The application is web-based and can be accessed through the internet as well as the organization's intranet. It is recommended that all institutions plug into this technology as it saves time, money and efforts. In the future, we hope to further improve on the system by extending the application to a mobile application with additional functionalities that take care of compelling attributes like convenience and usability and performance.

Acknowledgement. The authors of this research appreciate the immense contribution of Covenant University Centre for Research, Innovation, and Discovery (CUCRID) for its support for this research.

References

1. Idachaba, F.E, Mbeh, K.E., Oshin, O.I., Oni, O.O.: Webportal applications: automated student clearance portal. In: Proceedings of the World Congress on Engineering, WCE 2015, London, U.K., 1–3 July 2015, vol. I (2015). ISBN 978-988-19253-4-3. ISSN 2078-0958 (Print); ISSN 2078-0966 (Online)
2. Ojo, T.O.: Design and implementation of Online University Information System (UIS). Covenant University, Ota (2009)
3. Scott Stud ham: "Web portals for Higher Education" Microsoft, 12th September 2012. http://www.microsoft.com/education/enus/solutions/pages/web_portals_higher_ed.aspx
4. Hagg, S., et al.: Management Information Systems for Information Age, 2nd edn. McGrawHill, Boston (2000). 5th Edition
5. Ayo, C.K.: Information Systems and Technologies, Mckay CONSULT (2011)
6. Cox, R.D: Online educational as institutional myth: rituals and realities at community colleges. Teach. Coll. Rec. **107**(8), 1754–1787 (2005)
7. Zuhaib, A.S.: QUEST Online Clearance System. A student project supervised by Zuhaib and submitted to CSE Department, QUEST, Nawabshah (2013)
8. Agbo-Ajala, O., Makinde, O.E.: A web-based database-driven students' clearance system. Int. J. Adv. Res. Comput. Sci. Softw. Eng. **5**(7), 65–69 (2015)
9. Ben, U.C., Henry, U.C., Iriaoghuan, A.I.: Design and implementation of online clearance system: a case study of Imo State University. Eur. J. Appl. Sci. **7**(1), 25–31 (2015). ISSN 2079-2077. https://doi.org/10.5829/idosi.ejas.2015.7.1.1128
10. Alan, D., Barbara, H.W., Roberta, M.R.: System Analysis and Design, 5th edn. Wiley, New York (2012)
11. Vetter, D.J., Kumar, P.D.: Overview of Systems Analysis & Design (2011). http://download.nos.org/cca/ccal.pdf
12. Hoffer, J.A., George, J.F., Valacich, J.S.: Foundation for Systems Development, Modern Systems Analysis and Design, 5th edn. Prentice Hall, Upper Saddle River (2008)
13. Mele, C., Pels, J., Polese, F.: A brief review of systems theories and their managerial applications. Serv. Sci. **2**(1–2), 126–135 (2010). https://doi.org/10.1287/serv.2.1_2.126
14. Kamalrudin, M., Sidek, S.: A review on software requirements validation and consistency management. Int. J. Softw. Eng. Appl. **9**(10), 39–58 (2015). http://dx.doi.org/10.14257/ijseia.2015.9.10.05
15. Jonathan, O., Azeta, A., Misra, S.: Development of prepaid electricity payment system for a university community using the LUHN algorithm. In: Kebe, C.M.F., Gueye, A., Ndiaye, A. (eds.) InterSol/CNRIA 2017. LNICST, vol. 204, pp. 107–114. Springer, Cham (2018). https://doi.org/10.1007/978-3-319-72965-7_9
16. Sparx: UML Structural Models (2011). Retrieved from Sparx Systems: http://sparxsystems.cpm/enterprise_architect_user_guide/9.3/standard_uml_models/structuraldiagram.html
17. Booch, G., Rumbaugh, J., Jacobson, I.: The Unified Modeling Language User Guide. Addison Wesley, Reading (1999)
18. Eriksson, H.E., Penker, M.: Business Modelling with UML Open Training (2008)
19. Martin, R.C.: UML Tutorial: Sequence Diagram. Engineering Notebook Column, pp. 1–5 (1988)

20. Azeta, A.A., Ikpefan, O.A., Ayo, C.K., Gberevbie, D.E., Omoregbe, N.A.: Closing institutional gaps through academic research management system and implications in Nigeria. Int. J. Pharm. Technol. **8**(4), 22906–22914 (2016)
21. Adewumi, A., Nwaoyo, C., Parejas, F.J., Misra, S., Crawford, B., Soto, R.: Mobile-based emergency report and response system for academic institutions of developing countries. Far East J. Electron. Commun. **16**(special volume 2), 139–145 (2016)
22. Sowunmi, O.Y., Misra, S., Farnandez-Sanz, L., Merodio, J.A.M.: A framework of academic Advise through Mobile Applications. In: Proceedings of 25th International Conference on Information System Development (ISD 2016, Poland) (2016)

Enhanced Sketchnoting Through Semantic Integration of Learning Material

Aryobarzan Atashpendar⬛, Christian Grévisse(✉)⬛, and Steffen Rothkugel⬛

Computer Science and Communications Research Unit,
University of Luxembourg, Esch-sur-Alzette, Luxembourg
aryobarzan.atashpendar.001@student.uni.lu,
{christian.grevisse,steffen.rothkugel}@uni.lu

Abstract. Within the transition from pen-and-paper to digital solutions, many tablet-based note-taking apps have been developed. In addition, sketchnoting, a highly visual form of note-taking, has gained in popularity, especially in teaching and learning. While current solutions already reduce the burden of organizing and searching through stacks of paper, they provide little support in finding additional information related to the notes, and search capabilities are mostly limited to textual queries and content. In this paper, we present a novel solution for digital sketchnoting aimed at enhancing the learning experience of students. In addition to common capabilities such as handwriting recognition, our note-taking app integrates semantic annotation and drawing recognition. Handwritten notes are recognized and passed through concept recognition and entity linking tools to enable a knowledge graph-based integration of contextually relevant learning resources. We extend traditional search capabilities by including the semantic metadata from the related material as well as enabling visual queries to find recognized sketches. Finally, resembling the exchange of paper notes among students, our app allows to share the semantically enhanced notes with other devices.

Keywords: Sketchnoting · Learning material · Handwriting recognition · Semantic annotation · Drawing recognition · Visual search

1 Introduction

The classroom is an environment requiring substantial multitasking skills from students. While following a lecture, they might take notes about the presented content. Terms that are unknown to them or that require further information than presented by the teacher can be looked up either at home or while in class. For instance, in history class about the Second Punic War, the teacher might mention the battles of Cannae and Lake Trasimene, without indicating where these places are situated; or in a physiology course, the teacher might mention a chemical compound, which the student wants to know the structure of. At home, students might struggle with going through their unorganized notes, especially

© Springer Nature Switzerland AG 2019
H. Florez et al. (Eds.): ICAI 2019, CCIS 1051, pp. 340–353, 2019.
https://doi.org/10.1007/978-3-030-32475-9_25

weeks later in preparation for an exam. Some overcome these hurdles by reorganizing their new notes at the end of the day and doing further research of their own on topics they did not quite understand, though this requires additional time, especially to get back into the context of the lecture. Still, finding a certain note if the location or exact phrasing is unknown is an issue.

If they decide to gather further information on an unknown term while in class, they are likely to lose track of the discourse of the teacher. In fact, looking up information that is outside of the current context would cause the *split-attention effect* [2,15] and increase the *extraneous cognitive load* [17]. When consulting digital solutions for finding related information, students might also suffer from *information overload*, caused by the vast set of heterogeneous resources available. The interruption might lead to distraction or even abandonment [9,18] of the original learning task, i.e., following the lecture and taking notes, in favor of, e.g., consulting social media, which has a negative impact on the learning and note-taking process [10]. It would be desirable to scaffold the search for additional information by integrating relevant related knowledge in the note-taking environment, which would reduce - to a certain extent - the risk of losing track of the lecture while going over a large set of resources.

The transition from pen-and-paper note-taking to digital solutions has been fostered by schools adopting tablet-enhanced curricula. For instance, the *Digital Classroom* program of the Luxembourgish government promotes the use of iPads in class. Naturally, many tablet-based note-taking apps have been developed recently. Their objective is to overcome the intrinsic limitations of paper-based note-taking, such as facilitating the organization and retrieval of notes. *Sketchnoting*, a neologism combining note-taking and sketches, is a highly visual note-taking method gaining in popularity and supported by many note-taking apps [4]. While digital solutions cause less burden in terms of searching a note than going through stacks of paper, search results are mostly limited to what has actually been noted, while not considering implicit additional information related to the content of a note. Although some apps enable searching through handwritten notes, the search is mostly limited to textual queries, without considering the expressiveness and semantics of sketches.

In this paper, we present a novel solution for digital sketchnoting aimed at further enhancing the learning experience of students. Our iPad app for digital sketchnoting, on top of a common capability such as handwriting recognition, uses concept recognition and entity linking tools in order to recognize concepts mentioned in the notes. These semantic annotations further allow to retrieve and integrate related information from knowledge graphs, avoiding that the user has to manually search for additional information and thereby lose track of the lecture. In addition, users can search for terms appearing in the information from a knowledge graph that were not explicitly mentioned in the notes. Furthermore, to promote sketchnoting, the proposed app also integrates drawing recognition to allow users to semantically enhance sketches and perform visual queries over a note collection. Finally, resembling the exchange of paper notes among students, our app allows to share the semantically enhanced notes with nearby devices.

The remainder of this paper is organized as follows. In Sect. 2, we discuss related work from different research directions, relevant for our solution. The features of our app are presented in Sect. 3. We conclude in Sect. 4, inclusive of ideas for future work.

2 Related Work

Paek and Fulton explored how students used a tablet-based note-taking app in science class [13]. Overall, the participants, including a teacher, responded positively to the app and did not have trouble adapting to its usage. Its various tools, such as audio recordings and photo importing, offered the students new ways to capture information in the classroom. Nevertheless, some of the functionalities ended up being less used or applied in a different manner than intended: While the handwriting method was used, most pupils did so only for drawing tables and opted for typing out their actual text using the on-screen keyboard. Participants indicated that the screen did not feel as natural as paper. Recent products such as *PaperLike*[1] might tackle this issue. The authors concluded that further research in this area is needed, as there are benefits of handwriting over typing, especially for young children [11]. Furthermore, though a note-sharing function was available, only 30% of the population used it: While the app relied on Google Drive, only few pupils had an account.

Guidera [7] focused on digital sketching as opposed to digital handwriting. The aim was to evaluate the replacement of physical sketchbooks, used in disciplines ranging from architecture to graphic design, with digital tablets. The participants' response was overwhelmingly positive to this transition: Firstly, the digital tablet offered the same type of lightweight mobility that sketchbooks are known for. Secondly, with the support for stylus input, the users relied on a sense of familiarity in usage, as it reminded them of traditional pen and paper.

Existing note-taking apps already integrate some of the features this work proposes, without taking advantage of their combination, though. Handwriting recognition is arguably the most prominent functionality found throughout most note-taking apps, including iPad's native *Notes* app and third-party apps like *Google Keep, Notability, GoodNotes, MyScript Nebo* or *Noteshelf*, to only name a few. Searching through handwritten notes is often possible, although limited to the verbatim, not including implicit information. *OneNote* offers an *Ink to Text* feature in the desktop version, enabling to convert handwritten notes into printed text, effectively replacing what's been handwritten on the canvas. Though it can be useful for some, users may prefer to keep their handwriting as the conversion may interfere with the sizing or styling of the words, which can bear its own semantics.

Semantic annotation of a resource can be done using concept recognition and entity linking tools, such as DBpedia Spotlight [12]. Information from a knowledge graph, such as DBpedia, allows to enhance the explicit content of a resource. This can be of interest for students, as additional information relevant

---

[1] https://paperlike.com.

for the current context may improve their learning [5]. *Google Docs* integrates the feature to recognize topics mentioned in a document and to allow users to access web search results directly within the app, similar to the *Smart Lookup* feature in *Microsoft Word*, which is albeit limited to literal, non-contextual lookup. *Google Keep* recognizes the concept type of the recognized topics in notes to enable type-based searches, e.g., regroup every note discussing music. The recent *SoLeMiO* Office Add-in enables contextual recognition of concepts to both semantically enhance a document and suggest related information from a knowledge graph [6].

Finally, drawing recognition is the more niche feature, as it is rarely found in popular note-taking apps. Shape recognition is offered in apps like *Lekh Diagram*, *Instaviz* or *OneNote*, to replace user-drawn lines, arrows and circles with cleaner versions. However, these apps focus more on easing graph drawings than the recognition of objects. *DeepSketch* uses convolutional neural networks to enable sketch recognition [16]. In particular, it does not only label finished drawings, but also recognizes in-progress drawings, thus allowing their automatic completion with an existing drawing of the recognized shape. Furthermore, Google's *Quick, Draw!* experiment[2] served as a major contributor to sketch recognition, allowing users to draw a given shape in their own style and thus help train a neural network with sufficient variations for each category. Consequently, its public dataset contains over 50 million drawings for 345 categories, e.g., *"light bulb"*, making it a powerful basis for building drawing recognition models. This data can also be used to train a recurrent neural network capable of completing an unfinished sketch of a shape or object [8]. While shape recognition is provided by several note-taking apps, the integration of true sketch recognition is still missing.

3   Enhanced Sketchnoting App

To effectively promote digital sketchnoting as an enhanced method for note-taking, people are more willing to make this digital transition as long as the respective apps provide familiarity known to them from physical note-taking. Thus, handwriting and sketching should be as accurate as possible with support for stylus input. Sharing notes should be as simple as physically handing a note to another person. Furthermore, semantic annotation and drawing recognition can enhance the user experience with respect to providing additional, relevant information for the current context, automatically organize notes and allow advanced search capabilities, including visual queries and implicit content.

In this section, we present how these different objectives are realized in our app. In Fig. 1, we present the different components of our app. A note is passed through both handwriting (Sect. 3.1) and drawing recognition (Sect. 3.2) mechanisms. The recognized textual content is analyzed by semantic annotators (Sect. 3.3) to extract the main concepts and suggest related resources. The enhanced note is now prepared for advanced search capabilities (Sect. 3.4). Finally, we discuss possibilities of sharing notes among nearby devices (Sect. 3.5).

---

[2] https://experiments.withgoogle.com/quick-draw.

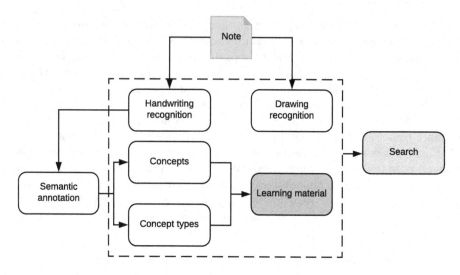

Fig. 1. Components of the proposed app

3.1 Handwriting Recognition

An important part of sketchnoting is the inclusion of handwriting as an input method: The familiarity of using a pen to write and sketch notes on paper can help bridge the transition from physical to digital note-taking. To that end, it is important that the offered handwriting tool works as seamlessly and as accurately as possible.

Our app integrates handwritten text recognition alongside its handwriting tool to provide several basic functionalities. These include being able to copy the handwritten text and to use it elsewhere, even outside the application. Additionally, recognizing the user's handwriting is crucial to allowing users to perform searches on their content.

Besides these general functions usually found in most other note-taking applications, the handwriting recognition is also necessary to enable the app's main proposed utility: By analyzing the user's handwritten text, semantically related resources can be provided to the user based on the concepts mentioned in the entire note.

Consequently, the app needs to recognize the user's handwriting as accurately as possible to provide this additional learning material. Hence, the app integrates Google Firebase's ML Kit[3] framework as its core OCR engine enabling text recognition. This engine is part of the mobile packaging of Google Cloud Vision offerings and it is suitable in three regards for this application. Firstly, as Firebase is mobile-oriented, the recognition engine and its underlying models have a small footprint on users' devices. Secondly, compared to its cloud version, the device-based variant is free and usable offline. Finally, as of late 2018[4], the engine also

---

[3] https://firebase.google.com/docs/ml-kit.

[4] https://cloud.google.com/vision/docs/release-notes.

supports handwriting in addition to printed text recognition, making it ideal for our sketchnoting app.

In addition to the usage of the ML Kit OCR engine, the app also integrates its own pre-processing and post-processing stages to improve the engine's recognition accuracy. The pre-processing consists of binarising the input image for the OCR engine, i.e., converting it to black and white: As the app has access to the user's individual strokes, the latter are redrawn in white and with a uniform thickness to a black canvas. Furthermore, drawings are hidden from the input image as they are not considered to contain text: This process is described in Sect. 3.2. The goal of the pre-processing stage is to highlight the text clearly and to hide everything else, i.e., sketches. The post-processing is based on a spell checker, namely Apple's UITextChecker[5] for iOS, which helps to correct some characters wrongly recognized by the engine because of similarities, e.g., "l" and "t".

3.2 Drawing Recognition

Drawing recognition implies recognizing the object(s) the user has hand drawn on the note's canvas, such as a light bulb. The app integrates this feature to expand its search functionality: By recognizing the user's drawings in a note, their labels (e.g., *"light bulb"*) can be stored for said note and be used for search results. Thus, the term *"light bulb"* would not only be searched for in the note's written text, but also in its recognized drawings.

To enable this feature, we rely on Google's Quick Draw[6] dataset, which contains 345 categories of objects (e.g., *"lightning"*, *"basketball"*), with multiple variations available for each category. The latter part is important, as the recognition process should be able to account for the unique drawing style of each user as much as possible: no drawing is ever drawn the same way by different people. Thus, by having several variations for each category, the model can be trained more broadly and it will be less sensitive to a single drawing variation of an object.

An existing convolutional neural network (CNN) model[7] trained on this dataset and available in iOS' CoreML format was used for the application. Similar to the handwriting recognition, the app pre-processes the drawings for this model: Each sketch is redrawn in white and with a uniform stroke thickness to a black, hidden canvas. Finally, this new image is resized to 28 × 28 pixels to conform to the drawing recognition model's input requirements.

As our app integrates both handwriting recognition and drawing recognition, it is necessary to know where to apply the correct recognition process for a given note: The user writes and draws by hand on the same canvas for a note, meaning the application needs a way to distinguish which user strokes are related to handwritten text and which are part of drawings.

---

[5] https://developer.apple.com/documentation/uikit/uitextchecker.

[6] https://quickdraw.withgoogle.com/data.

[7] https://github.com/hetelek/GuessMyDrawing-ios.

The chosen approach is to assume every stroke is text-related, unless the user has manually designated a specific region of the canvas as a drawing. In the latter case, the application will know where to check for drawings and only apply the drawing recognition process for strokes which are contained in these designated regions.

This also means that when the handwriting recognition is processed, strokes within the boundaries of drawing regions inserted by the user are ignored, i.e., hidden. This naturally improves recognition results by the engine as it is not trying to make out words from drawing strokes.

3.3 Semantic Annotation

Students often rely on switching between multiple apps while studying to look up information related to their notes, risking the previously mentioned split-attention effect, an increase of the extraneous cognitive load and information overload. To reduce these risks, our app uses semantic annotation of notes in order to retrieve related information from knowledge graphs serving as additional learning material and integrates it directly within the note-taking app.

The previously recognized content of a handwritten note is passed through concept recognition and entity linking tools to extract mentioned concepts. In addition, if the used knowledge graph provides such information, the type of recognized concepts can be used to classify notes. For instance, the sentence *"Johannes Bach was a composer of Baroque music"* contains the concept *"Johannes Bach"*, whose type is *"Person"*. With this additional information available, we can provide relevant resources based on the concepts and their respective types: While Wikipedia articles can be retrieved for concepts of type *"Person"*, maps would be more appropriate for concepts concerning locations. Thus, the type of suggested additional material can benefit from the type of recognized concept.

By using semantic annotators from different disciplines and taking advantage of the alignment of ontologies through the Linked Open Data cloud, results can be combined and further enhanced for a more accurate suggestion of domain-specific resources, such as knowledge base articles in chemistry. While the Wikipedia-based DBpedia can provide domain-general articles on many concepts, the BioPortal[8] can in turn deliver details on, e.g., chemical compounds. Similarly, GeoNames[9] can return locations from its geographical database that would be shown in a map.

Figure 2 shows a note on the Second Punic War. The app has so far recognized two concepts, namely *"Second Punic War"* and *"Lake Trasimene"*. For the former concept, the app has displayed the abstract of the associated Wikipedia article, while a map of Lake Trasimene is displayed, as the semantic annotator has labelled it as a location. It is important how this learning material is shown to the user. To avoid distracting the student during the note-taking, the app

---

[8] https://bioportal.bioontology.org.

[9] https://geonames.org.

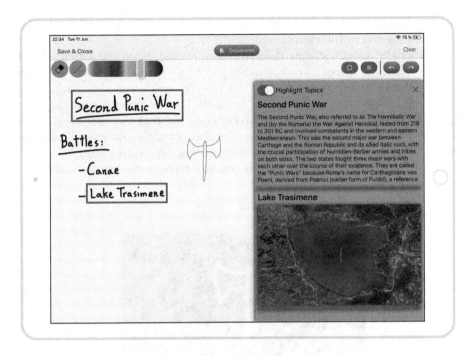

Fig. 2. Related resources found for a note on the Second Punic War

takes a reactive approach by only fetching and displaying related resources for a note when the user requests them. Furthermore, to better inform the user which concepts have been recognized in her handwritten text and which resources they are related to, the app highlights the words directly in the handwritten text, as indicated by the red borders.

3.4 Advanced Search Capabilities

In an effort to facilitate organizing notes and searching through them, the app firstly expands the sources for search results and secondly offers a visual approach to performing searches.

Traditionally, note-taking applications base their search results on the body, i.e., textual content, of notes. Alternatively, some apps also allow users to manually assign user-created labels to notes to group them together.

In turn, the proposed app goes beyond the textual content of notes and additionally uses their semantic information. Thus, users can search for concepts and their respective types recognized in a note's body. This information can help users quickly regroup all notes based on a concept, e.g., *"Johannes Bach"*, or based on the concept's type, e.g., *"Person"*. This approach eliminates the need for users to rewrite several notes as a single note, in case they want to consolidate related notes which were taken spontaneously and which are scattered throughout the user's notes collection. A use-case for searching by concepts would be for students who are reviewing for an exam and who need to find all their notes related to the exam's topics.

Additionally, by also storing the abstract of related Wikipedia articles found for these concepts, more indirect searches can be performed. Consider that the teacher mentioned a concept that is not directly written in the user's note, but is somehow related. For instance, he might have mentioned that the Lake Trasimene is quite close to the city of Perugia, and that the user recalls this mention of Perugia. With access to the entire abstract of the concept's Wikipedia article, the user can instead perform a search using the indirect term *"Perugia"* which does not appear in a note's body, yet still retrieve the relevant note.

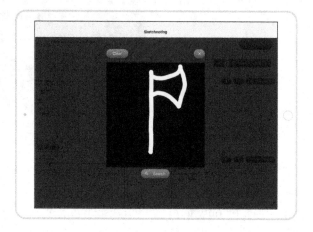

Fig. 3. Visual search for the drawing *"axe"*

Furthermore, the app provides visual searches as an alternative to text-based searches. By integrating drawing recognition, notes can be further classified by the sketches drawn on their canvas. Thus, users can for example draw symbols, such as a lightning shape, to mark sections of notes as important. Later on, by simply searching for the term *"lightning"*, these respective notes would be retrieved. Additionally, to reduce the need for using the on-screen keyboard, the user can also draw the shape or object they are looking for, e.g., a lightning, and by recognizing this drawing, the app will in turn use its label as a search term. Again during the preparation for an exam, it could be useful to quickly retrieve all notes that include a certain sketch, such as a lightning.

Figure 3 shows an example of a visual search, where the user draws a shape that is contained in the note(s) they are looking for. This drawing will be recognized as *"axe"* and this term will consequently be used as a search term. The note previously showcased in Fig. 2 would be a matching search result. Note that the two axe sketches in Figs. 2 and 3 differ in drawing style, but the app still recognizes both as the same object.

Our app thus uses the body, the recognized drawings and the semantic information (concepts, concept types and related resources) of notes as sources for finding matches to search terms. Naturally, this expanded approach can lead to too many notes as search results, in case the search terms are not very specific. To that end, users can combine search terms to gradually narrow down the number of search results.

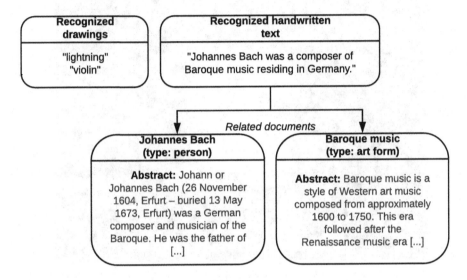

Fig. 4. Example of a note's information available for search results

To illustrate this search functionality, we can consider the search scenario in Fig. 4 where the user enters multiple search terms. The figure shows all the information a note holds and which can be used for search results. To find this note, the user can enter either of the following search terms:

"Lightning" This term will be found in the note's recognized drawings.
"Bach" This term will be found in the note's recognized handwritten text.
"Renaissance" This term will be found as a match in the related document *"Baroque music"*, specifically its abstract text.
"Person" This will be found as a match in the related document *"Johannes Bach"*, specifically its concept type.

3.5   Sharing of Sketchnotes

The objective of the sharing feature is to make it as simple and as straightforward as the typical scenario of two students exchanging physical notes in person. Consequently, the application proposes device-to-device sharing: A user can discover nearby devices likewise running the application and share notes with them. To prevent unwanted notes being sent to a user's device, recipients have to explicitly allow their device to be visible to others. If enabled, a screen as in Fig. 5 is shown.

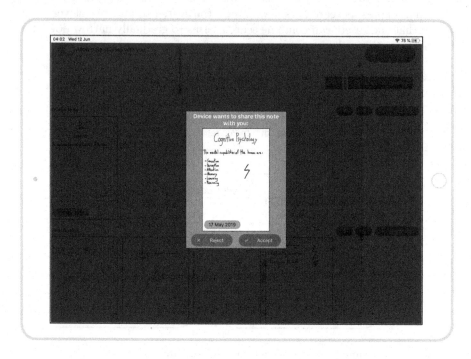

Fig. 5. Receiving a shared note from a nearby iPad

To make this process as quick as possible, the app does not rely on any third party service, e.g., Google Drive, requiring a user to have an account [13]. Instead, by integrating Apple's Multipeer Connectivity[10] framework for iOS, the sender and recipient just need to have Bluetooth or WiFi enabled, even if they have no Internet access. This framework allows sending the same note to up to seven other devices at the same time.

Our app does not exclusively rely on a universal format, such as PDF, or even an image to transfer a note to another device. Instead, by using the app's own encoding and decoding for notes, the recipient can receive a note in the same format as their existing notes. This preserves the shared note's semantic information, i.e., recognized concepts and related resources, as well as the ability to undo the original author's strokes. The former is important to enable annotation sharing, which can call the student's attention to an important concept that was mentioned [3]. The latter can be useful for a student to get feedback from her teacher: By using the same tools as the student, the teacher can add her remarks or corrections to the note and send it back to the student. Sharing

---

[10] https://developer.apple.com/documentation/multipeerconnectivity.

of notes can also be beneficial when used as a way to actively engage students in creating their own learning material and thereby co-constructing knowledge in a cooperative way. A generative note-taking method called *communal notes* based on social constructivism has been described in [1].

Still, the app provides the traditional method of generating a PDF or image from a note, in order to save or share it to a different application or cloud service. Furthermore, the idea of sharing notes using the app's internal encoding format can be extended beyond offline device-to-device sharing: By exporting the note in a custom file format known to the app, the file could be shared via email and the recipient could import this file into her own app.

4   Conclusions and Future Work

In this paper, we presented an enhanced digital sketchnoting app aimed at enhancing the learning experience of students. Leveraging the power of semantic annotation and sketch recognition, the proposed app extends the capabilities of traditional note-taking apps and provides an integrated solution. In addition to common handwriting recognition, our solution suggests related, heterogeneous resources, both domain-general and domain-specific, to the student during the note-taking process, avoiding the need to manually search for it and thereby reducing the risk of losing track of the lecture. Search capabilities are extended by including the semantic metadata from the related material as well as enabling visual queries to find recognized sketches. Finally, sharing notes among nearby devices is as easy as sharing their paper-based counterparts. Our solution expects less organization effort from a student. Instead, it allows them to focus on their note-taking and learning activities.

We have several ideas for future work. First, by further including semantic annotators and ontologies from different fields, the diversity of suggested resources can be promoted, with disciplines ranging from chemistry to architecture. Furthermore, the proposed iPad app could integrate Apple's ClassKit[11], opening its doors to the native *Schoolwork* app. This would facilitate the teacher's job of receiving students' assignments written in the proposed app and they would have a central view on every student's progress. Distinguishing between handwriting and drawing could be facilitated by taking advantage of the double tap feature of the Apple Pencil (2nd Generation). Porting the app to the Android platform would broaden the audience. An evaluation with students similar to the one in [13] could show the strong and weak points of our app. The evaluation will assess technical criteria such as usability, efficacy and accuracy [14], but also pedagogical criteria such as acceptance and learning performance. This could be done through log-file analysis, user surveys and semi-structured interviews. The results of the evaluation will help to prepare the app for general public release. Finally, we could imagine the integration of more interactive resources in the app, such as augmented reality (AR). This could incite more interest in a lecture's content, e.g., by featuring an AR display of a battle in

---

[11] https://developer.apple.com/classkit.

the Second Punic War directly within the app, providing students with a more visual and memorable experience.

References

1. Ahn, R., Ingham, S., Mendez, T.: Socially constructed learning activity: communal note-taking as a generative tool to promote active student engagement. Transform. Dialogues Teach. Learn. J. **8**(3), 1–15 (2016)
2. Chandler, P., Sweller, J.: The split-attention effect as a factor in the design of instruction. Br. J. Educ. Psychol. **62**(2), 233–246 (1992). https://doi.org/10.1111/j.2044-8279.1992.tb01017.x
3. Chang, M., Kuo, R., Chang, M., Kinshuk: Online annotation system and student clustering platform. In: 2015 8th International Conference on Ubi-Media Computing (UMEDIA), pp. 202–207, August 2015. https://doi.org/10.1109/UMEDIA.2015.7297455
4. Dimeo, R.: Sketchnoting: an analog skill in the digital age. SIGCAS Comput. Soc. **46**(3), 9–16 (2016). https://doi.org/10.1145/3024949.3024951
5. García-González, H., Gayo, J.E.L., Paule-Ruiz, M.: Enhancing e-learning content by using semantic web technologies. IEEE Trans. Learn. Technol. **10**(4), 544–550 (2017). https://doi.org/10.1109/TLT.2016.2629475
6. Grévisse, C., Manrique, R., Marino, O., Rothkugel, S.: SoLeMiO: semantic integration of learning material in office. In: Proceedings of E-Learn: World Conference on E-Learning in Corporate, Government, Healthcare, and Higher Education 2018, pp. 1524–1532. Association for the Advancement of Computing in Education (AACE), Las Vegas, NV, United States, October 2018. https://www.learntechlib.org/p/185123
7. Guidera, S.: The digital sketchbook: perceptions of the effectiveness of tablet-based sketching apps for design drawing. In: Proceedings of 10th Annual International Conference of Education, Research and Innovation, ICERI 2017, IATED, pp. 8498–8504, November 2017. https://doi.org/10.21125/iceri.2017.2299
8. Ha, D., Eck, D.: A neural representation of sketch drawings. In: Proceedings of the Seventh International Conference on Learning Representations (2018). https://openreview.net/pdf?id=Hy6GHpkCW
9. Krieger, K.: Creating learning material from web resources. In: Gandon, F., Sabou, M., Sack, H., d'Amato, C., Cudré-Mauroux, P., Zimmermann, A. (eds.) ESWC 2015. LNCS, vol. 9088, pp. 721–730. Springer, Cham (2015). https://doi.org/10.1007/978-3-319-18818-8_45
10. Kuznekoff, J.H., Munz, S., Titsworth, S.: Mobile phones in the classroom: examining the effects of texting, twitter, and message content on student learning. Commun. Educ. **64**(3), 344–365 (2015). https://doi.org/10.1080/03634523.2015.1038727
11. Longcamp, M., Zerbato-Poudou, M.T., Velay, J.L.: The influence of writing practice on letter recognition in preschool children: a comparison between handwriting and typing. Acta Psychologica **119**(1), 67–79 (2005). https://doi.org/10.1016/j.actpsy.2004.10.019
12. Mendes, P.N., Jakob, M., García-Silva, A., Bizer, C.: DBpedia spotlight: shedding light on the web of documents. In: Proceedings of the 7th International Conference on Semantic Systems, I-Semantics 2011, pp. 1–8. ACM, New York (2011). https://doi.org/10.1145/2063518.2063519

13. Paek, S., Fulton, L.A.: Elementary students using a tablet-based note-taking application in the science classroom. J. Digit. Learn. Teach. Educ. **32**(4), 140–149 (2016). https://doi.org/10.1080/21532974.2016.1206491
14. Prat, N., Wattiau, I., Akoka, J.: Artifact evaluation in information systems design-science research - a holistic view. In: Proceeding of the 19th Pacific Asia Conference on Information Systems, PACIS 2014, June 2014
15. Schmeck, A., Opfermann, M., van Gog, T., Paas, F., Leutner, D.: Measuring cognitive load with subjective rating scales during problem solving: differences between immediate and delayed ratings. Instr. Sci. **43**(1), 93–114 (2015). https://doi.org/10.1007/s11251-014-9328-3
16. Seddati, O., Dupont, S., Mahmoudi, S.: Deepsketch 3. Multimedia Tools Appl. **76**(21), 22333–22359 (2017). https://doi.org/10.1007/s11042-017-4799-2
17. Sweller, J., van Merrienboer, J.J.G., Paas, F.G.W.C.: Cognitive architecture and instructional design. Educ. Psychol. Rev. **10**(3), 251–296 (1998). https://doi.org/10.1023/A:1022193728205
18. Winter, J., Cotton, D., Gavin, J., Yorke, J.: Effective e-learning? Multitasking, distractions and boundary management by graduate students in an online environment. Res. Learn. Technol. **18**(1) (2010). https://doi.org/10.1080/09687761003657598

Robotic Autonomy

Comparative Analysis of Three Obstacle Detection and Avoidance Algorithms for a Compact Differential Drive Robot I N V-Rep

Chika Yinka-Banjo[1], Obawole Daniel[1], Sanjay Misra[2]([⊠]) [iD],
Oluranti Jonathan[2], and Hector Florez[3] [iD]

[1] Department of Computer Sciences, University of Lagos, Lagos, Nigeria
cyinkabanjo@unilag.edu.ng, obawoledaniel@gmail.com
[2] Covenant University, Ota, Nigeria
{sanjay.misra,
jonathan.oluranti}@covenantuniversity.edu.ng
[3] Universidad Distrital Francisco Jose de Caldas Bogota, Bogota, Colombia
haflorezf@udistrital.edu.co

Abstract. The aim of this research is to build a compact differential drive robot using the Virtual Robotics Experimentation Platform. Sensors are embedded in the Pioneer 3-dx mobile robot to provide necessary data from the real world to the robot. The main purpose of the mobile robot is its ability to arrive at a given destination (goal) precisely and astutely, hence, significantly reducing the risk of human mistakes. Many existing algorithms like obstacle detection, lane detection is combined to provide the essential and basic control functionalities to the car. The mobile robot controller model runs on a series of benchmark tasks, and its performance is compared to conventional controllers. During the scope of this project, comparisons between different algorithms, hardware and tools have been made to choose the best-fit for the project. The results are obstacle detection algorithms and a terrain handling feature, that works very well in simulations and real-life situations. The major tailbacks during the development of this project were limitations caused by low hardware computational power, the presence of stronger processors would exponentially increase the throughput and consequently improve the accuracy of the scene objects and the obstacle detection algorithms.

Keywords: Bug · Pioneer 3-DX · VREP · Sonar · API · OS · Scene

1 Introduction

Deriving motivation from natural world, mobile robots can adjust and transform its step patterns to efficiently navigate and maneuver difficult topography in the environment, such as, slippery, high hill slopes, or soft grounds, fissures, and especially the detection and avoidance of static or moving obstacles [1]. These features describe a mobile robot as a convenient machine suitable on various environments, exhibiting extra

© Springer Nature Switzerland AG 2019
H. Florez et al. (Eds.): ICAI 2019, CCIS 1051, pp. 357–369, 2019.
https://doi.org/10.1007/978-3-030-32475-9_26

significance than a legged robot for some specific operations like sensing its immediate surroundings, moving around its environment, and the ability to imitate intelligent human behavior to move from start to target through a guide track [2]. Furthermore, a robot with a symmetric layout, built on the Pioneer 3-DX (a compact differential-drive mobile robot, Fig. 1), has established an approach similar to insects, that these robots significantly lack the ability to survive in unfavorable environments or extreme conditions.

Fig. 1. Simulated model on V-rep.

The endless exploration and advancements of novel approaches and methods to achieve a robotic system that efficiently adapts its motion patterns with respect to the Pioneer 3-DX environment as a research object in the Virtual Robotics Experimentation Platform (VREP), has several benefits while handling these steadiness and more flexible requirements. It is conventional that at least a small lightweight two-wheel, two-motor differential drive robot is ideal for stability in the walkway configuration, leaving the world's most popular intelligent mobile robots for research and education. The characteristics which the robot possesses, including; dependability, versatility and stability, have made them the preferred development environment for advanced robotics [3].

2 Obstacle Detection

Obstacle detection is the method of using sensors, algorithms, and data structures to detect objects or environmental components that impede motion. Obstacle detection is applicable to any object that moves, as well as robot manipulators and manned or unmanned vehicles for land, air, sea, and space; these are all called *vehicles* here for conciseness.

The ultrasonic sensor is another example of obstacle detection sensor also called 'sonar'. The unique attributes that the sonar possesses makes it the most extensively used sensor for obstacle detection. The features include ease of use, convenient to operate and it is relatively cheap [4]. The major applications of sonar are during robot navigation and routing respectively, surveying a particular area for an obstacle through close range inspection [5].

Unfortunately, a significant disadvantage of ultrasonic sensors is the one to one module of sensors with respect to distance reading; i.e., in order to attain an acceptable picture of a robot traversing its environment, multiple sensors must be utilized together. It is ideal to have several rings of sonar sensors on Omni-directional vehicles as the mobile robot can traverse in any route to arrive at the destination. However, the number of sensors essential for a fitting field of view is not the only downside to sonar [9]. This clarifies that "Despite the fact that ultrasonic sensor ranging devices are highly significant and play a pivotal role in structural mobile robot applications, only the minority faction of researchers give attention to its drawbacks."

2.1   The Bug Family

This section explores the differences and similarities in the various outlined Bug Algorithms, specifically with respect to the techniques and conditions used to ensure termination criterion stands. The numerous variations of the Bug algorithms are extremely related, they vary in their mode of implementation to certify termination. Therefore, it was noted that every one of the Bug algorithms contain one of five unique approaches that will allow it to guarantee termination. The specific aim of examining the methods used is to establish the exact techniques and approaches implemented for reduction of path length (the distance covered from the point of initiation to the target) or algorithm complexity, whilst guaranteeing termination.

2.1.1   The Bug1 Algorithm

The Bug1 algorithm was proposed by Lumelsky et al. [10], as an easy and optimum resolve to the path planning drawback. This is the earliest Bug's family algorithm, hence, its solution to the motion planning difficulty is demonstrated in this section. Bug 1 algorithm is arguably the simplest algorithm discussed in this work. It arrives at the destination almost at every iteration, hence, exhibiting a high level of consistency. The instant drawback with this process is the state or quality at which the robot arrives at its destination. The robot moves on the shortest route, joining robot's starting position, (X) and destination, (Y), up until it bumps into a hurdle in its path. When the robot confronts an obstacle, it revolves around its surface and computes the distance from the goal. Subsequently, once the robot successfully completes a revolution around the obstacle, it figures out the point of exit that is next to the goal position. It maintains or changes direction of motion, depending on the distance of the leaving point from the hit point. This process can be shown in three phases:

(1)   Proceed to the destination.
(2)   Circumnavigate the obstacle if encountered, and record the distance to the goal.
(3)   Revisit the nearest position and advance.

The robot orbits around each obstacle as it advances towards the goal, thereby increasing computational efforts. The simplicity of execution makes it worth it; hence, it completes the task required regardless of time. Its implementation typically follows, as shown in Fig. 3 below (Fig. 2).

1. Set variable j to 0.
2. Increase j then advance towards the goal resulting to either of the two options:
    a. If we arrive at the goal, then End
    b. Once we reach an obstacle. Mark the position H_j and advance to phase 3.
3. We follow the obstacle boundary by maintaining the obstacle always to the right. At the same time we note Pdist (H_j, y) of the position(s) where P(y, T) is smallest and estimate if the robot is capable of reaching the goal at y.

   Record the lowest points as L_j. Immediately the robot arrives again at the higher points P_j, observe if the goal is attainable by checking if it can arrive at L_j. Once the robot doesn't reach exit state, we conclude that the goal is unattainable. If it terminates, observe the wall following approach P_{dist} (H_j, L_j) and traverse to L_j. Proceed to stage 1 at Lj.

Fig. 2. The Bug1 algorithm.

The Bug1 algorithm will definitely search through every obstacle, in search of the position that is closest to the goal (destination). Afterwards, the autonomous robot calculates and checks if it can advance towards the target position. In a case where the robot cannot, we then conclude that we cannot reach the target. The moment the robot advances and exits at that position, it would not encounter that obstacle moving forward.

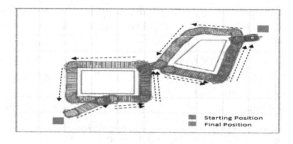

Fig. 3. The Bug1 algorithm in environment A

2.1.2   The Bug2 Algorithm

The Bug2 is a direct development that emerged from the Bug1 and it was also proposed by Lumelsky et al. [10]. As an alternative to obtaining the point at which the robot's path length is minimum, the Bug2 algorithm emphasizes on continuing the route of motion towards the destination, by calculating the slope of the line linking the initial position and the desired destination. The moment the robot advances towards an obstacle, it begins to move along the border of any obstacle ahead until it finds a point with the same slope. This algorithm is simple to implement and consequently more efficient than the Bug1 algorithm in most cases. The robot does not need to circum-navigate around the object as in the Bug1 algorithm. In this approach, the robot constantly makes an effort to travel along a line that links the initial (X_I) and goal (target) positions (X_G), the line called the m-line. The implementation of the model is shown as explained in Fig. 4:

---

1. To begin, you have to construct a virtual line, V, right from beginning to the goal and
   initialize j to 0.
2. Increase j and move towards the V line in the direction of the goal position resulting to one of the following:
   a. The goal position is attained, then Exit
   b. Tag the position you encounter the barrier as Hj advance to stage 3.
3. Constantly maintaining the traversal on the right position, you move forward around the borderline of the obstacle. Repeat the stage until:
   a. We arrive at the target and exit.
   b. The position along V is attained and dist(y, T) < dist(Hj, T). If the robot is able to advance towards the goal. Mark this point Li. Go to step 1. Otherwise, update d(Hi, T) with d(x, t).
   c. The robot returns to Hi. The target is unreachable. Stop.

Fig. 4. The Bug 2 algorithm

There has been some explanation in the collected works for path planning [11] about the leaving conditions for Bug2. Bug2+ was proposed by Antich and Ortiz [12], and the algorithm cleared every uncertainty, however this explains that the algorithm is related to Bug2 with a leaving condition. A precise explanation of the approach gives the Bug2 the feature to outline an exit position [13]. The implementation of the Bug2 algorithm emphasizes the straightforward nature, as shown in Fig. 5 below.

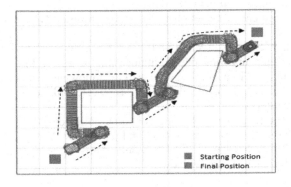

Fig. 5. The Bug2 algorithm in environment A

However, it is not good judgement when the robot is given an exit condition, if it cannot traverse to the goal directly after exit. Consequently, the exit condition is only fulfilled if it can advance towards the goal position.

As illustrated earlier in subclasses, you define the Bug1 as too precautious, although operative. However, Bug2 tends to be ineffective sometimes, such as crossings and native cycles, although it typically produces better enhanced paths whenever it is related to Bug1 [14].

The Bug2 approach was selected for evaluation because of its distinct, however straightforward, circumnavigation behavior that functions both with local or global motion planning drawbacks, and unlike the Bug1, it generates more improved routes. The standard Bug2 was also selected to the disadvantage of the DistBug as being the easiest algorithm that sustains the key features required for comparison.

2.1.3   The Distbug Algorithm

Kamon and Rivlin developed the DistBug algorithm [15]. The DistBug makes use of a proximity sensor to detect an obstacle and makes use of it in its leaving condition. The robot travels comparatively shorter distances than prior versions of the Bug algorithm, thereby ensuring that the robot to reach its destination in less time. This algorithm exhibits different obstacle avoidance behaviors. When the robot encounters an obstacle, it begins to follow the edge of the obstacle, simultaneously estimating and updating the path length from its existing and next position to the goal. The leaving point, which prompts a behavioral change from 'obstacle avoidance' to 'move to goal' paradigm, is selected based on the condition that the distance of the destination from its next position is greater than the equivalent path length from its current position. The robot keeps establishing its obstacle avoidance behavior otherwise. The algorithm is shown in Fig. 6 and an illustration is shown in Fig. 7.

1. Set variable $j = 0$ to estimate the thickness of the wall (which is the smallest width obtained from a barrier from the environment. It is defined and inputted by the user and is a major limitation exhibited from this algorithm).
2. Increase j and move towards the goal pending the occurrence of the instances:
    a. You arrive at the goal. Exit.
    b. You encounter an obstacle. Tag the position Hj. Advance to stage 3.
3. Move to the leftmost direction and move along the border of the obstacle, while constantly updating the minimum value of dist(y, T) and denote this value distmin (T). Repeat this until one of the following occurs:
    a. The goal is visible: $dist(y, T) - F \leq 0$. Record the position as Lj. Go to step 1.
    b. The range based leaving condition holds: $dist(y, T) - F \leq distmin (T) - Step$. Denote the position Lj. Advance to stage 1.
    c. This robot has finished a cycle and arrived at Hj. The goal cannot be reached, Hence, Exit.

Fig. 6. The DistBug algorithm

The DistBug algorithm has also exhibited its unique feature as it increases path-length execution in Sect. 3 and the motivation for this are extensively described in Sect. 4 consequently. In a nutshell, it is as a result that each time the DistBug calculate its exit criterion, it is range based and it considers two factors.

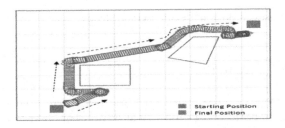

Fig. 7. The DistBug algorithm in environment A

First, if the robot can detect the closest position that precedes any other position moving towards the goal. The second factor is the STEP condition that always prevents the occurrence of the Class1 scenario, this can occur when the robot fulfils the exit condition, once it is at the closest position to the goal than any other position visited prior to the advancement to the goal.

3 Comparisons of the Bug Algorithms

After discussion of various methods of object avoidance, we will list the merits and demerits of each algorithm, which can be useful in choosing one for a specific application. The selection of the best method depends on specific requirements and resources.

3.1 The Bug1 Algorithm

(a) Merits
    i. It is a complete algorithm i.e. in finite time, it finds a path if such a path exists or terminates with failure if it does not.
(b) Demerits
    i. Large memory and computation is required in Bug 1, which results in lesser efficiency.
    ii. It is an exhaustive search algorithm

3.2   The Bug2 Algorithm

(a) Merits
    i. It is a greedy search algorithm i.e. it takes the first thing that looks better
    ii. It requires less computation also it is easy to implement
(b) Demerits
    i. In some cases, it does not exhibit completeness

4   Results and Evaluation

To verify the proposed method, extensive experiments were conducted in different terrain environments based on our differential drive robot, as shown in Fig. 5. The obstacle detection results in three different scenes are presented, to test the obstacle performance of the proposed method. Subsequently, the feasibility and efficiency of the Bug algorithms are evaluated in later sections.

4.1   Scene 1: Static Cuboid in the Center of a Wall in the Environment

This environment is a specific scene of a ground with a static cuboid placed in the center of a back wall. The ground is very flat, and the cuboid is placed as the obstacle at the center of the scene. In addition, some obstacles were overlapped in the intensity image. According to the proposed method, the whole obstacle detecting process is shown in Fig. 8, where the behavior of the Pioneer 3-DX robot was tested. Therefore, it is shown how the robot successfully exhibits its obstacle avoidance properties and also how it avoided the cuboid enclosed in the center of the wall and arrived safely at its target.

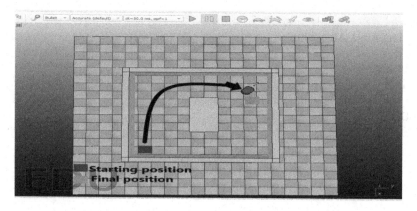

Fig. 8. Robot avoids obstacle and arrives at target in SCENE 1

4.2 Scene 2: Three Static Cuboid Placed Symmetrically

The second scene consists of a ground with three cuboids. The cuboid is positioned on a flat ground as an obstacle. It is strategically aligned at three different locations in a manner that is almost unavoidable and it uses the obstacle detection and avoidance module to reach its target. In addition, some obstacles were overlapped in the intensity image. The traversal of the robot from the starting position till it arrives at its target using the proposed method is illustrated in Fig. 9 where the behavior of the Pioneer 3-DX robot was tested and it shows how the robot successfully implements its obstacle avoidance module and avoids the static cuboids placed symmetrically in the environment.

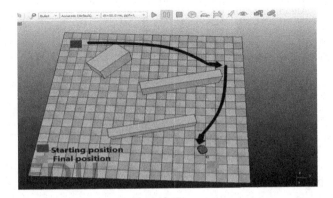

Fig. 9. Robot avoids obstacle and arrives at target in SCENE 2

4.3 Scene 3: D-Shaped Cuboid in the Environment

The third environment consists of four cuboids of which, three cuboids have been fused together to form a D-shaped object similar to a triangle in the V-REP environment with an additional cuboid positioned as an obstacle close to the final position of the robot.

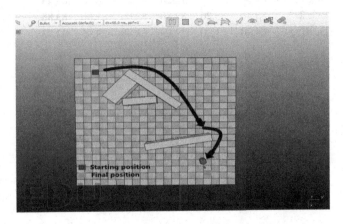

Fig. 10. Robot avoids obstacle and arrives at target in SCENE 3

The robot effectively avoids the obstacle and arrives at the target. The representation of how the robot demonstrates the avoidance functionality by maneuvering from the start position to the goal is shown in Fig. 10. The obstacle avoidance methods take inputs from the sensors and traverses till it successfully arrives at its proposed target.

4.4   Performance Comparison of Bug1, Bug2 and Distbug Algorithms

The experimental data obtained from each Bug1, Bug2 and DistBug algorithms are given in the tables below (Tables 1, 2, 3 and 4).

Table 1. Average time comparison data for scene 1

Algorithm	Time (s)					
	1	2	3	4	5	Average
Bug 1	55.80	59.20	53.50	57.20	58.90	**56.92**
Bug 2	22.25	24.63	21.86	25.91	23.58	**23.65**
DistBug	20.70	39.73	25.30	22.48	23.59	**26.36**

Table 2. Average time comparison data for scene 2

Algorithm	Time (s)					
	1	2	3	4	5	Average
Bug 1	143.40	147.00	178.80	135.60	171.00	**155.16**
Bug 2	65.40	75.00	61.20	71.40	76.80	**69.96**
DistBug	60.60	59.87	67.20	64.20	58.73	**62.12**

Table 3. Average time comparison data for scene 3

Algorithm	Time (s)					
	1	2	3	4	5	Average
Bug 1	183.00	154.80	172.20	163.80	168.60	**168.48**
Bug 2	83.40	85.20	82.80	87.00	81.00	**83.88**
DistBug	64.20	61.20	59.89	68.40	59.96	**62.73**

Table 4. Path length of the bug algorithms

Algorithm	Path Length (mm)		
	Scene 1	Scene 2	Scene 3
Bird-Eye View	8602.33	6702.35	9985.43
Bug 1	29021.92	20794.86	30112.85
Bug 2	16193.65	9563.87	18286.16
DistBug	12794.79	8941.83	16584.75

4.5   Average Time Comparison of the Bug Algorithms

The experimental data obtained from each Bug1, Bug2 and DistBug algorithms given in tables above, are duly represented in the chart below to show the correlations between the three bug algorithms and the varying speed and distance covered each of the algorithms exhibit during the simulations. The graph of the comparisons of path length and average time of the bug algorithms are therefore shown in Figs. 11 and 12 below.

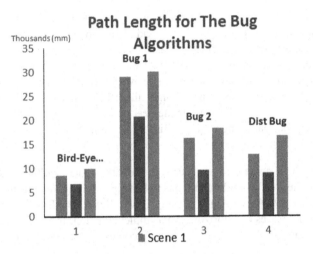

Fig. 11. Path comparison

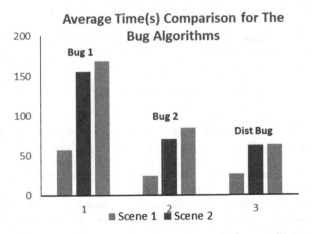

Fig. 12. Average time comparison

5   Conclusion

This paper presents a method for real-time obstacle detection and recognition in unstructured environments based on the use of vision and motion sensors of the Pioneer 3-DX robot. V-REP is introduced as a versatile and scalable simulation framework. By offering a multitude of different programming techniques for its controllers, and by the allowance for controllers to be embedded, as well as functionalities in simulation models, it eases the programmers' task and reduces the deployment complexity for the users.

It is therefore shown based on the necessary computations we can hereby compare the Bug1, Bug2, and DistBug algorithms and their modes of implementation. The operation of the approach described in earlier sections function on a Pioneer 3-DX robot and the simulation setup is by V-REP. Due to necessary comparisons of the three modules, a single scene is used. The results show that Bug1 is the worst one, with its path length approximately 3.37 times longer than the path length of the Bird-eye's view. On the other hand, the DistBug is the best option, as its path length is only 1.49 times longer than the path length of the Bird-eye's view.

Future Work

The future work will contain several scenes to test the functionalities and to show its effectiveness of the Bug's family and it has to highlight at least three of the other Bug's algorithms which are Alg1, Alg2, Class1, Rev1, Rev2, OneBug, LeaveBug, TangentBug, etc. it increases our horizon. After implementation, the algorithms should be tested on real pioneer robots to see the live outcomes of the real world.

Acknowledgement. The authors gratefully acknowledge the support of African Institute for Mathematical Sciences (AIMS), Alumni small research grant (AASRG), the Organisation for Women in Science for the Developing World (OWSD), and L'oreal-Unesco for Women in Science.

The authors of this research also appreciate the immense contribution of Covenant University Centre for Research, Innovation, and Discovery (CUCRID) for its support for this research.

References

1. Günther, M., Weihmann, T.: Climbing in hexapods: a plain model for heavy slopes. J. Theor. Biol. **293**, 82–86 (2011). Jena, Germany, Copyright © 2011 Elsevier Ltd. All rights reserved
2. Ferrell, C.: A comparison of three insect-inspired locomotion controllers. Robot. Autom. Syst. **16**, 135–159 (1995). Cambridge, Copyright © 1995 Published by Elsevier B.V.
3. Misra, S., Alfa, A.A., Olaniyi, M.O., Adewale, S.O.: Exploratory study of techniques for exploiting instruction-level parallelism. In: GCSIT 2014 – Global Summit on Computer and Information Technology, Tunisia, pp 1–6 (2014)
4. Navarro-Serment, L.: A beacon system for the localization of distributed robotic teams. In.: Proceedings of the International Conference on Field and Service Robotics (1999)

5. Omichi, T.: Hierarchy control system for vehicle navigation based on information of sensor fusion perception depending on measuring distance layer. In: Proceedings of the International Conference on Field and Service Robotics (1999)
6. Soto, A.: Cyber-ATVS: dynamic and distributed reconnaissance and surveillance using all terrain UGVS. In: Proceedings of the International Conference on Field and Service Robotics (1999)
7. Prassler, E.: Maid: a robotic wheelchair roaming in a railway station. In: Proceedings of the International Conference on Field and Service Robotics (1999)
8. Thrun, S.: Experiences with two deployed interactive tour-guide robots. In: Proceedings of the International Conference on Field and Service Robotics (1999)
9. Borenstein, J.: Obstacle avoidance with ultrasonic sensors (1999)
10. Guruprasad, K.R.: A real time path planning algorithm for a mobile robot in an unknown environment. In: Advanced Computing, Networking and Security (ADCON) (2011)
11. Sankaranarayanan, A., Vidyasagar, M.: Path Planning for Moving a Point Object Amidst Unknown obstacles in a plane (1991)
12. Okewu, E., Misra, S.: Applying metaheuristic algorithm to the admission problem as a combinatorial optimization problem. Front. Artif. Intell. Appl. **282**, 53–64 (2016)
13. Noborio: Evaluation of path length made in sensor-based path-planning with the alternative following. In: Proceedings of the IEEE International Conference of Robotics and Automation (2001)
14. Buniyamin, N.: A simple local path planning algorithm for autonomous mobile robots. Int. J. Syst. Appl. Eng. Dev. **5**(2), 151–159 (2011)
15. Kamon, I., Rivlin, E.: Sensory-based motion planning with global proofs. IEEE Trans. Robot. Autom. **13**(6), 814–822 (1997)
16. ASSIS: A Scalable Constructive Path Planning for Mobile Agents based on the Compact Genetic Algorithm (2017)
17. Kanehiro, F.: Open HRP: open architecture humanoid robotics platform. J. Robot. Res., Int (2004)
18. Ng, J.: An Analysis of Mobile Robot Navigation Algorithms in Unknown Environments (2010)
19. Pallottino, P.L.: Distributed Robotic Systems (2015)
20. Freese, M.: Collision detection distance calculation and proximity sensor simulation using oriented bounding box trees. In: 4th International Conference on Advanced Mechatronics (2004)
21. Pandya, H.V.: Mobile Manipulator based Framework for Dataset Generation and Algorithm Testing (2015)
22. Ramli, N.R.: An Overview of Simulation Software for, pp. 3–5 (2015)

Security Services

A Secured Private-Cloud Computing System

Modebola Olowu[1], Chika Yinka-Banjo[1], Sanjay Misra[2(✉)] [iD],
and Hector Florez[3] [iD]

[1] Department of Computer Sciences, University of Lagos, Lagos, Nigeria
mdblanne20@gmail.com, cyinkabanjo@unilag.edu.ng
[2] Covenant University, Ota, Nigeria
sanjay.misra@covenantuniversity.edu.ng
[3] Universidad Distrital Francisco Jose de Caldas Bogota, Bogota, Colombia
haflorezf@udistrital.edu.co

Abstract. The advent of internet and rapid growth of digital media has vastly increased concerns of cloud computing as source of data and information storage ever than before. It allows users to setup their own private clouds since the public clouds available, can't surpass their expectations at affordable costs. With private cloud computing, users do not need to be in a physical location when accessing personified cloud resources, thus; leading to cost reduction, improved user experience (ux), staff effectiveness, and file sharing with organizational collaborations from remote sites. Despite lots of benefits offered, there have been constant challenges associated with cloud computing from Data loss & breaches, service vulnerabilities, insufficient due diligence, identity, access and credential management, poor footprint tracking for threats & malicious insider attacks etc. which threatens network security. This proposed application is set out to provide immediate solution to help fight against cloud insecurity, particularly in private cloud domains through restriction of access to cloud resources, giving access to only trusted members to prove their identities through Footprint Notifications, Logging Encryption and activities of the authenticated users, as it is essential to monitor information flow on the cloud for information assessment purposes. The implementation of a secured Private-Cloud Computing System is the central focus of this project; the application is designed by using advanced features of HTML, CSS, JAVASCRIPT, & JQUERY for the frontend interface while PHP & MYSQL were used to design the backend of the application and its log encryption.

Keywords: HTML (Hypertext Markup Language) · (CSS) Cascading Style Sheet · JSON (JavaScript object Notation)

1 Introduction

Cloud computing is an innovative approach to the world of computing whereby sturdily accessible and virtual resources are made as services available across the Internet. It has led to an era of important technological trends, which is expected to redefine the processes and marketplaces involved in information technology, and marketplace [1]. Users can use diverse devices imbibing the technology of cloud

© Springer Nature Switzerland AG 2019
H. Florez et al. (Eds.): ICAI 2019, CCIS 1051, pp. 373–384, 2019.
https://doi.org/10.1007/978-3-030-32475-9_27

computing which includes smart phones, pc's and laptops to utilize available resources like storage, software design platforms and programs via the Internet as service rendered by the service providers for cloud computing. The internet's advent and rapid growth of digital media has vastly increased concern for cloud computing ever than before. Cloud computing has turned out to be a technological innovation that has transformed the activities of businesses and people today [2, 11]. It is the evolution and convergence point of numerous notions covering grid, enterprise IT management, virtualization, and distributed application design to provide an effective approach for scaling and installing applications [3, 12]. The cloud simply refers to Network or Internet. It can also be referred to as something that is located at remote location which is readily available to provide services over public, and private networks such as LAN, WAN, and VPN. Web conferencing, email and customer relationship management (CRM) can route on cloud. It has able to remove need for various organizations, individual cloud user and IT companies now moving their services from their private networks to the clouds since public available clouds can now surpass their expectations at affordable costs.

With private cloud computing, users do not need to be in a physical location when accessing cloud resources, thus; leading to cost reduction, improved user experience (ux), staff effectiveness, and file sharing with organizational collaborations from remote sites. In simple definition, cloud computing is the utilization of many services like storage, software development platforms, servers, and software over the internet. In the era of enterprise server and personal computer, hardware remained essential commodity criteria for processing capabilities that rely mainly on hardware configuration of server. Of particular interest is the Cloud computing feature that offers platform independency; software is not needed to be installed locally on individual PC or connecting devices; therefore, it enhances mobility and collaborative among connecting client devices [4, 13].

Up till recent time, Gafunk [Nig] Limited has never been interested in moving her services to cloud. The company data and their clients have been stored on her customized private network and traditional storage media which are usually unsecured and restricted to local domain. In existing system, office daily tasks at Gafunk are perform locally within premises of her private server equipment, instead of moving it to public cloud where daily tasks can be performed synchronously irrespective of her workers locations across the globe. Security issues of company and clients' information have been one of the reasons why Gafunk has been afraid of moving her services to cloud.

The deployment of secured cloud infrastructure within the company will go a long way to position the company among leading IT companies around the world. With this deployment, IT officers/workers can carry out their daily office routines synchronously from anywhere they are provided there is internet service to access cloud information storage in a secured manner.

2   Literature Review

2.1   Historical Development of Secured Cloud Computing

According to [5], the concept of cloud computing had been evolving since the 1950's; the organizations were using composite mainframe systems to process their useful data. In those early days, these systems were at high cost and very huge. As a result of this, most organizations started purchasing few machines and activate schedules for time-sharing so they can make profits as much as possible. Time sharing allows users have access to mainframe computers from non-processing linked power stations; this type of computational power shared became the birth of Cloud. [6]; emphasized that during 1955, John McCarthy, the first to name the word 'artificial intelligence', a phenomenon created to save the cost of getting too many computers by simply sharing among a whole number of users the computing time. Most start-ups couldn't purchase small computers which stalled their automation migration; McCarthy's theory suddenly brought about the solution most organizations have been clamouring for, especially for those who couldn't purchase as much computer systems as they should. So, as technology progressed, the notion of secured cloud computing advanced through the years unto the 1960s when foremost improvements began. Then in the 1960's mid, an American computer scientist called Licklider started with the concept of interrelated computer systems.

2.2   Understanding Information Security

Information security is concerned about information confidentiality, integrity, availability and data protection from unauthenticated users to disclose; access, modify, inspect, record or destroy information [7]. Most times, the information assurance, information security and computer security are usually misuse, even though they are related, and they all protect integrity, availability, and confidentiality information. However, the difference among the three of them has to do with methodology adopted, subject approach and part of concentration. So many institutions such as hospitals, banks, government, corporations, police and private establishments collect and possess sensitive employee information, product information, services, inquiries, financial and customer position. The computer system emergence has now made it possible to collect; process and store information before transmitting across the network to the target computer.

2.3   Types of Secured Cloud Computing Based on Architecture Models

The architecture of cloud computing is basically on cloud services highly accessible in demand and with multi-users. The growth rate of data and its usage as rapidly increased, as well as cloud computing. At the moment, archived data is making waves as the most recognized and suitable one for secured cloud computing; when considering metrics such as access frequency, integrity, availability, cost, frequency of access, protection and availability [8].

Cloud computing can be classified into three architecture types which are hybrid, private and public.

2.4   Characteristics of Secured Cloud Computing

According to [9], Secured cloud computing can be described by the following characteristics (Table 1):

Table 1. Features of secured cloud computing

Characteristics	Descriptions
Manageability	Capability of managing systems with marginal properties
Access Method	Protocols wherein the exposure of cloud computing is shown
Performance	Latency & Bandwidth metrics are used to measure the performance
Multi-tenancy	Allows multi tenants and users
Scalability	Capability of scaling to satisfy demands and loads higher in request
Data Availability	Availability of data and system to work
Control	Capability of controlling a computer system, its cost configuration, features and performance
Storage Efficiency	Shows and measures how properties from the raw storages utilized
Cost	Accounts for the cloud computing cost and expenses, usually measured in dollars per gig

2.5   Importance of Cryptography in Secured Information

Cryptography is about encryption and decryption; secured information utilizes cryptography to encrypt information into a form that is difficult to comprehend and readable by human standard and can as well be decrypted back to readable format. The aim of cryptography is to secure information and data from unauthenticated users during transmission and storage. Cryptography can also work along with other security application such as digital signature, information logging, access control, and encrypted network to improve secured information of cloud or local server data. Most old applications like FTP and telnet that are less secured are now rapidly being replaced with encrypted applications. WPA, WPA2 or WEP protocols are being used to secure wireless communication devices and applications while AES, X.1035 are being used in the encryption of wire devices and applications. So many other applications like PGP or GnuPG can encrypt email and data files as part of information security measure.

2.6   Application of Secured Cloud Computing

Secured cloud computing has been recognized with rising competitiveness through cost reduction, optimal resource utilization, greater flexibility and elasticity. Benefits of cloud computing isn't just about data storage or emails, rather these scalable cloud solutions have become medium of choice for software development, testing and deployment as well. Its relatively applied in Communication, Big Data Analytics, Storage, Synchronized workspace, allows Scalable usage, etc.

2.7   Limitations/Challenges in Secured Information in Cloud Computing

Irrespective of organization size, cloud computing still offers many benefits like any-where accessibility to data, affordable hosting, information security, overall discount for cost of investment, though clients and users will still pass through the security and technicality problems at different stages [10, 11].

3   System Analysis and Design

Here, the section explains in specific terms, techniques and tools employed in this research work. The methodologies and tools adopted, also touches the following parts of the study: Analysis of the Existing System, System Coding, System Design, Design Consideration and Architecture etc.

3.1   Analysis of the Existing System

A critical analysis of the present mode of handling information security in cloud computing at Gafunk (Nig) Ltd, reveals that the present system does not make use of any automation. Protection of data and information system from unauthenticated users to disclose; access, modify, inspect, record or destroy information are too weak to secure traditional cloud computing in use at Gafunk (Nig) Ltd from being attacked and hacked. In existing system, Gafunk (Nig) Ltd uses secret passphrase, blank or weak password as a form of security and authentication system to protect cloud computing resources from being tampered with. However, password choice will always be an argumentative point as long as users have to choose one. Cloud users have to struggle with remembering their precise passwords with a lot to choose from when initiating one from their special days and ones, leading to weakness in the existing cloud computing system by giving cloud hackers good chance to guess the correct password. Acute scrutiny for the existing system shows it's a system not effective for securing 21st century cloud resources due to inherent security challenges, lack of confidentiality, integrity and availability of data can occur due to use of blank or weak password.

3.2   Problem of Existing System

Some of the problems identified in existing secured cloud computing includes the following:

Hacks, Lack of confidentiality, integrity and availability of data, Lack of effective-ness in existing information security and Data loss & breaches; Service vulnerabilities & Insufficient due diligence, Insufficient identity, access and credential management; Poor footprint tracking for threats & malicious insider attacks, Misplacement of information on storage devices can occur, which can lead to chaos between management and cus-tomers. Etc.

3.3   Description/Analysis of New System

The main features of the new system being proposed will incorporate features like accuracy, reliability, rapid retrieval of information, ease of operation, security, data protection etc.

3.4   System Design

3.4.1   Output Design

It is made up of emerging conditions and measures for data preparation, also the required steps to route the right inputs and super desired user friendly outputs. Errors can also be controlled by providing to users suitable messages and apt direction.

3.4.2   Input Design

It is the method of changing user-initiated inputs, to computer-constructed forms. Essentially, it must be involved in the expansion and creation methods, as erroneous data inputs turn out to be the root-cause of mistakes in the processing of data.

3.4.3   Database Design

Creating a defined database is an essential stage in systems designing, here data essentials and structures are recognized and analyzed promptly to give an output of the storage and retrieval systems.

3.4.4   Functional Requirements for the Proposed System

These are the useful necessities that clients are looking to when using an application. Below stands some of the functional requirements for this proposed application:

i. A cloud user can sign up new account by admin as part of information needed for future login into secured cloud computing
ii. Logging of events at background for monitoring cloud activities

3.4.5   Non-functional Requirements for Proposed System

Non-functional requirement is described as parts of the system that deals with its development over time focusing on how its maintained, documented and if its extensible and not how it is been implemented.

3.5   System Coding Tools and Techniques

The system coding tools consist of the code and the environment used in designing this secured cloud computing for the use of Gafunk (Nig) Limited, Lagos. The coding tools used various types of programming languages to develop the cloud computing application, which includes: Hypertext Markup Laanguage (HTML), CSS (Cascading style sheet), JAVASCRIPT, PHP, JSON, MYSQL.

3.6   PHP Library Methods for Encryption

Cryptography has got everyone on their feet when it comes to the future trend of cloud security. In the case of PHP, bcrypt, Argon2 and Sodium were introduced for both data and password encryption on the PHP platform, which covers a whole lot of security areas in coding or criteria's for infusing security into third party applications and features. As such I will be making use of this internal libraries to make my private cloud more secured in the case of hashing passwords and encrypting it for safety.

Below are the major three (3) methods involved in PHP encryption modes; but we will be concentrating more on Hashing as our method of encryption.

i. **Secret Key Encryption:** It's also called a symmetric encryption that employs only a single key to carry out both encryption and decryption of data. It's launched using sodium on PHP. An encryption key will be the initial thing to be generated, with function- random_bytes(),which will be stored as an environmental variable.

ii. **Envelope Encryption:** It's a higher method of encryption as it is more secured than other methods, it is the process whereby keys will be encrypted with another key, like a double protection. It's used mostly when we want to avoid sending our confidential plaintext information to an intermediary/receiver, no matter how secured we think the platform may be.

iii. **Hashing:** A hashing algorithm receives an input value or commonly what is called a plain text or message and alters it; a lot of times into a fixed length hash, which will only be authenticated by transferring the original value to the hashing algorithm. This in turn, perfectly makes hashing the best for storing user credentials on the cloud.

The swift SHA1 and effectual MD5 are quite popular for check summing and file verification. Although, not suitable for hashing a user's password or username due to their incompatible speed. Nowadays passwords can be cracked by brute force in a matter of minutes, revealing the plaintext password or username. Thus, purposely algorithms with slower hashing will be used, e.g. bcrypt or Argon2, from password_hash() to PASSWORD_ARGON2I

3.7   Evaluation of Major Encryption Algorithms in Cloud Computing Cryptography and Their Weaknesses

The integration of cryptography in cloud computing can bring lasting security solution to cloud computing application, but this can be achieved if only the right encryption and decryption algorithm is used. There are several cryptographic algorithms that can be used with cloud computing to improve its security features; among them include: RSA algorithm, RC4 algorithm, Blowfish algorithm, Brie algorithm etc. In order to identify the algorithm that is most appropriate to give lasting security solutions, the strengths and weaknesses of each cipher in terms of security, speed, direct monetary cost, and ease of implementation are considered before considering appropriate security in smart cards. Here are general discussions relating to the advantages and disadvantages of RC4 and RSA which are most popular cryptographic algorithms used in cloud computing applications as presented below in this research work.

4   System Implementation Ad Documentation

This is the exact chapter that is concerned with the implementation and research evaluation. The implementation was finally achieved based on the input outcome from chapter three. The inputs were used to achieve the result enumerated as output design from chapter three. The central focus of this chapter is to enlighten application users on necessary software and hardware requirements needed to run developed application.

4.1   System Implementation

Now that the implementation of our proposed system (Secured Cloud Computing) has been achieved and functional, there is a need for total integration of this application to replace existing (old method) in use presently at Gafunk (Nig) Limited. The users of this application will need to be carried along until they are fully familiar with the new system. Several changeover methods are available for the management to adopt without affecting the management and application users in their present working environments.

4.2   Changeover Recommendation

After careful considerations, a parallel changeover method was recommended for Gafunk (Nig).

4.3   System Installation and System Run

System Installation works in conjunction with evaluation and documentation of new system. Having designed and implemented this cloud computing application for Gafunk, it is time to highlight how to run the program on computer so that one will be able to understand the approach and the environment on which the application is intended to run the software for the use of Gafunk (Nig) Limited to achieved target objectives.

4.3.1   Hardware Specification

For the proper implementation of new system, author recommends the following minimum hardware requirements for environment where this application will run: Pentium 4 processor and speed of 3.20 GHz, RAM of 448 megabytes (MB), 500 megabytes (500 MB) of hard disk space, A simple-enhanced windows keyboard and mouse, A color video graphics array or super video graphics array monitor, Speakers, CD-ROM or DVD-ROM drive, Sound card, HP Laser Jet printer for report generations & Uninterrupted Power Supply (UPS).

4.3.2   Software Specification

This includes a web browser (Opera, Google Chrome etc.), Wamp Server: if the application needs to be implemented on a local system, The system should be running windows XP or any higher Microsoft windows operating system, HTML, CSS, JAVASCRIPT for front-end Graphical User Interface design, PHP & MYSQL for back-end database design, Macromedia flash & not necessarily a private cloud saas.

4.4   System Documentation

Documentation is the complete facts about a system's scheme and description, showing its inner mechanisms, and functionalities.

4.4.1   User's Guide

After successful implementation, you are now ready to operate the application.

- Double click on the Wampserver icon on the desktop to start the local server
- Go to start and click on internet explorer
- From the address bar, type: http://localhost and press enter key to start navigation
- Welcome to home page of application

After successful testing, application must be moved to cloud to achieve the purpose for which it was created.

4.4.2   System Maintenance

System maintenance involves all the numerous parts involved in an IT maintenance, covering the computers, servers and all that is necessary to keep the system working efficiently and effectively. It is a continual event carried out periodically, covering the removal of obsolete programs, document updates, design and program errors, data testing data as well as apprising user support. Maintenance is made up of three (3) divisions which are:

(i)   Corrective
(ii)   Adaptive
(iii) Perfective

However, out of all the categories of maintenance system methods listed above, perfective maintenance method is recommended to enhance optimum performance (Fig. 1).

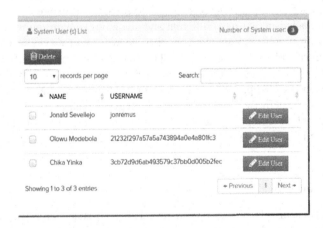

Fig. 1. Results of the encrypted credentials via the WAMP server.

5   Summary, Recommendation and Conclusion

5.1   Summary

These systems have passed through all the activities and process of a software life cycle from the developmental stages down to the implementation stages and testing. The secured cloud application has been developed bearing in mind the availability and improvement in network coverage of internet services that can boost safe cloud services within the organization. This research work has showcased important approaches towards cloud computing application, challenges and future prospects used by other researchers, cloud vendors, IT experts including users of this professions industrially, in order to carry out an appraisal on the secured cloud. There is a long list of challenges, in which cloud service providers will need to address to compel major acceptance [12, 13]. Due to complication of securing cloud computing environments, so many companies and organizations are now using hybrid cloud environments that include private and public clouds. The cloud vendors possess self-approaches of security management, which usually conflict with individual or company's rules [14, 15]. Having implemented this research, definite problems were noted from the existing systems which were improved upon during the course of this research. Now, secured cloud computing system has made authentication on the cloud more secured, foot print notifications and loggings more resilient.

5.2   Recommendation

Although the recorded successes in improving security of public cloud computing services through ICT in recent years have been commendable, yet there are still challenges and hindrances to organization internal security of their networks against public cloud vulnerabilities [18].

Before implementing security plan, the cloud users need to make sure that it will complement service provider's plan instead. In as much as cloud users relish the cost-effective advantage of cloud computing, the only thing to join hands to overcome is the challenges-security risks poses against cloud computing. The threats, safety issues, exposures and hacks surface from different and situations. According to [17], pointed out the following useful recommendations that are worthy of note for creating cloud computing security plans. Using licensed IT protection experts, agents and professionals to routinely evaluate the organizations network securities & policies and cloud services subscribed to. Approaching cloud security from a risk management point of view, will see the enterprise's risk management expert's plan & involvement. Before the new private cloud computing service is utilized in an organization, relevant competence training must be recommended for employees and top-management of Gafunk (Nig.) Limited.

5.3   Conclusion

A careful analysis of this project would reveal that all stated objectives have been achieved. Gafunk (Nig.) Ltd and the customers, have moved from an use cured zone to a more resilient one. The future appears promising for the Private Cloud Computing platform, despite a lot of challenges facing its development, its benefits and applications outweighs its challenges. Secured cloud computing offers many useful services that can benefit organizations as well as individual cloud users. In bigger IT firms the development and creation of private clouds always produces the best results, saving cost and improving generally efficiency in the enterprise; All to provide computing infrastructures at lowest possible cost using concepts of resource pooling, virtualization, dynamic provisioning, utility and commodity computing to create private secured cloud computing that meet their needs [19]. As many physical data will be stored off in the cloud by various cloud users, organizations and individual users will need to take drastic steps to ensure data security by employing strict security policies, regulatory compliance, disaster recovery, user access control policies and procedures and business continuity are all essential factors a cloud user should consider when moving to public cloud services offered by any cloud service provider in order to benefit from what future holds for secured cloud computing. However, the researcher has carried out explorative research and developed Secured Cloud Computing application framework to serve as prototype to experts, researchers, developers, inventors and academician to see opportunities, challenges as well as future prospects that can be explored through secured cloud computing and resource sharing collaboration for future development of our world.

5.4   Further Research

Moreover, there is no system with perfection in its specifications, thus, for future trends and research work, it is recommended that the scope of study must be beyond present scope of study covered while other features to add should include the following:

  i. A 2MFA form of protective logging.
 ii. The in-house cloud application should be developed to run on other platforms other than Web to incorporate users using other different platforms running on different Operating Systems.
iii. There should be future research work done on how the cloud computing can employ facial recognition and fingerprint biometric to improve cloud security

Acknowledgement. The authors of this research appreciate the immense contribution of Covenant University Centre for Research, Innovation, and Discovery (CUCRID) for its support for this research.

References

1. Zhou, J.: Analysis of Cloud Computing Security Problem. In: APSEC 2013 Cloud Workshop; Sydney, Australia (2013)
2. Yang, Y.: 'State of the Public Cloud: The Cloud Adopters' Perspective (2014). http://thecloud.appirio.com/rs/appirio/images/State_of_the_Public_Cloud_Results_FINAL-102910.pdf

3. Pallis, G.: Cloud computing: the new frontier of internet computing. IEEE Internet Comput. **14**(5), 70–73 (2010). ISSN 1089 7801

4. Dhamija, R., Dusseault, L.: Seven flaws of identity management: usability and security challenges. IEEE Secur. Priv. **6**, 24–29 (2008)

5. Zhang, G.: Toward a unified ontology of cloud computing environments. Int. J. Comput. Eng. (IOSRJCE), **1**(1), 1–8 (2015)

6. Wolman, N.: An intro to cloud computing for contemporary business environment. (IOSRJCE), **1**(1) (2013)

7. John Wiley: Cloud Computing Footprints, pp. 22–27. Hoboken, New Jersey, USA (2014)

8. Dennis, Y.: A History of Cloud Computing, p. 23 (2016)

9. Gopalakrishnan, H.: Dispersed identity for secure service interaction. In: IEEE, Piscataway, New Jersey, United States, pp. 56–59 (2013)

10. Grance, C.: Enhancing user authentication in claim-based identity management. In: (CTS), International Symposium IEEE, Piscataway, New Jersey, United States, pp. 75–83 (2013)

11. Ibrahim, B.: Auditing Cloud Computing: a Security and Privacy Guide, vol. 21 (2014)

12. Mambo, B.: CA Technologies Predicts Key Trends for Identity and Access Management (2016). http://www.ca.com/us/news/press-releases/na/2014/ca-technologies-predicts-key-trends-for-identity-and-access-management-in-2014.aspx. Accessed 2 June 2016

13. Meier, P.: How Cloud Computing Works, HowStaffWoks.com. http://howstuffworks.com/cloud-computing/cloudcomputing3.html Accessed 24 Nov 2014

14. Paul, P.: Security and cloud computing: identity management infrastructure for collaborative enterprises. In: 11th IEEE, Piscataway, New Jersey, United States, pp. 26–29 (2013)

15. Ranchal, K.: Evolution of cloud storage as cloud computing infrastructure. Int. J. Comput. Eng. (IOSRJCE), **1**(1) (2015)

16. Sharma, Q.: A proposed architecture of cloud computing for education system in bangladesh and the impact on current education system. IEEE, Int. J. Comput. Sci. pp. 21–27 (2014)

17. William, K.: Above the Clouds: a Berkeley View of Cloud Computing. Dept. Electrical Eng. and Comput. Sciences, University of California, Berkeley, pp. 2–5 (2018)

18. Odun-Ayo, I., Misra, S., Omoregbe, N., Onibere, E., Bulama, Y., Damasevicius, R.: Cloud-based security-driven human resources management system. Front. Artif. Intell. Appl. **295**, 96–106 (2017)

19. Jambhekar, N.D., Misra, S., Dhawale, C.A.: Cloud computing security with collaborating encryption. Indian J. Sci. Technol. **9**(21), 1–7 (2016)

Comparative Evaluation of Techniques for Detection of Phishing URLs

Oluwafemi Osho[1] (ID), Ayanfeoluwa Oluyomi[1], Sanjay Misra[2](✉) (ID),
Ravin Ahuja[3], Robertas Damasevicius[4], and Rytis Maskeliunas[4]

[1] Federal University of Technology, Minna, Nigeria
femi.osho@futminna.edu.ng,
ayanfeoluwaoluyomi@gmail.com
[2] Covenant University, Ota, Nigeria
sanjay.misra@covenantuniversity.edu.ng
[3] Vishwakarma Skill University Gurugram, Gurgaon, Hariyana, India
ravinahujadce@gmail.com
[4] Kaunas University of Technology, Kaunas, Lithuania
{robertas.damasevicius, rytis.maskeliunas}@ktu.lt

Abstract. One of the popular cyberattacks today is phishing. It combines social engineering and online identity theft to delude Internet users into submitting their personal information to cybercriminals. Reports have shown continuous increase in the number and sophistication of this attack worldwide. Phishing Uniform Resource Locator (URL) is a malicious web address often created to look like legitimate URL, in order to deceive unsuspecting users. Many algorithms have been proposed to detect phishing URLs and classify them as benign or phishing. Most of these detection algorithms are based on machine learning and detect using inherent characteristics of the URLs. In this study, we examine the performance of a number of such techniques. The algorithms were tested using three publicly available datasets. Our results revealed, overall, the Random Forest algorithm as the best performing algorithm, achieving an accuracy of 97.3%.

Keywords: Internet · Phishing · Uniform resource locator · URL · Random forest

1 Introduction

The Internet is increasingly used by individuals and organizations to perform different activities, such as personal, transactions and other business-related tasks. Today, more individuals, organizations, and governments are increasingly adopting and maintaining online presence. Consequently, this, among other benefits, has contributed to the growth of many businesses [1–4].

On the other hand, the Internet can be employed for malicious purposes. One way is to exploit the Internet to perpetrate offline attacks. For instance, terrorists use the Internet to plan and coordinate their attacks [5]. There are also attacks that are perpetrated on the Internet. These include spreading of malware, fake news and hate speeches, online scams, identity and intellectual property theft, and cyberbullying.

© Springer Nature Switzerland AG 2019
H. Florez et al. (Eds.): ICAI 2019, CCIS 1051, pp. 385–394, 2019.
https://doi.org/10.1007/978-3-030-32475-9_28

These have resulted in loss of confidential information, huge financial losses, reputational damages, to mention but few [2, 3].

One other common attack Internet users are susceptible to is phishing. Coined in 1996 [6], it combines the methods of social engineering and online identity theft and is used to lure vulnerable Internet users into giving out their sensitive information [7, 8]. With the information gathered, further cybercrimes, such as blackmailing and identity thefts, can be perpetrated.

Over the years, the number of phishing attacks have been on an upward surge. According to the Anti-Phishing Working Group (APWG), the number of detected phishing sites in the second quarter of 2010 was 85,062. By 2014, in the same quarter, the number had increased by around 52% to 128,978 [9].

Perpetrators of phishing use different vectors to exploit both technical and social vulnerabilities of the web and users respectively [7, 8, 10]. One of the commonly used vectors is phishing URL.

Phishing URLs are usually crafted by attackers to look like legitimate and benign URLs, to deceive unsuspecting Internet users. The goal is to gain the trust of such users to click the URLs and reveal their sensitive information. The intention of the attacker could also be to download malware to victims' computers [11–15]. In this case, the downloaded malicious application can steal information from the computers of the victims, which are then forwarded to the attacker. The malware could also be used to download other malicious files or create a backdoor to the infected system, which would allow the attacker to remotely control it. Other potential goals are deleting or modifying victims' information; and encrypting the entire files, in which case, the victim is requested to pay a ransom.

In the past, detection of phishing sites were relatively easy for users due to their design and look. However, with advancement in technology, they are becoming more sophisticated and refined and, consequently, very difficult to identify [13, 15]. Another detection technique employed the concept of visual similarity. It computes the visual similarity between a requested website, considering its visual appearance or images, and a known trust site [12, 13, 15]. A third method of detecting phishing sites entailed the use of whitelist, a list of real and trusted URLs. Any URL not in the list is flagged as malicious. While the technique was successful in reducing the rate of false positive, it had its own limitations. It became impractical to keep up with the pace at which newly trusted sites were being deployed [16]. To get around this, a list, known as blacklist, of all previously detected URLs was compiled instead. These were implemented in DNS-based browser toolbars and network appliances. Whenever a user requested a page, the web link is checked against the database. The success rate of this technique significantly relied on the quality of the list [3, 9, 17–19]. One of the limitations of the blacklist method is its inability to detect zero-hour phishing URLs, which are new and unknown URLs (Basnet et al. 2012; Khonji et al. 2013).

To detect zero-hour phishing URLs, different heuristic techniques have been developed. These techniques detect by identifying the inherent characteristics in phishing URLs. Existing heuristic methods proposed in various studies are based on different techniques, including support vector machine (SVM), ranking, logistic regression, decision trees, and Naïve Bayes [4, 8, 19–21].

In this study, we compare the performance of different techniques used to detect phishing URLs. To achieve the objective, in the next section, we summarise some related studies. In section three, the materials and methods used in the study are described. Section four presents the findings. The study is concluded in section five.

2   Related Works

A number of studies have sought to compare the performance of existing and proposed techniques used for detecting malicious contents users can be vulnerable to. Such studies include comparing methods for detecting mobile SMS spams [22] and email spam [23–26].

On malicious phishing sites, the study by Aburrous et al. [27] focused on e-banking phishing websites. Existing data mining association and classification algorithms, including PRISM, C4.5, PART, JRip, CBA, and MCAR were analyzed. Similar techniques were evaluated in the research by Aburrous et al. [28, 29].

Some authors concentrated on detecting websites that were generally malicious, without focusing on any particular malicious intent. One of such studies is that by Ma et al. [30]. Machine learning methods were used to identify lexical and host-based properties of the malicious websites. The performance of four techniques: Naïve Bayes, SVM with both linear and RBF kernel, and ℓ_1-regularized logistic regression were analyzed.

A similar research, where both versions of SVM were also tested, was conducted by Basnet et al. [31]. The study, however, focused on phishing websites. Other techniques examined were RF, J48, MLP, LR, and NB.

Another work on phishing websites was conducted by Gupta [32]. The author considered the efficacy of Random Forest, Nearest Neighbour Classification, and Bayesian Classifier. Results obtained showed varied levels of performance by the different techniques as a result of different percentage splits of the training dataset.

Nawafleh et al. [33] demonstrated the efficacy of associative classification techniques at detecting phishing websites compared with classification algorithms that employ rule induction, statistical, and probabilistic approaches. Specifically, the authors assessed the performance of the MAC algorithm against SVM, RIPPER, PRISM, and NB.

Ali [34] examined machine learning-based phishing detection techniques. Specifically, the author demonstrated the capacity of wrapper feature selection mechanisms to improve the performance of several detection techniques. Using five-fold cross-validation, results showed significant improvement in the performance of the BPNN, NB, RBFN, SVM, kNN, C4.5 and RF algorithms when the wrapper-based feature selection approach was used.

Our study was motivated by the recommendation by Oluyomi et al. [35]. Their study entailed the comparison of both commonly and scarcely used machine learning techniques for phishing detection. Using dataset from UCI Machine Learning Repository [36], Random Forest was found to outperform the rest of the techniques. The authors, however, suggested that other datasets should be considered, to confirm if the performance of Random Forest was dataset-specific.

3   Materials and Methods

3.1   Datasets Description

Three public available phishing datasets were used in this study. They comprised the UCI machine learning repository phishing websites dataset [36] and two from the University of Huddersfield repository [37], which were named Huddersfield_1 and Huddersfield_2.

The UCI dataset contained a total of 11,055 instances. Those of Huddersfield_1 and Huddersfield_2 were made up of 2,456 and 2,670 rows of data respectively. A description of the phishing website datasets are presented in Table 1.

Table 1. Description of the phishing website datasets

Description	Dataset		
	UCI	Huddersfield_1	Huddersfield_2
#Instances	11,055	2,456	2,670
#Phishing websites	4,898 (44%)	1,094 (45%)	1,485 (56%)
#Legitimate websites	6,157 (56%)	1,362 (55%)	1,185 (44%)

The datasets consisted of 30 attributes, segregated into 4 categories. Table 2 presents the list of categories and corresponding number of attributes.

Table 2. Categories and corresponding number of attributes

Category	Number of attributes
Address Bar based Features	12
Abnormal Based Features	6
HTML and JavaScript based Features	5
Domain based Features	7

3.2   Phishing Detection Techniques

We examined the performance of 35 classification techniques available on WEKA. In determining the list of techniques to be selected, we considered both popular and not so commonly used algorithms. Consequently, the techniques assessed include Ada-BoostM1, Attribute Selected Classifier, Bagging, Bayes Net, Classification via Regression, Decision Stump, Decision Table, Filtered Classifier, Hoeffding Tree, IBK, Iterative Classifier Optimizer, J48, JRIP, KStar, LMT, Logit Boost, Logistic, LWL, MLP, and Multiclass Classifier. Others were Multiclass Classifier Updateable, Naive Bayes, Naïve Bayes Updateable, OneR, PART, Random Committee, Randomizable Filtered Classifier, Random Forest, Random Subspace, Random Tree, REP Tree, SGD, Simple Logistic, SMO, and Voted Perceptron.

3.3 Performance Evaluation

To evaluate each technique, we used both 10-folds cross validation and 66% split. First, the UCI phishing dataset was loaded to WEKA (version 3.8.2) and then classified using each of the 35 techniques. The best 10 performing techniques in terms of accuracy were selected. We finally evaluated the performance of each of the 10 techniques on both Huddersfield phishing datasets. The entire experiments were performed on an HP laptop (x-64-based processor, Intel(R) Core(TM) i3-3120 M CPU @ 2.50 GHz, 8 GB RAM, Windows 10).

The performance of each technique was measured in terms of accuracy, precision, recall, F-measure, ROC area, and RMSE.

4   Results

The accuracy values of the 35 classification techniques under 10-folds cross validation and 66% split for the UCI phishing website dataset are presented in Table 3. From results obtained, Random Forest produced the highest accuracy value. Other high performing techniques were IBK, Kstar, RandomCommittee, MLP, LMT, PART, RandomTree, Bagging, and J48. With the exception of the ROC Area, where the best performing algorithm was Kstar, Random Forest also had the best precision, recall, F-measure, Kappa statistic, and RMSE values (Tables 4 and 5).

Table 3. The accuracy of the thirty-five algorithm under UCI phishing website dataset

S/N	Algorithm	Accuracy	
		10 Folds	66% Split
1.	RandomForest	0.973	0.973
2.	IBK	0.972	0.969
3.	Kstar	0.972	0.968
4.	RandomCommittee	0.972	0.967
5.	MultiLayerPerceptron	0.969	0.964
6.	LMT	0.969	0.964
7.	PART	0.968	0.958
8.	RandomTree	0.964	0.951
9.	Bagging	0.962	0.952
10.	FilteredClassifier	0.959	0.951
11.	J48	0.959	0.951
12.	ClassificationViaRegression	0.954	0.952
13.	REPTree	0.953	0.948
14.	Jrip	0.95	0.948
15.	RandomSubspace	0.949	0.948
16.	AttributeSelectedClassifier	0.944	0.941
17.	RandomizableFilteredClassifier	0.942	0.926

(continued)

Table 3. (*continued*)

S/N	Algorithm	Accuracy	
		10 Folds	66% Split
18.	Logistic	0.94	0.943
19.	SGD	0.94	0.938
20.	MultiClassClassifier	0.94	0.943
21.	MultiClassClassifierUpdateable	0.94	0.938
22.	SimpleLogistic	0.939	0.941
23.	SMO	0.938	0.935
24.	VotedPerceptron	0.938	0.938
25.	HoeffdingTree	0.936	0.924
26.	DecisionTable	0.932	0.928
27.	NaivesBayes	0.93	0.929
28.	NaiveBayesUpdateable	0.93	0.929
29.	BayesNet	0.93	0.929
30.	IterativeClassifierOptimizer	0.927	0.924
31.	LogitBoost	0.927	0.924
32.	AdaBoostM1	0.926	0.928
33.	LWL	0.889	0.889
34.	OneR	0.889	0.889
35.	DecisionStump	0.889	0.889

Table 4. Results from UCI repository dataset using 10 folds

S/No.	Algorithm	Accuracy	Precision	Recall	F-Measure	ROC Area	Kappa statistics	RMSE
1.	RandomCommittee	0.972	0.972	0.972	0.972	0.992	0.944	0.144
2.	PART	0.968	0.968	0.968	0.968	0.988	0.9343	0.1646
3.	J48	0.959	0.959	0.959	0.959	0.984	0.9162	0.1853
4.	LMT	0.969	0.969	0.969	0.969	0.991	0.9367	0.1599
5.	MLP	0.969	0.969	0.969	0.969	0.995	0.9372	0.1568
6.	IBK	0.972	0.972	0.972	0.972	0.989	0.9427	0.1443
7.	Kstar	0.972	0.972	0.972	0.972	**0.997**	0.943	0.1472
8.	Bagging	0.962	0.962	0.962	0.962	0.993	0.9228	0.1727
9.	RandomForest	**0.973**	**0.973**	**0.973**	**0.973**	0.996	**0.9444**	**0.1436**
10.	RandomTree	0.964	0.964	0.964	0.964	0.976	0.9264	0.1748

Analysis of the 10 techniques for the Huddersfield_1 dataset (Tables 6 and 7) also revealed Random Forest as the best performing algorithm. Under 10-folds cross validation, Random Forest achieved similar accuracy, precision, recall, and F-measure value of 0.947. For the 66% split option, the recorded value was 0.946. For the RMSE, the lowest value of 0.2088 (for 10-folds cross validation) and 0.2083 (for 66% split) were recorded.

Table 5. Results from UCI repository dataset using 66% split

S/No.	Algorithm	Accuracy	Precision	Recall	F-Measure	ROC Area	Kappa statistics	RMSE
1.	RandomCommittee	0.967	0.967	0.967	0.967	0.967	0.967	0.1561
2.	PART	0.958	0.958	0.958	0.958	0.958	0.958	0.1818
3.	J48	0.951	0.951	0.951	0.95	0.95	0.95	0.1999
4.	LMT	0.964	0.964	0.964	0.964	0.964	0.964	0.1744
5.	MLP	0.964	0.964	0.964	0.964	0.964	0.964	0.168
6.	IBK	0.969	0.969	0.969	0.969	0.969	0.969	0.1534
7.	Kstar	0.968	0.969	0.968	0.968	0.968	0.968	0.1533
8.	Bagging	0.952	0.952	0.952	0.952	0.952	0.952	0.1823
9.	RandomForest	**0.973**	**0.973**	**0.973**	**0.973**	**0.973**	**0.973**	**0.1524**
10.	RandomTree	0.951	0.951	0.951	0.95	0.95	0.95	0.2062

Table 6. Results from Huddersfield_1 using 10 folds

S/No.	Algorithm	Accuracy	Precision	Recall	F-Measure	ROC Area	Kappa statistics	RMSE
1.	RandomCommittee	0.941	0.941	0.941	0.941	0.971	0.8814	0.2191
2.	PART	0.94	0.94	0.94	0.94	0.964	0.879	0.2249
3.	J48	0.94	0.94	0.94	0.94	0.964	0.8783	0.2281
4.	LMT	0.939	0.939	0.939	0.939	0.981	0.8605	0.2409
5.	MLP	0.932	0.933	0.932	0.932	0.977	0.8633	0.2409
6.	IBK	0.916	0.936	0.934	0.934	0.969	0.8673	0.2345
7.	Kstar	0.941	0.943	0.941	0.941	**0.985**	0.8812	0.2152
8.	Bagging	0.941	0.941	0.941	0.941	0.98	0.8799	0.2101
9.	RandomForest	**0.947**	**0.947**	**0.947**	**0.947**	**0.985**	**0.8937**	**0.2088**
10.	RandomTree	0.906	0.907	0.906	0.906	0.909	0.8108	0.3023

Table 7. Results from Huddersfield_1 using 66% split

S/No.	Algorithm	Accuracy	Precision	Recall	F-Measure	ROC Area	Kappa statistics	RMSE
1.	RandomCommittee	0.938	0.938	0.938	0.938	0.976	0.8731	0.2226
2.	PART	0.921	0.922	0.921	0.921	0.961	0.8391	0.2583
3.	J48	0.941	0.941	0.941	0.941	0.964	0.88	0.2228
4.	LMT	0.932	0.932	0.932	0.932	0.972	0.8605	0.2392
5.	MLP	0.932	0.932	0.932	0.932	0.977	0.8602	0.2377
6.	IBK	0.926	0.929	0.926	0.926	0.961	0.85	0.2479
7.	Kstar	0.933	0.936	0.933	0.94	0.979	0.8644	0.2271
8.	Bagging	0.937	0.937	0.937	0.937	0.976	0.8706	0.2231
9.	RandomForest	**0.946**	**0.946**	**0.946**	**0.946**	**0.985**	**0.89**	**0.2083**
10.	RandomTree	0.921	0.921	0.921	0.921	0.921	0.8383	0.2806

In the case of Huddersfield_2 dataset, Random Forest and Kstar were the two best performing algorithms, with the former at best when 10-folds cross validation was used (accuracy = 0.957) and the latter producing the best results under 66% split (accuracy = 0.953). The performance of the 10 techniques are presented in Tables 8 and 9.

Table 8. Results from Huddersfield_2 using 10 folds

S/No.	Algorithm	Accuracy	Precision	Recall	F-Measure	ROC Area	Kappa statistics	RMSE
1.	RandomCommittee	0.948	0.948	0.948	0.948	0.974	0.8937	0.2035
2.	PART	0.945	0.945	0.945	0.945	0.971	0.8886	0.2187
3.	J48	0.945	0.946	0.945	0.945	0.966	0.8896	0.218
4.	LMT	0.951	0.951	0.951	0.951	0.987	0.9006	0.1945
5.	MLP	0.951	0.951	0.951	0.951	0.985	0.9	0.2108
6.	IBK	0.946	0.946	0.946	0.946	0.973	0.891	0.213
7.	Kstar	0.949	0.953	0.953	0.953	0.988	0.8074	0.1986
8.	Bagging	0.948	0.948	0.948	0.948	0.986	0.894	0.1983
9.	RandomForest	**0.957**	**0.957**	**0.957**	**0.957**	**0.989**	**0.9128**	**0.1905**
10.	RandomTree	0.92	0.92	0.92	0.92	0.922	0.8372	0.2772

Table 9. Results from Huddersfield_2 using 66% split

S/No.	Algorithm	Accuracy	Precision	Recall	F-Measure	ROC Area	Kappa statistics	RMSE
1.	RandomCommittee	0.943	0.943	0.943	0.943	0.978	0.8827	0.208
2.	PART	0.939	0.939	0.939	0.939	0.962	0.8765	0.2309
3.	J48	0.939	0.939	0.939	0.939	0.949	0.8764	0.2273
4.	LMT	0.934	0.934	0.934	0.934	0.978	0.8653	0.2271
5.	MLP	0.932	0.932	0.932	0.931	0.986	0.86	0.237
6.	IBK	0.943	0.943	0.943	0.943	0.97	0.8834	0.213
7.	Kstar	**0.953**	**0.953**	**0.953**	**0.953**	**0.988**	**0.904**	**0.198**
8.	Bagging	0.935	0.935	0.935	0.935	0.985	0.8675	0.2218
9.	RandomForest	0.949	0.95	0.949	0.949	**0.988**	0.8963	0.2026
10.	RandomTree	0.921	0.921	0.921	0.921	0.923	0.838	0.2757

5 Conclusion

Researchers have continued to develop techniques to keep up with the increasing number and sophistication of phishing websites. Our study set out to examine the capacity of some of such techniques. Selecting thirty five of the commonly referenced and unpopular techniques, our findings revealed Random Forest as the best performing algorithm.

It is essential that Internet users are made to enjoy online experience that is devoid of malicious actors. This is critical for the survival of the Internet. Our study underscores, therefore, the need for more improved detection techniques.

References

1. Moghimi, M., Varjani, A.Y.: New rule-based phishing detection method. Expert Syst. Appl. **53**, 231–242 (2016)
2. Mohammad, R., Thabtah, F., Mccluskey, L.: Predicting phishing websites based on self-structuring neural network. Neural Comput. Appl. **25**(2), 443–458 (2014)
3. Sahoo, D., Liu, C., Hoi, S.C.H.: Malicious URL detection using machine learning: a survey. 1–21 http://arxiv.org/abs/1701.07179 (2017)
4. Feroz, M.N., Mengel, S.: Phishing URL detection using URL ranking. In: IEEE International Congress on Big Data Phishing, pp. 635–638 (2015)
5. Oluwafemi, O., Adesuyi, F.A., Abdulhamid, S.M.: Combating terrorism with cybersecurity: the nigerian perspective. World J. Comput. Appl. Technol. **1**(4), 103–109 (2013)
6. Garera, S., Provos, N., Chew, M., Rubin, A.D.: A framework for detection and measurement of phishing attacks. In: Proceedings of the 2007 ACM workshop on Recurring malcode - WORM 2007, pp. 1–8 (2007)
7. Huang, H., Qian, L., Wang, Y.: A SVM-based technique to detect phishing URLs. Inf. Technol. J. **11**(7), 921–925 (2012)
8. Abu-Nimeh, S., Nappa, D., Wang, X., Nair, S.: A comparison of machine learning techniques for phishing detection. In: Proceedings of the Anti-phishing Working Groups 2nd Annual eCrime Researchers Summit, pp. 60–69 (2007)
9. Lee, J., Kim, D., Lee, C.-H.: Heuristic-based approach for phishing site detection using URL features. In: 3rd International Conference on Advances in Computing, Electronics and Electrical Technology - CEET 2015, pp. 131–135
10. Jagatic, T.N., Johnson, N.A., Jakobsson, M., Menczer, F.: Social phishing. Commun. ACM **50**(10), 94–100 (2007)
11. Basnet, Ram B., Sung, Andrew H., Liu, Q.: Feature selection for improved phishing detection. In: Jiang, H., Ding, W., Ali, M., Wu, X. (eds.) IEA/AIE 2012. LNCS (LNAI), vol. 7345, pp. 252–261. Springer, Heidelberg (2012). https://doi.org/10.1007/978-3-642-31087-4_27
12. Fu, A.Y., Wenyin, L., Deng, X.: Detecting phishing web pages with visual similarity assessment based on earth mover's distance (EMD). IEEE Trans. Dependable Secure Comput. **3**(4), 301–311 (2006)
13. Khonji, M., Iraqi, Y., Jones, A.: Lexical URL analysis for discriminating phishing and legitimate websites. In: Proceedings of the 8th Annual Collaboration, Electronic messaging, Anti-Abuse and Spam Conference, pp. 109–115 (2011)
14. Marchal, S., Saari, K., Singh, N., Asokan, N.: Know your phish: novel techniques for detecting phishing sites and their targets. In: Proceedings - International Conference on Distributed Computing Systems 2016, vol. 2016–August, no. Sect. V, pp. 323–333 (2016)
15. Khonji, M., Iraqi, Y., Jones, A.: Phishing detection: a literature survey. IEEE Commun. Surv. Tutorials **15**(4), 2091–2121 (2013)
16. Bergholz, A., Paaß, G., Reichartz, F., Strobel, S., Birlinghoven, S.: Improved phishing detection using model-based features. In: Fifth Conference on Email and Anti-spam, CEAS (2008)
17. Khonji, M., Jones, A., Iraqi, Y.: A novel Phishing classification based on URL features. In: IEEE GCC Conference and Exhibition (GCC), pp. 221–224 (2011)
18. Ma, J., Saul, L.K., Savage, S., Voelker, G.M.: Learning to detect malicious URLs. ACM Trans. Intell. Syst. Technol. (TIST) **2**(3), 30 (2011)

19. Miyamoto, D., Hazeyama, H., Kadobayashi, Y.: An evaluation of machine learning-based methods for detection of phishing sites. In: International Conference on Neural Information Processing, pp. 539–540 (2009)
20. Zhang, J., Wang, Y.: A real-time automatic detection of phishing URLs. In: 2nd International Conference on Computer Science and Network Technology (ICCSNT), pp. 1212–1216 (2012)
21. Miyamoto, D., Hazeyama, H., Kadobayashi, Y.: An evaluation of machine learning-based methods for detection of phishing sites. In: International Conference on Neural Information Processing, pp. 539–546 (2008)
22. Abdulhamid, S.M., et al.: A review on mobile SMS spam filtering techniques. IEEE Access 5, 15650–15666 (2017)
23. Blanzieri, E., Bryl, A.: A survey of learning-based techniques of email spam filtering. Artif. Intell. Rev. 29(1), 63–92 (2008)
24. Panigrahi, P.: A comparative study of supervised machine learning techniques for spam E-mail filtering. In: Proceedings - 4th International Conference on Computational Intelligence and Communication Networks, CICN 2012, pp. 506–512 (2012)
25. Abdulhamid, S.M., Shuaib, M., Osho, O.: Comparative analysis of classification algorithms for email spam detection. Int. J. Comput. Network Inf. Security 1, 60–67 (2018)
26. Iqbal, M., Abid, M.M., Ahmad, M., Khurshid, F.: Study on the effectiveness of spam detection technologies. Int. J. Inf. Technol. Comput. Sci. 01, 11–21 (2016)
27. Aburrous, M., Hossain, M.A., Dahal, K., Thabtah, F.: Associative classification techniques for predicting e-banking phishing websites. In: International Conference on Multimedia Computing and Information Technology (MCIT), pp. 9–12 (2010)
28. Aburrous, M., Hossain, M.A., Dahal, K., Thabtah, F.: Intelligent detection system for e-banking phishing websites using fuzzy data mining. Expert Syst. Appl. 37(12), 7913–7921 (2010)
29. Aburrous, M., Hossain, M.A., Dahal, K., Thabtah, F.: Predicting phishing websites using classification mining techniques with experimental case studies. In: Seventh International Conference on Information Technology: New Generations (ITNG), pp. 176–181 (2010)
30. Ma, J., Saul, L.K., Savage, S., Voelker, G.M.: Beyond blacklists: learning to detect malicious web sites from suspicious URLs. In: 15th ACM SIGKDD International Conference on Knowledge Discovery and Data Mining, pp. 1245–1254 (2009)
31. Basnet, R.B., Sung, A.H., Liu, Q.: Learning to detect phishing URLs. IJRET: Int. J. Res. Eng. Technol. 3(6), 11–24 (2014)
32. Gupta, R.: Comparison of classification algorithms to detect phishing web pages using feature selection and extraction. Int. J. Res. Granthaalayah 4(8), 118–135 (2016)
33. Nawafleh, S., Hadi, W.: Multi-class associative classification to predicting phishing websites. Int. J. Acad. Res. 4(6), 302–306 (2012)
34. Ali, W.: Phishing website detection based on supervised machine learning with wrapper features selection. Int. J. Adv. Comput. Sci. Appl. 8(9), 72–78 (2017)
35. Oluyomi, A., Osho, O., Shuaib, M.: Evaluation of classification algorithms for phishing URL detection. In: 2nd International Conference on Information and Communication Technology and Its Applications, pp. 243–249 (2018)
36. UCI Machine Learning Repository: Phishing Websites Data set (2018). https://archive.ics.uci.edu/ml/datasets/phishing+websites. Accessed 03 May 2018
37. Mohammad, R., Thabtah, F.A., McCluskey, T.L.: Phishing Websites Dataset. University of Huddersfield Repository (2018). http://eprints.hud.ac.uk/id/eprint/24330/. Accessed 04 Oct 2018

Socio-technical Systems

Cultural Archaeology of Video Games: Between Nostalgic Discourse, Gamer Experience, and Technological Innovation

Simone Belli[1](✉) and Cristian López Raventós[2](✉)

[1] Complutense University of Madrid, Madrid 28040, Spain
sbelli@ucm.es
[2] Universidad Autónoma Nacional de México, Morelia, Mexico
clopezr@enesmorelia.unam.mx

Abstract. This paper presents a history of video games as innovation form beyond entertainment, offering reasons to establish why it is important to know and study their history with regards its social and cultural contexts: making emphasis in the importance that the users have when creating video games through experience. The social and cultural context in which those video games were born is fundamental to understand the diffusion and popularity that video games had throughout the '80s and especially in the '90s. The objective of this study is to identify the communication and information strategies of video games prior to the arrival of the Internet, especially the way in which this information was shared in the Spanish context. In the first part of the paper, we introduce the theoretical and methodological framework in which this research is based, through the concept of cultural archeology. In the second part, we present stories created by the users to analyze the gaming experience and how to share it, using the concepts of playformance and play-world, to finish questioning the gamer's identity as a white, young, middle-class male subject. Finally, we want to point out the importance of sharing knowledge and strategies as a fundamental part of the social interaction of the gamer's experience. We observed video games as a tool to identify something beyond: the society and the uses that move around a cultural product.

Keywords: Video games · Cultural archeology · Gamer experience · Retrogaming

1 Introduction

In this article, we will identify how video games were played, talked about, and how information about them was shared in the Spanish context prior to the arrival of the internet.

For this reason, we are not talking about a traditional history of video games, but rather a guided history through the gaming experience and by sharing the game with others. We hereby present a narrative and experiential route of what it was like to play video games prior to the arrival of the Internet and the popularization of gaming consoles in Spanish families.

© Springer Nature Switzerland AG 2019
H. Florez et al. (Eds.): ICAI 2019, CCIS 1051, pp. 397–409, 2019.
https://doi.org/10.1007/978-3-030-32475-9_29

In the first part of this paper, we introduce the theoretical and methodological frameworks in which this research is based, through the concept of cultural archeology (Foucault 1969) to reexamine the discourses about the past to reorder the present; this is to say, the history of video games from a current point of view. Thus, we use the concept retrogaming (Souminen 2008, 2012; Juul 2009) constructed through nostalgic discourses and the appropriation of new technologies. Through ethnographic research, consisting in interviews made to twenty-four gamer experts of the '90s, we draw one history of video games in a personal, intimate way, constructed through the emotions and shared experiences of gamers.

In the second part, we present one of many histories constructed by the users. To analyze the game experience and the way of sharing it, we will use the concepts playformance and play-world (Frasca 2001a, b). We will also focus on the so-called Golden Age of the Spanish software and the post-golden era in the Spanish context to settle the panorama of our investigation. The identity of the gamer as a male, white, young, middle-class subject is also questioned in order to make space for new ways to identify the gamer from that time period.

1.1 Making Cultural Archeology in the Video Game Field

Our work here is to draw a cultural archaeology through nostalgic discourses and the appropriation of new technologies; a cultural archaeology based on the examination of discourses and the arrangement of the past in order to write down a history of the present. For Bolter and Grusin (2000) new technologies adapt the uses and dynamics of the old technology in the sense in which their development can be conceptualized with more precision through correction.

This experience can be analyzed in the discourses generated by the gamers of a very specific timeframe: the '90s. This decade has been called retrogaming by some experts (Suominen 2008, 2012; Juul 2009): an era which generated many of the video games we still play nowadays, a period of time in which some of the most successful video game sagas of all time were developed. According to a newspaper article on the 20 most successful video game sagas published in The Independent (2014), eight of them originally appeared in the '80s, number 1 being the Super Mario series, created in 1981.

Retrogaming is a phenomenon capable of having an impact in our contemporary lives.

The retrogaming phenomena impacts many aspects of our daily lives and the cultural products surrounding us—cinema, music, literature, fashion—. There was a time, according to Suominen (2012), in which video games generated a social and cultural impact in transnational generations. In his study based on the three big companies from the '90s—Nintendo, Microsoft, and Sony—, certain elements of the video games from that era can be identified in many aspects of our present lives. Soumeinen uses the aforementioned circles to categorize this presence. There are products that occasionally flirt with retro video games, products that have similar aspects with the video games of a previous era, and there are video games which are very heavily influenced by the retro. These three circles touch different aspects related to video games, from playability to graphical elements.

These nostalgic discourses are key to identify the gamer experience. Middle-ager nostalgia from what video games used to be in the '80s and '90s, is the same from those who listen to 70's rock music. It's not that every previous time was better than now, but the time in which it started was the very birth of the product itself before it became popular, and even before it covered an alternative category, a non-mainstream one, transformed as well into nostalgia (Suominen 2012).

Therefore, Michel Foucault is key to understand nostalgic discourses. Cultural archeology can be defined as the unconscious level of a culture that allows the real perceived forms of our everyday lives. The archeological approach allows the objects, ideas, thoughts, experiences, and so on, to offer a new specific historic paradigm (Foucault 1969). Making cultural archeology does not only include the totality of the cultural discourses of a time period, but also the laws, practices, conditions and, functioning that regulate the construction of specific cultural phenomena.

In the Game Studies, Huhtamo (2007) applied the archeologic method to map the prehistory of video games, dating back to the 19th century and the culture surrounding proto-interactive machines and devices. Järvinen (2001) presents as well his own video game archeology, which we take especially into account since it is an archeology of the users, the gamers. Järvinen recognizes that the gamers' practices must be looked for in the history of the first computer video games and consoles. For him, the game's situation is mostly an aesthetic phenomenon in which certain perceptions, affects, and emotions come into play upon the subject. This places the gamer in a specific position of use determined always by the historic characteristics of the biggest length in the video game. There is a vast literature in Spanish regarding the gamer's experience, but this is usually done from an educative and pedagogic point of view, focused on justifying the role of video games as a key element in the learning process, not as leisure.

It is necessary to mention that in the retrogaming context not only cultural archeology has been made, but also actual excavations and with the help of expert anthropologists; this is the case of Atari and the unsold gaming cartridges in the early '80s that were buried in Alamogordo, New Mexico. Around Christmas, 1983, five million E.T. the Extraterrestrial gaming cartridges, a ludic transposition of Steven Spielberg's movie. The video game was a complete commercial failure due to the little time given for its development—five weeks—, and for this reason, Atari shut down the activity and hurried thousands of these cartridges. In 2014, an archeologic expedition was organized to retrieve these retrogaming treasures.

2 Methodology

We made ethnographic research through interviewing twenty-four game experts from the '90s, with the objective of tracing one history of video games in a personal, intimate way, constructed through the emotions and shared experiences of gamers. This is to say, a biographic outlook on video games.

We used two main sources to carry out these stories: first, the in-depth interviews through audio recordings and their transcriptions; second, the textual productions related to the video game world in that particular timeframe in Spain. Both forms of texts must be understood as discursive practices (Foucault 2001). To Foucault, discourse is more a social practice than a sign system which represents reality with more or less fidelity. This is why it is often talked about discursive practices to emphasize on the speech as a constructor of objects, and not only a way of naming in a representational act. Those discursive practices generate a regulative framework that establishes objects, rules, and communities in each moment of history; these practices make possible to talk about the concrete elements in each moment of time. This social practice—discourse—sets up what can be named and what can't. Discourses become social practices that create objects that can be named and talked about (Foucault 2001).

The discourse's analysis provided by Foucault presents four different stages: First, the object described by the discourse is questioned; second, the inner logic that allows the construction of said objects is analyzed; third, a search for the subjects that generate and benefit from this discursive construction is set in motion; finally, it searches for the implicit objectives found deep within discursive practices. This whole discursive entanglement must be understood within a sociocultural process, in which organizing normative systems and knowledge field practices appear, intertwined through a constitutive, object-generator discourse.

The in-depth interviews were chosen utilizing the snowball method, due to the difficulty upon finding subjects with the specific profiles. This in-depth interview had a script intended to focus upon certain central notions on the narrative construction process upon gamer experience. The script's main topics where the places, where, how, and with what the video games began to be played, the mass-media that used to spread information all around the world, the preferred game genres and why were they chose, the bridges between these video games, the reality, and the perception about them from the rest of society.

The written material of that timeframe was selected due to its relevance with regards to the performed interviews. These materials are composed of gaming-specialized media up to the most relevant gaming manuals from back then. Therefore, the selection of this material does not end up being an in-depth analysis of the texts, but rather an amalgam of intertwined texts, generating and giving coherence to the gamer's experience narrations.

3   The Golden Age and Post-golden Age of the Spanish Software

For this investigation, we took into consideration the narratives made by some gamers of the post-golden age, this is to say, what comes immediately after the so-called Golden Age of the Spanish software. Mention should be made that this timeframe is set approximately between 1983 and 1992, time in which Spain was between the top hosts of European video game developers, headed only by the United Kingdom. We invite the reader to check out the articles by Portalo (2009), Gutiérrez (2012), Pedja and Spidey (2015) for further development on this timeframe. Loguidice and Barton (2009) offer a profound and thorough analysis of the '80s and '90s video games that surely came in handy to make archeology of many of the video games here mentioned. We name here only some of the most representative video games of the connection between them and the Spanish society. It must be pointed out that the term Golden Age of the Spanish software was coined by specialized magazines of the time which we will be analyzing further on and which we find fundamental to understand how information was distributed and shared back then. One of the most representative video games of that timeframe was Bugaboo (The Flea), from 1984, and Crazy Climber, from 1984.

There are certain video games of that time that teach us not only that they do have an impact on society, but also that society has an impact on video games. For this reason, the golden age is not limited only to the decontextualized video game production; on the contrary: it produces video games that touch themes directly related to that moment of Spanish society. El Golpe is a representative case since it reflects this aforementioned bidirectional phenomena, which allows the video game to be considered as a cultural product in the anthropologic sense of the word.

El Golpe is a 1984 video game which parodies the failed Spanish coup d'état from February 23rd, 1981. As we can see on the cover itself, it was quite colorful and it depicted cartoonish versions of the very protagonists of that historical event from Spanish society. More examples of this bidirectional impact can be found in Bull Fight (1984), Olé, Toro (1984) and, although out of the golden age, Chorizos de España (2013) (Navarrete 2014). This video game's spaniardness teaches us how often cultural models are exported through mass products.

It must be pointed out that the so-called Golden Age coincides with the booming decade of the 8-bits, and the post-golden age refers to the jump made to 16-bits consoles, which unleashed the dissolution of many Spanish companies in the early '90s. This 16-bits consoles implied a huge technological jump that many Spanish companies were unable to make.

3.1   At Home, at the Bar, or at Gaming Lounges?

The place in which the gaming act took place is the first observable category that comes into account in the narrations. There is a gaming aspect based upon the experience of playing in public spaces, which no longer hold the same impact from the '80s and '90s. Playing at bars or at gaming lounges was a subterfuge for socialization amongst gamers and video games.

Oriol—People used to play a lot on recreative slots at bars and at gaming lounges, the fandom sprung from there.

They shared these offline fiscal spaces in the same sense in which we now share digital online spaces thanks to the internet. The fact of sharing these spaces meant also getting in touch with the machine, a physical representation of that video game, which more than was more than one machine, as we can see below.

Emotions as well as the interactions experimented in the gaming lounges differed from the domestic versions of the game, the distance between the domestic and the coin-op versions were huge (Livingstone 2002; Newman 2004). Doing, touching, moving, ways in which our organism gathers information and shares lived experiences.

This is how the concept playformance is formed: for playing video games a series of actions named in the play-world is needed, which generates a concrete gaming experience. Doing, touching and moving are not only actions but rather ways of understanding the world, ways in which our organism acquires information and understands the world (Frasca 2009: 43).

Another relevant factor was the enormous distance between domestic 8-bit consoles and the machines one could find at gaming lounges:

Jorge—Playing video games at bars was very different from domestic gaming. Domestic consoles were less potent.

Cost and presentation were the key motivations for the gamers to attend these places instead of staying at home with their 8-bits. It must be mentioned that these—home, bars, gaming lounges—were not the only existent gaming places that appear in nostalgic discourses, but there is a fourth space: a friend's home.

Ferran—I used to hang with my friends Albert and Santi, my hometown friends. They had the best of '90s video games: the SNES Wildcard.

This refers to key nodes developed by gamers in these networks. In their stories, key figures such as Albert and Santi appear, popular for having a SNES emulator for all the games: a Wildcard. It is an emotional journey through childhood, the bonds cast when we were kids, through a technologic narrative. Making cultural archeology takes us back to SNES Wildcard for the construction of our first socialization decades. We found out that humankind prefers to play together and share leisure as a group (Pujol 2010). Once again, video gaming is a social and not an alienated phenomenon.

Ludology ceases not to point the fact that narration is not the only way of telling things, but that discourses are transmitted in diverse ways accordingly to the rules, structures, and gaming experiences. To this, two warnings must be made to all video game researchers: one, gaming is a social, physical experience (Frasca 2009: 42). Two, gaming always occurs with another; physical presence or not, gaming implies some kind of performative action.

Through these nodes, information about video games was distributed. Nodes had changed by the late '90s: being up to date didn't mean any more to be friends of the most upbeat kids from town; the arrival of the internet became the central outlet for information sharing.

Valeria—To be informed about video games I used EresMas, Telnet Spain. I used the IRC, MSNGroups and some of the first primitive Terra chatrooms.

Viviana—I used the Meristation forum or the TrucoTeca webpage in the 96.

The context in which gamer experience was shared shifted from physical to digital, from a friend's house to the online forum. The expert gamer digitalizes and shares his knowledge in a much wider and open space; gamer cooperation is born thanks to social gaming. The social experience of playing video games is no longer the activity of playing together on the same screen, but trying to get to the next level through sharing acquired knowledge. Therefore, gaming cheat codes are shared and the information is widespread through the net. Cheat codes are essential parts of video games, part of the unwritten rules by which a game is played.

Our study approach upon video games questions the traditional vision on the gamer as an impacted subject through its gaming practice and proposes an active role in which we read our surroundings. We are transformed into seekers and creators of meaning, interpreted in our surroundings, subjects capable of rewriting it and relocate the product in our everyday lives. We must approach video game studies as a relation-tool and not an alienation-tool, this is to say, the entanglement of dialogue relations and emotions can be enforced through gaming practices, without it being important if it's a familiar space or elsewhere. In this fashion, video games are objects in which the gamer's experience is based. Through video games, we can explain society and the social and cultural dynamics of a given moment. Through the object and its use, we talk about the subject. The gamer-subject experience allows sharing information between the community beyond the video game-object.

3.2 Information Distribution: Specialized Magazines

Talking about video games sometimes means going down memory lane, talking about our toys, but in a social way: through friends, gaming lounges, and cassette and cheat code sharing. It's something that comes from the experience of how we learned to use this machines that our parents before us didn't know how to use and therefore couldn't help us, unlike when we learned to ride a bike or to kick a ball. These are competencies that they couldn't offer us, which we had to learn on our own, with those around us, a familiar perhaps. For this reason, magazines were fundamental; they helped out beating a level, not to die over and over again in the same jump, not to make the same mistake time after time.

Ignacio Abril, Navy Moves programmer—The mines from the first stage were hellish. Even today I find them difficult. That was another time. Putting something like that in a current video game would make 99% of the players to bail in the act (Pedja and Spidey 2015).

Many of the video games from back then were—in Ignacio's words—hellish. Due to inexperience or the fact that these machines were originally thought as recreational within public spaces, based upon the Insert Coin logic (this means utilizing the bigger number of coins in the smallest amount of time possible) it would be pretty hard to find this typology in today's video games. Ancient video games didn't allow to save in-game progress, it was limited to three lives per game, without any possibility of continuing after that. The Atari 2600 console synthesizes this non-friendly aspect from the video games of back then.

For these reasons, in the times before wi-fi, gamers learned how to beat difficult levels in magazines; in them, one could learn how to overcome a difficult level, cheat codes and many more. There were also guides—not to be mistaken with game instructions—a sort of walk-through manuals for gamers (Consalvo 2007).

Gaming magazines represented one of the main bridges between video games and the public. It must be taken into consideration that those magazines spoke about video games in a wider spectrum, talking about social reality and its cultural products. An article writer from back then confirms it:

El Raffo—Reading a review was decisive, specially for those games in the middle or low range.

A review did not talk only about the game, but also about the public, the society, the experience of playing with others that worked at the magazine, etc. The very editorial committee was conformed by young people passionate for video games, that more often than not hadn't even finish high school. They were the only available experts of the time, quick-playing teenagers that could talk about the topic in an informal and direct style for the readers to understand what they were being told. This aspect has changed in actual magazines, more technical and formal each time.

Victor—I clearly remember two Spanish gaming magazines from back then: Micromania and Hobby Consolas. The first one was mostly for PC games and most times it included a CD with game demos so people could try them out. The second one focused mostly on gaming consoles. I'm sure that I must have some old numbers of both magazines back home—perhaps more from the '2000s than from the '90s.

In Spain, the informants agree upon the fact that the two most influential magazines were Micro Mania and Hobby Consolas. Each one had different objectives: while one focused mainly on PC gamers, the second one focused on console players. Interestingly, these magazines were usually kept and shared. Many times, the games or cheat codes mentioned were for video games not owned yet, but this information will surely come in handy in the future.

Miguel—From my hardcore-gamer times I remember the most mythical magazine was Hobby Consolas. This one was a must-buy because of the final pages, which had all the games being released sorted by consoles; we could fantasize about which games we were going to buy. Other popular magazines were Micro Mania and PC Mania, but this last one was mostly for nerds because every now and then you would find the occasional hardware article that did not interest anyone.

Hobby Consolas was the top magazine from back then, and it is interesting that the communication and distribution of video games were based on the new releases. This allowed the gamers to think and imagine the experience of acquiring the advertised video game, creating a wish-list of those to buy in future purchases. Reviews usually followed the same structure: screen frames from the game with complementary text. At the end of the written review the results were quantified in a scale from 0 to 10—or from 0 to 100—aspects such as playability, graphics quality, play time, sound effects, and an overall score.

Juan—There are two big Spanish classics from the '80s and '90s: the totemic magazines Micro Mania and Hobby Consolas; one of them focussed mainly on PCs (first tapes, then game cartridges and PCs), while Hobby Consolas was dedicated to consoles—as you might have deduced yourself—. I think Micro Mania is still being published, so it must be over 25 years old. Micro Mania was fundamental, and its format was like a '90s newspapers, brutal.

This differs from the previous narrative, in which the gamer expresses his negativity towards PC magazines; We have here a more positive experience, pointing out that the magazine was brutal. Therefore, through cultural archeology, we can find one of the many possible histories of cultural products. The emotions presented in each of the two narratives is totally different but valid enough to trace a history of video games.

Specialized magazines were relevant not only because they distributed information between video game development companies and gamers, but also to launch cultural products belonging to the context in which they were produced. An emblematic case of this is represented by the Spanish magazines and the Golden Age of Spanish software. As an example, the first number of Micro Mania—released in 1988—depicted one of the most talked about games from the Golden Age: Turbo Girl.

This is the embodiment of a fundamentals synergy to compete with other countries, for example, the United Kingdom, the United States, and Japan. To have a technologic company in the video game sector it's very important having a good information distribution in the context in which it's produced, in order to give more visibility to the product, and a bigger commercial impact, in the same fashion in which other countries push their products to the local market before releasing them to the international market. It is fundamental to understand the importance that these magazines had to the Golden Age sector.

In an international scale, there is a pioneer magazine in sharing and distributing information to different markets, the Nintendo Club magazine. Through yearly subscriptions, gamers had delivered to their homes a new issue of the magazine each month.

Viviana—I remember having a good collection of the TodoSega magazine, and some numbers of MicroHobby. Many of them were gifted to me because I was quite young back then (around 6 years old in 1994). When I grew up I started buying Hobby Consolas and PlayManía. There was also Nintendo Acción, although I didn't have any home console until 2000.

What comes to our attention in this excerpt is that the gamer's path narration about his experience as a specialized magazines reader, but as a gamer as well. This journey goes through the impact that multiplatform magazines had in their day, this is to say, magazines that informed about video games from various consoles opposed to magazines focused on a single console.

Viviana—Load'n'run was a magazine that included Spectrum gaming cassettes. Stars was quite similar. Input covered three gaming platforms. Nintendo Acción became Revista Oficial Nintendo, and it belonged to the same editorial that latter published Play Mania, Todo Sega, and Super Juegos.

Nintendo magazine was the first one to have the objective of analyzing only the video games released for that console. After that, many magazines dedicated to a single platform appeared in the market, dividing the public among consoles. The video game market started to have different sectors divided into specialized clients. The market shifted from a general one, where the reader was interested in the video game disregards the console it was being distributed through, to a market in which the gamer wants to know about the video games that are released exclusively for his machine. It must be added that the marker stretched notoriously in the '90s when more gamer profiles appeared and the video game industry began to be the huge empire of the cultural industry we know today.

Julia—In Spain, Nintendo Acción was one of the most popular magazines and, although the title says Nintendo, there were news about all the consoles and upcoming games, as well as tips at the end of the magazine on how to do certain things to unlock a secret level.

It is interesting how Nintendo Acción went from a multiplatform magazine to and up focusing on the video games of a single console. This first approach was due to a marketing strategy to catch the public from other consoles to then redirect them to the Nintendo console.

After this Golden Age of the video game magazines—from the year 2000 onwards —, the readers started to center solely upon the magazines deeply specialized in a specific console. Gamers were not interested in the games developed for other platforms, which caused the magazines to became specialized and technical. There were no longer articles about video games and society, and the journalists became video game technicians, utilizing an elevated language and a technical analysis of said game. The spontaneity was lost, and so was that rebel approach that characterized the journalist when they first came into notice, becoming the video game institutionalization as a mass media product, something serious. There's no longer space for the elements surrounding the video game—social, cultural, etc.—.

Some of the previous magazines mentioned in the narratives no longer exist, some continue in both digital and printed formats, and some only digitally.

4 Discussion: Social Innovation and Impact of Video Games in Spain

Ludology ceases not to alert us about narration not being the only way of telling things since discourses are transmitted through diverse ways as rules, structures, and game experiences. To this it must be added two warnings that all video game researchers must keep in mind: the game is always social and physical (Frasca 2009: 42). The game occurs always with someone else, physical presence or not, and it always involves some sort of performance. All these lines should alert about the fact of there is always some kind of produced discourse being transmitted in video games, and that these generate diverse actions. The social impact that video games have had—and still have —in society is undeniable: My friends and I used to play video games as an excuse to be together (Sherry 2001). But back then, the timeframe mentioned in this cultural archeology, this wasn't so evident. Video games had a marginal aspect in the media and research. Gamers were a minority and were very far to be considered a mainstream group; nevertheless, in the narratives gathered this importance of playing video games and the impact they had in the lives of the gamers and the society in general emerges.

Julia—Back then, 1998–1999, it wasn't that common to see gamer girls, as they are called now, so they didn't have someone to share it with since boys didn't see it all right. Still, at school, I had a group of 3 or 4 friends to talk about upcoming releases and speculated on how they would be like, etc.… I used to be the most trained, since I had my own PC and gained my own money, so I used to read the news in Meristation's webpage, which is still up since 1997, and in Trucoteca, which was basically the same but with cheat codes and gaming guides.

This gamer girl helps us understand how playing video games does not exist in an empty social space, there is always a time and a place where this action occurs. The construction of distant relation of patriarchal and conservative society in the Spain of that timeframe is also important. It was not only a boy's activity, but there was also a little group of gamer girls existing and functioning with the same dynamics boys used. The information circulated in the same way, even when looking for cheat codes. Only in the inside of the group could be shared cheat codes, information, and strategies. The social group is fundamental for gamers (Jessen 1999).

One of the first critics from this perspective came from Selnow (1984) in an essay in which he defended a hypothesis about playing video games being basically a solitary activity. Therefore, the longest a gamer spent immersed in video games the more he detached and drifted from their friends and other social interactions. Also, this dynamic generated in the gamer the loss of social abilities necessary to his everyday life. As it has been observed in this review through the research in the psychological field, the same results show how prejudices about the effects of video games have very little to do with the gamer's reality.

The works done about the influence of video games in social surroundings have found data that contradicts the idea of social alienation. For starters, gamers prefer to play with friends or other players (Tejeiro 1998; De Waal 1995) rather than playing alone in the PC or gaming console. Also, the video game transforms into an element that makes new relations with other users possible, from sharing the same fandom with new friends or generating friendships with other players. The development of collaborative gaming through the internet has facilitated this subject interconnection of people with the same likings (Kline 1998). This is to say, contrary to what is usually believed, users prefer to do this activity in the company of other users of the same video games, generating new social relations thanks to their likings.

We have also researched the possible influence of aspects that could show a social alienation in relation with video games, as is the number of friends or people that conform a surrounding (Estalló 1995), without mentioning significative results. In other researches, it has been tried to prove if there was a relation between playing video games and personal situations like solitude, popularity, or social status. Furthermore, most of the people that start in the video game practice do it thanks to a friend or family member (Griffiths and Hunt 1995). As told by Estalló (1995), gamers don't feel like their hobby affects their personal relations.

5 Conclusions

What has been described here is not a history of video games, but rather a history of the experience of playing and sharing the game with others; a narrative and experiential journey of how it was to playing video games and—perhaps—how has it changed. Therefore, this essay proposes to fill a void present in the Game Studies, studying the gamer's experience and the exchange of it. Thanks to the cultural archeology here described, we have been able to trace a history out of the many possible about video games seen as an interaction between nostalgic discourses, gamer experience, and technology innovation. We have traced the evolution of the perception of the games and their impact.

Making cultural archeology on video games is a nostalgic journey, it means talking about our toys and games in a more social way, sharing our experience of how we learned to use these machines. This approach to gamer studies tries to avoid classifications and game categories as technological products. Most of the times gamers themselves trace video game stories that cannot be encapsulated within traditional categories without having to hear first their discourse and tracing an epistemic journey throughout the gamer.

In the analyzed time frame it was difficult to imagine the full extent of the console's potential, video games were completely different back then. Their narratives ware the same over and over again, and the characters were constructed in a very simple manner, but playability was the most important thing. It's very likely—as it was pointed out in many interviews—that this was the very reason why they became the most influential cultural products from said timeframe. Nintendo, and his most known character, Mario, are still in the market today, having a huge market success, something that cannot be said about many consoles from back then. Therefore, we think it's important to consider these aspects to understand the brief but intense history of video games.

Finally, we want to point out the importance of sharing knowledge and strategies as a fundamental part of the social interaction of the gamer's experience. Only then, we can understand video games as a tool to identify something beyond: the society and the uses that move around a cultural product such as video games.

References

Belli, S., López, C.: Breve Historia de los Videojuegos. Athenea Digit. **14**, 159–179 (2009)

Bolter, J.D., Grusin, R.: Remediation. Understanding New Media. The MIT Press, Cambridge, London (2000)

Consalvo, M.: Cheating. MIT Press, Boston (2007)

De Waal, B.: Motivation for video game play: a study of social, cultural and physiological factors. Doctoral thesis, Simon Fraser University, Canada (1995)

Estalló, J.A.: Videojuegos. Efectos a largo plazo. Unpublished text, Institut Psiquiàtric, Barcelona (1995)

Foucault, M.: Las palabras y las cosas. Siglo XXI, Mexico (2001)

Foucault, M.: La arqueología del saber. Siglo XXI, Mexico (1969). (2010)

Frasca, G.: The Sims: Grandmothers are cooler than trolls. Game Stud. **1**(1) (2001a)

Frasca, G.: Ludology meets narratology: similitude and difference between (video)games and narrative (2001b)

Frasca, G.: Juego, videojuego y creaciónn de sentido. Una introducción. Comunicación **1**(7), 37–44 (2009)

Gutiérrez, J.: 8 Quilates. Una historia de la edad del software español. Polifemo, Madrid (2012)

Griffiths, M., Hunt, N.: Computer game playing in adolescence: prevalence and demographic indicators. J. Community Appl. Soc. Psychol. **5**, 189–193 (1995)

Huhtamo, E.: Máquinas de diversión, máquinas de problemas. Artnodes **7**, 43–60 (2007)

Järvinen, A.: Quake goes the environment: game aesthetics and archeologies. Digit. Creat. **12**, 2 (2001)

Jessen, C.: Children's Computer Culture. Three Essays on Children and Computers. University of Southern Denmark Press, Odense (1999)

Juul, J.: A Casual Revolution: Reinventing Video Games and Their Players. MIT Press, Cambridge (2009)

Kline, S.: Video Game Culture: Leisure and Play Preferences of B.C. Teens. Simon Fraser University, Burbany, Canada (1998)

Livingstone, S.: Young People and New Media: Childhood and the Changing Media Environment. Sage, London (2002)

Loguidice, B., Barton, M.: Vintage Games: An Insider Look at the History of Grand Theft Auto, Super Mario, and the most Influential Games of All Time. Focal Press, New York (2009)

Navarrete, L.La: imagen romántica de España en el Videojuego. Rassegna iberistica **37**(102), 215–228 (2014)

Newman, J.: Video Games. Routledge, New York (2004)

Pedja, Spidey: Génesis, guía esencial de los videojuegos españoles de 8 bits. Héroes de Papel, Madrid (2015)

Portalo, F.: Bugaboo, un hito en la Historia del Software Español. Universidad de Extremadura, Cáceres (2009)

Pujol, G.: Enriching online board games: An anthropological perspective. In: Riha, D. (ed.) Video Game Culture and the Future of Interactive Entertainment. Inter-Disciplinary Press, Oxford (2010)

Selnow, G.: Playing video games. The electronic friend. J. Commun. **34**(2), 148–156 (1984)

Sherry, J.L.: The effects of violent video games on aggression. Hum. Commun. Res. **27**(3), 409–431 (2001)

Suominen, J.: The past as the future? Nostalgia and retrogaming in digital culture. Fibreculture **11** (2008)

Suominen, J.: Retrogamers. Communal memory and discourses of digital history. Digit. Mem. **9** (2012)

Tejeiro, R.: La práctica de videojuegos en niños del campo de Gibraltar. Asociación de Jugadores de Azar en Rehabilitación del Campo de Gibraltar, Algeciras (1998)

Van Tejeiro, E., Weigman, O.: Children and video games: leisure activities, aggression, social integration, and school performance. J. Appl. Soc. Psychol. **27**(13), 1175–1194 (1997)

Vitali, D.: From bullies to heroes: homophobia in video games. Stud. Pulse **2**(2), 1–8 (2010)

Effects of Digital Transformation in Scientific Collaboration. A Bibliographic Review

Simone Belli$^{(\boxtimes)}$

Complutense University of Madrid, Madrid 28040, Spain
sbelli@ucm.es

Abstract. In this paper, we present a bibliographic review that contains the most important aspects of the digital transformation in scientific collaboration. We reviewed 162 scientific papers where authors have identified and analysed the digital changes in scientific research and the impact they have generated in the scientific community.

The main research question for this bibliographic review is the following: What are the key dimensions of digital transformation in scientific collaboration? The objective is to explain the changes in design practices in the science assessment criteria and ways of sharing knowledge through new techniques and software arising from stabilization of new tools. We will observe the most important aspects of the digital transformation in science, with the main contributions from the most representative authors in this area.

We show how open access and open science can solve the digital divide in science to create new modes of scientific communication.

Keywords: E-science · Open access · Open science · Scientific digital divide · Digital collaborations

1 Introduction

Nowadays our lives have introduced digital practices in daily activities. This change is also reproduced in professional settings, like the scientific one.

Research practices have been modified from this transformation, from communication with other researchers to the analysis of data. In every discipline, we observed the so-called "digital turn" or the digital transformation in scientific collaboration.

In this paper, we present a bibliographic review that contains the most important aspects of this transformation. We reviewed 162 scientific papers where authors have identified and analysed the digital changes in scientific research and the impact they have generated in the scientific community.

The study makes a step forward in explaining the relations between digital infrastructures, digital collaboration, and open access practices. The digital transformation represents a new strategy for sharing knowledge between scientific collaboration.

This project has received funding from the European Union's Horizon 2020 research and innovation programme under grant agreement No 693781 – "Giving focus to the Cultural, Scientific and Social Dimension of EU – CELAC Relations".

© Springer Nature Switzerland AG 2019
H. Florez et al. (Eds.): ICAI 2019, CCIS 1051, pp. 410–422, 2019.
https://doi.org/10.1007/978-3-030-32475-9_30

We are interested in identifying which are the digital mechanisms that account for success in scientific collaborations and the principles of co-evolution of the digital infrastructures in scientific communities.

The main research question for this bibliographic review is the following: What are the key dimensions of digital transformation in scientific collaboration? The objective is to explain the changes in design practices in the science assessment criteria and ways of sharing knowledge through new techniques and software arising from stabilization of new tools. We will observe the most important aspects of the digital transformation in science, with the main contributions from the most representative authors in this area.

This review is pertinent to identify the effects of the digital transformation in scientific collaboration, identifying digital communication elements and innovative processes to explain the relationships at work, communication patterns, the use of technological tools and the cognitive products that come out of this interactive process.

The evolution of disciplinary scholarly practices has transformed knowledge production, with the introduction of technology in research being one of the major drivers of changes. These changes must consider some aspects. The first one is the transformation from physical to digital journals, and the second is the promotion of Open Access to break social barriers such as legal, economic, or technological.

Open Access has been redefined in many occasions. In 1993 at Budapest, Open Access was defined as the free availability of the Internet to read, copy, distribute, add, or use material for any legal purpose to break economic and technological barriers. Another declaration of Open Access was in Berlin 2003, emphasizing the contributions of scientific investigation; it refers to data, photos, or graphics. Moreover, the Salvador Declaration 2005 is focused on the development, access, and use of science information.

Open Access gives freedom to use scientific publications under some conditions. This tool allows to use, publish, edit, and produce derivative research of the original work with the agreement of the original authors. In this sense, Open Access contributes to building knowledge society by promoting information and communication. However, each region needs to create politics to promote, develop and limit Open Access. For example, in Latin America, Copyright results in a barrier which obstructs the uses of data and limits the use of publication. A lot of Open Access journals in Latin America keep restrictive copyright policies, which is inconsistent with the values of Open Access.

However, Open Access is an essential instrument by which Open Science is based on the new strategies to diffuse knowledge and cooperative work using digital technologies. Open Science encompasses some instruments for openness as Open Data that focuses on fomenting the open publication of raw data and Open source that foments the openness of research prototypes and software.

Open Science development is showing the world that investigators are achieving attempts that otherwise would not be possible without collaborative networks and technological tools combined together. Some of the remarkable examples are significant in biology and medicine, such as drug development strategies getting better thanks to the addition of open strategies. The resulting changes are reshaping the industry. The relevant studies include drug development in malaria and tropical disease. Despite the risks that open science can have, this process is working better than traditional ways of co-working and at least for now it's a more efficient and fair way to make real science with global impacts.

Through time, a lot of advantages have been shown taking into account the powerful effects of Open Science and Open Access in the ways individuals tend to form collaborative teams, sharing profiles and creating a diversity of knowledge. This process changes local realities with the promotion of collaborations, including providing low-resource groups access to global resources and information In consequence, it's important to learn about these wide strategies to deal with persistent challenges.

Since Open Science and Open Access are seen as a strategy of knowledge production and dissemination that opposes the traditional closed strategies of knowledge production and dissemination, the purpose of this paper is to analyze the arguments treated by scientists in the dispute over whether to use it or not.

2 Digital Infrastructure

Digital transformation causes a change of space where research is conducted; researchers work in online and offline space at the same time. This mixed infrastructure is also called "e-Infrastructure" or digital infrastructure and it refers to research environment, regardless of their location in the world [1].

Leigh Star [2] has studied infrastructures in different research laboratories through ethnography, to understand the details of work practice, extensive prototyping, and user feedback. The use of digital infrastructure by researchers, tools, and communities requires organizations negotiating and positioning the implication of networks. Digital infrastructure is built on new types of scientific and engineering information settings, and pursuing research in new ways and with improved effectiveness [3], demands a re-engineering of the scientific system.

This concerns network infrastructure, where hardware and software platforms and tools and applications provide creative technology environments. Dreyfus [4] suggests that the way that we communicate to other people and actions in the connected world is not the same as the way we conduct ourselves in the physical world.

Digital computation, data, information, and networks enable people to reduce barriers of location, time, institution, and discipline [3]. Such environments enable researchers to distribute and cooperate over time and geographical, structural, and disciplinary distance. The digital infrastructure should be shaped and achieved in a way that allows research projects to adapt effective application –specific, yet interoperable [3]. Authors present this infrastructure for areas of knowledge because each field needs a digital infrastructure built ad hoc for specific needs.

For Tilson, Lyytinen, and Sorensen [5] the ubiquity of digital computers and connecting those computers through a digital transmission structure represent the revolution in scientific settings. Digital infrastructure includes dimensions like bandwidth, characteristic of facility, potential, ubiquity, flexibility, style, radio rate, power supplies, and sharing methods.

We can recreate a research environment using a digital tool, for example in myExperiment [6]. Another example is the Living Labs method to user-centric ICT. For Eriksson, Niitamo, and Kulkki [7], the implementation of Living Labs is built on the connection of the user in the innovation development, thus creating the innovation scheme user-centric, as contrasting to technology-centric. These are shaped and authenticated in cooperative multi-contextual experiential real-world settings. For example, the Living Labs in Paraguay [8]. For Katzy, Baltes, and Gard [9] this space – which involves actors – meets the purpose to co-create and experiment.

Digital infrastructure is also understood as digital libraries that contain not only the digital equivalent of published documents, but also pictures, videos, programs and any extra kind of multimedia objects that a group may describe as suitable to its working and communication requirements [1]. All disciplines identify the value of digital information being accessible at all times and from any place [10]. Friedlander [11] establish that scholars in the US used many on- and offline sources to support their research. In the UK, generic web search engines were valued 'very significant' by 45% of academics [10].

3   Digital Collaborations

We have observed that E-science in digital infrastructure is composed of interactions and knowledge between researchers using digital tools. Atkins et al. [3] present how many researchers were academically trained mainly with conventional tools; they have since incorporated digital tools into their professional career.

For Heimeriks, Horlesbergerm and Van der Besselaar [12], the emergence of digital information, online open database, and ICT have allowed a fundamental decreasing of the prices associated to cooperation, communication, and information distribution within the science organization and between information creators and users, with new patterns of communication and collaboration emerged. Communication networks are relevant indicators for the emergent configurations of collaboration, composed by actors involved (nodes), structure of the network (relations), and knowledge (content) [12].

Academic web networks are crucial to share research with other institutions and researchers. Smith and Thelwall [13] identify how academic domains tend to be better linked than commercial domains, and how university and research groups web pages are essential. Fenner and Haak [14] introduce the unique identifiers for research like ORCID to create a unique identity for a researcher to use in many scientific digital environments.

One of the most significant changes in e-science are scientific publications. Digital transformation has changed the way researchers publish their research, from an offline journal to an online journal. Successively it has changed the way researchers write a scientific paper. The tendency in the last years is to publish a paper as the result of the collaborative work in a research project and scientific networks. Dynamic publications and collaborative authoring are another form to understand the digital transformation in Science and Technology [15]. Authors say that publication can now change with the expansion of digital tools, such as cooperative authoring and writing instruments [15]. Circulation of drafts, presentations of papers, and sharing of citations and positions are cooperative initiatives that offer a social aspect to the private action of writing [16].

One of the most extraordinary transformations in the last years is the cloud, a way of arranging cooperation [15]. Before we used emails with text and the track changes option activated. Nowadays, we use cloud instruments that synchronize files within the workgroup and generate a backup of archives, operating a collaborative authoring tool to work simultaneously on documents. Dropbox and Google Drive are two of the most popular cloud storage solutions.

Also, if we have different environments to collaborate with our colleagues, email is still one of the most popular means on the Internet in science [17]. In academic communication, mailing lists and discussion groups transfer information and are a appreciated instrument for academics to gain access to knowledge [18]. These groups can generate new relations or strengthen current links between researchers. Weller and Puschmann [19] define Twitter as a instrument to direct users to significant works and as a font for unconventional influence.

The stabilization of digital technology as part of the collaborative process is transforming tools used as epistemic objects from models to surgery technology, or the robotized arm of a production chain [20]. This process modifies, at different levels and depending on the type of research group, the phases of the innovative process. Possible patterns of innovation based on distributed cognition will be pinpointed [21].

Digital tools are part of the action of researchers. Brassac [22] observe how the creative process is not simply intellectual, but that takings place within a connection to the world that is made up of analogic and digital units. These tools are intermediary objects that connect human actors [23]. Digital tools fund a canal for innovative processes, conveying information. Brassac et al. [22] argue that objects can help actors to solve problems. For Brassac et al. [22], displaying objects is a potent mode of making evidence. Objects are not defined only by their design, but also for the use, gestures and talk.

For Edmonds [24] the advent of digital media and computational instruments has unlocked innovative possibilities for ingenious practice, but digital tools themselves are not the only factors to be considered. Creativity can be manipulated by the circumstances in which it takes place like environment, tools, and actors.

4   The Dark Side of Digital Transformation: The Digital Divide

ICTs can benefit and move a country forward in social and economic growth. But ICT have been disproportionately distributed in most emerging countries [25].

For Rice [26] the global digital divide is indicated to as the technological gap, the ethnic digital gap, and the absence of digital insertion. Many authors [27–30] advance the notion of social growth and equal access to information as distributive integrity. Part of the motives for the small profile of researchers in developing countries is the modest access to scientific journals from developed countries, aggravated by the organization of copyright [31].

So digital transformation produces digital gap among developed and least developed countries, where access to the ICT is not distributed in the same way. The consequence of this is that many researchers from least developed countries cannot have access to scientific publications, books, grants, and scientific networks, which is basically knowledge.

Information in developing countries is not clearly available or public, and academics can not have access to it like in many developed countries, and it is more valuable than everything else. Difference of access to knowledge and technical advantages between scientists become a key aspect in science. Various academics are not participants in digital scientific networks. The implication of digital transformation needs to be comprehended more profoundly because of the mode in which advances in digital tools are giving to the use and circulation of power in society [32].

ICT is a suitable and effective way to manage information, have developed a crucial element to refining scientific performance [33–35]. Molloy [36] assesses the current journal structure which works in contradiction of the dissemination of data; barriers inherent in the current journal system.

Aguado-Lopez and Vargas [37] analyze the idea that the dominant scientific communication model involves a system of colonization of information. Harris [38] says that simply moving knowledge and instrumentation is not sufficient to support developing countries shape their research base. Scientists must have easy access to the digital instruments from commercial and innovative research areas [3]. Harnad [39] argued that value ranks of commercial publishers build most digital journals inaccessible to possible readers, thus increasing this digital divide and the barriers.

5   Open Access and Open Science

One of the most innovative solutions to solve the digital divide in science is Open Access (OA). The effects of OA in science can decrease existing asymmetries and the digital divide. OA solves information famine and helps countries to bridge the digital divide. We identify the step in which OA is a digital transformation that solves the access to scientific knowledge.

Phelps et al. [40] concern OA to scientific publications as a facilitator for growth, while restricted access to a minor subset of people with a subscription is a limitation to growth. OA can re-appropriate scientific knowledge as a device of political action of science in developing countries, such as in the LAC region [37], ensuring that knowledge is part of the extension of human rights, social equity and democratization of knowledge [41]. OA thus constitutes a political move toward a decolonization and the re-appropriation of knowledge, allowing the "return" of publicly-funded research. For Piedra et al. [42] OA is a direct reaction to knowledge privatization.

OA be able to restore information as a free good on a worldwide scale [29]. It is an umbrella term that incorporates a multitude of conventions about the future of information dissemination [43], a mode to improved the "developing world" [44] to the organization of knowledge by offering access to scientific production available in the "developed world" [45–50].

Agreeing with Murray-Rust [51], it is frustrating that journals privilege copyright for supporting information of an article. Information should not be 'free', but open for re-use in studies expected. In the OA movement many libraries and universities are starting to take direct actions to high-prices journals. Digital transformation also gives easy to access to millions of people to illegally-copyrighted scientific publications.

OA may provide an opportunity to develop a supportable infrastructure for both modes of information production [52].

Alperin, Fischman, and Willinsky [53] have focused on the growing OA movement in scientific organizations in Latin America and the Caribbean countries (LAC). In these countries, Internet usage grew at a 603% between 2000 and 2008, but the level of ICT expansion has been weaker than in other parts of the world. In LAC countries we do not have many scientific collaborations due to a deficiency of subsidy and imperfect facilities to check the principal journal in an area, which confronts potentials to conduct leading-edge high-grade investigation [54].

We have a huge difference between the presence of the OA publications in LAC countries and Europe and the US. Gomez et al. [55] found that most LAC countries developed their DOI indicator with Argentina, Brazil, and Chile. A study of peer-reviewed papers circulated in 2008 [56] found that approximately 20% were obtainable online, with alterations in scientific fields: Earth Science 25.9%; Physics and Astronomy 20.5%; Chemistry 7.4%. Lawrence [57] investigated that highly cited papers in applied informatics matched were freely accessible on the Web.

The mutual strengths of LAC institutes and scholars resulted in 13% of all Latin American journals being accessible and 51% of the amount of online journals [44]. LAC journals are using the OA publishing model to increase the sense of public missions about LAC universities to share knowledge [53]. Gomez and Bongiovani [29] have recognized the growth of OA publications between 2007 and 2010 in Argentina (236%), Brazil (12%) and Chile (85%). Authors say that territory is mobilized, working and knowledge about access to information and its effects. LAC countries are moving onward and becoming a principal strength behind access to information. The development of free, publicly accessible journal article collections has confirmed methods in which networks can change academic communication [58].

Tenopir et al. [56] identify that researchers are reticent to the public accessibility of their data: only 36% of researchers approved that others could access their data easily.

European countries have launched activities to promote their Open Data (OD) policies and portals. EU countries have successfully developed a basic OD policy, with 20 countries having an integrated and dedicated OD policy [59].

Neelie Kroes [60] says that in order to achieve development in science, we need to be share and open. Pampel and Dallmeier-Tiessen [61] introduce the OA to study data as the base of academic knowledge. To promote data sharing in public repositories, it is essential to recognize the difficulties that influence researchers concerning the sharing of their data.

Nicholas et al. [62] discussed that we need to observe information search and access in the broader setting of research. The Transparency and Openness Promotion (TOP) [63] promotes public archiving of data, computer code, etc. These authors suggest a pre-registration process before planning the work. Journals can attach badges to a paper that meet certain transparency standards of open data, open materials and preregistration. In computational science, Stodden [64] explains that incompetence to access scientific information and code standpoints as a obstacle to confirmation and knowledge transfer.

OA also works for grants and project funding. Many agencies have adopted strategies that hold open knowledge. The National Institutes of Health, the Wellcome

Trust, the European Research Council, and the European Commission Framework Horizon 2020 also necessitate subsidized projects to realize project-related research data freely obtainable [65]. For these authors, democratization of research sponsoring does not necessarily lead to a decrease in dependence but rather to an increase in reciprocity. Also in medical research, we are in an open data challenge [66]. Fecher and Friesike [43] show how the 'representative school' is worried with the concept of access to information, focusing on the principal access to the products of research.

Murray-Rust [51] conveys the connotation of the prefix 'open' to the shared meaning of open source software. Open source instruments open access to academic communication as the Public Knowledge Project [67]. For Harris [38], technology is a basis of scientific research, and frequent unsatisfying obstacles occur once acting experiments under the difficult environment found in laboratories in most developing countries. In many developing countries, we need to find advanced methods to overcome equipment insufficiency.

Open innovation is another topic in OA that intensified communication and interaction between scientists and corporations [68]. At the moment, we have several platforms to innovate together between problem solvers that contribute to different challenges like Innocentive, Inpama, and Presans.

6 Discussion

Nowadays our lives have introduced digital practices in daily activities. This change is also reproduced in professional settings, like the scientific ones. Research practices have been modified from this transformation, from communication with other researchers to the analysis of data. In every scientific discipline, we observe the so-called "digital turn". This term identifies a series of new professional practices to access and share knowledge between researchers. Digitalization has opened up new possibilities for researchers in their handling of information and knowledge.

Unlike previous generations, researchers today have a seemingly endless variety of potential scientific collaborations and research networks available through the digital tools. Indeed, the internet has become a powerful social and professional intermediary. It has partially displaced the role of physical institutions, such as laboratory, office and colleagues from the same department. Thanks to Internet, it requires less time and efforts to beginning and managing a scientific collaboration. As we observed, recent studies have shown that Internet-mediated collaboration is generally thought to increase scientific productivity.

Professional activities are being eroded by the proliferation of extensive 'networks' of professional possibility. 'Liquid science' has transformed scientific activities into a type of practices where researchers can do research with colleagues from different part of the World.

This article explored how information and communication technologies in this specific professional setting have affected the way in which research teams are related. In particular, this investigation explores the extent to which the scientific networks are composed and how they obtain and manage information thanks to the digital transformation. Observing the ways of communication and collaboration of research teams, information search and access to the knowledge, and the majors trends and changes they have perceived in the last years.

Cooperation in science has become increasingly important due to research networks and a shared vision that key societal challenges can only be addressed through science cooperation. Joint research endeavors are another factor enhancing scientific collaboration between countries and international institutions.

The future challenges of scientific research are in successful collaborations that can benefit scientific development in less developed countries. Regional collaboration is known to be especially important for countries whose scientific infrastructure and capacity can benefit from forging alliances with researchers from institutions abroad.

In the 2003 OCDE meeting, it was declared that cooperation in science and technology, in national and international settings, is considered a necessary condition to achieve the socioeconomic independence of the developing country to improve the number of scientific co-publications. International co-publications are most cited and there is a positive relation between the number of authors per document and the number of quotes received. Cooperation in Science is associated with better quality and scientific relevance; and from here, the tendency of the governments is to promote cooperation in research through bilateral and multilateral collaborations.

7 Conclusion

We have observed how digital transformation makes knowledge open; new dynamics are drawing a new era. The digital turn, meaning the replacement of conventional tools with digital ones at the academic level, has changed the way researchers work together. Digital transformation has revolutionized not only science and e-science, but other settings too: e-Business, e-Government, and e-Life [69].

The key point is to construct a "horizontal" infrastructure through technology to draw an innovative scientific community. Peer-to-peer processes are the beginning of this horizontal infrastructure based on open knowledge for everybody, through collaborative networks easy to manage [70]. Innovative methods of communication and value mechanism that trial the conventional scientific communication structure have developed within a handful of disciplines whose work association turns their perceived benefits.

Firm guidelines, transnational criteria, and top practices should be approved to incorporate digital transformation worldwide. Researchers think this transformation can give access to knowledge faster and easily, to collaborate, share, and advance regionally, mostly for less developed countries. We agree with Houghton [52] that it is important to take a complete method to 're-engineer' the organization, which involves the creation, production and distribution of scientific knowledge and the organization of rights, access, evaluation methods, and research knowledge organization.

Open Science and Open Access have a special potential to be more efficient, innovative and to democratize knowledge, and its production, management and dissemination towards the community. In the case of science-related knowledge and data, there are some aspects that are limiting the acceptance of this idea among scientists. These problems include: (1) a lack of information that can help to use and understand the open data published, (2) the quality of the data available due to the easy access for anyone to publish it and (3) the fear of scooping or using one's data without addressing its original creator. Nonetheless, if these problems are solved, Open Science can benefit the scientific community. It can allow researchers to publish their research and get feedback from a wider audience that can include professionals from areas not related to science. It can help to infer and obtain more knowledge from research results increasing the efficiency and the return of investment. Finally, it can help to preserve data that would otherwise be forgotten.

References

1. Candela, L., Castelli, D., Pagano, P.: History, evolution and impact of digital libraries. E-publishing and digital libraries: legal and organizational issues. In: Iglezakis, I., Synodinou, T., Kapidakis, S. (eds.) E-publishing and digital libraries, pp. 1–30. Information Science References, New York (2011)
2. Star, S.L.: The ethnography of infrastructure. Am. Behav. Sci. **43**(3), 377–391 (1999)
3. Atkins, D., et al.: Revolutionizing Science and Engineering Through Cyberinfrastructure: Report of the National Science Foundation Blue-Ribbon Advisory Panel on Cyberinfrastructure. National Science Foundation, Washington, DC (2003)
4. Dreyfus, H.L.: On the Internet: Thinking in Action. Routledge, New York (2001)
5. Tilson, D., Lyytinen, K., Sørensen, C.: Research commentary—Digital infrastructures: The missing IS research agenda. Inf. Syst. Res. **21**(4), 748–759 (2010)
6. Lazer, D., et al.: Computational social science. Science **323**(5915), 721–723 (2009)
7. Eriksson, M., Niitamo, V.-P., Kulkki, S.: State-of-the-art in utilizing Living Labs approach to user-centric ICT innovation-a European approach. Center for Distance-spanning Technology. Lulea University of Technology Sweden: Lulea, Lulea (2005)
8. De Arias, A.R., Masi, S.D., Dorigo, D., Rojas, F.A., Vega, M.C., Rolon, M.: Living Labs, spaces for open innovation and technology transfer. An alternative to the solution of social problems in Paraguay. Soc. Sci. **3**(3), 74–79 (2014)
9. Katzy, B.R., Baltes, G.H., Gard, J.: Concurrent process coordination of new product development by Living Labs–an exploratory case study. Int. J. Product Dev. **17**(1–2), 23–42 (2012)
10. Education for Change Ltd., SIRU University of Brighton and The Research Partnership. Researchers' Use of Libraries and other Information Sources: current patterns and future trends, Research Support Libraries Group (2002)
11. Friedlander, A.: Dimensions and Use of the Scholarly Information Environment, Digital Library Federation and Council on Library and Information Resources, Washington D.C. (2002)
12. Heimeriks, G., Hoerlesberger, M., Van den Besselaar, P.: Mapping communication and collaboration in heterogeneous research networks. Scientometrics **58**(2), 391–413 (2003)
13. Smith, A., Thelwall, M.: Web impact factors for Australasian universities. Scientometrics **54**(3), 363–380 (2002)
14. Fenner, M., Haak, L.: Unique identifiers for researchers. In: Bartling, S., Friesike, S. (eds.) Opening Science, pp. 293–296. Springer, Cham (2014). https://doi.org/10.1007/978-3-319-00026-8_21
15. Bartling, S., Friesike, S. (eds.): Opening Science. Springer, Cham (2014). https://doi.org/10.1007/978-3-319-00026-8

16. Brockman, W.S., Neumann, L., Palmer, C.L., Tidline, T.J.: Scholarly Work in the Humanities and the Evolving Information Environment. CLIR, New York (2001)
17. Lenhart, A., Horrigan, J.B.: Re-visualizing the digital divide as a digital spectrum. IT&Society 1(5), 23–39 (2003)
18. Matzat, U.: Academic communication and Internet Discussion Groups: transfer of information or creation of social contacts? Soc. Networks 26(3), 221–255 (2004)
19. Weller, K., Puschmann, C.: Twitter for scientific communication: how can citations/references be identified and measured? In: Proceedings of the ACM WebSci 2011, pp. 1–4. ACM Publishers, Koblenz (2011)
20. Knorr Cetina, K.: Epistemic Cultures. Harvard UP, Cambridge (1999)
21. Hutchins, E.: Cognition, Distributed. In: Smelser, N., Baltes, P. (eds.) International Encyclopedia of the Social and Behavioral Sciences. Elsevier, Amsterdam (2006)
22. Brassac, C., Fixmer, P., Mondada, L., Vinck, D.: Interweaving objects, gestures, and talk in context. Mind Culture Act. 15(3), 208–233 (2008)
23. Latour, B.: Science in Action: How to Follow Scientists and Engineers Through Society. Harvard University Press, Cambridge (1987)
24. Edmonds, E.A., Weakley, A., Candy, L., Fell, M., Knott, R., Pauletto, S.: The studio as laboratory: combining creative practice and digital technology research. Int. J. Hum Comput Stud. 63(4), 452–481 (2005)
25. Ahmed, A.: Open access towards bridging the digital divide–policies and strategies for developing countries. Inf. Technol. Dev. 13(4), 337–361 (2007)
26. Rice, M.F.: The digital divide and race in the United States. Polit. Adm. Change 36(July–Dec), 20–31 (2001)
27. Benkler, Y.: The Wealth of Networks: How Social Production Transforms Markets and Freedom. Yale University Press, New Haven (2006)
28. Balkin, J.: Foreword. In: Shaver, L.B., Rizk, N. (eds.) Access to Knowledge in Egypt: New Research on Intellectual Property, Innovation and Development. Bloomsbury Academic, London (2010)
29. Gómez, N., Bongiovani, P.C.: Open Access and A2 K: Collaborative Experiences in Latin America. De Gruyter, Berlin (2012)
30. Shaver, L.: Defining and measuring access to knowledge: towards an A2 K index. J. Law Policy Inf. Soc. 4(2), 64–87 (2008)
31. Tagler, J.: Recent steps toward full-text electronic delivery at Elsevier science. Ser. Librarian 28, 171–179 (1996)
32. Silverstone, R.: Why Study the Media?. Sage, London (1999)
33. Chataway, J., Wield, D.: Industrialization, innovation and development: what does knowledge management change? J. Int. Dev. 12, 803–824 (2000)
34. Garavelli, A.C., Gorgoglione, M., Scozzi, B.: Managing knowledge transfer by knowledge technologies. Technovation 22, 269–279 (2002)
35. Prez-Bustamante, G.: Knowledge management in agile innovative organisations. J. Knowl. Manage. 3(1), 6–17 (1999)
36. Molloy, J.C.: The open knowledge foundation: open data means better science. PLoS Biol. 9(12), 100–195 (2011)
37. Aguado-López, E., Arbeláez, E.J.V.: Reapropiación del conocimiento y descolonización: el acceso abierto como proceso de acción política del sur. Revista Colombiana de Sociología 39(2), 69–78 (2016)
38. Harris, E.: Building scientific capacity in developing countries. EMBO Rep. 5(1), 7–11 (2004)
39. Harnad, S.: Minotaur: six proposals for freeing the refereed literature online: a comparison. Ariadne 28, 1–23 (2001)

40. Phelps, L., Fox, B.A., Marincola, F.M.: Supporting the advancement of science: open access publishing and the role of mandates. J. Transl. Med. **10**, 13 (2012)
41. Banerjee, I., Babini, D., Aguado-López, E.: Tesis a favor de la consolidación del Acceso Abierto como una alternativa de democratización de la ciencia en América Latina. In: P. Suber (ed.) Acceso Abierto, pp. 13–48. Universidad Autónoma del Estado de México, Toluca (2005)
42. Piedra, N., Chicaiza, J., López, J., Tovar, E., Martínez, O.: Open educational practices and resources based on social software, UTPL experience. In: Proceedings of the 2009 Euro American Conference on Telematics and Information Systems: New Opportunities to increase Digital Citizenship, p. 34 (2009)
43. Fecher, B., Friesike, S.: Open science: one term, five schools of thought. In: Bartling, S., Friesike, S. (eds.) Opening Science, pp. 17–47. Springer, Cham (2014). https://doi.org/10. 1007/978-3-319-00026-8_2
44. Haider, J.: Of the rich and the poor and other curious minds: on open access and "development". In: Bawden, D. (ed.) Aslib Proceedings, vol. 59, no. 45, pp. 449–461 (2007)
45. Kirsop, B., Arunachalam, S., Chan, L.: Access to scientific knowledge for sustainable development: options for developing countries. Ariadne **52**, 3 (2007)
46. Arunachalam, S.: Information and knowledge in the age of electronic communication: a developing country perspective. J. Inf. Sci. **25**(6), 465–476 (2002)
47. Ramachandran, P.V., Scaria, V.: Open access publishing in the developing world: making a difference. J. Orthop. **1**(1), e1 (2004)
48. Weitzman, J.B., Arunachalam, S.: Open access in the developing world. Open Access Now **15**, 96–132 (2003)
49. Tenopir, C., et al.: Data sharing by scientists: practices and perceptions. PLoS ONE **6**(6), 211–231 (2011)
50. Durrant, S.: Overview of initiatives in the developing world. In: Open Access and the Public Domain in Digital Data and Information for Science: Proceedings of an International Symposium. National Academies Press, Washington, DC, US National Committee for CODATA, Board on International Scientific Organizations, Policy and Global Affairs Division, pp. 122–126 (2004)
51. Murray-Rust, P.: Open data in science. Ser. Rev. **34**(1), 52–64 (2008)
52. Houghton, J., Steele, C., Henty, M.: Changing research practices in the digital information and communication environment. Doctoral dissertation, Department of Education, Science and Training (2003)
53. Alperín, J.P., Fischman, G., Willinsky, J.: Open access and scholarly publishing in Latin America: ten flavours and a few reflections| Acesso livre e publicação acadêmica na América Latina: dez sabores e algumas reflexões. Liinc em Revista **4**(2), 172–185 (2008)
54. Terra-Figari, L.I.: Diseminación del conocimiento académico en América Latina. UNESCO, Montevideo (2008)
55. Gómez, N., et al.: Open access indicators and information society: the Latin American case. OCLC Syst. Serv. **25**(2), 82–92 (2009)
56. Björk, B.-C., et al.: Open Access to the scientific journal literature: situation 2009. PLoS ONE **5**(6), 11–27 (2010)
57. Lawrence, S.: Online or invisible? Nature **411**(6837), 521 (2001)
58. Lynch, C.A.: Institutional repositories: essential infrastructure for scholarship in the digital age. ARL **226**, 1–7 (2003)
59. European Data Portal (2016). https://www.europeandataportal.eu/. Accessed 16 June 2017
60. Kroes, N.: Opening Science Through e-infrastructures. Pergamon, Oxford (2012)

61. Pampel, H., Bertelmann, R., Hobohm, H.-C.: 'Data librarianship" Rollen, Aufgaben, Kompetenzen. In: Hohoff, U., Schmiedeknecht, C. (eds.), Ein neuer Blick auf Bibliothe en, pp. 159–176. Olms 2010, Hildesheim (2010)

62. Nicholas, D., et al.: Digital journals, big deals, and online searching behaviour: a pilot study. In: Aslib Proceedings, vol. 55, no. (1/2), pp. 84–109 (2003)

63. Nosek, B.A., Alter, G., Banks, G., Borsboom, D., Bowman, S., Breckler, S., Christensen, G.: Transparency and Openness Promotion (TOP) Guidelines (2016)

64. Stodden, V.: Intellectual property and computational science. In: Bartling, S., Friesike, S. (eds.) Opening Science, pp. 225–235. Springer, Cham (2014). https://doi.org/10.1007/978-3-319-00026-8_15

65. Eisfeld-Reschke, J., Herb, U., Wenzlaff, K.: Research funding in open science. In: Bartling, S., Friesike, S. (eds.) Opening Science, pp. 237–253. Springer, Cham (2014). https://doi.org/10.1007/978-3-319-00026-8_16

66. Floca, R.: Challenges of open data in medical research. In: Bartling, S., Friesike, S. (eds.) Opening Science, pp. 297–307. Springer, Cham (2014). https://doi.org/10.1007/978-3-319-00026-8_22

67. MacGregor, J., Stranack, K., Willinsky, J.: The public knowledge project: open source tools for open access to scholarly communication. In: Bartling, S., Friesike, S. (eds.) Opening Science, pp. 165–175. Springer, Cham (2014). https://doi.org/10.1007/978-3-319-00026-8_11

68. Schildhauer, T., Voss, H.: Open innovation and crowdsourcing in the sciences. In: Bartling, S., Friesike, S. (eds.) Opening Science, pp. 255–269. Springer, Cham (2014). https://doi.org/10.1007/978-3-319-00026-8_17

69. Berman, F., Fox, G., Hey, T.: Grid Computing: Making the Global Infrastructure a Reality. Wiley, Chichester (2003)

70. Belli, S., Aceros, J.C.: When technology draws society: distributed trust in horizontal infrastructure. Int. J. Actor-Network Theory Technol. Innov. **8**(2), 32–43 (2016)

glossaLAB: Co-creating Interdisciplinary Knowledge

José María Díaz-Nafría[1,2(✉)], Teresa Guarda[2,3], Mark Burgin[4],
Wolfgang Hofkirchner[5], Rainer Zimmermann[5,6], Gerhard Chroust[2,5],
and Simone Belli[7]

[1] Madrid Open University, Madrid, Spain
jdian@unileon.es
[2] BITrum-Research Group, León, Spain
[3] Universidad Estatal Península de Santa Elena, La Libertad, Ecuador
[4] University of California, Los Angeles, CA, USA
[5] Institute for a Global Sustainable Information Society, Vienna, Austria
[6] Institute for Design Science, Munich, Germany
[7] Universidad Complutense de Madrid, Madrid, Spain

Abstract. The paper describes the glossaLAB international project as a contribution to confront the urgent need of knowledge integration frameworks, as required to face global challenges that overwhelm disciplinary knowledge capacity. Under this scope, glossaLAB is devised to make contributions in three main aspects of such endeavor: (i) development of a sound theoretical framework for the unification of knowledge, (ii) establishment of broadly accepted methodologies and tools to facilitate the integration of knowledge, (iii) development of assessment criteria for the qualification of interdisciplinarity undertakings. The paper discusses the main components of the project and the solutions adopted to achieve the intended objectives at three different levels: at the *technical level*, glossaLAB aims at developing a platform for knowledge integration based on the elucidation of concepts, metaphors, theories and problems, including a semantically-operative recompilation of valuable scattered encyclopedic contents devoted to two entangled transdisciplinary fields: the sciences of systems and information. At the *theoretical level*, the goal is reducing the redundancy of the conceptual system (defined in terms of *"intensional performance"* of the contents recompiled), and the elucidation of new concepts. Finally, at the *meta-theoretical level*, the project aims at assessing the knowledge integration achieved through the co-creation process based on (a) the diversity of the disciplines involved and (b) the integration properties of the conceptual network stablished through the elucidation process.

Keywords: Knowledge co-creation · Knowledge integration · Systems sciences · Information studies · Interdisciplinarity · Transdisciplinarity

© Springer Nature Switzerland AG 2019
H. Florez et al. (Eds.): ICAI 2019, CCIS 1051, pp. 423–437, 2019.
https://doi.org/10.1007/978-3-030-32475-9_31

1 The Co-creation of Knowledge in Historical Perspective. Problems and Challenges

As a consequence of the constant development of information and communication technologies, the capacity to interact in an ever stretching milieu of data, information and knowledge producers offers a constantly evolving landscape of knowledge acquisition and creation, characterized by new possibilities and challenges.

In both ancient and modern perspectives, knowledge has been primarily seen as an individual activity. Indeed, it is the Platonic soul which acknowledges the eternal forms, and the Cartesian cogito which offer the first pillar of certainty. However, since the past century several views conceive knowledge as a social activity which is primarily carried out through social interaction [20]. In the case of the strong constructivist perspective, reality itself "is both revealed and concealed, created and destroyed by our [social] activities" [2, 18]. But even in the most classical tradition, in which the role of the individual plays the crucial part in the unveiling of reality, the importance of social interaction in the construction of knowledge has also been stressed throughout times. The Academy and the Lyceum, the medieval schools and universities, the Royal Society and the Republic of Letters, the Saint Simonians and the Positivist Schools, represent a few but highly relevant examples of institutionalized social relations for the development of knowledge in the most classical traditions. Therein, the communication, exchange and confrontation of ideas (as it happens for instance in the platonic dialectics) is fundamental to the creation of knowledge. Thus, it is possible to speak generally of co-creation of knowledge mediated by networks of knowledge agents, the same who develop the network of concepts used for the representation of reality (or, as the radical constructivist would rather state, the construction of reality) [7].

Yet the qualification of knowledge agents and relations (i.e. adequate interactions) in the process of justification of truthful believes is significantly different in each tradition.[1] In the historical development that leads to the constitution of positivism, it is the individual agent that follows the basic principles of the scientific method and adheres to the basics of her discipline who properly creates new knowledge in her domain and field of expertise. Here the assumption that our questioning of reality can be analytically broken down (which is in the core of modern epistemology since Descartes) provides a basic guiding for the structuring of knowledge networks: a treelike structure may suffice [7]. Aristotle himself provides a master guide to deploy the tree of knowledge through the posing of appropriate questioning: from the most general categories to the more specific ones, the endeavor of knowledge can be articulated in branches whose nodes are disconnected from other nodes at the same level [1, 35]. When the knower or a group of well-connected knowers end up, so to say, at the level of the leaves, it is possible to relink, in a synthetic effort, the parts which were previously divided in the analytical moment, grasping the tree in its full unity. This synthetic moment which was actually appreciated in the Cartesian epistemology [7], was unfeasible when the analytical mode was generalized from an individual

---

[1] In the case computer science, Millo and Lipon offers an interesting discussion about the social process involved in the justification of belief, particularly with respect to mathematics [32].

researcher to science as a whole, as it particularly happened in the 18th century. The path to the division of science into specialized disciplines was the natural consequence, despite the concerns stated by a few, and in particular, by Leibniz' caveat against breaching the necessary unity of science [29]. From the network perspective, the tree-like-structured disciplines started to be further apart, reducing the interaction among them. In the nineteenth and twentieth century, this division of science into separate disciplines grew to a much larger degree as the positivist tree of knowledge keep on growing.

1.1 Knowledge Co-creation in Network Perspective

The network perspective offers a suitable framework to analyze the problem of co-creation and integration of knowledge, as some of the authors have argued elsewhere [9, 10]. To this purpose, it suffices to draw on the abstract network, which is just comprised of a set of nodes and links [3, 8]. Indeed, the definition of *conceptual systems,* provided in another contribution to this volume [4], as a set of concepts and relations between them, is actually a network theoretical definition. However, as suggested above, the network perspective enables us to map not only the network of concepts (Fig. 1a), but also the networks of knowledge agents (Fig. 1b) as two sides of the same coin. This can be better seen for knowledge within a given discipline.

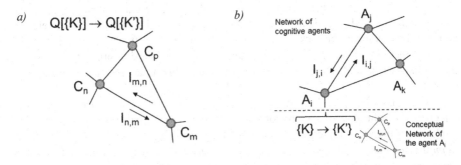

Fig. 1. Dynamics of the conceptual network evolving as: (a) passive network of concepts; (b) active network of interacting peers.

The dynamics of disciplinary knowledge correspond to the evolution of the *conceptual network* and, at the same time, the evolution of the interaction among the scientist whose joint undertaking corresponds to the continuous process of falsification, verification, and theoretical re-structuration [28]. Therefore, the knowledge of a discipline and its evolution can also be expressed by means of the communicative interaction among scientists, which can be mapped by an actor network [8]. The conceptual network is internalized by every peer, though in a slightly differ way. At the same time, the conceptual network as a whole can be taken as the one comprising the predicative relations supported by the community. A parallel representation of the passive network of concepts, on the left, and the active network of agents (peers), on the right, is represented in Fig. 1. The (individualized) conceptual networks, mostly shared by all peers, is represented at the lower part of the agent network. K → K' represents the evolution of individual knowledge, while Q{K} → Q{K} represents the evolution of knowledge qualified by the scientific community. The situation is different when we step out of a single discipline.

1.2   The Challenge of Reconciling Scientific Disciplines

As referred above, the process of fragmentation of the scientific enterprise derived from the epistemological groundings of modernity had as a consequence that the tree-like-structured disciplines started to be further apart. Hence, the interaction among disciplines and their respective conceptual networks was gradually reduced.

The concerns regarding the consequent mutilation of fundamental relations through the process of fragmentation of the reality under-study emerged since the second half of the twentieth century [21]. Appeals for reunification of science arose in different arenas caused by the necessity to address the fundamental complexity of the reality and the problems to be solved. The emergence of systems science, cybernetics, information theory, and the broad quest for interdisciplinarity belong to this trend [5, 19].

The relevance of this concern can also be observed in the pleas made by international institutions, as UNESCO and OECD, since the 1970s to merge scientific disciplines into integrated frameworks. However, despite the national and international endeavours to boost interdisciplinary research in the past decades, several barriers have significantly blocked its establishment. According to several studies, the most relevant barriers correspond to the lack of: (i) appropriate theoretical frameworks, (ii) broadly accepted methodologies and (iii) assessment criteria for interdisciplinarity [6, 14–16, 33]. As shown below, these constitute the main problems addressed by glossaLAB project.

As discussed in [9], the situation is actually different in the various trends to integrate scientific knowledge. According to UNESCO's classification [21], there is a gradation of theoretical integration that goes from the mere juxtaposition of disciplines in *multidisciplinary* settings, whose conceptual networks stay apart from each other, to *transdisciplinary* setting which "assumes conceptual unification between disciplines" and the sharing of a consistent conceptual network at a higher level of abstraction, as it is the case of systems science. The diverse situations in between correspond to *inter-disciplinarity* of different degree.

The network perspective (and Fig. 1 in particular) can also be applied to represent the case of interdisciplinarity. To this end, we can add a level of abstraction in the network of agents, taking as an agent one entire discipline. In this case, the conceptual network among disciplines is more heterogeneous than among disciplinary peers. However, if a good transdisciplinary setting is achieved, the corresponding conceptual network will be of a higher level of abstraction. The communication between disciplines (agents) will be mostly done using the more abstract conceptual network, while disciplinary concepts are used within the cluster of peers (abstracted as a single agent).

In intermediate situations, most of the communication will be done within the clusters of peers, while the interaction between clusters will be less dense and less consistent. The lack of interdisciplinary understanding among interacting disciplines results in the relative disconnection among the corresponding clusters. The structural properties of the conceptual system reveal, as we will see in Sect. 3, its capacity to integrate knowledge. In sum, the network representations of knowledge systems and communities can be used as a proxy for the qualification of the integration of knowledge in interdisciplinary settings.

2 Project glossaLAB: Background and Objectives

GlossaLAB project stems from several endeavours to provide a more robust toehold to the unification of knowledge through the strengthening of the *general studies of systems and information*. These fields offer in themselves a broad framework for the unification of knowledge in virtue of the conceptual abstraction of systems, information and related concepts with respect to the nature of the reality involved (which can be of physical, biological, social, technological or symbolic nature) [27]. However, the development of disciplines within the broader field of information and systems has resulted in the deployment of conceptual networks and perspectives which are not fully consistent (*ibidem*).

As it was essayed in the encyclopaedic projects which conforms the background of glossaLAB project, the establishment of good foundations for the integration of knowledge implies tackling, on the one hand, the challenge to reduce the distance within the network of related knowledge agents, on the other, the distance within the network of concepts. Just two sides of the same problem [9, 27].

More specifically the **goal** of the project is stated as "the development of an interactive open platform for conceptual elucidation and its application to the interdisciplinary co-creation, learning, dissemination and assessment of the knowledge underpinning interdisciplinary frameworks (in particular, the general study of systems and information). This development comprises: at the *technical level*, the semantically interoperable recompilation of valuable scattered encyclopedic contents; at the *theoretical level*, the reduction of conceptual redundancy (defined in terms of "*intensional performance*" of the contents recompiled) and the further elucidation of concepts; and at the *meta-theoretical level*, the assessment of knowledge integration based on diversity and conceptual network integration". The solutions adopted at these three levels will be shown in Sect. 3.

2.1 Facilitating the Co-creation of Knowledge

The way to achieve project objectives takes the form of developing the *Encyclopaedia of Systems Science & Cybernetics Online* (ESSCO) using the corpus of the *International Encyclopedia of Systems and Cybernetics* [17], the *Principia Cybernetica* [22] and *glossariumBITri* [11]. Among the methodological groundings it is worth mentioning the concept of *interdisciplinary-glossaries* developed within BITrum project as elucidation tools devoted to the clarification of concepts, methods, theories and problems in interdisciplinary settings, which at the same time are used as proxies for the evaluation of the related knowledge integration [9].

Underneath ESSCO, glossaLAB is also devised to host other focused *interdisciplinary-glossaries* devoted to specific research and innovation projects and frameworks. A subsidiary integration of these interdisciplinary-glossaries implies that those articles sufficient general as to become of general interest for the study of information and system can escalate to the level of ESSCO.

According to the aforementioned complementarity between the conceptual network and the agent network, the purpose of strengthening the capacity of systems science for the integration of knowledge implies not only analyzing and fortifying the network of concepts, but also the network of agents. Therefore, one of the dimensions of the projects concerns the development of communication and impact mechanisms linked to the glossaLAB platform for knowledge co-creation.

Figure 2 offers an overview of the project as a whole, highlighting the flow of content from the corpus to the glossaLAB platform and from here to other dissemination pathways.

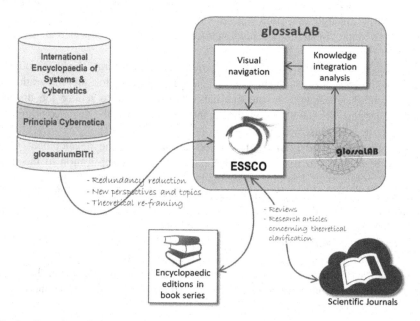

Fig. 2. Overview of glossaLAB project as regards ESSCO's development and content flow.

3   glossaLAB: A Three-Dimensional Endeavor

3.1   Technical Level: Integrating Scientific Networking

Network technologies facilitate encompassing the participation of the scientific community in the theoretical venture envisaged, keeping quality control and avoiding the multiplication of unnecessary redundant terminology. To this purpose, MediaWiki technology offers a panoply of tools and applications that enable the development of an editorial policy for *ESSCO*, driven to the achievement of high quality standards and its subsequent acknowledgement by the scientific community at large [31]. At the same time, MediaWiki framework offers a wide set of open resources in constant evolution which facilitate the development of visualization and semantic navigation tools based on the same network approach that is used at the theoretical and metatheoretical levels (s. Fig. 2, shadowed area). This specific target is intended to increase the utility, outreach and impact of *ESSCO*, which, as discussed above, is fundamental for the achievement of project's general objective. The currently ongoing development for the actualization of the glossariumBITri interactive platform [11] using MediaWiki technology, started in a previous project, offers a toehold for the development of glossa-LAB platform.

The current design follows a number of blue-prints for an article page, homepage, index pages, submission form, etc., devised in accordance with the objectives at the theoretical and meta-theoretical levels (Sects. 3.2 and 3.3). Figure 3 shows the blue-print of an article page for *ESSCO*, indicating for instance where the different contents come from. The publication record shown on the upper right side of the article summarizes the edition, curation and review process that the article has gone through. The upper tabs give access to the discussion (peer-review records) and edition history.

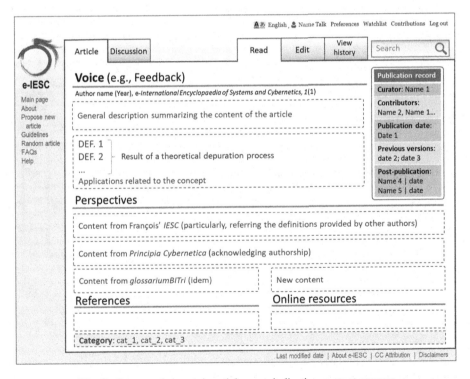

Fig. 3. Layout of a generic article page indicating content sources

Figure 4 describes in detail the parts of an article page of a Scholarpedia's article that has been taken as a model for the *ESSCO* lay-out in virtue of the parallelism between their respective editorial policies and the scientific quality and impact of Scholarpedia's articles, which are indexed as a regular journal articles [24]. In a large extent, the functionality is derived from MediaWiki open-source components customized to glossaLAB objectives, while some Scholarpedia's components have also been taken as a model, and often as code source, for the development of the platform. In addition, visual navigation tools based on semantic network analysis and representation (using the approach shown in the following sections) are currently under development.

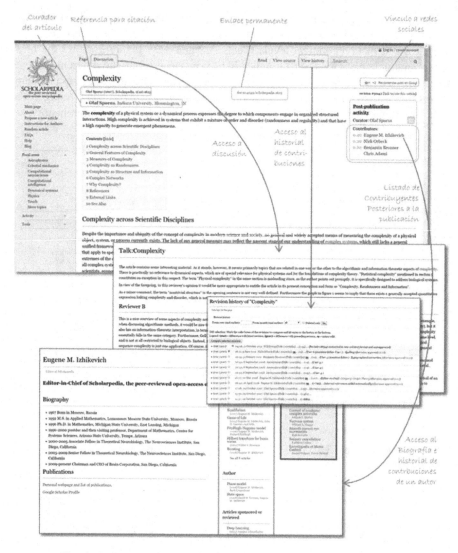

Fig. 4. Layout and functionality of article components in Scholarpedia.

3.2 Theoretical Level: Leveraging a Rich Legacy

The work that has been carried out over decades for the development of the *International Encyclopedia of Systems and Cybernetics* (directed by Charles François) [17] as well as the *Principia Cybernetica* [22] and *glossariumBITri* [11], represents an excellent platform to fulfil the theoretical purposes of the project. Charles François' enthusiasm, dedication and work quality constitutes an invaluable legacy capable to show the insight variety and penetration of the systems science community. Such a sweeping compilation of perspectives, understandings and theoretical frameworks, requires, within the scope of the project, being properly disseminated and actualized in order to encompass the on-going research. Thus, the theoretical target of the project concerns the effort to: (i) eliminate the redundancy usually observed in the varied usage of scientific terminology, (ii) incorporate new concepts, perspectives, theoretical frameworks and research topics, (iii) reframe the network of concepts and focus theories in the simplest possible way.

Targets (i) and (iii) can be rephrased in terms of the increase of *intensional performance*

Definition 3.1. *Intensional performance* is the capacity of a conceptual system C to refer a knowledge field K. The larger the relation between the extensions of K and C the larger the intentional performance of C.

Definition 3.2. The *relative intensional performance* of a set of definitions (re-framed) with respect to an original set is the relation between the number of definition in the original set with respect to the second, provided that K is preserved.

Thus, the intensional performance is better if a smaller set of definitions captures the same internal content as the original set.

In order to obtain guidance to increase performance at the theoretical level, a metatheory of knowledge systems, as addressed in Sect. 3.3, offers a cornerstone. To this end, a formal theory for the analysis and representation of knowledge integration is being developed [4, 9]. Its relevance, applied to the field of systems science was highlighted by Klir [27]: "The comparison of individual conceptual frameworks used in individual approaches to general systems theory appears to be very difficult. A metatheory must be used to decide whether one concept is identical to, is different from, or is a proper subset of a concept drawn from another theory".

Figure 2 illustrates the theoretical undertaking in the passage from the contents of the original corpora into *ESSCO*. An editorial team is committed to this work assisted by a scientific council. At the same time, this team is in charge of leveraging the participation of the systems science community and the proper integration of the new contributions into *ESSCO*.

Strengthening the Agent Network. As a measure to ensure participation of the scientific community (the counterpart of the fortification of the conceptual network), the contents of *ESSCO* (in continuous development) are linked to other dissemination and exploitation pathways (see Fig. 2 lower part), in particular, to scientific journals, encyclopedic editions, and scientific social networks [36]. In addition, a stakeholder engagement strategy contributes to leverage both scientific contributions from the community and dissemination of results.

3.3   Metatheoretical Level: Assessing Knowledge Integration

Using and advancing the methodology developed for the glossariumBITri [9, 10], glossaLAB aims at escorting this knowledge integration with the assessment of its performance (s. top right corner of Fig. 2). Just this achievement, concerning the qualification of knowledge integration, is considered by international institutions in charge of regional and global scientific policies as a necessary condition to strengthen the position of interdisciplinary and transdisciplinary research [6, 13–16].

The activity at this level is of two types: (i) the development of formal approaches to represent and analyze knowledge conceptualization and integration [4, 9], (ii) the application of these approaches to assess the achievements of knowledge integration at the theoretical level using the contents of the elucidation platform as proxies of the conceptual network [9].

Interdisciplinary-Glossary as Proxy of Knowledge Networks. In order to obtain a network of concepts corresponding to the theoretical framework already clarified, we follow a simple idea: the semantic network structure is derived from the meaning relations stablished by the authors in their own texts dedicated to the clarification of the conceptual network [9, 12].

In so far as an author's sentence implies a unit of sense, the syntactic co-occurrence of words (properly arranged in groups of derivative words) in the space of a sentence stablishes a semantic association to be explored in terms of link frequency [25]. For instance, if we observe a high co-occurrence degree between "link" and "connection", on the one hand; or "feedback" and "regulation", on the other, this is derived from the semantic proximity between these terms. In the first case, due to a relation of equivalence, in the other, due to a causal relation. In brief, the occurrence of terms and links enables the examination of the relevance of different categories and their semantic connection. Figure 5 shows the co-occurrence network corresponding to the glossariumBITri edition of 2016, filtered to relatively high frequency of terms and links (for more details about how to derive this network and the analysis of results derived from the network cf. [9, 10]). Besides the application to the assessment of knowledge integration, discussed in the referred literature, other applications of the co-occurrence networks, worth considering for future work, concerns the retrieval of definition statements in corpora [26] or the detection of semantic similarity [23].

Bi-Dimensional Assessment of Knowledge Integration. So far we have addressed the problem of assessing how far an interdisciplinary knowledge network is from the extremes of multidisciplinarity and transdisciplinarity. However, we have dismissed the relevance of the amplitude of the knowledge that is being integrated, i.e., the number and diversity of the disciplines convened. To bridge this gap, the qualification of knowledge integration concerns a double assessment:

- The **diversity of the contributing disciplines** (the more disciplines contributing the more diverse the knowledge integrated), and
- The **integration effectively achieved** through the collaboration of disciplines (the integration is weak if each discipline handles different aspects separately; the integration is sound if the theoretical constructs gets to merge into a general understanding of all the concept domain).

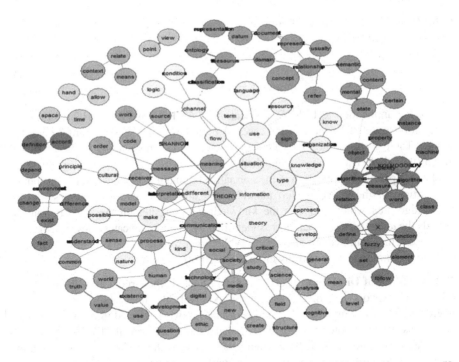

Fig. 5. Co-occurrence network of glossariumBITri edition of 2016 [11]. Term frequency >50 (130 most frequent concept-words); Most frequent links (thickness proportional to frequency); Colors: semantic clusters determined by intermediation measurements.

A. Discipline Diversity Index. To the purpose of evaluating this diversity, we draw on the Universal Decimal Classification (UDC) which has the virtue of covering all knowledge fields y a broadly accepted categorization of disciplines. But in order to apply it, we need first determining the granularity level in the distinction of disciplines. In a first approximation, this can be carried out determining the number of relevant UDC digits used to distinguish the knowledge areas involved in a particular research [30, 35, 37]. However an adaptive implementation of the UDC categories need to be introduced in our categorisation of *Knowledge Domains* (KD): (i) some UDC categories should be disregarded, for example, the ones not related to knowledge but to document typologies, (ii) some categories are scaled from a lower granularity level because of their relevance for the subject field, and (iii) some category groups have to be merged since correspond to different aspects of the same knowledge, for example, applied and theoretical.

Taking *N* as the number of considered KD, the diversity of participating disciplines is determined using *Shannon Diversity Index* weighted by the maximal value of diversity, which is attained by an equal participation of all the KD, that is $\log_2 N$. After normalization, the diversity index of an equalized participation of all the KD is 1, while for a single participant KD is 0. In general, the more KD and the more equal the participation, the index is closer to 1.

Definition 3.3. Calling p_i the frequency of occurrence of a contribution from the KD i the *diversity index* is:

$$DI = \frac{1}{\log_2 N} \sum_{i=1}^{N} p_i \log_2(1/p_i) \tag{1}$$

For the application to ESSCO, a selection of 67 KD have been selected from the UDC, corresponding in most of the cases to 2 digits of UDC code (about 7 per UDC group). Table 1 shows the first 10 categories selected corresponding to the first UDC group (the whole list has been published in [9]).

For the practical application of the normalized domain categories, each contribution (e.g. article of the encyclopedia) identifies the domain categories that best fits the knowledge area which supports the knowledge represented in the contribution. As regards the *agent network* each peer is identified by the domain categories matching her expertise. This identification also serves to the organization of the peer-review process and other communication and dissemination activities.

B. Integration of Disciplines. As discussed in Sect. 1, the structural properties of the conceptual network and of the actor network revels the integration capacity of the interdisciplinary setting at stake. A co-occurrence network derived from the elucidation corpus, as the one represented in Fig. 5, enables the assessment of integration properties (as shown in [9, 10]). To this purpose we use both quantitative and qualitative assessment. Regarding **quantitative assessment**, a good integrated conceptual network exhibits at a time, as discussed in Sect. 1.2 and [9]: low *average minimal distance* (between any two concept-words) and relatively high *clustering* (for an effective

Table 1. Knowledge Domain Categories selected for the classification of contributions.

i	Knowledge Domain (EN)	UDC code	Additional UDC fields covered by domain i + Clarifications
0	Generalities. Science and Knowledge. Organisation. Information. Documentation	0	# types/group: 10
00	Science and knowledge in general	001	
01	Documentation and Writing systems	002/003	
02	Computer science	004	
03	Management (including Knowledge management)	005	Do not confuse with 658 (business management)
04	Standardisation	006	
05	Activity and organizing. Control theory generally (systems science)	007	Do not confuse with the technical domain "Automatic Control" 681.5
06	Communication theory generally (incl. Information theory)	007	Do not confuse with the technical domain "Telecommunication and telecontrol" 654
07	Civilization. Culture	008	
08	Librarianship	02	01 + 03 + 05 + 07 / 09 01: bibliographies | 03: reference works | 05: serial publicat. | 07: newspapers | 08: polygraphed | 09: manuscripts
09	Organisations of a general nature	06	
⋮	⋮	⋮	

referencing of the concept domain, which can be smaller if the size of the network size is small). Thus, high *clustering coefficient, C*, and low *average minimal distance, L*, provides an indication of integration reached. Indeed, its ratio compared with the equivalent ratio for random networks correspond to the *small-world coefficient* which reflects the two factors contributing to the increase integration: $\sigma = {C}/{C_{rand}} \cdot {L_{rand}}/{L}$ which is used to measure knowledge integration.

In addition, the network analysis enables the **qualitative** identification of integration issues (as discussed in [9] for the case of glossariumBITri). This assessment provides specific and valuable guidance for the forward planning of the theoretical work.

4 Conclusions

In Sect. 1, we have presented the background problem addressed by glossaLAB project, namely, the fragmentation of knowledge derived from the epistemological grounding of modernity and the extension of the scientific enterprise. We have analyzed this problem using a network perspective applied to the levels of the conceptual network and the actor network in order to characterize the structural properties of poor and sound knowledge integration. In Sect. 2, we observed that project objectives focus on three big challenges: (i) the development of a sound theoretical framework for the unification of knowledge, (ii) the establishment of broadly accepted methodologies and tools to facilitate the integration of knowledge, (iii) the development of assessment criteria for the qualification of knowledge integration. In Sect. 3, we have seen the means adopted to address these challenges. To cope with (i), the project draws on systems sciences, which have been proven to provide a sound platform for the integration of knowledge in general, but requires overcoming differences between sub-disciplines, which is done departing from sound corpora. To cope with (ii), the project draws on well experienced methodologies derived from systems science, the interdisciplinary-glossaries developed in the past for similar endeavors, and technical solutions applied to numerous projects on knowledge co-creation. And finally to cope with (iii), a novel methodology to assess knowledge integration is devised, based on sound theoretical underpinnings.

Acknowledgements. The authors wish to dedicate this work to the memory of Charles François. His work represents an invaluable and everlasting contribution to the integration of knowledge to which glossaLAB project is devoted. We are indebted to his legacy. This contribution has been carried out under support of glossaLAB project, co-founded by the Universidad Estatal Península de Santa Elena, Ecuador, and an international consortium of academic institutions.

References

1. Ackrill, J.L. (eds): Aristotle: Categories and De Interpretatione. Clarendon Press, Oxford (1963)
2. Aguado, J.M.: Endogenous Information. In: Díaz-Nafría, J.M.; Salto, F.; Pérez-Montoro, M. (coord.): glossariumBITri: Interdisciplinary Elucidation of Concepts, Metaphors, Theories and Problems concerning Information, pp. 76–80. UPSE-BITrum, La Libertad (Ecuador)-León (Spain) (2016). Book edition: https://goo.gl/QnJpQ4. Accessed 1 June 2019

3. Barabási, A.-L.: Linked: The New Science of Networks. Perseus, Cambridge (2002)
4. Burgin, M., Díaz-Nafría, J.M.: Introduction to the mathematical theory of knowledge integration: Conceptual systems and structures. In: Proceedings of the Second International Conference on Applied Informatics. Communications in Computer and Information Science (2019, in Press)
5. Burgin, M., Hofkirchner, W. (eds.): Information Studies and the Quest for Transdisciplinarity: Unity through Diversity. World Scientific, New York (2017)
6. DEA-FBE: Thinking Across Disciplines – Interdisciplinarity in Research and Education. Danish Business Research Academy (DEA) & Danish Forum for Business Education (FBE), Copenhagen (2008). http://cordis.europa.eu/news/rcn/118314_en.html. Accessed 1 Dec 2017
7. Descartes, R.: Discourse on the method of rightly conducing the reason and seeking for truth in the sciences. In: Adler, M. (ed.) Great Books of Western World, vol. 31, pp. 41–68. Encyclopaedia Britannica, Chicago (1952)
8. Díaz-Nafría, J.: Cyber-subsidiarity: toward a global sustainable information society. In: Carayannis, E., Campbell, D., Efthymiopoulos, M. (eds.) Handbook of Cyber-Development, Cyber-Democracy, and Cyber-Defense, pp. 1–30. Springer, Cham (2017). https://doi.org/10.1007/978-3-319-06091-0_39-1
9. Díaz-Nafría, J.M.; Burgin, M.; Rodríguez-Bravo, B.: Evaluation of knowledge integration through knowledge structures and conceptual networks. In: Dodig-Crnkovic, G., Burgin, M. (eds.) Philosophy and Methodology of Information, pp. 457–489. World Scientific Publishing, Singapore (2019). https://doi.org/10.1142/9789813277526_0021
10. Díaz-Nafría, J.M., Guarda, T., Coronel, I.: A network theoretical approach to assess knowledge integration in information studies. Smart Innov. Syst. Technol. **94**, 360–371 (2018). https://doi.org/10.1007/978-3-319-78605-6_31
11. Díaz-Nafría, J.M., Salto, F., Pérez-Montoro, M. (coord.): glossariumBITri: interdisciplinary elucidation of concepts, metaphors, theories and problems concerning information. UPSE-BITrum, Libertad, Ecuador/León, Spain (2016). E-book: https://goo.gl/QnJpQ4. Accessed 1 Aug 2019. Interactive version: http://glossarium.bitrum.unileon.es/glossary. Accessed 1 Aug 2019
12. Drieger, P.: Semantic network analysis as a method for visual text analytics. Procedia Soc. Behav. Sci. **79**, 4–17 (2013). https://doi.org/10.1016/j.sbspro.2013.05.053
13. EC: New societal challenges for the European Union – New challenges for social sciences and humanities. Thinking across boundaries – Modernising European Research. Publication Office of the EU, Luxembourg (2009). https://ec.europa.eu/research/participants/portal/doc/call/fp7/fp7-ssh-2013-1/32839-booklet-new-societal-challenges_en.pdf. Accessed 1 June 2019
14. EC: Communication from the Commission: Horizon 2020 - The Framework Programme for Research and Innovation. COM/2011/0808 final, European Commission, Brussels (2011). http://eur-lex.europa.eu/legal-content/EN/TXT/?uri=CELEX:52011DC0808. Accessed 1 June 2019
15. EURAB Interdisciplinarity in Research. Final Report. European Commission - European Research Advisory Board (EURAB). European Commission, Brussels (2004). https://ec.europa.eu/research/eurab/pdf/eurab_04_009_interdisciplinarity_research_final.pdf. Accessed 1 June 2019
16. EURAB: The new Renaissance: will it happen? Innovating Europe out of the crisis. Third and Final Report of the European Research Area Board. European Commission-European Research Area Board, Brussels. European Commission, Brussels (2012). http://ec.europa.eu/research/erab/pdf/3rd-erab-final-report_en.pdf. Accessed 1 June 2019

17. François, C. (dir.): Internacional Enciclopaedia of Systems and Cybernetics. K.G. Saur, Munich (2004)
18. Fairhurst, G.T., Grant, D.: The social construction of leadership: a sailing guide. Manag. Commun. Q. **24**(2), 171–210 (2010)
19. Frodeman, R., Klein, J.T., Mitcham, C. (eds.): The Oxford Handbook of Interdisciplinarity. Oxford University Press, Oxford (2010)
20. Goldman, A.; Blanchard, T.: Social epistemolog. In: Zalta, E.N. (ed.) The Stanford Encyclopedia of Philosophy. Stanford University, Stanford, California (2018). https://plato.stanford.edu/archives/sum2018/entries/epistemology-social/. Accessed 28 June 2019
21. d'Hainaut, L.: Interdisciplinarity in General Education. UNESCO, Paris (1986)
22. Heylighen, F., Joslyn, C., Turchin, V. (eds.): Principia Cybernetica Web. Principia Cybernetica Project, Brussels (2016). http://cleamc11.vub.ac.be/REFERPCP.html. Accessed 1 June 2019
23. Islam, A., Inkpen, D.: Semantic text similarity using corpus-based word similarity and string similarity. ACM Trans. Knowl. Discov. Data. **2**(2), 10.1–10.25 (2008). https://doi.org/10.1145/1376815.1376819
24. Izhikevich, E.M.: Scholarpedia. Scholarpedia the peer-reviewed open-access encyclopedia **1**(2), 1 (2006). https://doi.org/10.4249/scholarpedia.1
25. Jackson, K.M., Trochim, W.M.: Concept mapping as an alternative approach for the analysis of open-ended survey responses. Organ. Res. Methods **5**(4), 307–336. https://doi.org/10.1177/109442802237114
26. Jiang, J, Allan, J.: Similarity-based distant supervision for definition retrieval. In: Proceedings of the 2017 ACM on Conference on Information and Knowledge Management (CIKM 2017), pp. 527–536. ACM, New York (2017). https://doi.org/10.1145/3132847.3133032
27. Klir, G.J. (ed.): Trend in General Systems Theory. Wiley, New York (1972)
28. Lakatos, I.: The Methodology of Scientific Research Programmes. Cambridge University Press, Cambridge (1978)
29. Leibniz, G.W.: New Essays Concerning Human Understanding. Cambridge University Press, Cambridge (1996)
30. McIlwaine, I.C.: Universal Decimal Classification: A Guide to Its Use, revised edn. UDC Consortium, The Hague (2007). Preprint: https://arxiv.org/abs/1705.07058. Accessed 11 Aug 2019
31. MediaWiki: MediaWiki.org. Wikimedia Foundation, Inc., San Francisco, CA (2016). https://www.mediawiki.org. Accessed 1 June 2019
32. de Millo, R.A., Lipton, R.J., Perlis, A.: Social processes and proofs of theorems and programs. Comm. ACM, **22**(5), 271–280 (1979)
33. NAS: Facilitating Interdisciplinary Research. National Academy of Sciences (NAS), National Academy of Engineering (NAE) and Institute of Medicine (IM). The National Academies Press, Washington (2005). https://www.nap.edu/catalog/11153/facilitating-interdisciplinary-research. Accessed 1 June 2019
34. Porphyry: On Aristotle Categories. Bloomsbury Publishing, London (2014). noor
35. Slavic, A.: Classification revisited: a web of knowledge. In: Foster, A., Rafferty (eds.) Innovations in Information Retrieval: Perspectives for Theory and Practice, pp. 23–48. Facet, London (2011)
36. Van Noorden, R.: Scientists and the Social Network. Nature **512**, 126–129 (2014). https://doi.org/10.1038/512126a
37. UDC Consortium: UDC Fact Sheet. In: UDCC website, UDC Consortium. The Hague (2017). http://www.udcc.org/index.php/site/page?view=factsheet. Accessed 1 June 2019

ICT and Science: Some Characteristics of Scientific Networks and How They Apply Information Technology

Simone Belli[1](✉) 🆔 and Ernesto Ponsot[2](✉) 🆔

[1] Universidad Complutense de Madrid, Madrid, Spain
sbelli@ucm.es
[2] Yachay Tech, Urcuquí, Ecuador
ernesto.pb@gmail.com
https://www.ucm.es/dep-antsocypssoc/cv-simone-belli

Abstract. In every discipline, we observed the so-called "digital turn" or the digital transformation in scientific collaboration. A survey was designed and applied to researchers within the framework of the H2020 project EULAC Focus. The researchers consulted embrace different disciplines and are located in different universities and research institutes. There are 305 different interviews and 159 variables or observed responses. The research explores how information and communication technologies in this specific professional setting have affected the way in which research teams are related. In particular, this investigation explores the extent to which scientific networks are composed and how they collaborate thanks to the applied informatics, observing the digital tools used by researchers to communicate and collaborate.

Keywords: Scientific collaborations · Digital transformation · Research groups · Scientific publications · Scientific networks

1 Introduction

Unlike previous generations, researchers today have a seemingly endless variety of potential scientific collaborations and research networks available through digital tools based on applied informatics. Thanks to the Internet, less time and efforts are required to begin and manage a scientific collaboration. Some studies have shown that Internet-mediated collaboration is generally thought to increase scientific productivity [1,2].

This article explores how information and communication technologies in this specific professional setting have affected the way research teams are related. A research team or group is conceived as any contact network integrated by at least 2 researchers, with a common purpose, regardless of whether or not they belong to the same institution, different institutions or even different countries. In particular, this investigation explores the extent to which scientific networks are

H. Florez et al. (Eds.): ICAI 2019, CCIS 1051, pp. 438–452, 2019.
https://doi.org/10.1007/978-3-030-32475-9_32

composed and how they obtain and manage information thanks to digital transformation. Observing the ways of communication and collaboration of research teams, information search and access to the knowledge, and the major trends and changes they have perceived in the last years.

In this paper, we are interested in identifying which are the digital mechanisms that account for success in scientific collaborations and the principles of co-evolution of the digital infrastructures in scientific communities. For this purpose, a survey was designed and applied to researchers within the framework of the EULAC Focus project. The researchers consulted embrace different disciplines and are located in different countries. The objective was to study how the new information and communication technologies have affected the way research groups are related. The first response was recorded on 12/16/2016 and the last on 2/13/2018. Members belong to both European and American countries. There are 305 different interviews and 159 variables or observed responses. As to date there is limited research specifically on digital tools based on applied informatics, this study aims to be an exploratory investigation that identifies the various affordances and transformations provided by the technologies, with the intent of also highlighting areas in need of further research.

These are the two hypotheses that have guided this research:

- *Hypothesis 1.* Scientists working in local research teams tend to have less scientific collaborations/publications.
- *Hypothesis 2.* Scientists tend to use online tools for the production of scientific collaborations/publications.

To test these hypotheses, we will observe the size of the networks of the researchers, its structure (local or global), the frequency of interactions and the modality (analogical or digital tool) in relation to the number of publications.

What follows is a brief review of the existing literature and the study's methodology, and then a more in-depth exploration of emerging patterns of usage and their professional consequences.

2   Methodology

2.1   Design and Measurements of the Survey

This is a quantitative research consisting of an online survey sent to a multi-stage random sample of European and Latin America and Caribbean university researchers in all disciplines via email from the accounts of the members of the EULAC Focus project (10 scientific institution in Latin American and Caribbean countries, and 9 in European Union) to their scientific networks connection and institutional colleagues.

The invitation was then subsequently shared via email and social networks (Twitter, Facebook, LinkedIn, ResearchGate, Academia.edu) by willing network connections in a 'snowballing' fashion [3]. While the 'snowball method' can have epistemological limitations with regards to generating statistically significant representative samples, the research method is nevertheless capable of collecting data indicative of broader social patterns and trends, especially when the survey reaches a broad cohort of participants [3–6].

The study population contains researchers, including Ph.D. students and postdoctoral researchers. The questionnaire contained items relating to digital transformation in science, detailed questions about digital communication and scientific production, in addition to questions about their research activities. In terms of statistics, the methodology includes a combination of descriptive and inferential analyses based on the data collected. For the inferences, the Poisson regression model [7] is used, in its variant that corrects the over dispersion present in the data, quasi Poisson. This model, a member of the family of generalized linear models [8], has a clear application when the response variable is the product of case counting and seeks to determine rates associated with a period of time (here, number of publications per year). All data processing was done in R Statistical Software [9].

The objective was to study how the new information and communication technologies have affected the way in which work teams are related through 159 variables or observed responses. The survey consisted of a combination of open-ended, multiple-choice and Likert-scale questions and took approximately 15–20 min to complete.

Only a subset of the variables collected in the survey are used for current analysis. There are three variables that are constructed from others:

- PubTotal: contains the total number of publications reported in the survey.
- PubScience: contains only the number of publications considered as scientific.
- Loc: Contains the grouping of locations of reported team members.

2.2   Data Collection

The first response to the survey was recorded on 12/16/2016 and the last on 2/13/2018. Members belong to both European countries and American countries, for a total of 18 countries. The survey had a total of 305 respondents, of whom most, but not all, answered all questions under consideration. In addition, for this research, the responses of those interviewed who indicated that they worked alone were not considered, only those who indicated that they were working as a team or both. In terms of gender, 4 people preferred not to inform (1%), 101 are female (34%) and 200 are male (66%). This leaves a total of 264 interviews to consider. Figure 1 shows the demographic pyramid of the surveyed.

The figure shows that those responding to the survey are mostly male, with ages between 33 and 45 years old. Moreover, female scientists face 'patrifocal' constraints in some developing world cultures that limit their access to new technologies and the ability to network outside the domestic arena [10]. Age is also a social factor that differentiates access to social networks (generally favoring experience and tenure) and technology adoption and use (generally favoring youth). In combination, unequal access to network and technology resources

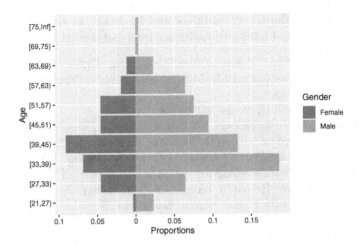

Fig. 1. Demographic pyramid of the sample

along regional, gender and age dimensions can be grouped together under the phrase 'geo-social asymmetries' [1].

Detailed demographic information was collected from the research participants, because it is one of the main objective of the EULAC Focus project. Researchers from 18 different countries were surveyed, 67% of the respondents work in an Ecuadorian university, followed by Mexican universities (14%) and Spanish universities (5%). There is an obvious bias towards Ecuador, because the principal researcher is based in this country. All other countries represent 13% of the sample. For regions, we have 1% from USA, 9% from European Union, and 90% from Latin American and Caribbean Countries.

The majority of participants work in universities (92%), where they are professors (68%), graduate students (13%), and post docs (5%). There is a balance between the surveyed who embrace scientific or technical careers and humanistic or artistic careers.

3   Results

3.1   Scientific Production

In this first section of our results, we will focus on the production of the researchers that have answered all the questions of the survey. Two response variables were constructed, considering the sum of the total (PubTotal) and the scientific production (PubScience) measured in publications count terms. Both are counting variables, suggesting the use of the Poisson distribution. In the data set the estimated mean for the total production is 10.06 and its estimated variance is 86.93. For scientific production, the estimated mean and variance are 7.99, 53.49, respectively. So, we note over-dispersion problems. For this reason, quasi-Poisson regression models are proposed for its analysis.

The following is the list of variables and its levels, in case it is not of a numerical type. The first level is the reference level and is written in italic letters.

- **Country**: *Argentina*, Brazil, Chile, Colombia, Cuba, Czech Republic, Ecuador, France, Germany, Italy, Mexico, Netherlands, Peru, Portugal, Spain, UK, USA, Venezuela.
- **Gender**: *Female*, Male, Prefer not to say.
- **Position**: *Academic technician*, Associate Professor/Reader, Director, Doctoral student, Head of Hospital Teaching, Lecturer/Fellow, Master, Masters student, Occasional Professor, Official Radiation Protection, Post Doc/Assistant, Private company worker, Professor, Project Manager, Research Assistant, Research technician, Researcher, Scientific Director, Senior Lecturer/Senior Fellow, Senior Researcher, Student.
- **InsType**: *Government*, Private Sector, Public Research Institute, University.
- **Discipline**: *Agricultural Sciences*, Astronomy And Astrophysis, Chemistry, Earth Sciences, Economic Sciences, Geography, History, Legal Sciences And Law, Life Sciences, Linguistics, Mathematics, Medical Sciences, Other, Pedagogy, Physics, Politic Science, Psychology, Science (Field Not Defined), Science Of Arts And Letters, Science of Earth And Space, Sociology, Technological Science.
- **AloneTeam**: *Alone*, Both, Team.
- **LocSameIns**: *FALSE*, TRUE.
- **LocDiffIns**: *FALSE*, TRUE.
- **LocDiffCou**: *FALSE*, TRUE.
- **FreqInt**: *Bi-weekly*, Daily, Less often, Monthly, No answer, Twice a week, Weekly.
- **ContactLetter**: *Essential*, No answer, Not Used, Used.
- **ContactPhone**: *Essential*, No answer, Not Used, Used.
- **ContactEmail**: *Essential*, No answer, Not Used, Used.
- **ContactList**: *Essential*, No answer, Not Used, Used.
- **ContactInsMess**: *Essential*, No answer, Not Used, Used.
- **ContactVideoC**: *Essential*, No answer, Not Used, Used.
- **Age**: (Numeric).
- **pubTotal**: (Numeric).
- **pubScience**: (Numeric).
- **TeamSize**: (Numeric).
- **Loc**: *DiffIns*, DiffIns/DiffCou, SameIns, SameIns/DiffCou, SameIns/DiffIns, SameIns/DiffIns/DiffCou.

A first, purely additive, quasi-Poisson regression model to study the association between the response variable (pubTotal) and the remaining explanatory variables is as follows:

$$\log(\lambda_1) = Country + Gender + InsType + Position \tag{1}$$
$$+ AloneTeam + Discipline + Loc + FreqInt + ContactLetter$$
$$+ ContactPhone + ContactEmail + ContactList + ContactInsMess$$
$$+ ContactVideoC + Age + TeamSize$$

where λ_1 is the rate of total publications per year.

Tables 1 and 2 contains the analysis of deviance of the model factors, with terms added sequentially (first to last). The reference level in each case is the first. In bold type are indicated the factors that are significant at $\alpha = 0.1$ (that is, with 90% confidence)[1].

Table 1. Analysis of deviance for total production (1).

	Df	Deviance	Resid. Df	Resid. Dev	Pr(>Chi)
NULL			263	1731.06	
Country	17	171.41	246	1559.66	**0.0228**
Gender	1	2.41	245	1557.25	0.5124
InsType	3	7.38	242	1549.87	0.7258
Position	18	201.36	224	1348.51	**0.0074**
AloneTeam	1	1.99	223	1346.52	0.5515
Discipline	19	230.27	204	1116.25	**0.0024**
Loc	5	51.75	199	1064.50	0.1008
FreqInt	5	29.72	194	1034.79	0.3813
ContactLetter	2	2.56	192	1032.23	0.7963
ContactPhone	2	43.90	190	988.33	**0.0201**
ContactEmail	2	1.61	188	986.71	0.8662
ContactList	2	39.29	186	947.42	**0.0302**
ContactInsMess	2	29.25	184	918.17	**0.0739**
ContactVideoC	2	51.21	182	866.96	**0.0105**
Age	1	10.11	181	856.85	0.1798
TeamSize	1	20.65	180	836.20	**0.0552**

Now, scientific production refers to the number of publications per year that take into account only those considered as scientific production, so that if λ_2 is the rate of annual scientific publications (pubScience), a second purely additive model proposed is:

$$\log(\lambda_2) = Country + Gender + InsType + Position \qquad (2)$$
$$+ AloneTeam + Discipline + Loc + FreqInt + ContactLetter$$
$$+ ContactPhone + ContactEmail + ContactList + ContactInsMess$$
$$+ ContactVideoC + Age + TeamSize$$

Comparing the results of Tables 1 and 2, it is important that the "Loc" factor is not significant when explaining the total publications, but it explains

---

[1] Hereafter, Df: Degrees of freedom. Resid: Residual. Dev: Deviance. Pr(>Chi) [or Pr(> |t|)]: p-value.

the scientific production. It is clear that the location of researchers in a team work has an impact on scientific production and not on all the publications. This activity can be done individually for the researcher with local and national means. Consequently, we will concentrate on scientific publications exclusively to analyze how liquid science is distributed in the scientific networks.

Table 2. Analysis of deviance for scientific production (2).

	Df	Deviance	Resid. Df	Resid. Dev	Pr(>Chi)
NULL			263	1325.94	
Country	17	118.50	246	1207.44	**0.0546**
Gender	1	0.43	245	1207.01	0.7534
InsType	3	8.46	242	1198.56	0.5839
Position	18	164.67	224	1033.88	**0.0040**
AloneTeam	1	3.31	223	1030.57	0.3827
Discipline	19	159.59	204	870.98	**0.0087**
Loc	5	43.12	199	827.86	**0.0777**
FreqInt	5	18.53	194	809.33	0.5126
ContactLetter	2	2.62	192	806.71	0.7399
ContactPhone	2	29.38	190	777.33	**0.0341**
ContactEmail	2	3.71	188	773.62	0.6527
ContactList	2	35.49	186	738.13	**0.0169**
ContactInsMess	2	16.60	184	721.53	0.1483
ContactVideoC	2	37.42	182	684.11	**0.0135**
Age	1	9.28	181	674.83	0.1442
TeamSize	1	22.79	180	652.04	**0.0221**

On the other hand, in Table 2, Gender, InsType, AloneTeam, FreqInt, ContactLetter, ContactEmail, ContactInsMess and Age factors are not significant, and will be excluded in the search for a more parsimonious model. This does not mean that they are not important, but that nowadays they do not seem to make a difference in scientific production, e.g. male or female essentially produce in the same way, and email and other forms of contacts excluded are valued by all of them in similar ways. Then the new model for pubScience is:

$$\log(\lambda_3) = Country + Position + Discipline + Loc + ContactPhone$$
$$+ ContactList + ContactVideoC + TeamSize \tag{3}$$

Table 3 contains the analysis of variance of the model, now considering the levels of the factors versus the reference level. For space reasons the table include only levels that were significant for factors Country, Position and Discipline.

Table 3. ANOVA for scientific production (3).

	Estimate	Std. Error	t value	Pr(> |t|)	Exp
(Intercept)	1.97	1.03	1.92	**0.06**	7.20
CountryPeru	1.57	0.70	2.24	**0.03**	4.79
PositionResearch technician	−3.28	1.56	−2.10	**0.04**	0.04
DisciplineOther	0.74	0.40	1.86	**0.06**	2.09
LocDiffIns/DiffCou	0.09	0.21	0.41	0.68	1.09
LocSameIns	−0.03	0.16	−0.17	0.86	0.97
LocSameIns/DiffCou	−0.19	0.31	−0.62	0.53	0.82
LocSameIns/DiffIns	−0.39	0.22	−1.77	**0.08**	0.68
LocSameIns/DiffIns/DiffCou	−0.06	0.16	−0.39	0.70	0.94
ContactPhoneNot Used	−0.36	0.19	−1.91	**0.06**	0.70
ContactPhoneUsed	−0.27	0.13	−2.13	**0.03**	0.76
ContactListNot Used	0.11	0.18	0.59	0.56	1.11
ContactListUsed	0.34	0.17	2.03	**0.04**	1.40
ContactVideoCNot Used	−0.55	0.19	−2.85	**0.00**	0.58
ContactVideoCUsed	−0.19	0.12	−1.61	0.11	0.83
TeamSize	0.02	0.01	2.44	**0.02**	1.02

Table 3 is produced by fitting a quasi-Poisson regression model, since we assume that there is over dispersion in the sample. We add a column Exp with the exponentiation of the parameters estimates. The dispersion parameter Φ is estimated in 4.31, so the estimated variance is $7.99 \times 4.31 = 34.44$, near that one estimated directly from the data (53.49). The model goodness of fit is poor, as can be seen from the residual deviance (715.12) and residual degrees of freedom (197). Nevertheless, this is to be expected since only a very small subset of all the variables that would explain the variability is used.

All the factors in Table 3 are significant because at least one of its levels is significant. Then, we can interpret the estimators obtained from the model. Because the model fits in a logarithmic scale, the explanation is clearer by returning to the linear scale. Then, in mathematical terms the model (3) is:

$$\log(\lambda_3) = \beta_0 + \beta_1 x_1 + \beta_2 x_2 + \beta_3 x_3 + \beta_4 x_4 + \beta_5 x_5 + \beta_6 x_6 + \beta_7 x_7 + \beta_8 x_8$$

where the estimated parameters are the $\beta_i, (i = 0, 1, \cdots, 8)$, β_0 is the intercept, and the values of the variables, x_i. The β_i are really vectors, because they accompany categorical variables that have one parameter for each level of the factor (minus the reference), except β_8 because TeamSize is a numerical variable and β_0. Then

$$\lambda_3 = \exp(\beta_0 + \beta_1 x_1 + \beta_2 x_2 + \beta_3 x_3 + \beta_4 x_4 + \beta_5 x_5 + \beta_6 x_6 + \beta_7 x_7 + \beta_8 x_8)$$

and if the other variables remain constant, the effect of the i-th variable on the mean λ_3 is $\exp(\beta_i x_i) = (e^{\beta_i})^{x_i}$ and every unit of increment in the variable x_i produces a multiplicative effect of e^{β_i} in the response λ_3.

In the next sub-sections we analyze each of the significant factors (levels) in relation to scientific publications productivity.

The Country: Figure 2 shows the box plot of pubScience by country. The highest median values in the sample correspond to Peru, Spain, and Venezuela, however, only the number of scientific publications in Peru is significantly different from the rest according to our model (3). This is because the reported with respect to Spain and Venezuela has a high variance.

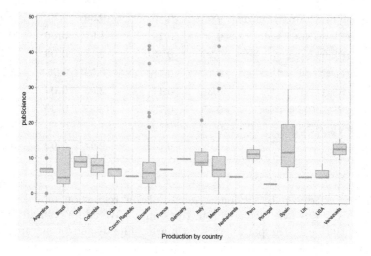

Fig. 2. Box plot of scientific publications by country

According to Table 3, the coefficient associated with Peru is 1.57, exponentiating 4.79, then a researcher from Peru has an estimated 4.8 times more scientific publications than a researcher from Argentina (reference level).

Position: The only significant level with respect to the position is Research technician. Its estimated coefficient is negative (-3.28), exponentiating 0.04, then research technicians have 0.04 times the number of publications that academic technicians (the reference level) and also that the rest of positions.

Discipline (Specialty): According to Table 3, the only significant level for discipline is Other. The scientific production is greater than the rest, but surely this is because in this category there are several different disciplines together. Consequently, the only interesting conclusion in this case is that there do not seem to be significant differences in the scientific production of the disciplines explicitly considered.

Location: In Fig. 3 the proportions of the research teams are shown, according to whether their members belong to the same institution (SameInst), to a different institution (DiffInst), to institutions of other countries (OtherCountry) or its combinations. The majority of their networks is located in the same institution (36%), 24% of the participants have colleagues in the same or in different institutions of the same country or in different countries. 20% of the sample report colleagues only from different institutions. The rest has similar interpretations. These proportions are useful to know the distribution of the research teams, and to know if the group is international or not.

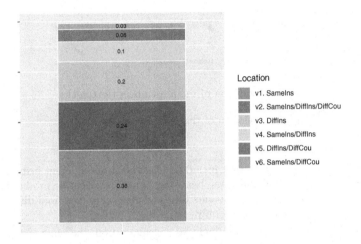

Fig. 3. Location of team members (proportions)

Figure 4 shows the box graphs for pubScience of each location level. The medians and variability displayed in figure do not show many differences for each level of location, however it is clear that those researchers who reported working mainly alone have the lowest productivity of the sample, while those who reported work both alone and with other institutions and other countries show the highest productivity.

According to our model, SameIns/DiffIns is the only factor that is significant. Its coefficient is -0.39, exponentiating 0.68, then the team that includes colleagues from the same institution and different institutions, has 0.68 times the scientific production than those teams that include colleagues from different institutions only (the reference level). Given the importance of these variables for the study, Table 4 contains similar explanations for the rest of the Location levels.

Then, it is interesting that the sample consulted reports a higher productivity if working in teams with different institutions only or different institutions and different countries. This result confirms Hypothesis 1 in the sense that productivity is estimated to increase when the research teams include members from

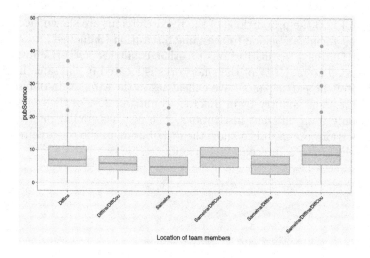

Fig. 4. Location of team members (boxplot)

Table 4. Location of the team members' analysis.

Level	exp(Est.)	Comment
DiffIns/ DiffCou	1.09	Teams that includes colleagues from different institutions and countries, has 1.091 times the scientific production that those teams that includes colleagues from different institutions only
SameIns	0.97	Teams that includes colleagues from the same institution only, has 0.97 times the number of scientific publications that those teams that includes colleagues from different institutions only
SameIns/ DiffCou	0.82	Teams that includes colleagues from the same institution and different countries, has 0.82 times the scientific production that those that includes colleagues from different institutions only
SameIns/ DiffIns/ DiffCou	0.94	Teams that includes colleagues from the same institution, different institutions and countries, has 0.94 times the scientific production that those teams that includes colleagues from different institutions only

different countries, and not just locals. This increase is slight but appreciable, as indicated by the first row of the Table 4.

Contact Means: The way we propose to analyze the scientific networks and how these networks work is to examine the construction of the links between researchers and the use of different technologies, analogical and digital. Researchers and analogical-or-digital devices constitute this network of a scientific community where everything is constantly under mediation and cooperation.

By focusing on the tools to communicate with the colleagues, we can observe how these have changed in the last years. Researchers have passed from analogical to digital tools to communicate with the rest of colleagues. The form to communicate in professional settings, and not, have changed strongly with the increase of the numbers of national and international networks. In Fig. 5, it can be possible to observe how researchers communicate with the rest of the nodes of their networks using analogical tools (Letters, Phone Calls) and digital tools based on applied informatics (Emails, Mailing Lists, Instant messaging, Video conference).

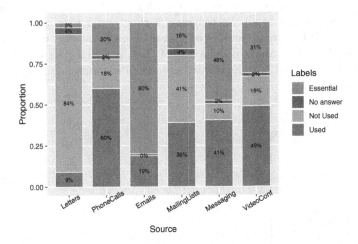

Fig. 5. All the mechanisms of contact the team members.

In Fig. 5, it can be observed how letters are not used by 84% (n = 256) of the researchers, converting it in an obsolete tool. A majority of researchers (80%, n = 244) agree that emails are essential in their professional tasks. This great agreement among the interviewees explains why these factors are not significant in our model.

In the last years messaging services via mobile have increased their impact to communicate between colleagues. For researchers, this service is considered essential and useful (89%, n = 269). Among the factors that are significant (see Table 3. The reference level is "essential"), we have:

- Phone: Respondents who say they have not used it have 0.7 times the scientific production than those who consider it essential. And those who say they have (but is not essential) has 0.76 times the scientific production than those who consider it essential. Clearly the use of the telephone is essential.
- Lists: Interviewees who say they have not used them have 1.11 times the scientific production than those who consider it essential. And who say they

have (but are not essential) have 1.4 times the scientific production than those who consider it essential. The use of lists is necessary but not essential.

– Video: Respondents who say they have not used them have 0.58 times the scientific production than those who consider it essential. And those who say they have (but is not essential) have 0.83 times the scientific production than those who consider it essential. Clearly the use of the video conference must be considered essential.

So, considering the use of the telephone and video conferencing as essential, as well as using the lists as a means of communication, increases the scientific productivity of the team. This affirms Hypothesis 2, since these mechanisms are characteristic of the digital era in communications.

The Size of the Network: One important question of the analysis is to understand if the researcher works in a collective way, if they prefer to work in a research team or alone. Only a small number of researchers, 6% (n = 19) work alone, and are excluded from this analysis. The size of their research groups is between 3 and 6 persons (63%), 34% of the researchers work in groups that have more than 6 researchers (see Fig. 6).

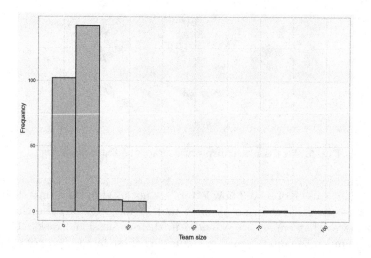

Fig. 6. Size of the research groups.

According to our model, each member that is added to the team increases 1.02 times the number of scientific publications. The importance of working in a team is evident.

4   Discussion

We have observed that more productive researchers work in medium and big research groups to achieve important results, and in consequence, to increase the number of scientific publications. Members of these research groups must come from different institutions and different countries to have advances in science. Heterogeneity of a research group is a determining variable to observe if the team can have a positive record or not.

It is surprising that in a digital era where the communication is instant and run to the screens, personal telephone conversations are considered essential to have great professional relations with the colleagues. Of course that emails and instant messaging are considered essential too, but phone conversations are needed to negotiate and to be clear between partners in order not to incur in misunderstandings caused by a text message. The use of this type of communication increases the number of scientific publications and scientific collaborations.

Video conferences are an evolution of phone conversations, where the body and facial expressions help to add more details to the voice, and for this it is considered essential to be more productive in science. This digital infrastructure based on applied informatics helps researchers to share and distribute scientific facilities regardless of their type and location in the world. Liquid science has increased collaborations between researchers, institutions and countries, creating a digital scientific infrastructure. In this new era, the effective and multimodal communication in teamwork is essential.

5 Conclusions

The most representative changes that digital communication in scientific networks has provided to the scientific community are mainly two: (1) The efficiency related to communication, and, (2) The information and knowledge flow.

The exploratory and explanatory findings offered by this study suggest that researchers view the digital transformation of science as welcome intermediaries to create and manage scientific networks. The majority of this study's participants believed that technology merely enhanced their abilities to work in scientific networks, increasing the number of their scientific publications.

Hypotheses 1 is confirmed since teams that include different institutions and countries show greater scientific productivity than teams composed only of local researchers. Hypothesis 2 is also confirmed as communications through digital media such as telephone, video conferencing or electronic lists are used and considered essential by those teams that show greater scientific productivity. A very clear recommendation is then that the research teams try to include among their members, researchers from different countries and get ready to use intensive media of the contemporary era.

Somewhat superficial and not specific, traditional views on the difference between analogic and digital tools is still largely prevalent. However, the conclusions that can be drawn from our analysis should be limited for three reasons. First, the lack of representatives of different countries; the research was carried out mainly in only three of them for the survey (Ecuador, Mexico, and Spain). Although, we have chosen these countries according to the availability of researchers that collaborate with the members of EULAC Focus project.

Thus, further research is needed. Second, the analysis related only to the uses of researchers from different disciplines and at different stages of their careers. These researchers can adopt and shape not shared perceptions of the digital tools that they use. Finally, data do not allow to test if these scientific networks generate some positive results to the research, or they are not competitive like other scientific networks, for example not build on digital technology. The project has bias that can conduct the researcher to respond in a positive way to the introduction of digital technology in their scientific activities and networks.

In the future, it is expected to improve the planning of the survey, seeking the prior construction of a specific sample framework. This, although difficult on a world scale, is worth it because it would allow to represent countries and different configurations of work teams in a better way.

Funding. This project has received funding from the European Union's Horizon 2020 research and innovation programme under grant agreement No 693781 – "Giving focus to the Cultural, Scientific and Social Dimension of EU – CELAC Relations".

References

1. Duque, R.B., Shrum, W.M., Barriga, O., Henriquez, G.: Internet practice and professional networks in Chilean science: dependency or progress? Scientometrics **81**(1), 239–263 (2009)
2. Olson, G.M., Zimmerman, A., Bos, N. (eds.): Science on the Internet. MIT Press, Cambridge (2008)
3. Hobbs, M., Owen, S., Gerber, L.: Liquid Love? Dating apps, sex, relationships and the digital transformation of intimacy. J. Sociol. **53**(2), 271–284 (2017)
4. Atkinson, R., Flint, J.: Sampling, snowball: accessing hidden and hard-to-reach populations. In: Miller, R.L., Brewer, J.D. (eds.) The A-Z of Social Research, pp. 274–280. Sage, London (2003)
5. Denscombe, M.: The Good Research Guide: For Small-scale Social Research Projects, 4th edn. McGraw-Hill, Maidenhead (2010)
6. Neuman, W.L.: Social Research Methods: Qualitative and Quantitative Approaches, 7th edn. Pearson, Boston (2011)
7. Agresti, A.: Foundations of Linear and Generalized Linear Models. Wiley, New Jersey (2015)
8. Nelder, J., Wedderburn, R.W.M.: Generalized linear models. J. R. Stat. Soc. A **135**, 370–384 (1972)
9. R Core Team: R: A Language and Environment for Statistical Computing. R Foundation for Statistical Computing, Vienna, Austria. https://www.R-project.org/. Accessed 4 Jan 2019
10. Palackal, A., Anderson, M., Miller, P., Shrum, W.: Internet equalizer? Gender stratification and normative circumvention in science. Indian J. Gend. Stud. **14**, 231–257 (2006)

ICTs Connecting Global Citizens, Global Dialogue and Global Governance. A Call for Needful Designs

Wolfgang Hofkirchner[1]([✉]), José María Díaz-Nafría[2], Peter Crowley[3], Wilfried Graf[4], Gudrun Kramer[5], Hans-Jörg Kreowski[6], and Werner Wintersteiner[7]

[1] Vienna University of Technology, Vienna, Austria
wolfgang.hofkirchner@tuwien.ac.at
[2] Madrid Open University (UDIMA), Madrid, Spain
josemaria.diaz.n@udima.es
[3] Paris Lodron University Salzburg, Salzburg, Austria
[4] Herbert C. Kelman Institute for Interactive Conflict Transformation, Vienna, Austria
[5] Austrian Study Centre for Peace and Conflict Resolution, Stadtschleining, Austria
[6] University of Bremen, Bremen, Germany
[7] Alpen-Adria Universität, Klagenfurt, Austria

Abstract. Humankind is on the transition to a supra-system of humanity, according to which social relationships – that organise the common good – are re-organised such that global challenges are kept below the threshold of a self-inflicted breakdown. In order to succeed, three conditions are imperative: (1) *Global governance* needs a *global conscience* that orients towards the protection of the common good. (2) Such global governance needs a *global dialogue* on the state of the common good and the ways to proceed. (3) Such a global dialogue needs *global citizens* able to reflect upon the current state of the common good and the ways to proceed to desired states. Each of these imperatives is about a space of possibilities. Each space nests the following one such that they altogether form the scaffolding along which institutions can emerge that realise the imperatives when proper nuclei are introduced in those spaces. Such nuclei would already support each other. However, the clue is to further their integration by Information and Communication Technologies. An *information platform* shall be launched that could cover any task on any of the three levels, entangled with the articulation of cooperative action from the local to the global, based on the cyber-subsidiarity model. This model is devised to ensure the percolation of meaningful information throughout the different organisational levels.

Keywords: Ethics and policies for a digitalized world · ICTs and society · Information society · Digital transformation of society · Global governance

© Springer Nature Switzerland AG 2019
H. Florez et al. (Eds.): ICAI 2019, CCIS 1051, pp. 453–468, 2019.
https://doi.org/10.1007/978-3-030-32475-9_33

1 Introduction

This proposal puts global governance in the **context of human evolution**. This is innovative and productive in two ways. First, the historical significance of the establishment of global governance can be imagined so as to allow a comprehensive picture. With the words of Edgar Morin [1], we are still living in the "prehistory of human spirit". **Global governance that transforms the global risks into challenges that can successfully be handled** would mark a decisive step in hominisation and usher in the **transition from humankind to humanity**. A proper world society could materialise as "Homeland Earth". The current crises turn out as coming-of-age problems of the human species. But the future is open. *Homo sapiens-demens* can succeed or fail.

Second, apart from visioning Homeland Earth as common goal, taking human evolution into account provides methodological hints on how to establish global governance in a realistic way. This is not a detailed blueprint for a determinate set of institutions to deal with one singular aspect of the many-faceted global challenges. At the contrary, it is an **evolutionary framework** of *enabling spaces* **that allows for a diversity of institutions to emerge such that they are set up to converge to an overall system of global governance**. The latter way goes over the **agents** of change, which are global citizens, and their **interaction**, which is a global dialogue, heading for **collective action** on the planetary level, which yields global governance.

The question to be answered here is how are those organisational relations of social information processes specified such that appropriate designs of supporting information and communication technologies can be developed.

2 Problem Statement

Systems emerge through organisational relations when co-operation of agents produces **synergy** effects [2]. The less friction is in the interaction of the agents as a consequence of relations promoting synergy, the more enduring are the systems. Natural systems we witness today succeeded in being most enduring in virtue of their ability to adapt to synergy requirements.

Social systems crystallise in social relations that allow the proliferation of the **common good**, the social synergy, for participant actors. Global challenges embody a crisis in the worldwide availability of the common good. They show that hominisation is an ongoing process. A re-organisation is needed as never seen before that is all about the common good.

Two major steps of **anthropo(socio)genesis** – the becoming of humans and society – can be distinguished so far [3]:

(1) The transition from a less developed state of co-operation among our animal ancestors to a state of sporadic, but ever-increasing co-operation in **dyads** of early humans **based on joint intentionality** (about a common goal, common initial conditions and a common strategy to achieve the goal). Dyadic co-operation guaranteed the common good for both actors.

(2) The transition from dyadic co-operation to an obligatory **triadic form of social relations** that mediate the interaction of individuals in the context of society. A common culture provides the ground for **collective intentionality**. The third of the triad is not another individual but rather the generalised other in the sense of George Herbert Mead. It is relations of society that relate individuals to each other with respect to the common good – even if the concrete content of the common good became a matter of disputation and conflict.

Today, another transition is about to start. A **third step of anthropo(socio)genesis** is in reach, by which the collectivity of human intention would be topped by a **cosmopolitan sharedness** on a planetary scale. The desired relationship is a **new triad**, materialising social synergy, so to speak, an omniad, when generalised onto the level of Homeland Earth.

There are three kinds of social relations:

(1) **Antagonistic relations** that make positions conflict with each other in a contradictory, mutually exclusive manner. They threaten humanity with extermination because there is only one solution – the elimination of one side of the antagonism.
(2) **Agonistic relations** that make different positions indifferent to, and co-exist with, each other in a compossible manner. They seem indispensable to social life [4], but do not suffice for collective action on a planetary scale.
(3) **Synergistic relations** that enable mutually supportive positions that complement each other for any goal and for the common good too, humanity-wide.

Antagonistic relations have to be reduced to a minimum, and agonistic relations have to be put in the service of truly synergistic relations to enact this third step of human evolution.

First of all, such a transition is **necessary**, since the social relations of any partition of humanity are based on the principle of othering of partitions that are considered outside of them, thus not doing justice to legitimate self-interests of the rest of the partitions. Frictions from which the global challenges emanate render the continuation of civilisation unsustainable. They are caused by the lack of relations that would be valid for all partitions from a bird's eye view, that is, from a meta-level perspective. The establishment of such relations would mean the abolition of those frictions by a new supra-system in which all existing systems take part and shape according to the new relations on a higher level, following the application of the *subsidiarity principle* (in its positive sense) as a basis for the preservation of diversity and autonomous agency [5, 6]. This needs not to mean a world government. But it means global governance by rules, regularities, resource regimes, eco- and techno-structures that in our time need to be transnational and trans-state in reach.

Furthermore, this step is not only needful but **also possible**. Despite some literature based on biologistic biases unable to imagine a transgression of the conceptual framework of the nation-state "we", transnational relations have been taking shape. There is empirical evidence of co-operation between culturally homogeneous groups several tens of thousands of years ago, between cities around five thousand years ago, and between modern states since the seventeenth century [7–9]. This co-operation between collective actors like groups, cities and states has already been paving the way for co-operation among the whole of humankind in the same way that dyadic, inter-personal co-operation between individual actors opened up the space of possibilities for triadic, societal co-operation. Examples are, as **top-down** models, a diversity of his-torical empires and contemporary regional federations with an economic or political focus like the EU as well as a diversity of organisations that fill the space beyond states, with the League of Nations as forerunner, and international organisations after 1945 like the UN family. Both supranational and international organisations turn rather in the direction of transnational organisations. Though they are still mirroring changing geopolitical balances of power, managers that have been running them developed an identity beyond the nation state, at a higher level [10]. Besides the top-down models, another model of transnational institution building has emerged that pays attention to **bottom-up** processes too. Examples are self-regulating communities, in particular in the economic field [11] as well as the large number of civil society organisations (CSOs), part of which are non-governmental organisations (NGOs), in particular, international NGOs (INGOs). And there have been social movements flashing up.

However, all those developments taken together will not accomplish the third transition in human evolution by themselves. Additional and specific efforts by the actors are needed for both quantitative and qualitative reasons.

Any transition from a state in which originally independent systems have become dependent on each other to a state in which a critical mass of them establish a suprasystem – a system of which they become elements that are able to complement each other for the sake of each of them and for the sake of the whole system – emerges not before a **quorum** of them catch up with the complexity of their interdependence that manifests in frictions. Any such suprasystem reduces these frictions. This is due to a reduction in the difference of complexity between a certain number of the suprasystem's elements-to-be and the challenges they face. They increase their com-plexity through the **generation of requisite information** to counterbalance the fric-tions [12]. The systems would remain in the old state as long as the conditions allow or would even disintegrate, if they failed to generate requisite information [13].

This is also true for a possible world society that steers itself. Faced today with the global challenges, all actors, whether individual or collective, if they were to survive and thrive in the foreseeable future, would need to adapt the actuality of their inter-action full of friction to the potentiality of harmonisation with proper social relations on a level beyond and above the contemporary global players. At least, a considerable number of actors are able to go ahead, raise their intelligence and institute those relations.

In that context, developments in the direction of global governance as listed above are, so far, lacking the **right balance of qualitative and quantitative features for coping with the complexity** of the current state of interdependence of the social systems populating the planet. Either the form of institutions is still missing the right **content** for a world society that takes successful measures to mitigate the global problems or, if the content is right, the **critical mass** to tackle the problems has not yet been accomplished.

Deficiencies hamper the full realisation of self-organised social information pro-cesses that would underpin the appropriate transformation of the social systems involved. As one of the authors has analyzed elsewhere from a network theoretical perspective, the **deficiencies of the current ICT networks,** powered by big-data technologies, as regards the generation of the requisite information to bring about the third step of social evolution [5]. Deficiencies appear in the fields of co-operation, communication and cognition. In each of the fields a potential can be identified the actualisation of which is **imperative** in order to execute the third step in social evolution.

(1) Co-operative information processes play the role of **consensualisation** on the social systems level, about the goal and the means to achieve the goals. The deficiency is that actors still do not explicitly **dedicate** the social relations they are (re)producing **to** the advancement of **the common good**. But, in principle, common intentionality can underlie the complex structure that administrates the commons. **Global conscience and global consciousness** can emerge in a hyper-"commonalist" vein, which means caring for the commons from the local to the planetary scales in a subsidiarity scaffolding, and can gain dominance over traditional relationships that cause violent global frictions.

(2) Communicative information processes convey **collaboration** between actors, that is, preparing support for the decisions upon goals and means by bringing together different perspectives as well as guiding and monitoring the process of achieving the goals, and preparing adjustments of means and goals. The deficiency is that actors do not yet **deliberate commonly** as much **upon possible goals** as upon possible means. But, in principle, there can be consilience about the larger picture. A **conversation on the design of another world**, open to any actor, can be carried out globally.

(3) Cognitive information processes conceive the **co-ordination** of possible activities according to the position in the social system a single actor finds herself placed on. The deficiency is that actors do not yet **discern** sufficiently the possibility of **extending their scope of action** that is currently restricted because of frictions and the lack of meaningful information, properly adapted to the action level. But, in principle, they are able to reflect upon the quality of social relations and understand that friction-free relations would benefit each actor. They are able to anticipate a meta-level of possible new social relations on a global scale and make improvements they **concern**.

Co-operative, communicative and cognitive information build a hierarchy in that co-operation builds upon communication and communication upon cognition. The imperative of hyper-commonalism on the co-operative level of information benefits from being underpinned by all-inclusiveness on the communicative level and the imperative of all-inclusiveness benefits from being underpinned by meta-reflexivity [14] on the cognitive level. The lower levels are necessary conditions for the higher ones so that the higher levels shape the lower ones.

3 Proposal

3.1 Starting Point

What follows is the proposal of how to bring about the emergence of a nested network of new civil society institutions at different levels, all based on cosmopolitan principles and the idea of the common good, which together form a task force for the needed societal change at a global level.

The institutionalisation of global governance that is targeted on a successful resolution of the social dysfunctions causing the global challenges would be doomed to failure if it ignored the **informational imperatives** described above. As a consequence of the analysis, these imperatives need to be taken into account to tackle the global challenges in a proper way:

(1) on the *systems* level, the imperative of a **commons-oriented global conscience/consciousness** that guides global action for the sake of the common good in an adequate subsidiary concert with the lower action levels;

(2) on the level of the *actors'* interaction, the imperative of an **all-inclusive global conversation** open to any local actor of any perspective with the aim of exchanging positions on possible solutions of how to deal with the global issues;

(3) on the level of an *individual actor's mind* as well as of organisational goals of a collective actor, the imperative of a **globally concerned meta-reflexion** about the transformation of social relations on which the fate of humanity depends.

Future-oriented global governance is based upon these conceptual cornerstones. How can these imperatives be met?

3.2 A Framework of Enabling Spaces

It is true that global challenges that threaten the survival of humanity in totality can be alleviated only by acts carried out as if humanity were united. But the success of global action depends on how fast the deficiencies identified in social information processes can be fixed and a critical mass of knowledgeable and determined actors can assemble as "spearhead of the willing" before a window of opportunity closes.

All actors today are **exposed to the three information imperatives**. Though all actors share a responsibility for the future of humanity, even if in different grading and often not wittingly, they are free to respond to the imperatives in different degrees and cannot be expected to be as responsive as they should. Since a critical mass of actors suffices, anyway, a framework needs to be designed that enables any actor to participate in the spirit of global conscience, global "conversability" and global concernedness and to form an emergent critical mass. Such framework functions as an environment of **"enabling spaces"** [15] that are accessible to any actor.

Enabling spaces are spaces of possibilities that are anchored in reality, namely, in the current realities of co-operative, communicative and cognitive information processes. The spaces of possibilities build a hierarchy of necessary conditions according to the hierarchy of real information processes and the informational imperatives. This hierarchy of the spaces of possibilities works as scaffolding along which new effective spaces can emerge.

To turn the order upside down, the following spaces of possibilities to be realised can be considered as enabling spaces building upon each other while giving successively room to each other:

(1) At the bottom is the cognitive field where meta-reflexive actors can raise concern about global issues, can develop a new cosmopolitanism and become ready to live **global citizenship**.

(2) Evolving global citizens can, on their part, populate multiple planetary communicative spaces in which they start to conduct an all-inclusive debate about global issues, a **global dialogue**, in particular, about facts and figures of global development and how to assess them, which, in turn, has repercussions on the cognitive field so as to solidify global citizenship and recruit new global citizens.

(3) The communicative spaces of the global dialogue in *statu nascendi* can, on their part, contribute, eventually, to the establishment of an all-embracing global public sphere at the top of the hierarchy at which **global governance** is to be completed – decision-making in the name of, and mandated by, the whole humanity as well as the implementation of measures to safeguard the commons and the common good for the world society, guided by an emerging conscience along with a consciousness on the global level, which, in turn, feeds back to the intermediary level so as to strengthen the multiplicity of planetary communicative spaces for the task of collaboration and, as preparation for decision-making, for the task of impact assessment as well as to create new such spaces if need be.

This framework enables the respect for the informational imperatives to the greatest extent without use of strict enforcement. The social space of global citizens helps attain global concerns, the social space of planetary communication furthers global dialogue, and the social space of the global public contributes to global consciousness with a global conscience.

According to that framework, global governance is **distributed** along nested information processes: every level provides a space for information processes that are conducive to the emergence of information processes that comply with the imperative on the next higher level and every level is a space that reinforces those information processes that it necessitates on the next lower level. The meta-reflexions taking place in the space of global citizens are conducive to the global dialogue and the space of the global dialogue that includes the former space shapes the reflective processes there as these are part of it; at the same time, global dialogue is conducive to global governance, while global governance demands global dialogue as part of it. Thus, the model proposed here conceptualises global governance as unfolding in time over levels of relative autonomy, as emergent product of a **punctuated bottom-up process** that entails a **top-down process** that re-organises the preconditions from which global governance arises and upon which it builds. Since individual actors reside on the bottom level, interact with each other on the intermediate level and produce social relations of synergy on the top level once they co-act, global governance is a process of social self-organisation in which agency is the driving force that is nudged by the structure it produces. Nevertheless, it is an open-ended process that scaffolds from the local to the global in a subsidiary manner.

3.3 Instituting Nuclei

The framework of enabling spaces for global governance addresses anybody without discrimination and shall provide an environment friendly to the emergence of changing institutions to safeguard the global common good. Given the right environment, right **nuclei** have to be instilled in those spaces as seeds for desired institutions. The nuclei work as **clues that can be taken up by any of the actors to make them consider global issues in any field of information processes they are involved in**, particularly if, according to the subsidiarity principle, they concern the global level, and make them turn into (1) "citizens of the earth" who engage with initiatives, movements, organisations in a (2) "communicative democracy" for a (3) "politics of humanity and civilisation", as Morin formulated [15].

The overall objective of providing such nuclei is to strengthen the forces that are already there and try to shift the balance towards Homeland Earth. They shall be supported to gain power through **integration without skipping their differentiation**. In a qualitative respect, a **screening and revisiting of the political aims** they pursue in the light of the global informational imperatives is compulsory. In a quantitative respect, an **aggregation in a common network** they join is mandatory as long as a critical mass shall be acquired.

Such a stepwise, piecemeal institutionalisation of global governance can comprise the building of particular, **new institutions** and the insertion and incorporation of particular, required **new traits in old institutions** as well. Nuclei can go either way.

A combination of nuclei described in the following paragraphs seems most advisable and feasible to concretise the enabling spaces framework. There are three suggestions to give existent institutions on the global citizens, global dialogue and global governance levels each a kick. And the suggestion to install germs of novel institutions for the technical integration across all levels must be based upon the analysis of the demand of new organisations of those social information processes. The suggestions here attend to the subsidiarity principle.

Reform of Thinking and Education for Citizens of the Earth. According to Morin, the reform of thinking together with a reform of education is the *conditio sine qua non* for any substantial change towards Homeland Earth [15].

What is needed is complexity thinking in every-day thinking, an understanding why trans-disciplinary approaches are required, a logic that stretches beyond deductive reasoning, systems and evolution literacy, ethical, inter-religious and inter-cultural education to build intellectual and emotional capacities of open-minded actors fit for a new planetary era.

Having said that, the organisational innovation to be supported by newly ICTs is as follows: to support initiatives in any country to reform the education systems to include **pedagogics for peace, global social justice and a thriving planet**, wherever applicable, from the kindergarten over the primary and secondary schools to universities and to continuing education. Artists shall be encouraged to write fiction, to write songs, to perform theatre plays, operas, musicals, dancing, to produce pieces of artwork, installations and exhibitions that are dedicated to the new way of thinking required or put given pieces into the context of today's challenges. Similarly, scientists should be stimulated to focus their research on such issues. A "Global Youth Exchange Programme" shall be planned [17]. Social impact foundations shall be asked to offer initiatives in the field the opportunity of applications for funding. These foundations could develop a co-ordinated programme.

Constructive News for Communicative Democracy. Communicative spaces enable humans to grasp the world they live in through exchange with, and adapt their views to, each other. What Morin calls democracy in that context is the insight that none of us owns the absolute truth but that we can converge to consilience by adding our individual perspectives until common pictures emerge. In the age of global challenges, it is mandatory not to exclude any perspective because it might prove precious to save civilisation.

Media are influential and condition the free intercourse. It is a fact that worldwide mainstream media are biased and convey partisan interests of elites [18]. Journalists maintain not only connections to INGOs like think tanks propagating a certain political agenda but also to governments and the so-called intelligence communities of certain states. Editorial offices gather to arrange how to label certain phenomena of the political and economic world like political leaders and groups or economic measures in a way that reminds of Orwell's Newspeak. Due to deteriorating working conditions, investigative journalism is hard to practice and P.R. industries that economically outbalance media industries feed the media with fabricated news that are not questioned. Commercialisation reinforces echo chambers that trigger off the public's most primitive instincts and even diversion plays a role in that topics relevant for a peaceful future of different cultures in harmony with nature are neglected.

"Transformation-oriented", "impact-oriented", "future-oriented", "solution-oriented", "constructive journalism" are denominations of a new genre. According to that, journalists shall not bring bad news but constructive news and direct their attention to problems and the attempts to solve them, including failures to learn from them. Already existing examples are medias like *Le Monde Diplomatique* or *Lettre Internationale*. Film-makers follow this trend, e.g. in the Austrian movie "Die Zukunft ist besser als ihr Ruf" or the French movie "Demain/Tomorrow – Take concrete steps to a sustainable future".

Having said that, the organisational innovation to be supported by newly designed ICTs is as follows: the establishment of a **constructive media fund** fed by social impact foundations to support media outlets that comply with the imperative of a global dialogue for the sake of civilisation. Only such an independent body can guarantee the production of communication free from private or state interests that tend to block interests of whole humanity. In addition, it shall provide materials for self-organised learning and teaching materials in the line of a **pedagogics for peace, global social justice and a thriving planet**.

An Addendum to the UN General Assembly for a Politics of Humanity and Civilisation. Now that globalisation has produced an infrastructure of a world society without a common consciousness, according to Morin, a regime of global governance, based upon a somewhat revised United Nations, would be required to produce a new civilisation [16].

There is a growing number of social entrepreneurs, philanthropists, retired politicians, professionals, intellectuals, artists and others, working in not-for-profit sectors, who have also become part of social movements or civil society organisations, from the local to the global, all of which – individuals or collective actors – anticipate in their actions, some values, norms and principles of social relations, that could be universalised for all of humanity. They would represent the vanguard of a global conscience. More often than not, however, they are scattered around the world, focusing sometimes on a narrow section of a global challenge and become blinded through such a routine, that they lose the larger picture, if they ever had one, and hence do not develop a common, comprehensive, single integrated strategy. Many of them refrain from programmatic work, developing political demands, entering political negotiations, and even when some of them, form independent forums, or when they are invited to join international meetings or the UN system, they are sometimes not treated as being on an equal footing with the policy makers. Their influence on politics is as a consequence, rather marginal. Some of the latest examples may be the Global Solidarity Summit in July 2017 in Hamburg, organised by a coalition of more than seventy organisation and initiatives, attracting more than 2.000 people, or those NGOs that had been operating rescue ships in the Mediterranean, to save refugees and migrants on their way to Europe, from being drowned.

On the other hand, there have been proposals to sidestep the UN by proclaiming a global parliament [19] or, if not, to reform the UN such that the present General Assembly (GA) would become one of a two chamber world-parliament. Whereby the second chamber should represent the world population by members of the national parliaments, if not through direct elections as Václav Havel proposed. Such a solution would create legislative powers for the whole parliament, which would replace the present *international law* – that, in principle, is only binding for those nation states that share a consensus. *Transnational law* would be binding on all subjects and promote world jurisdiction on a par with a world government of a world state [20]. Since current governments are so far not inclined to give up sovereignty, these plans for a world parliament are, in effect, stalled. This is especially the case since re-nationalisation is taking place on a worldwide scale, sometimes even comparable to the international political situation a hundred years ago.

Having said that, the organisational innovation to be supported by newly designed ICTs is as follows: The idea of using the momentum of global civil society movements and organisations that enact global ethics shall be taken up, along with the idea of designing an addendum to the UN GA to finally outbalance some of the negative effects of national sovereignty. The transnational, avant-gardist civil society momentum needs to better translate into international politics and international politics, in turn, needs to receive an impetus to go transnational. Thus, the UN shall establish a **permanent expert group (PEG) of global civil society representatives** that have expertise and valuable performance of work in transnational fields. These representatives shall not represent the people of the world, as it is, but, so to speak, the future population of a united world. They would represent CSOs and global movements that act for a viable and flourishing future, guided by an emergent global conscience, or would be persons who as eminent persons make outstanding contributions to the betterment of the world. All those persons would be chosen by the UN in due consideration of the criteria are outlined above. This PEG shall be endowed with the right to elaborate, in constructive sub-groups, on **proposals on any aspect of dealing with the global challenges to be presented to the UN GA**, which, for its part, can prepare resolutions and reach consensus decisions incorporating those proposals. Thus, the PEG at the UN GA would, in the course of a third generation of UN-CSOs relations, enjoy consultative status with the GA itself, as well as with diverse UN agencies.

This suggestion would confirm the agreement at the Millennium NGO Forum in May 2000 that a permanent assembly of CSOs should be established to meet before annual sessions of the GA. The important point here is that there is no need to change the basic mechanism of current procedures of the UN GA. The state representatives are free to vote in favour or against such resolutions or abstain, or simply absent themselves from voting. The civil society representatives that would enjoy an enhanced status, by being accredited members of an official UN body, could build up political pressure at a higher level and could achieve this, the more reasonable their proposals are. Progress could also be achieved through states that are willing to form coalitions and implement measures, without waiting for all states to take part. Such an example is the Treaty on the Prohibition of Nuclear Weapons that was negotiated through the adoption of a mandate of the GA and signed by a group of member states.

What occurs at a United Nations Organisation, complemented in such a manner, would deserve proper media coverage. Apart from traditional media, the *constructive media fund* could make a specific focus of media coverage of the activities of the PEG of global society representatives and its sub-groups.

4   ICTs for Homeland Earth

The suggestions above concentrate on the promotion of an eventual "global mind" – global consciousness with global conscience – as the essential feature of global governance. A global mind needs a "global brain" [21]. The penetration of societies with Information and Communication Technologies (ICTs), the Internet and further advancements, are looked upon as the technical requisites for the global brain of humanity. ICTs mediate all social information processes – cognition, communication and co-operation. Also, social media can be designed and used for the support of cognition (through, e.g., websites) of communication (through, e.g., online news portals) and of co-operation (through, e.g., wikis) [22].

Having said that, the technical recommendation for the support of the re-organisation of social information processes from the world level down to the most local level along the nuclei discussed above in relation to the imperatives of our time is as follows: An **information platform** shall be launched that provides applications that serve the growth of any of the aforementioned nuclei – first, the pedagogics for peace, global social justice and a thriving planet, second, the constructive media fund, and third, global civil society's PEG at the UN. That is:

(1) On the *cognitive level*, online materials and online courses, video recordings of artistic performances and pieces of art, electronic fiction books that abide by the pedagogical principles in question shall be offered.
(2) On the *communicative level*, the participation in producing and using constructive news and in events of deliberating on which path societies should take shall be offered.
(3) And on the *co-operative level*, the PEG shall be offered online tools that facilitate their tasks of working out solutions.

Moreover, synergy effects would arise that reinforce the *integration of the three levels* and boost global governance.

To serve the purposes of global governance on all levels of information processing, this platform must be, on the one hand, run by some non-for-profit structure instead of classical private for-profit-corporations to keep it free from private interests, on the other hand, modelled in such a way that very strong **consistency conditions** are satisfied including, for example, (a) an easy and fair access of meaningful information for all involved actors, (b) a quality control making sure that all content is serious and true-to-fact, as well as properly and transparently related to the various tasks and goals, filtering out hate-filled, discriminating, sexist, racist, and inhuman contributions, (c) a security regime that prevents any manipulation and corruption, and (d) an adaptable information management architecture, described below, based on the subsidiarity principle from the local to the global levels, through which the information flow is substituted by synthetic information percolating 'meaningfully' across organisational levels.

4.1 ICT Architecture Based on Cyber-Subsidiarity

Though so far we have focused our attention to the level of global governability, this shall be based on the participation of citizens dealing with issues scaling up from the local to the global. However, the very common citizen has a very restricted autonomous capacity to move through the digital network gathering the information which is mostly meaningful to the issues at stake, as discussed in [5]. At the same time, the capacity to manage relevant information, from our-selves and the environment we are living in, offers new avenues to deal with issues of significant social concern.

If we compare the information management model within the living organism with respect to the model that corresponds to the internet powered by current big-data technologies, we observe a significant difference [6]. Concerning their respective sizes, the information volume in living beings is interestingly much larger for the time being. However, while the internet is notably characterized by the overload of information agents (among which we can mostly find information dwarfs and a few information giants), the former is based on the minimization of information management requirements at the higher levels and the recursive coordination of autonomous agency (*ibid*). This is a result of the application of the aforementioned subsidiary principle to the organisation of living beings, and a natural pathway to the emergence of sustainable systems from the local to the global, as intended hereby [5].

As argued in [5, 23], the *free-scale network* structure exhibited by the Internet routing network offers a sound footing for the instantiation of the subsidiarity principle. However, the real structure of the internet, particularly when it is powered by current big-data technologies in the present situation of strong inequality, represents an important breach in the subsidiarity principle. Moreover, current big-data technologies seem to intensify the already intolerable inequality, pushing the periphery outwards and consequently increasing cultural and social exclusion (*ibid*), thus hampering the necessary transition discussed in Sect. 2. To overcome this issue, we propose a **cyber-subsidiarity model** for the organisation of human cooperation backed up by subsidiary information management following the *Viable System Model* proposed by Stafford Beer [24]. This model, consisting of a decentralised multi-layered organisation of autonomous operational units, offers at a time a means to preserve autonomy, identity, environmental and social sustainability at different levels, from the local to the global.

The *Viable Systems* (VS) model, devised from the analysis of the necessary and sufficient conditions of viability of living organisms as a paradigm of sustainable autonomous organisation, is based on three fundamental principles: (i) The *principle of recursion*, stating that any VS is composed of nested VS (s. Fig. 1a); (ii) The *principle of requisite variety*, stating that the variety of a system must be greater than the variety of the issues the systems is facing; (iii) The *principle of subsidiarity*, stating that the variety is resolved at the lowest (recursive) level, so that only the residual variety percolates to the upper organisational level (firstly to the metasystem or system's management bodies; secondly, to the upper recursive level).

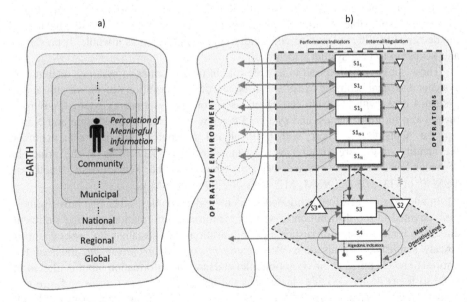

Fig. 1. Cyber-subsidiarity model: (a) Vertical nesting, (b) Horizontal organisation.

The viability of each nested system means that it is able to autonomously manage the variety of its operational context (namely, solving the problems related to its own activity and subsistence), by means of a proper information management to coordinate cooperation, facilitate meaningful communication, and enable the development of meta-reflexivity. To ensure the necessary and sufficient conditions of system's sustainability, VS must be composed of five subsystems that interact with each other, represented in Fig. 1b:

(**S1**) Every VS embraces several primary activities of which different operative units take care. Each operative unit is a VS itself, according to the principle of recursion and performs at least one of the fundamental functions of the organisation.

(**S2**) represents the information channels and functions that allow the primary activities in S1 to communicate and cooperate with one another while facilitating S3 to supervise and coordinate activities in S1. It is responsible for the immediate programming and sharing of resources to be used by S1, conflict resolution and stability.

(**S3**) encompasses the structures and controls arranged to establish S1 rules, resources, rights and responsibilities. It guarantees internal regulation, optimize capacities and resources and looks after synergy at the operational level. It has a panoramic view of the processes developed in S1 used to carry out strategic planning, while it offers an interface for S4/S5 to comply with and facilitate forward planning and preserve system's identity. Within S3, an audit subsystem, System 3* (S3*) is devoted to assess sporadically overall performance.

(**S4**) has the function of giving account of environmental changes in order to forecast forthcoming scenarios. At the same time, it takes care of how the organisation has to adapt to preserve its viability in the long-term, developing forward planning.

(**S5**) is responsible for political decisions in the organisation as a whole, balancing the demands of different parties and guiding the organisation as a whole. It preserves and keeps up-to-date system's identity.

These subsystems respond to a triple role in the dynamics of system's adaptation: systems 1–3 deal with the "Inside and Now" of the operations of the organisation; system 4 deals with "Outside and Then" as a strategic response to external, environmental and future demands; and system 5 deals with balancing the "Inside and Now" and the "Outside and Then" with political and axiological directives that maintain the identity of the organisation as a sustainable entity. According to the principle of recursion, VS is composed of VS, which can be symbolically stated as: $VSM \stackrel{\text{def}}{=} \{\{S1\}, M|S1 \stackrel{\text{def}}{=} VSM; M \stackrel{\text{def}}{=} \{S2, S3, S3*, S4, S5\}\}$.

In addition to the aforementioned fundamental principles, other regulative principles, devoted to the distribution of variety, action and information, provide sufficient directives for the design of sustainable organisations and sustainability assessment of already stablished organisations. As regards *information management*, most of the information is handled at the operational level. Here, the information input is filtered in order to focus on the activities and issues the unit is devoted to (to this end, group's ontology play an important role). Since this approach holds at any organisational level, only the information that is needed in order to handle the issues not solved at a given level will percolate to the upper level. More details are provided in [25, 26], describing the application of the model to the dealing of issues of planetary concern.

5   Conclusion

This paper shows that the design of IT need not be restricted to technical considerations alone that promise high returns on the markets. It can take social factors into consideration when it comes to questioning the underlying design objectives, which is an asset of integrated technology assessment and technology design, and it needs to do so if and because the evolution of humanity is facing threats of exterminism that renders profitable efficiency secondary. The deliberation of design objectives requires, furthermore, an extension of the focus of research and development towards social sciences and humanities – hence an inter- if not transdisciplinary account. Transdisciplinarity itself is best carried out with the help of systems thinking.

This paper demonstrates how the inclusion of social and human science issues can work in a systems perspective to provide a sound basis for the alignment of IT design issues with humane goals. It provides an example of how such a collaboration can work out in the case of finding ways to implement global governance, based on the cyber-subsidiarity model to articulate cooperative action from the local to the global.

References

1. Morin, E.: Homeland Earth. Hampton Press, Creskill (1999)
2. Corning, P.A.: The Synergism Hypothesis. McGraw-Hill, New York (1998)
3. Tomasello, M.: A Natural History of Human Thinking. Harvard University Press, Cambridge (2014)
4. Mouffe, C.: Agonistics. Verso, London (2013)
5. Díaz-Nafría, J.M.: eSubsidiarity: an ethical approach for living in complexity. In: Hofkirchner, W., Burgin, M. (eds.) The Future Information Society: Social and Technological Problems, pp. 59–76. World Scientific Publishing, Singapore (2017)
6. Díaz-Nafría, J.M.: Cyber-Subsidiarity: towards a global sustainable information society. In: Carayannis, E.G., Campbell, D.F., Efthymiopoulos, M.P. (eds.) Handbook of Cyber-Development, Cyber-Democracy and Cyber-Defense, pp. 1–30. Springer, Berlin (2017). https://doi.org/10.1007/978-3-319-06091-0_39-1
7. Messner, D., Weinlich, S.: The evolution of human cooperation. In: Messner, D., Weinlich, S. (eds.) Global Cooperation and the Human Factor in International Relations, pp. 3–46. Routledge, London (2016)
8. Neumann, I.: Diplomatic cooperation. In: Messner, D., Weinlich, S. (eds.) Global Cooperation and the Human Factor in International Relations, pp. 225–245. Routledge, LDN (2016)
9. Grimalda, G.: The possibilities of global we-identities. In: Messner, D., Weinlich, S. (eds.) Global Cooperation and the Human Factor in International Relations, pp. 201–224. Routledge, London (2016)
10. Menasse, R.: Der Europäische Landbote. Zsolnay, Wien (2012)
11. Djelic, M., Quack, S.: Transnational communities and governance. In: Djelic, M., Quack, S. (eds.) Transnational Communities, pp. 3–36. CUP, Cambridge (2010)
12. Ashby, W.R.: An introduction to cybernetics. Chapman and Hall, London (1956)
13. Beniger, J.R.: The control revolution. Harvard University Press, Cambridge (1986)
14. Archer, M.S.: The Reflexive Imperative. CUP, Cambridge (2012)

15. Peschl, M.F., Fundneider, T.: Spaces enabling game-changing and sustaining innovations. OTSC **9**(1), 41–61 (2012)
16. Morin, E.: Der Weg. Krämer, Hamburg (2012)
17. Fischer, D.: United Nations Reform. In: Fawcett, E., Newcomb, H. (eds.) United Nations Reform, pp. 59–77. Science for Peace, Toronto (1995)
18. Krüger, U.: Mainstream. C. H. Beck, München (2016)
19. Falk, R., Strauss, A.: Toward global parliament. Foreign Affairs, 8(1) (2008). https://doi.org/10.2307/20050054
20. Leinen, J., Bummel, A.: Das demokratische Weltparlament. Dietz, Bonn (2017)
21. Heylighen, F.: Conceptions of a global brain. In: Grinin, L.E., Carneiro, R.L., Korotayev, A.V., Spier, F. (eds.) Evolution, pp. 274–289. Uchitel Publishing, Volgograd (2011)
22. Fuchs, C.: Social Media. Sage, London (2014)
23. Díaz-Nafría, J.M., Guarda, T.: Is the structure of our digital world suited for a fair intercultural life? Cult. – Commun. Cooper. **22**, 243–276 (2018)
24. Beer, S.: Diagnosing the System for Organizations. Wiley, New York (1985)
25. Díaz-Nafría, J.M., Alfonso, J., Panizo, L.: Building up eParticipatory Decision-Making from the local to the global scale. Comput. Hum. Behav. **47**, 26–41 (2015)
26. Guarda, T., Díaz-Nafría, J.M., Augusto, M.F., Vitor, J.A.: Territorial intelligence in the impulse of economic development initiatives for artisanal fishing cooperatives. Smart Innov. Syst. Technol. **94**, 105–115 (2018)

Introduction to the Mathematical Theory of Knowledge Conceptualization: Conceptual Systems and Structures

Mark Burgin[1] and José María Díaz-Nafría[2]([envelope])

[1] University of California, Los Angeles, CA, USA
[2] Madrid Open University, Madrid, Spain
jdian@unileon.es

Abstract. The paper departs from the general problem of knowledge integration and the basic strategies that can be adopted to confront this challenge. With the purpose of providing a sound meta-theoretical framework to facilitate knowledge conceptualization and integration, as well as assessment criteria to evaluate achievements regarding knowledge integration, the paper first reviews the previous work in the field of conceptual spaces. It subsequently gives an overview of structural tools and mechanisms for knowledge representation, recapped in the *modal stratified bond model* of global knowledge. On these groundings, a novel formalized representation of conceptual systems, structures, spaces and algebras is developed through a set of definitions which goes beyond the exploration of mental knowledge representation and the semantics of natural languages. These two components provide a sound framework for the development of the glossaLAB international project with respect to its two basic objectives, namely (i) facilitating knowledge integration in general and particularly in the context of the general study of information and systems; (ii) facilitating the assessment of the achievements as regards knowledge integration in interdisciplinary settings. An additional article tackles the solutions adopted to integrate these results in the elucidation of the conceptual network of the general study of information and systems.

Keywords: Knowledge conceptualization · Knowledge integration · Conceptual systems · Conceptual structures · Conceptual spaces · Conceptual algebras

1 Introduction

Knowledge of people in general and scientific knowledge in particular has become an extensively large system, which is continuously growing. Even various big knowledge domains, such as mathematics, physics or information sciences, are so huge that an expert in one subdomain (say, group theory) does not know and understand what is going in another subdomain (say, probability theory). This brings scientists to the problem of *knowledge integration*. There are different approaches to this problem. One of the most powerful approaches to knowledge integration is *abstraction*. Another useful method of knowledge integration is *algorithmization*. The third tactic is

© Springer Nature Switzerland AG 2019
H. Florez et al. (Eds.): ICAI 2019, CCIS 1051, pp. 469–482, 2019.
https://doi.org/10.1007/978-3-030-32475-9_34

conceptual knowledge integration. It consists of two major steps: *domain knowledge conceptualization* and *systemic integration.* In domain knowledge conceptualization, the existing domain knowledge is transformed into the conceptual form. There are three key goals of this process. The first goal is to bring diverse forms of knowledge representation to a synthesized description in a unified format. The second goal is simplification of existing advanced knowledge making it comprehensible to a much wider audience in comparison with the top experts in a specific domain. The third goal is preparation of knowledge for the subsequent knowledge integration.

The glossaLAB project, to which the present work is contributing, aims at enabling knowledge integration through the utilization of *interdisciplinary glossaries* [23–25]. In these glossaries, not to be confused with usual glossaries, the meaning of concept names used in interdisciplinary settings (particularly devoted to the study of systems and information, as well as application problems that requires strong interdisciplinarity) are simultaneously elucidated from the different disciplinary perspectives summoned. Its ultimate purpose is contributing to the development of sound *transdisciplinary* settings in which the integration of knowledge is effectively achieved (*ibidem*). In the first place, the commitment to the study of systems and information offers good groundings for knowledge integration in general, in virtue of the abstraction of the concepts involved. On the other hand, its form, as an online hypertext in continuous development by an interdisciplinary community of users, offers the means to carry out the theoretical work required for knowledge integration and meta-theoretical assessment of the integration effectively achieved. To both purposes, we need modelling conceptual systems as well as addressing the problem of knowledge integration. We concentrate our attention here in the first part, the modelling of conceptual systems, while the specific problems of knowledge integration have been analyzed in previous works [22, 23] and is further addressed in another work [24].

To build, explore and utilize a mathematical model of this process, we apply the *representational model of a concept* [10], hypertexts, hypermedia [6, 44] and *named set theory* [13, 18]. In a conceptual knowledge system, each concept is represented by a *hypertext* (hypermedia) and is mathematically modeled by syntactic and model logical varieties [8, 12], which is a system of interconnected named sets. Here we construct the base for knowledge conceptualization and integration developing formalized representation of conceptual systems, structures, spaces and algebras. That is why in Sect. 2, we give an overview of the previous work in this area. However, our overall goal, in which this paper is only the first step, is to develop a theory of conceptual knowledge integration, which demands taking into account all forms of knowledge representation and not only the conceptual one. That is why in Sect. 3, we give an overview of structural tools and mechanisms of knowledge representation coming to the conclusion that although these tools and mechanisms are highly developed in contemporary epistemology, methodology and AI, they do not pay enough attention to the conceptual level of knowledge systems. This demands developing new tools for knowledge conceptualization and integration. Construction of the first level of tools and mechanisms for knowledge conceptualization and integration is the main purpose of this paper.

With this in mind, in Sect. 4, we build a mathematical model of conceptual systems in the form of conceptual spaces and algebras. It is necessary to remark that our theory is essentially different from the previous research due to the following reasons. The aim of the conceptual spaces constructed before was exploration of mental knowledge representation and reconstruction of conceptual semantics. Our goal is exploration of textual knowledge representation and construction tools, structures and mechanisms for conceptual knowledge integration in the textual form. Finally, a conclusive section summarizes results as regards the objectives of the work.

2 Conceptual Spaces as Tools for Learning Theory and the Semantics of Natural Languages

The concept of *conceptual space* was introduced and studied by Peter Gärdenfors in his theory of conceptual representation in the mind, aiming at building foundations of learning theory and the semantics of natural languages [29, 30, 32, 33]. In his works, Gärdenfors further developed the approach of Osgood, Suci and Tannenbaum to the measurement of meaning [45].

According to Gärdenfors, *conceptual spaces* are defined as systems of quality dimensions of different types. Quality dimensions based on perception can be, for instance, temperature, brightness, color, weight, pitch and the three ordinary spatial dimensions. The dimensions represent perceived similarity and dissimilarity in the following sense: the closeness between any two points of the conceptual space corresponds to the similarity judged through perception. Points in a conceptual space denote objects, while regions of similar points represent concepts [29].

This makes it natural to call these structures by the name *attributive conceptual spaces*. In contrast to this, spaces introduced and studied in this paper are called *structural conceptual spaces*.

Properties correspond to convex regions in the conceptual space. For instance, a sour taste corresponds to a convex region in the five-dimensional space of basic tastes. As a result, a concept, according to Gärdenfors, is a bundle of properties joined to information about the way how these properties correlate to each other [32]. For instance, the concept of an orange encompasses properties corresponding to regions of color space, shape space, taste space, nutrition space, and other spaces.

One of the most important applications of conceptual spaces concerns the modeling of the semantic processes involved in language acquisition. According to the main assumption in this application new words are never learnt separately as single words, but rather as words within the same domain. For example, once the child learns a color, other color words are learnt at the same time. On the other hand, they learn them in connection to objects which are colored, and through the uttering of color relations while stating sentences about the world, be it real or imagined. These links establish correlations among dimensions of the concept space which determine the convex region of the concepts involved.

Based on his theory, Gärdenfors describes a linguistic learning process in the following way.

"What is it that you know when you know a language? Certainly, you know many words of the language (its lexicon), and you know how to put the words together in an appropriate way (the syntax). More important, you know the meaning of the words (the semantics of the language). If you do not master the meaning of the words you are using, there is no point in knowing the syntax (unless you are a parrot). You can communicate in a foreign language with some success just by knowing some words and without using any grammar. In this sense, semantic knowledge precedes syntactic knowledge." [34].

Operations in conceptual spaces such as concept composition were formalized and studied in [1, 41, 48]. Method of utilization of grammatical structures within conceptual spaces in categories were developed and studied in [7].

All this clearly demonstrates that the existing theory of conceptual spaces is essentially oriented on mental processes of conceptual information processing [16]. At the same time, conceptual information and knowledge representation in encyclopedia and dictionaries as well as text formation for these sources have dissimilar regularities and conditions. That is why to develop a theory having in mind our purpose, we need different types of conceptual spaces and other structures, which we construct in this paper.

3 Structural Tools and Mechanisms of Knowledge Representation

There are three main areas where researchers explored and developed knowledge representation with the modern emphasis on formal structures, methods and techniques: epistemology as field of philosophy, methodology of science and artificial intelligence [17].

Studies of knowledge started with the beginning of philosophy. Great Greek philosophers Plato and Aristotle paid considerable attention to problems of knowledge. Knowledge was enthusiastically studied in ancient Indian teachings and doctrines such as Samkhya, Nyaya, Jaina, Buddhist and other school of Hindu philosophy [47].

However, philosophers made the main emphasis on mundane knowledge developing logic as a tool for cognition in the form of knowledge acquisition and justification. Researchers started to study and develop knowledge representation when people tried to make their computers intelligent, teaching computers to solve problems people can solve. The reason was that mundane knowledge was represented by notions and texts of natural languages, which computers were not able to understand. Orientation on computers brought force formal methods with orientation on structural tools and mechanisms of formalized knowledge representation.

As a consequence, the most widespread model of knowledge is the *standard (positivist or logical) model*, in which knowledge is represented by logical propositions and/or predicates (cf. [20, 46, 51]). Another popular approach is the *structuralist model of knowledge*, in which knowledge is represented by collections of models utilizing means of set theory (cf. [4, 52, 54]).

Some researchers treat knowledge as a collection of devices for the formulation and resolution of problems, modeling knowledge through systems of propositions and queries, sometimes including several types of problem representation, as well as, guidelines to address the problems using erotetic logic in order to analyze problems thoroughly and to solve them. This representation was consolidated in the *interrogative model of knowledge* (cf., for example, [35]). Another approach treats knowledge as assemblies of highly organized guidelines, concepts and solutions to problems [53].

The first unified approach to formalized knowledge representation was achieved in the *structure-nominative model* [11]. The unified character of this model resides in the fact that other formalized models of knowledge became subsystems of the structure-nominative model, at the time the structures employed within each model are named sets of systems of named sets [18]. In this vein, the aforementioned standard model of knowledge corresponds to a logic-linguistic subsystem of the unified model, while the structuralist model corresponds to a model-representing subsystem.

3.1   The Modal Stratified Bond Model of Global Knowledge

Later on this unified model was broadened and improved by one of the authors [18] moving further in the modeling of global knowledge. Nowadays, the state-of-the-art to this regard is the **modal stratified bond model of global knowledge** developed by the same author [17], virtually capable to embrace any other system model of scientific knowledge and knowledge in general.

In accordance with this model, general knowledge has three basic dimensions – the modal, the systemic and the hierarchical dimension – although separate knowledge items may only have one or two of these dimensions.

The *modal dimension* reflects the three types of knowledge modality referred to in Table 1.

Table 1. Modal dimension of global knowledge.

Knowledge modality	Its epistemic structures are explicit or implicit expression of
Assertoric	Being knowledge
Hypothetic or heuristic	Being possible knowledge
Erotetic	Knowledge deficit

We can find examples of assertoric knowledge in logical propositions or statements, for instance, "the Sun is a star". Examples of hypothetic knowledge can be found among beliefs whose certainty is weak, for instance, "there is a lot of water in the shadowed craters of the moon." On the other hand, questions and problems, such as "how can the water be conserved on the moon surface?", constitute basic forms of erotetic knowledge.

Knowledge modalities shape strata of knowledge systems determining their *horizontal structure*, while its *vertical structure* is determined by the **hierarchical dimension** whose levels are referred to in Table 2. These levels are in themselves comprised of layers and sections.

Finally, the *systemic dimension* of knowledge is composed by the three categories referred to in Table 3.

Table 2. Hierarchical dimension of global knowledge.

Knowledge level	It is comprised of
Componential	Elements and groups of elements upon which structures of the attributive level of knowledge are assembled
Attributive	The static knowledge structures which are built up by the elements of the componential level
Productive	The dynamic knowledge structures which includes the means of acquiring, producing and transmitting knowledge

Table 3. Systemic dimension of global knowledge.

Knowledge category	It is comprised of	Examples
Descriptive (declarative or propositional)	Knowledge about properties and relations of objects	"A cat is white" "Two is less than three"
Representational	The set of representations (through knowledge structures) of an object	The image of Jose that Alex has of his friend
Operational	Knowledge about how to perform actions, how to organize behavior and how to regulate and control system's operation	Algorithms, regulations, instructions, procedures, guidelines, etc.

4   Conceptual Systems, Structures, Spaces and Algebras

In this section, we build a formalized representation of conceptual systems. The basic element (block) of this representation is the concept, which itself has a certain structure. Construction of conceptual spaces and algebras is based on definite models of concepts. Let us consider some of these models as a basis for the subsequent consideration of conceptual systems, spaces, algebras and structures.

4.1   Models of Concepts

The first known model of a concept belongs to Gottlob Frege, who treated concepts as ways of thinking of objects, properties and relations [28]. Formally, this is represented by the following diagram.

In this triadic structure, the *denotation* of a concept is a set of all objects denoted by the concept, while the *sense* of a concept accounts for its cognitive significance being the way by which people conceive of the denotation of this concept.

Bertrand Russell conceived concepts as constituents of propositions, whereas his model of concept is similar to the model of Frege [49].

In this triadic structure, the *denotation* of a concept consists of particular exemplifications of the concept, while the *meaning* comprises the set of propositions describing the concept.

Cohen and Murphy consider four types of existing concept models: *extensional, fuzzy set-theoretical, prototypical* and *semantic* models [21].

Hampton describes that five broad classes of models have been proposed by different researchers [36]:

1. The *classical model* takes concepts as clearly and entirely determined by a system of necessary and sufficient features as the system attributes, which later were divided into two groups: *defining features* and *characteristic features*.
2. The *prototype model* represents a concept by an object with the most common attributes of the category or the system of these attributes, which is called the prototype. Objects are denoted by the concept if the similarity to the prototype suffices.
3. The *exemplar model* is similar to the prototype model but instead of being based on one prototype, it is based on a set of exemplifications.
4. The *theory-based model* has the form of a structured frame or schema, comprising theoretical knowledge about the relations between these attributes, as well as their causal and explanatory links.
5. The *psychological essentialism model* agrees with the classical "core" definition of concept, though admitting among its determinations empty "place holders", as it can be, for instance, further attributes which are still unknown.

It is also worth mentioning the novel *quantum model* of concepts, which has the form of the triad state-context-property. Here the states of a concept correspond to unitary vectors within a Hilbert space, affected by a linear operator modelling the influence of the context [2].

The Representational Model. Currently the most general model is the *representational model* of a concept which was co-introduced and studied by one of the authors [10] and was later developed by the same author [15]. Within this model a particular type of named sets or fundamental triads constitute its surface structure [18]. In this model, whose higher specification level is illustrated in Fig. 3, the concept name can either be a word or a text.

As it has been proven, this model, as a structure of a higher abstraction degree, comprises virtually any other concept model [15]. In this regard, the aforementioned concept model from Frege (Fig. 1) can be derived from the representational model considering "sense" and "denotation" as conceptual representatives. Similarly, the

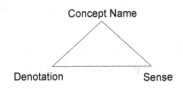

Fig. 1. Frege's *concept triangle*

concept model from Rusell (Fig. 2) can be derived from the representational model considering "meaning" and "denotation" as conceptual representatives.

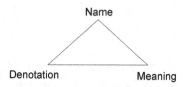

Fig. 2. Russel's *concept triangle*

Concept Name ——————➤ Conceptual Representative

Fig. 3. Higher specification level of a concept in the *representational model.*

In a lower specification level, the conceptual representative is differentiated in the three components referred to in Table 4.

Table 4. Components of the *conceptual representative* in the representational model.

Component	Corresponds to	Equivalent to
Concept Domain (D_C)	The domain of reality referred to by the concept C	*Denotation* in the models of Frege and Russell
Meaning (or *broad-spectrum concept knowledge*)	Knowledge about the concept domain D_C	*Sense* in Frege's concept model
Representation	A set of representations of the knowledge about the concept domain D_C	(it includes) *meaning* in Russell's concept model

In addition, the collection of all knowledge about the concept domain D_C is called the *abundant domain knowledge*.

In the case of being "knowledge" the name of the concept at stake, an article about knowledge within an encyclopedia or a dictionary is a representation of the concept knowledge. In other words, while one concept may have several representations, the union of representations of this concept is also a representation of the same concept.

4.2   Conceptual Systems

However, concepts, as consider in the previous paragraphs, do not exist separately but form conceptual systems.

Definition 4.1. A *conceptual system* is composed of concepts and relations of different levels.

Within the conceptual systems, we can find concept of three different types, systemic, emphasized and background concepts, as referred to in Table 5.:

Table 5. Types of concept within a conceptual system.

Concept type	Consist of	They have descriptions within the conceptual system (definitions)
Primary or *Systemic*	Knowledge items from a given knowledge domain	Yes
Secondary or *Emphasized*	Concepts which are used in descriptions of primary/systemic concepts	Yes
Tertiary or *Background*	Concepts which are used in descriptions of primary/systemic concepts	No

Considering concepts, it is necessary to distinguish properties of concepts and properties that define concepts. For instance, states of concepts in the quantum model are properties of concepts [2] while quality dimensions in the model of Gärdenfors are properties that define concepts [32].

4.3   Conceptual Spaces, Algebras and Structures

To define conceptual spaces and algebras, we discern relations of two types: *pure relations* and *operational relations*.

For instance, properties are pure relations. Relations between elements in a network are also pure relations. Operational relations define operations. In essence, any operation can be presented by a relation. For instance, we can define $R_+(a, b, c)$ is true if and only if: $a + b = c$. In particular, $R_+(2, 2, 4)$ is true while $R_+(2, 3, 4)$ is false in the conventional arithmetic.

Definition 4.2. A conceptual system is a *conceptual space* or more exactly, a *structural conceptual space*, if it is a logical model, i.e., it has only pure relations.

In other words, a structural conceptual space consists of formal (abstract) representations of concepts, e.g., of prototype, exemplar or representational models, and formal relations between these models.

For instance, in the quantum model of concepts, referred to above, concepts are mapped by vectors within a Hilbert space [2].

A conceptual space in the theory of Gärdenfors, referred to above, is a multidimensional feature space, in which vectors denote objects and regions denote concepts [31, 32]. The basis of a conceptual space is comprised of *quality dimensions*, which denote basic features, such as *weight, color, taste* and so on, used for the definition and comparison of concepts and objects of concepts and objects.

A different kind of semantic spaces found useful applications for building a theory of meaning and its measurement [45].

Different kinds of operators are acting in conceptual spaces. For example, in the quantum model, linear operators acting on the Hilbert space of concepts model contextual impact [2].

Operations with concepts convert conceptual spaces into conceptual algebras.

Definition 4.3. A conceptual system is a *conceptual algebra* if it is a conceptual space with operations.

Note that concepts can include physical elements. For instance, if we take the model of Frege, then the concept *dog* includes all real dogs as its denotation. However, theoretically we study only formal concepts, in which form names are used instead of physical or mental objects.

Definition 4.4. A *conceptual structure* consists of formal concepts and abstract relations of different levels.

It means that on the top level with only binary relations a conceptual structure is a *network of concepts* [5, 25, 37, 39, 40, 42].

Structural conceptual spaces and conceptual algebras are special cases of conceptual structures.

Because properties (features) form intermediate structures, in accordance with the general theory of structures [15], attributive conceptual spaces of Gärdenfors [31, 32] also are special cases of conceptual structures. Another special case of conceptual structures was studied in the theory of meaning and its measurement [45].

At the same time, abstract conceptual spaces form an important type of semantic spaces [17]. As a result, *networks of concepts* represent a principal category of *semantic networks* [9, 14, 50].

In turn, semantic spaces are a significant form of knowledge spaces [3, 17, 19, 26, 38]. In this case, semantic networks shape a noteworthy sort of *knowledge networks* [55]. Interestingly, as the authors have argued elsewhere [22], the network of knowledge agents represents a counterpart of the semantic networks [43].

There are two categories of conceptual spaces: mixed and abstract conceptual spaces.

Definition 4.5. A conceptual system is a *mixed conceptual space* if it has physical and/or mental elements.

Mental spaces are examples of mixed conceptual spaces. They consist of small conceptual bundles associated, on the one hand, to long-term schematic knowledge, named "frames"; on the other to long-term specific knowledge [27].

Conceptual spaces have their structures.

Definition 4.6. A conceptual structure is an *abstract conceptual space* if it is a logical model, i.e., it has only pure relations.

Abstract conceptual spaces are used for exploration of arbitrary conceptual spaces and belong to the World of Structures [15]. All conceptual spaces studied in scientific literature are abstract.

There are two sorts of conceptual algebras: mixed and abstract conceptual algebras.

Definition 4.7. A mixed conceptual space with operations is a *mixed conceptual algebra*.

This shows that it would be useful to study not only mental spaces as in [27] but also mental algebras for the modeling and investigation of human mentality and mental conceptualization of knowledge.

Definition 4.8. A conceptual structure is an *abstract conceptual algebra* if it is an algebraic system, i.e., it contains both pure and operational relations.

There are various operations in (abstract) conceptual algebras. Many of them are used for formation of new concepts or transformation of existing concepts. Operation of the first type is conceptual combination. For instance, concepts *Pet* and *Bird* are combined into the conjunction *Pet-Bird*. Operation of the second type is conceptual abstraction. For instance, the concept *Cat* is transformed into the concept *Animal*.

These componential and abstraction procedures (among conceptual levels) are actually widespread in science and global knowledge, and include more complex process than the stated above, as it is, for instance, the case of metaphorization. Indeed, they represent some of the most fruitful processes in knowledge creation (at the productive level). For its analysis, it is worth mentioning the utilization of category theory as proposed by several authors who have developed formal approaches to analyze the general problem of abduction and metaphorization [56].

To conclude, it is necessary to remark that conceptualization converts assorted knowledge systems described in Sect. 3 into conceptual spaces and algebras, which provide better knowledge comprehension and more efficient knowledge integration [22, 24].

5   Conclusion

Thus, we have explored the field of conceptual knowledge representation and constructed new tools, structures and mechanisms as the base (foundation) for knowledge conceptualization and conceptual knowledge integration in the textual form such as conceptual structures, structural conceptual spaces and conceptual algebras. It is demonstrated that these tools give and adequate picture of textual knowledge representation in the form of concept networks, which pave the way for the integration of knowledge aimed at the glossaLAB project. The next step is exploration of existing and creating new operators in structural conceptual spaces and operations in conceptual algebras.

Acknowledgment. This contribution has been carried out under support of glossaLAB project, co-founded by the Universidad Estatal Península de Santa Elena, Ecuador, and an international consortium of academic institutions. The authors wish to dedicate this work to the memory of Charles François whose work represents an invaluable and everlasting contribution to the integration of knowledge.

References

1. Adams, B., Raubal, M.: A metric conceptual space algebra. In: Hornsby, K.S., Claramunt, C., Denis, M., Ligozat, G. (eds.) COSIT 2009. LNCS, vol. 5756, pp. 51–68. Springer, Heidelberg (2009). https://doi.org/10.1007/978-3-642-03832-7_4
2. Aerts, D., Gabora, L.: A state-context-property model of concepts and their combinations II: a Hilbert space representation. Kybernetes **34**(1/2), 176–204 (2005)
3. Albert, D., Lukas, J. (eds.): Knowledge Spaces: Theories, Empirical Research. Applications. Lawrence Erlbaum Associates, Mahwah (1999)
4. Balzer, W., Moulines, C.U., Sneed, J.D.: An Architectonic for Science: The Structuralist Program. Reidel, Dordrecht (1987)
5. Barabási, A.-L.: Linked: The New Science of Networks. Perseus, Cambridge (2002)
6. Barrett, E. (ed.): Text, Context and Hypertext: Writing with and for the Computer. MIT Press, Cambridge (1988)
7. Bolt, J., Coecke, B., Genovese, F., Lewis, M., Marsden, D., Piedeleu, R.: Interacting conceptual spaces: grammatical composition of concepts. In: Kaipainen, M., Zenker, F., Hautamäki, A., Gärdenfors, P. (eds.) Conceptual Spaces: Elaborations and Applications, pp. 11–19. Springer, Cham (2017). https://doi.org/10.1007/978-3-030-12800-5_9
8. Burgin, M., de Vey Mestdagh, C.N.J.: Consistent structuring of inconsistent knowledge. J. Intell. Inf. Syst. **45**(1), 5–28 (2015)
9. Burgin, M., Gladun, V.: Mathematical foundations of semantic networks theory. In: Demetrovics, J., Thalheim, B. (eds.) MFDBS 1989. LNCS, vol. 364, pp. 117–135. Springer, Heidelberg (1989). https://doi.org/10.1007/3-540-51251-9_9
10. Burgin, M., Gorsky, D.P.: Towards the construction of a general theory of concept. In: The Opened Curtain, pp. 167–195. Oulder, San Francisco, Oxford (1991)
11. Burgin, M., Kuznetsov, V.: Introduction to Modern Exact Methodology of Science. International Science Foundation, Moscow (1994). (in Russian)
12. Burgin, M.: Logical varieties and covarieties. In: Methodological and Theoretical Problems of Mathematics and Information and Computer Sciences, Kiev, pp. 18–34 (1997). (in Russian)
13. Burgin, M.: Named sets as a basic tool in epistemology. Epistemologia, **XVIII**, 87–110 (1995)
14. Burgin, M.: Named sets in the semantic network theory. In: Knowledge - Dialog - Decision, pp. 43–47. Leningrad (1991). (in Russian)
15. Burgin, M.: Structural Reality. Nova Science Publishers, New York (2012)
16. Burgin, M.: Theory of Information: Fundamentality, Diversity and Unification. World Scientific Publishing, Singapore (2010)
17. Burgin, M.: Theory of Knowledge: Structures and Processes. World Scientific, New York/London/Singapore (2017)
18. Burgin, M.: Theory of Named Sets. Mathematics Research Developments. Nova Science, New York (2011)
19. Burgin, M.: Weighted e-spaces and epistemic information operators. Information **5**(3), 357–388 (2014)
20. Carnap, R.: The Logical Syntax of Language. Humanities, New York (1937)
21. Cohen, B., Murphy, G.L.: Models of concepts. Cogn. Sci. **8**(1), 27–58 (1984)
22. Díaz-Nafría, J.M., Burgin, M., Rodriguez-Bravo, B.: Knowledge structures and conceptual networks for evaluation of knowledge integration. In: Dodig-Crnkovic, G., Burgin, M. (eds.) Philosophy and Methodology of Information: The Study of Information in the Transdisciplinary Perspective, pp. 457–489. World Scientific, Singapore (2019)

23. Díaz-Nafría, J.M., Guarda, T., Coronel, I.: A network theoretical approach to assess knowledge integration in information studies. In: Rocha, Á., Guarda, T. (eds.) Smart Innovation, Systems and Technologies, vol. 94, pp. 360–371. Springer, Cham (2018). https://doi.org/10.1007/978-3-319-78605-6_31

24. Díaz-Nafría, J.M., et al.: glossaLAB: Co-creating Interdisciplinary Knowledge. In: Proceedings of the Second International Conference on Applied Informatics. Communications in Computer and Information Science (2019). [In Press]

25. Díaz-Nafría, J.M.: Cyber-subsidiarity: toward a global sustainable information society. In: Carayannis, E.G., et al. (eds.) Handbook of Cyber-Development, Cyber-Democracy, and Cyber-Defense, pp. 1–30. Springer, Cham (2017). https://doi.org/10.1007/978-3-319-09069-6_39

26. Doignon, J.-P., Falmagne, J.-Cl.: Knowledge Spaces. Springer, Heidelberg (1999). https://doi.org/10.1007/978-3-642-58625-5

27. Fauconnier, G., Turner, M.: The Way We Think: Conceptual Blending and the Mind's Hidden Complexities. Basic Books, New York (2002)

28. Frege, G.: Über Sinn und Bedeutung. Zeitschrift für Philosophie und philosophische Kritik **100**, 25–50 (1892)

29. Gärdenfors, P., Löhndorf, S.: What is a domain? Dimensional structures vs- meronymic relations. Cogn. Linguist. **24**, 437–456 (2013)

30. Gärdenfors, P.: Cognitive semantics and image schemas with embodied forces. In: Krois, J. M., Rosengren, M., Steidele, A., Westerkamp, D. (eds.) Embodiment in cognition and culture, pp. 57–76. Benjamins, Amsterdam (2007)

31. Gärdenfors, P.: Conceptual spaces as a framework for knowledge representation. Mind Matter **2**(2), 9–27 (2004)

32. Gärdenfors, P.: Conceptual Spaces: On the Geometry of Thought. MIT Press, Cambridge (2000)

33. Gärdenfors, P.: Geometry of Meaning: Semantics Based on Conceptual Spaces. MIT Press, Cambridge (2014)

34. Gärdenfors, P.: Semantic Knowledge, Domains of Meaning and Conceptual Spaces. In: Meusburger, P., Werlen, B., Suarsana, L. (eds.) Knowledge and Action. Knowledge and Space, vol. 9. Springer, Cham (2017). https://doi.org/10.1007/978-3-319-44588-5_12

35. Garrison, J.W.: Hintikka, Laudan and Newton: an interrogative model of scientific discovery. Synthese **74**(2), 45–172 (1988)

36. Hampton, J.A.: Concepts and natural language. In: Concepts and Fuzzy Logic, pp. 233–258, MIT Press, Cambridge (2011)

37. Hempel, C.G.: Fundamentals of concept formation in empirical science. In: International Encyclopedia of Unified Science, vol. 2, no. 7. University of Chicago Press, Chicago (1952)

38. Jago, M.: Logical information and epistemic space. Synthese **167**(2), 327–341 (2009)

39. Kuhn, T.: The Structure of Scientific Revolutions. The University of Chicago Press, Chicago (1970)

40. Lakatos, I.: The Methodology of Scientific Research Programmes. Cambridge University Press, Cambridge (1978)

41. Lewis, M., Lawry, J.: Hierarchical conceptual spaces for concept combination. Artif. Intell. **237**, 204–227 (2016)

42. Losee, J.: A Historical Introduction to the Philosophy of Science. Oxford University Press, New York (2001)

43. Muyeba, M., Rybakov, V.: Knowledge Representation in Agent's Logic with Uncertainty and Agent's Interaction, Preprint in Computer Science, 1406.5495 [cs.LO] (2014). Electronic edition in: http://arXiv.org. Accessed 10 Aug 2019

44. Nielsen, J.: Hypertext and Hypermedia. Academic Press, New York (1990)

45. Osgood, C.E., Suci, G.J., Tannenbaum, P.H.: The Measurement of Meaning. University of Illinois Press, Urbana (1978)
46. Popper, K.R.: Objective Knowledge: An Evolutionary Approach. Oxford University Press, New York (1979)
47. Rao, V.S.: Theories of knowledge: Its Validity and its Sources. Sri Satguru Publications, Delhi (1998)
48. Rickard, J., Aisbett, J., Gibbon, G.: Reformulation of the theory of conceptual spaces. Inf. Sci. **177**(21), 4539–4565 (2007)
49. Russell, B.: On denoting. Mind **14**, 479–493 (1905)
50. Sowa, J.F.: Semantic networks. In: Encyclopedia of Artificial Intelligence. Wiley, New York (1987)
51. Suppe, F.: The Positivist Model of Scientific Theories, in Scientific Inquiry. Oxford University Press, New York (1999)
52. Suppes, P.: What is a scientific theory? In: Philosophy of Science Today, pp. 55–67. Basic Books, New York (1967)
53. Thagard, P.: Computational Philosophy of Science. A Bradford Book, Oxford (1988)
54. van Frassen, B.: The semantic approach to scientific theories. In: Sklar, L. (ed.) The Nature of Scientific Theory, pp. 175–194. Garland, New York (2000)
55. Zhuge, H.: The Knowledge Grid: Toward Cyber-Physical Society. World Scientific Publishing, Singapore (2012)
56. Zimmermann, R.E.: New Ethics Proved in Geometrical Order. Spinozist Reflections on Evolutionary Systems. Emergent Publications, Litchfield Parz (2010)

Software Design Engineering

Dynamic Interface and Access Model by Dead Token for IoT Systems

Jorge Hernandez[1], Karen Daza[1], Hector Florez[1(✉)] ⓘ, and Sanjay Misra[2] ⓘ

[1] Universidad Distrital Francisco Jose de Caldas, Bogotá, Colombia
`jehernandezrodriguez@gmail.com, kgiselledaza@gmail.com,`
`haflorezf@udistrital.edu.co`
[2] Covenant University, Ota, Nigeria
`sanjay.misra@covenantuniversity.edu.ng`

Abstract. Communication between users and intelligent devices is normally done through a graphical user interface. In addition, devices that communicate using Bluetooth are also implementing a control interface. Thus, most of the devices in an enclosure such as home or work can be remotely controlled. This implies that each device can have an interface and an IP assignment for its own control. In this way, users must learn and manage several communication interfaces. In this paper, we present a model of a general graphical user interface to control different smart devices that can consume HTTP requests or that are controlled by Bluetooth. In addition, we present an authentication approach for the Internet of Things that uses the proposed model.

Keywords: Internet of Things · Dynamic Graphical User Interface · HTTP Security Model

1 Introduction

Nowadays, Internet of Things (IoT) is very important for the technology evolution because it embraces multiple technological services that solves daily problems. This concept focuses on the idea that each device can process internet data connections to other devices in real time. Thus, in the same way in which humans use internet, devices will be the main users in the ecosystem of IoT [3]. The application of IoT technologies are numerous and diverse due IoT solutions are expanding to a lot of areas of daily life [14].

IoT involves the combination of hardware and software. Currently, there are a lot of IoT devices with a specific function such as video cameras, switches, actuators, etc. Thus, IoT emerges with the responsibility of controlling different devices through internet [1]. Then, it is necessary the design and development of standards to admit a great amount of applications in order to face the common requirements of several industrial areas, environment, society, and people [2].

When users develop smart devices, they must use multiple Graphical User Interfaces (GUI) to control each element of the device. For instance, it is possible

© Springer Nature Switzerland AG 2019
H. Florez et al. (Eds.): ICAI 2019, CCIS 1051, pp. 485–498, 2019.
https://doi.org/10.1007/978-3-030-32475-9_35

to find in a smart house doors and lights control [23], fire alarm [9], and smart windows shades [11]. Each IoT provider offers their own control interface provoking a problem for final users for managing all this kind of resources at once. Another problem is that when using several devices there are several authentication requests, which generates a security issue because not all people or devices should have access to all devices.

In this work, we propose a conceptual model for graphical user interfaces to provide IoT developers a standard to deploy and configure control elements for their devices. Thus, providers of IoT devices can save time in the development process because they just need to focus on the hardware and software for controlling the device.

The paper is structured as follows. Section 2 presents the main concepts of model dynamic interface. Section 3 presents the security a review. In Sect. 4, we illustrate the model Security for HTTP systems. Section 5 presents the related work. Section 6 presents a case study. Finally, Sect. 7 concludes the paper and proposes the future work.

2   Model for Dynamic GUI

The aim of this section is to present the design of a model for GUIs that can be used by IoT developers for configuring elements and control of the device. With this in mind, a device could be remotely controlled and could act as a physical access point to the services available in Internet [14,22].

2.1   Communication Control (Interface - Thing)

We propose two ways to control the device: sending parameters via Bluetooth or managing HTTP requests. It is necessary to establish a bidirectional communication with the device in order to manage its behavior. Figure 1 presents the interaction between the interface and the device. The component **Interface - GUI** consists mainly of control buttons of two types. The former is designed to send codes by Bluetooth to the device that must previously be paired with a smartphone. The latter is designed for objects that work with web services; then, when the button is pressed, the URL previously configured by the IoT provider will be consumed. Regardless of the button, an order is sent to the device. In the interface there is a component called **Request To** which checks the structure of the button and sends the HTTP request or the message via Bluetooth. Upon receipt of the command by the component **Handle request** on the device, the task **Process operation** is performed. The device will be in the disposition to respond the status of the task or some message to the interface by the same connection method. In this case the component **Request To** will also be listening to messages from the device confirming bidirectional communication with GUI. The message will be shown in the interface by the component **Monitor output** that will be able to display or embed HTML tags.

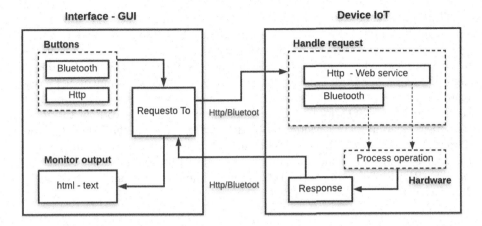

Fig. 1. Communication GUI with device

2.2   Interface Configuration by WebHook

IoT providers will complete the entire configuration process through a Web-Hook[1], which is a web service that has custom callbacks and listens HTTP requests to respond with another request. Its main advantage is to provide services to third parties in the flow of an application. It is done through this system because there is no need to (a) have a configuration system for the elements of the interface and (b) provide the business logic for security. Initially, provider must register their device in the WebHook so that the user can search for the smart device.

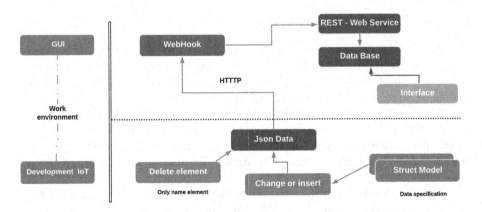

Fig. 2. Model configuration for GUI

---

[1] https://www.webhooks.org/.

The GUI will show control buttons that are the main elements. Said buttons will be managed by the IoT developer through the WebHook independent of the interface. Each time the user chooses the device in the app. Then, the elements managed by the IoT provider will be loaded by consulting the providers database. Figure 2 shows two work environments in the GUI and development IoT configuration process. The IoT provider must send the element's data through a HTTP request in JSON format. It must also provide a unique code or token for the object as an authentication method that will be given at the moment of the device creation. In the GUI, the WebHook (after validating the data) must map the code or token and depending on the case, the WebHook must send them to the API-REST of the interface. Table 1 shows the data that should be sent in JSON format.

Table 1. Data for create button

Index	Example value	Required
type	"bluetooth", "url"	Yes
codBluetooth	"A1"	Yes (if type is bluetooth)
conectionKey	"123456"	Yes (if type is bluetooth)
url	"http://domain.com"	Yes (if type is url)
verbHttp	"POST", "DELETE", "GET", "UPDATE"	Yes (if type is url)
data	array or object	Yes (if type is url)
color	"color hex."	Yes
shape	"round, square, clasic"	Yes

2.3   Dynamic Interface in IoT

The interface of a dynamic web application can change depending on the needs of users, which is inferred by the (relatively) frequent modification of the source code [12]. The proposed structure of the dynamic interface is focused on the ability to change its elements in execution time. There must be two mechanisms in the dynamics of an emerging interface. The first is code mobility, which allows moving an active program fragment (along with its status) from one site to another during execution. The second is a tracking service, which allows the components to meet and interact with each other despite their movement (possibly uncoordinated) during the lifetime of the application [8].

Figure 3 presents the main elements in the proposed interface. The architecture shows two main components: Abstract Devices and Layout Interaction.

- **Abstract Devices.** As mentioned before, the main idea is to bring the elements of each IoT device from the database. For this, the first thing that the interface does is to consult the component **Data Filter** to save the associated devices in the storage space of the smartphone. In any case where the

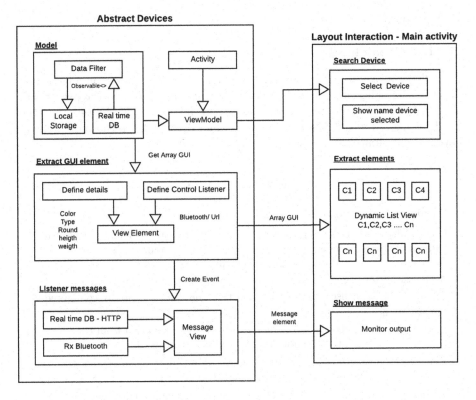

Fig. 3. Dynamic architecture GUI

developer changes the elements of a device, in real time **Data Filter** will be listening for changes in the database. The device is the main model of the architecture. An array of the elements associated with the device is created, where the structure of the element is defined with attributes such as color, size (height - width), shape and the associated event according to the type of connection to control the device. In this component we also find **Listener messages** that depending on the connection with the device creates an element called **Message View**, where is extracted in HTML format to show it in the interface.

– **Layout Interaction.** In the main activity of an app, the layout consists of three elements: the first one called **Search device**, which will be responsible for selecting the device or changing it by the user. The second element called **Extract elements**, which is responsible for extracting the elements in the view dynamically. The last one is **Show Message**, which is responsible to print text in the device after communication embedding HTML tags in the view.

3 Security in IoT

3.1 IoT Capabilities

The collection of data from the devices should be used to offer intelligent services to users. The interconnection of equipment and the network represents in IoT one of the greatest responsibilities. There are some capabilities that the IoT developers apply depending on the scope. Table 2 shows the most general concepts that smart things should have [14].

Table 2. IoT capabilities

Capabilities	Description
Communication and cooperation	Devices are able to connect to Internet resources or even to connect to other devices on order to make use of services and data as well as to update their state
Addressability	Based on IoT, devices can be automatically located by discovery services and thus the can be remotely configured
Identification	Devices can be identified in a unique manner. This identification allows to retrieve information from the internet and be connected to the network
Sensing	Devices can collect all desirable information of their environment using sensors
Actuation	Devices can include actuators to manipulate some specific elements in their environment
Embedded information processing	Devices have a processor or microcontroller as well as storage capacity. These resources are used to process all services included in the devices
Localization	Based on Global Position Systems (GPS), smart devices can be located
User interfaces	Smart devices can provide dynamic ways to communicate with people in an appropriate manner

3.2 Security Architecture

The Internet is the physical layer that connects different devices. Its main responsibility is to transport information from one node to another. World Wide Web or (web) is an application layer that operates over the Internet and provides an interface for information. Data on the Internet is integration, privacy, and availability [7]. For IoT, security is a very important issue to take into account since smart devices that are deployed can be vulnerable. Cyber attacks on IoT-based systems are critical as they can cause physical damage [19]. As IoT is part of the internet, it is likely to have vulnerabilities. Even there is no universal architecture, different authors have raised and discussed the architecture with which IoT should operate in a context. This work is based on a three-layer architecture [20]: the perception layer, network layer, and application layer. In terms of security, the security of all layers must be guaranteed.

- **Perception Layer.** It is in charge of obtaining data either from the user or from the system on which it is acting. The main actuators are the sensors that are integrated into the IoT technologies capable of uploading the data to the cloud by means of Amazon AWS. With this in mind, in this layer the best work options are Arduino[2] or Raspberry[3] devices.
- **Network Layer.** It is responsible for connecting one device to other IoT devices, use the corresponding tools which allow the transmission of data between devices, and process the data.
- **Application Layer.** It is the layer for users' applications. In this layer, there are industrial or home applications that use IoT making possible smart homes or smart cities.

These layers are known as IoT three-layer architecture, plus there is a five-layer architecture that collects information from the three layers mentioned above and two more layers such as the transport layer and the processing capacity. In addition, IoT security must also include the security of the entire system that crosses the perception layer, the transport layer, and the application

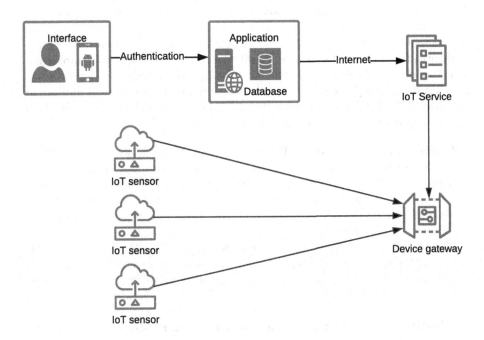

Fig. 4. IoT devices connection

---

[2] https://www.arduino.cc/.
[3] https://www.raspberrypi.org/.

layer [21]. In some applications, such as AWS from Amazon Web Services[4], where the security is based on the use of certificates when registering a device in the application, the user is the only one who knows said certificate and the keys that it generates. Each connected device must have credentials to access the message agent or the Device Shadow service. The AWS security protocols protect the data when it goes from AWS to IoT and viceversa.

Figure 4 shows the connection between devices that implement IoT and cloud in order to keep information secure, which is generated by smart devices such as sensors, cameras, smartphones, etc. Then, users can use an application through a smartphone after the corresponding authentication using a username and password, which is encrypted with a hash method. Later, users can consume the available IoT services, which are linked to the application IoT sensors avoiding linking to unknown sensors. The device gateway allows creating a secure access point from the sensor to the internet connection in order to consume the corresponding services. Finally, requests are sent between the sensor and the mobile device through HTTP or bluetooth.

3.3   IoT Authentication

The security is based on an identity between a device and IoT platform. As we mentioned, IoT can be operate in a three layers architecture to guarantee the security of the information. Each layer might have to a business authentication. This work is focused in the application layer; however, the perception Layer should encrypt data and sensors or actuators should present its identity. Authentication in the network layer could take advantage if there is a third agent that provides key parameter services for the application layer [6]. A protocol is a standard to define a process. The end-device communication could implement a protocol. Then, we present some that have been used depending on needs of the communication between device and IoT platform.

- **Constrained Application Protocol (CoAP)**[5]**.** The protocol HTTP in IoT communication allows low overhead and multi-cast support. CoAP depends on REST, which is a principle adopted from HTTP and embedded in UDP (User Datagram Protocol) for the transaction [17]. Additionally, CoAP was designed to request-response and uses synchronous and asynchronous responses. The reason to implement it is a reduced bandwidth.
- **The Representational State Transfer (REST).** REST uses methods POST, GET, PUT, DELETE, and HTTP offering a system oriented to the resources. Thus, all asynchronous operations request-response can be done through the HTTP command. In addition, REST can handle JSON or XML content.
- **XMPP: Extensible Messaging and Presence Protocol.** It is an extensible messaging protocol that was designed to exchange messages and is one

---

[4] https://aws.amazon.com.
[5] https://coap.technology/.

of the most used protocols on the internet. However, being an old protocol, it is not enough to provide the necessary services for some of the new emerging data applications. Nevertheless, it is a communication protocol suitable for IoT. It has integrated TLS/SSL security.

- **AMQP: Advanced Message Queuing Protocol.** It is a transport protocol that provides asynchronous communication. Unlike other protocols, AMPQ can send massive messages per second. It is one of the most used protocols by large companies to send their millions of messages per day.
- **MQTT: Message Queue Telemetry Transport.**[6] It is a TCP communication protocol, which works asynchronously publishing/subscribing. These protocols have the IoT requirements better than others of request/response since they require less computer resources. The MQTT protocol is designed to use low bandwidth and battery use [10]. For security, authentication uses password and mail and TLS/SSL may be required.

4   Model Security for HTTP Systems

A security scheme represents the permission to the actions of the system. Registered users must provide the appropriate identification for their access [5]. The presented model defines a central node between a device and a GUI. The request to know if the device can be controlled can be requested from any end, but the other end will have a dead access because the control has the end that requests it. Users of the interface are saved in the database.

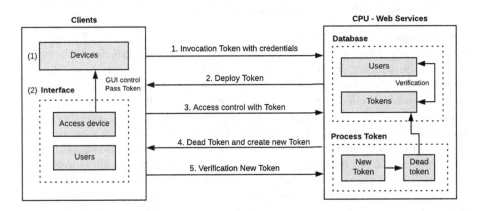

Fig. 5. Model token design

Moreover, a token is a set of unique characters in the system, which identify clients and have a time of use. Systems that consume application services are generally authenticated with a previously requested security token with credentials through an HTTP request. This section shows a security system for

---

[6] http://mqtt.org/.

multiple applications or systems called dead access. When any action is taken, the token dies. Figure 5 shows the design of the security model for the control of the devices. In the GUI, an authentication thread (user login) occurs on the user side, where it is consulted in the Central Processing Unit (CPU), when the user exists. Thus, the CPU corresponds to the services provided by the web services for all the authentication in the business logic. The control is a cyclical process between both clients. Each client notifies and prolongs the authentication of the other. Both clients must perform the authentication process to obtain their active token, which corresponds to *Invocation Token with Credentials* and *Deploy Token* (see Fig. 5). If the user asks the interface to control some device, after the generation of the token in GUI, it must send an HTTP request to the CPU to kill the token of the device and generate a new one. After the response *Access control with Token* and *Dead Token and create new Token*, it sends a new token to the device and it verifies the new token (through *Verification New Token*) in the CPU to be able to perform the operation. The opposite case is when the device is executed manually by the user where it performs the whole process of calls to the CPU.

5   Case Study

In this section, we present an implementation of the interface model, which is controlled by the proposed communication.

5.1   Context and Device to Control

We built a prototype for controlling window shades activated by HTTP requests or messages by Bluetooth to test the two connections of the interface. The operation of the window shade is based on two circular movements (up - down). Figure 6 presents the components of the prototype. Mainly, this is made up of an Arduino-based microcontroller that is composed of other components such as Arduino Ethernet, HC-05 device to manage communication by Bluetooth and an actuator for movement. A servomotor was implemented as an actuator that performs two movements. The arduino is configured as a web server listening for GET requests for its operation. In addition, it is also listening Bluetooth messages to control movements. Then, movements can be performed by Bluetooth and Http; however, the goal is controlling the devices through an interface.

5.2   System Interface

Figure 7 shows the main components of the interface together with the two communication protocols proposed for the control. First of all, there is a selector which shows the devices that the user already has added to the application. In the GUI, we validate the main process, which is the communication with the device. We create buttons with the same functionality but with a different event call according to the communication. In this case, the green buttons will work

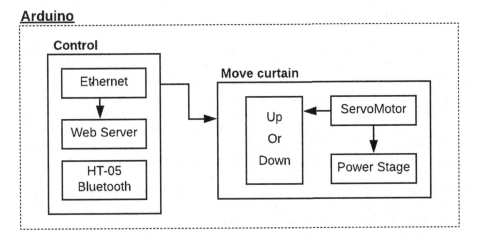

Fig. 6. Electronic prototype

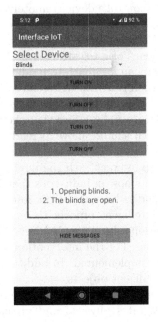

Fig. 7. Dynamic interface

when the device to be controlled (i.e., window shade) is connected by Bluetooth, which will make the window shade get up when the *Turn On* button is pressed or get down when the *Turn Off* button is pressed. In the HTTP communication, we use the blue buttons, which send HTTP requests to get up or get down the window shade. Finally, a button called *Hide Messages* allows hiding the messages generated by the monitor.

6   Related Work

To design the dynamic model of the interface, it is necessary to analyze the context and review the related work, where an interface with several devices is developed or modeled.

Castillejo et al. [4] presents an application in which WSN (Wireless Sensor Network) is implemented where the data collected by the application is sent by portable devices. The main problem is that the system requires Bluetooth connection due to the heterogeneity of the network to integrate different platforms and introduce a service-oriented solution in a single application where the user manipulates multiple hardware systems from this single application. In this application, the main idea is to include services in the application without having any external intervention. In our proposed interface, we also seek to be able to manipulate several applications from a single interface to improve the user experience.

Amazon Web Services (see Footnote 4) presents an application called AWS IoT which allows IoT users to control a device remotely. This application provides bidirectional communication between the devices and the AWS application. In addition, it allows users to control these devices from their cell phones or tablets. The application works by means of a registration in AWS.

Prehofer et al. [16] presents an approach to model systems for IoT using sensors and UML modeling to then generate REST interfaces. From the structured models, it shows how RESTFULL interfaces can be generated mainly functional for IoT manipulation. One of the main issues that should be taken into account is the uniform interfaces which should allow to read and manipulate resources through HTTP operations. This project focuses on obtaining optimal RESTFULL interfaces to be able to interact with the intelligent devices properly.

Kortuem et al. [13] presents how in industries they implement the use of the IoT in order to overcome the disadvantage of the infrastructure. In this project, they turn their tools into intelligent objects through devices with integrated sensors and wireless connections. Intelligent objects interpret sensor data and are capable of making decisions. For the intervention of the user, an application with integrated buttons was implemented. In addition, a remote interface was developed to operate the intelligent objects.

ur Rehman et al. [18] present the use of a cyber-physical system (CPS), which is a system that integrates physical and virtual capabilities communicated through the network. Attributes of CPS includes real-time, fault-tolerance, security, safety, scalability, reliability, distributed, adaptability and heterogeneity. For this system, security is very important due to its constant connection to the web. Then, they search threats surrounding the CPS. Finally, this security model is implemented in a smart home for its validation.

Odusami et al. [15] present different methods to detect malware in mobile applications. The study carried out a survey on malware detection techniques towards identifying gaps providing the basis for improving and effective measure for unknown android malware. Similar to this work, the security problem and the consequences of a failure are analyzed. The main objectives of the implemented study is to observe the stopping of malware on android and to propose a more efficient method.

7   Conclusions and Future Work

In this work, we have implemented two models: representation of dynamic interface and design of a security model for the systems in the devices that handle HTTP. The main problem faced was the use of various graphical interfaces in IoT for each device. IoT represents the evolution of technology therefore has a high degree of interest in society. Implementing solutions to IoT problems helps this emerging revolution.

Based on the validation, we show that the interface model complies with the problem solution. Apart of the development of the device, the interface controls its events. For the security model, hacking tests were carried out. These tests need to be carried out by external consultants.

As future work, we will create a model or technique for the user to temporarily schedule the control events of the device as well as control other devices made by other IoT developers. Another task we have is to extend the security model to authenticate devices that only use Bluetooth as a control connection. In this way the access for people will be guided only by the GUI.

References

1. Arévalo-Gómez, M.Á., Carrillo-Zambrano, E., Herrera-Quintero, L.F., Chavarriaga, J.: Water wells monitoring solution in rural zones using IoT approaches and cloud-based real-time databases. In: Proceedings of the Euro American Conference on Telematics and Information Systems, p. 39. ACM (2018)
2. Bandyopadhyay, D., Sen, J.: Internet of things: applications and challenges in technology and standardization. Wirel. Pers. Commun. 58(1), 49–69 (2011)
3. Bello, O., Zeadally, S.: Intelligent device-to-device communication in the internet of things. IEEE Syst. J. 10(3), 1172–1182 (2016)
4. Castillejo, P., Martínez, J.F., López, L., Rubio, G.: An internet of things approach for managing smart services provided by wearable devices. Int. J. Distrib. Sens. Netw. 9(2), 190813 (2013)
5. Florez, H., Sánchez, M., Villalobos, J.: A catalog of automated analysis methods for enterprise models. SpringerPlus 5(1), 406 (2016)
6. Gan, G., Lu, Z., Jiang, J.: Internet of things security analysis. In: 2011 International Conference on Internet Technology and Applications, pp. 1–4. IEEE (2011)
7. Hamidi, H.: An approach to develop the smart health using internet of things and authentication based on biometric technology. Future Gener. Comput. Syst. 91, 434–449 (2019)
8. Holder, O., Ben-Shaul, I., Gazit, H.: System support for dynamic layout of distributed applications. In: icdcs, pp. 403–411 (1999)
9. Kang, D.H., et al.: Room temperature control and fire alarm/suppression IoT service using MQTT on AWS. In: 2017 International Conference on Platform Technology and Service (PlatCon), pp. 1–5. IEEE (2017)

10. Karagiannis, V., Chatzimisios, P., Vazquez-Gallego, F., Alonso-Zarate, J.: A survey on application layer protocols for the internet of things. Trans. IoT Cloud Comput. **3**(1), 11–17 (2015)
11. Karmakar, G., Roy, S., Chattopadhyay, G., Xiao, Z.: Dynamically controlling exterior and interior window coverings through IoT for environmental friendly smart homes. In: 2017 IEEE International Conference on Mechatronics (ICM), pp. 487–491. IEEE (2017)
12. Kollar, L.: GUIML, creating dynamic GUI objects using XML. Math. Comput. Model. **38**(7–9), 893–901 (2003)
13. Kortuem, G., Kawsar, F., Sundramoorthy, V., Fitton, D., et al.: Smart objects as building blocks for the internet of things. IEEE Internet Comput. **14**(1), 44–51 (2009)
14. Mattern, F., Floerkemeier, C.: From the internet of computers to the internet of things. In: Sachs, K., Petrov, I., Guerrero, P. (eds.) From Active Data Management to Event-Based Systems and More. LNCS, vol. 6462, pp. 242–259. Springer, Heidelberg (2010). https://doi.org/10.1007/978-3-642-17226-7_15
15. Odusami, M., Abayomi-Alli, O., Misra, S., Shobayo, O., Damasevicius, R., Maskeliunas, R.: Android malware detection: a survey. In: Florez, H., Diaz, C., Chavarriaga, J. (eds.) ICAI 2018. CCIS, vol. 942, pp. 255–266. Springer, Cham (2018). https://doi.org/10.1007/978-3-030-01535-0_19
16. Prehofer, C.: Models at rest or modelling restful interfaces for the internet of things. In: 2015 IEEE 2nd World Forum on Internet of Things (WF-IoT), pp. 251–255. IEEE (2015)
17. Rahman, R.A., Shah, B.: Security analysis of IoT protocols: a focus in COAP. In: 2016 3rd MEC International Conference on Big Data and Smart City (ICBDSC), pp. 1–7. IEEE (2016)
18. ur Rehman, S., Iannella, A., Gruhn, V.: A security based reference architecture for cyber-physical systems. In: Florez, H., Diaz, C., Chavarriaga, J. (eds.) ICAI 2018. CCIS, vol. 942, pp. 157–169. Springer, Cham (2018). https://doi.org/10.1007/978-3-030-01535-0_12
19. Sadeghi, A.R., Wachsmann, C., Waidner, M.: Security and privacy challenges in industrial internet of things. In: 2015 52nd ACM/EDAC/IEEE Design Automation Conference (DAC), pp. 1–6. IEEE (2015)
20. Sethi, P., Sarangi, S.R.: Internet of things: architectures, protocols, and applications. J. Electr. Comput. Eng. **2017**, 25 pages (2017)
21. Suo, H., Wan, J., Zou, C., Liu, J.: Security in the Internet of Things: a review. In: 2012 International Conference on Computer Science and Electronics Engineering, vol. 3, pp. 648–651. IEEE (2012)
22. Wanumen, L., Moreno, J., Florez, H.: Mobile based approach for accident reporting. In: Botto-Tobar, M., Pizarro, G., Zúñiga-Prieto, M., D'Armas, M., Zúñiga Sánchez, M. (eds.) CITT 2018. CCIS, vol. 895, pp. 302–311. Springer, Cham (2019). https://doi.org/10.1007/978-3-030-05532-5_22
23. Windarto, Y.E., Eridani, D.: Door and light control prototype using Intel Galileo based Internet of Things:(case study: embedded and robotics laboratory, department of computer engineering, Diponegoro University). In: 2017 4th International Conference on Information Technology, Computer, and Electrical Engineering (ICITACEE), pp. 176–180. IEEE (2017)

Evaluation of the Performance of Message Routing Protocols in Delay Tolerant Networks (DTN) in Colombian Scenario

Nazhir Amaya-Tejera[1], Farid Meléndez-Pertuz[1(✉)],
Rubén Sánchez-Dams[2], José Simancas-García[1], Iván Ruiz[3],
Hermes Castellanos[3], Fredy A. Sanz[3], César A. Cárdenas R.[3],
and Carlos Collazos-Morales[3]

[1] Departamento de Ciencias de la Computación y Electrónica,
Universidad de la Costa, Barranquilla, Colombia
fmelendel@cuc.edu.co
[2] Facultad de Minas, Universidad Nacional de Colombia, Medellin, Colombia
[3] Vicerrectoría de Investigaciones, Universidad Manuela Beltrán,
Bogotá, Colombia

Abstract. Certain vehicles need to send information to their monitoring stations constantly, this information is usually sent by the vehicles, through the cellular network. The use of these wireless networks depends on coverage that it is not usually available in all geographic areas. This is the case of road segments where the coverage of data service of cellular networks is partial or zero, making transmission impossible. A particular case is the roads between the municipality of Juan de Acosta and the city of Barranquilla in Atlántico department (Colombia). As a solution, Delay-Tolerant Networks (DTN) emerge, which allow the transmission of data to the monitoring stations when there is no cellular network coverage. In this work, a simulated evaluation of the performance of some message routing protocols for DTN is performed, in the Juan de Acosta – Barranquilla scenario. Using *"The Opportunistic Networking Environment"*, we determined the performance of these message routing protocols. The results show that the *first contact* message routing protocol, presents the highest rate of delivery messages *(delivery rate)* and the lowest delivery latency *(delivery latency)*. In addition, the *Spray and Wait* protocol presents better results in System message overload *(overhead)* than the first one. *The Opportunistic Networking Environment* simulator, the performance of these message routing protocols was determined in this scenario. The results show that the *Firstcontact* message routing protocol presents the highest rate of delivery *(deliveryrate)* and the *lowest delivery delay (deliverylatency)*. In addition, the *Spray and Wait* protocol has a better result in system overhead than the first one.

Keywords: Routing protocols · Delay Tolerant Networks (DTN) · Direct delivery · Epidemic · First contact · Spray and wait

© Springer Nature Switzerland AG 2019
H. Florez et al. (Eds.): ICAI 2019, CCIS 1051, pp. 499–516, 2019.
https://doi.org/10.1007/978-3-030-32475-9_36

1   Introduction

Networks are groups of computing devices connected each other that allow the accomplishment of a task. Additionally, a group of networks can form a network, as is the case of "internet" which is a network of networks. To have several interconnected devices, it is necessary to ensure the transmission of messages from the sender to the destination. In some networks, an information package may pass through several intermediaries before arriving at its destination. The assurance of this transmission is made by means of routing algorithms [1].

According to the mode of communication, networks can be classified into: infrastructure networks in which there is an access point or base station through which the communications are made, or the AD hoc type, in which two Devices communicate directly with each other without any intermediary [1]. Cellular networks (*GSM, Global System for Mobile communications*) are that type of infrastructure, as all communications between devices pass through the base stations distributed by the connection area. In places where there are no base stations, or they are out of reach of wireless devices, information exchange is not possible.

Connections in infrastructure networks (such as the Internet, which uses *Transmission Control Protocol/Internet ProtocolTCP/IP* for message routing) have characteristics such as: established and constant bidirectionality between sender and receiver, delay in Milliseconds when requesting and receiving information and low loss or corruption data [2, 3]. However, there are networks that not accomplish with the aforementioned characteristics. In such networks, protocols such as TCP/IP does not work. These networks are known as Delay-Tolerant and Disruption Networks (DTN) [4]. Finally, the reliability of transmission is low in DTN networks, unlike those using TCP/IP [4].

DTN networks consist of nodes that seek to communicate in scenarios in which the connection between them fails or is null. A particular case of DTNs is the *VehicularDTN (VDTN)*. In this type of networks, the vehicles are used to retransmit messages moving in the network, and to collect messages from origin nodes [5]. Indeed, DTNs can be used in several application. For example, Montoya *et al.* [6] have implemented a monitoring system for agriculture. This study does not implement a DTN but it can be a solution in zones with poor coverage.

In a system of vehicles monitored by GSM, it is necessary to have a connection between the nodes and the base stations to have knowledge of the vehicle information (position, speed, acceleration, fuel levels and oil). In cases where there is no base station, it is not possible to know the status of the vehicles, generating uncertainty in the monitoring operation, until by its displacement, the vehicle re-enters a coverage area of a base station *GSM* and it can deliver the information to its supervisory center.

The VDTN architecture is presented as a solution to a system as described above. With the help of the message routing protocols, it is possible to maintain communication with the monitoring center. However, according to the scenario, some protocols present better performance than others, in terms of the probability of message delivery, the time it takes the message to go from node to node, and the number of messages to be transmitted so that there is successful delivery to the destination.

For the evaluation of performance in routing protocols, several authors are developing hardware implementations called testbed, these allow to demonstrate and evaluate applications of VDTN and validation of the results of simulated evaluations [7]. Developed a prototype of a testbed VDTN in the laboratory using robotic cars, combining LEGO MINDSTORM NXT, desktop computers and laptops. On the other hand in [8] a testbed is presented using real cars developed with the objective of validating technical concepts in a controlled environment. Finally [9] presents a routing protocol called RAPID and for its evaluation are used simulations and a testbed. The testbed consists of 40 buses that travel in an area of 250 square kilometers.

On the other hand, the evaluation by simulation of different routing protocols is a resource used by several authors through the use of simulation software such as *NS-2* (Network Simulator), *NS-3* u *ONE* (*The Opportunistic Networks Environment*) [10], And few authors use real scenario maps with these tools. [11] uses the NS-2 software to evaluate the performance of a routing protocol based on probabilistic gradients. In [12] the NS-3 software is used to evaluate the design of a new routing protocol in a map of the city of Valencia comparing with existing protocols. Another way to evaluate the performance of different routing protocols is through the use of grids, although these do not provide realistic or very frequent scenarios as is the case [13, 14]. In [15] synthetic maps are used for the evaluation of *Epidemic* y *Spray and Wait* routing protocols.

The simulator ONE is a discrete event simulation engine where the main agents of the simulation are the nodes that move on a map. Each node generates, transmits, and delivers messages to other nodes when come into contact For protocol performance evaluation, many authors use the map that loads by default ONE (a portion of the city of Helsinki - Finland), as is the case of [15] that compares the performance of the routing protocols *Epidemic, Spray and Wait, Prophet* y *Maxprop*. [16] evaluates the performance of the protocols, such as *Epidemic, First contact, Direct delivery, Prophet, Spray and Wait* y *Maxprop*. [17] proposes a scheme to avoid nodes which not forward messages and/or delete messages received. Performs a simulation using the *Spray and Wait* routing, improving with its proposal the probability and reducing the overhead in the network. [18] proposes a mobility model that represents the movement of vehicles and population after a disaster that affects the network of transport. Finally [19] proposes two routing protocols based on contact information between nodes, these are compared with protocols such as *Maxprop, Prophet* y *Spray and Wait*.

Few authors have performed real scenario mapping in ONE such as [20], which evaluates the performance of the *Epidemic, Spray and Wait* y *Maxprop* routing protocols on the map of the city of Tirana, capital of Albania.

The work presented in this article is carried out with the objective of determining the characteristics of the message routing protocols in *VDTN* in the Juan de Acosta – Barranquilla route and that could serve as an alternative for the monitored vehicles that transit it, seeking to reduce the uncertainty about its status in areas where *GSM* coverage is not available. It is organized in the following way, in the first section a definition of the delay-tolerant networks, the routing protocols used in this evaluation and the evaluation metrics is made. This is followed by defining the software used in this simulation and the used methodology. Finally, simulation results and conclusions are presented.

2   Delay-Tolerant Networks (DTN)

Delay Tolerant Networks or *DTN* are those that experience intermittent or often zero connections and have a delay in delivering long information. DTNs were proposed as part of the interplanetary network, where satellites do not have a constant line of sight between them or the earth.

In DTNs the senders and receivers of messages are nodes. Nodes can represent vehicles, cell phones or any device that could wirelessly exchange messages, information processing, and storage space. The DTNs base their operation on "routing" a message through a series of nodes, being stored and forwarded by each one. The operation is performed when two nodes are within their communication ranges, until the message reaches the destination node. This process is known as "*store, carry, forward*" [21].

In recent years, the use of DTNs has been of interest to researchers since they allow communication in adverse environments where there is no constant connection between nodes [8]. For this reason, the current applications of DTNs include satellite communications [22], deep space communications [23], submarine communications [24], communications in emergency and disaster situations [11] and communications for Vehicular networks [25].

2.1   Routing Protocols

The development of new routing protocols is a constant activity, in the review of the literature of this article we found numerous routing protocols. They base their operation on the "*store, carry, deliver*" paradigm, however they can be grouped depending on (a) the way make such copies, based on the information known by the nodes and (b) the number of copies it generates. For the first group, there are stochastic and deterministic protocols [26]. The stochastic routing protocols assume that the behavior of the nodes is totally random and is not possible to determine the future encounters of a node in this way when delivering a copy to a node operating under one of these protocols is done without regard if the node has a high probability of delivery.

On the other hand, deterministic protocols assume that future encounters of a node can be predicted based on factors such as the history of encounters, geographical location, among others, making possible to copy messages only to nodes that have a certain probability of to meet the destination node to increase the message delivery rate. On the other hand the routing protocols can generate a single copy of the message, a certain number of copies or an unlimited number of messages; however as more messages are generated, more resources will be used, for example, storage space. Following are the routing protocols that were evaluated are detailed, all these are stochastic protocols that generate different numbers of copies.

2.2   Direct Delivery

It is a protocol that handles a single copy of the message in the whole network, it bases its operation in that the node that generates the message only transmits it when it comes in contact with the destination node. *Direct delivery* is characterized by not excessively occupying the storage space, however, it can make the delivery time of the messages variant, depending on the location of the sending and receiving node. The operation of *Direct delivery* is represented in Fig. 1.

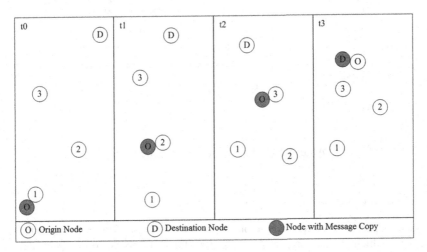

Fig. 1 Direct delivery protocol. Based in [26].

2.3   Epidemic

It was the first proposal for DTN networks made by [27]. Each node in generating a message creates an ID to each message, when two nodes come in contact, exchange the list of IDs to determine which messages are common between the two nodes and which are not. When detecting the non-common messages, the messages are copied so that at the end of the transmission both nodes have the same messages, if the node receiving the new copies of a message has the space to store those copies. In this way, it is sought to create copies of a message on all the nodes to ensure that one of them is delivered to the destination.

However this proposal makes an excessive consumption of storage space making it ideal to use when there is a storage space of considerable size. The following, is the pseudo code of the Epidemic protocol at the moment two nodes come into contact:

```
 1: Procedure Name: OnContact
 2: Input: node a, node b, integer ContactDuration
 3: DropExpiredPackets(a,b) /* Drop packets with their
lifetime expired in both nodes */
 4: ExchangeSummaryVector(a,b)
 5: if ContactDuration > 0 then
 6:          pkt=GetPacket(a)
 7:          if pkt then
 8:                    if NotReceivedBefore(pkt,b) then
 9:                         if IsDestination(pkt,b) then
10:                              SendPacket(pkt,a)
11:                              ConsumePacket(pkt,b)
12:                         else
13:                              SendPacket(pkt,a)
14:                              StorePacket(pkt,b)
15:                         end if
16:                         ContactDuration=ContactDuration-
size(pkt)
17:                    end if
18:          end if
19: end if
```

Algorithm 1. Epidemic Pseudocode [27].

2.4   Firstcontact

This routing protocol bases its operation on delivering a copy of the message to the first node with which it has contact. After the transfer is made the message is deleted, maintaining a single copy in the network. The process is repeated until the message reaches its destination. This process not ensure the delivery of the messages in all cases, since the transference can be made to a node that is not in the path of the destination node. The operation of *Firstcontact* is shown in Fig. 2.

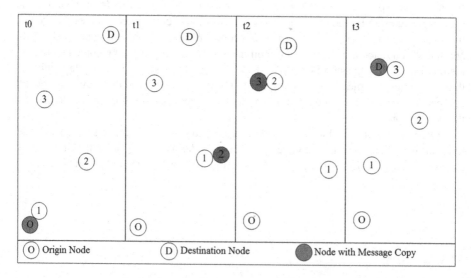

Fig. 2 First contact protocol based in [27].

2.5   Spray and Wait

The routing protocol was proposed by [28] with the objective of ensuring the delivery of messages, creating a certain number of copies but controlling not consume resources such as storage space. It consists of two phases, first to spread (Spray) and then to wait (Wait), hence its name.

In the first phase the sending node creates a message from which a certain number of copies are generated. These copies are delivered to the first nodes with which contact is made. If the message is delivered to the destination in this phase, the route is terminated. If the delivery of the message to the destination is not met in the first phase, then each node maintains a copy of the message and retains it until it is delivered Direct to the destination node.

The two phases of *Spray* and *Wait* are in operation like *Epidemic* with a controlled number of copies and *Direct delivery* respectively. This routing protocol is also characterized by having two types of functions called *Vanilla* and *Binary* in their *Spray* phase. In the first mode, N copies are generated, and a single copy is delivered to the first N-1 nodes to be contacted (the sending node keeps a copy).

In *Binary* mode the first node delivers half of the copies to the first node it comes in contact with (N/2), then each of these nodes delivers at the next contact the half of copies with which it counts and so on until each node only retains a single copy of the message. The following is the pseudo-code of the *Spray and Wait* protocol in *Binary* mode, right in the moment the nodes come in contact:

```
 1: Procedure Name: OnContact
 2: Input: node a, node b, integer ContactDuration
 3: DropExpiredPackets(a,b) /* Drop packets with their
          lifetime expired in both nodes */
 4: ExchangeSummaryVector(a,b)
 5: if ContactDuration > 0 then
 6:         pkt=GetPacket(a)
 7:         if pkt then
 8:                 if NotReceivedBefore(pkt,b) then
 9:                         if IsDestination(pkt,b) then
10:                                 SendPacket(pkt,a)
11:                                 ConsumePacket(pkt,b)
12:                         else
13:                                 NrOfCopies=GetNrOfCopies(pkt,a)
14:                                 if NrOfCopies > 1 then
15:                                         SendPacket(pkt,a)
16:                                         StorePacket(pkt,b)
17:                                         SetNrOfCopies(pkt,a,NrOfCopies/2)
18:                                         SetNrOfCopies(pkt,b,NrOfCopies/2)
19:                                 endif
20:                         endif
21:                         ContactDuration=ContactDuration-size(pkt)
22:                 endif
23:         endif
24: endif
```

Algorithm 2. *Spray and Wait Binary* Pseudo-code [28].

2.6   Evaluation Metrics

When a new protocol is created or evaluated the performance of several existing protocols in a specific scenario, it is important to demonstrate which one is better. In this sense, to make this comparison, an evaluation metrics are necessary, here are some of the most used [19]:

Deliveryrate (DR) or "delivery index", specifies a quantity of delivered messages to their destination with respect to all created messages, is calculated by the following Eq. (1):

$$DR = \frac{N° \text{ of delivered messages}}{N° \text{ of created messages}} \tag{1}$$

The DR result is more favorable when it is equal to 1 (or 100% if it is represented by percentages), since the number of messages delivered should be as close as possible to the number of messages created.

Deliverylatency (DL) or "delivery latency", also known as *Averagedelay (AD)* or "average delay" [20]. It is calculated as the average time the delivered messages arrive at their destination using the following formula (2)

$$DL = \frac{\Delta \text{ Delivery time}}{N° \text{ of created messages}} \tag{2}$$

When comparing different protocols through its *DL*, a better result is obtained when approaching zero, since the delivery time of the messages should be the smallest possible.

Overhead (O), represents the overhead of the system and is calculated as the difference in total messages transmitted and delivered over the total delivered (messages transmitted are those that are copied between nodes) as shown in Eq. (3):

$$O = \frac{N° \text{ of created messages} - N° \text{ of delivered messages}}{N° \text{ of delivered messages}} \tag{3}$$

In the evaluation of *DTNs* routing protocols, *O* is expected to approach zero (or 0% if it is represented by percentages), since it represents the overload of messages that have been created but not delivered in the network and occupy resources such as storage space and energy. This metric is fundamental for the evaluation of *DTNs* since it can saturate quickly the network with message overload [20].

2.7   The Opportunistic Networks Environment

DTNs message routing protocols can be evaluated in a simulation before implementation, so software has been designed for this purpose has been developed. The simulator *ONE (The Opportunistic Networks Environment)* [9] is a discrete event simulation engine where the main agents of the simulation are the nodes. There are mobile and static nodes. A node represents an element that can fulfill the DTNs "store, carry, deliver" paradigm. Nodes have different characteristics to model the behavior of a real node. These characteristics can be the routing protocol, the storage capacity for messages, a communication interface, the communication range, the speed transfer speed on the communication interface, and others.

In *ONE* simulator to ensure communication and messages exchange between nodes, there are equal communication interfaces. A communication interface is determined by the name of the interface, the transfer rate and the communication range.

In addition, the nodes have mobility models, algorithms that define how each node moves on the map. Among the mobility models implemented by *ONE* are the "*Shortest Path Map Based Movement*" or *SPMBM* that chooses a random point on the map and moves to it using the shortest route established by the streets or map routes. There is also the *Stationary movement* model that is used when nodes without mobility are required.

In this article a simulated evaluation of a rural environment between a city and a municipality is carried out. It is a scenario that focuses on the road that communicates the two communities. The monitored vehicles that follow this route, suffer disconnection due to lack of GSM coverage, due to the shortage of base stations. The motivation of this work is due to the obvious need to provide connectivity to an area of low cell phone network coverage. It is a fairly busy municipal interconnection route and a work like the one proposed establishes a starting point for an implementation aimed at solving the problem. The evaluation will determine the performance of message routing protocols by changing the number of nodes and their storage capacity. The protocols to be evaluated are *Direct delivery*, *Epidemic*, *First contact* and *Spray and Wait*.

3 Materials and Methods - Description of the Evaluation

The present study arises due the necessity to track vehicles in rural areas where the lack of network coverage is a problem, then a simulation which recreate the conditions in a real road is necessary.

The first step to develop the simulation was the selection of the software to perform the evaluation. Meléndez *et al.* [29] has been used LabVIEW as software to simulate the process. Nevertheless, ONE was chosen [9] as a tool validated by the scientific community due the multiple jobs that are supported; consequently, Juan de Acosta – Barranquilla scenario is represented considering the following factors.

3.1 Juan de Acosta – Barranquilla Scenario

To use the Juan de Acosta – Barranquilla scenario map, the following procedure was performed:

- From the Open Street Map website, the area of interest in OSM format was selected and downloaded.
- Using the Java Open Street Map (JOSM) tool, filtering was performed, eliminating those elements that were not relevant such as mountains, peaks, lakes, etc., leaving only the vehicular routes of the Juan de Acosta – Barranquilla scenario.
- Finally, the OSM format is converted to a. WKT file to be used with ONE.

3.2   Generation and Reception of Messages

In the DTN there is sending and receiving messages between the nodes that compose it. For this test it has been established that mobile nodes (which pretend to be vehicles) are the message emitters. Also on the map are distributed static nodes that pretend to be base stations of cellular telephony, which will be the receivers of the messages. These base stations are distributed considering the location of the existing base stations that are in the evaluated scenario.

In establishing the nodes in this way, we seek to emulate the real-world behavior of supervised vehicles that consistently generate and send messages when there is coverage. In the simulation these messages are considered successfully sent when the vehicle finds coverage of a base station.

3.3   Mobile Nodes

In the simulation there are three groups representing mobile nodes, each with a minimum and maximum speed. These groups simulate different types of vehicles that travel on the map. The speeds of the groups are from 3 to 70 km/h, 50 to 100 km/h and 50 to 80 km/h.

Number of Mobile Nodes: The number of nodes in each of the three groups of nodes is set at 10, 20, 30 and 40 for a total of nodes in the simulation of 30, 60, 90 and 120.

Range of Communication Between Nodes: The mobile nodes have a single communication interface with a transfer speed set at 1 MB/s and a range of 100 mts. The static nodes or base stations have two communication interfaces, the first is the same used by the mobile nodes and the second with a transfer rate of 1 MB/s and a range of 35,000 mts.

3.4   GSM Communication Coverage

The objective of this work is to determine the performance characteristics of the protocols evaluated in an environment where due to the lack of coverage in the whole route that the nodes (vehicles) must meet, there are intermittences on communications. In the simulator *ONE*, a group of fixed nodes representing the base stations were established. The location of the base stations was determined by the following procedure:

- The OpenSignal application was installed available for Android and IOS devices. This application allows to determine the position of the base stations and the level of GSM communication coverage.
- Trips from the city to the municipality by the two main routes were made, in this process the application registered information of the state of the base stations. Parallel to this was a direct observation of the base stations that were visible from the route.

- Once the above steps were taken, it was determined that the coverage zones in the Juan de Acosta – Barranquilla route are in the urban centers next to the road where they have a base station. The coordinates of these base stations are obtained from the OpenSignal application.

The base stations were then located on the *ONE* map, representing the study scenario. The location of the base stations was adjusted to less than 100 meters of the route, because in the *ONE* simulator sending messages between nodes is possible if they have identically configured communications interfaces.

4   Consolidating Simulation Parameters

The application ran sixteen times for each of the following routing protocols: First contact, Direct delivery, Epidemic, and Spray and Wait. For the Spray and Wait protocol a number of copies were used in the first six phase of Binary type.

The consolidation of the simulation parameters is shown in Table 1. For each run application the values of "storage capacity" and the number of mobile nodes where modified. The parameters for the simulation, were selected taking into account the previous works developed in this same subject.

Table 1. Simulation parameters.

Parameter	Value
Time	24 h
Simulation Map	Juan de Acosta – Barranquilla Route
Number of groups	4 (3 mobile groups and a group of base stations)
Number of nodes	30, 60, 90, 120
Storage capacity	5 Mb, 10 Mb, 15 Mb, 20 Mb
Mobility Models	SPMBM
Speed	3 km/h–100 km/h
Message lifespan	5 h
Message size	500 Kb–1 Mb
Generating time messages	60 s
Routing Protocol	Direct delivery, Epidemic, First contact, Spray and Wait.

5   Results

Due to the different metrics that are evaluated by varying parameters, the results are presented divided by metrics and from Presented from smaller to greater number of nodes (30 and 120); In each graph the storage capacity is varied. *Delivery rate* and *overhead* are presented in percentage, *delivery latency* is presented in minutes.

5.1 Delivery Rate Evaluation Results

According to Figs. 3 and 4 it is observed that *First contact* and *Spray and Wait* present greater *DR* in all the scenarios when the number of nodes is varied. In the case of *Spray and Wait*, a direct relationship between the storage capacity and the *DR* is observed, this is due to the number of copies generated by the *Spray* phase when there is a new message, causing it to occupy large storage space in the nodes and it is impossible for new copies to be received when they are filled out.

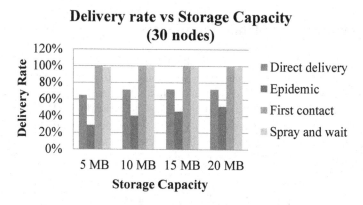

Fig. 3 *Delivery rate* of 30 nodes vs Storage capacity.

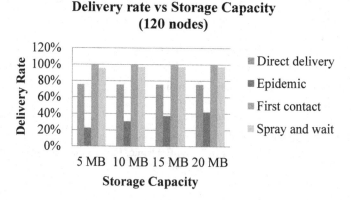

Fig. 4 Delivery rate of 120 nodes vs Storage capacity.

The Direct delivery protocol presents better results when the number of nodes increases. On the other hand, the *Epidemic* protocol presents the worst results in *DR*, although for each scenario of 30, 60, 90 and 120 nodes a better result is obtained as the storage capacity is increased, however the *DR* decreases as there are more nodes. This is due to *Epidemic* way of operating, which generates unlimited copies of the message, making it possible for more storage capacity to receive more copies, but there comes a point where copies of a message must be rejected because there is no storage capacity. In the same way, when the number of nodes increases, more messages are produced that saturate the network

5.2 Delivery Latency Evaluation Results

Based on Figs. 5 and 6 it is observed that the routing protocol with higher *DL* is *Direct delivery*, on the other hand *First contact* presents the lowest *DL*; Although both routing protocols are single copy, the transfer between several nodes of *First contact* favors the delivery time of the messages even increasing the number of nodes increases *DL*.

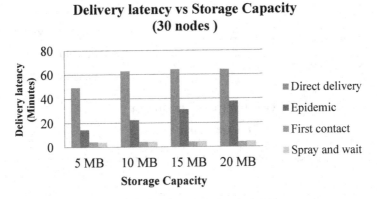

Fig. 5 *Delivery latency* of 30 nodes vs Storage capacity.

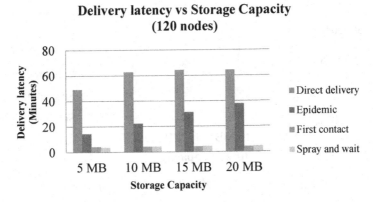

Fig. 6 Delivery latency of 120 nodes vs Storage capacity.

The *Epidemic* protocol presents a *DL* that varies depending on the number of nodes and the storage capacity. When observing its progress, it can be affirmed that *Epidemic* decreases *DL* when the number of nodes is increasing. On the other hand, *Spray and*

Wait although the scenario of smaller numbers of nodes and less storage capacity presents the lowest *DL* of all scenarios, this number increases when these two parameters increase. This is due to the *Spray* phase, which delivers a limited number of copies to the nodes which is contacted regardless.

5.3   Overhead Evaluation Results

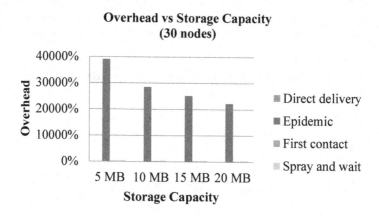

Fig. 7 *Overhead* of 30 nodes vs Storage capacity.

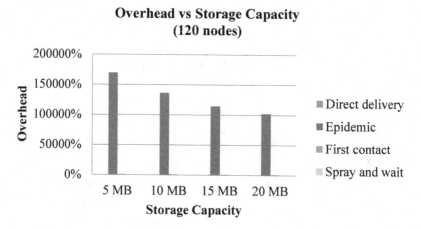

Fig. 8 Overhead of 120 nodes vs Storage capacity.

Figures 7 and 8 show that *Epidemic* is a protocol which generates overload in the system by creating unlimited copies of the message to all the nodes contacted, for this reason when increasing the number of nodes major tends to be *O*, Resulting in the highest value in all scenarios for all protocols. Because the value of *O* is significantly higher for the *Epidemic* protocol, making difficult the interpretation of the graph, the following images show the performance of the *First contact*, *Direct delivery* and *Spray and Wait* protocols.

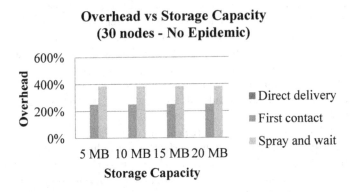

Fig. 9 *Overhead* of 30 nodes vs Storage capacity.

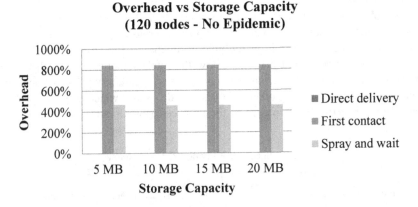

Fig. 10 Overhead 120 nodes vs Storage capacity.

Figures 9 and 10 show that *First contact* presents greater *overhead* when there are more nodes, this is because the message is delivered to any node no matter that it may or not be suitable to deliver the message to the faster receiver, in this way a single message can be delivered multiple times until it reaches to its destination. The *Direct delivery* protocol does not generate *overhead* because for each delivered message a single transfer is made to the destination node.

6 Conclusions

It is clarified that the base stations were not located in the actual positions on the map. This is because the simulator *ONE* does not allow the transmission of messages between nodes with communication interfaces of different characteristics. This prevents different communication ranges for the base stations representing the *GSM* communication coverage. However, the new location of the stations does not affect the results of the simulation, because they are placed in places close to the main roads and/or roads that serve to enter and exit urban centers, in this way the mobile nodes will have contact with the base stations and the message transfers will be made, if applicable. Since other *GSM* coverage services are not considered, the location of the base stations is adjusted for the simulation.

Based on a balance between the three metrics considered (*delivery rate, delivery latency* y *overhead*), and according to the performance results of routing protocols, it is stated that the protocol with better performance to be implemented in the *DTN* network in the Juan Acosta – Barranquilla scenario is *First contact*, followed by *Spray and wait*. It is clarified that the results of this evaluation correspond to values of the parameters "number of nodes" and "storage capacity" used in this article. In this way different results can be obtained by having a more crowded scenario than the one represented here or in the opposite case.

Non-probabilistic protocols were used in this article. For future work, it is desired to perform further evaluations with other types of protocols, in addition to adding protocols to the message feature to multiple destinations. Similarly, it was observed that the mobility model used does not allow the total emulation of a realistic rural environment and situations such as slowing down at mandatory stops, or accidents, detours or roadblocks, among others. Tables 2 and 3 show which protocol performs better in the selected metrics in each of the two scenarios (30 and 120 nodes).

Table 2. Scenario: 30 nodes. * No epidemic

	5 MB	10 MB	15 MB	20 MB
Delivery rate	First contact	First contact	First contact	First contact
Delivery latency	First contact	Spray and wait	Spray and wait	Spray and wait
Overhead*	Direct delivery	Direct delivery	Direct delivery	Direct delivery

Table 3. Scenario: 120 nodes. * No epidemic

	5 MB	10 MB	15 MB	20 MB
Delivery rate	First contact	First contact	First contact	First contact
Delivery latency	First contact	Spray and wait	Spray and wait	Spray and wait
Overhead*	Direct delivery	Direct delivery	Direct delivery	Direct delivery

References

1. Tanenbaum, A.S., Wetherall, D.J.: Redes De Computadoras (2012)
2. Socolofsky, T.J., Kale, C.J.: TCP/IP tutorial. RFC Editor (1991)
3. Warthman, F., et al.: Delay-and Disruption-Tolerant Networks (DTNs). A Tutorial. V.. 0, Interplanetary Internet Special Interest Group, pp. 5–9 (2012)
4. Rodrigues, J.J.P.C., Soares, V.N.G.J.: An introduction to delay and disruption-tolerant networks (DTNs). In: Advances in Delay-Tolerant Networks, pp. 1–21. Elsevier (2015)
5. Soares, V.N.G.J., Farahmand, F., Rodrigues, J.J.P.C.: A layered architecture for vehicular delay-tolerant networks. In: Proceedings - IEEE Symposium on Computers and Communications, pp. 122–127 (2009)
6. Montoya, F.G., Gómez, J., Cama, A., Zapata-sierra, A., Martínez, F., Luis, J., et al.: A monitoring system for intensive agriculture based on mesh networks and the android system. Comput. Electron. Agric. **99**, 14–20 (2013)
7. Paula, M.C.G., Isento, J.N., Dias, J.A., Rodrigues, J.J.P.C.: A real-world VDTN testbed for advanced vehicular services and applications. In: 2011 IEEE 16th International Workshop on Computer Aided Modeling and Design of Communication Links and Networks, CAMAD 2011, pp. 16–20 (2011)
8. Dias, J.A., Isento, J.N., Soares, V.N.G.J., Rodrigues, J.J.P.C.: Impact of scheduling and dropping policies on the performance of vehicular delay-tolerant networks. In: IEEE International Conference on Communications (2011)
9. Balasubramanian, A., Levine, B., Venkataramani, A.: DTN routing as a resource allocation problem. ACM SIGCOMM Comput. Commun. Rev. **37**(4), 373 (2007)
10. Keränen, A., Ott, J., Kärkkäinen, T.: The ONE simulator for DTN protocol evaluation. In: Proceedings of the Second International ICST Conference on Simulation Tools and Techniques (2009)
11. Chenji, H., Stoleru, R.: Delay-tolerant networks (DTNs) for emergency communications. In: Advances in Delay-Tolerant Networks, pp. 105–136. Elsevier (2015)
12. Martínez, S., Director, T., Manzoni Director, P., Vicente, C.G., Tornell, S.M.: Diseño de un protocolo para redes tolerantes a retardos: RTaDAP (2011)
13. Honda, T., Ishikawa, S., Ikeda, M., Barolli, L.: A message suppression method for vehicular delay tolerant networking. In: Proceedings of the 2014 9th International Conference on Broadband and Wireless Computing, Communication and Applications, BWCCA 2014, pp. 351–356 (2014)
14. Ishikawa, S., Honda, T., Ikeda, M., Barolli, L.: Investigation of message suppression method considering TCP in vehicular-DTN. In: Proceedings of the IEEE 29th International Conference on Advanced Information Networking and Applications Workshops, WAINA 2015, pp. 370–375 (2015)
15. Robles, D.G.: Evaluación de algoritmos de propagación de mensajes en redes oportunistas, Universitat Politècnica de Catalunya (2013)
16. Spaho, E., Barolli, L., Kolici, V., Lala, A.: Performance evaluation of different routing protocols in a vehicular delay tolerant network. In: 2015 10th International Conference on Broadband and Wireless Computing, Communication and Applications (BWCCA), pp. 157–162 (2015)
17. Abdelkader, T., Naik, K., Nayak, A., Goel, N., Srivastava, V.: A performance comparison of delay-tolerant network routing protocols. IEEE Netw. **30**(2), 46–53 (2016)
18. Páez Bencomo, M.I.: Análisis y evaluación de prestaciones de protocolos de encaminamiento en Redes Tolerante al Retardo, Universidad Politécnica de Madrid (2013)

19. Chakrabarti, C.: A dynamic two hops reputation assignment scheme for selfish node detection and avoidance in delay tolerant network. In: 2015 IEEE International Conference on Research in Computational Intelligence and Comunication Network, pp. 345–350 (n.d.)
20. Uddin, Y.S., Nicol, D.M., Abdelzaher, T.F., Kravets, R.H.: A post-disaster mobility model for delay tolerant networking. In: Proceedings of the Winter Simulation Conference, pp. 2785–2796 (2009)
21. Chen, H., Lou, W.: Contact expectation based routing for delay tolerant networks. Ad Hoc Netw. **36**, 244–257 (2016)
22. Caini, C.: Delay-tolerant networks (DTNs) for satellite communications. In: Advances in Delay-Tolerant Networks, pp. 25–47. Elsevier (2015)
23. Clarke, N.L., Ghita, B.V., Furnell, S.M.: Delay-tolerant networks (DTNs) for deep-space communications. In: Advances in Delay-Tolerant Networks, pp. 49–60. Elsevier (2015)
24. Rahman, R.H., Frater, M.R.: Delay-tolerant networks (DTNs) for underwater communications. In: Advances in Delay-Tolerant Networks, pp. 81–103. Elsevier (2015)
25. Soares, V.N.G.J., Rodrigues, J.J.P.C.: Vehicular delay-tolerant networks (VDTNs). In: Advances in Delay-Tolerant Networks, pp. 61–80. Elsevier (2015)
26. Amah, T.E., Kamat, M., Moreira, W., Abu Bakar, K., Mandala, S., Batista, M.A.: Towards next-generation routing protocols for pocket switched networks. J. Netw. Comput. Appl. **70**, 51–88 (2016)
27. Vahdat, A., Becker, D.: Epidemic routing for partially connected ad hoc networks. Technical report Number CS-200006, Duke University (CS-200006), pp. 1–14 (2000)
28. Spyropoulos, T., Psounis, K., Raghavendra, C.S.: Spray and wait: an efficient routing scheme for intermittently connected mobile networks. In: SIGCOMM, pp. 252–259 (2005)
29. Meléndez, F., Vélez, J., Caicedo, J.: Modelado y prueba de desempeño en tasa de errores de bits de un sistema de comunicaciones con modulación QAM y codificación Reed-Solomon utilizando LabVIEW para la enseñanza en pre... Revista Técnica de La Facultad de Ingeniería **40**(3) (2017)

Recovering Fine Grained Traceability Links Between Software Mandatory Constraints and Source Code

Alejandro Velasco[✉] and Jairo Hernan Aponte Melo[✉]

Departamento de Ingeniería de Sistemas e Industrial,
Universidad Nacional de Colombia, Bogotá, Colombia
{savelascod, jhapontem}@unal.edu.co

Abstract. Software traceability is a necessary process to carry out source code maintenance, testing and feature location tasks. Despite its importance, it is not a process that is strictly conducted since the creation of every software project. Over the last few years information retrieval techniques have been proposed to recover traceability links between software artifacts in a coarse-grained and middle-grained level. In contexts where it is fundamental to ensure the correct implementation of regulations and constraints at source code level, as in the case of HIPAA, proposed techniques are not enough to find traceability links in a fine-granular way. In this research, we propose a fine-grained traceability algorithm to find traces between high level requirements written in human natural language with source code lines and structures where they are implemented.

Keywords: Software traceability · Information retrieval · Static code analysis · Software maintenance · Program slicing · Natural language processing · Healthcare

1 Introduction

Software traceability is a research area in software engineering that aims to recover traces and links between high-level artifacts (e.g. documentation, use case diagrams, requirements specifications) and source code artifacts (e.g. classes and methods) [12, 26]. Due to its nature, the traceability of the code constitutes an imperative role in code comprehension and helps to perform a wide variety of tasks such as bug tracking, feature location, and software testing. Traceability focuses on making easier the assurance of stakeholder's needs and the correct implementation of functional and non-functional requirements in any software system [33].

Although traceability should be carried out from the beginning of any software project [37], in practice, it is an unusual activity. Developers usually center their efforts more on building the software system than on making documentation artifacts. Similarly, it is a common practice of developers to face the documentation of the system in the final stages of any project to fulfill deadlines [37]. These practices may cause serious problems when assuring the quality of the constructed artifacts as well as the verification of the compliance of final products with the initial requirements and needs of stakeholders.

© Springer Nature Switzerland AG 2019
H. Florez et al. (Eds.): ICAI 2019, CCIS 1051, pp. 517–532, 2019.
https://doi.org/10.1007/978-3-030-32475-9_37

In the context of critical software systems, it is crucial that the software products comply with security, privacy, and safety regulations (e.g., HIPAA law for healthcare information systems). Software companies and regulatory entities, such as the HHS (U. S. Department of Health and Human Services) Office for Civil Rights, must assure regulatory compliance of software systems [3]; typically, regulators conduct manual inspection of the source code to achieve such purposes [14, 17, 35]. To support people on critical mandatory constraint's verification (which is a difficult and error-prone traceability task), research has devoted to develop automated techniques on traceability links recovery. However, existing techniques only go down to link classes and methods with high-level constraints. Mandatory constraint's compliance requires going to deeper granularity levels in order to confirm and assure that software systems implement mandatory regulations and requirements.

Fine-grained traceability link recovery is intended to fully support requirement compliance of software, by linking critical mandatory constraints to specific code structures such as statements, conditions, variable assignments and basic code blocks. To accomplish such objective, we developed a software traceability technique which based on heuristics, IR techniques and static software code analysis, is able to identify traces between software mandatory constraints and source code structures.

2 Related Work

Requirement mapping is an expensive task that is required to ensure the software compliance of constraints and features given by stakeholders and organizations [14]. In the particular case of HIPAA [1], there are several studies conducted to classify the statutes by topology in order to make the validation process a more comprehensive task. HIPAA law is divided in three principal sets of regulatory constraints, in the particular case of healthcare software systems, HIPAA establish a set of standards and rules that must be covered and taken into account in order to protect the security and confidentiality, and ensure the correct management of all patients' data [3]. Breaux [15, 17], defined a semantic model by identifying language patterns to extract rights and obligations from HIPAA statutes, the requirement classification was conducted for privacy rules on HIPAA regulations. Based on the Breaux methodology, two frameworks were constructed and evaluated [16, 27, 38]. Alshugran et al., proposed as well a process to extract privacy requirements from HIPAA, since the law regulations are written in a complex and dense format, authors proposed a set of methods to analyze, extract and model privacy rules [9]. There are also studies that intend to find the best way to evaluate the legal compliance of HIPAA requirements in software healthcare systems. Maxwell et al. proposed a production rule model to encourage requirement engineers to keep trace between law and high level artifacts across every development process [30], authors validated the proposed technique against iTrust, an HIPAA compliant healthcare system.

2.1   Traceability Links Recovery

Most techniques for traceability link recovery between software requirements and source code operate at coarse-grained and middle-grained levels of granularity [2, 10, 11, 13, 18, 21, 24, 28, 29, 31]. Fasano [24] proposes ADAMS, a tool for automatic traceability management; the recovery link technique proposed, uses Latent Semantic Indexing (LSI) as an improvement of the Vector Space Model technique [20, 23], under the assumption that almost every software system has high level software artifacts with well-defined hierarchical structure. ADAMS is able to recover traceability links between software high level documentation and classes in the source code.

Marcus and Maletic [29] address the problem of recovering traceability links between methods and documentation, using LSI, which extract the meanings (i.e., semantics) of the documentation and source code, using all the comments and identifier names presents in the source code.

Paloma et al. [31] designed a tool called CRYSTAL (Crowdsourcing RevIews to SupporT App evoLution) to create traceability links between commits, issues (given a software release) and user reviews, using IR techniques with some adaptations to remove useless words, calculate the textual similarity of the artifacts, and select the candidate links according to a criterion (i.e., a threshold value).

De Lucia et al. [28] adopt the use of smoothing filters to reduce the effects of noise in software artifacts. By an empirical study, the authors describe a significant improvement of the IR techniques Vector Space Model and Latent Semantic Indexing.

Diaz et al. [21] proposed the usage of code ownership to improve the candidate links generation under the assumption that if a developer authored code that is linked to a particular high level artifact, then other code developed by the same author is likely to be associated with the same artifact. This technique was adopted to tackle the problem of vocabulary mismatch present in the associated artifacts. Their solution was named TYRION (TraceabilitY link Recovery using Information retrieval and code OwNership).

2.2   Alternative Methods and Improvements for Traceability Link Recovery Techniques

There are also approaches that aim to produce results at a fine-grained granularity level, between features and specific source code structures like statements, decisions and basic blocks [22]. Those strategies, mainly take advantage of the execution traces of defined features in a software system, heuristics, and source code static analysis techniques [19, 32, 34–36]. Wong et al. [36] propose a technique based on execution slices, which takes as an input set of test cases that exercise and a set of test cases that do not exercise the feature of interest. Using dynamic information extracted by running the instrumented software system (i.e., list of statements executed), the technique is able to distinguish between code that is unique to a feature, and code that is common to several features.

Dagenais and Robillard [19] propose a model based on heuristics and source code static analysis, to recover traceability links between the software documentation, and the software API documentation. The authors designed a meta-model representation of the involved artifacts (i.e., documentation, source code and support channels) to understand the context in which a code-like term is used.

Sharif and Maletic [5, 34] developed an approach to support the evolution of traceability links. The process to update and evolve traceability links is supported by the differentiation between versions of the involved artifacts in a traceability link. The authors compare XML tags to address the new locations and evolve the links.

2.3   Limitations of Adopted Strategies

Current IR-based techniques for recovering traceability links, designed to associate software requirements to code, have focused on coarse-grained granularity (i.e., files and classes), they trace high-level software artifacts to files, classes, up to methods. The reason for this is that granular source code structures (e.g., if-statements or exception handling statements) usually do not contain enough textual information that matches the vocabulary of high-level artifacts [23]. This leads to low accuracy of IR-based techniques. Therefore, it is necessary to define new techniques or improve the existing ones if we want to generate traceability links between high-level documents (such as software mandatory constraints) and code structures (e.g., conditionals, assignations, method calls).

3   Dataset Description

In order to trace high level constraints into source code by using a software traceability technique, we define a taxonomy to classify HIPAA statutes that are more concerned with software implementation standards and regulations. Not all sections written in the HIPAA rules are related to software healthcare management systems; since in this study we aim to trace regulations related to software implementations, we filtered the most related HIPAA statutes and user data security regulations (as stated in the privacy rule); then, we extracted a set of law statutes that apply for our particular problem. Table 1 summarizes the HIPAA administrative simplification, in this study we decided to analyze the Security and Privacy rule of HIPAA since it contains the major part of regulations related to the implementation of healthcare management systems.

We take as input those statutes derived from HIPAA security and privacy rules as were defined in the administrative simplification; then we identified those that are suitable to associate with source code implementations and configurations in healthcare systems. As a result, we defined a taxonomy of rules in which we classified the law constraints according to three categories.

The first category (A) defines the rules that could be easily traced into code. It consists of regulations that mainly refer to functional requirements that must be implemented in every HIPAA compliant healthcare system. The second category (B) has those statutes that define constraints related to software implementation and non-functional requirements, still suitable to be traced to code. Finally, the third category (C) groups statutes and standards related to the way in which organizations and health care providers assume practices and methods to interact with healthcare systems in order to protect the private information of patients, and that therefore are unsuitable

Table 1. Taxonomy of HIPAA Security and Privacy regulations.

ID	Category	Subpart	Statutes samples
A	Potentially suitable to trace into code	Security Standards: General Rules Administrative safe guards Technical safeguards	164.306(a)(1), 164.306(a)(2), 164.306(a)(3), 164.308(a)(1)(ii)(D), 164.308(a)(5)(ii)(C), 164.308(a)(5)(ii)(D)
B	Moderate suitable to trace into code	Administrative safe guards	164.308(a)(1)(i), 164.308(a)(1)(ii), 164.308(a)(4)(ii)(A), 164.308(a)(4)(D)(B)
C	Indirectly related to health care software systems	Security Standards: General Rules Administrative safe guards Physical safeguards	164.306(a)(1), 164.306(a)(2), 164.306(a)(3), 164.306(c), 164.306(d), 164.306(d)(1), 164.306(d)(2), 164.306(d)(3)

to be traced to code. Table 1 shows a summary of the HIPAA taxonomy from privacy and security rules that we considered in this study.

3.1 Healthcare Systems

In order to design a fine-grained traceability algorithm with the ability to trace and associate links between high level artifacts and software source code structures, we identify healthcare software systems whose source code is available. Thus, we focused in java open source healthcare systems with available documentation (e.g. use cases, user stories, user manuals). It is also important to mention that such health care systems were explicitly defined as HIPAA compliant in official pages.

Our search process identified four candidates: iTrust [5, 7], OpenMRS [4], OSCAR [6] and TAPAS [8]. These open source projects have available documentation that describes in different ways the features and characteristics implemented by each system. Table 2 summarizes the main characteristics of these four health care systems.

Table 2. Summary of open source health care systems chosen to analyze in this study.

Name	Repository	Version
TAPAS	https://sourceforge.net/projects/tap-apps/	v. 0.1
iTrust	https://sourceforge.net/projects/it	v. 21
OSCAR	https://sourceforge.net/projects/scarmcmaster	v. 14.0.0
OpenMRS	https://github.com/openmrs	v. 1.12.x

Each of the health care systems have conventional features that implement standards defined in HIPAA law. The features that we could evidence in all systems by observing the deployed applications include user authentication, patient historical data management, appointments definitions, diseases reports, audit controls and data encryption.

We observed the extension of files that interact with the source code in some way from each system, as described in Table 3. For source code analysis we took into account .java .js and .jsp extensions. Such files contain statements written in java and javascript, and also html and custom tags; .xml and .properties files have relevant information about constants and variables that are used within the source code, hence were also relevant for our purpose. Finally, .sql files contain sql sentences with significant information about data and entities related to the application domain and are referenced in the source code.

Table 3. Summary of source code artifacts that were taken as the corpus of the traceability algorithm

	iTrust	OpenMRS	OSCAR	TAPAS
JAVA	936	1545	3810	221
JSP	266	447	1655	0
JS	3636	416	875	0
XML	14	820	193	14
SQL	192	2	711	0
PROPS	7	39	39	2
TOTAL SC ARTIFACTS	5051	3269	7283	237

3.2   Extracting Requirements from High Level Artifacts

Since we want to associate high level requirements with source code, one of the problems that we had to face is the extraction of specific requirements from the available documentation on each health care system.

We setted apart several phrases and paragraphs from requirements explicitly declared in the software high level artifacts (query of our algorithm). Then, we extracted software requirements embedded in sentences from the documentation of all four systems, according to the next format:

$$[Article] + [Subject] + [ObligationVerb] + [Complement]$$

The extracted requirements were textually taken from documentation without any modification. In some cases, following the precise definition of the format leads to the extraction of phrases with no sense or context. For that reason, in such particular cases, we included in the extraction additional information (i.e. terms that were not taken into account when the filter was applied) from the surrounding text of such phrases complete them. Table 4 shows some examples of specific requirements extracted from artifacts of each system.

Finally, we selected all the extracted requirements that were more suitable to trace into code according to the proposed taxonomy of HIPAA Security and Privacy regulations. To put it another way, we associated each extracted requirement with a HIPAA statute and focused on those in the categories (A) and (B) of the proposed classification (Table 2).

4 Fine Grained Traceability Algorithm

Different approaches have been adopted to conduct a traceability link recovery process. In order to support regulatory compliance verification at a granular level, we proposed a technique that involve information retrieval (IR) techniques, static code analysis and heuristics derived from observations after a process of manual analysis of source code implementations.

The proposed algorithm takes advantage of search algorithms developed in information retrieval techniques as well as heuristic derived from observations and static analysis of source code. Figure 1, shows a summary of our proposed technique.

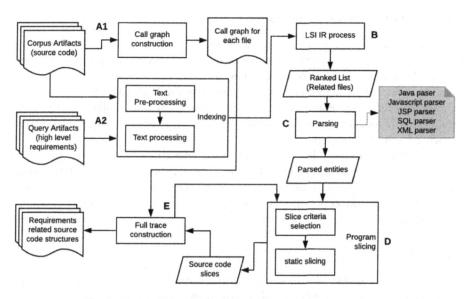

Fig. 1. Proposed fine-grained traceability link recovery process

4.1 A1: Call Graph Construction from Source Code Files

The files and artifacts that contain the source code and relevant structures present in the implementation of a system are all of a very different nature. Java classes are constituted by attributes and methods, javascript code files are batch processing files that are stored in plain text, JSP files are a combination of java code, javascript code, tomahawk and html tags. The process of A1 as depicted in Fig. 1, can be summarized in the generation of a plain text file with the information of methods headers (i.e. access modifier [optional], return type, name, parameter list, exception throws [optional]) and their path in the different source code artifacts.

4.2   A2: Indexing Phase

Before going through the algorithm of information retrieval, several processing tasks are performed on the text for both the corpus and the query. The query is a list of requirements writing in natural human language to be traced into the corpus, which is the source code of a selected system.

When dealing with two entries of a different nature, the treatment of the terms that make up the corpus and the query is essentially different in both cases. With respect to the treatment performed on the query, tokenization, stemming, stopword removal, part of speech (a.k.a. POS) tagging, punctuation removal, number spell out and word embedding [3, 5, 8, 16, 25] task are performed. On the other hand, the tasks carried out with the terms that make up the corpus include stop word removal, splitting by camel case, punctuation removal and tokenization.

4.3   B: Information Retrieval Process

Once the corpus and the query are indexed, they are treated as entries for the information retrieval algorithm to obtain a ranked list of the possible corpus files that are most likely related to the text of the query requirements.

After executing the algorithm of information retrieval, k files are obtained in order of relevance for each requirement; that is, if the query file contains a set of n requirements in total, the list of ranked links will contain a total of kn most related files to each entry in the query file.

The determination of the number of links taken into account (k) for each requirement was determined empirically. In other words, after several tests of execution we determined that the optimal value for k fluctuates between 25 and 30 files per requirement. This number is sufficient to obtain the most strictly relevant files, ignoring those that are least related to requirements.

4.4   C: Parsing Phase

Once the list of possible files more related to a given requirement based on textual similarity is obtained, the next phase of the algorithm consists of analyzing source code implementations and perform abstractions through program slicing, to find structures at source code level that are related to the implementation of a particular requirement. In order to correctly extract different structures within the code, we use parsers for each type of file that was included in the corpus file. The parsers statically analyze code elements present in .java, .js, .jsp, .xml, .sql, .properties and plain text files. Parsers receive as input a source code fragment and give us an Abstract Syntax Tree (AST) representation of it in a way that make it easier to process.

4.5 D: Program Slicing Process

After executing the parsers for each type of source code file, it is possible to extract code fragments of interest since we are able to perform an exhaustive static analysis of source code. For each of the files that were identified by the information retrieval algorithm (LSI), slicing criteria were defined taking into account the subjects present in the description of each requirement. Within the source code there are terms (e.g. subjects, adjectives, verbs) of the problem context and therefore it is possible to define slicing criteria from the names of variables, objects, classes and methods. To illustrate this point, let's assume that a requirement r1 contains a total of 4 subject names; so it is possible to define 4 slicing criteria to conduct a program slicing process in each file obtained from the retrieval information algorithm for r1 after executing the process defined in B (Fig. 1). For each source code file, a slicing process is performed to obtain the code lines within each file that affect or are affected by a particular criterion. The result of this operation is a set of slices for each file ranked in B.

4.6 E: Full Trace Construction Phase

The information given by the process of abstraction of the source code through program slicing is not enough to build entirely the trace of a requirement. To put it another way, consider a slice of source code obtained after applying the process defined in D; it is highly likely that such fragment of code contains calls to other methods within the system that do not necessarily contain terms in common with a high level requirement but that fulfill a very important role in the implementation. This problem can also be seen as a consequence of delegation.

In this phase of the algorithm the fragments of code obtained in the slices are analyzed and, for each call to an external method that is not defined in the parent file, a search process is carried out according to the definition header of the method that is invoked with the support of the mapping file obtained in A1. Each of the methods that are referenced are also included in the trace of the requirement and recursively, a slicing process D is performed.

To carry out the process of evaluation and testing of our approach, we developed a tool in Java that implements the traceability technique previously exposed. It was named Fine Grained Traceability Hunter (FGTHunter). We implemented a set of tools designed for static analysis of source code, as well as information retrieval algorithms.

Table 4. Some specific requirements extracted from the available documentation of selected healthcare systems

ID	Requirement	System	Documentation
ITRUST-1	"An HCP is able to create a patient [S1] or disable a selected patient [S2]. The create/disable patients and HCP transaction is logged (UC5)"	iTrust	http://agile.csc.ncsu.edu/iTrust/wiki/doku.php?id=requirement

(*continued*)

Table 4. (*continued*)

ID	Requirement	System	Documentation
OSCAR-1	"Your password is stored in an encrypted format such that even the system administrator cannot find out what it is. If you have forgotten your user name and/or password, your administrator can reset the password for you but he/she cannot tell you what the original password was"	OSCAR	http://oscarmanual.org/oscar_emr_12/General%20Operation/access-preferences-and-security/accessing-oscar
TAPAS-1	"The system must have the ability to manage users in the system. Like clinical data, users should not be able to be deleted from the system as they will be tied to activities in a record"	TAPAS	http://tap-apps.sourceforge.net/docs/use-cases.html#UCSYSADM-01

5 Results

We executed the traceability algorithm implemented in the FGTHunter tool for each of the open source systems. We collected the results and evaluated the precision of our technique to find traceability links between high level artifacts and source code lines. The algorithm was able to successfully find a large number of the high-level requirements filtered for this study, along with new traceability links that were not originally found by the manual construction of traces.

To evaluate the performance of our technique, we calculated the F1 score for each extracted requirement that was associated with a HIPAA statute; then, we calculated the average of F1 scores obtained in each statute. Results were grouped for each of the analyzed systems. Table 5 summarizes our findings.

The audit management is a fundamental part of any software system that aims to keep track of all the operations that are performed by every actor that use the system. Table 5 shows the average of the harmonic mean (average of F1 score) for the requirements in each healthcare system that are related to HIPAA statute 164.312 (b). The precision of FGTHunter for iTrust and OSCAR systems had an approximate value of 0.4 whereas in TAPAS the precision was much lower. In the process of observation that was made when performing the manual code inspection, we noticed that very few code lines in TAPAS handled the audit control; this may explain the low precision for this case.

The access control of the information within a system ensures the correct manipulation of the data. In the four systems that we analyzed, the access of the information was restricted by the definition of roles and user permissions to see, read, modify or eliminate the data. Table 5 shows the F1 score means of FGTHunter obtained after executing the algorithm to find the lines of code that most are related to the requirements associated with the statute 164.312 (a) (1) of HIPAA in each system. The

Table 5. Summary of results for all healthcare systems analyzed in this study.

HIPAA statute	Description	Average F1 score
164.312(b)	"Implement hardware, software, and/or procedural mechanisms that record and examine activity in information systems that contain or use electronic protected health information"	iTrust: 0,39 OSCAR: 0,39 TAPAS: 0,15
164.312(a)(1)	"Implement technical policies and procedures for electronic information systems that maintain electronic protected health information to allow access only to those persons or software programs that have been granted access rights as specified in §164.308(a)(4)"	iTrust: 0,25 OSCAR: 0,39 OPENMRS: 0,66 TAPAS: 0,39
164.312(a)(2)(i)	"Assign a unique name and/or number for identifying and tracking user identity"	iTrust: 0,43 OSCAR: 0,65 OPENMRS: 0,77
164.312(d)	"Implement procedures to verify that a person or entity seeking access to electronic protected health information is the one claimed"	iTrust: 0,6 OSCAR: 0,87 TAPAS: 0,46
164.312(a)(2)(iii)	"Implement electronic procedures that terminate an electronic session after a predetermined time of inactivity"	iTrust: 0,30 OSCAR: 0,32 TAPAS: 0,46
164.308(a)(5)(ii)(C)	"Procedures for monitoring log-in attempts and reporting discrepancies"	iTrust: 0,48 OSCAR: 0,73 OPENMRS: 0,66
164.308(a)(1)(ii)(D)	"Implement procedures to regularly review records of information system activity, such as audit logs, access reports, and security incident tracking reports"	iTrust: 0,4 OSCAR: 0,39
164.312(e)(2)(i)	"Implement security measures to ensure that electronically transmitted electronic protected health information is not improperly modified without detection until disposed of"	iTrust: 0,41
164.308(a)(5)(ii)(D)	"Procedures for creating, changing, and safeguarding passwords"	iTrust: 0,53 OSCAR: 0,69
164.312(a)(2)(iv)	"Implement a mechanism to encrypt and decrypt electronic protected health information"	OSCAR: 0,83
164.308(a)(7)(ii)(A)	"Establish and implement procedures to create and maintain retrievable exact copies of electronic protected health information"	OSCAR: 0,96 TAPAS: 0,58
164.308(a)(4)(i)	"Establish and implement procedures to create and maintain retrievable exact copies of electronic protected health information"	TAPAS: 0,32
164.312(c)(2)	"Implement electronic mechanisms to corroborate that electronic protected health information has not been altered or destroyed in an unauthorized manner"	TAPAS: 0,63
164.312(c)(1)	"Implement policies and procedures to protect electronic protected health information from improper alteration or destruction"	TAPAS: 0,51

average harmonic mean has an acceptable level (greater than 0.4 points) in OPENMRS, OSCAR and TAPAS; on the other hand, for iTrust the algorithm had the lowest performance. According to our observations, the access control by roles in iTrust was handled by access restrictions defined in the configuration .xml files for the TOMCAT server.

Assigning a unique identifier to each entity of a system ensures the correct manipulation of the data and facilitates the control of the information integrity. According to our observations, the restrictions of non-repetition were always defined at the database level, that is, the traceability of the requirements associated with the Statute 164.312 (a)(2)(i) of HIPAA was carried out analyzing .sql files with thousands of code lines impacting negatively on the precision of our technique. However, according to the results, for OSCAR and OPENMRS systems the algorithm reaches its highest performance, probably because at the application level, the uniqueness of the identifiers for each entity was also validated.

Ensuring the correct implementation of access control mechanisms is a fundamental aspect in any system that manipulates critical information. Such control strategies range from verification of passwords and access codes to role management within the system. Considering the wide spectrum of artifacts in each system that may be related to HIPAA Statute 164.312 (d), it is natural that the accuracy tend to be very high; however in TAPAS that value is low, maybe because the access control in this application is not clearly defined at the application level (i.e. there is no login forms or access restrictions) and externally they must control the access to the information by applying restrictions policies.

Finishing the session after a period of inactivity is a measure of additional protection that usually exists to avoid improper manipulation of the data. The session time limit for a given user is usually specified in a particular line of code within the application, either through a property file, a database record or a global variable. Considering the quantity of artifacts analyzed and the reduced number of code lines in which the requirements related to statute 164.312 (a)(2)(iii) of HIPAA are implemented, for iTrust and OSCAR the level of precision was very low. According to Table 5, TAPAS is the exception probably because in many parts of the code the mechanisms of termination of sessions are repeated, once a particular operation has started.

As a security measure, many information systems keep a record of unsuccessful attempts prior to login for a particular service. Depending on the number of failed attempts, an account is blocked for a period of time or indefinitely until an administrator decides to unblock it. Table 5 summarizes the traceability results for the requirements related to HIPAA Statute 164.308 (a)(5)(ii)(C). iTrust was the system with less precision in this aspect, probably because there are very few code lines where the control of failed attempts is made.

When a user of the system views or edits the information of a particular patient, the audit information should be able to be consulted to follow the detail of the modifications in critical data, as is established by the statute 164.308 (a)(1)(ii)(D) of HIPAA. Table 5 shows the average of the harmonic mean for the systems that implemented control mechanism of visualization for audit data. In general, the performance of the traceability algorithm was acceptable, above 0.4.

As a measure of securing information in the event of a disaster, data security should be periodically generated from the information contained in the database in order to be effectively restored. The HIPAA statute 164.308 (a)(7)(ii)(A) refers to this topic. OSCAR was the system in which our algorithm reached a higher precision, while TAPAS was the opposite case. This particular behavior can be proved when we compare the source code artifacts from both systems that were involved in the implementation of such statute, from our findings in the GOLDSET we can observe that OSCAR contains more lines of code associated with data backups and database restoration than TAPAS.

6 Conclusions

Traceability in software systems is a necessary and important process that must be conducted from the beginning of any project where a large number of people work and delegate tasks. Especially in contexts where it is required to follow strict and critical rules to ensure the correct treatment of data in sensitive information, such is the case of medical health systems that obey written legal regulations such as HIPAA.

From the results it was possible to appreciate that the precision of FGTHunter obtained an acceptable performance (in general, more than 0,4 F1 score mean for each requirement) when in the code there were present good design practices and conventions to name entities according to the context of the problem.

Techniques of static code analysis play a predominant role in the construction of a totally autonomous technique to recover traceability links between high level requirements and source code artifacts. An information recovery technique alone would not achieve a level of precision adequate enough to build the full trace of a requirement.

The restrictions and standards written in legal texts are usually described in a very technical language and detached from a particular context. For this reason, as a step prior to the execution of the algorithm, it was necessary to filter and extract official documentation requirements for each software system that had a relationship with some HIPAA statute within the taxonomy that we defined.

Although it is not a mandatory task in the execution of our technique, when starting from requirements that are defined from a specific context (i.e. system domain) the precision of the technique would improve.

Regulations related to audit control standards and session expiration in the implementation of healthcare systems were in general terms the ones that achieved less precision when analyzed with our traceability algorithm (over 0,35 F1 score mean for each related system). Very few lines and source code structures related with these requirements were successfully mapped by our algorithm for each system; This may be explained probably due to the few places within the source code where these requirements were implemented, increasing in that way the recall of our technique and decreasing the precision. With respect to the other statutes defined in the privacy and security rule of HIPAA, the performance of our algorithm was acceptable (over 0,4 F1 score mean) and in some cases excellent (over 0,8 F1 score mean).

Although, it is very difficult to reach a perfect degree of precision in a traceability technique based on an information retrieval algorithm without the help of an external person to delimit the list of ranked links, our proposal would undoubtedly facilitate the work of those people who seek to certify a system compliance with rules and standards at a source code level, as in the case of HIPAA.

7 Future Work

Our technique was designed for projects written in JAVA EE; future work may require to improve our traceability algorithm so that it would be generic in any programming language independently of the syntax and particular rules. For this purpose we could use controlled techniques of machine learning, and train models constantly with the new trends in programming and design patterns. We could also follow the original approach of our technique and define syntactic analyzers for each programming language in such a way that the source code slicer and code analysis algorithms can be applied.

To evaluate the performance of our technique in other regulations different to HIPAA, we would have to conduct an adequate study of the structure of such regulations and find software systems whose source code and documentation is available for analysis.

An empirical study to assess the performance of our tool with real users and regulation reviewers would give us an important feedback for real situations. This point should be boarded in future improvements for our algorithm.

References

1. Health Insurance Portability and Accountability Act of (1996)
2. Huang, J., Gotel, O., Zisman, A. (eds.): Software and Systems Traceability, p. 27. Springer, London (2012). https://doi.org/10.1007/978-1-4471-2239-5
3. HIPAA Compliance & Enforcement (2018). http://www.hhs.gov/hipaa/for-professionals/compliance-enforcement/. Accessed 27 Sept 2018
4. Home - Documentation - OpenMRS Wiki (2018). https://wiki.openmrs.org/. Accessed 11 Nov 2018
5. iTrust — Medical Free/Libre and Open Source Software (2018). www.medfloss.org/node/542. Accessed 11 Nov 2018
6. OSCAR EMR — Site (2018). http://oscarmanual.org/oscar_emr_12. Accessed 11 Nov 2018
7. start [iTrust] (2018). https://152.46.18.254/doku.php. Accessed 11 Nov 2018
8. TAPAS Home (2018). http://tap-apps.sourceforge.net/docs/srs.html. Accessed 11 Nov 2018
9. Alshugran, T., Dichter, J.: Extracting and modeling the privacy requirements from HIPAA for healthcare applications (2014)
10. Antoniol, G., Canfora, G., Casazza, G., Lucia, A.D.: Information retrieval models for recovering traceability links between code and documentation, San Jose, CA, pp. 40–49 (2000)
11. Antoniol, G., Canfora, G., Casazza, G., Lucia, A.D., Merlo, E.: Tracing object-oriented code into functional requirements. In: Program Comprehension, Proceedings, Limerick, pp. 79–86 (2000)
12. Antoniol, G., Canfora, G., Casazza, G., Lucia, A.D., Merlo, E.: Recovering traceability links between code and documentation. IEEE Trans. Softw. Eng. 28(10), 970–983 (2002)

13. Antoniol, G., Canfora, G., Lucia, A.D., Merlo, E.: Recovering code to documentation links in OO systems. In: Reverse Engineering, Atlanta, GA, pp. 136–144 (1999)
14. Avancha, S., Baxi, A., Kotz, D.: Privacy in mobile technology for personal healthcare. ACM Comput. Surv. 3(1), 1–3 (2012)
15. Breaux, T., Antón, A.: Analyzing regulatory rules for privacy and security requirements. IEEE Trans. Softw. Eng. 34(1), 5–20 (2008)
16. Breaux, T.D., Antón, A.: A Systematic Method for Acquiring Regulatory Requirements: A Frame-Based Approach (2007)
17. Breaux, T.D., Vail, M.W., Anton, A.I.: Towards Regulatory Compliance: Extracting Rights and Obligations to Align Requirements with Regulations (2006)
18. Capobianco, G., Lucia, A.D., Oliveto, R., Panichella, A., Panichella, S.: Improving IR-based traceability recovery via noun-based indexing of software artifacts. J. Softw. Evol. Proc. 25(7), 743–762 (2013)
19. Dagenais, B., Robillard, M.P.: Recovering traceability links between an API and its learning resources (2012)
20. Deerwester, S., Dumais, S.T., Furnas, G.W., Landauer, T.K., Harshman, R.: Indexing by latent semantic analysis. J. Am. Soc. Inf. Sci. 41(6), 391–407 (1990)
21. Diaz, D., Bavota, G., Marcus, A., Oliveto, R., Takahashi, S., Lucia, A.D.: Using code ownership to improve IR-based Traceability Link Recovery (2013)
22. Dit, B., Revelle, M., Gethers, M., Poshyvanyk, D.: Feature Location in Source Code: A Taxonomy and Survey (2011)
23. Dumais, S.T.: Improving the retrieval of information from external sources. Behav. Res. Methods Instr. Comput. 23(2), 229–236 (1991)
24. Fasano, F.: Fine-Grained Management of Software Artefacts, Paris (2007)
25. Goldberg, Y., Levy, O.: word2vec Explained: deriving Mikolov et al.'s negative-sampling word-embedding method, arXiv:1402.3722 [cs, stat] (2014)
26. Gotel, O.C.Z., Finkelstein, C.W.: An analysis of the requirements traceability problem. In: Requirements, pp. 94–101. Springs, CO (1994)
27. Kiyavitskaya, N., et al.: Automating the extraction of rights and obligations for regulatory compliance. In: Li, Q., Spaccapietra, S., Yu, E., Olivé, A. (eds.) ER 2008. LNCS, vol. 5231, pp. 154–168. Springer, Heidelberg (2008). https://doi.org/10.1007/978-3-540-87877-3_13
28. Lucia, A.D., Penta, M.D., Oliveto, R., Panichella, A., Panichella, S.: Improving IR based Traceability Recovery Using Smoothing Filters (2011)
29. Marcus, A., Maletic, J.I.: Recovering documentation-to-source-code traceability links using latent semantic indexing. In: Software Engineering. Proceedings, pp. 125–135 (2003)
30. Maxwell, J.C., Antón, A.I.: Checking Existing Requirements for Compliance with Law Using a Production Rule Model (2009)
31. Palomba, F., et al.: User reviews matter! Tracking crowdsourced reviews to support evolution of successful apps (2015)
32. Qusef, A., Bavota, G., Oliveto, R., Lucia, A.D., Binkley, D.: Recovering test-to-code traceability using slicing and textual analysis. J. Syst. Softw. 88, 147–168 (2014)
33. Ramesh, B., Jarke, M.: Toward reference models for requirements traceability. IEEE Trans. Softw. Eng. 27(1), 58–93 (2001)
34. Sharif, B., Maletic, J.I.: Using fine-grained differencing to evolve traceability links. In: TEFSE/GCT 2007, pp. 76–81, March 2007
35. Shen, W., Lin, C.L., Marcus, A.: Using traceability links to identifying potentially erroneous artifacts during regulatory reviews (2013)

36. Wong, W.E., Gokhale, S.S., Horgan, J.R., Trivedi, K.S.: Locating program features using execution slices, pp. 194–203 (1999)
37. Yadav, V., Joshi, R.K.: Evolution traceability roadmap for business processes, vol. 20, pp. 1–20. ACM, New York (2019)
38. Zeni, N., Mich, L., Mylopoulos, J., Cordy, J.R.: Applying GaiusT for extracting requirements from legal documents (2013)

Using Graph Embedding to Improve Requirements Traceability Recovery

Shiheng Wang, Tong Li$^{(\boxtimes)}$ ⓘD, and Zhen Yang

Beijing University of Technology, Beijing 100124, China
yeweimian21@163.com, {litong,yangzhen}@bjut.edu.cn

Abstract. Information retrieval (IR) is widely used in automatically requirements traceability recovery. Corresponding approaches are built based on textual similarity, that is, the higher the similarity, the higher possibility of artifacts related. A common work of many IR-based techniques is to remove false positive links in the candidate links to achieve higher accuracy. In fact, traceability links can be recovered by different kinds of information, not only the textual information. In our study, we propose to recover more traceability links by exploring both textual features and structural information. Specifically, we use combined IR techniques to process the textual information of the software artifacts, and extract the structural information from the source code, establishing corresponding code relationship graphs. We then incorporate such structural information into the traceability recovery analysis by using graph embedding. The results show that combined IR techniques and using graph embedding technology to process structural information can improve the recovery traceability.

Keywords: Requirements traceability recovery · Graph embedding · Structural information

1 Introduction

Software projects usually consist of many software artifacts, such as requirements documents, source code. The traceability recovery can get the relationships between these artifacts [5]. Traceability links is critical role for software comprehension. Usually, it need to create and maintain traceability links in whole software lifecycle. Unfortunately, in most cases, traceability links recovered from current artifacts. The creation and maintenance of traceability links are primarily manual. It consume lots of work and easy to make mistake. A completely manual traceability approach is usually only applicable to small projects. Although many researches attempt to automate the work, it has encountered a lot of difficulties due to the poor accuracy and too many false positives traceability links. Since most software artifacts contain textual data, many approaches are based on IR techniques. This kind of approach considered that the artifacts have high textual similarity are related. The source and target artifacts form candidate

© Springer Nature Switzerland AG 2019
H. Florez et al. (Eds.): ICAI 2019, CCIS 1051, pp. 533–545, 2019.
https://doi.org/10.1007/978-3-030-32475-9_38

links. The software engineer can discriminate the right or wrong links in the candidate links [2].

If the word used in the source artifacts are same to the word used in the target artifacts, IR-based techniques will have a good performance. But researchers often encounter the lexical mismatches problem due to artifacts developed by different software engineers. Therefore, IR-based approaches suffer from the lexical mismatches [1]. In addition, some artifacts usually are short, most IR techniques cannot get the suitable similarity values between them. This leads to many correct links fall to the end of the candidate list. These problems limit the traceability recovery.

Some approaches [1] focus on lexical transformations to solve problem. While others utilize different types of information to recover the links between artifacts [6], such as structural information of the code.

In our research, we propose to use textual information and structural information of software artifacts in combination to enhance the traceability recovery. We propose to utilize the structural information more effectively by using graph embedding.

Specifically, the contributions of our research are as follows:

1. Embedding code relationship graph by using the graph embedding technology, effectively expressing and utilizing the structural information of the code.
2. Analysis and extraction of various structural relationships such as inheritance, implement, parameters, and return values between the source code.
3. Comprehensive use of textual information and structural information to enhance the traceability recovery.

The paper is structured as follow. The second part discusses related work. The third part describes the background information of traceability recovery. The fourth part describes the approach we proposed. The fifth part describes the evaluation of the experiment. The sixth part analysis the effectiveness of the experiment. The seventh part summarizes the paper. The eighth part is discussion and future work.

2   Related Work

Information retrieval is a widely adopted technology in traceability recovery. [7] using the IR methods: vector space model (VSM), probabilistic Jensen and Shannon (JS) models, and relational topic modeling (RTM). [8] Statistically analysis of widely used IR methods: JS, VSM, Latent Semantic Index (LSI) and Latent Dirichlet Allocation (LDA). [4] proposes a simple method that only uses the nouns in the artifacts to improve the accuracy of the traceability recovery method. [5] proposed an automation technique that using machine learning techniques for LDA. The approach saves traceability links and learns probabilistic topic model. The learning model achieves semantic classification and visualization themes. Although [4–7] continues to improve the IR method and extract more semantic information, it is one-sided to focus on textual information only, and the results in implementation are not ideal.

The structural information between source code is also very useful in traceability recovery. [3] introduced a way for traceability recovery in requirement document by using textual and structural information. [3] speculated that the relevant requirements share relevant source code elements. Building Evolving Interoperation Graph (EIG) using the JRipples [11] structural analysis tool. The traceability link graph (TLG) is proposed that encodes requirements and source code into nodes, and edges between nodes are recovery links. [1] proposed to use the textual information of the verb-object phrase in the requirement and source comments and the structural information of the source code to perform traceability link recovery. They process the natural language text, such as requirements and code comments, and source code separately. They use WordNet to handle synonym problems. [2] proposed to use feedback from software engineers to classify links to enhance the effect structural information. Specifically, they utilize structural information only when the engineer verifies the traceability link and classifies it as the correct link. Although the results of [1–3] have improved, structural information has not been fully explored.

There are other ways to come up. [6] proposed to use code ownership information to capture the relationship of source code. [9] proposed a neural network architecture that uses word embedding and RNN techniques to automatically generate traceability links. [10] proposed a traceability recovery method called Trustrace to identify traceability links by building VSM in the CVS/SVN change log. [12,13] proposed to use closeness analysis of code dependency. These methods improve the results, but limited.

3   Background

This section outlines the techniques involved in the traceability recovery process.

3.1   IR-Based Traceability Recovery Process

The IR-based traceability recovery firstly indexes the artifacts by extracting terms from their content. The text normalization phase is required before the indexing process. The output of the indexing process is an $m \times n$ matrix (term-by-document matrix). The widely used weighted mode is TF-IDF, which places more emphasis on words appear many times in the document and contain in minority documents, so it has high discriminative weight.

Engineers can use IR methods to compare artifacts after artifacts are indexed, and sort the similarities of all artifacts.

3.2   Latent Dirichlet Allocation

LDA is a generative probabilistic model. Each document has multinomial distribution over T topics, and each topic has multinomial distribution over the words of the corpus.

To compare the similarities of the documents, we use the Hellinger Distance, which is a measure of symmetric similarity between two probability distributions. Previous research on topical modeling also used it as a means of capturing similarities between documents. The Hellinger distance is defined as (1).

$$H(P,Q) = \sum_{x \in X} \left(\sqrt{P(x)} - \sqrt{Q(x)} \right)^2 \tag{1}$$

The number of topics is key, and how to choice the correct number is undecided.

3.3   Graph Embedding

Information networks are common in society. Analysis of large information networks has attracted more and more attention from academia and industry. Graph embedding is a representation learning technique that maps nodes in a graph to real number vectors, and expresses the relationship in the graph by the relationship between the vectors.

The main purpose of Graph Embedding is to map the nodes to the vectors. These vectors are used to represent the relationship in the original graph.

This paper uses the LINE (Large-scale Information Network Embedding) [14]. After defining the objective function, LINE use a new edge-sampling which samples according to the probabilities of the edges weight. The first-order approximation can map directly connected nodes to closer distances, and the second-order approximation can map nodes with the same neighbor to a closer distance. Therefore, the first-order approximation can retain more local structural information, while the second-order approximation can retain more global structural information. As shown in Fig. 1, the node 6 and node 7 have a very high weight edge connection between them, and the node 5 and node 6 have many identical neighbor nodes. Considering the two approximations, the nodes 5, 6, and 7 are all Map to a closer distance in the embedding space.

4   Approach

4.1   Overall Process

The overall process is as shown in the Fig. 2. We extracting the textual information of the document and source code, and calculating the text similarity between the software artifacts. In our case, the document is use case. For the source code, we also analyses the structural information between the source codes besides extracting the textual information, organizes the source code into a graph, embeds it using the graph embedding algorithm, and the get the embedding vector of the code nodes, calculates the distance between the code nodes. The candidate links are generated based on the textual similarity and distance, and we set a threshold to filter the candidate links.

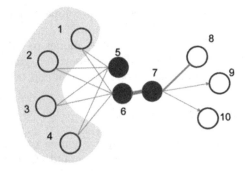

Fig. 1. An example of information network

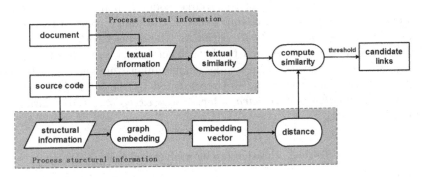

Fig. 2. The overall process

4.2   Process Textual Information

The software artifacts usually contain a large amount of semantic information, so the text information of the software artifacts can be extracted and processed by using the IR technology.

It need to preprocess the text of the software artifacts. All software artifacts need to: Segmentation of words: Dividing words according to separator. (ii) Morphological analysis: conversion of word case, conversion of nouns singular and plural, recovery of abbreviations, extraction of stems. (iii) Deletion of stop words, key words and most non-text marks.

The identifier of the source code, such as the class name, method name, contains important information, so we must handle the identifier appropriately. Identifiers often use Camel-Case and consist of several different words, distinguished by the case of the first letter of the word. So we need to split the source code identifier into separate words based on the letter case.

Then indexing the processed document. The $m \times n$ matrix (term-by-document matrix) will be gotten after the indexing process. The widely used weighted mode is TF-IDF, which places more emphasis on words often appear in the document and contain in minority documents.

Then the engineers can use IR methods to compare artifacts and rank the similarities.

Firstly, we use the TF-IDF and the LDA model to calculate the textual similarity, and the similarities of the artifacts are sorted to generate the candidate links. We use the use case and source code as source and target artifacts.

4.3 Process Structural Information

The Construction of the Code Graph. Source code artifacts not only contain textual information, but also inheritance and other structural relationships between source code, and such structural information between source code is very valuable for recovering traceability links of software artifacts. Therefore, we should not simply treat the source code as plain text, but rather to discover the structural relationship between the source code to help recovery traceability links of the software artifacts. The dataset software repository selected in this paper is developed by Java. Therefore, we propose the following six relationships between source code, namely inherit, implement, attribute, parameter, return and exception, and represented by the set $Relationship = \{Inherit, implement, attribute, parameter, return, exception\}$. The relationship is shown in Table 1.

Table 1. Relationship between source code

Relationship	Description	Weight
Inherit	Class A inherit class B	1
Implement	Class A implement interface B	1
Attribute	Class A has a class B type attribute	1
Parameter	Class A has a method whose argument type is Class B	1
Return	Class A has a method whose return type is Class B	1
Exception	Class A has a method whose exception type is Class B	1

We can organize the source code as a graph. The nodes in the graph are the source code classes, and the edges represent the relationships between the code elements. The graph structure is a natural and effective representation of the structural relationship of the source code. The code relational structure diagram can fully reflect the relationship between the source code. For the software project selected in this article, we can use existing tools to parse its source code.

There are many tools for parsing Java source code. These tools can parse Java software projects and extract code elements and the relationship between them. This article uses Eclipse JDT, a lightweight code analysis tool that can quickly builds Java code to a DOM structure's Abstract Syntax Tree (AST). Each element in the code corresponds to a node on the AST. By traversing the

AST, you can get all the code elements and the relationships between them to build a software code structure diagram.

We use Eclipse's JDT tool to parse the source code, get the structural information, and construct the corresponding relationship graph of the structural information.

The graph $G(C, E)$ a directed weighted graph that shows the relationship between code classes, where the vertex set $C = \{c_1, ..., c_n\}$ is a collection of code classes, and the edge set $E = \{(c_i, c_j),$ the relationship between c_i and $c_j\}$ is a collection of edges. The S is the collection of source artifacts. The $List = \{(s, c)\}$ is the candidate links.

In software projects, the closeness of relationship between different source code classes is different, and there are more relationship types and relationship numbers between source code classes with more closely related relationships. Therefore, we believe that if there are multiple relationship types or multiple relationships between two source code classes, the relationship between the two source code classes should be closer. Therefore, the edges (c_i, c_j) in the code graph $G(C, E)$ are weighted, and the weights represent the closeness of the relationship between the source code classes. The specific definition of the weight is as follows: for each relationship between two source code classes, the weight of the edge between them is incremented by one. For example, if there is one attribute relationship between the code nodes c_i and c_j, two parameter relationships, and two return value relationships, the weight between the edges (c_i, c_j) between them is 5.

Embedding the Code Graph. The main purpose of graph embedding is mapping the nodes to low dimension vectors. The structural information here can be different levels order. The first-order structural information can keep the distance between the adjacent nodes in the embedding space is still very close, and the higher-order structural information can keep the distance of the nodes with similar contexts in the embedding space still very close.

In this paper, we use LINE which can work for any type of information network: undirected, oriented, unweighted or weighted. This method optimizes the objective function and preserves the network structure. The algorithm is very efficient in practice.

We use the LINE graph embedding technology to embed the code nodes, and map them into low-dimensional space. If the two source code classes have a close relationship, the distance between the vectors of the two source code classes will be closer. Therefore, the closeness of relationship between the source codes can be expressed according to the distance between the vectors corresponding to the code nodes, that is, if the two source code classes have closer distances, the relationship between them is closer.

The reason why the graph is embedded in this paper is that when using the structural information between the codes to calculate the similarity between use case and source code, the distance between any two vertices on the graph needs to be calculated. By using the graph embedding technique to obtain the vector corresponding to the source code node, the distance between the source code nodes can be calculated. There are many kinds of distances between two vectors in the representation space. In our study, the Euclidean distance (2) is used to represent the distance between two source code nodes.

$$d(x,y) := \sqrt{(x_1 - y_1)^2 + (x_2 - y_2)^2 + \cdots + (x_n - y_n)^2} = \sqrt{\sum_{i=1}^{n}(x_i - y_i)^2} \quad (2)$$

4.4 Calculate the Similarity by Combining the Textual and Structural Information

We have calculated the textual similarity between artifacts and the distance between nodes, and then we will update the candidate links with textual information and structural information.

We proposed that if a text artifact d(use case) has a high similarity to the source code c_i, and the source code c_j is associated with the source code c_i in the structural information, then the similarity between d and c_j should be improved. On the contrary, if a textual artifact d(use case) has a low similarity to the source code c_i, and the source code c_j is associated with the source code c_i in the structural information, then the similarity between d and c_j should be reduced. Follow the same idea, we update the similarity between the text artifact d and the source code c_j according to the following formula (3), (4).

$$Sim(d, c_j) = Sim_{Text}(d, c_j) + \frac{Sim_{Text}(c_i, c_j)}{dist(c_i, c_j)} \quad (3)$$

$$Sim(d, c_j) = Sim_{Text}(d, c_j) - \frac{Sim_{Text}(c_i, c_j)}{dist(c_i, c_j)} \quad (4)$$

Finally, we will filter the generated candidate connections. There are usually two ways to do this. You can sort the generated candidate joins and pick the top k links with the highest similarity. Instead, we set a threshold for the candidate connection and filter out the links above the threshold.

5   Experiment Evaluation

In this section, we describe the evaluation the proposed method.

5.1   Dataset

The software repository of our research is eTour which is an electronic touristic guide. It contains 58 Use Cases, 174 classes and 366 correct links. The artifact language for the eTour systems is English. The correct traceability links which called oracle is restored to analyze the proposed experimental method.

5.2   Research Questions

In our research, we have proposed questions:

1. Whether combining the textual information and structural information of the software artifacts can improve the traceability link recovery work? Whether the structural information contributes to traceability links recovery work?
2. Whether use graph embedding technology to indicate the structural information of the source code can help the software artifact traceability recovery work?
3. Whether the combination of different IR methods can improve the traceability recovery method? Specifically, can a combination of different IR technologies achieve better accuracy and recall than using only one IR technology?

In response to our research questions, we compared only using the IR-based method with the combination of IR technology and graph embedding technology in the traceability recovery. For obtaining the experimental results of traceability recovery by combining different IR methods, we apply TF-IDF and LDA model combination to the recovery of artifact traceability links.

5.3   Metrics

Our research uses precision and recall metrics to evaluate proposed approach (5), (6).

$$precision = \frac{|correct \cap retrieved|}{|retrieved|}\% \tag{5}$$

$$recall = \frac{|correct \cap retrieved|}{|correct|}\% \tag{6}$$

We evaluate the result by comparing precision and recall.

5.4   Analysis of the Results

The Fig. 3 shows the number of correct links found in traceable link recovery. It can be seen from the figure that the combination of TFIDF and LDA, and using graph embedding technology for traceable link recovery can improve the number of correct connections captured, thus indicating that the combination of IR and graph embedding technology can improve traceability link recovery.

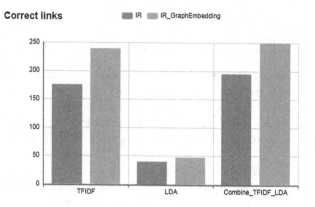

Fig. 3. The retrieved correct links

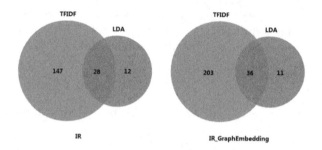

Fig. 4. The correct links captured by each method

The Fig. 4 shows the correct links captured by each method. Using graph embedding technology can capture more correct links. We also found that most of the correct links are captured by the TF-IDF method, but the LDA method also captures many correct links that ignored by TF-IDF.

The Fig. 5 shows the accuracy obtained in traceable link recovery. It can be seen from the figure that the use of combined IR method and Graph Embedding technology for traceable link recovery does not significantly improve accuracy, even with LDA technology, the accuracy is slightly reduced.

The Fig. 6 shows the recall obtained in traceable link recovery. It can be seen from the figure that using graph embedding technology for traceable link recovery can greatly improve the recall. In the case of using TFIDF and Combine TFIDF and LDA, the recall is significantly improved. In the LDA case, the recall has also increased slightly. This shows that graph embedding technology can significantly improve the recall of traceable links, and graph embedding helps traceability link recovery.

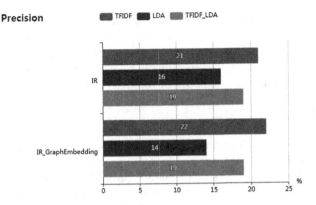

Fig. 5. The precision of traceability recovery

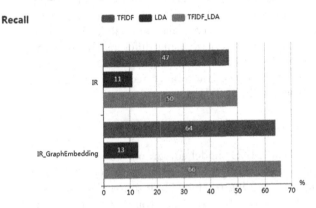

Fig. 6. The recall of traceability recovery

In conclusion, using graph embedding technology can capture more correct links and significantly increase the recall of traceability links, so graph embedding technology is helpful. And using multiple IR technologies can achieve better results than using one IR technology alone.

6   Threats to Validity

The repositories used in our research is difficult to compete with actual industrial projects. But it is near to the repository used in other research. ETour has been used as a benchmark repository for TEFSE 2011 traceability recovery challenges. Nonetheless, we plan to use other artifact repositories to replicate the experiment to confirm our findings.

Regarding the calculation of the distance between source code nodes, we use the Euclidean distance. Although Euclidean distance is useful, it has limitations. It treats the differences between the different properties of the sample as equivalent, which sometimes does not satisfy the actual situation. Therefore, the

Euclidean distance is applied to the case where the metrics of the components of the vector are unified.

We use LDA to calculate the text similarity of software artifacts. Although LDA is very useful, but it is very difficult to select the appropriate number of topics T. The inappropriate number of topics T will reduce the result.

7 Conclusion

Maintaining the traceability links often is an time-consuming work. The research strive for reducing manual work and increase productivity partly. The use of IR technique for recovering links has achieved promising results. But it often suffer the terms mismatch problem of artifacts developed by different people. In addition, some data have a lot of noise. In this case, this problem suppresses the IR technique to distinguish between related and unrelated artifacts. This article combines the textual information of the software artifacts with the structural information to recover the traceability link. Textual information of the software artifacts is processed by using different IR techniques, and the structural information of the source code is represented by using the graph embedding technology. We Improve the traceability recovery by comprehensively utilizing textual and structural information.

8 Discussion and Future Work

Our study uses the LINE model for graph embedding of source code nodes, which is applicable to any type of information network. In the future, we will use other graph embedding to embedding source code nodes.

Our study implementation on the eTour software repository. In the future we will try to recover traceable links for more software repository.

Our research focuses on the inheritance, implement, class attributes, function parameters, function return, and exceptions thrown by functions. These features are crucial for program comprehension and traceability recovery. We plan to utilize these and more features in other effective ways in the future.

Furthermore, the domain knowledge of software engineering is also significant for traceability recovery according to our empirical research. Therefore, we plan to utilize the logical reasoning to recover traceability links directly in the future.

Acknowledgement. This work is supported by National Key R&D Program of China (No. 2018 YFB0804703), International Research Cooperation Seed Fund of Beijing University of Technology (No. 2018B2), and Basic Research Funding of Beijing University of Technology (No. 040000546318516).

References

1. Zhang, Y., Wan, C., Jin, B.: An empirical study on recovering requirement-to-code links. In: 2016 17th IEEE/ACIS International Conference on Software Engineering, Artificial Intelligence, Networking and Parallel/Distributed Computing (SNPD). IEEE (2016)

2. Panichella, A., et al.:. When and how using structural information to improve IR-based traceability recovery. In: European Conference on Software Maintenance and Reengineering. IEEE (2013)
3. Mcmillan, C., Poshyvanyk, D., Revelle, M.: Combining textual and structural analysis of software artifacts for traceability link recovery. In: Workshop on Traceability in Emerging Forms of Software Engineering. IEEE (2009)
4. Capobianco, G., De Lucia, A., Oliveto, R., Panichella, A., Panichella, S.: On the role of the nouns in IR-based traceability recovery. In: IEEE International Conference on Program Comprehension. IEEE (2009)
5. Asuncion, H.U., Asuncion, A.U., Taylor, R.N.: Proceedings of the 32nd ACM/IEEE International Conference on Software Engineering - ICSE 2010 - Software Traceability with Topic Modeling, Cape Town, South Africa, 1–8 May 2010, vol. 1, p. 95. ACM Press (2010)
6. Diaz, D., Bavota, G., Marcus, A., Oliveto, R., Takahashi, S., Lucia, A.D.: Using code ownership to improve IR-based Traceability Link Recovery. In: IEEE International Conference on Program Comprehension. IEEE (2013)
7. Gethers, M., Oliveto, R., Poshyvanyk, D., Lucia, A.D.: On integrating orthogonal information retrieval methods to improve traceability recovery. In: IEEE International Conference on Software Maintenance, The College of William and Mary. IEEE (2011)
8. Oliveto, R., Gethers, M., Poshyvanyk, D., Lucia, A.D.: On the equivalence of information retrieval methods for automated traceability link recovery. In: 2010 IEEE 18th International Conference on Program Comprehension (ICPC). IEEE (2010)
9. Guo, J., Cheng, J., Cleland-Huang, J.: Semantically enhanced software traceability using deep learning techniques. In: 2017 IEEE/ACM 39th International Conference on Software Engineering (ICSE). IEEE Computer Society (2017)
10. Ali, N., Gueheneuc, Y.G., Antoniol, G.: Trust-based requirements traceability. In: 2011 IEEE 19th International Conference on Program Comprehension (ICPC). IEEE (2011)
11. Buckner, J., Buchta, J., Petrenko, M., Rajlich, V.: JRipples: a tool for program comprehension during incremental change. In: International Workshop on Program Comprehension. IEEE Computer Society (2005)
12. Kuang, H., Nie, J., Hu, H., Lü, J.: Improving automatic identification of outdated requirements by using closeness analysis based on source code changes. In: Zhang, L., Xu, C. (eds.) Software Engineering and Methodology for Emerging Domains. CCIS, vol. 675, pp. 52–67. Springer, Singapore (2016). https://doi.org/10.1007/978-981-10-3482-4_4
13. Kuang, H., Nie, J., Hu, H., Rempel, P., Lü, J., Egyed, A., Mäder, P.: Analyzing closeness of code dependencies for improving IR-based Traceability Recovery. In: 2017 IEEE 24th International Conference on Software Analysis, Evolution and Reengineering (SANER), February 2017, pp. 68–78. IEEE (2017)
14. Tang, J., Qu, M., Wang, M., Zhang, M., Yan, J., Mei, Q.: Line: large-scale information network embedding. In: Proceedings 24th International Conference on World Wide Web (WWW 2015), pp. 1067–1077 (2015)

Author Index

Printed in the United States
By Bookmasters